The Twenties in America

The Twenties in America

Volume 3
Racial discrimination—
Zworykin, Vladimir
Appendixes
Indexes

Editor
Carl Rollyson
City University of New York,
Baruch College

SALEM PRESS
A Division of EBSCO Publishing
Ipswich, Massachusetts
Hackensack, New Jersey

Cover photos (pictured left to right, from top left): Bathing beauty posing in red bathing suit (©Trolley Dodger/Corbis); F. Scott Fitzgerald by David Silvette (© Bettmann/Corbis); Man smashing keg of beer (© Bettmann/Corbis); Close-up of Chrysler Building spire (©Hoberman Collection/Corbis)

Title page photo: A pensive Babe Ruth poses for photographers in Yankee Stadium before a game in May of 1926. (© Getty Images)

Copyright ©2012, by Salem Press, A Division of EBSCO Publishing, Inc.

All rights reserved. No part of this work may be used or reproduced in any manner whatsoever or transmitted in any form or by any means, electronic or mechanical, including photocopy, recording, or any information storage and retrieval system, without written permission from the copyright owner. For permissions requests, contact proprietarypublishing@ebscohost.com.

∞ The paper used in these volumes conforms to the American National Standard for Permanence of Paper for Printed Library Materials, Z39.48 1992 (R1997).

Library of Congress Cataloging-in-Publication Data

    The twenties in America / editor, Carl Rollyson.
       p. cm.
    ISBN 978-1-58765-855-6 (set) — ISBN 978-1-58765-856-3 (vol. 1) — ISBN 978-1-58765-857-0 (vol. 2) — ISBN 978-1-58765-858-7 (vol. 3)
    1. United States—History—1919-1933. 2. United States—Social conditions—1918-1932. 3. United States—Social life and customs—1918-1945. 4. Nineteen twenties. I. Rollyson, Carl E. (Carl Edmund)
    E784.T84 2012
    973.91–dc23

                                                                           2011051370

PRINTED IN THE UNITED STATES OF AMERICA

Contents

Complete List of Contents ix

Racial discrimination 707
Radio 710
Radio Act of 1927 713
Radio Corporation of America (RCA) 714
Railroads 715
Railway Labor Act of 1926 719
Randolph, A. Philip 720
Rayon stockings 721
Recession of 1920-1921 722
Red Scare, The 723
Reed, John 726
Refrigerators 727
Reid, Wallace 728
Religion in Canada 729
Religion in the United States 732
"Return to Normalcy" 735
Revenue Acts of 1924, 1926, and 1928 736
Rhapsody in Blue 737
Ringling Bros. and Barnum & Bailey Circus 738
Rin Tin Tin films 739
Roach, Hal, Sr. 739
Roaring Twenties 741
Robeson, Paul 742
Robinson, Edwin Arlington 743
Rocketry 745
Rockne, Knute 746
Rockwell, Norman 748
Rodgers, Jimmie 749
Rogers, Will 749
Romberg, Sigmund 751
Roosevelt, Franklin D. 752
Rosenfeld, Fanny "Bobbie" 754
Ross, Harold 755
Ross, Nellie Tayloe 755
Route 66 757
Royal Canadian Air Force 758
Rural Life 759
Russian Famine Relief Act of 1921 762
Ruth, Babe 762

Saarinen, Eliel 765
Sacco and Vanzetti case 766
Safety Last 767
Saint Valentine's Day Massacre 768
Sandburg, Carl 770

Sanger, Margaret 771
Sarnoff, David 773
Sartoris 774
Schiaparelli, Elsa 774
Schindler, Rudolph 775
Scholastic Aptitude Test (SAT) 776
Scholz, Jackson 777
Schultz, Dutch 778
Science and technology 779
Science fiction 784
Scopes trial 786
Sears, Roebuck and Co. 788
Sennett, Mack 789
Sesquicentennial Exposition 791
Sex and sex education 792
Sexually transmitted diseases 795
Sheik, The 797
Shenandoah airship disaster 797
Sheppard-Towner Act 799
Show Boat 800
Shuffle Along 800
Sinclair, Upton 801
Slang 802
Smith, Alfred E. 804
Smith, Bessie 806
Soccer 807
Social sciences 809
Société Anonyme 812
Sound and the Fury, The 812
Southern Agrarians 813
Soviet Union and North America 815
Speakeasies 816
Spiritualism 818
Sports 819
Spring and All 822
Steamboat Willie 823
St. Francis Dam disaster 824
Stein, Gertrude 825
Stella Dallas 827
Stieglitz, Alfred 827
Stock market crash 829
Stone, Harlan Fiske 831
Strange Interlude 833
Student Prince, The 834
Studies in Classic American Literature 835
Sturtevant, Alfred H. 835
Suburbs 836

Sun Also Rises, The	838
Supreme Court, U.S.	839
Swanson, Gloria	841
Taft, William Howard	843
Tales of the Jazz Age	845
Talking motion pictures	845
Tarkington, Booth	847
Taylor, William Desmond	848
Teapot Dome scandal	849
Teasdale, Sara	851
Telephone technology and service	852
Television technology	853
Ten Commandments, The	855
Ten Days That Shook the World	856
Tennis	857
Theater in Canada	859
Theater in the United States	861
Thief of Bagdad, The	864
This Side of Paradise	864
Thompson machine gun	865
Thorpe, Jim	866
Three Soldiers	868
Tilden, Bill	868
Tin Pan Alley	869
Tomb of the Unknown Soldier	870
Tong Wars of Chinatown, San Francisco	871
Toomer, Jean	872
Traffic signals	874
Transportation	875
Travel	877
Tunney, Gene	880
Unemployment	881
Unionism	883
United Artists	886
United States v. Ninety-Five Barrels Alleged Apple Cider Vinegar	887
United States v. United States Steel Corp	887
Universal Negro Improvement Association (UNIA)	888
Urbanization	889
Valentino, Rudolph	893
Vallée, Rudy	894
Van Der Zee, James	895
Vaudeville	896
Vidor, King	899
Vitamin D discovery	899
Voting rights	900
Walker, Jimmy	903
Wallace, DeWitt	903
Waller, Fats	904
Warner, Harry	905
Warner, Sam	906
Warner Bros.	907
Washington Naval Conference	908
Waste Land, The	910
Weissmuller, Johnny	911
West, Mae	912
West Virginia mining disaster	912
Wharton, Edith	913
What's O'Clock	915
Whiteman, Paul	915
Wilder, Thornton	916
Williams, William Carlos	918
Wilson, Edith	919
Wilson, Edmund	920
Wilson, Woodrow	921
Wings	922
Women in college	923
Women in the workforce	925
Women's rights	927
Workers' education	931
World War I veterans	932
Wright, Frank Lloyd	934
Wylie, Elinor	936
Yo-yos	937
Ziegfeld, Florenz	939
Ziegfeld Follies	940
Zworykin, Vladimir	941

Appendixes

Entertainment: Major Broadway Plays and Awards	945
Entertainment: Major Films	949
Entertainment: Radio Programs, Personalities, and Firsts	957
Legislation: Major U.S. Legislation	963
Legislation: Major U.S. Supreme Court Decisions	967
Literature: Best-Selling Books in the United States	972
Music: Popular Musicians	975
Music: Top-Selling U.S. Recordings	981
Sports: Winners of Major Events	985

Time Line 991
Bibliography 1000
Glossary 1008
List of Entries by Category 1013

Indexes
Photo Index 1025
Personages Index 1029
Subject Index 1037

■ Complete List of Contents

Volume 1

Contents v
Publisher's Note ix
Contributors xi
Complete List of Contents xix

Academy Awards 1
A. C. Nielsen Company 2
Adams, Franklin P. 3
Adding Machine, The 4
Adkins v. Children's Hospital 5
Advertising in Canada 6
Advertising in the United
  States 7
African Americans 11
Age of Innocence, The 14
Agricultural Marketing Act
  of 1929 15
Agriculture in Canada 16
Agriculture in the United
  States 18
Aiken, Conrad 21
Air Commerce Act of 1926 21
Airmail 22
Air Mail Act of 1925 23
Air pollution 24
Airships 26
Alberta Sexual Sterilization
  Act 28
Alexander, Grover Cleveland .. 29
Algonquin Round Table 30
Ali, Noble Drew 31
Alice Adams 32
All God's Chillun Got Wings 33
American Civil Liberties
  Union (ACLU) 34
American Federation of
  Labor (AFL) 35
American Mercury, The 37
Anderson, Marian 38
Anderson, Sherwood 39
Andrews, Roy Chapman 41
Anna Christie 42
Anti-Semitism 43
Appalachian Trail 45

Arbuckle, Fatty 45
Archaeology 47
Architecture 49
Armstrong, Louis 52
Art Deco 53
Art movements 54
Asia 57
Asian Americans 59
Astronomy 61
Automobiles and auto
  manufacturing 63
Auto racing 67
Aviation 68

Babbitt 73
Bailey v. Drexel Furniture Co. 73
Baker, Josephine 74
Band-Aids 76
Banking 77
Bánky, Vilma 80
Banting, Frederick Grant 81
Bara, Theda 82
Barrymore, John 82
Baseball 83
Bathing suits 86
Bathtub gin 87
Baylor Plan 87
Beiderbecke, Bix 88
Bell, James "Cool Papa" 89
Bell Labs 90
Ben-Hur 91
Berlin, Irving 91
Better Homes in America
  movement 93
Birdseye, Clarence 94
Birth control 95
Black-and-tan clubs 96
Black Swan Records 97
Bobbed hair 98
Bonus Act of 1924 99
Book clubs 100
Bookman, The 101
Book publishing 102
Border Patrol, U.S. 105

Bose, Sudhindra 105
Bow, Clara 106
Boxing 107
Bread slicer 109
Bridge of San Luis Rey, The 110
Broadway musicals 111
Brooks, Louise 113
Brotherhood of Sleeping
  Car Porters 114
Bryan, William Jennings 115
Bubble gum 116
Buck v. Bell 116
Bulldozer 117
Bungalows 118
Bunion Derby 119
Bureau of Chemistry and
  Soils, U.S. 120
Burns and Allen 120
Bushman, Francis X. 121
Business and the economy 122
Byrd, Richard E. 125

Cabell, James Branch 127
Cable Act of 1922 128
California Institute of
  Technology (Caltech) 129
Canada and Great Britain 130
Canadian minority
  communities 132
Canadian nationalism 136
Cancer 137
Capablanca, José Raúl 140
Capone, Al 140
Carmichael, Hoagy 142
Carr, Mary 143
Carter Family 143
Cascade Tunnel 144
Castle Gate, Utah, mining
  disaster 145
Cather, Willa 146
Cellophane 147
Censorship 148
Chain stores 150
Chandler, Harry 151

- Chanel, Coco ... 152
- Chaney, Lon ... 154
- Chaplin, Charlie ... 155
- Charleston, The ... 157
- Chemistry ... 158
- Chinese Immigration Act of 1923 ... 161
- Chrysler, Walter P. ... 162
- Chrysler Building ... 163
- *Circus, The* ... 164
- Cities ... 165
- *City, The* ... 169
- Civil rights and liberties ... 170
- Classical music ... 172
- Cline, Genevieve R. ... 175
- Cloche hats ... 176
- Cobb, Ty ... 177
- Cocoanut Grove ... 178
- *Cocoanuts, The* ... 179
- Cohan, George M. ... 180
- Coleman, Bessie ... 181
- Colman, Ronald ... 182
- Comic strips ... 183
- *Coming of Age in Samoa* ... 184
- Communism ... 185
- Compton, Arthur Holly ... 187
- Coney Island ... 188
- Congress, U.S. ... 189
- Coogan, Jackie ... 192
- Coolidge, Calvin ... 193
- Coolidge, Grace ... 196
- Copland, Aaron ... 197
- *Corrigan v. Buckley* ... 198
- Corrupt Practices Act of 1925 ... 198
- Cotton Club ... 199
- Cotton swabs ... 200
- Cox, Ida ... 201
- Cox, James M. ... 202
- Credit and debt ... 203
- Crimes and scandals ... 206
- Crooners ... 209
- Crosby, Bing ... 210
- Crossword puzzles ... 211
- Cummings, E. E. ... 212
- Currency and coinage ... 214
- Curtis, Charles ... 215

- Dance and choreography ... 217
- Dances, popular ... 219
- Darrow, Clarence ... 220
- Daugherty, Harry M. ... 222
- Davis, John W. ... 223
- Dawes, Charles G. ... 224
- Dawes Plan ... 225
- *Death Comes for the Archbishop* ... 227
- Debs, Eugene V. ... 228
- DeMille, Cecil B. ... 229
- Demographics ... 231
- Dempsey, Jack ... 234
- Demuth, Charles ... 236
- Denby, Edwin ... 237
- Denishawn School of Dancing and Related Arts ... 238
- *Desire Under the Elms* ... 239
- Detroit-Windsor Tunnel ... 240
- Dewey, John ... 241
- *Dial, The* ... 242
- Differential analyzer ... 243
- Disney, Walt ... 244
- Doolittle, Hilda ... 245
- Douglas Aircraft Company ... 246
- Du Bois, W. E. B. ... 247
- Duncan, Isadora ... 249
- Durant, Will ... 250
- Dyer antilynching bill ... 251

- Earhart, Amelia ... 253
- Eastman, George ... 254
- Ederle, Gertrude ... 255
- Education ... 256
- Einstein, Albert ... 259
- Elections, Canadian ... 260
- Elections, midterm, U.S. ... 262
- Elections of 1920, U.S. ... 264
- Elections of 1924, U.S. ... 266
- Elections of 1928, U.S. ... 269
- Electrical recording ... 271
- Electrification ... 272
- Eliot, T. S. ... 273
- Ellington, Duke ... 274
- *Elmer Gantry* ... 275
- *Emperor Jones, The* ... 276

- Equal Rights Amendment ... 277
- Eskimo Pie ... 278
- Eugenics movement ... 279
- Europe ... 280
- Evangelism ... 283

- Fads ... 285
- Fairbanks, Douglas, Sr. ... 288
- *Farewell to Arms, A* ... 289
- Farm subsidies ... 290
- Fashions and clothing ... 292
- Faulkner, William ... 294
- Faust, Frederick ... 296
- Federal Aid Highway Act of 1921 ... 298
- Federal highway system ... 298
- Federal Power Act of 1920 ... 300
- Federal Radio Commission (FRC) ... 301
- Felix the Cat ... 302
- Ferber, Edna ... 303
- Fields, W. C. ... 305
- Film ... 305
- Fitzgerald, F. Scott ... 308
- Fitzgerald, Zelda ... 310
- Flagpole sitting ... 312
- Flappers ... 313
- *Flesh and the Devil* ... 314
- Fokker, Anthony ... 315
- Food, Drug, and Insecticide Administration, U.S. ... 316
- Food trends ... 318
- Football ... 321
- Forbes, Charles R. ... 323
- Foreign policy, U.S. ... 324
- Four Horsemen of Notre Dame ... 327
- Fox, William ... 327
- Foxx, Jimmie ... 329
- Freon ... 330
- *Frontier in American History, The* ... 331
- Frost, Robert ... 332
- Frozen foods ... 333
- *Fugitive, The* ... 334
- Fugitive Poets ... 335

Volume 2

Contents v
Complete List of Contents ix

Gambling 337
Garbo, Greta 338
Garvey, Marcus 340
Gehrig, Lou 342
General, The 343
Gentlemen Prefer Blondes 343
Gershwin, George 344
Gila Wilderness Area 345
Gilbert, John 346
Gipp, George 347
Girl Scout cookies 348
Gish, Dorothy 348
Gish, Lillian 349
Gitlow v. New York 350
Goddard, Robert 351
Gold Diggers of Broadway 353
Gold Rush, The 353
Goldwyn, Samuel 354
Golf 355
Gompers, Samuel 357
Graham, Martha 358
Grand Ole Opry, The 359
Grange, Red 360
Grauman's Chinese Theatre ... 361
Great Gatsby, The 362
Great Migration 363
Great Mississippi Flood
  of 1927 364
Greed 366
Griffith, D. W. 367
Gross national product
  of the United States 368
Group of Seven 370
Grove, Lefty 371

Hair dryers 373
Hairstyles 373
Halibut Treaty of 1924 375
Hallelujah! 376
Hall-Mills murder case 377
Hammerstein, Oscar, II 378
Hammett, Dashiell 379
Hardin, Lillian 379
Harding, Warren G. 380

Harlem Renaissance 383
*Harp Weaver and Other Poems,
  The* 386
Hart, Lorenz 387
Haywood, Big Bill 388
Health care 389
Hearst, William Randolph 392
Hearst Castle 393
Hemingway, Ernest 395
Hester v. United States 397
Historiography 397
Hobbies and recreation 400
Hockey 404
Holland Tunnel 405
Hollywood Bowl 406
Hollywood sign 407
Holmes, Oliver Wendell, Jr. ... 407
Home furnishings 408
Homosexuality and gay
  rights 411
Hood ornaments 413
Hoover, Herbert 414
Hoover, J. Edgar 416
Hopper, Edward 417
Hornsby, Rogers 419
Horse racing 419
Houdini, Harry 421
Housing 422
Hubble, Edwin Powell 424
Hughes, Charles Evans 426
Hughes, Howard 427
Hughes, Langston 429
Hurston, Zora Neale 431

I'll Take My Stand 433
Immigration Act of 1921 433
Immigration Act of 1924 435
Immigration to Canada 437
Immigration to the United
  States 439
In the American Grain 442
Ince, Thomas H. 442
Income and wages 443
Indian Citizenship Act
  of 1924 447
Installment plans 448
Insulin 449

International Business
  Machines (IBM) 450
International trade 451
Inventions 454
Iron lung 457
Isolationism 458
Izaak Walton League
  of America 459

Jannings, Emil 461
Japanese American Citizens
  League 462
Jazz 463
Jazz Singer, The 466
Jews in Canada 468
Jews in the United States 469
Jim Crow in the U.S. South 471
John Brown's Body 472
John Keats 472
Johnson, Jack 473
Johnson, James Weldon 474
Johnson, Judy 476
Jolson, Al 476
Jones, Bobby 477

Kahanamoku, Duke 479
Kane, Helen 479
Keaton, Buster 480
Keller, Helen 482
Kellogg, Frank B. 483
Kellogg-Briand Pact
  of 1928 484
Kern, Jerome 486
King, William Lyon
  Mackenzie 487
King of Kings, The 490
Kirby, Rollin 490
Knickerbocker Storm 491
Koko the Clown 493
Kool-Aid 494
Ku Klux Klan 494

Labor strikes 497
La Follette, Robert M. 500
Landis, Kenesaw Mountain ... 501
Lang, Eddie 502
Langdon, Harry 503

Langley, John W. 504
Lardner, Ring 505
Lasky, Jesse L. 506
Latin America and the
  Caribbean 507
Latinos 509
Laurel and Hardy....................511
League of Nations...................513
League of United Latin
  American Citizens 515
League of Women Voters.......515
Leopold-Loeb murder case 518
Lewis, John L. 519
Lewis, Sinclair........................520
Lincoln Memorial 521
Lindbergh, Charles.................522
Lindsay, Vachel 524
Lindy Hop 525
Lippmann, Walter...................525
Literature in Canada...............526
Literature in the United
  States 529
Little Blue Books....................533
Lloyd, Harold 534
Lodge, Henry Cabot 535
Look Homeward, Angel 536
Los Angeles Aqueduct
  dynamiting........................537
Los Angeles Memorial
  Coliseum 538
Lost generation 539
Loudspeakers 541
Lowell, Amy 542
Luce, Henry R. 543
Lynching................................545

MacLeish, Archibald 547
Macy's Thanksgiving Day
  Parade 548
Magazines 549
Mah-Jongg 551
*Main Currents in American
  Thought* 552
Main Street..............................553
Man o' War 553
Marathon dancing 554
Marin, John 555
Marriage and dating 556
Marx Brothers 557
McFadden Act of 1927...........559

McKinsey, James Oscar 560
McPherson, Aimee Semple....561
Mead, Margaret 563
Medicine................................564
Meighen, Arthur 567
Mellon, Andrew......................568
Mencken, H. L. 569
Menuhin, Yehudi 571
Merry Widow, The 572
Metro-Goldwyn-Mayer
  (MGM) 572
Mexico 574
Meyer v. Nebraska 576
Micheaux, Oscar 577
Migrations.............................578
Millay, Edna St. Vincent.........580
Millikan, Robert Andrews......581
Miss America pageants...........583
Mitchell, Billy 584
Mix, Tom 585
Model A Fords 586
Montessori method 587
Moody, Helen Wills................588
Moore v. Dempsey 589
Morgan, Thomas Hunt...........590
Morton, Jelly Roll 591
Motels 592
Mount Rushmore 593
Movie palaces 594
Museum of Modern Art
  (MoMA) 594
Music, popular 595

Nanook of the North 599
National Association for the
  Advancement of Colored
  People (NAACP) 599
National Broadcasting
  Company (NBC) 601
National Conference on
  Street and Highway
  Safety................................603
National debt of the United
  States 604
National Football League
  (NFL) 605
National Parks of the United
  States 607
Native Americans 608
Natural disasters....................611

Natural resources,
  exploitation of 614
Negro History Week...............616
Negro League Baseball 617
Newberry v. United States 619
New Criticism 620
Newspapers, U.S....................621
New Yorker, The........................624
New York Yankees 626
Nightclubs 627
Nineteenth Amendment 628
Nixon v. Herndon 631
Nobel Prizes..........................632
Normand, Mabel...................633
Novarro, Ramón....................635

Oil Pollution Act of 1924........637
Okeechobee Hurricane
  of 1928..............................638
O'Keeffe, Georgia...................639
Oliver, Joe "King" 640
Olmstead v. United States 642
Olympic Games of 1920
  (Summer) 643
Olympic Games of 1924
  (Summer) 645
Olympic Games of 1924
  (Winter) 647
Olympic Games of 1928
  (Summer) 648
Olympic Games of 1928
  (Winter) 651
O'Neill, Eugene 652
Organized crime 654
Orphans of the Storm................657
Ott, Mel..................................657
Ouija boards 658
Our Gang comedies...............659
Ozawa v. United States..............661

Paddock, Charles 663
Palmer raids..........................664
Parker, Dorothy 665
Parrish, Maxfield...................665
Paul, Alice 666
Peanut butter and jelly
  sandwiches 667
Pershing Map 668
Phillips, C. Coles 669
Philosophy and philosophers...669

Photography 672	Political parties......................686	*President's Daughter, The* 696
Physics 675	Polygraph...............................689	Progressive Party of
Pickford, Mary......................678	Pornography..........................690	1924......................................696
Pierce v. Society of Sisters............679	Post, Emily 691	Prohibition 698
Piston, Walter 680	Postage stamps 692	*Prophet, The*..............................701
Player pianos 681	Pound, Ezra 694	Psychology, psychiatry,
Poetry....................................682	President's Conference	and psychoanalysis............702
Polio......................................684	on Unemployment 695	*Public Opinion*..........................705

Volume 3

Contents v	Rosenfeld, Fanny "Bobbie"......754	Sheppard-Towner Act 799
Complete List of Contents ix	Ross, Harold 755	*Show Boat*................................800
	Ross, Nellie Tayloe 755	*Shuffle Along* 800
Racial discrimination 707	Route 66 757	Sinclair, Upton 801
Radio......................................710	Royal Canadian Air Force......758	Slang 802
Radio Act of 1927..................713	Rural Life...............................759	Smith, Alfred E......................804
Radio Corporation of	Russian Famine Relief Act	Smith, Bessie 806
America (RCA) 714	of 1921..............................762	Soccer 807
Railroads................................715	Ruth, Babe..............................762	Social sciences 809
Railway Labor Act of 1926.....719		Société Anonyme 812
Randolph, A. Philip 720	Saarinen, Eliel 765	*Sound and the Fury, The*...........812
Rayon stockings.....................721	Sacco and Vanzetti case 766	Southern Agrarians................813
Recession of 1920–1921.........722	*Safety Last* 767	Soviet Union and North
Red Scare, The 723	Saint Valentine's Day	America............................815
Reed, John 726	Massacre 768	Speakeasies............................816
Refrigerators..........................727	Sandburg, Carl 770	Spiritualism 818
Reid, Wallace 728	Sanger, Margaret....................771	Sports.....................................819
Religion in Canada 729	Sarnoff, David 773	*Spring and All*..........................822
Religion in the United States ... 732	*Sartoris*....................................774	*Steamboat Willie*.......................823
"Return to Normalcy" 735	Schiaparelli, Elsa 774	St. Francis Dam disaster........824
Revenue Acts of 1924, 1926,	Schindler, Rudolph 775	Stein, Gertrude 825
and 1928...........................736	Scholastic Aptitude Test	*Stella Dallas*.............................827
Rhapsody in Blue 737	(SAT) 776	Stieglitz, Alfred......................827
Ringling Bros. and Barnum	Scholz, Jackson 777	Stock market crash................829
& Bailey Circus 738	Schultz, Dutch 778	Stone, Harlan Fiske...............831
Rin Tin Tin films....................739	Science and technology..........779	*Strange Interlude*......................833
Roach, Hal, Sr........................739	Science fiction 784	*Student Prince, The*..................834
Roaring Twenties 741	*Scopes* trial 786	*Studies in Classic American*
Robeson, Paul 742	Sears, Roebuck and Co. 788	*Literature* 835
Robinson, Edwin	Sennett, Mack........................789	Sturtevant, Alfred H..............835
Arlington 743	Sesquicentennial	Suburbs..................................836
Rocketry 745	Exposition 791	*Sun Also Rises, The*..................838
Rockne, Knute.......................746	Sex and sex education 792	Supreme Court, U.S..............839
Rockwell, Norman 748	Sexually transmitted	Swanson, Gloria....................841
Rodgers, Jimmie....................749	diseases.............................795	Taft, William Howard............843
Rogers, Will 749	*Sheik, The* 797	*Tales of the Jazz Age*..................845
Romberg, Sigmund................751	*Shenandoah* airship	Talking motion pictures 845
Roosevelt, Franklin D. 752	disaster 797	Tarkington, Booth 847

Taylor, William Desmond 848
Teapot Dome scandal 849
Teasdale, Sara 851
Telephone technology
    and service 852
Television technology 853
Ten Commandments, The 855
*Ten Days That Shook the
    World* 856
Tennis 857
Theater in Canada 859
Theater in the United
    States 861
Thief of Bagdad, The 864
This Side of Paradise 864
Thompson machine
    gun 865
Thorpe, Jim 866
Three Soldiers 868
Tilden, Bill 868
Tin Pan Alley 869
Tomb of the Unknown
    Soldier 870
Tong Wars of Chinatown,
    San Francisco 871
Toomer, Jean 872
Traffic signals 874
Transportation 875
Travel 877
Tunney, Gene 880

Unemployment 881
Unionism 883
United Artists 886
*United States v. Ninety-Five
    Barrels Alleged Apple
    Cider Vinegar* 887
*United States v. United States
    Steel Corp* 887

Universal Negro Improvement
    Association (UNIA) 888
Urbanization 889

Valentino, Rudolph 893
Vallée, Rudy 894
Van Der Zee, James 895
Vaudeville 896
Vidor, King 899
Vitamin D discovery 899
Voting rights 900

Walker, Jimmy 903
Wallace, DeWitt 903
Waller, Fats 904
Warner, Harry 905
Warner, Sam 906
Warner Bros. 907
Washington Naval
    Conference 908
Waste Land, The 910
Weissmuller, Johnny 911
West, Mae 912
West Virginia mining
    disaster 912
Wharton, Edith 913
What's O'Clock 915
Whiteman, Paul 915
Wilder, Thornton 916
Williams, William Carlos 918
Wilson, Edith 919
Wilson, Edmund 920
Wilson, Woodrow 921
Wings 922
Women in college 923
Women in the workforce 925
Women's rights 927
Workers' education 931
World War I veterans 932

Wright, Frank Lloyd 934
Wylie, Elinor 936

Yo-yos 937

Ziegfeld, Florenz 939
Ziegfeld Follies 940
Zworykin, Vladimir 941

Appendixes
Entertainment: Major
    Broadway Plays and
    Awards 945
Entertainment: Major Films 949
Entertainment: Radio
    Programs, Personalities,
    and Firsts 957
Legislation: Major U.S.
    Legislation 963
Legislation: Major U.S.
    Supreme Court
    Decisions 967
Literature: Best-Selling Books
    in the United States 972
Music: Popular Musicians 975
Music: Top-Selling U.S.
    Recordings 981
Sports: Winners of Major
    Events 985
Time Line 991
Bibliography 1000
Glossary 1008
List of Entries by
    Category 1013

Indexes
Photo Index 1025
Personages Index 1029
Subject Index 1037

The Twenties
in America

Racial discrimination

Racial discrimination in 1920s America continued as it had for decades, based on the assumed superiority and desirability of white Anglo-Saxon Protestant culture. While African Americans faced most of the same hardships that they had since Reconstruction, immigrants, because of their swelling numbers, began to encounter a new upsurge of nativist sentiment that resulted in the passage of harsh new anti-immigration laws. Also during this time, racial discrimination fed most viscerally by economic competition found support from such ostensibly reputable academic theories as eugenics.

Racial discrimination occurred at all levels of American society in the 1920s, from the actions of individuals to the passage of discriminatory national legislation. On the individual level, racial and ethnic minorities were routinely denied jobs, housing, and other social goods, and the racial hierarchy, especially in the South, was often enforced through acts of vigilantism, including the lynching of blacks and occasionally other minorities suspected of crimes against white society. On the regional level, the South's Jim Crow laws continued to mandate the formal racial segregation of public facilities, aimed at keeping blacks and whites separate. Meanwhile, the 1920s saw the implementation of strict federal immigration restrictions based on national origin, with the intention of curbing, if not halting, the influx of immigrants from specific countries. Behind much of this policy making lay not only concern for the economic well-being of native-born white Americans but also the then-popular social scientific concept of eugenics, which promoted the notion that society could be strengthened through selective breeding.

Race Riots

During and after World War I, many African Americans were able to take advantage of jobs at factories, railroads, and docks, but they experienced a great deal of discrimination, especially from the poor whites with whom they competed for work. In the South in particular, blacks were subject to extensive discrimination and the terrorist violence of the Ku Klux Klan; this, along with the hope of better economic opportunities, contributed to the Great Migration, in which many blacks left the South for urban areas of the North, such as New York, Detroit, and Chicago. In 1919, social tensions between whites and African Americans led to deadly urban riots in multiple American cities, and incidents of racial unrest continued into the 1920s.

A notable example is the Tulsa, Oklahoma, race riot of 1921. There, rising tensions between blacks and whites culminated in an ill-fated racial incident on May 31, 1921. On that day, a crowd of blacks, including soldiers who fought in World War I, descended on the local jail after learning that a young black man was being held there for allegedly assaulting a white woman and that a white mob was planning to lynch him. Shots exchanged between black and white mobs exploded into violence across the city, with extensive burning and looting, especially of Tulsa's prosperous and predominantly black Greenwood neighborhood. By the time order was restored by four companies of the Oklahoma National Guard, over $1 million worth of property had been destroyed, and thirteen whites and at least twenty-six blacks had been killed, with several hundred wounded; many consider the unofficial death toll to be much higher.

Revival of the Ku Klux Klan

In 1915, the Ku Klux Klan was resurgent, and by the 1920s, it was by far the most powerful white supremacist group in the country. To maintain white social dominance, the Klan used a variety of terrorist tactics, including cross burnings, beatings, and lynchings. The primary targets of terrorist violence by the Klan remained African Americans, but the 1920s incarnation of the group also targeted immigrants,

Catholics, communists, and other minorities. By the middle of the decade, the Klan had, by some estimates, around 3 million members and had strengthened its presence in the South. Most noteworthy, however, was that the organization had expanded significantly in states outside the South, including Oklahoma, Oregon, Indiana, and Colorado. From Indianapolis, Indiana, the Klan published their newsweekly, the *Fiery Cross*, whose readers were told that darkness and dark-skinned people signified sin and that all nonwhite people, including southern and eastern European immigrants, should leave the country.

The people who swelled the ranks of the Klan in the 1920s represented a wide cross section of white America. Under the banner of "100 percent Americanism," the Klan was able to recruit laborers, businesspeople, judges, social workers, and physicians. The Klan marketed itself as a civic organization whose members upheld traditional American values, which they believed were being threatened by immigrant culture and economic competition from immigrants and blacks who were asserting themselves in the postwar era. Women could join the Klan's women's auxiliaries, where they advocated for social policies that blended racism and political Progressivism: They advocated for women's rights, child welfare measures, public education, good citizenship, morality, temperance, and Protestant fundamentalism. Through vigilantism and political mobilization of the white community, the Klan was able to attack African Americans, Jews, Catholics, feminists, and communists.

Discrimination Against Immigrants

Immigrants from southern and eastern Europe, as well as the Irish, did not suffer the same level of discrimination as blacks, but the discrimination directed at them was racialized in that they were seen by many whites as racially inferior. The Irish, for example, were depicted as brutish, apelike creatures, and many immigrant groups were thought to be more likely to be involved in crime. Discrimination led to the enactment of legislation intended to reduce the numbers of immigrants entering the United States, and in some cases, effectively prevented entire nationalities—especially Asians—from entering the country. Attempts to limit immigration had been made before the 1920s, but during that decade, organizations such as the Klan and legislators

---

Tulsa Race Riot

The race riot in Tulsa, Oklahoma, of May 31–June 1, 1921, known as "the night Tulsa died," stands as one of the more disgraceful episodes in American history. The riot was sparked by a rumor that a black man had sexually assaulted a white woman in an elevator. The story was picked up and sensationalized by a city newspaper, and events quickly spiraled out of control as angry mobs gathered outside the courthouse. On the night of May 31 and continuing until noon the following day, gangs of white citizens were seen shooting black citizens in public and torching and vandalizing homes and businesses in Tulsa's predominantly black Greenwood district. Roughly thirty-five blocks in Greenwood, including more than twelve hundred homes and numerous businesses, were destroyed by fire, and some ten thousand people were left homeless. According to an American Red Cross investigation, the number of deaths was at least three hundred, and some investigators place the number much higher, perhaps in the thousands. Suspicions remain that many of those killed in the rioting were buried in mass graves.

---

sympathetic to anti-immigration sentiments were able to get particularly harsh legislations passed that cut the flow of immigration to a trickle.

The Immigration Act of 1921, known as the Emergency Quota Act, established the first immigration quotas in U.S. history. Under the act, the number of immigrants permitted to enter the United States from a given country each year was limited to a percentage of the number of residents from that country already living in the United States in 1910. Under pressure from anti-immigration activists, Congress tightened these restrictions further in the Immigration Act of 1924, which both lowered the quota percentage and pushed the baseline for measurement back to 1890. In addition, the 1924 law banned immigration from most Asian countries entirely. These laws slashed the overall rate of immigration to the United States, drastically reducing in particular the numbers entering from eastern and southern Europe and Asia.

Immigrants were seen as threatening to the social

and biological fabric of the country and as morally and physically inferior to Americans of northern and western European origin. Of the various immigrant groups, Italians were arguably singled out for discrimination. Many white Americans viewed Italians as particularly prone to criminality, and there was a widespread belief that most Italians were involved in one way or another with criminal organizations like the Mafia.

The most famous example of what some regard as prejudice and discrimination directed against Italians in the 1920s is the case of Sacco and Vanzetti. In 1920, two Italian immigrants, Nicola Sacco and Bartolemeo Vanzetti, were convicted of robbery and murder outside Boston, Massachusetts. In addition to being immigrants, both were anarchists, adhering to a political ideology widely associated with violence and nefarious foreign influence. Despite a series of appeals and widespread allegations that their trials were unfair, Sacco and Vanzetti were executed in 1927. Whether they were truly guilty of their crimes is still a matter of dispute, but their radical beliefs and Italian background are seen by many as ensuring that Sacco and Vanzetti would not receive a fair trial.

Anti-Semitism, or anti-Jewish prejudice, was also common in the 1920s, espoused by groups like the Ku Klux Klan and prominent individuals such as noted industrialist Henry Ford. Through his Michigan publication the *Dearborn Independent*, Ford oversaw an anti-Semitic program that lasted from 1920 to 1927. The *Independent* published numerous stories propagating the racist belief in a global Jewish conspiracy to take over the world by controlling international banking and finance. Though not everyone subscribed to such extreme views, anti-Semitism was prevalent enough that Jews were often excluded from various areas of American social life, including clubs, resorts, neighborhoods, schools, and even certain professions. Elite educational institutions such as Harvard University and Columbia University had policies that limited the number of Jews that could be admitted. Medical and law schools throughout the country established quotas of their own for the number of Jews that could be admitted in any given year.

Eugenics

Much of the discrimination directed at blacks, immigrants, and other minorities was supported by the eugenics movement, which had many educated followers in the 1920s. Eugenicists believed that the way to improve society was to encourage the reproduction of people with socially desirable traits and discourage the reproduction of those with undesirable traits. Though seen by many at the time as a socially progressive viewpoint, there was little to distinguish eugenics from scientific racism, as white Anglo-Saxon Protestants in general were seen to typify the category of "socially desirable" in terms of mental and physical ability and basic disposition. Among those typically seen to possess socially undesirable traits—such as lack of intelligence or a perceived inherent tendency toward criminality—were darker-skinned peoples, as well as people with mental or physical disabilities. Eugenicists argued that if the genetically "fit" interbred with these sorts of people, American society as a whole would be weakened over time. Thus, the eugenic viewpoint discouraged intermarriage between whites and nonwhites and favored policies such as sexual sterilization for people with disabilities, either real or perceived, and those seen as immoral. Eugenicists successfully lobbied for laws implementing compulsory sterilization programs for the "unfit" in several states as well as parts of Canada. Some of the eugenic polices of the 1920s remained in place for decades.

Impact

To cope with some of the adverse effects of racial discrimination, many of the affected groups established organizations that advocated on their behalf or provided social services to their members. Immigrants, for example, established parallel institutions such as schools, newspapers, and insurance companies run by and for people of the same national or ethnic background. They also formed unions that fought to advocate on their behalf in the labor market. Blacks created civil rights organizations such as the National Association for the Advancement of Colored People (NAACP) that sought to instill a sense of positive racial identity among blacks as well as combat discrimination through legal and political means. However, many of these groups would have to wait decades to see their efforts at social change bear fruit.

O. Nicholas Robertson

Further Reading

Blee, Kathleen M. *Women of the Klan: Racism and Gender in the 1920s.* 2d ed. Berkeley: University of California Press, 2009. Explores the rise of the second Ku Klux Klan in the 1920s, especially the inclusion of women in a previously all-male organization.

Goldberg, David Joseph. *Discontented America: The United States in the 1920s.* Baltimore: Johns Hopkins University Press, 1999. Provides an overview of the 1920s and includes significant discussion about racial discrimination during the decade.

King, Desmond S. *Making Americans: Immigration, Race, and the Origins of the Diverse Democracy.* Cambridge, Mass.: Harvard University Press, 2002. An analysis of U.S. immigration policy in the twentieth century, with a focus on the legislative debates of the 1920s and the role of eugenics.

Lombardo, Paul A. *Three Generations, No Imbeciles: Eugenics, the Supreme Court, and* Buck v. Bell. Baltimore: Johns Hopkins University Press, 2010. An examination of one of the most important Supreme Court cases pertaining to eugenics and compulsory sterilization laws.

See also: African Americans; Anti-Semitism; Asian Americans; *Buck v. Bell;* Civil rights and liberties; Eugenics movement; Immigration Act of 1924; Ku Klux Klan; Lynching; Sacco and Vanzetti case

Radio

In the 1920s, radio provided a new means of communication that could reach people throughout the United States more quickly than any other medium. The release of wireless technology from government control and the development of new technological and business systems transformed the medium into a nationwide pastime. By the end of the decade, nearly fourteen million households owned a radio, and more than six hundred licensed stations broadcast information and entertainment.

During World War I, the United States government had assumed control over all radio production and broadcast channels, as well as all patents owned by radio equipment manufacturers, in order to facilitate military communications. With the end of hostilities, the government no longer had a justifiable need to control the industry but was hesitant to return control to any foreign-owned companies. Consequently, the Radio Corporation of America (RCA) was established on October 17, 1919, to hold all seized patents. With national control ensured, major blocks of stock in RCA were divided among industry competitors American Telephone & Telegraph (AT&T), General Electric (GE), Western Electric Company, and the Westinghouse Electric and Manufacturing Company. On March 1, 1920, the U.S. Navy officially released all stations from government control, and a number of amateur stations began broadcasting.

Industry Growth

Frank Conrad, a Westinghouse engineer who made regular amateur broadcasts from his garage in Pittsburgh, had garnered considerable public attention, and on October 27, 1920, Westinghouse obtained the first public broadcast license from the Department of Commerce to support Conrad's broadcasts. Days later, Conrad would make history with an experimental broadcast that focused on presidential election results and announced the landslide victory of Republican candidate Warren G. Harding over his Democratic opponent, James M. Cox, long before the news reached print. Still largely perceived as a special-interest hobby with cumbersome equipment, the industry was initially slow to grow, even as companies developed new patents and broadcasters explored content.

By the end of 1921, multiple stations were broadcasting market and weather reports, music, concerts, lectures, and sporting events. Interest boomed over the first half of 1922 as the Department of Commerce issued more than two hundred public broadcast licenses. With no restrictions on ownership, nearly four hundred department stores, electric companies, colleges, religious institutions, corporations, newspapers, and local and state governments were licensed to broadcast by the end of the year.

As the commercial viability and potential for profitability of radio became clear, conflicts followed. Agreements made in 1920 and 1921 that pooled patents and assigned various rights among the major corporations proved unworkable as corporations declared an intercompany patent war to control manufacturing and distribution of equipment. RCA, for instance, refused to sell transmitting tubes to competitors, and AT&T attempted to levy licensing fees against stations using AT&T equipment. Federal Trade Commission monopoly investigations in 1923 ultimately led to arbitration and reinstatement of cross-licensing agreements. In 1922, the American Society for Composers, Authors, and Publishers initiated legal action against stations that broadcast

> ### Amos 'n' Andy
>
> At ten o'clock on the evening of March 19, 1928, the radio station WMAQ, broadcasting from its studio in Chicago's Merchandise Mart, aired the first episode of the *Amos 'n' Andy* comedy series, primarily for Chicago-area listeners but also for a number of smaller stations elsewhere by means of recordings. The show immediately proved popular and was quickly bought by the National Broadcasting Company's (NBC) Blue Network. NBC began broadcasting the show nationwide beginning on August 19, 1929. At the height of its popularity in the early 1930s, the daily broadcast claimed an audience of over forty million listeners.

music without paying licensing fees. A small group of broadcasters formed the National Association of Broadcasters in 1922 to resist but would soon enter into settlement negotiations, establishing a new system of fees.

The brokered peace refocused attention on the creation of networks. The broadcast of political conventions and campaigns across chains of stations had proved networking was viable. Further, AT&T station WEAF in New York had employed the mutually beneficial concept of corporate sponsorship, despite a governmental ban on direct advertising, to develop quality programming to share with other stations. Late in 1926, RCA established the National Broadcasting Corporation (NBC) with backing from GE and Westinghouse to capitalize on these concepts. Under the supervision of managers such as David Sarnoff, NBC endeavored to produce and distribute quality programming across affiliated stations. In 1927, NBC divided programming into two networks: the NBC Red Network, with established sponsored programming, and the NBC Blue Network, with less expensive and experimental programming. NBC dominance of the airwaves resulted in the formation of its primary competitor, the Columbia Broadcasting System (CBS), originally the United Independent Broadcasters, in 1927.

Simplification of receiving equipment provided ready-to-use products for the average citizen, and ownership consequently grew at an astonishing rate. Sales of radio equipment rose from $60 million in 1922 to nearly $900 million by 1929, when hundreds of thousands of radios were being produced annually and more than ten million households owned a radio set.

Programming

Music programs proved extremely popular with radio audiences, and stations introduced the nation to a variety of performers and genres. The NBC Red Network distributed the *Music Appreciation Hour*, hosted by conductor Walter Damrosch, which broadcast works from the classical canon along with commentary. In addition to broadcasting the program during school hours, NBC provided textbooks and worksheets to teachers to further enhance acculturation. *The Grand Ole Opry*, also carried by the NBC Red Network, began as a one-hour program hosted by George D. "Judge" Hay. In contrast to Damrosch's program, the *Grand Ole Opry* featured performances of country music and would become one of the longest-running music programs in the United States. Musical programming also included weekly broadcasts from the famed Cotton Club in Harlem that featured jazz performances by such talented musicians as pianist and bandleader Duke Ellington. Despite the restriction of direct advertisements, sponsors' names often appeared in the program titles. For instance, one such program on New York's WEAF was *The Ipana Troubadors*, a Latin music program sponsored by Ipana toothpaste. Other similarly named programs included the *Armstrong Quakers Orchestra*, *Champion Sparkers*, and the *Lucky Strike Dance Orchestra*.

Early sports programs often consisted of a simple reading of baseball scores from local newspapers. Pioneer station KDKA in Pittsburgh, however, began providing sporadic experiments in sports broadcasting, beginning with a noteworthy broadcast of the Johnny Dundee and Johnny Ray boxing match at the Motor Square Garden by local sportswriter Florent Gibson on April 11, 1921. The Jack Dempsey and Georges Carpentier heavyweight bout in July 1921 was described over the phone, transcribed, and read over the airwaves to a wide audience. KDKA subsequently broadcast the first baseball game, during which the Pittsburgh Pirates beat the Philadelphia Phillies, and first college football game, during which the University of Pittsburgh beat West Virginia University, in August and October of 1921, respectively, with announcer Harold W. Arlin offering play-by-play commentary. WJZ in Newark, New Jersey, followed suit and became the first station to broadcast the Major League Baseball World Series in 1921. Sportswriter Sandy Hunt attended the series between the New York Giants and New York Yankees and announced the game over the phone to Tommy Cowan, who re-created the game for listeners in the broadcast studio. By 1927, both the CBS and NBC networks broadcast the World Series live through network affiliates across the country. By the end of the decade, announcers such as Graham McNamee and Edward Britt "Ted" Husing had distinguished themselves as sportscasters, and regular broadcasts of sports events included baseball, boxing, auto racing, and football.

In 1923, stations began featuring original dramatic content, such as Fred Smith's *When Love Wakens*. Two comedy actors from early radio, Freeman Gosden and Charles Correll, broke ground with *Sam 'n' Henry*, a situation comedy that ran from 1926 to 1928 and centered on two African American characters inspired by minstrel stereotypes. In 1928, Gosden and Correll launched a similar program, the highly influential and retrospectively controversial series *Amos 'n' Andy*. The franchise would attract millions of listeners at its peak and spawn a film, cartoon appearances, and a television program before its end in 1960.

On February 8, 1922, President Harding installed the first radio in the White House, and on June 14, he spoke over the radio from a dedication service honoring Francis Scott Key, the poet who penned the American national anthem. On February 22, 1924, President Calvin Coolidge delivered the first White House address over the radio, and later that year the national conventions for the Republican and Democratic Parties were broadcast to the nation. Coolidge listened to a signal emanating from a radio as he received the Republican nomination at the convention. By the 1928 presidential election, both Republican and Democratic budgets included funding for radio time, and presidential candidates Herbert Hoover and Al Smith turned to the microphone to earn votes. During his presidency, Hoover would make about eighty broadcasts from the White House to a troubled nation.

Federal Regulation

As radio stations multiplied, it became apparent that the rules established by the Radio Act of 1912, which had required federal licensing of operators, were inadequate to address myriad challenges presented by the growing medium. For instance, when Hoover, then secretary of commerce, rejected the Intercity Radio Company's application for license renewal in 1921 over concerns about wavelength interference, the company successfully sued to overturn his decision.

Hoover led a series of four radio conferences between 1922 and 1925 to establish control through a cooperative blueprint for growth. Conference attendees, consisting of government officials, station owners, and corporate leaders, discussed issues ranging from frequency and signal strength to programming content and station ownership. The conferences mandated more control for the Department of Commerce; established Class A, B, and C station designations; provided guidelines for frequencies and signal strength to prevent interference; encouraged networking; formed regional advisory committees; and called for self-governance of content to avoid government censorship. Such recommendations eventually led to the passage of the Radio Act of 1927 and formation of the Federal Radio Commission. The act divided the country into five regions, with equal allocation of licenses, station power, and operating hours. Each region was to be represented by a commissioner, who had jurisdiction to grant or deny licenses and assign frequencies.

Impact

Radio served to homogenize American culture in the 1920s by providing a practical means of connecting citizens to a common experience, nationalizing entertainment, and transforming politics. The institutions established during the decade, including the National Association of Broadcasters, the NBC and CBS radio networks, and the Federal Radio Commission, would continue to shape the industry throughout the following decades.

Gary Galván

Further Reading

Benjamin, Louise. *Freedom of the Air and the Public Interest: First Amendment Rights in Broadcasting to 1935*. Carbondale: Southern Illinois University Press, 2006. Provides an examination of the fine line between freedom of speech and censorship in the infancy of the radio industry.

Cox, Jim. *American Radio Networks: A History*. Jefferson, N.C.: McFarland, 2009. Recounts the formation, originators, outlets, history, and programming of major radio networks across the nation.

Craig, Douglas B. *Fireside Politics: Radio and Political Culture in the United States, 1920–1940.* Baltimore: Johns Hopkins University Press, 2006. Addresses the change in American politics propagated by the development of radio.

Douglas, George H. *The Early Days of Radio Broadcasting.* Jefferson, N.C.: McFarland, 2002. Explores the rapid development of radio from infancy to its venture into politics, sports, and entertainment.

Slotten, Hugh Richard. *Radio and Television Regulation: Broadcast Technology in the United States, 1920–1960.* Baltimore: Johns Hopkins University Press, 2000. Discusses the forty years that guided the complex relationship between broadcasters and legislators in the burgeoning electronic media.

See also: Federal Radio Commission (FRC); Hoover, Herbert; National Broadcasting Company (NBC); Radio Act of 1927; Radio Corporation of America (RCA); Sarnoff, David

■ Radio Act of 1927

The Law: Federal legislation establishing the Federal Radio Commission (FRC) and regulating the use of airwaves for radio broadcasting
Date: Enacted on February 23, 1927

The Radio Act of 1927 authorized government control over radio broadcasting through the establishment of the Federal Radio Commission (FRC), a body of five commissioners each charged with regulating one of five geographically determined radio zones. The primary objective of the Radio Act of 1927 was to eliminate signal interference and restore order to the airwaves by establishing requirements for broadcasters regarding licensing procedures, frequency allocations, and public service obligations.

Passed after the fourth in a series of radio conferences convened by Secretary of Commerce Herbert Hoover, the Radio Act of 1927 superseded the Radio Act of 1912, which required radio operators to have licenses. The earlier law had considered point-to-point communications only, such as those from ship to shore, and its creators had not anticipated radio broadcasting as a mass medium. The new act was a direct response to the rapid development of radio broadcasting stations by amateurs as well as commercial and noncommercial entities. With its passage, the government and large commercial operators such as the Radio Corporation of America (RCA) sought to eliminate the resultant excessive signal interference to ensure the profitability and continuing cultural impact of the new medium.

Provisions of the Law

Under the auspices of the Radio Act of 1927, the FRC was created as a temporary body responsible for evaluating license applications and restoring order to the airwaves, a responsibility previously charged to Secretary of Commerce Herbert Hoover. Each of the five FRC members was appointed by the president to oversee one of five specific radio zones covering the United States.

The majority of the regulations contained within the Radio Act of 1927 established procedures for the granting and revocation of licenses. Those applying for a license had to prove that they were citizens of the United States, of upstanding character, and financially qualified. Applicants also had to specify the frequencies and time of day during which they wished to operate, as well as the general purpose of the station. Licenses would not be granted to any foreign government or its representative or to any company whose stock was more than 20 percent owned or controlled by a foreign entity. License revocation could occur if any single broadcaster attempted to monopolize the airwaves.

The Radio Act of 1927 contained few regulations related to content. Self-regulation was preferred by the large commercial broadcasters, such as RCA and American Telephone & Telegraph (AT&T), and encouraged by the government. Content-specific regulations were limited to an equal-time rule, which required broadcasters to offer equal time to any political candidate running for public office who wished to respond to a candidate who was already afforded airtime. Broadcasters were not required to give any candidates airtime, however, as this would be a violation of their First Amendment rights. The law also stipulated that broadcasters could not interfere with the free speech rights of others and could not censor material, though the use of obscene, indecent, or profane language over the airwaves was prohibited.

The Public Interest

Although content-specific regulations were few, the

Radio Act of 1927 contained one of the most significant mandates related to the general mission of telecommunications industries in the United States. Borrowing a phrase from public utility law, the Radio Act of 1927 stipulated that all broadcast licensees were required to serve the "public interest, convenience, or necessity." License renewal was based upon how well licensees fulfilled this mandate.

The interpretation of the public interest was, and continues to be, a source of great debate. The trusteeship and marketplace models of broadcasting best exemplify how the public interest has been defined through history. The trusteeship model identifies the airwaves as a public resource, and as such, broadcasters must provide audiences with programming that is entertaining as well as educational and informative. The marketplace model interprets the public interest as being determined by the public's desire for certain programs over others. In this model, market demand is considered the best arbiter of the public interest.

The public service mandate contained within the Radio Act of 1927 supported aspects of both models, as it privileged the development of the largest commercial broadcasters. Such stations were able to provide the public with the type of high-quality, diverse programming that smaller stations could not because of their financial, geographical, or philosophical positions.

Impact

Plagued by staff turnover and debate in Congress regarding the public interest criterion, the FRC was superseded by the permanent Federal Communications Commission (FCC), established through the Communications Act of 1934. The Radio Act of 1927 in effect created the regulatory environment that would enable the nation's largest commercial broadcasting networks—the National Broadcasting Company (NBC), Columbia Broadcasting System (CBS), and later American Broadcasting Company (ABC)—to consolidate their power and control of the radio and then television industries through the late 1970s. This approach inhibited the growth of small, independent, and noncommercial stations. In the early twenty-first century, debates about new media technologies continue to be influenced by the policies set forth in this act.

Sharon Zechowski

Further Reading

Aufderheide, Patricia. *Communications Policy and the Public Interest.* New York: Guilford Press, 1999. Evaluates the Telecommunications Act of 1996 within the context of the public interest mandate that became law in the Radio Act of 1927.

Barnouw, Eric. *A History of Broadcasting in the United States.* 3 vols. New York: Oxford University Press, 1968. Chronicles the development of the American system of commercial broadcasting.

Douglas, Susan J. *Inventing American Broadcasting, 1899–1922.* Baltimore: Johns Hopkins University Press, 1989. A cultural history of radio's evolution as a mass medium.

McChesney, Robert. *Telecommunications, Mass Media, and Democracy: The Battle for Control of U.S. Broadcasting, 1928–1935.* New York: Oxford University Press, 1995. A revisionist history of American broadcasting, highlighting the roles of government, industry, and reformers.

Slotten, Hugh Richard. *Radio's Hidden Voice: The Origins of Public Broadcasting in the United States.* Urbana: University of Illinois Press, 2009. A history of the public service tradition as implemented by noncommercial providers.

See also: Federal Radio Commission (FRC); Hoover, Herbert; National Broadcasting Company (NBC); Radio; Radio Corporation of America (RCA)

■ Radio Corporation of America (RCA)

Identification: Electronics and communications company
Date: Established on October 17, 1919

In the 1920s, the Radio Corporation of America (RCA) played a leading role in the development of the wireless communication and radio broadcasting industries in the United States. In addition to working to develop existing technologies such as radio transmitters and create new technologies, RCA facilitated rapid development in the fields of communications and popular media through its establishment of the National Broadcasting Company (NBC).

After the end of World War I, which had highlighted the importance of radio communications technology in warfare, the U.S. government sought to establish an American-owned company to administer and further develop the existing technology in the country. In late 1919, the Radio Corporation of America (RCA) was organized, absorbing the Marconi Wireless Telegraph Company of America, formerly owned by a British parent company; the rights to radio patents registered by manufacturers such as the General Electric Company; and radio equipment and facilities used by the U.S. military during the war.

During the 1920s, RCA continued to develop radio transmission technology, working in areas such as international communication and home radio. The company also moved into radio broadcasting, establishing the National Broadcasting Company (NBC) in 1926. NBC operated several networks, including the Blue Network and the Red Network, which could be heard throughout the United States. These networks broadcasted sports games such as the 1927 Rose Bowl and music such as jazz bandleader Duke Ellington's performances at the Cotton Club in Harlem, as well as news reports.

Until 1929, RCA primarily sold radios and records manufactured by related companies such as General Electric. That year, expanding the manufacturing and developmental capabilities of the company, RCA acquired the Victor Talking Machine Company, which had manufactured phonographs such as the Victrola and phonograph records for more than two decades. Renaming the division RCA Victor, RCA began manufacturing its own products for sale.

Impact

Through the technology produced and radio broadcasting system put in place during the 1920s, the Radio Corporation of America brought music, sports, and news to radios across the United States, allowing people throughout the country to share a collective listening experience. In later decades, RCA played a major role in the development of television, video and music recording, and computing, continuing its work in the field of mass communication.

C. Alton Hassell

Further Reading

Balk, Alfred. *The Rise of Radio: From Marconi Through the Golden Age.* Jefferson, N.C.: McFarland, 2006.

Sobel, Robert. *RCA.* New York: Stein & Day, 1986.

Wenaas, Eric P. *Radiola: The Golden Age of RCA, 1919–1929.* Chandler, Ariz.: Sonoran, 2007.

See also: Federal Radio Commission (FRC); National Broadcasting Company (NBC); Radio; Radio Act of 1927; Sarnoff, David; Zworykin, Vladimir

Railroads

For American railroads, the 1920s were a decade of comparatively normal operations and productivity sandwiched between two extremes: the expanded traffic demands of the World War I years and the contracting economic environment of the Great Depression. There were some advances in technology and operating efficiencies on the railroads, but there was also increasing competition from other forms of transportation. Some railroad lines were facing severe financial problems well before the beginning of the Great Depression.

American railroads had done tremendous service moving goods and people during the World War I years. In the Army Appropriations Act of 1916, Congress had authorized a government takeover of the railroads in times of national emergency, and in December 1917, President Woodrow Wilson had ordered that all American railroads be brought under government control. The United States Railroad Administration (USRA) was created to oversee the operations of the railroads, although the ownership and actual management of the lines remained in private hands. The government exercised unprecedented power in forcing cooperation on the American railroads and the system generally functioned well to meet the needs of war production and transportation.

Return to Private Control

At the end of the war, there were some in the government who wanted to maintain federal control of the American railroad system. William G. McAdoo, who left his position as director general of the railroads and head of the USRA when the armistice was signed in November 1918, recommended that the government continue to operate the railroads for five more years. However, the mood of Congress and the country seemed to demand a return to private control as soon as possible. The Esch-Cummins Act, also called the Transportation Act of 1920, was passed in February of that year and returned control of the railroads to their corporate owners as of March 1, 1920.

The corporate managers of the American railroads were generally unsatisfied with conditions as they took back direct control of their lines. Heavy wartime traffic had worn out tracks and equipment, while regulated rates had kept the railroads' profits low. Railroad labor had received significant wage increases during the war and overall operating costs remained high, reaching a record 94 percent of total revenue in 1920. With the end of war production, railroad traffic had begun to decline almost immediately.

Attempts at Consolidation
Iowa Republican senator Albert Cummins, a cosponsor of the Esch-Cummins Act, had wanted a more radical redesign of the American railroad system after the war years. His original bill would have mandated the consolidation of all U.S. railroads into a fixed number of lines roughly equal in size and earnings potential. Ultimately, the Esch-Cummins Act did not go this far: It authorized the Interstate Commerce Commission (ICC) to draw up a proposal to consolidate the railroads into about twenty lines, with the question of formal adoption to be decided later (a plan was drawn up by the end of the decade, but later dropped). The ICC was also empowered to assess the value of railroad property and equipment, set both minimum and maximum shipping rates, oversee the regulation of operations and services, and approve the issue of new railroad securities. In addition, the bill created the Railroad Labor Board to deal with relations between the workers and the railroad companies.

There was relatively little consolidation of lines in the United States during the 1920s, but in Canada, several lines that were either operated by the government or had come under government control because of bankruptcy were merged into the Canadian National Railway. This process, which began in 1917 and was completed by 1925, left the government-owned Canadian National and the privately held Canadian Pacific Railway as the only major railroads in Canada, although several regional short lines still continued to operate.

Railroad Labor
In general, the 1920s were not kind to organized labor, with railroad workers no exception. U.S. trade union membership in all industries had peaked at about 5 million workers in 1920, partly as a result of World War I, but declined to about 3.5 million by 1929. An antiworker attitude among many business leaders and disunity among labor organizations contributed to this decline, as did the general prosperity of the early 1920s, which led many workers to believe they had no need for union protection. On the railroads, a downturn in business after the end of World War I quickly turned a labor shortage into a labor surplus, and some railroad managers saw an opportunity to break the unions and gain more control over labor conditions.

The Progressive Era had inspired widespread interest in efficiency. In industry, the ideas of Frederick Winslow Taylor, author of *The Principles of Scientific Management* (1911), influenced many business leaders to seek greater productivity from their workers. Many of Taylor's principles were not directly applicable to operating crews in the railroad industry, however; efficiency in train operation was more a function of technology, train length, and other factors apart from worker productivity. Nonetheless, in the maintenance shops, railroads began to move toward paying the shopmen (maintenance workers) on a piecework basis rather than an hourly wage. Some railroads, notably the Pennsylvania and the Erie Railroads, also began to contract maintenance to outside businesses.

In June 1922, the Railroad Labor Board authorized a seven-cent reduction in shopworkers' hourly wages. This, combined with the above factors, led to the Shopmen's Strike of 1922. On July 1, the day the wage reductions went into effect, shopworkers around the country walked off the job. The strike was peaceful and orderly in the beginning, but after the Railroad Labor Board allowed the railroads to hire workers to cross the picket lines and break the strike, increasing hostilities eventually led to violence against the strikebreakers and attacks on the strikers by railroad police and security guards. In addition to attacking strikebreakers, union members occasionally sabotaged railroad equipment. Members of the operating personnel's unions, such as engineers and switchmen, sporadically stopped work in sympathy with the shopmen's strike.

In response to this strike, John Weeks, the secretary of war, declared martial law in Texas at the end of July and sent in federal troops to break the strike. On September 1, President Warren G. Harding's attorney general, Harry Daugherty, obtained an injunction against the strikers that was one of the most far-reaching antilabor decisions ever issued by a federal judge, making even speaking out in support of the strike a crime. Over time, as public support for the strikers waned and the unions ran short of funds to support them, the workers went back to work. Some railroads made minor reforms and allowed returning strikers to retain their seniority, while other lines made virtually no compromises. The strike ended on most lines within a few months, but workers held out longer against some companies; on the Pennsylvania Railroad, for example, strike action continued until 1928.

The Shopmen's Strike of 1922 was the last U.S. railroad strike to involve significant violence. In its wake, Congress revisited the issue of railroad labor law and passed the Railway Labor Act of 1926, which guaranteed the right of railroad workers to organize for collective bargaining and required that both workers and management negotiate in good faith. It also created a Board of Mediation, later the National Mediation Board, that would intervene to try to head off strikes. If this board could not reach a settlement, a Presidential Emergency Board could be assembled as a last resort. After the passage of this act, railway labor matters usually led to a confrontation of lawyers and mediators, rather than gangs of striking workers confronting railroad officials and security forces.

Retrenchment
After the years of heavy traffic during World War I, the railroads entered a long period of decline due to competition from the automobile for passenger traffic and trucks for freight service. In 1920, the number of railroad passengers reached an all-time high, with around 1.27 billion passengers riding 47.4 billion passenger miles on the American rail system. By 1930, total passenger counts had dropped to a little over 700 million, and passenger miles to 26.9 billion. Initially, automobiles were suited primarily for local transportation needs and did not seem to pose a threat to railroad passenger traffic for long-distance travel due to the lack of a nationwide highway system. During and after World War I, however, major highway construction programs added more and more mileage to the nation's roadways. The number of registered automobiles in the United States, which stood at 6.7 million in 1919, would grow to 23 million by 1929, an increase of over 340 percent in just ten years.

Likewise, trucks at first seemed merely to supplement railroad freight service, taking freight from railroad yards and freight houses to local businesses. But improvements in technology allowed the development of larger trucks, and more paved roads led to much short- and intermediate-distance freight traffic being lost to the trucking industry, which was largely unregulated in the early days and operated on streets and highways subsidized by taxation. Because of increasing government regulation, the railroads no longer had as much latitude to raise rates on freight traffic in order to absorb losses on passenger service. In addition to the trucking industry and the private automobile, the railroads were also facing increased competition from barge traffic, as the U.S. Army Corps of Engineers increased its efforts to improve inland water transportation, and from new pipelines that took away much of the traffic in bulk oil and other petroleum products.

The total mileage of the American railroad system had peaked in 1916 at approximately 259,000 miles. By that point, the rail system was overbuilt, with branch lines reaching out to many small communities that would not generate sufficient traffic to sustain the railroad's long-term presence, especially when trucks and automobiles began to compete for the limited traffic. In most years after 1916, more miles of track were being abandoned than built, as the system began to shed excess mileage and concentrate operations on lines that remained viable.

During the 1920s, common railroad stocks slowly began to lose value as their yields failed to keep pace with inflation. Generally, throughout the decade, railroad stocks averaged an annual return in the range of 4 to 7 percent. Even 1929, the year of the stock market crash, saw an average yield of 4.29 percent on railroad stocks.

Advances
Despite the general trend of retrenchment and decline, there were some notable achievements on American railroads during the 1920s. The Shopmen's Strike of 1922, the ongoing shortage of freight cars, and operating problems brought on by an especially severe winter in 1922–1923 all led railway management to explore new ways to increase efficiency. The year 1923 saw the creation of the Northwest Shippers Advisory Board, headquartered in Minneapolis, Minnesota, an organization of shippers and customers of the railroads that coordinated the use of freight cars

to make railroad transportation more productive. Within a few years, there were thirteen such regional boards around the country, which made significant progress in making more efficient use of equipment and avoiding car shortages.

While few new lines were built in the 1920s, major improvements were made on some existing lines, with new facilities being built in many places. In 1925, a new Union Station for passenger service opened in Chicago, the nation's major railroad hub; within a few years, it was handling over fifty thousand passengers per day. In 1929, the Great Northern Railway opened its new Cascade Tunnel at Stevens Pass, traversing the Cascade Mountains in the state of Washington. At 7.8 miles long, it was for many years the longest railroad tunnel in the Western Hemisphere; today, still in operation as part of the BNSF Railway, it remains the longest railroad tunnel in the United States.

Over a seven-year period, from 1923 to 1930, the railroads spent $6.7 billion on capital improvements. This amount included $765 million for new locomotives, $1.7 billion on new freight cars, $398 million on passenger equipment, and $1.3 billion on track and right-of-way improvements. Because of these new purchases, by 1930, more than one-fourth of all locomotives in service were less than eight years old, as were 40 percent of the freight cars.

In 1925, the first diesel-electric locomotive was put into service as a switch engine in the Central Railroad of New Jersey rail yards in New York City, where it was used for assembling and disassembling trains and moving cars around the yard. While steam locomotives would remain the main source of motive power for some time, by the early 1930s, several dozen diesel-electric locomotives were in use around the country. The Canadian National Railroad ran a diesel railcar from Montreal to Vancouver in a record seventy-two hours in November 1925, and in August 1929, it put the first diesel locomotives into passenger service on its Montreal to Toronto trains. In the summer of 1923, the Canadian National began its radio service to provide broadcasts for the entertainment of travelers on their long-distance passenger trains, which other people along the railroad lines could listen to as well. When radio companies began to complain about the competition, it led to the Canadian National radio department being incorporated into the Canadian Broadcasting Corporation in 1936.

While the U.S. government's plans for a major consolidation of the railroad system never came to fruition, in the late 1920s, several major lines expanded by either buying up small regional competitors or purchasing a substantial amount of the stock in neighboring lines. These purchases reached a peak in what became known as the "scramble of 1929." The bull market on Wall Street made it easy to borrow money for such purchases. The New York Central Railroad bought heavily into the Lackawanna Railroad, and the Baltimore and Ohio Railroad increased its holdings of stock in the Reading Railroad. The Pennsylvania Railroad created a holding company, Pennroad, which was owned not by the railroad corporation but by its stockholders. Pennroad made major acquisitions of stock in the Wabash Railroad and the Lehigh Valley Railroad, and eventually bought the Detroit, Toledo and Ironton Railroad line from Henry Ford. Many of the railroads involved in this scramble borrowed money to do so, and when the Great Depression hit, it left these lines overextended on credit at a time when revenues were falling dramatically.

Impact

The 1920s were a tumultuous decade for American railroads. Following the government takeover of the railroads during the war years, the lines were returned to private control in March 1920. The first signs of serious competition from the automobile and the freight trucking industry began to affect revenues, and railroads began to shed excess trackage, while at the same time, considerable sums were spent on improvements to equipment, track and roadbed, and other types of facilities. The Railway Labor Act of 1926 marked a significant milestone for relations between workers and management. However, no measure of farsighted management or wise reinvestment of revenues into improvement of the physical plant could prepare the railroads for the catastrophic decline in business following the onset of the Great Depression in late 1929.

Mark S. Joy

Further Reading

Douglas, George H. *All Aboard! The Railroad in American Life.* New York: Smithmark, 1996. A social history of the impact of the railroads on many aspects of American life.

Goddard, Stephen B. *Getting There: The Epic Struggle Between Road and Rail in the American Century.* New

York: Basic Books, 1994. Includes good information on the 1920s, the decade in which the automobile began to offer significant competition to the railroads for passenger travel and the long-distance freight-trucking industry saw significant growth.

Grant, H. Roger. *Twilight Rails: The Final Era of Railroad Building in the Midwest*. Minneapolis: University of Minnesota Press, 2010. A series of case studies of midwestern lines built in the early twentieth century.

Martin, Albro. *Railroads Triumphant: The Growth, Rejection, and Rebirth of a Vital American Force*. New York: Oxford University Press, 1992. A major study of American railroads from the early days of heady growth, through the era of stifling regulations and increasing competition, and to the rebirth of a more specialized and focused railroad system.

Saunders, Richard, Jr. *Merging Lines: American Railroads, 1900–1970*. DeKalb: Northern Illinois University Press, 2001. A history of the American rail system and the struggle for political and commercial control of the industry.

Schwantes, Carlos A., and James A. Ronda. *The West the Railroads Made*. Seattle: University of Washington Press, 2008. Looks at the image of the American West that the railroads created in order to stimulate travel to the region and addresses some of the efforts to combat automobile competition in the 1920s.

Stover, John F. *American Railroads*. Chicago: University of Chicago Press, 1961. A general overview of the history of the railroads in the United States.

See also: Brotherhood of Sleeping Car Porters; Cascade Tunnel; Labor strikes; Railway Labor Act of 1926; Transportation; Travel

■ Railway Labor Act of 1926

The Law: Federal legislation granting railroad workers the right to organize and bargain collectively

Also known as: Federal Railway Labor Act; RLA

Date: Enacted on May 20, 1926

The Railway Labor Act of 1926 was the first federal collective bargaining statute enacted in the United States. Although the law established mechanisms for resolving most labor disputes in the railroad industry during the late 1920s, not all its provisions were effective.

The Transportation Act of 1920 ended the federal government's World War I operation of the nation's railroads and returned them to private control. However, a nationwide railway strike in 1922 demonstrated the inadequacy of the act's provisions for handling labor disputes. In 1924, President Calvin Coolidge invited railroad management and labor to recommend legislation that would ensure labor peace. Two years later, railroad executives and union representatives agreed upon and presented a draft bill, which was passed by Congress with no substantive changes and signed by President Coolidge.

The Railway Labor Act of 1926 created three mechanisms to promote healthy labor relations. First, it gave labor the right to freely organize unions and for them to bargain collectively with management. Second, the act mandated that unresolved contract disputes be submitted to a Board of Mediation. If mediation failed and the board was unable to convince labor and management to submit to binding arbitration, the act granted the president of the United States authority to create an emergency board to make nonbinding recommendations to resolve disputed issues. Third, the act permitted railroads and unions to create boards of adjustment to arbitrate grievances involving the interpretation or application of contracts generated through collective bargaining.

Impact

The Railway Labor Act was reasonably successful in promoting labor peace during the 1920s. The Board of Mediation was able to resolve most contract disputes and avert all but a few minor railroad strikes. However, the act failed to provide adequate protection for unions' organizing rights, and its mechanism for grievance dispute resolution was ineffective. It did not dissolve company-sponsored unions or penalize their continued existence, nor did it deter railroads from actively interfering with labor's right to organize. Moreover, individual railroads agreed to establish local boards to adjudicate grievances with their company-sponsored unions but frequently opposed the use of a national board, preferred by labor organizations, because it would undermine management's control of grievance settlement. When Congress amended the Railway Labor Act in 1934, it addressed these failures by barring company-sponsored unions and creating the National Railroad Adjustment Board to resolve grievances submitted by either labor or management.

The Railway Labor Act was subsequently amended multiple times and later extended to include the airline industry. Early in the twenty-first century, it continues to serve as the basis for relations in both transportation industries.

William Crawford Green

Further Reading

Aaron, Benjamin, et al. *The Railway Labor Act at Fifty: Collective Bargaining in the Railroad and Airline Industries.* Washington, D.C.: National Mediation Board, 1977.

Wilner, Frank N. ed. *Understanding the Railway Labor Act.* Omaha, Neb.: Simmons-Boardman Books, 2009.

See also: Coolidge, Calvin; Labor strikes; Railroads; Unionism

■ Randolph, A. Philip

Identification: African American labor leader and civil rights activist
Born: April 15, 1889, Crescent City, Florida
Died: May 16, 1979, New York City, New York

Born the son of a minister, A. Philip Randolph was a multitalented man who organized the Brotherhood of Sleeping Car Porters, the first African American–led labor union. He was later instrumental in desegregating the U.S. military and in the Civil Rights movement.

Asa Philip Randolph was an accomplished athlete, actor, and activist who advocated for working people and African Americans through much of the twentieth century. He came to prominence in the 1920s, when he led the first serious effort to unionize railway workers at the Pullman Company.

Randolph had joined the Socialist Party in 1910; with its help, he and fellow Socialist Chandler Owen started to publish the *Messenger* magazine, which campaigned for unionization and racial integration and against lynching and World War I. In 1920 and 1922, he unsuccessfully ran for New York public office as a Socialist. After organizing a union for

A. Philip Randolph. (Getty Images)

elevator operators in 1917 and serving on the National Brotherhood Workers of America's board of directors from 1919 to 1920, Randolph helped launch the Brotherhood of Sleeping Car Porters (BSCP).

On August 25, 1925, hundreds of railroad porters gathered in Harlem to organize a union at the Pullman Company, which had thus far resisted unionization. Randolph was elected president of the new union, partly for his proven leadership ability and partly because, as he was not a Pullman employee, he could not be threatened or coerced. The all-black BSCP adopted the slogan "Fight or Be Slaves."

While the BSCP did not see immediate results, Randolph and the union persevered through the remainder of the decade, the stock market crash, and the Great Depression. The Railway Labor Act of 1926, which had established official channels through which to resolve railway labor disputes, was amended in 1934 to cover porters, and in 1935, Pullman finally began to negotiate with the BSCP. The union signed a collective bargaining agreement with Pullman in 1937.

Impact

In the 1940s, Randolph successfully pressured the government to ban racial discrimination in war industries. In the 1950s, he became the first African American vice president of the American Federation of Labor and Congress of Industrial Organizations (AFL-CIO), and in the 1960s, he helped organize the March on Washington for Jobs and Freedom and lobbied for the Civil Rights Act. Throughout his life, Randolph used his leadership and oratory skills to bring together and influence African Americans suspicious of organized labor, employers resistant to negotiating with workers, labor reluctant to embrace African American unionists, and a government hesitant to change racist policies. He was a leader who crossed lines of class, race, and geography.

Bill Knight

Further Reading

Anderson, Jervis. *A. Philip Randolph: A Biographical Portrait.* Berkeley: University of California Press, 1986.

Kersten, Andrew Edmund. *A. Philip Randolph: A Life in the Vanguard.* Lanham, Md.: Rowman & Littlefield, 2007.

Pfeffer, Paula F. *A. Philip Randolph, Pioneer of the Civil Rights Movement.* Baton Rouge: Louisiana State University Press, 1996.

See also: African Americans; Brotherhood of Sleeping Car Porters; Civil rights and liberties; Du Bois, W. E. B.; Labor strikes; Railroads; Railway Labor Act of 1926; Unionism

■ Rayon stockings

Ease of mobility and sexual expression became key priorities for women during the Roaring Twenties, including in the realm of fashion and style. The transition from plain, opaque cotton stockings to sheer rayon stockings offered the wearer a sexier, more intimate look and provided more freedom of movement.

Prior to the 1920s, American women were not likely to show their feet or legs in public; they usually wore long dresses or skirts with black or white cotton stockings that came to the knee. Corsets and cotton knickers were the mainstays of women's undergarments during the first two decades of the twentieth century.

However, by the 1920s, women's fashion expectations and needs had changed as American society shifted both in terms of common activities and social mores. The popularity of leisure activities such as social dancing and sports grew during this era of economic prosperity, and Americans wanted lighter-weight clothes to facilitate their active lifestyles. Gaining suffrage in 1920 and beginning to drink alcohol outside the home during Prohibition, women became increasingly independent in political and social spheres during this decade.

As a result of these dramatic changes in attitude, demand for shorter, knee-length dresses and skirts increased in the early 1920s, bringing with it changes in the design of women's footwear, undergarments, and hosiery. Cotton was replaced with the lighter materials silk and rayon (then frequently termed "artificial silk") in undergarments and stockings. Intimate apparel made of silk, previously associated with prostitution by some, became sought-after luxury items, and rayon stockings provided a similar look and feel for half the cost. Another part of their appeal was that rayon stockings came in a variety of shades and colors, with beige or tan being the most popular because of their nude look. Even their color names displayed an underlying interest in sensuality and luxury: Champagne, Pearl Blush, French Nude, Moonlight.

Thigh-high sheer rayon stockings held up by garter belts above the knee became the prevailing fashion. Some women began rolling their stockings down to their knees in order to enable them to dance more freely. This became a signature part of the flapper look, considered scandalous by many. Despite this reputation, flappers would apply powder to their knees in a nod to the common belief that exposing bare knees was indecent.

Impact

During a period of dramatic political and social change, women chose to break free from restrictive clothing and began to wear more loose-fitting, comfortable garments. Lightweight, attractive, easy to wash, and affordable, rayon stockings exemplified the shifts in attitude about women's social roles during the 1920s. The popularity of rayon likely encouraged the development of later synthetic fibers, including nylon, polyester, and acrylic, which would become common clothing materials beginning in the 1940s. In fact, nylon supplanted silk and rayon in stocking production to the point where "nylons" became the generic term used for women's hosiery.

Macey M. Freudensprung

Further Reading

Allen, Frederick Lewis. *Only Yesterday: An Informal History of the 1920s.* Reprint. New York: Perennial Classics, 2000.

Blum, Stella, ed. *Everyday Fashions of the Twenties as Pictured in Sears and Other Catalogs.* Mineola, N.Y.: Dover, 1981.

See also: Dances, popular; Fashions and clothing; Flappers

■ Recession of 1920–1921

The Event: Economic downturn characterized by severe deflation
Date: January 1920 to July 1921

Only the second recession to hit the United States following the creation of the Federal Reserve in 1913, the economic downturn of the early 1920s saw the federal government playing a more central role in dealing with the financial crisis. The efforts of the Federal Reserve and, to a lesser extent, the President's Conference on Unemployment set the stage for the federal government to take greater responsibility for dealing with the impact of economic downturns.

Although often characterized as a period of economic growth and prosperity, the 1920s started as they ended: with a recession. Less famous than the 1929 recession, later known as the Great Depression, the recession of 1920–1921 stands out more for its large drop in prices, or deflation, than for its drop in output. As with most recessions, experts generally agree about its impact on employment, output, and prices, but disagree about its causes.

In common usage, a recession is said to have occurred if a country's total output, or real gross domestic product (GDP), has declined for two or more consecutive quarters (six months or more). However, the National Bureau of Economic Research (NBER) uses a more sophisticated definition, identifying a recession as having occurred if there is a "significant decline in economic activity," with economic activity being defined by broad economic measures such as real output, income, and employment.

Using their definition, the NBER has identified the 1920 recession as having begun in January 1920 and ended in July 1921. This means that economic activity reached a peak in January of 1920 and a trough in July of 1921, at which point the economy began to grow again. From its peak, real output has been estimated to have dropped by roughly 3 percent or more, while unemployment increased from 5.2 percent to between 8.7 and 11.7 percent.

What distinguishes the 1920–1921 recession from other severe recessions is its sharp drop in prices. An economic slowdown creates downward pressure on prices as businesses try to reduce their inventories and generate sales in order to employ idle resources. From a high in May 1920, wholesale prices dropped by 45 percent by June 1921, while consumer prices dropped by more than 10 percent. The falling prices hit the agricultural sector particularly hard.

Causes

Recessions are generally caused by a sudden reduction in the demand for output. The trigger for that change in demand is important to know in order to avoid recessions in the future. While it is not a universally accepted theory, many economists name the Federal Reserve as a primary cause of the severity of the 1920–1921 recession. Created in 1913, the Federal Reserve is the central bank of the United States, in which capacity it influences the country's money supply and interest rates. Lowering interest rates makes it cheaper to borrow money, so businesses tend to increase their demand for capital goods such as equipment and machinery, and consumers tend to increase their demand for goods typically purchased on credit, such as new homes. This increase in demand causes the economy to expand. Increasing interest rates—an action normally taken to head off inflation—has the opposite effect of lowering demand, causing the economy to grow more slowly or even to shrink.

Starting in November 1919, in response to postwar inflation, the Federal Reserve began raising the discount rate, which is the interest rate it charges on the money it lends to banks. By June 1920, the discount rate had increased from 4 percent to 7 percent. This in turn resulted in higher interest rates charged to businesses and consumers, thereby causing a reduction in their purchases.

While the Federal Reserve may have played a role in the severity of the recession, its main cause was likely global economic adjustments following the end of World War I. As a result of the disappearance of war-related expenditures, the federal government went from having a deficit to having a surplus, which meant that less money was in the hands of businesses and consumers, leading to reduced demand. At the same time, other factors allowed for an increase in supply or output in the economy, which put further downward pressure on prices. As the economies of other countries rebuilt, this resulted in a decline in U.S. exports, and the demobilization of U.S. troops and rising immigration rates meant an increase in the labor supply. All of these factors created the expectation of lower prices in the future, which further decreased demand and depressed economic activity.

Impact

Although painful in its severity, the 1920–1921 recession did not last very long, and the U.S. economy quickly recovered. By 1922, real output had returned to its prerecession level, and the unemployment rate had also declined. However, this turnaround was not yet evident in September 1921, when President Warren G. Harding's secretary of commerce, Herbert Hoover, convened the President's Conference on Unemployment. This move was a first step toward the government taking on a larger role in mitigating the pain of unemployment that accompanies recessions.

Randall Hannum

Further Reading

Eichengreen, Barry. *Golden Fetters: The Gold Standard and the Great Depression, 1919–1939*. New York: Oxford University Press, 1992. Contains a discussion of the 1920–1921 recession and Federal Reserve policy in the context of the return to the gold standard following World War I.

Friedman, Milton, and Anna J. Schwartz. *A Monetary History of the United States, 1867–1960*. Princeton, N.J.: Princeton University Press, 1963. Presents details of the 1920–1921 recession in the context of a study of the post–Civil War U.S. economy, including the role the Federal Reserve may have played in the crisis.

Garraty, John A. *Unemployment in History: Economic Thought and Public Policy*. New York: Harper & Row, 1978. Provides a brief discussion of the President's Conference on Unemployment and the economic conditions that led to it.

Kindleberger, Charles P., and Robert Aliber. *Manias, Panics, and Crashes: A History of Financial Crises*. 5th ed. Hoboken, N.J.: John Wiley, 2005. Puts the 1920–1921 recession into historical perspective within the context of other economic crises, along with lessons learned.

Knoop, Todd A. *Recessions and Depressions: Understanding Business Cycles*. Santa Barbara, Calif.: Praeger, 2010. An overview of recessions and the factors that lead to them.

See also: Gross national product of the United States; Income and wages; President's Conference on Unemployment (1921); Unemployment

■ Red Scare, The

The Event: A yearlong panic about the possibility of a communist revolution in the United States, resulting in thousands of arrests and hundreds of deportations
Date: April 1919–June 1920
Place: The United States

The Red Scare was symptomatic of the rapid change in national mood during the transitional period following the end of World War I. Americans' obsession with the German threat became an obsession with the threat of radicalism, leading to widespread violence and total disregard of civil liberties.

On January 2, 1920, four thousand Americans were arrested in major cities throughout the nation. By mid-January, the Justice Department had arrested or interrogated over ten thousand people suspected of being communists or communist sympathizers. Media headlines warned of an imminent communist takeover of the United States, while state and local governments passed a plethora of legislation violating basic constitutional rights. By the summer, however, this national hysteria had all but evaporated.

Causes

The United States' participation in World War I greatly magnified issues that had been brewing since the turn of the century. First, there was a long series of strikes by ever-growing labor unions. In all, nearly thirty-six hundred separate strikes took place in 1919. Fear of radicalization of labor was heightened by a major dock strike in Seattle in January 1919, followed by a general strike in February. Federal troops were sent to quell the strike, which was labeled by newspapers as the work of communists and anti-American anarchistic ideas brought in by recent immigrants. In September 1919, a steelworkers' strike crippled the nation's steel production, and during the same month, a strike by the Boston Police Department resulted in widespread looting after the suspension of police functions. By November, 400,000 members of the United Mine Workers were out on strike. Aware that a general strike had caused the fall of the czarist regime in Russia, leading to the execution of the czar and his family, and that American labor unions such as the Industrial Workers of the World (IWW) were urging general strikes, a significant segment of American society feared for the future.

Another factor was the race riots that abounded during the summer of 1919 in urban areas such as Chicago, Philadelphia, Charleston, and Washington, D.C. This time, unlike in the major East St. Louis riot of 1917, African Americans fought back. Again, the Bolshevik movement was blamed for instigating a racial civil war.

A third factor was the emotional excesses caused by wartime propaganda. Preoccupation with the evil "Huns" incited anti-German demonstrations across the United States, culminating in the lynching of a German immigrant in 1918. Even after the war was over, the threat of Germany was still linked with the threat of communism; after all, the German government had financed the Bolsheviks in Russia, helping to bring Communist leader Vladimir Lenin to power, and Karl Marx, the father of communist thought, was himself a German.

The immediate cause of the Red Scare was an anarchist conspiracy centered around May Day, 1919. In late April, thirty mail bombs were sent to prominent politicians, judges, and business executives, including John D. Rockefeller and J. P. Morgan. The mail bombs were intended to arrive on May 1. Of the thirty, only two were actually delivered and only one exploded, injuring the wife and the housekeeper of Georgia senator Thomas Hardwick. In cities such as Boston, New York, and Cleveland, large May Day parades turned violent, largely due to police overreactions.

A second wave of attacks took place in June, when eight fragmentation bombs, each triggered by 20 pounds of dynamite, exploded in several major U.S. cities. The bombings' sole victim was one of the bombers himself, Carlo Valdinoci, who stumbled and was killed in the explosion near the front porch of his intended victim, U.S. attorney general A. Mitchell Palmer. Though all the bombings were tied to a small group of anarchists called the Galleanists, the public made little distinction between anarchists, socialists, communists, and labor organizers.

Palmer Raids

In August 1919, Attorney General Palmer organized a special intelligence unit within the Justice Department to be headed by recent law school graduate J. Edgar Hoover. One of the unit's immediate goals was to construct an intelligence file on tens of thousands of radicals who could potentially be jailed and resident aliens who could be deported. While this was being done, both popular media and the U.S. Senate demanded immediate action.

On November 7, 1919, the second anniversary of Lenin's Bolshevik Revolution, Hoover's federal agents worked in conjunction with local police to seize over three thousand alleged radicals. Targeted in twelve major cities were schools and organizations dedicated to serve the needs of recent immigrants from Russia. Overnight, Palmer became an American hero who had extinguished the fires of communist revolution before they had become an inferno. Following interrogation, beatings, and jailing in makeshift prisons, 249 resident aliens were put on the *Buford*, a dilapidated army transport ship, and shipped to Russia via Finland, guarded by 250 armed soldiers.

For Palmer, the November raid was a rehearsal for a larger raid, organized in secret, to take place six weeks later. Three days before the raid, immigration rules were changed so that aliens did not have to be informed of the charges against them or their right to legal representation. To speed extradition, three thousand letters of arrest were printed, each with a blank space to fill in the name of the arrestee. In defiance of mathematics, those three thousand warrants would be used to arrest between five thousand and ten thousand resident aliens.

The second Palmer raid began on the evening of January 2, 1920. Federal agents working with police seized suspected radicals in the major cities of the East, the Midwest, and the western states of Washington, Oregon, and California. Such suspects included all diners at a foreign restaurant in Detroit and an entire choral society in Philadelphia, as well as amazed onlookers, friends or relatives of those arrested, and many victims of mistaken identity. The only weapons located, after the seizure of thousands of suspects across thirty-three American cities, were three target pistols. In the end, only 556 resident aliens were ever deported.

> **Palmer Raids**
>
> *In a 1920 article, U.S. attorney general A. Mitchell Palmer offered this explanation for his insistence on rooting out "Reds" and deporting them from the United States:*
>
> Behind, and underneath, my own determination to drive from our midst the agents of Bolshevism with increasing vigor and with greater speed, until there are no more of them left among us, so long as I have the responsible duty of that task, I have discovered the hysterical methods of these revolutionary humans with increasing amazement and suspicion. In the confused information that sometimes reaches the people they are compelled to ask questions which involve the reasons for my acts against the "Reds." I have been asked, for instance, to what extent deportation will check radicalism in this country. Why not ask what will become of the United States government if these alien radicals are permitted to carry out the principles of the Communist Party as embodied in its so-called laws, aims, and regulations?
>
> There wouldn't be any such thing left. In place of the United States government we should have the horror and terrorism of bolsheviki tyranny such as is destroying Russia now. Every scrap of radical literature demands the overthrow of our existing government. All of it demands obedience to the instincts of criminal minds—that is, to the lower appetites, material and moral. The whole purpose of communism appears to be a mass formation of the criminals of the world to overthrow the decencies of private life, to usurp property that they have not earned, to disrupt the present order of life regardless of health, sex or religious rights. By a literature that promises the wildest dreams of such low aspirations . . . communism distorts our social law. . . .
>
> The Department of Justice will pursue the attack of these "Reds" upon the Government of the United States with vigilance, and no alien, advocating the overthrow of existing law and order in this country, shall escape arrest and prompt deportation.
>
> It is my belief that while they have stirred discontent in our midst, while they have caused irritating strikes, and while they have infected our social ideas with the disease of their own minds and their unclean morals we can get rid of them! and not until we have done so shall we have removed the menace of Bolshevism for good.
>
> *Source:* A. Mitchell Palmer, "The Case Against the Reds," *Forum* 63 (February, 1920).

The popular media and the public reacted positively to the Palmer raids, as national sentiment at the time was in favor of such strong measures. Thirty-two states made it illegal to display the red flag, and the New York state legislature expelled five assembly members for belonging to the Socialist Party. In Congress, a large number of anti-sedition bills were introduced. In February 1920, attempting to capitalize on his national esteem, Palmer announced his candidacy for the Democratic Party's presidential nomination.

However, the excesses of the Palmer raids also produced a slowly growing negative reaction. Twelve of the nation's leading lawyers, including future Supreme Court justice Felix Frankfurter, denounced the raids as violating four of the ten amendments in the Bill of Rights. To offset criticism, Palmer warned that a communist seizure of power was being planned for May 1, 1920. When the day passed without incident, the national mood began to turn against him, and he failed to secure the Democratic presidential nomination. In June, he was questioned by the House of Representatives for misuse of power; the following January, he appeared before the Senate Judiciary Committee to answer the same charges. By this time, public interest in the Red Scare had faded.

Impact

The Red Scare of 1919–1920 was a brief prelude to the McCarthy-era Red Scare of the 1950s, when the nation would become preoccupied with mostly imagined domestic revolutionary enemies. The first Red Scare ended the career of Attorney General Palmer but launched the forty-eight-year-long career of J. Edgar Hoover, who had organized the logistics of the Palmer raids. The atmosphere of repression and persecution put serious limitations on the growth of the Communist Party in the United States during the 1920s and stifled the future growth of the IWW. It caused trauma for thousands whose civil rights were violated by unwarranted arrest and imprisonment and for the over eight hundred deported to Russia. For millions of recent immigrants, the Red Scare instilled in them the very real fear that their loyalty might be questioned on spurious grounds and they could be punished as enemies of the state.

Irwin Halfond

Further Reading

Ackerman, Kenneth D. *Young J. Edgar: Hoover, the Red Scare, and the Assault on Civil Liberties.* New York: Da Capo Press, 2008. An in-depth study of the extralegal measures employed in the Red Scare raids and the effort to create national hysteria.

McCormick, Charles H. *Seeing Reds: Federal Surveillance of Radicals in the Pittsburgh Mill District, 1917–1921.* Pittsburgh, Pa.: University of Pittsburgh Press, 2003. A scholarly case study of the unfolding of the Red Scare in a major American industrial city.

Murray, Robert K. *Red Scare: A Study in National Hysteria, 1919–1920.* 1955. Reprint. Westport, Conn.: Greenwood Press, 1980. A landmark scholarly study of the event.

Pfannestiel, Todd J. *Rethinking the Red Scare: The Lusk Committee and New York's Crusade Against Radicalism, 1919–1923.* New York: Routledge, 2003. Looks at the expression and the effects of the Red Scare in New York.

Schmidt, Regin. *Red Scare: FBI and the Origins of Anticommunism in the United States.* Copenhagen: Museum Tusculanum Press, 2000. Deals with the 1919–1920 period and the role of the nascent Federal Bureau of Investigation during the crisis.

See also: Civil rights and liberties; Communism; Elections, U.S., of 1920; Hoover, J. Edgar; Palmer raids; Sacco and Vanzetti case; Soviet Union and North America; Unionism

■ Reed, John

Identification: American journalist
Born: October 22, 1887, Portland, Oregon
Died: October 17, 1920, Moscow, Russia

John Reed was a left-wing journalist and activist who helped found the Communist Labor Party of America, which would become the Communist Party USA. Although he died in 1920, his account of the October Revolution, Ten Days That Shook the World, *influenced American leftists throughout the decade.*

John Silas Reed was raised in a wealthy Oregon family and graduated from Harvard before moving to New York City to pursue a career in journalism. Beginning in 1913, Reed worked as a journalist and commentator for the *Masses* newspaper, a significant journal of the Left that attracted radical writers and artists. During this time, Reed became known for his coverage of labor disputes. In addition to writing articles about the plight of the nation's workers, he often actively participated in strikes and demonstrations, forming an association with the International Workers of the World (IWW). He was jailed for his role in one such protest.

In 1917, he traveled to Russia with his wife, journalist Louise Bryant, to cover the revolutions of that year. While there, they witnessed the October Revolution, during which the Bolsheviks assumed control of Petrograd. Returning to the United States, Reed wrote his account of the Bolshevik victory, *Ten Days That Shook theWorld* (1919). The October Revolution prompted an ideological dispute within the Socialist Party of America, leading Reed and a number of his fellow radicals to split from the party in the summer of 1919. This group split as well, and Reed's faction founded the Communist Labor Party of America, which would merge with the Communist Party of America to form the Communist Party USA in the 1920s.

Reed returned to Russia in late 1919 and again in 1920, representing the Communist Labor Party of America at the second congress of the Communist International (Comintern). He died shortly thereafter and was buried with honors in Moscow, at the Kremlin Wall Necropolis.

Impact

Although John Reed died early in the decade, his work continued to influence leftist thought throughout the 1920s and beyond. In the late 1920s and early 1930s, the *New Masses* created chapters of the John Reed Club in various cities, serving as an organization of leftist writers and artists. *Ten Days That Shook the World* remained one of few direct accounts of the

October Revolution, providing insight into the events of the period, and despite political pressure, the Communist Labor Party that Reed helped to found eventually became the enduring Communist Party USA.

Frederick B. Chary

Further Reading

Homberger, Eric. *John Reed*. Manchester, England: Manchester University Press, 1990.

Newsinger, John, ed. *Shaking the World: John Reed's Revolutionary Journalism*. London: Bookmarks, 1998.

Reed, John. *Ten Days That Shook the World*. Reprint. London: Penguin, 2007.

See also: Communism; Debs, Eugene V.; Haywood, Big Bill; Lippmann, Walter; Palmer raids; Red Scare, The; Soviet Union and North America; *Ten Days That Shook the World;* Unionism

■ Refrigerators

The refrigerator became an essential household appliance in the 1920s as advancing technology and widespread access to electricity led to the development, production, and sale of refrigerators for home use. The number of refrigerators produced increased dramatically throughout the decade as companies such as General Electric and General Motors capitalized on the era's widespread prosperity and moved toward more convenient methods of food preparation and storage.

The years after World War I brought a period of economic and technological progress to the United States, resulting in the development and sale of various technologies for home use. Refrigerators entered American homes in increasing numbers throughout the decade as refrigeration techniques became safer and more efficient and the machines themselves became modern in both function and appearance. As electrification spread beyond urban areas, the use of refrigerators became both possible and advantageous.

Development

For much of human history, food was generally cooled by placing it, along with naturally formed ice, in an icebox or a similarly enclosed and insulated space. However, the second half of the nineteenth century brought great technical advances in the development of mechanical refrigeration, in which heat is removed from the area being cooled by one of several kinds of processes. Two systems of powering such refrigerators were perfected, one using natural gas as the energy source to drive the cooling process and the other using electricity; the latter would eventually become the dominant system. In the late nineteenth century, commercial applications of refrigeration flourished in the brewing and ice-making industries and began to develop in the fruit, vegetable, and meat production and storage industries as well.

The biggest change to the refrigeration industry that occurred in the 1920s was the development of household units. Although a few manufacturers had begun to produce refrigerators for the home prior to 1920, most of the technical advancements that made household refrigerators relatively safe and reliable were perfected between the early 1920s and the mid-1930s. Safety and reliability were two of the most important concerns of the industry. Before the 1930s, when the use of chlorofluorocarbons began, many refrigerators used refrigerants that were toxic or flammable. In addition, many early refrigerators were effectively modified iceboxes and prone to leaking such hazardous refrigerants. This was an especially important issue for companies producing refrigerators for home rather than commercial or industrial use, as many Americans were wary of purchasing a potentially dangerous device that might endanger home and family. Also, commercial refrigeration had relied on water-cooling, but this was impractical and unreliable in a domestic setting. Manufacturers of the 1920s sought to ameliorate these problems through the development of sealed compression units, air-cooled systems, and all-in-one designs.

Production and Sale

Producing improved refrigerators was a costly project that required large investments in research and development and in the construction of assembly lines for mass production. Due to these large capital requirements, two of the largest U.S. corporations of the time, General Motors (GM), through its purchase of Frigidaire, and General Electric (GE), played a significant role in the development of household refrigerators. As technological advancements were incorporated into the design of refrigerators, consumer demand began to rise quickly, and the returns on these investments began to emerge.

Refrigerators of the 1920s were expensive, generally costing several hundred dollars, a significant portion of the average annual household income. The cost of repairs and relatively heavy use of electricity incurred further expenses. Nevertheless, production of household refrigerators in the United States rose from five thousand units per year in 1921 to about one million units per year by the end of the decade. General Electric created its "Monitor Top" refrigerator in 1925 and sold fifty thousand units by 1929 and one million units by 1931.

Impact

The household refrigerator emerged as an essential domestic appliance in the 1920s, with the design and sale of domestic refrigerators becoming an important business for such companies as General Electric, Westinghouse, and General Motors. Throughout the decade and afterward, these developments in refrigeration had a significant impact on general nutrition, rates of illnesses caused by eating spoiled food, and consumption patterns for perishable foods.

Carmen James Schifellite

Further Reading

Anderson, Oscar E. *Refrigeration in America: A History of a New Technology and its Impact.* Princeton, N.J.: Princeton University Press, 1953. Traces the history of refrigeration from the 1600s to 1950.

Craig, Lee A., Barry Goodwin, and Thomas Grennes. "The Effect of Mechanical Refrigeration on Nutrition in the United States." *Social Science History* 28, no. 2 (Summer, 2004): 325–336. Estimates the effects of mechanical refrigeration on nutrition and ultimately on the population of the United States.

Donaldson, Barry, and Bernard Nagengast. *Heat and Cold: Mastering the Great Indoors.* Atlanta, Ga.: Ashrae Publications, 1994. Traces the development of heating and cooling from prehistoric times to the 1930s.

Nye, David E. *Electrifying America: Social Meanings of a New Technology, 1880–1940.* Cambridge, Mass.: MIT Press, 1992. Explores the effects of the introduction of electricity and related technology, including refrigerators, into American homes.

Schwartz Cowan, Ruth. "How the Refrigerator Got its Hum." In *The Social Shaping of Technology,* edited by Donald MacKenzie and Judy Wajcman. Milton Keynes: Open University Press, 1985. Discusses the competition between gas-powered and electric-powered refrigeration technologies in the early decades of the twentieth century.

See also: Electrification; Food trends; Frozen foods; Inventions; Science and technology

■ Reid, Wallace

Identification: American silent film actor, screenwriter, and director
Also known as: William Wallace Reid
Born: St. Louis, Missouri, April 15, 1891
Died: January 18, 1923, Los Angeles, California

Wallace Reid was among the most prolific and marketable film stars of the 1910s and early 1920s. His death in 1923, the result of several years of morphine addiction, caused a major scandal in an already-embattled film industry and called new attention to the dangers of narcotics.

Wallace Reid was a prominent actor of the silent film era, appearing in hundreds of films between 1910 and 1922 and writing or directing a number of others. His films ranged from dramatic works such as *Carmen* (1915) and *The Birth of a Nation* (1915) to car-racing films such as *Double Speed* (1920). In 1919, Reid was injured in an accident either while filming or traveling to film *The Valley of the Giants.* Due to his injuries, Reid was prescribed morphine for pain relief. When filming was complete, Reid was rushed into another film production, leaving little time for rest or recovery.

By the start of the 1920s, Reid's screen image of robust health and fitness was a fiction. He completed more than twenty feature-length films between 1920 and 1922, all the while taking daily doses of morphine. Going without the drug debilitated Reid, causing increased pain, weakness, insomnia, and irritability. In 1922, Reid entered a rehabilitation facility for detoxification. Years of drug abuse had weakened his body and immune system, and in mid-January of 1923, Reid died. The Hollywood community blamed narcotics for Reid's death, and his widow, fellow film star Dorothy Davenport, embarked on a national antidrug campaign. Davenport coproduced a melodramatic film about the dangers of opiates,

Wallace Reid. (Hulton Archive/Getty Images)

Human Wreckage (1923), and lectured on the subject throughout the United States.

Impact
Wallace Reid's death was one of several crippling scandals, including the Fatty Arbuckle manslaughter trials and the murder of actor and director William Desmond Taylor, that drew negative attention to Hollywood in the early 1920s. Such scandals played a significant role in convincing the American public of the immorality of the film industry, and this perception led to the foundation of the Motion Pictures Producers and Distributors Association and the development of the Motion Picture Production Code, also known as the Hays Code. Under the code, cinema in the United States would face censorship for several decades.

Michael R. Meyers

Further Reading
Fleming, E. J. *Wallace Reid: The Life and Death of a Hollywood Idol.* Jefferson, N.C.: McFarland, 2007.

Jonnes, Jill. *Hep-Cats, Narcs, and Pipe Dreams: A History of America's Romance with Illegal Drugs.* Baltimore: Johns Hopkins University Press, 1999.

See also: Arbuckle, Fatty; Censorship; Crimes and scandals; Film; Taylor, William Desmond

■ Religion in Canada

Religion in 1920s Canada was marked by ongoing divisions between Protestant and Catholic Canadians, as well as conflicts between conservatives and progressives in Christianity and Judaism. In response to social changes in Canada following the end of World War I, social reform activism and pacifism emerged as major movements in both Protestantism and Catholicism. Due to immigration restrictions, Judaism remained a much smaller religious presence in Canada throughout the decade.

As the 1920s opened, Canada was emerging from its identity as a British colony. The end of World War I in 1919 ushered in a period of dramatic changes in Canadian life, as Canadian cities became more populous and skyscrapers were built in many Canadian cities. Motion pictures, growing telephone networks, and increased air travel began to influence Canadian society in the 1920s. Although most personal travel was still by train, automobiles were becoming more numerous on Canadian roads. Most Canadians lived in cities by the 1920s. A serious economic depression in Canada in 1920 and 1921 started a wave of discontent with previous Conservative administrations and led to the election of Liberal politician William Lyon Mackenzie King as prime minister. Canada's gross national product rose again after 1921 as the nation increased its export sales to the United States rather than Great Britain or Europe.

One of the most important perennial social factors of Canadian life was the division between generally Roman Catholic Canadians of French background and Protestant Canadians of largely English heritage. Canadian politics often involved conflicts over national policies that favored the more numerous English Canadians over French Canadians or English culture and tradition over French influence. This may have been partly to blame for French Canadians' somewhat tepid attitudes toward national participation in World War I. Roman Catholic hierarchy likely encouraged a strong national unity, and

Roman Catholicism may also have been an encouraging refuge for Canadians who felt distinctly in the minority.

The Social Gospel
The combination of a strong rural farming sector and increasing urbanization fed into social strains that could also be traced in the United States. Generally tending toward conservative viewpoints and interested in national policies easing financial strains on agricultural life, the farming sector embraced any number of religious traditions willing to face the harsh realities of northern prairie farming. Canada thus played host to a few Christian sects willing to engage in isolated, arduous agricultural life, such as the Russian Doukhobors, who went to British Columbia, or the Hutterites and Mennonites, who went to the central plains as well as urban centers such as Winnipeg.

In Canadian cities, a resurgent labor movement that attracted many soldiers returning from World War I led to the rise of the social gospel movement in Canada. This was a combination of Christian piety and socialist zeal for reform. In the 1920s, especially after the labor protest known as the General Strike in Winnipeg, there arose various fusions of liberal Protestantism and labor union activism. These fusions resulted in the short-lived Labor Churches, where progressive theorists would preach financial and political reform as a direct expression of conscientious religious devotion. Early in the 1920s, these experiments combining Christian ethics, social criticism, and labor reform were quite popular, and some initiatives had to move from their modest original buildings into local cinemas on Sunday mornings to accommodate high attendance. Significant leaders included clergymen and theologians William Ivens, who was briefly imprisoned for his support of labor activism, and Salem Bland, whose preaching skills helped fuel the movement.

A significant Roman Catholic component of the spirit of social reform was expressed in the influence of Catholic Action, a movement that began among Roman Catholics in Belgium in 1924 but quickly arrived in Quebec. Belgian priest Joseph Cardijn named his movement Jeunesse ouvrière chrétienne (JOC) and encouraged his followers to become actively involved in education and in the encouragement of fellow Catholics in workplaces and schools. This quickly sparked renewed applications of older Catholic social teachings in the new industrial contexts, giving rise to a Catholic version of the social gospel expressed in its own terms.

The entire movement, Catholic and Protestant, began to wane toward the end of the 1920s, however. Some churches began to be suspicious of aggressive labor tactics and responded with a conservative backlash. Another factor in the waning of the Catholic Action movement may have been its successful support of secular social work initiatives on the provincial level. The movement, however, spawned a related youth group that remained active throughout the decade, and its impact on Canadian society can be seen in the vibrant religious life of both Catholic and Protestant movements before World War II.

The horrors of World War I also led to the growth of a pacifist movement among some Canadian churches in the early 1920s. While nonviolence was always an aspect of Quaker and Mennonite Christian piety, the political pacifist movement grew especially among Methodists, and when their influential work, *The Christian and War* (1924), was published, it was heralded as a progressive step for peace, even though it represented a range of opinions on war and Christian military participation. At this time, many churches responded to hopeful steps toward the League of Nations, an international peacekeeping organization that became the immediate precursor to the later United Nations.

Jewish Communities
By 1920, approximately 125,000 Jews were living in Canada. Some eastern European Jewish groups had attempted to form farming colonies in the Canadian prairies, as had Christian groups such as Mennonites. Because few of these Jewish immigrants had limited farming experience, many of these settlements failed. The majority of the Jewish population in the 1920s settled in major cities such as Montreal, Toronto, and Winnipeg. In the early 1920s, the Canadian Jewish Congress (CJC) was formed to assist Jewish groups with immigration and settlement issues in Canada. Despite limitations placed on immigration from non-western European nations in the early twentieth century, the Jewish population in Canada would grow to become the fourth largest in an industrialized nation in the twenty-first century.

Conservative and Liberal Religious Traditions
The decade of the 1920s saw considerable turbulence between progressives and conservatives in various re-

ligious traditions. Progressive liberal religious groups sought change and pushed for the modernization of attitudes and ideas. At the same time, conservatives sought to preserve what they perceived as traditional values, even though some of these values had only recently been recognized as traditional. This conflict affected Canadian Judaism as much as it did Christianity. It is difficult to find similar tensions within Canadian Islam during the early 1920s, however, since Canadian Muslims only developed as a significant population during the second half of the twentieth century, especially in Toronto. Elements of the conservative-progressive conflict even affected debates in indigenous cultures as Amerindians struggled to define their native identities and communities in the growing economic context of a modernizing Canada.

Christianity and Indigenous Religion

Christian missions were active among Canadian indigenous peoples as early as the seventeenth and eighteenth centuries, beginning with early Jesuit missions and continuing with the Anglican Communion's Church Missionary Society. Such missionary work continued throughout the twentieth century and beyond. One notable result of historical Christian missions to indigenous Canadian peoples was the often highly creative synthesis achieved between ancient native customs, ideas, and roles, and the newly adopted Christian faith. In the northern Inuit camps of Ingnertoq and Igloolik, for example, an elder known as Umik initiated a religious movement complete with hymns that he wrote, the centralized distribution of food, and meetings at which he incorporated Christian themes into his teaching. Later, when a Roman Catholic mission was sent to Igloolik, the Inuit living there had already incorporated foundational Christian beliefs into their religion. The 1920s saw many new Anglican missions founded in the north as well, with many mission personnel reporting recent synthetic movements fusing aspects of traditional Inuit practice and orally transmitted traditions of Christianity. The spread of Inuit Christianity was facilitated by the fact that local shamans and tribal leaders often adopted aspects of Christian belief and prayer as a source of increased power and authority, thus inspiring entire villages to follow their lead.

Conservative Movements

Conservative Christian revival movements emerged among European Canadians and especially in Protestant Canada during the early twentieth century. The Canadian Fundamentalist revival movement of the 1920s focused on the work of evangelist Oswald J. Smith. Although initially associated with the Presbyterian Church, Smith had difficulties with Presbyterian educational requirements for leadership and soon found a home with the more conservative and evangelical movement known as the Christian and Missionary Alliance (C&MA), founded in 1887 by Canadian clergyman Albert Benjamin Simpson. Smith's revivalist preaching borrowed heavily from dramatic forms of live stage entertainment, especially as pioneered by his Canadian revivalist predecessors in the late nineteenth century: Hugh Crossley and John Hunter. Smith's preaching emphasized an emotional and personal commitment to Jesus Christ, and it consciously turned away from all forms of biblical analysis that Smith saw as reducing the Bible's authority as the literal, inerrant, and inspired word of God. Smith was also staunchly opposed to the growing influence of Darwinian ideas that many liberal clergymen were trying to reconcile with a more modern form of the Christian faith. Although he initially emphasized faith healing among his revivalist meetings, Smith soon became disillusioned with the faith healing movement spreading rapidly in the United States in the 1920s. He developed a strong emphasis on the pending end of the world and the Second Coming of Jesus, which gave him a sense of urgency in the task of evangelizing. American evangelist Billy Graham considered Smith among the most important evangelical preachers of his time. Smith inaugurated his Cosmopolitan Tabernacle, later renamed the People's Church, in Toronto in the mid-1920s, and it soon became a significant evangelical group in Canada.

Impact

Far more technically sophisticated than liberal Modernist movements, Christian Fundamentalists made full use of the latest technology of the 1920s, such as making religious movies, magazines, radio, stage, and contemporary music. Revivalist Fundamentalism was also important in terms of its financial and institutional creativity. Involved in the founding and financing of organizations and educational institutions, Fundamentalist Christianity continues to have a strong presence in North American society in the twenty-first century.

The 1920s was a decade of difficult transitions for

Canadian religious groups, from differences between conservative and liberal Christianity to social gospel Christian activists giving way to secular reformers. Later, as a result of World War II, which is generally believed to have contributed to the rise of secularism in North America, the major religious concerns and conflicts of the 1920s lost a great deal of salience for many Canadians.

Daniel L. Smith-Christopher

Further Reading

Allen, Richard. *The Social Passion: Religion and Social Reform in Canada, 1914–1928*. Toronto: University of Toronto Press, 1990. Discusses the relations between religious groups and social improvement initiatives in early twentieth century Canada.

Bothwell, Robert. *The Penguin History of Canada*. Toronto: Penguin Canada, 2007. Provides a broad overview of Canadian history, including notes on the religious developments of the early twentieth century.

Choquette, Robert. *Canada's Religions: An Historical Introduction*. Ottawa: University of Ottowa Press, 2004. Examines the relationship between conservative and liberal perspectives in Canada's religious traditions.

Gauvreau, Michael, and Ollivier Hubert, eds. *The Churches and Social Order in Nineteenth and Twentieth Century Canada*. Montreal: McGill-Queens University Press, 2006. Compares Roman Catholicism and Protestantism in Canadian history, noting the impact of society, culture, economics, and politics on each church.

Kee, Kevin B. *Revivalists: Marketing the Gospel in English Canada, 1884–1957*. Montreal: McGill-Queens University Press, 2006. Discusses the contributions of individual evangelists to the age of commercialized religion in Canada.

See also: Canadian minority communities; Immigration to Canada; Jews in Canada

■ Religion in the United States

Religion played a major role in Americans' search for peace and stability during World War I. As the unifying force of the war ended, however, contention increased among religious groups in the United States.

American religion in the 1920s reflected the complexity of a nation struggling to find peace in a decade full of upheaval. Although American religion took a generally pacifistic turn after the violence of World War I, intense conflict arose among groups such as Fundamentalists, Modernists, Protestants, Roman Catholics, Jews, creationists, and evolutionists.

Postwar Religious Discord

The Interchurch World Movement (IWM) was a Protestant post–World War I campaign to connect all missionary and benevolent societies. In April of 1920, the group implemented domestic and foreign activities within all denominations. These activities included evaluating worldwide needs, producing educational programs, recruiting personnel, and raising large sums of money. The IWM's financial goals were never met, and the movement rapidly collapsed as its liberal leadership alienated conservative Protestants. By 1922, the IWM had failed, and its debts were turned over to member denominations to pay them off in full.

The 1918 congressional elections gave Republicans a large victory as World War I brought American patriotism to new heights and increased prejudice against foreigners, Communists, or nonconformists. In May of 1921, President Harding and Congress passed a law limiting immigration to quotas based on the 1910 census. A 1924 law limited immigrant quotas even more, while academic universities instituted quotas of their own to limit Catholic and Jewish presence on campuses.

The 1920s marked a large increase in the membership and activities of the extremist organization known as the Ku Klux Klan (KKK). The organization had been reestablished in 1915 by William J. Simmons. While maintaining the antiblack emphasis of the old Klan, Simmons was able to broaden the platform of targeted groups to include Roman Catholics and Jews, thereby widening the Klan's base of support. During the 1920s, the Klan became a Protestant militant organization complete with chaplains and revival service hymns. By 1923, the Klan had over three million members nationwide, allowing it to wield significant political power.

Prohibition

The ban on alcohol production and consumption in the United States dominated the Protestant agenda during the 1920s. Prohibition, as the ban was known,

> **Evangelist Aimee Semple McPherson Claims She Was Kidnapped**
>
> In May of 1926, the popular thirty-five-year-old Christian evangelist Aimee Semple McPherson walked into the Pacific Ocean and disappeared. The founder of the Foursquare Gospel Church and the Angelus Temple in Los Angeles, California, was presumed dead. A month later, she was found in a hospital in Douglas, Arizona, claiming she had been kidnapped. Skeptics, doubting her story, demanded a grand jury investigation, and many people believed she fabricated the story and had instead run away with a lover. McPherson and her mother were subsequently charged with obstruction of justice, corruption of public morals, and conspiracy to manufacture evidence, but these charges were dismissed in January 1927 for lack of evidence.
>
> McPherson's life and the scandal unwittingly increased the popularity of Pentecostal Christianity, as it exacerbated the schism between the conservative, fundamental Protestant Church and the moderate Protestant Church. In addition to the journalists looking to develop news stories for their papers, McPherson's opponents were eager to malign her. While she kept some loyal followers, from the famed Baltimore journalist H. L. Mencken to the Ku Klux Klan, she was widely portrayed as a fraud and hypocrite.

became the social issue around which liberal and conservative Protestants rallied in order to crusade for a return to moral order. In October of 1919, the Eighteenth Amendment was ratified, and Congress passed the Volstead Act over President Wilson's veto, providing enforcement for the Amendment and resulting in Prohibition becoming a reality on January 16, 1920. Maintaining this law became a major Protestant effort throughout the 1920s. Revivalist Billy Sunday was a notable figure of the time, having preached about the evils of alcohol in major cities since 1909.

The biggest threat to Prohibition came during the 1928 presidential election when the Democrats nominated Alfred E. Smith Jr., a Roman Catholic from New York who was in favor of legalizing alcohol. To Protestants, Smith embodied urban wickedness; many Protestant leaders accused him of leading America into great immorality. Republican presidential candidate Herbert Hoover defeated Smith, and Prohibition survived until the stock market crash of 1929 weakened its political and social support. The 1932 election of Franklin D. Roosevelt brought an end to Prohibition as he immediately began the repeal process. On December 5, 1933, the Twenty-First Amendment was ratified, repealing the Eighteenth Amendment.

Social Gospel and Pacifism

World War I served to intensify American religious leaders' critique of social injustice, and their dissatisfaction with American society increased with the growing moral complacency characterizing the 1920s. Denominational publications consistently contained social criticisms, attacks on national isolationism, and calls for the United States to join the League of Nations, an international peacekeeping organization. This push for a more just social order and international accountability was born out of traditional Christian arguments for peace and justice. It was an American cultural trend that aided Hoover in his ascent to the presidency in 1928; Hoover was raised as a Quaker and had become famous for his efforts to aid Europe after World War I. One major problem with the popularity of pacifism, however, was that it delayed American efforts to oppose totalitarian threats in the 1930s.

Protestant Conservatives and Evolution

Pacifism is sometimes considered to be linked to theological liberalism. However, even with the popularity of pacifism after World War I, theological liberalism did not have a monopoly on the religious scene in America during the 1920s. Many Americans were disoriented by the modernist movement spreading in intellectual and artistic domains and wanted to conserve the past. These Protestant conservatives became known as Fundamentalists. The teaching of the theory of evolution in schools became the primary issue of conflict between Fundamentalists and liberal Modernists during the 1920s. Conservatives during this decade tried to stop public schools and universities from teaching evolution, since it contradicted literal readings of the Bible. In July of 1925, the Scopes trial pitted Presbyterian politician William Jennings Bryan against lawyer Clarence Darrow.

Darrow defended John Scopes, a teacher who was on trial for teaching evolution in Tennessee schools. Scopes was found guilty; however, the Tennessee Supreme Court rejected the verdict on a technicality. This trial became a national event that demonstrated the divisions within American Protestantism in the 1920s.

Tennessee was not the only state that attempted to shut down the teaching of evolution. In 1923, Oklahoma passed the nation's first law banning evolution from school curricula. Later that same year, Florida passed a similar law. In 1926 and 1927, Mississippi and Arkansas, respectively, passed laws against the teaching of evolution in schools. Antievolution conservatives also made some inroads in Northern cities such as Minneapolis, where the pastor of the First Baptist Church, William Bell Riley, headed the World's Christian Fundamentals Association. In spite of some local and state successes, Fundamentalists were unable to gain national support or nationwide control over denominations. The struggle between Fundamentalists and Modernists did not begin or end in the 1920s; however, the decade brought about an aggressive confrontation between Protestant conservatives and liberals. Following the 1920s, Fundamentalists continued to grow in certain denominations, but their influence diminished within mainstream American culture.

Protestant Leaders
Reverend Harry Emerson Fosdick became one of the most famous liberal ministers from the 1920s to the 1940s and was a prominent character within the Fundamentalist-Modernist controversy of the 1920s. In May of 1922, as pastor of the First Presbyterian Church, he preached his historic sermon "Shall the Fundamentalists Win?" In his sermon, he defended scientific modernism and claimed that the Bible, as the unfolding will of God, should not be taken literally. These positions were considered heretical by the General Assembly of the Presbyterian Church. Fosdick resigned as pastor in 1924. He was immediately hired in a Baptist church where wealthy philanthropist John D. Rockefeller Jr. was a member. Rockefeller funded the new pastor's building project that became the Riverside Church in New York City.

J. Gresham Machen was a professor of New Testament at Princeton Seminary from 1915 to 1929. He led the conservative attack against Modernism, claiming that liberal theology was a completely different religion from Christianity, which he famously asserted in his book *Christianity and Liberalism* (1923). In the late 1920s, Machen's Fundamentalist position on scriptural inerrancy was challenged in Princeton, which led to a shakeup of the seminary. Machen left Princeton to start Westminster Seminary in Philadelphia.

William Jennings Bryan, a devout Presbyterian, was a dominant force in the liberal wing of the Democratic Party. He ran for president three times, in 1896, 1900, and 1908, and also served as secretary of state under President Woodrow Wilson from 1913 to 1916. He became a voice of Fundamentalist thought in the 1920s, advocating for peace, Prohibition, and creationism. In 1925, he was victorious in the *Scopes* trial and died shortly after the trial ended.

Roman Catholic Church
The Catholic Church in America faced a radically different situation from American Protestantism, since a large percentage of its members lived in urban centers and were recent immigrants to the United States. Catholicism was deeply involved in the labor movement and provided a liberal influence as Catholic bishops pushed for a social welfare state in their agenda entitled "Social Reconstruction: A General Review of the Problems and Survey of Remedies." Throughout the 1920s, Catholics had to contend with Protestant hostilities stemming from the changing American population. In 1860, Catholics only made up 8 percent of the population, but by 1926, they had doubled to 16 percent.

In spite of militant Protestants' intense hatred of Catholics, by 1928, the Democratic Party was willing to nominate a Roman Catholic, Alfred E. Smith Jr., for president. Although Smith lost to Hoover by a large margin in presidential electoral ballots, he did manage to win 60 percent more votes than any previous Democratic candidate, and his candidacy pointed to a new diverse religious reality. American culture could no longer be viewed as completely dominated by white Protestants.

Judaism
In 1860, Jews in the United States did not even constitute 1 percent of the total American population. By 1930, the Jewish population had increased to around 3 percent. During the 1920s, the majority of American Jews took the middle religious path of Conservative Judaism, which was a compromise between Reform

and Orthodox Judaism. American Reformed Judaism promoted such religious reforms as changing the language of sermons to English, using shorter prayers in worship services, and instituting family seating rather than seating separated by gender. These practices became common in the majority of Jewish religious services. Many Protestant social gospel activities were also integrated into Jewish religious life. However, cultural Judaism was in general more successful as a binding force than religious Judaism. This was demonstrated by Jewish Reconstructionism, a form of cultural Judaism developed in 1922 by Mordecai Kaplan, a rabbi, writer, and educator. Kaplan founded the Society for the Advancement of Judaism in an attempt to combine cultural Judaism with nonstructured worship.

Impact

Religion in the United States during the 1920s sought stability and peace in a tumultuous decade sandwiched between the end of World War I and the stock market crash of 1929. The intense conflict between a diminishing Protestant majority and a rapidly growing Catholic minority can be seen in the push for new laws limiting immigration and the growth of the KKK during the 1920s. Prohibition and the social gospel demonstrated that mainline Protestantism still maintained a large cultural influence during the decade, at the same time as Fundamentalists attacked Modernism in general and evolution in particular. The nomination of Al Smith as a presidential candidate revealed the growing influence of Roman Catholics in America, while the development of Jewish Reconstructionism displayed the adaptability of Judaism in American culture.

Robert A. Britt-Mills

Further Reading

Abrams, Douglas Carl. *Selling the Old-Time Religion: American Fundamentalists and Mass Culture, 1920–1940*. Athens: University of Georgia Press, 2001. Discusses the relationship between American Fundamentalists and the cultural norms of the 1920s and 1930s.

Ahlstrom, Sydney E., and David D. Hall. *A Religious History of the American People*. 2d ed. New Haven, Conn.: Yale University Press, 2004. A religious history of the American people narrating the history of the European Reformation up to the 1960s. Contains a chapter dedicated to the 1920s.

Hankins, Barry. *Jesus and Gin: Evangelicalism, the Roaring Twenties, and Today's Culture Wars*. New York: Palgrave Macmillan, 2010. An account of evangelicalism in the 1920s and its role during Prohibition, with insights into how evangelicals participated in the shaping of American culture.

Martin, Marty E. *The Noise of Conflict, 1919–1941*. Vol. 2 in *Modern American Religion*. Chicago: University of Chicago Press, 1991. Details American religious history during the interwar period.

Noll, Mark. *A History of Christianity in the United States and Canada*. Grand Rapids, Mich.: W. B. Eerdmans, 1992. A North American religious history that includes a significant section on the 1920s, also including information about the religious history of Canada.

See also: Anti-Semitism; Bryan, William Jennings; Evangelism; Immigration to the United States; Jews in the United States; Ku Klux Klan; McPherson, Aimee Semple; Prohibition; *Scopes* trial (1925); Smith, Alfred E.; Spiritualism

■ "Return to Normalcy"

The election of Warren G. Harding to the U.S. presidency in 1920 signified Americans' rejection of the dynamic idealism and political reforms of the Progressive Era. During his electoral campaign, Harding promised a "return to normalcy," by which he meant the more traditional approach to politics and governance practiced prior to World War I. He won in a landslide victory, and his Return to Normalcy philosophy would set the American political agenda for the decade.

American voters in 1920 rejected what they saw as the Woodrow Wilson administration's legacy of failure. Dissatisfaction with Wilson's wartime policies was aggravated by the difficult transition to peace, as rapid demobilization and the cancellation of war contracts contributed to a period of economic turmoil. During 1919, some four million workers went on strike, while inflation caused the cost of living to increase to 82 percent more than in 1914. Then, in 1920, the United States was struck by a severe recession. The most extreme deflation on record gutted commodity prices, hitting farmers especially hard, and unemployment surged to around 10 percent. Other sources of national stress were the politically acrimonious Red Scare of 1919–1920 and the debate over U.S. participation in the League of Nations, an international peacekeeping organization.

Warren G. Harding, the Republican presidential nominee for the 1920 election, responded by championing a comfortably old-fashioned style of politics. This came naturally to Harding, a longtime supporter of Ohio politicians William McKinley and William Howard Taft; like McKinley, he conducted his presidential campaign from his front porch, appearing affable, calm, and competent as he greeted visitors in his hometown of Marion, Ohio. Harding articulated an attractive political platform rooted in time-honored Republican values, including cuts to government spending, reduced taxes, and better management of the federal budget. He also called for increased tariffs and new economic protections for farmers, while remaining studiously vague on the League of Nations issue.

Harding's "return to normalcy" rhetoric proved irresistible to voters of the postwar era. He won a stunning political victory, receiving 60.2 percent of the popular vote, while the Republicans increased their majorities in Congress by sixty-three seats in the House of Representatives and ten seats in the Senate.

Impact

Once in office, Harding carried through on his promises. He reduced federal spending, created the Bureau of the Budget (later the Office of Management and Budget), cut tax rates, and signed legislation that reformed agricultural policy and increased tariffs. With regard to foreign policy, Harding kept his distance from the League of Nations but played a leading role in world affairs through such initiatives as the Washington Naval Conference. The nation's rapid return to booming prosperity seemed to validate Harding's policies, so that even after his death, his ideal of normalcy continued to define the policies of the presidency, which remained in Republican hands throughout the decade.

Daniel P. Murphy

Further Reading

Dean, John W. *Warren G. Harding*. New York: Times Books, 2004.

Murray, Robert K. *The Harding Era: Warren G. Harding and His Administration*. Minneapolis: University of Minnesota Press, 1969.

_____. *The Politics of Normalcy: Governmental Theory and Practice in the Harding-Coolidge Era*. New York: W. W. Norton, 1973.

See also: Congress, U.S.; Elections, U.S., of 1920; Farm subsidies; Foreign policy, U.S.; Harding, Warren G.; Labor strikes; League of Nations; Political parties; Recession of 1920–1921; Red Scare, The

■ Revenue Acts of 1924, 1926, and 1928

The Law: A series of federal acts altering tax rates
Date: Enacted on June 2, 1924; February 25, 1926; and May 29, 1928

The Revenue Acts of 1924, 1926, and 1928 made a number of modifications to personal and corporate income taxes, gift and inheritance taxes, and excises, steadily reducing taxes from high wartime levels.

While the United States' involvement in World War I had necessitated an increase in revenue, the federal government sought to lower tax rates from wartime levels during the 1920s. To that end, Andrew Mellon, secretary of the Treasury during the presidencies of Warren G. Harding, Calvin Coolidge, and Herbert Hoover, wanted to reduce the maximum income tax rate and eliminate various minor taxes, but in return, he was willing to accept a small increase in the corporate tax rate and increased personal exemptions.

The Revenue Act of 1924 lowered the maximum income tax rate, which combined the base rate and the surtax, from 58 percent on incomes greater than $200,000 to 46 percent on incomes over $500,000. The Revenue Act of 1926 further reduced the maximum tax rate to 25 percent on incomes over $100,000. The 1926 act also increased personal exemptions from $1,000 to $1,500 for individuals and from $2,500 to $3,500 for married couples, thus reducing the amount of taxable income.

As Mellon supported higher tax rates for unearned income, or money accumulated through investments or inheritance rather than wages, the Revenue Act of 1924 increased the maximum estate tax rate from 25 percent to 40 percent of the amount in excess of $10 million, although the 1926 act lowered the rate to 20 percent. The corporate income tax rate increased from 12.5 percent to 13.5 percent with the Revenue Act of 1926 before decreasing to 12

Political cartoon illustrating the Revenue Act of 1924. (Getty Images)

percent in 1928. The 1926 act also eliminated a number of excise taxes and a gift tax that had been added in 1924.

In addition to altering tax rates, the 1924 act permitted the Treasury to reveal private tax returns to the public. The Senate had asked for the tax returns of several corrupt Harding administration officials while investigating the Teapot Dome scandal and other financial wrongdoing, but Coolidge had refused because revealing private tax returns was then illegal. After a brief period of public access, the 1926 act removed this provision, restoring the privacy of tax returns.

Impact
Maximum tax rates were drastically reduced, and exemptions increased during the 1920s, thus encouraging the period's overall economic growth. The passage of the Revenue Acts of 1924, 1926, and 1928, combined with limited spending, significantly reduced the national debt during the decade. However, the stock market crash of 1929 put an end to this prosperity, and tax rates increased throughout the 1930s.

Timothy Lane

Further Reading
Brownlee, W. Elliot. *Federal Taxation in America: A Short History.* 2d. ed. New York: Cambridge University Press, 2004.

Cannadine, David. *Mellon: An American Life.* New York: Vintage Books, 2008.

See also: Coolidge, Calvin; Harding, Warren G.; Mellon, Andrew

■ Rhapsody in Blue

Identification: Landmark orchestral work combining elements of jazz and classical music
Composer: George Gershwin
Date: February 12, 1924

Popular bandleader Paul Whiteman commissioned composer George Gershwin to write a new piece for his orchestra in 1923. In February 1924, with Gershwin himself at the piano, Rhapsody in Blue *premiered in New York City's Aeolian Hall as part of a program titled "An Experiment in Modern Music." The composition was an instant success and continues to be recognized as an American musical masterpiece.*

Gershwin was a noted composer by his early twenties, having established his reputation among the collective of songwriters and sheet music publishers known as Tin Pan Alley and also composing Broadway musicals and such vocal hits as "Swanee" for entertainer Al Jolson. Gershwin once remarked to Whiteman that he hoped to create a major jazz composition someday. Soon afterward, newspapers reported that Gershwin's new work was to be premiered in an upcoming concert. This announcement surprised the composer, because he had not even begun to write the composition. Despite his hectic schedule, Gershwin began planning his new work. During a train ride to Boston, the incessant rhythmic clatter of the train on the tracks heavily influenced his conception of the new jazz rhapsody. When completed, *American Rhapsody* was a score for two pianos in one movement that Gershwin submitted to Whiteman's chief arranger, Ferde Grofé. Gershwin's brother Ira, a lyricist, felt *American Rhapsody* was an ineffective title. Inspired by the use of color in titles of paintings by artist James McNeill Whistler, Ira renamed it *Rhapsody in Blue.*

Familiar with the special talents of orchestra members, Grofé adapted the score to magnify individuals' talent and increase the piece's musical impact. The revised score was finished just eight days before the premier, which was attended by notable celebrities such as Sergei Rachmaninoff, John Phillip Sousa, and Jascha Heifetz, along with numerous music critics. The opening clarinet glissando left listeners spellbound and eager to hear what followed.

Impact

Rhapsody in Blue was the first crossover jazz and classical composition to receive national attention and to be premiered in a prestigious concert hall. In a decade when jazz was generally performed by small Dixieland-style musical groups in New Orleans, New York, and Chicago, Gershwin's *Rhapsody in Blue* featured a big band jazz arrangement augmented with strings and specialty instruments: The use of "blue" notes, along with jazz-oriented instruments such as saxophone, banjo, and accordion, characterized Gershwin's concept of jazz in the 1920s. Written at a time when jazz and "serious" music were not considered compatible, *Rhapsody in Blue* successfully combined them and became an enduring piece of American music history.

Douglas D. Skinner

Further Reading

Hyland, William G. *George Gershwin: A New Biography*. Westport, Conn.: Praeger, 2003.

Peyser, Joan. *The Memory of All That: The Life of George Gershwin*. New York: Simon & Schuster, 1993.

See also: Classical music; Jazz; Tin Pan Alley; Whiteman, Paul

■ Ringling Bros. and Barnum & Bailey Circus

Identification: American traveling circus
Date: Formed in 1907

During the 1920s, the Ringling Bros. and Barnum & Bailey Circus represented an immense traveling entertainment unit in the United States that made it possible every year for thousands of Americans to be both educated and entertained.

The Ringling brothers from Baraboo, Wisconsin, founded a circus in 1882 that eventually became the famous Ringling Bros. Circus. By the turn of the century, Albert, Otto, Alfred, Charles, and John Ringling had put themselves in fierce competition with the Barnum & Bailey Circus. John, the leading Ringling, decided in 1907 to buy out the Barnum & Bailey Circus and to put the two major circuses on the road together. The Ringlings also bought out a number of smaller circuses in financial trouble. Despite a few family arguments regarding the arrangement and operation of the circuses, as well as the deaths of Albert and Alfred, the Ringlings had become circus kings by 1920.

Often referred to as the "Big One," the Ringling Bros. and Barnum & Bailey Circus forfeited its usual lease to open the circus season at the Madison Square Garden in New York City to circuses from the American Circus Corporation in 1929. John Ringling responded by buying out the entire American Circus Corporation, amounting to five circuses for nearly $2 million. John now had a circus empire of over one hundred railroad cars, herds of horses and elephants, a gigantic menagerie of many species of wild animals seldom seen across the United States, and over one thousand performers and workers. In short, John Ringling now owned every circus of any note in America. Throughout the remainder of the 1920s and into the 1930s, the Ringlings continued to send out several railroad circuses every year.

Putting a railroad circus on the road was expensive and exhausting, involving the organization and care of performers, workers, and herds of exotic animals. After an extended stay at a large city, the circus would move out on the road for six to seven months, exhibiting its show twice each day wherever its trains stopped.

Impact

Throughout the 1920s, the Ringling Bros. and Barnum & Bailey Circus presented a tented world of romance and glamour to the American public, populated by clowns, acrobats, equestrians, aerialists, and exotic animals. Although financial and familial problems in the 1930s forced John Ringling from his role as circus director, the circus itself went on to greater success and popularity over the decades that followed. The circus survived the Great Depression, the transition from tent performances to circus arena shows, and multiple changes in ownership and direction. Ringling Bros. and Barnum & Bailey Circus continues to give performances in the early twenty-first century.

Wilton Eckley

Further Reading

Apps, Jerold W. *Tents, Tigers, and the Ringling Brothers.* Madison: Wisconsin Historical Society Press, 2008.

Plowden, Gene. *Those Amazing Ringlings and Their Circus.* Caldwell, Idaho: Caxton Printers, 1968.

See also: Hobbies and recreation; Roaring Twenties

■ Rin Tin Tin films

The wildly popular Rin Tin Tin films reportedly saved a struggling Warner Bros. studio from bankruptcy in the early 1920s. Thanks to several scripts written by staff writer Darryl Zanuck, the films became Warner Bros.' first truly successful franchise.

On September 15, 1918, American soldier Lee Duncan found a mother dog and litter of German shepherd puppies in the ruins of a bombed-out building in Lorraine, France. Duncan rescued the animals and claimed two of the pups, a male and a female, for his own. He named the male dog "Rin Tin Tin" and the female dog "Nanette," after small puppets that French children gave the soldiers for good luck. Though Nanette died soon after Duncan returned to the United States, Rin Tin Tin survived.

After training Rin Tin Tin to do stunts, Duncan decided that the dog belonged in films and approached Hollywood with a script he had written called *Where the North Begins*. Though no production company would take on his script, Duncan did talk a Warner Bros. crew into allowing Rin Tin Tin to fill in for an uncooperative wolf in a scene for the 1922 film *The Man from Hell's River*. He claimed his dog could complete the scene in one take; the dog was true to his owner's word and was hired for the rest of the shoot.

In the following eight years, Rin Tin Tin starred in twenty-six Warner Bros. productions, alongside such acclaimed actors as Myrna Loy, John Barrymore, and Douglas Fairbanks Jr. His first major role was in the film *Where the North Begins* (1923), adapted from Duncan's original script. Subsequent movies included *Find Your Man* (1924), the script that won screenwriter Darryl Zanuck his first job at Warner Bros.; *The Lighthouse by the Sea* (1924), another Zanuck-penned film; and *Clash of the Wolves* (1925), which has since been entered into the National Film Registry in the Library of Congress.

Rin Tin Tin died at Duncan's home in Los Angeles on August 10, 1932. It is commonly rumored that film star Jean Harlow, who lived across the street, held the dog's head in her lap as he died. He was later buried in France.

Impact

Following Rin Tin Tin's death, his legacy was carried on by his descendants, who provided Warner Bros. with numerous hits over the next several decades. Rin Tin Tin was one of the most admired film stars of the period, receiving thousands of fan letters every week and eventually becoming one of a small number of animals given a Hollywood Walk of Fame star. The popularity of his movies spawned three radio serials, only the first of which starred the original Rin Tin Tin, and led to the 1950s television series *The Adventures of Rin Tin Tin*.

Theresa L. Stowell

Further Reading

Elwood, Ann. *Rin-Tin-Tin: The Movie Star.* Seattle, Wash.: CreateSpace, 2010.

English, James W. *The Rin Tin Tin Story.* New York: Dodd, Mead, 1958.

Orlean, Susan. *Rin Tin Tin: The Life and the Legend.* New York: Simon & Schuster, 2011.

See also: Film; Warner Bros.

■ Roach, Hal, Sr.

Identification: American filmmaker and producer
Born: January 14, 1892, Elmira, New York
Died: November 2, 1992, Los Angeles, California

Hal Roach Sr. influenced the film industry of the 1920s through the comedy films he wrote, directed, and produced. His collaboration with actors such as Stan Laurel, Oliver Hardy, and Harold Lloyd helped propel their film careers.

The film career of Harold Eugene Roach began when he formed the Rolin Film Company in 1915. In order to get official credit for his films, Hal Roach renamed the company the Hal E. Roach Studios in 1920. Roach's studio boasted a family environment and often used family members and friends as extras in films. The atmosphere on the studio lot was so

Hal Roach Sr. (Popperfoto/Getty Images)

warm and friendly it was known as Hollywood's "lot of fun." Roach wrote, directed, and scripted gags for his films. Although he made all kinds of motion pictures, Roach preferred making short films rather than feature-length ones because he believed comedy should be brief.

Roach's Stars

Roach's first success was with comedian Harold Lloyd. Lloyd established both himself and Roach as formidable players in the film industry. The films made by Lloyd and Roach in the 1920s became some of the top-grossing films of the decade. Stan Laurel and Oliver Hardy were perhaps Roach's most famous stars, however. After Roach teamed the pair as a comedic duo in the late 1920s, they became successful and made sixty-six shorts and fourteen feature films for Roach through 1938. Another of Roach's great successes came in 1922, with a group of child actors at first called "Hal Roach's Rascals," but later known simply as "Our Gang" (and known still later as the "Little Rascals"). These films became the longest-running shorts series in Hollywood history and continued to be produced through 1944.

Of all the stars he employed, however, Roach was friendliest with Western film actor Will Rogers, as they shared interests in aviation and polo. Although the two men were close, they only made a handful of films together in the 1920s, because Roach felt silent cinema did not adequately showcase Rogers's talents.

Morality Code and Success

In 1922, Roach created a morality code that insisted his studio make movies appropriate for all audiences, including no content that might offend women or children. The Roach Studio code stated that a movie should only be made if it was clean and free of questionable material.

Roach's success as a filmmaker surpassed that of rival filmmaker Mack Sennett. While Sennett used excessive slapstick comedy, Roach's comedies featured restrained humor that included emotion, visual gags, strong plots, and technical superiority. This style was seen in many of Roach's short films as well as his features, including Lloyd's 1923 film *Safety Last!*

Roach's success helped him secure a distribution deal with Metro-Goldwyn-Mayer (MGM) in 1927. This business agreement carried Roach's filmmaking career from the silent era to the sound films that quickly became standard fare by the end of the 1920s.

Impact

Roach was a pioneering filmmaker in the 1920s whose vision for comedy helped establish the careers of stars such as Lloyd, Laurel and Hardy, and the Our Gang actors. Roach influenced Hollywood as a writer, director, producer, and film industry mogul. Roach's talent was especially evident in his comedic insights and ability to work with known and unknown stars to create entertaining films. Roach produced nearly one thousand movies and won three Academy Awards during his career, including an honorary Oscar in 1984 for his lifetime achievements in the film industry. Roach died of pneumonia in 1992, just months before his 101st birthday.

Kimberly Miller

Further Reading

Bengtson, John. *Silent Visions: Discovering Early Hollywood and New York Through the Films of Harold Lloyd.* Solana Beach, Calif.: Santa Monica Press, 2011. Considers Lloyd's early career with Roach, along with Lloyd's later studio work.

Cerra, Julie Lugo, and Marc Wanamaker. *Movie Studios of Culver City.* Charleston, S.C.: Arcadia, 2011. Presents the role of Culver City, California, as an early film studio location that influenced the development of Hal Roach Studios.

Maltin, Leonard, and Richard Bann. *The Little Rascals: The Life and Times of Our Gang.* New York: Three Rivers Press, 1992. Contains a chapter on Hal Roach Studios, giving insight into the creation and operation of the production company; also includes biographies of all members of the Little Rascals, as well as reviews and a synopsis of the declining years of the franchise.

Skretvedt, Randy, and Jordan R. Young. *Laurel and Hardy: The Magic Behind the Movies.* Beverly Hills: Moonstone Press, 1987. Contains information gleaned from employees of Hal Roach Studios about the studio itself, as well as the Laurel and Hardy comedy team, including a chronological analysis of Laurel and Hardy films that notes Roach's influence.

Ward, Richard Lewis. *A History of the Hal Roach Studios.* Carbondale, I.L.: Southern Illinois University Press, 2005. A chronological consideration of the creation and operation of Hal Roach Studios that elaborates on its humble beginnings as the Rolin Film Company, also discussing its more modern dealings with the television industry, with insights into Roach's far-reaching impact.

See also: Film; Laurel and Hardy; Lloyd, Harold; Normand, Mabel; Our Gang comedies; Sennett, Mack; Talking motion pictures

■ Roaring Twenties

The decade of the 1920s, also known as the Roaring Twenties or the Jazz Age, represented a unique period in American society, reflecting momentous cultural, economic, political, and technological changes.

The 1920s in the United States have been referred to as the Roaring Twenties because of the many changes, crises, and challenges of the time. A liberal lifestyle emerged that promoted decadence, optimism, and enthusiasm. This lifestyle contrasted with the national banning of alcohol, known as Prohibition. Organized crime flourished during Prohibition as gangsters such as Al Capone benefited from illegal liquor production and distribution. Scandals and violence emerged in large urban centers like Chicago, where the Saint Valentine's Day Massacre took place between Capone's and a rival gang in 1929. Corruption reached even the White House during President Warren G. Harding's administration, as demonstrated by the Teapot Dome Scandal involving bribery and government-owned oil repositories.

The emerging musical genre of jazz captured the attention of many Americans. Women were now able to vote and projected their new freedoms by dressing in unconventional "flapper" style and by maintaining a presence in "speakeasies," or establishments that illegally sold alcohol. Many Americans devoted themselves to breaking records in athletic events and performing feats of endurance and transportation; aviator Charles Lindberg, for example, made the first solo nonstop transatlantic flight from New York to Paris. Henry Ford's introduction of the assembly-line method in automobile production substantially increased the number of cars in the United States and sparked efforts to expand and improve traffic infrastructure. The movie entertainment business blossomed with film stars, as silent cinema gave way to talking pictures by the end of the decade. The stock market's success before 1929 suggested there was no limit to economic expansion.

American cities were also changing in a number of ways. Many cities developed vibrant ethnic communities resulting from a significant wave of immigrants. The growing economic and industrial prosperity to be found in urban areas also attracted many rural Americans, as well as African Americans from the South.

The 1920s were was an era of hope, aspiration, and achievement. However, the decade also had negative characteristics, such increased activity by the extremist Ku Klux Klan organization. White Americans and the government demonstrated prejudice against African Americans, Jews, Catholics, and immigrants. Toward the end of the decade, the country faced one of its greatest challenges with the stock market crash and resulting economic downturn.

Impact

The Roaring Twenties represented a vibrant and eventful period of American life, bookended by World War I and the Great Depression. The decade increased the American people's confidence in their society's ability to change. Many Americans felt that their lives were improved by the economic, political, and cultural changes of the decade. The period also enhanced the belief that the United States offered better opportunities for its residents than other nations.

William E. Kelly

Further Reading

Allen, Frederick Lewis. *Only Yesterday: An Informal History of the 1920s.* New York: Harper, 1957.

Gray, James H. *The Roar of the Twenties.* Toronto: Macmillan of Canada, 1975.

Kyvig, David E. *Daily Life in the United States, 1920–1939: Decades of Promise and Pain.* Westport, Conn.: Greenwood Press, 2002.

See also: Aviation; Crimes and scandals; Demographics; Fads; Film; Flappers; Jazz; Lindbergh, Charles; Prohibition; Urbanization; Women's rights

■ Robeson, Paul

Identification: American athlete, performer, author, and civil rights activist
Born: April 9, 1898, Princeton, New Jersey
Died: January 23, 1976, Philadelphia, Pennsylvania

Paul Robeson became an African American scholar, athlete, multilingual singer, actor, and the first artist-activist in the United States. His groundbreaking acting performances were a unique achievement in cinematic history and helped pave the way for later African American actors.

Paul Leroy Robeson was born to William Drew Robeson, an escaped slave who became a Presbyterian minister, and Maria Louisa Bustill, a teacher who died when Paul was only six years old. As a child, he heard ragtime, hymns, gospel songs, blues, and spirituals, all of which influenced his concert repertoire in later years. His father instilled in him values that informed his artistry and activism, including the concept that all human beings, no matter how diverse, are equal members of a single family. The third African American student accepted to Rutgers University, he became known as "Robeson of Rutgers," attaining fourteen varsity letters and two all-American titles as a football star equally adept at offensive and defensive positions. In 1920, enamored with the African American intellectual, cultural, and artistic movement known as the Harlem Renaissance, he earned a degree from Columbia Law School. After playing professional football to pay for his education, he chose not to practice law. Instead, with the encouragement of his wife, Eslanda Cardozo Goode, he focused on a theatrical career, both as a stage actor and concert singer.

There was no organized civil rights movement when Robeson began acting in 1922. He spent many years in Great Britain and Europe, attempting to find opportunities unavailable in his homeland. Like Josephine Baker, Louis Armstrong, and other black artists, he retreated to Europe to escape the racial prejudice that was still pervasive in the United States. Around the same time the talking motion picture *The Jazz Singer* (1927) was released, Robeson was starring in the original British stage version of Oscar Hammerstein II's and Jerome Kern's musical *Show Boat* in London's West End. Robeson ultimately appeared in the 1932 American stage version and 1936 film version of the musical, in which he performed his signature song "Ol' Man River." Robeson later rewrote a portion of the song's lyrics. His knowledge of many languages also allowed him to perform concerts for packed houses in countries across the globe.

Robeson's other stage successes included the all-black revue *Shuffle Along* (1922), Eugene O'Neill's plays *The Emperor Jones* (1924–1925) and *All God's Chillun Got Wings* (1924), and Dorothy and DuBose Heyward's play *Porgy* (1928). He made his feature-film debut playing two radically different characters in African American filmmaker Oscar Micheaux's independently produced *Body and Soul* (1925). Later that year, he cut his first music recordings, accompanied by pianist Lawrence Brown, at Victor Records in Camden, New Jersey, and posed in the Greenwich Village studio of Italian sculptor Antonio Salemme, who immortalized his physique in a life-size statue titled *Negro Spiritual*.

Closing the decade with his critically acclaimed performances in the British version of *Show Boat*, Robeson became the first African American performer to attain top billing in mainstream motion pictures. One U.S. film he appeared in, *The Emperor*

Jones (1933), was followed by several in Britain, including *Sanders of the River* (1935), *Song of Freedom* (1936), and *King Solomon's Mines* (1937). He also became the first black actor in one hundred years to play the title role in Shakespeare's tragedy *Othello* opposite a white cast. Robeson played Othello in the 1930 London production, as well as in a 1943–1944 Broadway smash, for which he was honored with the Spingarn Medal by the National Association for the Advancement of Colored People.

Impact

Robeson was greatly admired for his achievements and considered as an important African American figure during the 1920s and beyond. During the Cold War and after, some viewed his unbending political principles as seditious and labeled him a communist. American and British intelligence forces carried out surveillance of Robeson from the beginning of U.S. involvement in World War II until his death. In 1949, he was blacklisted and deprived of his passport, negatively affecting his life and career for many years. Robeson survived assassination threats and attempts and has been compared to Presidents Abraham Lincoln and John F. Kennedy, as well as prominent civil rights activists Medgar Evers and Martin Luther King Jr. as an individual who championed human unity and equality at the cost of his own individual well-being. His most visible public valediction occurred in 2004 when the United States Postal Service honored him on a Black Heritage Commemorative postage stamp.

Scott Allen Nollen

Further Reading

Duberman, Martin. *Paul Robeson.* New York: New Press, 2005. Provides biographical information about Robeson.

Robeson, Paul. *Here I Stand.* Boston, Mass.: Beacon Press, 1958. Robeson's memoir presenting his sociopolitical views.

———. *Paul Robeson Speaks: Writings, Speeches, Interviews, 1918–1974.* Edited by Philip Sheldon Foner. New York: Citadel Press, 2002. Includes original material written by Robeson.

Robeson, Paul, Jr. *The Undiscovered Paul Robeson: An Artist's Journey, 1898–1939.* New York: John Wiley & Sons, 2001.

———. *The Undiscovered Paul Robeson: Quest for Freedom, 1939–1976.* Hoboken, N.J.: John Wiley & Sons, 2010. A two-volume set, written by Robeson's son, covering Robeson's development as an athlete, singer, actor, and the nation's first artist-activist.

See also: African Americans; American Civil Liberties Union (ACLU); Armstrong, Louis; Baker, Josephine; Broadway musicals; Civil rights and liberties; Communism; Harlem Renaissance; Micheaux, Oscar; *Show Boat*; *Shuffle Along*

■ Robinson, Edwin Arlington

Identification: American poet
Born: December 22, 1869, Head Tide, Maine
Died: April 6, 1935, New York, New York

Over the course of his lifetime, Edwin Arlington Robinson was esteemed as one of America's greatest living poets. During the 1920s he was awarded three Pulitzer Prizes for poetry, and his reputation as a major writer of the early twentieth century remains strong.

Robinson is considered one of the foremost poetic voices of the early twentieth century. Born in 1869, he understood the profoundly unsettling changes of industrialization and Progressive reform on nineteenth- and early-twentieth-century American life and culture. As a young man, he rejected lucrative career opportunities to become a poet. While a fledgling poet, he took odd jobs and lived in various cities in Maine, New Hampshire, and New York. He returned to New York in 1899 and stayed there for the rest of his life, also partaking in regular summer retreats at the MacDowell Colony for artists in Peterborough, New Hampshire, and at the homes of friends in Connecticut and Boston.

Work

He self-published his first volume of poems, *The Torrent and the Night Before*, in 1896, following it with *The Children of the Night* in 1897 and *Captain Craig* in 1902. Over his lifetime Robinson published nineteen major works and collections of poems. Tilbury Town, the fictitious locale of several of his poems, is reminiscent of the New England towns of his youth.

Fame came slowly during the post–World War I period, as Robinson continued to publish and collect his poems. During the 1920s, however, his literary

> **Edwin Arlington Robinson on His Poems**
>
> *In a letter to Harry de Forest Smith, dated May 13, 1896, Robinson describes what he hoped his poems would do for his readers:*
>
> If printed lines are good for anything, they are bound to be picked up some time; and then, if some poor devil of a man or woman feels any better or any stronger for anything that I have said, I shall have no fault to find with the scheme or anything in it.
>
> *Writing to Smith again in February 3, 1897, Robinson reaffirmed his position:*
>
> I also make free to say that many of my verses [were] written with a conscious hope that they might make some despairing devil a little stronger and a little better satisfied with things—not as they are, but as they are to be.

career picked up speed when he received three Pulitzer Prizes for Poetry: His first prize was awarded in 1922 for his *Collected Poems*; his second in 1924 for *The Man Who Died Twice*; and his third for *Tristram* in 1927. In 1929 he was awarded a gold medal by the National Institute of Arts and Letters.

Style

Robinson's poetry blended terse New England realism and spirituality with classic forms of comedy and tragedy. Common themes in his writing include failure, unrealized potential, and the relationship between the artist and society. His poetic works from the 1920s include "Avon's Harvest," "Roman Bartholomew," and "Dionysus in Doubt." Robinson worked in traditional poetic forms like the sonnet, blank verse, the villanelle, and the ballad. He was known for using iambic pentameter and a variety of tightly woven syntactic line styles.

Robinson was disciplined in assimilating into his own work the classic and contemporary literary traditions. The performing arts also had a profound impact on the form and content of Robinson's poetry. In particular, his writing was influenced by the works of William Shakespeare and Henrik Ibsen, along with composer Richard Wagner. Further theatrical works that found resonance in Robinson's writing and played important roles in his characters and imagery included the light operas of W. S. Gilbert and Arthur Sullivan, as well as the classical Greek tragedies and comedies. His ability to sustain an emotional intensity and the provocative interplay of his characters set him apart from his peers. These qualities are most evident in his extended works such as "Isaac and Archibald," "Rembrandt to Rembrandt," and "The Man Who Died Twice." His Arthurian poems "Merlin," "Lancelot," and "Tristram" are preeminent among others of their genre. "Tristram" was especially popular during the Great Depression; nearly 100,000 copies were sold during Robinson's lifetime. Robinson led a notably solitary life, dying in New York in 1935 at age sixty-five.

Impact

Robinson's writing has undergone cycles of critical acclaim and neglect. During his lifetime he was considered one of America's greatest living poets. Serious twenty-first-century writers consider him one of the great masters of the early twentieth century. No mention of Arlington's success would be complete without acknowledging the profound cultural contributions of the MacDowell Colony, a thriving retreat community for artists created by musicians Edward and Marian MacDowell at a farm in Peterborough, New Hampshire. Robinson is one of many artists whose works were completed in the studios provided by the colony.

Victoria M. Breting-Garcia

Further Reading

Baym, Nina. *Between the Wars 1914–1945*. Vol. D in *The Norton Anthology of American Literature*. 6th ed. New York: Norton, 2003. A critically acclaimed anthology of major works representing American literature between the world wars.

Donaldson, Scott. *Edwin Arlington Robinson: A Poet's Life*. New York: Columbia University Press. 2007. A biography of the poet's life and the lives of those who influenced his work.

Fussell, Edwin S. *Edwin Arlington Robinson: The Literary Background of a Traditional Poet*. Berkeley and Los Angeles: University of California Press, 1954. A carefully researched series of essays on the literary foundations of Robinson's poetry.

Gale, Robert L. *An Edwin Arlington Robinson Encyclopedia*. North Carolina: McFarland & Company, Inc. 2006. Considered a companion to the Donaldson biography; provides excellent background summaries describing the influential people in Robinson's career and short analytic summaries of Robinson's poems.

Robinson, Edwin Arlington, and James P. Carley. *Arthurian Poets: Edwin Arlington Robinson*. Rochester, N.Y.: Boydell Press, 1990. Collects Robinson's Arthurian poems, including "Merlin" (1917), "Lancelot" (1920), "Tristram" (1927), and "Modred: A Fragment" (1929).

See also: Literature in the United States; Poetry

■ Rocketry

In the 1920s, rocketry graduated from a tradition-based technical craft producing little more than fireworks to a formal engineering research and development discipline aimed at achieving record-breaking altitudes. Extravagant publicity about possible flights to the moon and other planets created a motivated community of spaceflight enthusiasts and fertilized the new literary genre of science fiction.

At the dawn of the 1920s, the mathematical theory of high-performance rocketry had reached an advanced state. Konstantin Tsiokolvsky of Russia, Robert Esnault-Pelterie of France, and Robert H. Goddard of the United States all independently derived the fundamental relationship between mass of a rocket without fuel, the mass of propellant onboard at launch, and the final velocity of the rocket when the engine ceases to operate. All three recognized that maximizing a rocket's performance requires the rocket to emit exhaust at high velocities, and all speculated on the superiority of liquid propellants over solid propellants.

Goddard, however, was the only one to follow theoretical work with experimental development. He began experimenting with solid fuel rockets in the 1910s, supported by a grant from the Smithsonian Institution. In December 1919, he published "A Method of Reaching Extreme Altitudes," an account of his accomplishments to date, including the first description of a multistage rocket (a rocket composed of multiple parts, each with its own engine and propellant). An offhand description of how a rocket could be used to reach the moon caught the attention of the public and made Goddard infamous, provoking widespread criticism of this allegedly preposterous claim.

Liquid Propulsion

In the early 1920s, Goddard shifted his focus from solid propellants to liquid propellants, specifically liquid oxygen as oxidizer and gasoline as fuel. Liquid propellants bring a much higher level of complexity to rocket design, as they need storage tanks, plumbing, valves, and seals. The liquids must be forced into the combustion chamber at high pressure, mixed evenly, and burned in a rapid, controlled manner.

On November 1, 1923, Goddard conducted the first successful static test (that is, a test with the engine tied down) of a liquid propellant engine. He continued to work on improving his design, mainly the fuel pump system, with which he was having difficulty. A subsequent test in June 1925 revealed that the pumps fed the propellants in surges, which caused the engine to thrust in pulses rather than continuously and smoothly. Improved pumps led to a more significant successful test in December of that year, in which a liquid propellant rocket engine lifted its own weight for the first time.

Goddard launched the first ever test flight of a liquid-fueled rocket at Auburn, Massachusetts, on March 16, 1926. The rocket was initially too heavy for the minuscule amount of thrust delivered by the engine, but the weight dropped as the propellants were consumed. After 20 seconds, the rocket rose and accelerated, reaching an altitude of 41 feet (12.5 meters) and a range of 184 feet (56.1 meters) during 2.5 seconds in the air.

The next flight took place on April 3, 1926. A rocket similar to the first flew for 4.2 seconds and traveled 50 feet (15.2 meters) away from the launch site. Two more flights were failures, as the nozzle of one and the combustion chamber wall of the other both burned through. Goddard's progress was halting until he began experimenting with injecting unburned fuel into the exhaust, creating a thin layer of cool gas that would insulate the walls of the combustion chamber and nozzle from the hot exhaust gases. Late in December 1928, his improved design flew to 204 feet (62.2 meters) in altitude.

Experiments with Instrumentation

By July 17, 1929, Goddard was ready to fly a barometer, thermometer, and camera. This latest rocket employed tail fins for aerodynamic stability and a parachute to return it safely to Earth. The camera was designed to snap a picture of the instruments at the instant the parachute deployed; the barometer reading would document the altitude at deployment, and the thermometer would document the ambient air temperature at that altitude. It was the first attempt to launch a rocket carrying scientific instruments.

The rocket lifted off 13 seconds after ignition, reached an altitude of 80 feet (24 meters), and hit the ground 171 feet (52.1 meters) away. The flight lasted 18.5 seconds. Although the test was a success, the gasoline tank exploded on impact, causing frightened neighbors to call the authorities to report a plane crash. The ensuing publicity brought Goddard's work to the attention of aviator Charles Lindbergh, who recommended it for funding from the Daniel Guggenheim Fund for the Promotion of Aeronautics. Secure long-term support from the fund allowed Goddard to move to Roswell, New Mexico, and work full time on rocketry research.

Impact

The publicity generated by Goddard's work in the 1920s inspired the scientists and engineers who would lead U.S. rocketry development in the 1940s and 1950s, and popular interest in rocketry and other scientific advances created a market for science-fiction film and literature. Although Goddard pioneered many advances in rocketry, his obsession with secrecy ultimately gave him little long-term influence on the field. German scientists and engineers independently made great advances in rocketry during World War II and passed their expertise on to the United States and the Soviet Union following Germany's defeat.

Billy R. Smith Jr.

Further Reading

Butrica, Andrew J. *Single Stage to Orbit: Politics, Space Technology, and the Quest for Reusable Rocketry.* Baltimore: Johns Hopkins University Press, 2003. A history of the concept of single-stage-to-orbit vehicles, beginning with the 1920s.

Clary, David A. *Rocket Man: Robert H. Goddard and the Birth of the Space Age.* New York: Hyperion Books, 2003. A biography of Goddard containing detailed descriptions of his test launches.

Goddard, Robert H. *Rockets: Two Classic Papers.* Mineola, N.Y.: Dover, 2002. Reprints Goddard's papers, "A Method of Reaching Extreme Altitudes" (1919) and "Liquid Propellant Rocket Development" (1936).

Gruntman, Mike. *Blazing the Trail: The Early History of Spacecraft and Rocketry.* Reston, Va.: American Institute of Aeronautics and Astronautics, 2004. An overview of rocketry from its early days to the space age.

Winter, Frank H. *Rockets into Space.* Cambridge, Mass.: Harvard University Press, 1993. Describes the evolution of space launch vehicles.

See also: Goddard, Robert; Lindbergh, Charles; Science and technology; Science fiction

■ Rockne, Knute

Identification: American football coach
Born: March 4, 1888, Voss, Norway
Died: March 31, 1931, Bazaar, Kansas

Knute Rockne has been recognized as one of the premier coaches in American college football history. His innovative approach to coaching and his dynamic personality made him a legendary figure in the early years of college football. Among his many achievements, Rockne has been credited with being the first coach to use the forward pass as a major component of his game plan.

Knute Rockne was born Knut Larsen Rokne in Voss, Norway, to Lars Knutson Rokne and Martha Pedersdatter Gjermo. When he was five years old, his family emigrated from Norway to Chicago, Illinois, settling in the largely Scandinavian neighborhood of Logan Square. It was here, in street games with the neighborhood children, that Rockne first learned to play football and baseball. In high school, he joined the football team and participated in several other sports as well, notably running and pole vaulting. After leaving high school, he worked at the Chicago post office until 1910, when, having earned enough money to attend college, he left his job and enrolled at the University of Notre Dame in South Bend, Indiana.

Notre Dame Football Legend

Rockne entered Notre Dame with the intention of pursuing a career in medicine. To help pay his tuition, he worked as a janitor in the chemistry department. He joined the Notre Dame football team in

Knute Rockne. (AP Photo)

1910, though he sat on the bench his first year and only became a starting player in 1911. In 1913, Rockne was elected team captain and led his team to their third undefeated and second perfect (undefeated and untied) season in a row.

Rockne graduated magna cum laude from Notre Dame with a degree in chemistry and applied to Saint Louis University's school of medicine. When he was rejected, he accepted an offer from Notre Dame to work as an assistant chemistry instructor and assistant football coach instead. In 1917, when head coach Jesse Harper retired, Rockne took over the position.

Rockne's first season as head coach, the 1918 season, was less than spectacular, with 3 wins, 1 loss, and 2 ties. The next two seasons, however, his team was undefeated, and his reputation as a coach began to grow. Throughout the 1920s, Notre Dame continued to perform at a consistently high level, becoming known as the team to beat. Rockne's most notable accomplishments included a victory in the 1925 Rose Bowl following another undefeated season in 1924, and two further undefeated seasons in 1929 and 1930. In his thirteen seasons as Notre Dame's head coach, he attained a record of 105 wins, 12 losses, and 5 ties. Rockne readily attributed much of his success to the ability of his players; in his 1924 championship season, he relied heavily on the skills of his "Four Horseman of Notre Dame," a backfield consisting of Harry Stuhldreher, Don Miller, James Crowley, and Elmer Layden.

Sportswriters were eager to work with Rockne because of his colorful and quotable public remarks. His inspirational phrases and speeches were often featured in newspapers, magazines, and radio programs. Perhaps most memorable was his famous "Win one for the Gipper" speech, delivered in honor of legendary player George Gipp, which was featured in the Hollywood movie *Knute Rockne, All American*.

Impact

Knute Rockne was one of the pioneering coaches in college football, helping to transform the sport from an extracurricular aspect of college life into the billion-dollar industry that it is today. Innovation was the key to Rockne's success: He changed the game of football from a test of brute strength and kicking ability to a more exciting game that relied on speed, deception, precision blocking, and long passes. He also realized the importance of creating a loyal following of Notre Dame supporters and played to the crowds both on and off the field. Rockne used his national popularity to financially benefit both himself and the University of Notre Dame through personal appearances, promotional endorsements, and commercial writing. He was at the height of his career when he was killed in an airplane crash in Kansas in 1931, and his legend has inspired new generations of football players ever since.

Paul P. Sipiera

Further Reading

Cavanaugh, Jack. *The Gipper: George Gipp, Knute Rockne, and the Dramatic Rise of Notre Dame Football.* New York: Skyhorse, 2010. Focuses on Gipp's career, his relationship with Rockne, and the influence of both men on the rise of Notre Dame football.

Maggio, Frank P. *Notre Dame and the Game That Changed Football: How Jesse Harper Made the Forward Pass a Weapon and Knute Rockne a Legend.* New York: Carroll & Graf, 2007. A detailed history of the beginnings of Notre Dame football and how two of its coaches, Harper and Rockne, brought the university to athletic prominence.

Robinson, Ray. *Rockne of Notre Dame: The Making of a Football Legend.* New York: Oxford University Press, 2002. Presents a more human picture of Rockne, in contrast to the mythological figure of Notre Dame legend.

Sperber, Murray A. *Shake Down the Thunder: The Creation of Notre Dame Football.* Bloomington: Indiana University Press, 2002. An account of the early days of Notre Dame football with heavy emphasis on Rockne, written with unprecedented access to the university's sports archives.

Steele, Michael R. *Knute Rockne: A Portrait of a Notre Dame Legend.* Champaign, Ill.: Sagamore, 1998. A detailed look at Rockne as both the man and the legend, based on extensive research and including statistics, interviews, and family and professional photos.

See also: Football; Four Horsemen of Notre Dame; Gipp, George; National Football League; Sports

■ Rockwell, Norman

Identification: American artist and illustrator
Born: February 3, 1894, New York, New York
Died: November 8, 1978, Stockbridge, Massachusetts

Norman Percevel Rockwell was America's iconic painter from the 1920s to the 1970s. His paintings were based on everyday life experiences and celebrated values such as human decency and integrity.

Norman Rockwell's paintings exemplified the best in American life and culture. He studied art at the Chase School (later the Parsons School of Design), the National Academy of Design, and the Art Students League, all in New York City, where he earned the nickname the "Deacon" for his serious work ethic. His early illustrations appeared in children's books such as *Tell Me Why Stories* (1912) and magazines such as the Boy Scouts publication *Boys' Life*. On May 20, 1916, Rockwell had his first cover on the *Saturday Evening Post*, titled *Boy with Baby Carriage*. He became the top cover artist for the *Post*, working with its editor George Horace Lorimer. Around this time, he married Irene O'Connor and they lived in New Rochelle, New York, where he built his first studio.

Rockwell published over three hundred *Post* covers in forty-seven years. On January 29, 1921, *Literary Digest* had his painting *Mother Tucking Children into Bed* on its cover, and Rockwell received additional commissions for covers on the magazines *Leslie's Weekly, Judge, Country Gentleman,* and *Life*. He illustrated the Boy Scouts' calendars annually from 1925 through 1976 and produced numerous advertising illustrations. His 1920s paintings included *Santa and Expense Book* (1920), *No Swimming* (1921), *Girl Reading Palm* (1921), *Santa and the Elves* (1922), and *Doctor and Doll* (1929). His *Literary Digest* covers included *Dreams in the Antique Shop* (1923).

Rockwell established his reputation and style by painting everyday situations as stories, often with humorous overtones. His art evoked a fundamental wholesomeness and often depicted youth, old age, dogs, and holiday celebrations. He painted life as he wanted it to be, idealizing family bonds. His characters appeared genuine, kind, and filled with common sense.

Rockwell also served as a judge for the second annual Miss America contest in Atlantic City in 1922. He enjoyed celebrity status during the 1920s, playing golf, sailing, and touring South America and Europe.

Impact

Inspired by President Franklin D. Roosevelt's speech of the same title, Rockwell painted his *Four Freedoms* (1943) series as *Saturday Evening Post* war covers. Rockwell's idealized work came to represent the finer qualities of the United States and Americans as exemplified by his painting *The Golden Rule* (1960), illustrating multicultural harmony. He was awarded the Presidential Medal of Freedom in 1977. The Norman Rockwell Museum in Stockbridge, Massachusetts, established as a trust in 1973, preserves his legacy.

Barbara Bennett Peterson

Further Reading

Buechner, Thomas S. *Norman Rockwell, Artist and Illustrator.* New York: Harry N. Abrams, 1970.

Claridge, Laura P. *Norman Rockwell: A Life.* New York: Random House, 2001.

Rockwell, Norman. *My Adventures as an Illustrator: An Autobiography.* Indianapolis: Curtis, 1979.

See also: Art movements; Magazines

■ Rodgers, Jimmie

Identification: American country music singer and songwriter
Also known as: James Charles Rodgers
Born: September 8, 1897, Meridian, Mississippi
Died: May 26, 1933, New York, New York

Incorporating traditional yodeling, jazz syncopations, and elements from the blues into his music, Jimmie Rodgers emerged as an early pioneer of country music in the 1920s. Commercially successful as a recording artist, he served as an archetype for future generations of country musicians and songwriters.

As a young child, Jimmie Rodgers lived with relatives in both Mississippi and Alabama after his parents' separation and his mother's death. He later lived with his father, a railroad foreman, and his stepmother. He displayed an interest in the entertainment industry at an early age, participating in amateur singing contests by the age of thirteen. However, family responsibilities required him to work with his father as a water boy for the railroad. Rodgers also worked as a brakeman and switchman. At twenty-seven, he contracted tuberculosis, forcing him to leave railroad work for a time, during which he briefly toured the Southeast in a traveling road show.

In 1927, he performed with musician Otis Kuykendall on the radio station WWNC in Asheville, North Carolina. Soon afterward, Rodgers began performing weekly with the Tennessee-based group known as the Tenneva Ramblers, appearing collectively on WWNC as the Jimmie Rodgers Entertainers. The newly formed group auditioned for Victor Records; however, internal disagreement led Rodgers to record "Sleep, Baby, Sleep" and "The Soldier's Sweetheart" alone. Moderate success with these first two songs led to further recordings with Victor Records, and of these later sessions, Rodgers's single "T for Texas," also known as "Blue Yodel No. 1," obtained remarkable commercial success.

Rodgers appeared in the 1929 movie short *The Singing Brakeman*, in which he sang his compositions "Waiting for a Train," "Daddy and Home," and "T for Texas." Rodgers later toured with cowboy and entertainer Will Rogers. In 1930, Rodgers recorded the song "Standin' on the Corner" with well-known jazz trumpeter Louis Armstrong. The country music star died of advanced tuberculosis in 1933.

Impact

In a relatively short period of time, Rodgers released 110 songs, popularizing country music for a growing American audience during the 1920s. By incorporating blues, jazz, and traditional American music, he helped shape a new approach to country music. Known as the "Father of Country Music," Rodger's pedal steel guitar playing and meter-free style of singing and yodeling was imitated by later generations of country musicians. Rodgers was inducted into the Country Music Hall of Fame, the Songwriters Hall of Fame, and the Rock and Roll Hall of Fame in the 1960s and 1970s.

Mark E. Perry

Further Reading

Mazor, Barry. *Meeting Jimmie Rodgers: How America's Original Roots Music Hero Changed the Pop Sounds of a Century.* New York: Oxford University Press, 2009.

Peterson, Richard A. *Creating Country Music: Fabricating Authenticity.* Chicago: University of Chicago Press, 1999.

Porterfield, Nolan. *Jimmie Rodgers: The Life and Times of America's Blue Yodeler.* Rev. ed. Jackson: University Press of Mississippi, 2007.

See also: Armstrong, Louis; Film; Grand Ole Opry, The (radio show); Music, popular; Railroads; Rogers, Will

■ Rogers, Will

Identification: American humorist, actor, and social commentator
Also known as: William Penn Adair Rogers
Born: November 4, 1879, Cooweescoowee District, Indian Territory (now Oologah, Oklahoma)
Died: August 15, 1935, Point Barrow, Alaska

Many have characterized Will Rogers as a humorist, but during his life, he was much more than that. It has been said that Rogers drew on his Cherokee roots to become a moral compass for the United States during the 1920s and 1930s. Rogers traveled the world, acting and speaking to thousands while projecting his view of life with a wry and instructive style of humor.

Will Rogers was an immensely popular entertainer, and he willingly shared his celebrity with up-and-coming actors. Tom Mix, who later became Hollywood's best-known movie cowboy, learned to perform rope tricks and ride horses from Rogers. Rogers also suggested to Oklahoma telegraph operator Gene Autry that he should audition for an acting role in Hollywood. Autry went on to become a successful actor and country singing legend after Rogers's death.

Born in 1879 to a Cherokee ranching family, William Penn Adair Rogers learned his roping and riding skills as a young boy on the ranch. These abilities would later serve him on stage for most of his professional life. As a young man, Rogers worked his way around the world as a cowboy, performing rope and riding tricks, but his career was solidified in vaudeville in 1904 when he added political commentary and humor to the trick roping act. Soon he was better known as a political philosopher and humorist than as a stage cowboy.

Rogers married Betty Blake in 1908 after an eight-year courtship. Together they had four children, including Will Rogers Jr., who became an actor but was also a decorated World War II combat veteran and a member of the United States Congress. Their second child, Mary Rogers, acted on Broadway. Jim Rogers had a few small acting parts in movies but mainly followed the family tradition of ranching and horse breeding. The youngest child, Fred Rogers, who was born in 1918, died of diphtheria at the age of eighteen months.

The Ziegfeld Follies

In 1918, Rogers joined the Ziegfeld Follies as one of its few male performers and the only performer to bring a horse onstage. Rogers's reputation as a political commentator and humorist spread rapidly during his vaudeville days. By the early 1920s, Rogers was also writing one of the most widely syndicated weekly newspaper columns in the United States for the McNaught Newspaper Service. After his first column appeared in the *New York Times*, Rogers traveled the world in order to report his observations. As a popular writer, Rogers covered a wide spectrum of political commentary. He also wrote frequently on the mistreatment of American Indians by the U.S. government. Rogers's commentaries were so popular that he was encouraged to run for president of the United States in the 1924, 1928, and 1932 elections.

Rogers's career with the Ziegfeld Follies hit its height during the 1920s. Gene Buck, Ziegfeld's

Will Rogers. (Getty Images)

chief writer, said that Rogers possessed the genius to write and to say aloud what many people thought but did not dare say. Rogers was a consummate student of the news and ordinary Americans' reactions to it. Rogers's nightly routine after each Follies appearance was to buy every newspaper he could find and then read them carefully while jotting notes for the next day's act.

Impact

Although he never ran for president, Rogers did master radio and film, which served to spread his fame worldwide. It has been said that the time when the U.S. population was 120 million people, Rogers was reaching over 40 million Americans each week through his newspaper columns and radio speeches. By the end of his movie career, Rogers starred or otherwise appeared in seventy-one films.

Rogers's desire to visit and write about Alaska led to his boarding a small airplane piloted by famed aviator Wiley Post. The plane crashed near Point Barrow, Alaska, on August 15, 1935, killing both men. News of Rogers's death dominated newspapers for days, and nearly 100,000 people visited his casket in Glendale, California.

The Dog Iron Ranch on the shores of Lake Oolagah, Oklahoma, where Rogers was born, became a public park, and parks and memorial museums throughout Oklahoma were also dedicated to him. Rogers's ranch at Pacific Palisades, California, is a state park, and the Oklahoma City airport was renamed the Will Rogers World Airport in his honor.

Bruce E. Johansen

Further Reading

Chavers, Dean. *Modern American Indian Leaders: Their Lives and Their Works.* 2 vols. Lewiston, N.Y.: Edwin Mellen Press, 2007. Includes information on Rogers's role as a social commentator and humorist, with emphasis on his impact near his home in Oklahoma.

Rogers, Betty Blake. *Will Rogers: His Wife's Story.* Rev. ed. Norman: University of Oklahoma Press, 1979. A biography of Rogers from his wife's point of view.

Rogers, Will. *The Writings of Will Rogers.* 21 vols. Stillwater: Oklahoma State University Press, 1973–1983. Contains nearly everything written by Rogers during his prolific literary career.

Wertheim, Arthur Frank, ed. *Will Rogers at the Ziegfeld Follies.* Norman: University of Oklahoma Press, 1992. Describes Rogers's career with the Ziegfeld Follies, which peaked during the 1920s.

White, Richard D., Jr. *Will Rogers: A Political Life.* Lubbock: Texas Tech University Press, 2011. Explores Rogers's political influence during the 1920s and 1930s.

Yagoda, Ben. *Will Rogers: A Biography.* Norman: University of Oklahoma Press, 2000. A biography of Rogers's life, including photographs.

See also: Aviation; Mix, Tom; Native Americans; Ziegfeld, Florenz; Ziegfeld Follies

■ Romberg, Sigmund

Identification: American composer
Also known as: Siegmund Romberg; Siegmund Rosenberg; Sigismund Romberg; Zsigmond Romberg
Born: July 29, 1887, Nagykanizsa, Austro-Hungarian Empire (now Hungary)
Died: November 9, 1951, New York, New York

Romberg was among the leading and most prolific Broadway composers of the 1920s, best known for his operettas and for establishing two distinct models for the American operetta.

Hungarian-born composer and conductor Sigmund Romberg arrived in New York in 1909 and found work as a restaurant pianist and orchestra leader. In 1914, theater owners J. J. and Lee Shubert hired Romberg as a staff composer of revues and adaptations of Central European operettas.

Romberg's first major success came from the operetta *Maytime* (1917). Produced by the Shuberts, *Maytime* established the first Romberg operetta model: sentimental storylines involving a romantic couple, a bittersweet ending, and a recurring waltz duet that unified the expansive score and constituted the basis for the finale.

Romberg wrote many successful operettas for the Shuberts during the 1920s, including *Blossom Time* (1921), a fictional tale of real-life composer Franz Schubert that includes the recurring waltz "Song of Love." *The Student Prince* (1924), Romberg's most successful original operetta, is the story of unrealized love between a prince and a commoner in nineteenth-century Germany and was the longest-running Broadway musical of the 1920s. *My Maryland* (1925) reimagines the American Civil War and includes the popular march "Your Land and My Land."

Romberg then worked with producers Laurence Schwab and Frank Mandel in the mid-1920s and simultaneously collaborated with lyricist Oscar Hammerstein II. The team scored the successful *The Desert Song* (1926), which signaled Romberg's second operetta model: Stories were no longer set in the past, no longer ended sadly, and waltzes, though still part of the production, were no longer the focal point of the work. *The Desert Song* is filled with what were then contemporary references to the Riff wars in North Africa, and it capitalized on the celebrity of silent film star Rudolph Valentino and on the stories of British soldier T. E. Lawrence ("Lawrence of Arabia"). The musical score includes "It" and "One Alone," the recurring ballad that ends the show. The same team was responsible for *The New Moon* (1928), which is set in eighteenth-century Louisiana and introduced some of the most popular songs of the decade, including "Wanting You," "One Kiss," and the choral march "Stouthearted Men."

In 1928, Romberg and George Gershwin collaborated on *Rosalie*, a show created to feature Ziegfeld star Marilyn Miller. Romberg provided the European-sounding operetta music (the title character was Romanian), while Gershwin contributed jazz-inspired musical comedy.

Impact
During his career, Romberg produced seventy-eight operettas, eight films, and close to two thousand songs. Romberg's music has remained popular through film adaptations of his operettas, amateur and professional stage productions, and studio recordings.

William A. Everett

Further Reading
Everett, William A. *Sigmund Romberg*. New Haven: Yale University Press, 2007.
Mordden, Ethan. *Make Believe: The Broadway Musical in the 1920s*. New York: Oxford University Press, 1997.

See also: Broadway musicals; Gershwin, George; Hammerstein, Oscar, II; *Sheik, The; Student Prince, The;* Theater in the United States; Valentino, Rudolph

Roosevelt, Franklin D.

Identification: American politician
Born: January 30, 1882, Hyde Park, New York
Died: April 12, 1945, Warm Springs, Georgia

During the 1920s, Franklin D. Roosevelt further established himself as a capable politician, building a political philosophy and career that would lead him to the presidency in the next decade. He overcame political defeat in 1920, coped with a serious and debilitating illness, and was elected governor of New York in 1928.

Franklin Delano Roosevelt was born into a wealthy family in the late nineteenth century. The Hyde Park Roosevelts were Democrats, unlike their relatives in Oyster Bay, New York, among whom was Theodore Roosevelt, Republican president of the United States between 1901 and 1909 and Franklin Roosevelt's fifth cousin. After attending Harvard, Roosevelt married Theodore's niece Eleanor Roosevelt in 1905. He became a lawyer, and was elected to the New York legislature in 1910 and 1912, resigning from his second term in 1913 to serve as assistant secretary of the U.S. Navy.

In 1920, Roosevelt received the Democratic vice-presidential nomination alongside presidential nominee James M. Cox, governor of Ohio. Roosevelt was young and charismatic, his ties to New York brought geographical balance to the ticket, and his last name evoked the political reputation of his cousin Theodore. However, Cox lost the election to Republican Warren G. Harding. After this defeat, Roosevelt became vice president of the New York office of the insurance firm Fidelity and Deposit Company of Maryland, which allowed him to pursue his political and philanthropic interests.

Polio
In August of 1921, while vacationing at Campobello Island in New Brunswick, Canada, Roosevelt lost feeling in his legs and became partially paralyzed. His condition was diagnosed as poliomyelitis, the disease commonly known as polio, although some researchers would later suggest other diagnoses. He was transferred to New York's Presbyterian Hospital, where the doctors were pessimistic that he would even sit up in the future. Roosevelt had always led an active life, and his physical impairment was discouraging, as was the possible effect of his partial paralysis on his political career. His mother, Sara, wanted him to return to Hyde Park, but Eleanor and his political advisor Louis Howe urged him to pursue his political and social interests to the best of his ability. Roosevelt was optimistic that the use of his limbs would soon return and found swimming an excellent exercise, as the water reduced the weight of his legs. He began to visit the town of Warm Springs, Georgia, for the possible therapeutic benefits of its hot springs; he later purchased land there, establishing the Warm Springs Foundation for the treatment of polio victims.

Business and Politics
Roosevelt continued his business and political activities in spite of his disability. He became chair of the American Construction Council and also invested in several prospective businesses related to the lobster market, taxi advertising, and "clerkless stores." He was a major force behind the election of Al Smith as governor of New York in 1922, and he nominated Smith for the presidency at the 1924 Democratic National Convention, referring to Smith as "the happy warrior." Although Smith did not receive the

Franklin D. Roosevelt. (Hulton Archive/Getty Images)

nomination and the Democrats lost to Calvin Coolidge, Roosevelt became an increasingly well-known and respected political figure. New technology contributed to Roosevelt's increased standing: both the Democratic and Republican conventions of 1924 had been broadcast on the radio. Unlike many of his contemporary politicians, who tended to shout into the microphones, Roosevelt's voice and manner of speaking were fitting for this new medium, and his radio speeches of the 1920s prefigured the famous "fireside chats" of his later presidency. After the convention, some of his admirers hoped that he would run for president in 1928. Meanwhile, through numerous letters and telephone calls, Roosevelt and Howe developed a nationwide network of political contacts.

After the disastrous Democratic defeat in 1924, Roosevelt called for unity, believing that the various factions of the party, including farmers and laborers, urban political machines such as New York's notoriously corrupt Tammany Hall, and the so-called Solid South, could be brought together under the banner of "Progressive Democracy." Roosevelt's definition of Progressivism was somewhat vague, but it included strengthening the central government for the purpose of assisting the common people. He was urged to accept the Democratic nomination for United States senator from New York, but refused; he was still committed to regaining his strength, and his goal was the presidency, not the Senate.

Governorship of New York

In 1928, New York governor Al Smith was the only major candidate for the Democratic presidential nomination. Roosevelt had supported Smith in the past, and he nominated him in 1928, as he had in 1924, again acclaiming Smith as "the happy warrior," though he was less enthusiastic about Smith's connections to large business interests and Tammany Hall. In addition, Smith faced substantial difficulties in winning over voters: He was the first Catholic to be nominated for president by a major political party, and he was "wet"—a politician opposed to Prohibition, which was still the law of the land and supported by many Americans.

Smith and his advisors pressured Roosevelt to run for governor of New York in the 1928 state election, in part to help Smith carry the state in the presidential contest against Republican Herbert Hoover. Roosevelt eventually succumbed to Smith's appeals and was narrowly elected governor by about twenty-five thousand votes out of more than four million cast. Smith, however, failed to carry the state and the nation, losing the presidential election to Hoover.

Roosevelt was inaugurated in early 1929. Initially he had no elaborate political program, but over time he worked to reform the state's prison system and strongly advocated for the development of a hydroelectric power plant on the St. Lawrence River. Roosevelt also worked to reduce political corruption, although for political reasons he did not confront New York City's Tammany Hall. Following the stock market crash of October 1929 and the subsequent Great Depression, Roosevelt initiated a state relief system and a public works construction program and urged the adoption of old-age pensions and unemployment insurance, programs he would advocate on a national scale as president.

Impact

Roosevelt was reelected governor in 1930, and two years later, the economic crisis had made Hoover so vulnerable that Roosevelt challenged him for the presidency and won. Roosevelt guided the United States through the Great Depression, building upon his concept of progressive democracy to alleviate the nation's economic distress through government intervention. Under the New Deal, Roosevelt created jobs, initiated public works projects, and established enduring social relief systems. By the time of his death in 1945, Roosevelt had been in office for twelve years, longer than any other U.S. president.

Eugene Larson

Further Reading

Davis, Kenneth S. *FDR: The Beckoning of Destiny, 1882–1928.* New York: Putnam, 1972. The first volume of a five-volume biography, focusing on Roosevelt's early life and career.

Freidel, Frank. *Franklin D. Roosevelt: The Apprenticeship.* New York: Little, Brown, 1952. The first volume of a multivolume study of Roosevelt.

Schlesinger, Arthur M., Jr. *The Crisis of the Old Order, 1919–1933.* Boston: Houghton Mifflin, 1957. An account of the 1920s with an extensive focus on Roosevelt.

Smith, Jean Edward. *FDR.* New York: Random House, 2007. A one-volume study of Roosevelt's life, both personal and political.

Ward, Geoffrey C. *A First Class Temperament.* New York: HarperCollins, 1990. The second volume of a multivolume biography that recounts Roosevelt's early political career and his struggle with partial paralysis.

See also: Cox, James M.; Elections, U.S., of 1920; Elections, U.S., of 1924; Elections, U.S., of 1928; Political parties; Smith, Alfred E.

■ Rosenfeld, Fanny "Bobbie"

Identification: Canadian athlete
Born: December 28, 1904 (sources vary), Yekaterinoslav, Russia (now Dnipropetrovsk, Ukraine)
Died: November 13, 1969, Toronto, Ontario, Canada

Fanny Rosenfeld, nicknamed Bobbie because of her bobbed hair, was the leading female Canadian athlete of the 1920s. She dominated many sports, broke national and world records, and won gold and silver medals in the 1928 Summer Olympics.

As an infant, Fanny Rosenfeld immigrated with her family to Barrie, Ontario. When she was nineteen, the family moved to Toronto, where she played baseball, hockey, and basketball in local leagues.

Rosenfeld came to national attention in 1923 when, while at a picnic, she entered a 100-yard dash competition and won, beating Canadian champion Rosa Grosse. Later that year, she competed in a track meet at the annual Canadian National Exhibition, where she beat both Grosse and Helen Filkey, the American world record holder.

Rosenfeld was an astounding natural athlete. In a single day at the 1925 Ontario Ladies' Track and Field Championships, she placed first in discus, long jump, low hurdles, shot put, and the 220-yard dash, and second in javelin and the 100-yard dash. She went on to set national records in discus, javelin, shot put, standing broad jump, and the 440-yard relay, and also excelled in ice hockey, softball, fastball, golf, speed skating, tennis, and lacrosse.

At the 1928 Summer Olympics, the first in which women were permitted to compete in track-and-field events, Rosenfeld's team won the 400-meter relay gold medal. In the 100-meter run, which ended in an apparent tie, she was given the silver. Perhaps more remarkably, in the 800-meter run, she ran alongside an injured teammate in order to provide encouragement and moral support, even holding back at the end so that her teammate could take fourth place. Observers noted that had she not done so, she might have won the bronze medal.

Severe arthritis led to Rosenfeld's retirement in 1933, after which she went on to coach women's track and softball. From 1937 to 1958, she wrote a regular column on women's sports for the *Toronto Globe and Mail* newspaper.

Impact

Rosenfeld defined athletic greatness in the 1920s, showing that great character could accompany great athleticism. She advocated for physical education and sports opportunities for women, writing with intelligence and humor in defense of female athletes. She was elected to the Canadian Sports Hall of Fame in 1949, and in 1950, was named by Canadian sportswriters as Canada's Female Athlete of the Half Century. Bobbie Rosenfeld Park was established in Toronto in 1991. Since 1978, the Bobbie Rosenfeld Award has been presented annually to Canada's female athlete of the year.

Leslie Friedman

Ross, Harold

Identification: American editor
Born: November 6, 1892, Aspen, Colorado
Died: December 6, 1951, Boston, Massachusetts

In the second half of the 1920s, editor Harold Ross gathered a staff of writers and illustrators, including Dorothy Parker, James Thurber, Robert Benchley, Ring Lardner, S. J. Perelman, and Ogden Nash, to turn The New Yorker *into one of the leading literary magazines in the United States.*

After serving in World War I and working on a number of newspapers, Harold Wallace Ross founded *The New Yorker* in February of 1925 with financial backing from yeast heir Raoul Fleishmann. The magazine floundered for two years before finding its own voice as a sophisticated weekly that reported on New York City culture and events with wit and style. Ross soon established the departments The Talk of the Town, which consisted of brief, often humorous and casually written insights into life in New York, and the informal biographical "Profiles" that would become the trademarks of the new journal.

By 1930, Ross had attracted some of the greatest talent in the country to work for the magazine, including artists such as Peter Arno and Helen Hokinson and writers and editors such as Alexander Woollcott and E. B. White. Ross was also a founding member of the Algonquin Round Table, a daily and informal lunch meeting in the dining room of New York's Algonquin Hotel, where well-known and highly respected writers and journalists of the period would trade wit and witticisms.

Ross was considered an anomaly as an editor of such a cosmopolitan magazine. Born in Colorado and raised in Utah, well outside the confines of New York City, Ross left high school before earning a diploma. He was said to be shy and prudish, but he also became the driving force behind what many consider the most sophisticated humor magazine in America.

Ross is said to have worked ten-hour days, seven days a week, and the magazine's popularity by the end of the decade attests to his dedication. By the late 1920s and into the 1930s, *The New Yorker* was known nationwide for its unique content and distinctive style. Ross would remain the magazine's editor until 1951.

Impact

Harold Ross was the editorial force who, in the mid-1920s, collected a talented staff at what would become the leading popular magazine in the United States in the twentieth century, a journal known for its fiction and nonfiction, cartoons and covers, and humor and urbanity.

David Peck

Further Reading

Kunkel, Thomas. *Genius in Disguise: Harold Ross of* The New Yorker. New York: Carroll & Graf, 1996.
Ross, Harold. *Letters from the Editor:* The New Yorker's *Harold Ross.* Edited by Thomas Kunkel. New York: Modern Library, 2001.
Thurber, James. *The Years with Ross.* 1957. Reprint. New York: Perennial Classics, 2001.

See also: Algonquin Round Table; Magazines; *New Yorker, The;* Parker, Dorothy

Ross, Nellie Tayloe

Identification: American politician
Born: November 29, 1876, Andrew County, Missouri
Died: December 19, 1977, Washington, D.C.

Nellie Tayloe Ross of Wyoming was the first woman to serve as governor of a U.S. state. She was thrust into the world of government policy and party politics after the sudden death of her husband, Wyoming governor William Bradford Ross, in 1924.

Nellie Tayloe was born on her family's plantation in Missouri. Previously a well-established family, the

Tayloes had lost much of their wealth and standing in the aftermath of the Civil War. Their house burned down when Nellie was seven years old, after which the family moved to Kansas. Once Nellie had finished high school, they moved to Omaha, Nebraska, where Nellie gave piano lessons to supplement the family finances; later, she completed a two-year teaching course and went on to teach kindergarten classes.

On a family visit to Tennessee in 1900, Nellie met William Bradford Ross. They married in 1902 and moved to Cheyenne, Wyoming, where William opened a law practice. William's practice flourished, and he became known for his consistent adherence to progressive Democratic ideals. He was nominated to run for governor in 1922, and with the dominant Republican Party weakened by scandal and badly divided, he won by a narrow margin. However, in October 1924, less than two years into his term, he died due to complications following an appendectomy, leaving Nellie Tayloe Ross a widow with three sons.

Nellie Tayloe Ross. (© Bettmann/Corbis)

Governorship

Wyoming's nickname, "The Equality State," refers to the fact that women there had been granted the right to vote and hold public office in 1869, twenty years before the territory became a state. Wyoming was also the home of the United States' first female justice of the peace, first all-female jury, first female court bailiff, and first woman to be elected to statewide office. Armed with this precedent and aware of the sympathy many in the sparsely populated state felt for Ross—and knowing that Texas was poised to elect Miriam Ferguson governor as a proxy for her impeached husband—Democratic Party leaders nominated Ross to stand in the special election in November 1924, hoping to beat Texas to another historical first. Ross did not campaign on her own behalf, saying only that she would continue her husband's work. However, her Republican opponent carried the stain of the Teapot Dome scandal, and she was elected by a wide margin. She was sworn in on January 5, 1925, as the first female governor in American history.

Though she came to office by what historians call the "widow's route" and had no formal experience in government, Ross dedicated herself to the task and quickly learned her role. In the forty-day legislative session that began within weeks of her swearing in, she faced Republican majorities in both houses. She did continue her husband's policies, which included strict economies of government, the permanent establishment of a loan program for farmers, and the firm enforcement of Prohibition. She also strengthened worker protections, especially in mining; furthered bank reform and instituted an early type of depositors insurance; and played a leading role in defending Wyoming's water rights, as guaranteed in the Colorado River Compact, in a hearing regarding the proposed construction of the Boulder Dam (later the Hoover Dam).

As a female official, Ross achieved great notoriety. She was swamped with requests for interviews, speeches, and articles. She traveled to Washington for the inauguration of President Calvin Coolidge and spoke at the National Women's Democratic Club in March 1925, attended the Woman's World Fair in Chicago in April, and participated in the National Governors' Conference in Maine in July. Never had a Wyoming official had such visibility, and Ross enjoyed the celebrity. She had, however, declined to attend the National Conference of the League of Women Voters in February.

Later Career

Ross stood for reelection in November 1926. Republicans, however, were now united behind candidate Frank C. Emerson, and they campaigned hard, blaming Ross for her failure to balance the state budget. Many of Wyoming's strongest feminists were Republicans, and the election elicited a good deal of discussion in newspapers about appropriate roles for women and whether Ross's activities and policies did or did not contribute adequately to women's advancement. Again, Ross chose not to travel the state to campaign, feeling that such a display of ambition would be unseemly. She lost the election.

Ross went on to work for the national Democratic Party in 1928 and 1932, organizing vigorous campaigns focused on unaffiliated women voters. In 1933, Franklin Delano Roosevelt named her the first female director of the U.S. Mint, a position she would hold for twenty years.

Impact

Ross was a groundbreaker for women's participation in politics. By assuming the governorship, she became a symbol of the potential of postsuffrage women. However, she never identified with the feminist movement in America, nor did she espouse the cause of women's rights. For Ross, good government had no gender.

Jean Owens Schaefer

Further Reading

Mackey, Mike. "Nellie Tayloe Ross and Wyoming Politics." *Journal of the West* 42, no. 3 (Summer, 2003): 25–34. Details Ross's rise to office, activities, and subsequent defeat in 1926.

Mayhead, Molly A., and Brenda DeVore Marshall. *Women's Political Discourse: A Twenty-First-Century Perspective.* Lanham, Md.: Rowman & Littlefield, 2005. A brief overview of women who have held U.S. political office.

Pierce, Jennifer Burek. "Portrait of a 'Governor Lady': An Examination of Nellie Taylor Ross's Autobiographical Political Advocacy." In *Navigating Boundaries: The Rhetoric of Women Governors,* edited by Brenda DeVore Marshall and Molly A. Mayhead. Westport, Conn.: Praeger, 2000. Analyzes Ross's 1927 presentation of her political career.

Ross, Nellie Tayloe. "The Governor Lady." *Good Housekeeping* 85, nos. 2–4 (August–October, 1927). Ross's own view of her gubernatorial career.

Scharff, Virginia. "Feminism, Femininity, and Power: Nellie Tayloe Ross and the Woman Politician's Dilemma." *Frontiers: A Journal of Women's Studies* 15, no. 3 (1995): 87–106. Uses Ross's letters and essays to analyze her ambivalences about women, careers, and politics.

Scheer, Teva J. *Governor Lady: The Life and Times of Nellie Tayloe Ross.* Columbia: University of Missouri Press, 2005. A detailed biography.

See also: League of Women Voters; Nineteenth Amendment; Political parties; Progressive Party of 1924; Prohibition; Teapot Dome scandal; Women's rights

■ Route 66

Route 66 was one of the first roads designed specifically for interstate automobile travel. Stretching from Chicago, Illinois, to Los Angeles, California, and passing through six states in between, it created new communities as small towns sprang up along its length to supply travelers with food, gasoline, and lodging.

The burgeoning popularity of automobiles in the early twentieth century created an increasing need for roads, as those that existed were mainly converted wagon trails, often little more than poorly marked dirt paths. By the mid-1920s, independent road clubs sponsored "auto trails," which they marked and mapped in a variety of ways. To establish a system of federal highways that would facilitate interstate travel, the Federal Aid Road Act of 1916 had appropriated funds for the improvement or new construction of such roads. Plans for a nationwide system of highways were underway by the early 1920s.

Cyrus Avery, a state highway commissioner and leader of the American Association of State Highway Officials, collaborated with members of a federally appointed committee to plan a road that would connect Chicago and Los Angeles. Originally designated U.S. Route 60, it was renamed U.S. Route 66 after a conflict with another proposed road. When complete, the highway spanned three time zones, running more than 2,000 miles through eight states from east to west: Illinois, Missouri, Kansas, Oklahoma, Texas, New Mexico, Arizona, and California.

In 1927, the U.S. Highway 66 Association was founded in Tulsa, Oklahoma, to promote the road as a major route, encouraging travel to California and the Southwest through advertisements and various promotional events. The association also advocated the paving of the entire highway, which, like others of the era, included significant stretches of unpaved dirt or gravel road. This task would not be completed until late in the next decade.

Impact

During the Great Depression of the 1930s, Route 66 served as a major artery for farmers leaving the Dust Bowl in search of work in California. In later decades, interstate highways were built to bypass the small towns and Route 66, causing the road to be decommissioned in 1985 and destroyed in some places. However, Route 66 went on to become a cultural landmark, with parts of it designated a National Scenic Byway, and it has inspired such works as the Bobby Troup-penned song "(Get Your Kicks on) Route 66," the 1960s television series *Route 66*, and the 2006 Pixar film *Cars*. By the 1990s, many Route 66 associations had been founded to preserve the remaining road and its landmarks, and in places it attracts significant tourist traffic.

Karen S. Garvin

Further Reading

Dedek, Peter B. *Hip to the Trip: A Cultural History of Route 66*. Albuquerque: University of New Mexico Press, 2007.

Wallis, Michael. *Route 66: The Mother Road*. New York: St. Martin's Press, 1990.

Witzel, Michael Karl, and Jim Hinckley. *Greetings from Route 66: The Ultimate Road Trip Back Through Time Along America's Main Street*. Minneapolis, Minn.: Voyageur Press, 2010.

See also: Automobiles and auto manufacturing; Federal Aid Highway Act of 1921; Federal highway system; Transportation; Travel

■ Royal Canadian Air Force

Identification: The branch of the Canadian armed forces responsible for aerial operations
Also known as: RCAF
Date: Established April 1, 1924

The Royal Canadian Air Force (RCAF) was initially responsible for all Canadian civil aviation and homeland defense, including law enforcement, mail delivery, and forest protection operations. It remained primarily responsible for civilian operations until 1936, when civil aviation came under the purview of the Department of Transport.

Following its inception as a full-time aviation force in 1924, the RCAF handled all defense and civil aviation missions throughout Canada. Among its other duties, the organization conducted law enforcement patrols and antismuggling operations, participated in forest conservation by providing aerial spraying and fire watch capabilities, conducted aerial photography and surveys, delivered mail, and provided flight training.

The RCAF was an amalgamation of several Canadian organizations formed after World War I. When the Canadian Expeditionary Force (CEF) was sent to the Europe's Western Front in 1914, a small unit called the Canadian Aviation Corps (CAC) was formed to accompany them. The CAC was soon disbanded, and Canadian volunteers instead served in Britain's Royal Flying Corps and Royal Naval Air Service. In late 1918, the Canadian Air Force was created in Europe, but it was disbanded in 1920 before ever flying an operation. Another Canadian Air Force (CAF) was formed a few months later as part of the regulatory Air Board and was used for surveying, aerial photography, forest fire patrols, and antismuggling operations. In January 1923, the Air Board, the Department of Naval Services, and the Department of Militia and Defence combined to form the Department of National Defence, and on March 12 of that year, King George V officially granted the CAF its "Royal" designation. However, the RCAF did not become a full-time professional service until April 1, 1924.

The new RCAF started with a group of 66 officers and 194 enlisted men in a Permanent Active Air Force, with a further 4 officers in a Non-Permanent Active Air Force, essentially a reserve unit. In 1927, the Directorate of Civil Government Air Operations (DCGAO) was created to control civil aviation, ostensibly leaving the RCAF a primarily military force. However, the RCAF continued to staff and operate the DCGAO until 1936, when responsibility for civil aviation was shifted to the Department of Transport.

Impact

The RCAF served as the primary civil aviation arm in Canada from its inception in 1924 to 1936. In the early years of civilian aviation, the organization provided key law enforcement functions in combating illegal alcohol smuggling between the United States and Canada, and its aerial surveys were vital to mapping portions of Canada's uncharted wilderness, including the area around the Hudson Strait. As the world moved closer to World War II, the RCAF began to focus more on its military role, ultimately fielding the world's fourth-largest air force during the war.

Michael W. Cheek

Further Reading

Greenhous, Brereton, and Hugh A. Halliday. *Canada's Air Forces, 1914–1999.* Montreal: Art Global, 1999.

Krayden, David. *On Windswept Heights: Historical Highlights of Canada's Air Force.* Ottawa: Department of National Defence, 2009.

Pigott, Peter. *Flying Canucks: Famous Canadian Aviators.* Toronto: Hounslow Press, 1994.

See also: Aviation; Canada and Great Britain

■ Rural Life

Rural life in the United States changed significantly during the 1920s. Farming communities experienced an economic downturn in the years after World War I despite widespread urban prosperity, and a significant portion of the rural population migrated to cities. The growing availability of technology such as automobiles, tractors, and radios further shaped rural life over the course of the decade.

Rural life in the United States during the 1920s was deeply affected by the economic and cultural changes that shaped the nation in the wake of World War I and the Progressive Era. The preceding decade of the 1910s was among the most prosperous in the history of American agriculture. The rapid expansion of internal markets and the war in Europe increased the demand for farm products, resulting in high prices. The recession following World War I, however, initiated one of the worst economic periods in the history of rural America. The end of the war sharply reduced demand from Europe, while urban unemployment resulted in lower domestic demand, drastically reducing prices and overall farm values. This began a rapid downward trend that would only worsen in the Great Depression of the following decade.

Economy

Between 1920 and 1921, prices of farm products dropped by about 50 percent, while farm output dropped by only a tenth and farm debt increased by a fifth. This sent farm prices into a nearly unstoppable downward spiral, reducing farm income. Farmers sought to compensate for lower prices by increasing production, but this furthered the problem of oversupply. Although farm prices recovered slightly by the middle of the decade, they did not return to pre-1920 levels. At the same time, farm debt continued to increase, as did property taxes. The effect of this crisis on small farms was significant, especially in the arid regions of the Great Plains and Upper Midwest that had been settled most recently and had the least productive soils. Many farming families barely survived the financial difficulties of the 1920s, and the economic crisis of the next decade would drive many of them off the land entirely.

Technology and Culture

The agricultural economic crisis of the 1920s coincided with a period of increasing productivity for rural America, which did not help falling commodity prices. New mechanized equipment, particularly tractors, and advances in the sciences of crop and livestock breeding helped American farmers produce more per acre than ever before. Rural extension services, educational organizations based in state land-grant universities, came of age in the 1920s. They sought to introduce new types of crops and farming techniques and to modernize the lives of rural families through improved health, hygiene, and food preparation techniques. The growth of new hybrid corn varieties and new crops such as soybeans also began in the 1920s, though the full impact of these changes would not be felt until later decades.

One of the most significant technological transformations of the 1920s, however, was in transportation. By 1920, most of the rural United States was served by a railroad network of main and branch lines, and throughout much of the Midwest and Great Plains, the creation of rail lines had preceded town building. Small towns were established along the railroad lines, allowing the railroad companies to capture the farm traffic from the surrounding region as completely as possible. Thus, most towns in the Upper Midwest were spaced six to seven miles apart, which was deemed the optimal distance for farmers to travel round trip with a wagonload of goods in one day.

The arrival of cars and trucks in large numbers in the 1920s dramatically changed this picture. Motor vehicles gave farm families greater mobility, allowing them to buy and sell goods over a wider area. This greatly benefited larger towns with more amenities, a wider selection of goods, and better prices than their smaller counterparts. Although rural families had long been exposed to national consumer markets through mail-order catalogs, the availability of cars and trucks brought them ever closer to the emerging mass-market culture.

Interwoven with the technological changes of the 1920s were important social and cultural shifts. The increasing mobility of farm families coincided with the expansion of mass marketing aimed at rural consumers. Although mail-order catalogs had been a fixture of rural life since the 1890s, the range and affordability of products and the exposure of rural Americans to urban marketing grew dramatically in the 1920s. Mass-produced consumer goods and changing notions of what constituted "the good life" drew rural Americans nearer to their urban counterparts in tastes and sensibilities.

Other than the automobile, no single item of technology did more to counter the geographic isolation of rural Americans than the radio. Between 1923 and 1930, about one-third of American households acquired radios, and while this rate of acquisition was necessarily slower in rural areas due to limited income, about 500,000 farm households owned a radio by 1925. By 1930, that number would grow to 1.4 million. Rural radio listening was encouraged by the United States Department of Agriculture (USDA), which began broadcasts for farmers on stations across the country early in the decade. The broadcasts included weather reports, crop forecasts, commodity prices, and practical information to improve the lives and livelihoods of farmers and their families. The USDA joined many early proponents of radio in assuming that farmers would be one of the primary beneficiaries of this new technology. The prevalence of the broadcasts and their growing rural audience opened new avenues for advertisers and those seeking to reach this relatively isolated population. One significant development was the successful effort to sell "country music" to a rural audience. This music, with its roots in the upland South and

Ralph S. Peer

In the early 1920s, the recording industry in the United States became interested in the rural market and therefore in rural music and performers, particularly in the South. "Old-time music" and "mountain music" were two of the terms often used to describe what the industry wanted, and the phrase "hillbilly music" was also coined at the time. In addition, new interest was growing in rural blues as performed by African American musicians. One of the pioneers in recording such music was Ralph S. Peer, who worked for a time at OKeh Records but, by 1927, was under contract with the RCA Victor Company. A staunch believer in field expeditions, Peer set out to find and record new talent from among performers already known in their local communities.

Anglo-Celtic folk music, was culturally alien to many rural Americans, but caught on due its frequent play on popular farm radio stations.

Demographics

The increase in mobility also coincided with and hastened an increasing migration from rural areas to cities. In 1920, the U.S. Census revealed for the first time that less than half of the nation's population lived in rural areas. Thereafter, the rural population underwent a gradual decline as the children of farmers migrated to larger towns and cities in search of economic opportunities unavailable on the farm or in small towns. Economically marginal areas were depopulated the fastest, but most rural areas were affected to some extent, leaving a growing number of abandoned farmsteads to testify to the economic realities of rural life during the decade.

The most dramatic impact of migration was felt in the smallest towns, many of which were at their economic and demographic apexes during the early 1920s and stagnated or declined thereafter. Most could no long offer the range of amenities required to remain a viable part of the modern mass market. Despite this, not all migration took place between rural and urban areas; movement between rural towns occurred as well. Population losses in some areas were masked by inbound migration from surrounding rural areas. The most successful rural towns were regional trade centers, which had a wider range of businesses and often some small commodity processing plants that provided additional employment opportunities.

One of the most dramatic rural to urban migration streams came from the South, as impoverished farmers and sharecroppers migrated to industrial cities such as New York, Chicago, and Detroit. This movement had begun during World War I, which cut off immigration from Europe and thus increased the demand for labor. Early in the 1920s, the United States enacted laws to prevent nearly all immigration from eastern and southern Europe and Asia, thus limiting the labor supply from overseas. Rural southerners responded to this continued demand for labor with a new surge of northward migration.

Although many white southerners migrated to the North during the 1920s, the era is particularly notable for the Great Migration of African Americans, who moved to the urban North in search of economic opportunity and freedom from legal segregation and often violent racial discrimination. While the North was not free of discrimination by any means, it offered expanded economic and social opportunities, and about one million African Americans moved from the rural South to northern cities and surrounding areas during the 1920s. The demand for labor also drew Mexican American migrants from rural Texas and the Southwest, as well as from Mexico itself, forming some of the first permanent Mexican American communities in the North.

Rural ethnic demographics in the Midwest and Great Plains were also affected by World War I and the new immigration laws. While many rural communities had been formed by immigrants from European nations such as Norway, Germany, and Poland, the war and the immigration restrictions of the 1920s greatly reduced the influx of new immigrants to such towns. The postwar decade provided new opportunities for established European immigrants and their children, and like many other Americans, they migrated to urban areas in significant numbers.

Impact
The rural population of the United States struggled during the Great Depression of the 1930s, although toward the end of that decade, federal aid programs brought electric power to many farms for the first time. In the farming communities of the southern Great Plains, poor economic conditions, along with a series of droughts and severe dust storms, drove countless families from their homes in search of work in California and other states. After the Depression, the trends of widespread industrialization and urbanization continued, and many rural communities continued to shrink; by the twenty-first century, more than 80 percent of the U.S. population was living in urban or suburban areas.

John Radzilowski

Further Reading

Atherton, Lewis. *Main Street on the Middle Border.* Bloomington: Indiana University Press, 1984. Chronicles the history of a midwestern town, including the developments of the 1920s.

Barron, Hal S. *Mixed Harvest: The Second Great Transformation in the Rural North, 1870–1930.* Chapel Hill: University of North Carolina Press, 1997. Discusses the agrarian communities of the northern United States in the 1920s and earlier.

Borchert, John R. *America's Northern Heartland: An Economic and Historical Geography of the Upper Midwest.* Minneapolis: University of Minnesota Press, 1987. Describes the characteristics of the rural upper Midwest, including the economic and geographic conditions that shaped the region.

Craig, Steve. "The Farmer's Friend: Radio Comes to Rural America." *Journal of Radio Studies* 8, no. 2 (2001): 330–347. Reviews the advent of radio and its effects on rural life.

Jellison, Katherine. *Entitled to Power: Farm Women and Technology, 1913–1963.* Chapel Hill: University of North Carolina Press, 1993. Explores the relationship between rural women and technology.

Nye, David E. *Electrifying America: Social Meanings of a New Technology, 1880–1940.* Cambridge, Mass.: MIT Press, 1992. Describes the effects of electricity and related technology such as the radio on both urban and rural areas of the United States.

See also: Agriculture in the United States; Electrification; Farm subsidies; Radio

Russian Famine Relief Act of 1921

The Law: Federal act providing funds to the American Relief Administration (ARA) to supply food to famine victims in the Soviet Union
Date: Enacted on December 22, 1921

This agreement allowed the European antifamine efforts of the American Relief Administration to include the Soviet Union. In one of the first major interactions between the United States and the Soviet Union following the Russian Revolution, Congress permitted the distribution of $20 million in surplus American agricultural goods to the Soviet Union to relieve the suffering caused by the famine of 1921.

After the United States entered World War I in 1917, President Woodrow Wilson appointed Herbert Hoover to oversee food supply and distribution for the United States and its European allies. This effort, known as the American Relief Administration (ARA), increased the available supply of food and encouraged domestic food conservation. After the war, the ARA was recreated as a private organization charged with European famine relief. Although it lacked stated political goals, the ARA is credited with helping prevent the spread of communism in Europe by providing material relief and thus a measure of social stability.

The Soviet Union did not benefit from the ARA's postwar operations until 1921. Many Soviet leaders were concerned that Western famine relief efforts would provide an implicit critique of Soviet political and economic policies. Hoover's elevation to the post of secretary of commerce in the Harding administration in 1921 further increased Soviet suspicion. However, as the famine intensified and deaths from starvation rose into the millions, the material suffering of the Soviet people overrode the political fears of the Bolshevik administration.

On August 20, 1921, the Riga agreement was signed between the ARA and the Soviet government, allowing the ARA to distribute food, medicine, and humanitarian aid to the Soviet people with minimal interference from Soviet authorities. This aid would be distributed without any distinction due to race, creed, or social status. In exchange, the Soviet government demanded a guarantee that no relief workers would be permitted to engage in political or social discussion in any way.

On December 22 of that year, Congress passed the Russian Famine Relief Act, which appropriated $20 million for the ARA to purchase food supplies from American farmers.

Impact

Although the Soviet secret police did interfere with food distribution operations, the ARA fed approximately eleven million people over the course of twenty-two months. Despite the use of American agriculture products in the relief effort, rapprochement between the United States and the Soviet Union remained out of reach, and the political potential of the relationship was not realized.

Patrick Callaway

Further Reading

Childs, J. Rives, and Jamie H. Cockfield. *Black Lebeda: The Russian Famine Diary of ARA Kazan District Supervisor J. Rives Childs, 1921–1923*. Macon, Ga.: Mercer University Press, 2006.

Weissman, Benjamin M. *Herbert Hoover and Famine Relief to Soviet Russia, 1921–1923*. Stanford, Calif.: Hoover Institution Press, 1974.

See also: Communism; Hoover, Herbert; Soviet Union and North America

Ruth, Babe

Identification: American baseball player
Also known as: The Bambino
Born: February 6, 1895, Baltimore, Maryland
Died: August 16, 1948, New York City, New York

Babe Ruth was one of the most successful athletes of the 1920s, leading the New York Yankees to six American League pennants and three World Series victories during the decade. A powerful hitter, he profoundly affected the way the game of baseball was played. Ruth's achievements in the game made him a cultural icon of the period.

For many Americans, George Herman "Babe" Ruth epitomized the classic rags-to-riches story. Growing up on the rowdy docks of Baltimore's "Pigtown" neighborhood, his childhood was one of poverty and petty crime. His adolescence was spent at a reformatory for delinquent boys, where he first learned the game that would make him famous. Ruth's career in baseball began when he signed with the minor-league Baltimore Orioles in 1914, joining the Boston Red Sox several months later as a pitcher.

After the 1919 season, Red Sox owner Harry Frazee sold Ruth to the New York Yankees for $125,000 and an additional loan of $350,000. It would later be suggested that the sale of Ruth cursed the Red Sox, as the team, which had won the 1918 World Series due in part to Ruth's pitching, did not win another series for more than eighty years. This transaction changed the course of baseball history, as the historically unsuccessful New York Yankees came into possession of a player who would become one of the most renowned batters in the history of professional baseball.

New York Yankees

At the start of the 1920s, Babe Ruth was a successful pitcher, having won more than twenty games for the Red Sox in the 1916 and 1917 seasons. He had also been a member of the World Series–winning Red Sox roster in 1915, 1916, and 1918. Although Ruth was mostly known as a pitcher, he set a major-league record of twenty-nine home runs in a single season while playing as a part-time outfielder in 1919. In contrast, the New York Yankees, founded in Baltimore in 1901 before moving to New York in 1903, had been largely unsuccessful as a franchise. By 1920, the team had yet to win an American League pennant and consequently had never appeared in a World Series.

Upon joining the Yankees, Ruth began to play as an outfielder exclusively, allowing New York to benefit from his powerful batting abilities. During the 1920 season, Ruth hit fifty-four home runs, a total greater than the number of home runs hit by the combined roster of all but one other major-league team. He broke this record the following year, hitting fifty-nine home runs and helping the Yankees win the team's first American League pennant. Ruth hit more than fifty home runs in two more seasons during the decade, 1927 and 1928, and he led the American League in the category eight times, only relinquishing the league's home run championship in 1922 and 1925, years in which he missed a significant portion of the season due to suspension and poor health, respectively. His sixty home runs in 1927 set a record that would not be broken until 1961. Ruth hit a total of 467 home runs during the decade.

Ruth was also successful in areas other than home runs. By the end of the decade, his number of runs batted in totaled 1,331, and he led the major leagues

Babe Ruth. (Getty Images)

in that category five times, sharing the distinction with teammate Lou Gehrig in 1928. He maintained a high batting average throughout the decade, ranging between a low of .290 in 1925 and a career high of .393 in 1923. His season batting average was the second highest in the major leagues on three occasions. By the end of the 1920s, Ruth had a cumulative batting average of .355 for the decade. In addition, while he played almost exclusively as an outfielder during the 1920s, Ruth returned to his roots as a pitcher for three games in his first two seasons with the Yankees, all New York victories.

Ruth's prowess at the plate had a profound effect on the way the game of baseball was played during the 1920s. In the previous decades, baseball strategy focused on pitching, defense, speed, and stealth on the base paths. That changed as Ruth began to hit numerous home runs, impressing spectators and changing the game's focus to batting. By the end of the decade, most teams had adjusted to this new style of play and developed their own power hitters. However, Ruth remained the home run champion for the majority of the decade. Meanwhile, the Yankees developed the talents of other powerful hitters, most notably Lou Gehrig. In 1927, Ruth, Gehrig, and several other hitters were grouped together in the Yankees' lineup; this string of strong batters became known as Murderers' Row.

The new strategy of play and the skills of players such as Ruth transformed the New York Yankees from an unsuccessful franchise to a major contender over the course of the decade. The team won its first American League pennant in 1921 and went on to win five more in 1922, 1923, 1926, 1927, and 1928. Ruth led the Yankees to three World Series titles, defeating the New York Giants in 1923, the Pittsburgh Pirates in 1927, and the St. Louis Cardinals in 1928.

Off the Field

Ruth had a charismatic personality, and fans were drawn to his humor, his folksy banter, and even his prodigious appetite for food and drink. Promoted by an expanding media, he became an American icon soon after arriving in New York. Success on the baseball field transformed Ruth into one of the decade's most identifiable personalities, and the emerging technology of the time only enhanced this effect. Throughout the 1920s, Ruth appeared in vaudeville acts as well as several films, ranging from silent comedies to short documentaries, garnering him further national fame.

Despite his fame and skill as a player, Ruth was involved in a number of conflicts with baseball authorities during the 1920s. He regularly became embroiled in high-profile arguments with the manager of the New York Yankees, Miller Huggins. On several occasions, such arguments resulted in suspension from play and hefty fines. After a series of arguments late in the 1925 season, Huggins suspended Ruth and refused to allow him to return to the team until he had apologized. Ruth also feuded with Ban Johnson, the president of the American League, during the 1920s. Johnson complained that Ruth was immature and had an utter disregard for all regulations.

Another authority figure displeased with Ruth's actions was Kenesaw Mountain Landis, a federal judge who had been appointed commissioner of baseball in 1920 in the wake of a series of baseball gambling scandals. Ruth and Landis came into conflict in 1921 over Ruth's barnstorming—playing in exhibition games—during the off-season, which was prohibited for players who had appeared in that year's World Series. Landis suspended Ruth and his fellow offenders until late May of 1922. Nevertheless, these clashes with baseball leadership and periods of suspension had little effect on Ruth's popularity with fans or success in the game.

Impact

Babe Ruth continued to play professional baseball until the mid-1930s, leading the Yankees to another World Series victory in 1932 and joining the Boston Braves as a player and vice president in 1935. By his retirement in the late spring of 1935, Ruth had achieved a career total of 714 home runs, setting a record that would not be broken until 1974. His success as a batter continued to shape the game of baseball throughout the subsequent decades, as powerful hitting continued to be an important strategy. For his contributions to the sport, Babe Ruth was inducted into the Baseball Hall of Fame in 1939.

Paul E. Doutrich

Further Reading

Creamer, Robert W. *Babe: The Legend Comes to Life.* New York: Simon and Schuster, 1974. Discusses Ruth's entire life, including his career during the 1920s.

Montville, Leigh. *The Big Bam: The Life and Times of Babe Ruth.* New York: Doubleday, 2006. Chronicles Ruth's life and career, with a significant focus on Ruth as a person.

Reisler, Jim. *Babe Ruth: Launching the Legend.* New York: McGraw Hill, 2004. Focuses on Ruth's sale to the Yankees and the subsequent 1920 baseball season.

Smelser, Marshall. *The Life That Ruth Built: A Biography.* New York: Quadrangle/New York Times Books, 1975. Provides a scholarly, historical take on Ruth's life.

Sobol, Ken. *Babe Ruth and the American Dream.* New York: Random House, 1974. Explores the more negative aspects of Ruth's upbringing, career, and personality.

See also: Baseball; Cobb, Ty; Gehrig, Lou; Landis, Kenesaw Mountain; New York Yankees (baseball); Sports

S

■ Saarinen, Eliel

Identification: Finnish American architect
Also known as: Gottlieb Eliel Saarinen
Born: August 20, 1873, Rantasalmi, Finland
Died: July 1, 1950, Bloomfield Hills, Michigan

Eliel Saarinen was a successful Finnish architect who immigrated to the United States in the early 1920s. He was known for his influence on American skyscraper design as well as his design of the architecture at the Cranbrook Educational Community in Bloomfield Hills, Michigan. As the first president of the Cranbrook Academy of Art, Saarinen guided the school to become one of the leading design schools in the United States.

While enrolled in Helsinki Polytechnic Institute to study architecture, Eliel Saarinen opened an architectural firm with fellow students Armas Lindgren and Herman Gesellius. Soon the partners were awarded commissions that called for designs using elements of the Finnish National Romantic movement, which represented an attempt to develop a distinctive national style of architecture.

Saarinen won first prize in 1904 for his Helsinki Railroad Station design. After controversy surrounding its purely National Romantic style, however, Saarinen revised the design in 1909 to incorporate more modernist innovations such as a central arch and reinforced concrete vaults. Saarinen's firm also designed the Finnish National Museum in 1912, which many believe marked the end of the National Romantic movement in Finland.

Saarinen's career in the United States began in 1922 with his second-place win in the Chicago Tribune Tower competition. His design drew the attention of American architects, and many believe it strongly influenced the future design of U.S. city skyscrapers. Using some of his prize money, Saarinen relocated his family to the United States the following year and began teaching architecture courses at the University of Michigan.

In 1925, Detroit newspaper publisher George Booth offered Saarinen the opportunity to design the buildings for an artist's colony on Booth's 350-acre estate outside of Detroit. The cluster of brick buildings, designed in the popular Arts and Crafts style, would become the nationally acclaimed Cranbrook Educational Community, and as an instructor in its art academy, Saarinen would teach and mentor burgeoning talents such as furniture designers Charles and Ray Eames and city planner Edmund N. Bacon. Saarinen's son Eero Saarinen, also a student at Cranbrook, would later gain prominence by designing the famous St. Louis gateway arch in 1947.

Impact

In 1932, Eliel Saarinen became president of the Cranbrook Academy of Art and head of the architecture department. He continued to design buildings at Cranbrook through the 1940s and collaborated with his son Eero on numerous projects, including the Smithsonian Art Gallery in Washington, D.C., which won the gold medal from the American Institute of Architects in 1947.

Daniel McDonough

Further Reading

Christ-Janer, Albert. *Eliel Saarinen: Finnish-American Architect and Educator.* Rev. ed. Chicago: University of Chicago Press, 1984.

Merkel, Jayne. *Eero Saarinen.* New York: Phaidon Press, 2005.

Wittkopp, Gregory, and Diana Balmori. *Saarinen House and Garden: A Total Work of Art.* New York: H. N. Abrams, 1995.

See also: Architecture; Chrysler Building; Wright, Frank Lloyd

Sacco and Vanzetti case

The Case: Court ruling on two anarchists accused of robbery and murder
Date: Decided on July 14, 1921

Accused of stealing a factory payroll and murdering two employees in Massachusetts in 1920, anarchists and Italian immigrants Nicola Sacco and Bartolomeo Vanzetti were tried and executed later in the decade. Their conviction raised the question of whether their trial was judicially fair or influenced by anti-immigrant bias and the widespread fear of anarchism in the United States.

The Sacco and Vanzetti case, decided early in the 1920s, called attention to the anti-immigrant sentiment and fear of anarchism that would persist in the United States throughout the decade. Although the crime was a relatively straightforward one, the trial took on a new significance due to the political stance and immigrant status of the accused men. Bartolomeo Vanzetti and Nicola Sacco were born in Italy late in the nineteenth century, and both immigrated to the United States in 1908. It is believed that they first met at an anarchist rally in the spring of 1917. To avoid being conscripted into the United States military during World War I, which conflicted with their political beliefs, Sacco and Vanzetti sought refuge in Mexico with a number of fellow anarchists shortly after their first meeting, returning to the United States in September of that year. The two were involved with the anarchist newspaper *Cronaca Sovversiva* (Subversive Chronicle) and participated in various demonstrations and anarchist meetings.

As anarchists, Sacco and Vanzetti faced significant opposition from the United States government and legal system. Socialist, anarchist, and other alternative political groups had existed in the country for decades, but the success of the Russian Revolution of 1917 exacerbated fears of a domestic political revolt. In a period known as the Red Scare, the federal government stressed patriotism and became suspicious of immigrants, particularly those who advocated radical or left-wing political, social, or economic ideas. Many leftists were jailed, and immigrants among them were deported. Anarchist bombing plots were uncovered, thus increasing the public perception of the danger of such groups.

On April 15, 1920, a payroll of $15,776 was stolen from two employees of the Slater and Morrill shoe factory in South Braintree, Massachusetts, a small community south of Boston. Frederick Parmenter, the company's paymaster, and Alessandro Berardelli, his guard, were shot and killed during the robbery. The two men who committed the crime escaped with at least two other men in a stolen Buick; the total number of individuals involved in planning or carrying out the crime remains unknown. Sacco and Vanzetti were arrested in May and charged with the murders of Parmenter and Berardelli; in addition, Vanzetti was charged with attempted robbery in an earlier incident in Bridgewater, Massachusetts, in 1919, for which he was promptly tried and convicted. Then, on May 31, 1921, a joint trial of both men began in Dedham, Massachusetts. Leading the prosecution was District Attorney Frederick Katzmann, while Fred H. Moore, a radical attorney from California, represented the defendants. Judge Webster Thayer, known as a vocal opponent of anarchism and radical politics generally, presided over the proceedings.

Evidence and Defense

The evidence against Nicola Sacco included numerous eyewitnesses who placed him in or near Braintree at the time of the crime. Bullets found at the site were alleged to have been fired from a Colt semiautomatic pistol, a model of gun that Sacco owned. A cap with a hole in it was also found at the crime scene, and a witness testified that the cap resembled one that Sacco owned. The Buick getaway car was later found near the home of anarchist Mario Buda, also known as Mike Boda, and both Sacco and Vanzetti were seen at a car repair shop with Buda after the crime. Because he initially lied about knowing Mario Buda, owning a gun, and supporting anarchist causes, it was difficult for Sacco to establish his credibility.

Eyewitnesses also placed Bartolomeo Vanzetti at the crime scene, with some testifying that he drove the getaway car. A gun in Vanzetti's possession proved to be the same make as one carried by Berardelli and that had gone missing from the scene of the shooting. The prosecution also used Vanzetti's previous conviction for the Bridgewater robbery attempt to undermine his credibility, and both men's anarchist activities were raised during the trial.

During the trial, the defense argued that the eyewitnesses and evidence collected from the crime scene had been tampered with or were otherwise unreliable. Defense testimony noted that some of the bullets could not have been fired from Sacco's gun. Sacco denied owning the cap, even trying it on to prove it did not fit. While Sacco admitted that he had not gone to work the day of the crime, his defense team produced several witnesses who testified he was in Boston at the time of the robbery, seeking a passport from the Italian consulate. Vanzetti claimed he had been selling fish in Plymouth, Massachusetts, on the day of the crime, and this alibi was confirmed by several witnesses.

Verdict and Appeals

On July 14, 1921, the jury found Sacco and Vanzetti guilty of murder in the first degree. The defense made a number of appeals to Judge Thayer, challenging specific testimony by alleged eyewitnesses or the circumstantial evidence introduced at trial. All motions for a new trial were denied. On May 12, 1926, an appeal to the Supreme Judicial Court of Massachusetts to set aside the convictions and hold a new trial was also denied. In 1925, a convicted murderer, Celestino Medeiros, confessed that he and a group called the Morelli gang, known for a series of robberies in southeastern Massachusetts and Rhode Island, had committed the crime; in late 1926, Thayer denied the motion for a new trial based on this confession as well, citing the unreliability of Medeiros's statements. Sacco and Vanzetti were sentenced to death on April 9, 1927.

After the sentencing, Massachusetts governor Alvan T. Fuller appointed Harvard University president A. Lawrence Lowell to lead a committee to review the case. The committee noted that eyewitness and ballistics evidence seemed to indicate Sacco and Vanzetti's guilt and further argued that the witnesses who had placed the defendants in Boston and Plymouth on the day of the crime were friends of the accused, and possibly fellow anarchists, and therefore were unreliable. Despite allegations from Sacco and Vanzetti's supporters that the trial had been influenced by political and anti-immigrant bias, Lowell and the committee ruled that the trial had been fair. Based on this report, Fuller declined to grant the defendants clemency. The courts refused any further motions for a new trial based on judicial bias or additional evidence, and Sacco and Vanzetti were executed on August 23, 1927.

Impact

After their deaths, Nicola Sacco and Bartolemeo Vanzetti came to represent for many the persecution faced by anarchists and other political radicals in the United States. Their supporters in the United States and around the world continued to argue that bias against immigrants and anarchists had driven an unfair conviction. Later analyses of the case explored the possible involvement of the Morelli gang and suggested that Sacco was guilty of the crime and Vanzetti innocent, but the facts of the South Braintree crime remain unclear. In a statement characterizing Sacco and Vanzetti as victims of intolerance, Governor Michael Dukakis of Massachusetts proclaimed the fiftieth anniversary of the executions, August 23, 1977, Nicola Sacco and Bartolomeo Vanzetti Memorial Day.

William A. Paquette

Further Reading

Allison, Robert, and Eli Bortman. *Sacco and Vanzetti.* Boston: Commonwealth Editions, 2005. A concise historical study of the case.

Avrich, Paul. *Sacco and Vanzetti: The Anarchist Background.* Princeton, N.J.: Princeton University Press, 1991. An analysis of the case that places Sacco and Vanzetti within an anarchist context.

Sacco, Nicola, and Bartolomeo Vanzetti. *The Letters of Sacco and Vanzetti.* New York: Penguin Classics, 2007. A collection of the personal correspondence of the two defendants that also includes a history of the case.

Topp, Michael M. *The Sacco and Vanzetti Case: A Brief History with Documents.* New York: Bedford/St. Martin's, 2004. An introduction to the case accompanied by key case documents.

Watson, Bruce. *Sacco and Vanzetti: The Men, the Murders, and the Judgment of Mankind.* New York: Viking Press, 2007. A comprehensive study of the case that examines whether the trial was fair.

See also: Civil rights and liberties; Crimes and scandals; Red Scare, The

■ Safety Last

Identification: Silent film about a man forced to climb the face of a twelve-story building
Directors: Fred C. Newmeyer and Sam Taylor
Date: 1923

In the early 1920s, "human flies" scaled the exteriors of skyscrapers and public buildings across the country, often as

publicity for products or businesses. The success of Safety Last, *one of the silent era's highest-grossing comedies, reflects Americans' fascination with these performers.*

The protagonist of *Safety Last*, impoverished department store clerk Harold (Harold Lloyd), is in a financial bind when his fiancée from back home, Mildred (Mildred Davis), pays him a surprise visit in the big city. Mildred believes Harold to be a wealthy businessperson and expects to be married immediately. Meanwhile, Harold's manager offers a $1,000 reward to anyone who can devise a way to draw new crowds to the store, so Harold convinces his roommate, "Limpy" Bill (human fly Bill Strother), to scale the exterior of the twelve-story building. When the day of the climb arrives, however, a police officer is waiting at the scene to arrest Bill. Harold is thus forced to climb the building himself, encountering numerous dangers along the way.

The inspiration for *Safety Last* came in the summer of 1922, when Lloyd witnessed Strother climbing the Brockman Building in Los Angeles. Lloyd's producer, Hal Roach, immediately contracted Strother to appear in the film, and *Safety Last* went into production in August 1922. The film's climactic sequence was conceived of first, with the incidents preceding the climb devised thereafter. For this sequence, no trick photography was employed. Four sets representing different sections of the fictional Bolton Building's exterior were constructed atop increasingly taller buildings around Los Angeles. Carefully framed shots of Lloyd climbing these sets, coupled with cutaways of Strother scaling the International Bank Building dressed as Lloyd, created the illusion that he was indeed ascending a twelve-story building.

Safety Last's distributor, Pathé Exchange, paid human fly Harry Young fifty dollars to climb the Hotel Martinique in New York City to promote the film's release. With the words "Safety Last" on his back, Young fell to his death in front of a crowd of thousands. As a result of this disastrous publicity stunt, within weeks, ordinances were put forth in New York prohibiting human fly performances.

Impact
The image of Harold Lloyd dangling from the hands of the Bolton Building's clock in *Safety Last* is one of the most famous of the silent film era. The film grossed more than $1.5 million at box offices nationwide and cemented Lloyd as one of the most popular screen comedians of silent film, rivaled only by Charlie Chaplin. Although Lloyd made only five "thrill" comedies throughout his prolific career, of which *Safety Last* was the fourth, the film's enormous success solidified the public's perception of him as a daredevil comedian. *Safety Last* was inducted into the National Film Registry in 1994.

Jef Burnham

Further Reading
McCaffrey, Donald W. *Three Classic Silent Screen Comedies Starring Harold Lloyd*. London: Associated University Presses, 1976.

Smith, Jacob. "The Adventures of the Human Fly, 1830–1930." *Early Popular Visual Culture* 6, no. 1 (April, 2008): 51–66.

See also: Advertising in the United States; Chaplin, Charlie; Film; Lloyd, Harold; Roach, Hal, Sr.

■ Saint Valentine's Day Massacre

The Event: Murder of seven Chicago gang members and associates
Date: February 14, 1929
Place: Chicago, Illinois

On Valentine's Day of 1929, five members of Chicago mobster George "Bugs" Moran's gang and two others were murdered by a group of men dressed as police officers. Known as the Saint Valentine's Day Massacre, the event was thought to have been orchestrated by rival gangster Al Capone in an attempt to consolidate his power over organized crime in Chicago.

Chicago was a major crime center during Prohibition as various gangs vied for control over the manufacture and sale of illegal alcohol, among other criminal enterprises. During the 1920s, the two primary criminal factions in Chicago were the North Side Gang and the South Side Gang, led by rival gang leaders George "Bugs" Moran and Al Capone, respectively. Each attempted to kill the other on several occasions, and this escalating violence was likely one of the causes of the Saint Valentine's Day Massacre.

Massacre
Around 10:30 A.M. on February 14, 1929, a black Cadillac similar to those driven by police stopped in front of a garage in Chicago. The garage was owned

by the SMC Cartage Company, a front for the Moran gang's illegal activities. Two of the four men in the car were disguised as police officers. Under the guise of a raid, the men entered the garage and instructed everyone inside to stand against a wall. The assailants opened fire with two Thompson submachine guns and a shotgun, killing or mortally wounding all seven men. Five of the men were members of Moran's gang: Peter and Frank Gusenberg, Albert Kachelleck, Adam Heyer, and Albert Weinshank. The other two were John May, a mechanic, and Reinhart Schwimmer, an optician and associate of the gang members.

Investigation
While some in Chicago initially believed that the shooting had, in fact, been perpetrated by corrupt police officers, suspicion soon shifted to Al Capone and his gang. Bugs Moran, the suspected target, was scheduled to be in the garage that morning but arrived late. Capone, who was vacationing in Florida at the time of the shooting, likely wanted Moran dead for a number of reasons, including his interference with Capone's bootlegging and dog-racing operations and role in the attempted murder of Jack McGurn, Capone's primary enforcer. The Cadillac used by the killers was partially burned in a garage fire on February 22, and Claude Maddox, a gang member and good friend of McGurn, had been seen in the vicinity of the garage beforehand.

The police detained several suspects, including McGurn and other Capone gang members. McGurn and John Scalise, another Capone gunman, were indicted in mid-March of 1929 for the massacre. Scalise was murdered before his trial, while McGurn's future wife, Louise Rolfe, provided him with an alibi. Charges against McGurn were eventually dropped, and he was charged with a lesser, unrelated crime. In December, police in Michigan raided the home of Fred Burke, another Capone gang member, after he killed a police officer. Several firearms were recovered, including two Thompson submachine guns that ballistics expert Calvin Goddard later identified as the weapons used in the massacre. Burke would be apprehended in 1931 but would not be extradited to Illinois or charged for his suspected role in the massacre. The case remained officially unsolved into the 1930s.

Impact
The biggest break in the case came in 1935, after the arrest of Byron Bolton for an unrelated crime. Bolton surprised authorities by confessing to several crimes, including the Saint Valentine's Day Massacre. Bolton alleged that Capone had ordered the murder of Moran, and he admitted to buying the Cadillac and serving as a lookout. According to Bolton, he had mistakenly identified one of the men in the garage as Moran, thus causing the massacre to begin before the real target arrived. He identified several gangsters as the murderers, including Fred Goetz, Gus Winkler, Fred Burke, and Claude Maddox. However, investigators noted significant flaws in Bolton's confession. Bolton had alleged that Capone wanted Moran dead because he and Frankie Yale were interfering with Capone's operations, but Yale had been killed the previous year. In addition, many of the men he named could no longer be prosecuted. Burke was already serving a life sentence in Michigan, and Winkler and Goetz were dead. Maddox was arrested but was soon released and never charged, as records and witnesses confirmed that he had been in court at the time of the massacre. Thus, despite Bolton's confession, the Saint Valentine's Day Massacre remained officially unsolved, becoming one of the most famous examples of gang violence in the United States.

Jennifer L. Campbell

Further Reading:

Eig, Jonathan. *Get Capone: The Secret Plot That Captured America's Most Wanted Gangster.* New York: Simon and Schuster, 2010. Argues that South Side gangster Jack "Three Fingers" White was the mastermind of the massacre rather than Capone.

Helmer, William, and Arthur Bilek. *The St. Valentine's Day Massacre: The Untold Story of the Gangland Bloodbath That Brought Down Al Capone.* Nashville: Cumberland House Publishing, 2006. Suggests that a group of gangsters from St. Louis were responsible for the massacre and that law enforcement ignored evidence that pointed to anyone except Capone.

Jacobs, David. *The Mafia's Greatest Hits.* New York: Citadel Press Books, 2006. Discusses the Mafia's ten most famous murders, including the Saint Valentine's Day Massacre.

McDonough, Daniel. "Chicago Press Treatment of the Gangster, 1924–1931." *Illinois Historical Journal* 82 (Spring, 1989): 17–32. Provides a summary of the massacre and investigation through newspaper reports, including direct quotes.

Schoenberg, Robert. *Mr. Capone: The Real—and Complete—Story of Al Capone.* New York: Harper Collins, 1993. Explores Capone's motivations and outlook on life, including a section on the massacre.

See also: Capone, Al; Crimes and scandals; Organized crime; Prohibition; Thompson machine gun

■ Sandburg, Carl

Identification: American poet, historian, and journalist
Charles Sandburg
Born: January 6, 1878, Galesburg, Illinois
Died: July 22, 1967, Flat Rock, North Carolina

Sandburg's love of the common people and his use of vernacular language in his poetry helped him express the dreams and ideals of millions of Americans. Drawing on his wide-ranging employment experiences and especially on his interest in socialism and journalism, Sandburg celebrated the overlooked and underappreciated.

Carl August Sandburg was born into a working-class Swedish immigrant family in Galesburg, Illinois. He quit school after eighth grade and worked various jobs, from milkman and ice harvester to bricklayer and blacksmith. He served briefly in Puerto Rico during the Spanish-American War, attended Lombard College in Galesburg for a time, wrote poetry, and did some newspaper work, including for the *Chicago Daily News*. He lived in Milwaukee, Wisconsin, from 1907 to 1912, becoming involved in socialist politics and marrying fellow socialist Lilian Steichen. The couple then returned to the Chicago area, eventually settling with their three daughters in the suburb of Elmhurst from 1919 to 1930, for what was arguably the most productive and varied decade of Sandburg's life and career.

Journalism, Poetry, and History

During the 1920s, Sandburg wrote for the *Chicago Daily News*, where he covered labor issues, reviewed films, and published personal essays and features. He released a number of poetry collections during this time as well, including *Smoke and Steel* (1920), *Slabs of the Sunburnt West* (1922), *Selected Poems* (1926), and *Good Morning, America* (1928).

Also during the 1920s, Sandburg published the

Carl Sandburg. (Getty Images)

first part of the project for which he is perhaps best remembered: his multivolume biography of Abraham Lincoln, whom Sandburg worked to portray as a human being rather than the larger-than-life myth he had become in the popular imagination. The groundbreaking two-volume *Abraham Lincoln: The Prairie Years* was published in 1926; it would be more than a decade before the final four volumes, *Abraham Lincoln: The War Years* (1939), came to print.

Children's Books and American Music

In addition to his journalism, poetry, and history, Sandburg published collections of children's stories inspired by tales he made up for his own daughters, set in the rural American Midwest: *Rootabaga Stories* was published in 1922, followed the next year by *Rootabaga Pigeons*. He also published a Lincoln biography for young readers, *Abe Lincoln Grows Up* (1928).

Sandburg was also a lifelong lover of American music, and he published one of the first collections of American folk songs, *The American Songbag* (1927), featuring hundreds of songs, including "Ain' Go'n' to Study War No Mo'," "Frankie and Johnny," "John Henry," and "Hallelujah, I'm a Bum!"

In 1930, Sandburg and his family moved to Michigan, where they lived until 1945, when they moved to Flat Rock, North Carolina, which would be the family home until Sandburg's death in 1967 at eighty-nine.

Impact

Sandburg was prolific for decades, writing countless poems, his six-volume Lincoln biography, the novel *Remembrance Rock* (1948), and the autobiography *Always the Young Strangers* (1953). In all, he published more than thirty books and received many writing awards, including three Pulitzer Prizes (for poetry in 1919 and 1951, and history in 1940). In 1959, Sandburg became the first private citizen to deliver an address to a joint session of Congress, in honor of the 150th anniversary of Lincoln's birth. In all his work, literary or political, Sandburg foregrounded his love of grassroots American culture and working people and his wish for their well-being. He was one of only a few American writers to succeed in so many areas: journalism, poetry, biography, fiction, and music.

Bill Knight

Further Reading

Callahan, North. *Carl Sandburg: His Life and Works.* University Park: Pennsylvania State University Press, 1987. Produced in cooperation with the Sandburg family, this biography features insight into Sandburg from friends and associates as well as archival material.

Niven, Penelope. *Carl Sandburg: A Biography.* New York: Scribner's, 1991. A comprehensive biography of Sandburg's writing and personal life.

Sandburg, Carl. *Always the Young Strangers.* San Diego: Harcourt, Brace & Jovanovich, 1991. Sandburg's first autobiography, focusing on his first twenty-one years.

_____. *The Letters of Carl Sandburg.* Edited by Herbert Mitgang. New York: Harcourt, Brace & Jovanovich, 1988. Comprised of Sandburg's correspondence with his wife as well as with well-known individuals such as Eugene Debs, Edward R. Murrow, Ezra Pound, and Franklin D. Roosevelt; includes an index, chronology, and explanatory notes.

_____. *"The Movies Are": Carl Sandburg's Film Reviews and Essays, 1920–1928.* Edited by Annie Bernstein. Chicago: Lake Claremont Press, 2000. A collection of Sandburg's work as movie critic for the *Chicago Daily News*, with commentary by the editor.

Yannella, Philip R. *The Other Carl Sandburg.* Jackson: University Press of Mississippi, 1996. Explores Sandburg's life and experiences apart from being a poet and biographer. Provides insight into Sandburg as a longtime newspaperman and an activist for social justice.

See also: Historiography; Lindsay, Vachel; Newspapers, U.S.; Poetry

■ Sanger, Margaret

Identification: American birth control activist
Born: September 14, 1879, Corning, New York
Died: September 6, 1966, Tucson, Arizona

Margaret Sanger was an advocate for birth control and women's health who believed that in order to achieve social and economic equality, women needed access to accurate health information and effective methods of contraception. In 1921, she founded the American Birth Control League, later known as Planned Parenthood. Sanger's work during the 1920s drew attention to the issue of reproductive rights and established birth control as a public health issue.

A feminist and reproductive rights activist, Margaret Higgins Sanger became aware of the need for accessible contraception at a young age. Her mother experienced eighteen pregnancies and eleven live births before dying at the age of fifty, and Sanger believed that the frequent pregnancies and numerous miscarriages had contributed to her mother's death. In 1912, Sanger began working as a nurse in New York City, where she cared for many women who suffered from complications due to frequent childbirth, miscarriages, and self-induced abortions and lived in extreme poverty due to their large families. This experience further convinced Sanger of the need to educate women about reproductive health and ensure their access to effective birth control methods.

Sanger distributed various informational publications throughout the 1910s and was indicted in 1914 for violating the Comstock Act of 1873, which prohibited the distribution of obscene materials through the mail, including information about birth control.

In 1916, Sanger opened the nation's first birth control clinic in Brooklyn, New York, offering women birth control information and contraceptives. Although Sanger was arrested nine days after opening the clinic, the event generated a great deal of publicity and financial support that helped Sanger promote birth control as a public health concern. In 1918, the New York Court of Appeals upheld Sanger's conviction but ruled that doctors had the right to prescribe contraceptives; overall the ruling was considered a victory for the birth control movement.

During the 1920s, Sanger worked to attract a wider range of supporters to the cause, lecturing on birth control before various women's groups and using personal stories to illustrate the importance of accessible contraception. She published books such as *Woman and the New Race* (1920) and *Motherhood in Bondage* (1928), the latter of which collected letters to Sanger written by women seeking advice about birth control.

Organizations

In 1921, Sanger founded the American Birth Control League, which distributed information about birth control to organizations and individuals and held conferences on the topic. The league also supervised the operations of the Clinical Research Bureau, a birth control clinic that Sanger founded in New York in 1923. Unlike her earlier facility, this clinic was legal, as it was staffed by doctors and distributed contraceptives for medical purposes in accordance with the 1918 ruling. The clinic also researched various birth control methods and documented their effectiveness.

Sanger resigned from the league in 1928 and established the clinic as a separate entity, renaming it the Birth Control Clinical Research Bureau. The following year, she formed the National Committee on Federal Legislation for Birth Control in an attempt to overturn the laws prohibiting the importation and distribution of contraceptives. The committee lobbied for government support for birth control, but these attempts failed.

Political and Social Views

Sanger participated in a variety of leftist causes, having supported the strikes led by the Industrial Workers of the World early in the 1910s. Many of her early activist writings appeared in socialist publications such as the *New York Call*, and she associated with influential socialists and anarchists. In the 1920s, however, Sanger sought to attract more mainstream supporters to the birth control movement, and she adjusted her political rhetoric accordingly.

In an attempt to gain widespread support for birth control, Sanger also allied with members of the eugenics movement, who supported birth control as a means of reducing the number of individuals with mental and physical disabilities and, in some extreme cases, sought to eliminate "undesirable" racial or ethnic groups. This association would make Sanger a controversial figure among supporters of birth control in later decades. However, Sanger was adamant that she did not support racially motivated eugenics efforts, and she would go on to open clinics in conjunction with prominent African American leaders.

Impact

Margaret Sanger continued to influence the birth control movement throughout the following decades, particularly through the organizations she founded. In the 1930s, the American Birth Control League merged with the Birth Control Clinical Research Bureau, forming the Birth Control Federation of America; this group was renamed the Planned Parenthood Federation of America in 1942. Sanger also helped obtain funding for the development of the birth control pill, which was introduced in the 1960s. Such legacies of Sanger's work have proven instrumental in the ongoing movement for reproductive rights in the United States.

Melinda Swafford

Sanger Opens First Birth Control Clinic in the United States

American reformer Margaret Sanger was able to open the first legal, doctor-staffed birth control clinic in the United States in 1923. It was the first of many such clinics. It was through Sanger's efforts that medical staffs were able to gain the skills necessary to operate the clinics and conduct the contraceptive research that would affect the lives of women and their families the world over. Because of Sanger's work, ordinary women eventually were able to limit the size of their families without stigma, without risking their health, and without violating the law.

Further Reading

Chesler, Ellen. *Women of Valor: Margaret Sanger and the Birth Control Movement in America.* Reprint. New York: Simon and Schuster, 2007. A biography of Sanger that discusses her personal life as well as her career.

Kennedy, David M. *Birth Control in America: The Career of Margaret Sanger.* New Haven, Conn.: Yale University Press, 1970. An account of the birth control movement and Sanger's role in its development.

Reed, Miriam. *Margaret Sanger: Her Life in Her Words.* Fort Lee, N.J.: Barricade Books, 2003. A biography of Sanger featuring numerous primary source documents.

Rossi, Alice. *The Feminist Papers: From Adams to de Beauvoir.* New York: Columbia University Press, 1988. A history of feminism and related movements and causes, including the birth control movement, over a period of two hundred years.

Sanger, Margaret. *The Autobiography of Margaret Sanger.* Reprint. Mineola, N.Y.: Dover, 2004. Sanger's own account of her life and career, first published in 1938, detailing the motivating factors behind her activism.

See also: Birth control; Eugenics movement; Health care; Medicine; Sexually transmitted diseases; Women's rights

■ Sarnoff, David

Identification: American media executive
Born: February 27, 1891, Minsk, Russian Empire (now Belarus)
Died: December 12, 1971, New York, New York

As head of the Radio Corporation of America (RCA) and then the National Broadcasting Company (NBC), David Sarnoff was a leading figure in the growth of the radio industry during the 1920s, and he also presided over early experiments in television broadcasting.

Having emigrated to the United States with his family at age nine, David Sarnoff began working in the fledgling radio industry as a teenager, operating wireless telegraph machines for the American Marconi Company. By the early 1920s, the self-educated Sarnoff had risen through the ranks to become general manager of the Radio Corporation of America (RCA). As general manager, Sarnoff oversaw the growth of the company's radio broadcasting operations into a two-network system that dominated the industry for the remainder of the decade, and in 1926 he presided over the transformation of these operations into NBC, the commercial radio network created by RCA. Known as much for his tireless self-promotion as for his leadership of NBC, Sarnoff became a powerful and charismatic figure in the rapidly-growing world of broadcast radio.

As a young radio executive in the early 1910s, Sarnoff had predicted the emergence of television as a revolutionary broadcast medium. As acting president of NBC in the 1920s, Sarnoff began directing a large portion of the network's resources toward the development of television, acquiring several key patents on behalf of NBC and underwriting the experiments of Russian engineer and inventor Vladimir Zworykin in electronic television. As a result, NBC led the transition from mechanical to electronic television technology and achieved an advantageous position in the race to set technological standards for commercial television broadcasting in the United States. Although television broadcast standards had not been finalized by the end of the decade, the early experiments in electronic television conducted on NBC experimental stations laid the groundwork for the eventual emergence of commercial television in the late 1930s and early 1940s.

Impact

The growth of commercial radio and developments in television technology at NBC under Sarnoff in the 1920s shaped the development of the prewar broadcasting industry and established Sarnoff as a leading figure in subsequent decades. An aggressive self-promoter and ruthless competitor, Sarnoff developed a reputation as a controversial and divisive figure in the broadcast business whose methods were often questioned and sometimes challenged in court. Nevertheless, Sarnoff played a formidable role in the industry's technological and economic development during the 1920s and beyond.

Michael H. Burchett

Further Reading

Bilby, Kenneth W. *The General: David Sarnoff and the Rise of the Communications Industry.* New York: Harper & Row, 1986.

Edgerton, Gary R. *The Columbia History of American*

Television. New York: Columbia University Press, 2007.

Sobel, Robert. *RCA*. New York: Stein and Day, 1986.

See also: National Broadcasting Company (NBC); Radio; Radio Corporation of America (RCA); Television technology; Zworykin, Vladimir

■ *Sartoris*

Identification: Novel about the decline of an aristocratic southern family and the return of World War I veterans to Mississippi
Author: William Faulkner
Date: 1929

William Faulkner's third novel, Sartoris, *is significant for its introduction of the fictional Yoknapatawpha County, a recurring setting for many of Faulkner's later works. The novel also launched many of Faulkner's stock characters and storylines. Critics see* Sartoris *as marking Faulkner's transition into the mature style and themes that would define his later writing.*

Sartoris, originally titled *Flags in the Dust*, was the first William Faulkner novel set in fictional Yoknapatawpha County, Mississippi. It tells the story of a once proud and important southern family attempting to come to terms with its circumstances in the twentieth century, haunted by memories of the family's glorious past.

Bayard Sartoris, the son of a Civil War hero, runs the local bank in the town of Jefferson and disparages modern ways while glorifying the past through frequent retellings of his grandfather's Civil War exploits. His grandson, the younger Bayard, has just returned from World War I after having lost his twin brother and fellow pilot in the war.

Emotionally scarred and racked with guilt for having survived the war when his brother did not, young Bayard is unable to find peace at home and continually engages in risky, self-destructive behavior. He eventually marries Narcissa Benbow, who also appeared in Faulkner's 1921 novel *Sanctuary*, and she becomes pregnant. After his grandfather's death, caused by young Bayard driving recklessly off the road, young Bayard flees Jefferson and is eventually killed after crashing a poorly built test airplane. He dies on the day of his son's birth.

Impact

Critics have pointed out that Faulkner wrote *Sartoris* as a commentary on the South's struggle to enter the modern world, and that just as the book's characters have difficulty separating themselves from their past, the South seemed to resist breaking with its traditions and customs in order to join modern times. Additionally, many of Faulkner's great themes, such as family, the weight of history, time as a means of narration, and the decline of status, are all introduced in *Sartoris*, as are numerous recurrent characters. A history of the Sartoris family, for instance, is chronicled in *The Unvanquished* (1938), and the amoral Snopes family, whose members also appear in *Sartoris*, is the subject of Faulkner's trilogy *The Hamlet* (1940), *The Town* (1957), and *The Mansion* (1959).

Scott D. Yarbrough

Further Reading

Brooks, Cleanth. *William Faulkner: The Yoknapatawpha Country*. Baton Rouge: Louisiana State University Press, 2002.

Kinney, Arthur F, ed. *Critical Essays on William Faulkner: The Sartoris Family*. Boston: G. K. Hall Press, 1985.

Towner, Theresa M. *The Cambridge Introduction to William Faulkner*. New York: Cambridge University Press, 2008.

See also: Faulkner, William; Literature in the United States; *Sound and the Fury, The*

■ Schiaparelli, Elsa

Identification: Italian fashion designer
Born: September 10, 1890, Rome, Italy
Died: November 13, 1973, Paris, France

Elsa Schiaparelli was a fashion designer who specialized in creating cutting-edge designs for the modern woman. Her popularization of sportswear and knit separates challenged gender identities and helped to define the appearance of a generation of women.

Born into an affluent and aristocratic Italian family, Elsa Luisa Maria Schiaparelli worked as a nanny in London before moving to New York City. There, Schiaparelli was inspired by the architecture of the Art Deco movement and the relatively liberated status of American women, who, by 1920, could vote, drive

Elsa Schiaparelli. (Gamma-Keystone via Getty Images)

cars, and participate in sports such as tennis, golf, swimming, and cycling. Schiaparelli's early designs catered to the modern woman's need for sportswear and included knit sweaters, which would become a signature part of her collections throughout her career. In the mid-1920s, she relocated to Paris to further establish herself as a designer.

Schiaparelli unveiled her first public collection in 1927, showcasing a small but successful selection of knitwear. Some designs featured an Armenian knitting technique in which a garment is composed of two separate yarns, one visible underneath the other. In addition to being aesthetically pleasing, the technique allowed sweaters to retain their proper shape when worn. A sweater featuring this Armenian technique as well as a large knit image that created the illusion of a bow on the neckline, introduced later that year, became incredibly popular in the United States. Building her reputation upon this type of innovation, Schiaparelli became known for her use of color, texture, beading, and embroidery in whimsical designs.

Throughout the 1920s, Schiaparelli gained recognition from fashion magazines for her innovations in sportswear, pairing rich color schemes with practical designs that had never before appeared on ski slopes or tennis courts. Later, she began to expand her collections to include eveningwear, accessories, jewelry, and perfume.

Impact

Schiaparelli experienced her greatest success in the 1930s, selling her designs despite the onset of the Great Depression. Her work during the period was inspired by avant-garde art, and she collaborated with artists such as Salvador Dalí. Her popularity waned during World War II and afterward. Nevertheless, her innovations, particularly in the realms of sportswear and knits, continued to influence fashion over the next several decades.

Shannon Oxley

Further Reading

Baudot, François. *Elsa Schiaparelli.* New York: Vendome Press, 1997.

Blum, Dilys E. *Shocking! The Art and Fashion of Elsa Schiaparelli.* New Haven, Conn.: Yale University Press, 2003.

White, Palmer. *Elsa Schiaparelli: Empress of Paris Fashion.* London: Aurum Press, 1995.

See also: Art movements; Fashions and clothing; Sports

■ Schindler, Rudolph

Identification: American architect
Born: September 10, 1887, Vienna, Austria
Died: August 22, 1953, Los Angeles, California

Rudolph Schindler was a pioneer of twentieth-century American architecture who began to gain recognition for his modern aesthetic in the early 1920s. Schindler's buildings, primarily residential structures in and near Los Angeles, California, were known for their open living spaces and incorporation of glass and concrete.

Rudolph Michael Schindler, known professionally as R. M. Schindler, studied architecture in Austria before immigrating to the United States in 1914. He was impressed with the work of modernist architect

Frank Lloyd Wright and persuaded Wright to hire him in 1918. Working from Wright's studio in Oak Park, Illinois, Schindler managed several of Wright's American projects while Wright completed a commission in Japan. In 1920, Schindler moved to Los Angeles to assist Wright and his son in creating a house for the oil heiress Aline Barnsdall. Schindler was credited with much of the work on the project, known as the Hollyhock House, which would later be designated a national landmark. Barnsdall was pleased with Schindler's work on her home and would later hire him for other projects.

Perhaps Schindler's most important work of the period was his 1922 Kings Road House, also known as the Schindler House, a building in West Hollywood designed to provide work and living space for two professional couples. This house became a long-term home for Schindler and his wife, and they were joined there by architect Richard Neutra and his family in 1925. The house had no separate living rooms or bedrooms and made creative use of concrete slabs and sliding glass panels, elements that would become signatures of Schindler's modern style. His houses also typically featured enclosed courtyards, rooftop sleeping areas, and integrated indoor and outdoor spaces.

Schindler completed several other notable projects in California during the 1920s, including the How House (1925) and the Manola Court apartment building (1926), both in Los Angeles, and a beach house in Newport Beach known as the Lovell House (1926). He began but did not complete a translucent beach house for Barnsdall and designed a building known as Wolfe House (1929) on Catalina Island.

Impact

After ending his partnership with Wright in 1931, Schindler worked independently for the next two decades, experimenting with such innovations as plaster skin construction and his own creation, the Schindler Frame. Designing or supervising more than two hundred buildings during his career, he became widely respected for his use of concrete, wood, and glass in ways that acknowledged California's unique climate and landscape. The Schindler House was eventually established as a center for art and architecture and opened to the public for tours.

Cynthia A. Bily

Further Reading

Darling, Michael, and Elizabeth A. T. Smith, eds. *The Architecture of R. M. Schindler*. New York: Harry N. Abrams, 2001.

Gebhard, David. *Schindler*. San Francisco: William Stout Publishers, 1997.

Sheine, Judith. *R. M. Schindler*. London: Phaidon Press, 2001.

See also: Architecture; Saarinen, Eliel; Wright, Frank Lloyd

■ Scholastic Aptitude Test (SAT)

Developed in the 1920s, the Scholastic Aptitude Test (SAT) has emerged as the premier college admissions test, taken by generations of high school students. SAT scores have become critical components of the scholarship and admissions procedures for many universities.

As the United States was about to enter World War I, American Psychological Association president Robert Yerkes spearheaded several programs to assist with the war effort, one of which was the development of an intelligence test for army recruits. Yerkes chaired a committee made up of other prominent psychologists of the time, including Henry Goddard, Lewis Terman, and a young Carl Brigham. The result was a group-administered multiple-choice intelligence test in two formats: the Army Alpha for literate recruits and the Army Beta for the illiterate. The Army Alpha test would provide the basis for the development of the SAT.

In the early 1920s, Brigham, now a professor of psychology at Princeton University, became chairman of the College Entrance Examination Board (CEEB), established in 1900 by a group of colleges in the Northeast in order to oversee college admissions testing. It was in this capacity that Brigham created the SAT, adapted from the Army Alpha test and designed to predict success in college. The SAT was first administered to high school students on June 23, 1926. It consisted of nine different types of problems and was primarily multiple choice. Taking the first test were approximately eight thousand students, about 60 percent of whom were male.

The SAT slowly gained in popularity, with scores increasingly being used to make scholarship and college admission decisions. The nine problem types were decreased to seven in 1928, then again to six the following year. In 1930, the test was formally divided into mathematics and verbal sections, with scores for each section ranging from 200 to 800, scaled to a mean of 500 and a standard deviation of 100.

Impact

In 1948, SAT development and administration duties were shifted from the CEEB to a new agency, the nonprofit Educational Testing Service (ETS), located in Princeton, New Jersey. In the late twentieth and early twenty-first centuries, the SAT underwent significant revisions and name changes; the Scholastic Aptitude Test became the Scholastic Assessment Test in 1990, the SAT I: Reasoning Test (as distinct from the SAT II: Subject Tests) in 1993, and finally the SAT Reasoning Test in 2004 (with the Roman numeral being dropped from the SAT Subject Tests as well). A writing section was introduced in 2005, and the verbal section was changed to the critical reading section. Since its introduction in the 1920s, the SAT has become the most widely used test of its kind, although some critics have disputed the test's accuracy and raised issues of potential bias.

Russell N. Carney

Further Reading

Gregory, Robert J. *Psychological Testing: History, Principles, and Applications.* 6th ed. Boston: Allyn & Bacon, 2011.

Lemann, Nicholas. *The Big Test: The Secret History of the American Meritocracy.* New York: Farrar, Straus and Giroux, 1999.

See also: Education; Psychology, psychiatry, and psychoanalysis

■ Scholz, Jackson

Identification: American sprinter and author
Born: March 15, 1897, Buchanan, Michigan
Died: October 26, 1986, Delray Beach, Florida

Jackson Scholz competed in the Olympic Games of 1920, 1924, and 1928 as a sprinter, winning two gold medals and one silver medal for the United States. During the late 1920s, Scholz also began a successful career as a writer of sports fiction.

Jackson Volney Scholz studied journalism and ran track at the University of Missouri, from which he graduated with a bachelor's degree in 1920. He made his first appearance in the Olympic Games that summer, competing as a member of the U.S. Olympic team in Antwerp. A sprinter, Scholz finished fourth in the 100-meter dash and joined three other Americans in winning the 4 × 100-meter relay in 42.2 seconds, setting a world record.

At the 1924 Summer Olympics in Paris, Scholz again reached the final round of the 100-meter race, finishing in second place with a time of 10.7 seconds, just behind the British sprinter Harold Abrahams. Two days later, Scholz won the 200-meter event, tying an Olympic record with his time of 21.6 seconds and winning his second gold medal. In the United States the following year, he won the 220-yard sprint in the Amateur Athletic Union National Championships.

In 1928, at the Olympic Games in Amsterdam, Scholz became the first sprinter to run in the finals of three consecutive Summer Olympics. Although he officially finished fourth in the 200-meter event, with a time of 21.9 seconds, he had tied for third place with the sprinter who was awarded the bronze medal and declined to participate in a runoff. Scholz effectively retired from competition after the 1928 Olympics, instead beginning a lengthy career as a writer of sports-themed novels and short stories. The first of Scholz's books, *Split Seconds: Tales of the Cinder Track*, a collection of short stories narrated by a coach, was published in 1927.

Impact

Scholz continued to write throughout the subsequent decades, publishing such sports novels as *Fielder from Nowhere* (1948) and *Backfield Blues* (1971) and contributing stories and articles to *Boys' Life* and other popular publications. He briefly returned to the public eye following the 1981 release of the film *Chariots of Fire*, which featured Scholz, portrayed by Brad Davis, as a minor character. For his contributions to the sport, Scholz was inducted into the National Track and Field Hall of Fame in 1977.

Victor Lindsey

Further Reading

U.S. Olympic Committee. *Olympism: A Basic Guide to the History, Ideals, and Sports of the Olympic Movement.* Torrance, Calif.: Griffin, 2001.

Wallechinsky, David. *The Complete Book of the Summer Olympics.* Wilmington, Del.: Sport Classic Books, 2004.

See also: Ederle, Gertrude; Kahanamoku, Duke; Literature in the United States; Olympic Games of 1920 (Summer); Olympic Games of 1924 (Summer); Olympic Games of 1928 (Summer); Paddock, Charles; Sports; Weissmuller, Johnny

■ Schultz, Dutch

Identification: American criminal
Also known as: Arthur Flegenheimer
Born: August 5, 1902, New York, New York
Died: October 24, 1935, Newark, New Jersey

Dutch Schultz was a notorious gangster and bootlegger based in New York City. Beginning the 1920s in relative obscurity, he rose to prominence as one of the city's most ruthless criminals over the course of the decade.

Dutch Schultz, born Arthur Flegenheimer, began committing crimes as a teenager, but it was the onset of Prohibition that allowed him to become one of the notable gang leaders of the 1920s. With legal sales channels for alcohol eliminated by the Eighteenth Amendment to the United States Constitution, the demand for illegal alcohol was significant, providing an opportunity for gangsters such as Schultz to profit financially from bootlegging operations.

After being released from prison early in the decade, Schultz spent the early 1920s working for more established gangsters, including his eventual adversary, Jack "Legs" Diamond. This gave Schultz the opportunity to observe how successful bootleggers operated, and he learned the importance of forging alliances, distributing efficiently, exploiting the indifference or corruption of the local judiciary and law enforcement, and eliminating competition. By 1928, Schultz and his friend Joey Noe had begun to establish their own bootlegging operation specializing in the distribution and sale of beer.

Throughout the late 1920s, Schultz earned a reputation for violence that was considered extreme, even by the standards of other gangsters. In one case, Schultz and his associates kidnapped a competitor and tortured and blinded him before holding him for ransom. His reputation intimidated the competition and forced other bootleggers to retire from the business or flee New York City. Schultz also cultivated relationships with public officials, including the powerful and corrupt New York politician James J. Hines.

Dutch Schultz. (Getty Images)

Although he would dabble in other crimes during the 1920s, Schultz made his mark through bootlegging. By the end of the decade, Schultz and his gang dominated the underground trade in alcohol throughout Harlem, the Bronx, and much of Manhattan.

Impact
Dutch Schultz continued to supervise the production and sale of illegal liquor into the early 1930s before turning to illegal lotteries and extortion schemes following the end of Prohibition. While facing charges of tax evasion, Schultz was assassinated under the orders of Mafia leadership, who feared that Schultz would murder his prosecutor and draw unwanted attention to their operations.

Michael R. Meyers

Further Reading

Currie, Stephen. "Dewey Defeats the Dutchman." *American History*, December, 2002, 38–46.

Sann, Paul. *To Kill the Dutchman!* New Rochelle, N.Y.: Arlington House, 1971.

See also: Capone, Al; Organized crime; Speakeasies

■ Science and technology

Most Americans appreciated scientists' and engineers' efforts to advance scientific knowledge and develop technological innovations during the 1920s. The Protestant religious movement known as Fundamentalism challenged the compatibility of scientists' ideas and work with religion. Funding resources shifted from those available in previous decades. During the 1920s, corporations, foundations, and philanthropists, more than governments, shaped the specific scientific and technological research goals of industrial and university laboratories, often deciding which projects to pursue and how to implement results.

After World War I ended, many American scientists and engineers resumed research in their fields of expertise. The post–World War I academic scientific community had been depleted of professionals who decided to continue wartime endeavors with industries or other employers rather than return to university laboratories. During the war, scientists and engineers had pursued innovations in manufacturing techniques and equipment to meet businesses' and consumers' needs through mass production. When the 1920s began, returning soldiers who had delayed educational training for military service enrolled in schools or sought out research opportunities. Conservative Republicans' dominance in executive and legislative positions resulted in most elected officials choosing not to interfere with established financial policies that encouraged scientific and engineering investments.

Professionalism and Public Roles

During the 1920s, various organizations supported either specific or broad scientific and technological research agendas. Two major groups established in the nineteenth century provided resources and recognition for many scientists and engineers in the 1920s. The American Association for the Advancement of Science (AAAS), formed in 1848, shaped many researchers' professional identities and helped them interact with colleagues sharing similar interests. In 1920, the association had 11,547 members; by 1930, their numbers had grown to 19,059 members. Diverse scientific interests were represented, and members collaborated with affiliated societies and state science academies. Another organization, the National Academy of Sciences (NAS), founded in 1863, continued to include distinguished North American research scientists and engineers among its members. Scientists and engineers of the 1920s also participated in groups formed to provide professional opportunities for specialized research or in scientific honorary societies such as Sigma Xi. Professionals in other fields also created organizations discussing science and technology; in 1924, scholars organized the History of Science Society (HSS). Some science professionals belonged to groups promoting science education, such as the American Nature Study Society.

Professional scientific organizations contributed to the professionalization and protection of several scientific disciplines in the United States. Such groups often created professional codes of ethics that guided members. During the 1920s, representatives of scientific associations sought the passage of laws relevant to their technical fields, lobbying legislators regarding issues such as enforcing the performance of rabies control work by licensed veterinarians. Many scientific societies also provided stipends and other incentives to encourage students and young investigators to attend academic programs and conduct research.

Many scientific and technological professional organizations published journals, conference proceedings, or books during this period. These publications reported news relevant to scientists and their fields, discussing controversies regarding research methods and findings, and containing members' articles, most of them edited by peers to assure accuracy and conformity to professional standards. Some organizations and scientific supporters maintained libraries of scientific and technical publications. For instance, the National Research Council of Canada established its library in 1924.

Examples of professional journals distributed during the 1920s included *Chemical and Metallurgical Engineering*, *Automobile Engineer*, and the *Canadian Journal of Research*, established by Canada's National Research Council in 1929. The Smithsonian Institution

> ### Sound Technology Revolutionizes Motion-Picture Industry
>
> In May 1928, the decision to incorporate sound into films transformed the American film industry almost overnight. Attendance at theaters doubled, and "talkies" became the rage around the world. The production of the first sound films required several stages of innovation. First, scientists had to develop apparatus to record and synchronize sounds and images, complete with a quality and tone that would permit the finished product to be shown before large audiences. Moreover, companies had to learn how to market sound films to the public, knowing the inherent risk in trying to sell something many critics said would not work. Finally, the major film companies had to decide to accept the new technology and to substitute it for the standardized silent film.

issued annual reports with papers by scientists. Edward W. Scripps, a prominent media figure in the United States, promoted the publicizing of scientific information, and by March 1920, the Science News Service, directed by NAS and AAAS members, released articles to mass media. The next year, the Science News Service printed the *Science News Letter*. By 1922, psychologist James M. Cattell incorporated the service's information in the AAAS magazine, *Scientific Monthly*, which he also edited. In the mid-1920s, Smithsonian curator Austin H. Clark created the AAAS Press Service to assure coverage of that association's conferences in newspapers and popular national magazines such as *Life*. Amateur scientists of the 1920s could also enjoy reading the *Scientific American* magazine.

Women and minorities found a lessening of discrimination within the scientific community during this period. Female scientists often dealt with gender discrimination, despite women gaining suffrage when the Nineteenth Amendment was passed in 1920. However, the NAS admitted its first female member, anatomist Florence Sabin, five years later. Women science writers, including Jane Stafford and Marjorie MacDill, were also employed by the Science News Service in the 1920s and contributed to the professionalization of science journalism, serving as examples for female readers interested in pursuing scientific and technical careers. Scientific circles increasingly accepted African American scientists, such as biologist Ernest E. Just, who delivered a presentation at the 1920 AAAS meeting in Chicago, Illinois.

Financial Support and Policies

The U.S. and Canadian National Research Councils evaluated and funded science and technology research during World War I, creating partnerships with universities, industries, and governments that would be maintained into the 1920s. After the armistice, both councils continued to determine which scientific and technological projects merited financial resources, such as grants and fellowships.

During the 1920s, North American industries financed research and development in hopes of creating lucrative patents, profitable commercial products, and more efficient manufacturing machinery and processes. In 1921, approximately 526 industries supported research laboratories, a figure that doubled within six years and tripled by the decade's close. Manufacturers identified scientists and engineers at universities for whom they financed research projects or hired as consultants. The number of researchers hired by North American industries increased by approximately 400 percent in the 1920s. The U.S. Bureau of Standards oversaw a research associates program that funded projects chosen by industry and government representatives to meet specific needs such as the improvement of construction materials.

Government policies helped corporations protect their intellectual properties with patenting processes and tax and interest rate reductions assured by Andrew Mellon, the U.S. secretary of the Treasury from 1921 through 1932. This allowed corporations to spend more on research and development initiatives. Corporations were able to purchase rival scientific and technical businesses without risking penalization for the violation of antitrust laws intended to prevent monopolies. Herbert Hoover, originally an engineer, encouraged science and technology programs while serving as U.S. secretary of commerce that decade, before becoming president in 1929.

During the 1920s, U.S. and Canadian governments supported agricultural experiment stations, often affiliated with colleges, to encourage research with economic benefits. The privatization of research and development for nonagricultural projects at universities expanded in the 1920s. Administrators sought financial donors to advance the quality of their schools' research. Private funding enabled these schools to hire elite researchers and achieve superb laboratory facilities, often resulting in their faculty and students attaining international recognition. Some 1920s academic researchers followed the pioneering example of biochemist Harry Steenbock, who developed a procedure to enrich food with vitamin D by irradiating it with ultraviolet light and then gave ownership of that patent to the University of Wisconsin, where he had performed his research.

The Rockefeller Foundation, Carnegie Corporation, John Simon Guggenheim Foundation, and Sigma Xi association were leaders in endowing fellowships for graduate and postdoctoral science and engineering education in addition to fellowships for research. In 1925, Carnegie Corporation head Frederick Keppel stated that at least fifteen hundred science education fellowships were annually financed by foundations. Fellowships helped students pursue advanced work, resulting in the number of science and engineering doctorates earned at North American schools increasing by almost 500 percent by 1940.

Philanthropists provided money to university researchers whom they believed could improve society with scientific and technological achievements. The *Bulletin of the National Research Council* identified donors giving more than $1,000 to fund university science and technology research in 1920, listing the AAAS, NAS, American Academy of Arts and Sciences, American Medical Association, Smithsonian Institution, Carnegie Institution, National Geographic Society, Engineering Foundation, and Elizabeth Thompson Science Fund. Foundations often specified how donated funds were to be used; for example, the Daniel Guggenheim Fund provided over $2 million from 1926 to 1930 for aeronautics research, enabling several universities to construct wind tunnels.

Some philanthropists chose to provide funds for creating research institutes that concentrated on specific scientific or technological fields such as physics, botany, or medicine. In 1921, the *Bulletin of the National Research Council* reported that sixteen institutes had spent almost $600,000 to conduct research that year. Notable research institutes established during the 1920s included the Food Research Institute, the Brookings Institution, and the Boyce Thompson Institute for Plant Research.

Public Health Risks

Scientific endeavors during the 1920s occasionally compromised people's safety. Motivated by profits generated by the expanding automobile industry, vehicle and petrochemical manufacturer executives ordered company scientists to develop higher-octane fuels to improve cars' performance. They aspired to achieve faster, quieter vehicles. In Dayton, Ohio, mechanical engineer Thomas Midgley Jr. led a General Motors research laboratory team in 1922 to experiment with fuel combinations. They mixed gasoline and tetraethyl lead to achieve increased compression in vehicle engines, resulting in greater driving speeds and less knocking. As a result, General Motors acquired tetraethyl lead made by the DuPont Corporation Chemical Company and Standard Oil Company and then combined it with automotive fuel.

Aware of this development, chemist William Mansfield Clark cautioned Assistant Surgeon General Arthur M. Stimson in October 1922, urging the Public Health Service's Division of Chemistry and Pharmacology to study health risks associated with tetraethyl lead. Division scientists suggested the investigation be conducted by relevant industries instead. Surgeon General Hugh S. Cumming contacted DuPont, resulting in money from the General Motors Research Corporation financing the recommended study using the Pittsburgh Field Station site belonging to the U.S. Bureau of Mines. General Motors spokesman Charles Kettering insisted that the investigators and government officials not release news of this study to the press. Graham Edgar, the General Motors director of research, told Paul Leech, a representative of the American Medical Association, that the study indicated ethyl gasoline was safe and was not connected to lead poisoning.

By February 1, 1923, fuel stations in some U.S. locations began selling leaded gasoline. In the next year, General Motors and DuPont executives established the Ethyl Corporation, with Midgley serving as its general manager, to make and distribute leaded gasoline. Some scientists and public health personnel worried about the toxins and possible poisoning that might result from lead gasoline exhaust polluting the air. In October 1924, approximately 80 percent of people employed at a Standard Oil Company refinery making tetraethyl gasoline additives suffered neurological damage, leading to the deaths of several employees. Although executives were able to conceal those casualties, the press became aware of other incidents, such as the lead poisoning of workers at a New Jersey chemical plant.

By early May 1925, Columbia University scientists who had examined tetraethyl gasoline warned of its health dangers, sending their results to Cumming, who arranged a May 20, 1925, meeting in Washington, D.C., to discuss this issue. Industry leaders defended their product and blamed workers' carelessness or preexisting conditions as the cause of illnesses. Public health and environmental supporters outlined hazards. Yandell Henderson, an applied physiology researcher at Yale, and Alice Hamilton, a Harvard University physician, stressed their belief that the contaminated fumes of tetraethyl gasoline were harmful to people and that substitutes should be developed.

Many attendees believed that evidence supporting the dangers of unleaded fuel was insufficient. One attendee, American Public Health Association president Henry F. Vaughan, appointed a committee to investigate the issue. The committee decided more evaluation was needed but that studies should only be conducted by industries and their scientists. *Chemical and Metallurgical Engineering* editor Howard C. Parmelee remarked that chemical manufacturers deserved to have additional testing of tetraethyl gasoline and not be deprived revenues due to what he considered the impulsive and emotional responses of some scientists. Ignoring possible hazards, the automotive industry demanded consistent access to tetraethyl fuel, which it considered essential to achieve sales. For several months that year, some states and cities enforced bans of gasoline containing lead, and plants briefly stopped making tetraethyl fuel before its distribution to North American motorists resumed.

Religion and Science
Spiritual issues complicated scientific activities in the 1920s because Fundamentalism, a conservative Protestant religious movement provoked by public awareness of Charles Darwin's theories, thrived during the decade. Conservative clergy urged their congregations to reject scientific assertions regarding evolution and natural selection that countered literal interpretations of the Bible. Many scientists emphasized the compatibility of religion and scientific research in their attempts to identify truth.

During the 1920s, AAAS, NAS, and Smithsonian representatives issued statements regarding evolution. In December 1921, Cambridge University geneticist William Bateson presented a paper at the Toronto AAAS meeting, in which he, like many of his scientific peers, pondered aspects of evolution without suggesting that the process did not exist. *Scientific Monthly* printed Bateson's commentary, "Evolutionary Faith and Modern Doubt," which creationists cited as proof of their antievolution claims. As a result, the AAAS Council named geologist and paleontologist Henry Fairfield Osborn and biologists Edwin Grant Conklin and Charles Davenport to devise a statement for the association. The NAS Council requested paleontologist Charles Doolittle Walcott, who then served as the society's president, to create a committee to craft a resolution on that issue.

William Jennings Bryan, a popular speaker of the 1920s, denounced evolution at public forums. In February, 1922, he wrote a *New York Times* editorial, "God and Evolution," in which he referred to Bateson when outlining his reasons for not believing in evolution and protested educational curricula that referred to evolution. Antievolution actions escalated. Many states and towns enacted legislation forbidding public schools to teach evolutionary theory. *The New York Times* printed essays, including "Bryan and Evolution," by Conklin and "Evolution and Religion" by Osborn, emphasizing evidence confirming evolution. That newspaper also published editorials supportive of evolution prepared by Harry Emerson Fosdick, a Union Theological Seminary professor, and Stuart L. Tyson, an Episcopal rector. In early March 1922, educators criticized Bryan at the National Education Association meeting, stressing their belief that antievolution legislation impeded science education.

Later that year, the American Institute of Sacred Literature (AISL), affiliated with the University of Chicago Divinity School, printed Conklin's and Fosdick's editorials as pamphlets. During the 1920s, the AISL asked notable scientists and religious leaders to write essays specifically for a pamphlet series examining the relationship of science and theology. Authors included such significant 1920s scientists as Nobel Prize–winning physicists Robert Millikan and Arthur Holly Compton, as well as astrophysicist Edwin Frost, physical chemist Michael Pupin, geologist

Kirtley Mather, and ornithologist Samuel Christian Schmucker. Schmucker's pamphlet *Through Science to God* explained how hummingbirds evolved through natural selection. Funded by scientists' donations, the Rockefeller Foundation, and the AAAS, the AISL distributed thousands of such pamphlets to educators, many of whom incorporated them into syllabi.

The AAAS Council approved its resolution by December 1922, printing it the next year in *Scientific Monthly*. That statement supported evolutionary theories associated with humans, animals, and plants, stating that scientific investigations had proven them valid. The AAAS statement criticized restrictions on instruction regarding evolution. John Mason Clarke, state paleontologist of New York, chaired the NAS committee, which prepared a statement summarizing the reasons scientists knew evolution occurred. Astronomer Charles G. Abbot and ornithologist Alexander Wetmore prepared the Smithsonian's statement, which identified eleven lines of scientific evidence validating evolution. None of the statements referred to Darwin.

During the 1925 *Scopes* trial, the AAAS distributed its statement with the Science News Service and printed it in *Scientific Monthly*. AAAS members, hoping to use the *Scopes* court case as an example of how religion and scientific theories can coexist, assisted Scopes in the preparation of his defense and contributed to a fund to finance his graduate science studies after the trial. Communications technology, especially radio, enabled global transmission of trial news. Afterward, Osborn wrote *Evolution and Religion in Education, Polemics of the Fundamentalist Controversy of 1922 to 1926*.

Impact

Science and technology developments achieved during the 1920s resulted in North American researchers gaining global recognition and respect for their competence as they became more competitive. The commercialization of technology produced through research funding strengthened consumer demand for technological goods, both domestically and in foreign markets. As resources expanded North American scientific opportunities, some European scientists, such as Albert Einstein, visited or relocated to North America, where they became prominent members of research faculties and participated in scientific organizations and activities. North American scientists and engineers equaled and, in many cases, surpassed their European peers who had previously represented the standard for scientific excellence.

Private funding and corporate support of research and development in the 1920s established a basis for financial aid in the following decades. Several subsequent generations of scientists and engineers have built careers based on 1920s discoveries such as quantum theory and technological advances in rocketry that inspired later programs such as aerospace exploration of the universe. Outstanding academic centers enriched with equipment and essential resources in the 1920s sustained the quality of those research communities and advanced their status for scientific accomplishments as new fields and theories evolved. Americans still benefit from access to products inspired by 1920s science and technology for medical treatment, communication, entertainment, and travel. While leaded gasoline was eventually removed from vehicle fuel markets, the evolution controversy remains an issue confronting twenty-first-century scientists and educators.

Elizabeth D. Schafer

Further Reading

Davis, Edward B. "Science and Religious Fundamentalism in the 1920s." *American Scientist* 93, no. 3 (May/June, 2005): 253–260. Examines the response of liberal scientists and theologians to attempts to stop public schools from teaching evolution.

Hart, David M. *Forged Consensus: Science, Technology, and Economic Policy in the United States, 1921–1953*. Princeton, N.J.: Princeton University Press, 1998. Focuses on conservative politicians who influenced 1920s tax, property, and other business legislation affecting corporations' investments, technical research, and production.

Kohlstedt, Sally Gregory. *Teaching Children Science: Hands-on Nature Study in North America, 1890–1930*. Chicago: University of Chicago Press, 2010. Provides details regarding 1920s field clubs, scouting groups, and American Nature Study Society leaders, including images of educators, participants, and educational materials.

Kohlstedt, Sally Gregory, Michael M. Sokal, and Bruce V. Lewenstein. *The Establishment of Science in America: 150 Years of the American Association for the Advancement of Science*. New Brunswick, N.J.: Rutgers University Press, 1999. Notes significant developments in 1920s leadership, conferences, publications, education, and professional interactions, including appendices listing officers, editors, meeting sites, and membership numbers for that decade.

Rosner, David, and Gerald Markowitz. "A 'Gift of God'?: The Public Health Controversy over Leaded Gasoline During the 1920s." *American Journal of Public Health* 75, no. 4 (April, 1985): 344–352. Discusses corporate pressure to control government and media reactions to scientists' warnings regarding the adverse aspects of tetraethyl.

Rossiter, Margaret W. *Women Scientists in America: Struggles and Strategies to 1940*. Baltimore: Johns Hopkins University Press, 1997. Chronicles obstacles females faced and alternatives they pursued while attempting to advance in 1920s research positions in academia, industries, and government.

See also: Automobiles and auto manufacturing; Chemistry; Inventions; Medicine; Nobel Prizes; Physics; Rocketry; *Scopes* trial (1925); Television technology

■ Science fiction

In the 1920s, science fiction followed science, or at least speculation based on science, along its path of new knowledge, innovation, and creativity. Its joining of the components of fiction with scientific and technological methods and content led to something new: stories based in a system of inquiry, facts, and theories that led in previously unimagined directions.

Science fiction of the 1920s well reflects the scope, range, vigor, and expectations of the period. The genre had been taking shape for decades in the writings of various authors, notably Jules Verne and H. G. Wells, as well as American writers such as Garrett P. Serviss and George Allan England. These writers generally wrote about marvelous inventions or discoveries, the results of which would reach beyond the observed world to provide unfamiliar backgrounds for human or nonhuman action, in any time or place or in parallel dimensions.

Authors of science fiction based their fictional premises on extensions of known science or ideas that they suspected might one day come to fruition. Their fiction depicted realistically altered settings involving an ever-growing range of topics, including space flight, time travel, discovery of other dimensions, artificial intelligence, extraterrestrial life, future wars, new inventions, and new power sources, notably atomic energy. It combined degrees of scientific rationalization with narrative components based in spectacular actions, extraordinary voyages, or exotic settings. These stories appeared in book form as well as in popular-fiction magazines, which could be acquired from American newsstands or via subscription. In magazine form, science fiction manifested itself as a distinct literary category in the mid-1920s, and the magazine would remain the genre's primary format for nearly twenty-five years.

Gradual Emergence

In particular, the popular general-fiction magazines *Argosy All-Story Weekly* and *The Blue Book Magazine* often published stories involving science or technology, featuring the work of such established or newly emerging authors as Edgar Rice Burroughs, Gertrude Barrows Bennett (as Francis Stevens), Garrett Smith, and Austin Hall. More specialized magazines such as *Weird Tales*, founded in 1923 and dedicated to publishing supernatural, fantasy, and occult stories, offered fiction by Otis Adelbert Kline, H. P. Lovecraft, Henry S. Whitehead, and A. Merritt. Magazines that included stories rooted in scientific and technological speculation found a ready audience and increasing sales, while surging population growth, rising literacy rates, and improved living standards drove magazine circulation and encouraged writers. Science-based stories accorded profoundly with the American character, the spirit of the frontier, the heroic explorer, the free-acting independent individual, and the ideals of progress, expansion, and growing knowledge.

Science and technology permeated daily life in the 1920s to an unprecedented degree. The public was exposed to changes brought by electricity, radio, telephone, motion pictures, automobiles, airplanes, household appliances, industrialization, mechanization, medical advances, and even television in its experimental stages. People were becoming increasingly aware of developing, unfamiliar, and unanticipated social and cultural conditions that would shape daily life in the near future. Meanwhile, scientists frequently made new, startling discoveries as they probed such unexplored frontiers as the universe, the atom, electromagnetism, and the space-time continuum. Greater knowledge and ability opened up even greater mysteries: Science revealed unsettling, staggering realities, and technology brought far-reaching changes. Together, they posed a challenge to established manners, morals, attitudes, values, beliefs, assumptions, and behaviors.

All these developments offered writers and publishers innovative points of departure for storytelling. Partly because they appeared in various magazines, stories of this kind acquired several names, including "invention stories," "impossible stories," "different stories," and "pseudo-science stories." The transition from the word "stories" to the word "fiction" marked a turning point in the history of science fiction.

Hugo Gernsback, Father of Science Fiction

In April 1926, Hugo Gernsback, a naturalized American born in Luxembourg, identified and distinguished this new, growing subcategory of popular fiction. He called it "scientifiction" and devoted an entire monthly magazine to it: *Amazing Stories*, the first science-fiction magazine.

By giving the genre a name, Gernsback also established its framework and defining characteristics. In his initial editorial, "A New Sort of Magazine," Gernsback explained what he meant by scientifiction, citing the works of Jules Verne, H. G. Wells, and Edgar Allan Poe, as well as contemporary writers G. Peyton Wertenbaker, George Allan England, and Austin Hall. He saw Poe, Verne, and Wells as forerunners of the new category, and this claim, along with reference to such well-established writers as England and Hall, lent credibility to his new specialized fiction magazine. Gernsback explained his intention of shaping a generation of writers who would explore the frontiers of science in entertaining ways. Frank R. Paul, Gernsback's illustrator, produced bright, bold cover illustrations that conveyed the spectacle and drama of the genre. His striking futuristic images initiated the development of science-fiction art.

Gernsback wanted science fiction to both entertain and provide some understanding or appreciation of the science involved. He saw the genre as a forerunner to genuine scientific innovation, suggesting new scientific or technological ideas that could then be achieved in reality. *Amazing Stories* would be the medium through which readers could enjoy the future now. Gernsback also asked for readers' responses to the stories, giving enthusiasts a voice and sense of community and fostering the free exchange of ideas.

For the next three years, Gernsback's *Amazing Stories*, along with its companions, *Amazing Stories Annual* (1927) and *Amazing Stories Quarterly* (launched 1928), published leading authors in the new genre. In addition to Verne and Wells, authors included William F. Jenkins (as Murray Leinster), Clare Winger Harris, Edmond Hamilton, David H. Keller, Edward E. Smith, and Philip Francis Nowlan. The August 1928 issue of *Amazing Stories* featured Nowlan's novella *Armageddon 2419 A.D.*, which introduced the character for which he would later become famous: Anthony "Buck" Rogers, a World War I veteran who is transported from the year 1927 to the far future. Buck Rogers would go on to become a pop-culture phenomenon, featuring in a long-lived newspaper comic strip that debuted in January 1929, and later starring in the first ever science-fiction radio program. The phrase "that Buck Rogers stuff" came to signify the entire genre of science fiction.

In February 1929, Gernsback lost control of *Amazing Stories* to another publisher, who continued the magazine. In June of that year, Gernsback began to publish *Science Wonder Stories*, the fourth science-fiction magazine; in July, *Air Wonder Stories*; and in the fall, *Science Wonder Quarterly*. In an editorial published in June 1929, he dropped the term "scientifiction" in favor of "science fiction."

Impact

Many science-fiction magazines followed those of Gernsback. His work and that of others in the 1920s made science fiction an important extension of popular literature, and later other arenas of popular culture such as film and television. The magazine science fiction of the 1920s inspired what would become the golden age of the genre, lasting from roughly the mid-1930s through the late 1940s. More than any other form of literature, and in a far shorter time, science fiction invested American culture with an awareness of new possibilities for human life in wider realms of space and time.

Timothy C. Miller

Further Reading

Ackerman, Forrest J., and Brad Linaweaver. *Worlds of Tomorrow: The Amazing Universe of Science-Fiction Art*. Portland, Oreg.: Collectors Press, 2004. Provides commentary on science-fiction artwork from the 1920s through the 1950s.

Ashley, Mike. *The Time Machines: The Story of the Science-Fiction Pulp Magazines from the Beginning to 1950.* Liverpool: Liverpool University Press, 2000. A comprehensive history of science-fiction magazines.

Clute, John. *Science Fiction: The Illustrated Encyclopedia.* London: Dorling Kindersley, 1995. Surveys all forms of the genre by decade, with charts, classifications, and commentary.

Del Rey, Lester. *The World of Science Fiction, 1926-1976: The History of a Subculture.* New York: Ballantine, 1979. Describes the growth of science fiction in America as cultural force.

Gunn, James. *Alternate Worlds: The Illustrated History of Science Fiction.* Englewood Cliffs, N.J.: Prentice-Hall, 1975. Analysis of the artistic, scientific, social, and intellectual influences associated with science fiction.

See also: Comic strips; Literature in the United States; Magazines; Science and technology

Scopes trial

The Event: The prosecution of a teacher from a Tennessee public school for teaching the biological theory of evolution
Date: July 10-21, 1925
Place: Dayton, Tennessee

Schoolteacher John T. Scopes was found guilty of violating Tennessee's anti-evolution law, but his fine was overturned by the state's supreme court, making it impossible for defense lawyers to appeal the ruling to the federal courts in hopes of getting the law itself overturned. Although the anti-evolution law remained on the books, the widespread ridicule of prosecutors in the trial tended to discourage enforcement of the law.

By the 1920s, a majority of biologists accepted the scientific validity of Charles Darwin's theory that all animal species had evolved gradually, primarily through the process of natural selection. Opponents of the theory were distressed that it was favorably discussed in most public school textbooks. The most significant opposition to Darwinism came from Christian Fundamentalists, religious conservatives who espoused a literal reading of the Bible, including its Creation narrative. Fundamentalist preachers and their allies insisted that departure from the biblical account would promote atheism and immorality, and they further argued that citizens in a democracy had the right to ban such teachings from schools financed by their taxes.

In February 1925 Tennessee legislators passed a bill sponsored by state representative John W. Butler, making it a misdemeanor to teach any theory that denied the biblical account of Creation. The punishment for violating the law was a minimum fine of one hundred dollars and a maximum of five hundred dollars. Although the law was often ignored, it acted as a deterrent to biology teachers. The American Civil Liberties Union (ACLU) announced that it would pay the legal expenses for any teacher prosecuted under the Butler Act.

Preparations for the Trial
When civic leaders in the small town of Dayton read about the ACLU's offer, they recognized that a trial to test the law's constitutionality would raise Dayton's profile and positively affect its economy. On May 4, they contacted John T. Scopes, a twenty-four-year-old educator who taught math, physics, and chemistry, occasionally substituting for the biology teacher. When asked if he had ever violated the Butler Act, he replied he had perhaps summarized the theory while standing in for a biology class in April. He pointed out that the state's approved text, George Hunter's *A Civic Biology: Presented in Problems*, had a section describing evolution. A religious skeptic, Scopes strongly opposed the law, and he agreed to stand trial for a test case. The next day the chairman of the school board obtained the ACLU's promise of support and announced the arrest of Scopes to the press.

The story of the impending trial quickly captured national headlines, especially after famed journalist and social critic H. L. Mencken labeled it the "monkey trial"—a reference to the notion that humans evolved from apes—in his coverage for the *Baltimore Sun*. On May 13, William Jennings Bryan, a former secretary of state and presidential candidate, agreed to represent the World Christian Fundamentals Association—an interdenominational group that supported the Butler Act—at the trial, and the state accepted him as a special prosecutor. This prompted Clarence Darrow and Dudley Field Malone, two of the most prominent libertarian lawyers in the country, to offer their services for the defense without fees. In June, Scopes traveled to New York

John Scopes (right) with his father, Thomas. (Getty Images)

to formulate a legal strategy with ACLU lawyers. Although the ACLU preferred another attorney, they agreed to honor Scopes's preference for Darrow as the lead lawyer, with the assistance of Arthur Garfield Hays and John R. Neal, among others.

The Trial

Both the proponents and opponents of evolutionary theory saw the trial as a showdown between two incompatible worldviews. Bryan and other Fundamentalists viewed the trial as a battle to save the country from atheism and immorality. Secular intellectuals and liberal scientists were shocked at the prospect of the government restricting scientific knowledge from classrooms. Responding to public interest, newspapers sent more than 120 journalists to report on the proceedings. Chicago radio station WGN dispatched announcer Quin Ryan to Dayton, and the case became the first U.S. trial to be broadcast live over national radio.

As its leaders had hoped, Dayton's economy improved with the trial. Merchants sold monkey dolls and featured monkey motifs in their advertisements. Hotel Aqua, the only true hotel in town, was fully occupied, and many visitors had to find housing in neighboring communities.

On July 10, presiding judge John Raulston opened the trial in the presence of nine hundred spectators. After the jury was impaneled, the defense tried unsuccessfully to quash the indictment on the grounds that the Butler Act violated the freedoms guaranteed in both the state and federal constitutions. Tennessee attorney general A. T. Stewart then presented an opening statement, alleging that Scopes was guilty of committing a misdemeanor. Defense attorney Malone responded that there was no evidence that Scopes had actually denied the biblical account of Creation, arguing that some Christian theologians interpreted the Bible as being consistent with evolutionary theory. Raulston, however, accepted the prosecution's evidence that Scopes had admitted to teaching evolution, thereby disobeying the literal words and intent of the statute.

Three students testified that Scopes had said in the classroom that humans had gradually evolved from single-celled organisms. When Scopes's lawyers attempted to call competent zoologists to testify in support of evolutionary theory, Raulston disallowed their testimony, explaining that scientific knowledge was irrelevant to whether or not Scopes had broken the law. Bryan gave a long speech defending the Bible and alleging that Darwin's ideas had inspired German militarism and motivated two murderers recently defended by Darrow. Malone countered that truth is always victorious and therefore needs no laws respecting free speech.

On the seventh day, the defense unexpectedly called Bryan to the stand as an expert witness. The ensuing confrontation between Darrow and Bryan was the highlight of the trial. Darrow forced Bryan to defend literal interpretations of biblical stories. Bryan admitted that the word "day" in the Genesis Creation story might denote a period of more than twenty-four hours. Darrow's supporters felt Bryan was made to look foolish, whereas Bryan's supporters were disappointed with his inability to give more persuasive answers.

Closing for the defense on July 21, Darrow asked for a verdict of guilty in order to allow the case to be appealed. The jury found accordingly, and Raulston fined Scopes one hundred dollars. Scopes appealed, maintaining that the Butler Act was a violation of his constitutional freedoms. Two years later, the Tennessee Supreme Court held in *Scopes v. State* (1927) that the Butler Act was consistent with the state's constitution, but it overturned Scopes's punishment on a technicality, because the law specified that the fine should have been decided by the jury rather than the judge. This decision prevented an appeal to the federal courts. The state's attorney general could have prosecuted Scopes in a second trial, but he declined to do so.

Impact

The Scopes trial demonstrated the great gulf that existed between Americans with secular views and those committed to traditional religious beliefs. Following the trial, partisans of both sides claimed victory. Although some historians have asserted that the trial marked the displacement of religious faith and rural values by secularism and scientific skepticism, the number of committed Fundamentalists continued to grow. During the next five years, twelve state legislatures debated bills with wording similar to the Butler Act, and efforts in Mississippi and Arkansas were successful. Although the laws were rarely enforced, they nevertheless encouraged teachers to avoid mentioning evolution in the classroom.

The Scopes trial failed to settle the most important legal issue of the case: whether the Butler Act violated the U.S. Constitution. A month before the trial began, the U.S. Supreme Court had declared in *Gitlow v. New York* (1925) that the First Amendment's upholding of religious exercise and freedom of speech was binding and further protected by the Fourteenth Amendment. The Tennessee legislature repealed the Butler Act in 1967. The next year, in *Epperson v. Arkansas*, the U.S. Supreme Court concluded that it was unconstitutional to prohibit the teaching of a scientific theory on religious grounds.

Thomas Tandy Lewis

Further Reading

Johnson, Anne Janette. *The Scopes Monkey Trial.* Detroit: Omnigraphics, 2007. A readable account of the trial, including biographies of key participants and a selection of primary-source materials.

Larson, Edward. *Summer for the Gods: The Scopes Trial and America's Continuing Debate over Science and Religion.* New York: Basic Books, 1997. Analyzes the trial as part of the continuing controversy between scientists and Fundamentalists.

Lienesch, Michael. *In the Beginning: Fundamentalism, the Scopes Trial, and the Making of the Antievolution Movement.* Chapel Hill: University of North Carolina Press, 2007. Discusses the trial as a significant event in the history of two antagonistic social movements.

Scopes, John T., et al. *The World's Most Famous Trial, State of Tennessee v. John Thomas Scopes: Complete Stenographic Report of the Court Test of the Tennessee Anti-Evolution Act at Dayton, July 10 to 21, 1925.* New York: Da Capo Press, 1971. A primary source for researchers interested in the exact words used in the trial.

Scopes, John T., and James Presley. *Center of the Storm: Memoirs of John T. Scopes.* New York: Holt, Rinehart and Winston, 1967. Corrects mistakes found in many secondary accounts of the trial.

See also: Bryan, William Jennings; Censorship; Darrow, Clarence; Education; *Gitlow v. New York* (1925); Mencken, H. L.; Religion in the United States

■ Sears, Roebuck and Co.

Identification: Retail department store
Date: Founded in 1886

During the 1920s, Sears, Roebuck and Co., a pioneer of the mail-order retail industry, shifted its focus to opening retail stores in response to changing urban markets. The resultant growth of the company established its position as a dominant economic force of the early twentieth century.

Richard W. Sears established the R. W. Sears Watch Company in 1886 in order to sell mail-order watches. The following year, he was joined in his business by watchmaker Alvah C. Roebuck, and they changed the company's name to Sears, Roebuck and Co. in 1893. Sears and Roebuck achieved early success by adopting the mail-order retail model pioneered by Montgomery Ward, which used newly constructed railroad networks to ship a variety of goods at low cost to small towns and rural areas. With an increasingly diverse collection of items in its annual catalogs, Sears, Roebuck and Co. provided consumers with an affordable alternative to relatively expensive general stores and dry-goods merchants. By the early twentieth century, Sears, Roebuck was far outstripping the sales volume of other mail-order retailers serving rural markets, and their catalogs offered a wide variety of items that ranged from everyday household goods to automobiles and home designs.

During the 1920s, as the populations of American cities grew and the proliferation of automobiles drew increasing numbers of shoppers into urban areas, Sears, Roebuck began making inroads into urban retail markets. The company opened its first department store in Chicago in February 1925 and then opened several more stores in the latter 1920s. By 1929, it was operating over three hundred stores in cities nationwide. This rapid growth allowed Sears, Roebuck to expand its practice of marketing certain products under exclusive store-owned brand names, contributing to the success of such brands as Craftsman tools and Kenmore appliances, both of which the company began selling in 1927.

Early Sears, Roebuck department stores proved successful but failed to match the market dominance of the company's mail-order business due to competition with numerous established urban retailers. Nevertheless, conventional retail sales grew steadily throughout the decade, overtaking mail-order sales by 1931.

Impact
Following an aggressive policy of diversification that would shape its business model for decades to come, Sears, Roebuck and Co. expanded its operations from an exclusively mail-order business to one offering hundreds of physical store locations during the 1920s. Although its new stores failed to equal the success of other department store retailers, Sears, Roebuck captured a significant share of the conventional retail market during the decade, which, combined with its still-thriving mail-order business, established the company as a stalwart of American retailing.

Michael H. Burchett

Further Reading
Katz, Donald R. *The Big Store: Inside the Crisis and Revolution at Sears.* New York: Penguin Books, 1988.
Martinez, Arthur C., and Charles Madigan. *The Hard Road to the Softer Side: Lessons from the Transformation of Sears.* New York: Crown Business, 2001.
Worthy, James C. *Shaping An American Institution: Robert E. Wood and Sears, Roebuck.* Urbana: University of Illinois Press, 1984.

See also: Automobiles and auto manufacturing; Chain stores; Urbanization

■ Sennett, Mack

Identification: Canadian-born American filmmaker
Also known as: Michael Sinnott
Born: January 17, 1880, Richmond, Quebec, Canada
Died: November 5, 1960, Los Angeles, California

Mack Sennett was a pioneer in the film industry and helped create over a thousand short and full-length films. Sennett was among the most prolific producers of film comedies in the silent era and discovered future film talents such as actors Charlie Chaplin, Gloria Swanson, Bing Crosby, and Carole Lombard, as well as director Frank Capra.

Mack Sennett was born Michael Sinnott to Catherine Foy and John Francis Sinnott, both descendants of Irish-Catholic immigrants who had immigrated to Quebec in the 1840s. His formal schooling ended in 1897 when the Sinnott family moved to East Berlin, Connecticut, and then to Northampton, Massachusetts, the following year. He worked in a boiler factory in Connecticut and a pulp mill in Massachusetts and took singing lessons in his spare time.

In 1900, Sennett moved to New York to break into show business as a singer. He found work in vaudeville, traveling chorus shows, singing quartets, and Broadway musicals, and adopted the stage name of Mack Sennett. In 1908, Sennett joined Biograph, an early movie producer, where he met future film director D. W. Griffith. While at Biograph, Sennett learned every aspect of filmmaking, and his first job was as an actor in the starring role of comic Frenchman Monsieur Dupont in the 1908 film *The Curtain Pole*. That same year, Sennett scripted the film *The Lonely Villa*, which was directed by Griffith. Mabel Normand, silent film actor and comedian, joined Biograph in 1909, and she and Sennett became good friends and, later, lovers. By 1910, Sennett was in charge of all comedy productions at Biograph, and his first role as director was for his 1911 screenplay *Comrades*, in which he also starred.

Keystone Pictures

In 1912, Sennett became the production head at Keystone Pictures Studios, an early film company in California. Many early film greats got their start with Sennett and Keystone, such as Roscoe "Fatty" Arbuckle, who began with the studio in 1913 starring in the popular slapstick Keystone Kops comedies. Charlie Chaplin got his start in films when he joined Keystone in 1913. Chaplin made thirty-five films before leaving Keystone the following year for a contract with Mutual Film Corporation. Sennett left Keystone in 1917 to form an independent film company, Mack Sennett Comedies.

Silent film comedian Ben Turpin joined Sennett's new company in 1917 and became its most reliable star, appearing in over fifty films through 1927. Turpin's movies with Sennett Comedies included *Down on the Farm* (1920), *Married Life* (1920), *A Small Town Idol* (1921), and *The Sheik of Araby* (1923). In 1920, Sennett hired Billy Bevan, who starred in over seventy films during the next nine years. Bevan's movies included *Love, Honor, and Behave* (1920), *The Lion's Roar* (1928), and *The Best Man* (1928), which featured nineteen-year-old Carole Lombard. Mabel Normand had left Sennett to sign with Samuel Goldwyn in 1917, but Sennett bought Normand's contract from Goldwyn and cast her in the feature-length films *Molly O'* (1921), *Suzanna* (1923), and *The Extra Girl* (1923).

Sennett discovered Harry Langdon in 1923. Langdon had appeared in two short films before signing with Sennett, and after joining Mack Sennett Comedies, he starred in more than twenty short films, the first of which was *Picking Peaches* (1924). In 1924, Frank Capra was hired by Sennett as a screenwriter and wrote several films starring Langdon, including the 1925 shorts *Plain Clothes*, *Lucky Stars*, and *There He Goes*.

The Jazz Singer, considered by many to be the first talking motion picture, was released in 1927 by Warner Bros., and Sennett raced to convert his studio to sound. Sennett borrowed money to begin producing sound pictures in 1928. After the stock market crash of 1929, however, banks refused to extend Sennett any credit, despite his producing several successful short sound films starring W. C. Fields and Bing Crosby. Sennett ran out of cash by 1933, declared bankruptcy, and was forced into premature

Mack Sennett. (Moviepix/Getty Images)

retirement. He received an honorary Academy Award in 1938 and appeared as himself in the 1939 film *Cavalcade*.

Impact

Mack Sennett was the most successful producer of comedies during the silent film era. Although he did not invent slapstick or the chase scene, many believe he took the two concepts to a higher level. He is credited with creating the Keystone Kops, and many believe Sennett's greatest gift was his sense of the absurd. Sennett was able to make stars out of such unconventional personalities as Fatty Arbuckle, Ben Turpin, and Harry Langdon, and he was also an innovator in the realm of special effects and trick photography in his use of a panoramic film set and of treadmills for chase scenes. Sennett discovered and helped launch the careers of such film industry greats as Charlie Chaplin, Frank Capra, Gloria Swanson, Carole Lombard, and Bing Crosby.

Thomas R. Feller

Further Reading

Fowler, Gene. *Father Goose: The Story of Mack Sennett*. New York: Covici-Friede, 1934. An authorized biography of Sennett.

Lahue, Kalton C. *Mack Sennett's Keystone: The Man, the Myth, and the Comedies*. New York: A. S. Barnes, 1971. A comprehensive biography of Sennett.

Louvish, Simon. *Keystone: The Life and Clowns of Mack Sennett*. New York: Faber and Faber, 2005. Examines film comedy with a focus on Sennett's studio and provides background on the studio's actors and directors. Includes photographs.

Sennett, Mack, and Cameron Shipp. *King of Comedy*. Reprint. San Francisco: Mercury House, 1990. Sennett's autobiography, including photographs.

Sherk, Warren M. *The Films of Mack Sennett: Credit Documentation from the Mack Sennett Collection at the Margaret Herrick Library*. Lanham, Md.: Scarecrow Press, 1998. Detailed listing of storylines, credits, cast and production information, and special notes for 855 Sennett films produced between 1912 and 1933.

Walker, Brent E. *Mack Sennett's Fun Factory: A History and Filmography of His Studio and His Keystone and Mack Sennett Comedies, with Biographies of Players and Personnel*. Jefferson, N.C.: McFarland & Co., 2010. An in-depth examination of Sennett, his films, and his independent studio, including photographs and biographies of actors and technical personnel.

See also: Arbuckle, Fatty; Chaplin, Charlie; Fields, W. C.; Film; Griffith, D. W.; *Jazz Singer, The;* Langdon, Harry; Normand, Mabel; Swanson, Gloria; Talking motion pictures

■ Sesquicentennial Exposition

The Event: World's fair held during the 150th anniversary of the signing of the Declaration of Independence
Date: May 31–November 30, 1926
Place: Philadelphia, Pennsylvania

Marking the 150th year of American independence, this second international fair showcased the United States as the wealthiest and most powerful nation in the world following the end of World War I. Although beautifully designed and built, it became the nation's forgotten fair.

In 1921, Philadelphia was designated as the site for the sesquicentennial celebration of American independence. A marsh on the south side of the city was transformed into a vast park where one could look forward into the future, while celebrating the best of the nation's revolutionary past. The fair was opened by President Calvin Coolidge, Philadelphia mayor W. Freeland Kendrick, Secretary of State Frank B. Kellogg, and Secretary of Commerce Herbert Hoover. Fifty million visitors were expected, but only around ten million passed under the 80-foot replica of the Liberty Bell that formed the entrance to the site. Adults paid fifty cents to enter, while the fee for children was a quarter. Perhaps the main reason for the poor attendance was that it rained on 107 of the 184 days the exposition was open.

Five major halls featured exhibitions centered on themes such as agriculture, education, fine arts, liberal arts, machinery, and transportation. The High Street area was a neighborhood with twenty historic structures from 1776, while the Gladway area provided a theater, restaurants, and varied amusements. Treasure Island was an area of the exposition designed especially for children. There was also an auditorium that accommodated 10,000 and a stadium for 100,000 spectators.

The exposition had to be self-supporting because the federal government provided no funding, apart from approving the minting of two commemorative coins: a silver half-dollar and a gold quarter eagle that was valued at $2.50. These coins were to be sold as souvenirs at the exposition. The dies were prepared by the newly appointed chief engraver of the United States Mint, John Sinnock. The obverse of the half-dollar, which was based on sketches by John Frederick Lewis of Philadelphia, consisted of side-by-side busts of George Washington and Calvin Coolidge, who was the first president to appear on a United States coin during his own administration. The half-dollar's reverse side showed the Liberty Bell. Philadelphia's Independence Hall was depicted on one side of the quarter eagle, while the coin's other side showed the Statue of Liberty. The exposition would have made significant profits had all the coins been sold at about twice their value. In the end, however, the exposition failed to meet its financial goals, and the U.S. District Court placed it under equity receivership in April 1927.

Impact
Although the Sesquicentennial Exposition of 1926 has largely been overlooked in later decades, the silver half-dollar and gold quarter eagle produced to

commemorate the event became collectible items, along with a series of other coins specially minted during this decade.

Clifton W. Potter Jr.

Further Reading

Austin, Erastus Long, and Odell Hauser. *The Sesquicentennial International Exposition.* New York: Arno Press, 1976.

Ristine, James D. *Philadelphia's 1926 Sesquicentennial Exposition.* Charleston, S.C.: Arcadia, 2009.

See also: Currency and coinage; Hobbies and recreation

Sex and sex education

In the wake of World War I, the United States faced growing promiscuity in its adolescent and young adult population and an attendant growth in cases of sexually transmitted diseases. The U.S. government and various social and religious organizations nationwide decided that remaining silent about sex was ineffective, and public schools began to offer some instruction about sexual development, hygiene, and reproduction.

In some ways, the 1920s marked a significant shift in the moral landscape of the United States. As the 1920s approached, the traditionally held belief that sexual intercourse was only meant for procreation began to be replaced by beliefs that sexual pleasure was also a legitimate reason to have sexual relations. A trend of increased promiscuity among American youth became more noticeable as soldiers began to return from World War I. This increase in sexual activity and the corresponding increase in sexually transmitted diseases (STDs) such as syphilis and gonorrhea were considered alarming and dangerous. Until then, American youth had generally received little or no education from their elders about sex, though many learned the "facts of life" from peers at a young age.

Theories of Sexual Development

During the 1920s, scientists began to discredit earlier theories of sexual development, particularly with regard to "self-stimulation," or masturbation. The dominant theory for centuries had been that self-stimulation to any degree was sharply detrimental to the development and function of the mind and body—even leading to blindness, insanity, or death—but by the mid-1920s, most physicians and psychologists had discarded these views.

However, some scholars, including sex education pioneer Maurice Bigelow, believed that self-stimulation in young children should be viewed in approximately the same light as thumb-sucking: as an understandable form of self-exploration that should nonetheless be discouraged before it becomes a long-term habit. For this reason, Bigelow published and lectured on the necessity of "prophylaxis," or prevention, of masturbation in children. To that end, he outlined several measures parents could take, such as keeping children clean; dressing them in loose-fitting clothing to avoid any chafing or friction on the sex organs; having them sleep on hard mattresses and bathe in cool water; keeping them physically and mentally active; giving them few opportunities for privacy; and educating children as early as possible about the basic purpose of the sex organs, to prevent them from asking their peers about sexual topics. When discussing masturbation, Bigelow advised parents not to get angry or scold their children, but to explain calmly that the behavior is unhealthy.

School-Based Sex Education

Bigelow was an early advocate for public sex education, in light of the rise of what he saw as preventable problems, including STDs, illegitimacy, promiscuity, sexual immorality, unsuccessful marriages, and dysgenic parenthood (reproduction that did not conform to the principles of eugenics). The efforts of Bigelow and other Progressive Era social reformers such as New York physician Prince A. Morrow resulted in the formation in 1914 of the American Social Hygiene Association, which soon formed local chapters to advise doctors, public health officials, and schools about the best ways to curb the spread of STDs and educate the public about safe sex—still defined at the time as abstinence until marriage. At the same time, the growing recognition of adolescence as a distinct phase of human development helped guide theories of sex education.

The first high school sex education classes were implemented in Chicago in 1913 by Ella Flagg Young, superintendent of the city's public school system. About twenty thousand students received instruction in subjects such as "personal sexual hygiene," "problems of sex instincts," and "prevention of venereal disease." The program faced community

The Case for Birth Control

Margaret Sanger's essay "The Case for Birth Control" first appeared on February 23, 1924, in Woman Citizen. *In it, she argued for the need for birth control:*

Everywhere we look, we see poverty and large families going hand in hand. We see hordes of children whose parents cannot feed, clothe, or educate even one-half of the number born to them. We see sick, harassed, broken mothers whose health and nerves cannot bear the strain of further child-bearing. We see fathers growing despondent and desperate, because their labor cannot bring the necessary wage to keep their growing families. We see that those parents who are least fit to reproduce the race are having the largest number of children; while people of wealth, leisure, and education are having small families.

It is generally conceded by sociologists and scientists that a nation cannot go on indefinitely multiplying without eventually reaching the point when population presses upon means of subsistence. While in this country there is perhaps no need for immediate alarm on this account, there are many other reasons for demanding birth control. At present, for the poor mother, there is only one alternative to the necessity of bearing children year after year, regardless of her health, of the welfare of the children she already has, and of the income of the family. This alternative is abortion, which is so common as to be almost universal, especially where there are rigid laws against imparting information for the prevention of conception. It has been estimated that there are about one million abortions in the United States each year.

To force poor mothers to resort to this dangerous and health-destroying method of curtailing their families is cruel, wicked, and heartless, and it is often the mothers who care most about the welfare of their children who are willing to undergo any pain or risk to prevent the coming of infants for whom they cannot properly care.

There are definite reasons when and why parents should not have children, which will be conceded by most thoughtful people.

First—Children should not be born when either parent has an inheritable disease, such as insanity, feeble-mindedness, epilepsy, or syphilis.

Second—When the mother is suffering from tuberculosis, kidney disease, heart disease, or pelvic deformity.

Third—When either parent has gonorrhea. This disease in the mother is the cause of 90 percent of blindness in newborn babies.

Fourth—When children already born are not normal, even though both parents are in good physical and mental condition.

Fifth—Not until the woman is twenty-three years old and the man twenty-five.

Sixth—Not until the previous baby is at least three years old. This gives a year to recover from the physical ordeal of the birth of the baby, a year to rest, be normal, and enjoy her motherhood, and another year to prepare for the coming of the next.

We want mothers to be fit. We want them to conceive in joy and gladness. We want them to carry their babies during the nine months in a sound and healthy body and with a happy, joyous, hopeful mind. It is almost impossible to imagine the suffering caused to women, the mental agony they endure, when their days and nights are haunted by the fear of undesired pregnancy.

Seventh—Children should not be born to parents whose economic circumstances do not guarantee enough to provide the children with the necessities of life.

A couple who can take care of two children and bring them up decently in health and comfort, give them an education and start them fairly in life, do more for their country and for mankind than the couple who recklessly reproduce ten or twelve children, some of them to die in infancy, others to survive but to enter the mill or factory at an early age, and all to sink to that level of degradation where charity, either state or private, is necessary to keep them alive. The man who cannot support three children should not have ten, notwithstanding all pleas of the militarists for numbers.

Eighth—A woman should not bear children when exhausted from labor. This especially applies to women who marry after spending several years in industrial or commercial life. Conception should not take place until she is in good health and has overcome her fatigue.

Ninth—Not for two years after marriage should a couple undertake the great responsibility of becoming parents. Thousands of young people enter marriage without the faintest idea of what marriage involves. They do not know its spiritual responsibilities. If children are born quickly and plentifully, people consider that the marriage is justified. I claim that this is barbaric and wrong. It is wrong for the wife, for the man, for the children.

It is impossible for two young people to really know each other until they have lived together in marriage. After the closeness and intimacy of that relation there often comes to the woman a rude awakening; the devoted lover becomes careless and dissatisfied. If she becomes pregnant immediately, she becomes physically disturbed, nervous, and irritable. The girl has changed, and the boy who knew her as a happy smiling sweetheart finds her disagreeable and disgruntled. Of course thousands of people learn to adjust themselves. Nevertheless, I maintain that young people should marry early and wait at least two years to adjust their own lives, to play and read together, and to build up a cultural and spiritual friendship. Then will come the intense desire to call into being a little child to share their love and happiness. When children are conceived in love and born into an atmosphere of happiness, then will parenthood be a glorious privilege, and the children will grow to resemble gods. This can only be obtained through the knowledge and practice of Birth Control.

P.S.—The American Birth Control League desires that the instruction in birth control should be given by the medical profession. Only through individual care and treatment can a woman be given the best and safest means of controlling her offspring. We do not favor the indiscriminate diffusion of unreliable and unsafe birth control advice.

and governmental opposition, however, and came to an end after only one year. Nonetheless, the "social hygiene movement" gained traction over time, and in the wake of World War I, sex education for young people became more of a priority. An estimated 75 percent of normal schools and 40 percent of public high schools surveyed after the war were offering some level of sex education.

Most schools split their sex education curriculum across several different subjects, as it was believed that devoting a single class to instructing students about sexual activity might create an unhealthy fascination with the subject. Under this integrated system, biology courses covered topics such as the physiology of the sex organs, reproduction, and eugenics (the then-popular movement promoting social improvement through encouraging reproduction among people with socially desirable traits). Physical education classes discussed puberty, menstruation, seminal emissions, and personal hygiene. Concurrently, social studies classes were enlisted to instruct students about the dangers of prostitution and STDs, the value of monogamy, and control of the impulses. Classes incorporating social hygiene topics were often segregated by gender, with adolescent girls being taught by female teachers and adolescent boys being taught by male teachers. Together, these courses sought to help young people understand sexual urges while shaping their moral development. This practice of moral education was extended to literature classes, where teachers often pointed to heroes and villains in literary works to illustrate that the virtuous were rewarded for their chastity, while the lustful and impulsive were punished for their sinful lifestyles.

The course materials and textbooks used for sex education were a topic of considerable debate among early sex educators. Some were apprehensive about giving students graphically illustrated textbooks to teach them about the physiology of sex, fearing such materials might provide too much information and be inappropriately arousing. Others believed that the textbook was the only medium that could accurately and effectively instruct students about these topics; they worried that if sex instruction was made too obscure or vague, it would not be truly effective, and students would then seek out answers from their peers, thus defeating the purpose of formal sex education. A great many other people felt—as some still do—that public schools are no place for any kind of sex education.

The Public Health Service
The federal government first became involved in sex education during World War I, when soldiers and sailors deployed overseas were instructed about the dangers of prostitution and STDs. After the war, the U.S. Public Health Service (PHS) became involved in some of the public education efforts espoused by the social hygiene movement, launching a multi-pronged attack of pamphlets, lectures, films, and exhibits about the dangers of STDs. This campaign focused on general good health practices, displayed the effects of disease, and emphasized self-control.

The initial target audience of the PHS campaign was white adolescent boys, who were seen as the most vulnerable population, but was soon expanded to include all young people, recent immigrants, and minorities. Target groups received specialized materials tailored to their perceived needs and values. *Keeping Fit*, a sex education exhibit for boys, and *Youth and Life*, a similar exhibit for girls, were widely used, and modified, by schools and local community organizations. In the mid-1920s, the PHS also produced and circulated the sex-education silent films *The Gift of Life* and *The Science of Life*.

Impact
The effectiveness of sex education efforts in the 1920s at reducing the rates of STDs such as syphilis and gonorrhea is difficult to determine. At the time, statistical data on such topics as STD rates were just beginning to be gathered, and early diagnostic tests could be grossly inaccurate. Making analysis more difficult is the fact that both the integrated sex education system and the PHS efforts lacked standardization and coordination. The PHS campaign continued through the 1920s, but by the decade's close, Congress had begun cutting appropriations for the agency's sex education efforts. Reasons for this went beyond any public backlash or difficulty in determining the program's effectiveness: As World War I became a more distant memory and contraception became more readily available and socially acceptable, alarm over the spread of STDs began to fade.

It is also unclear how many schools nationwide actually offered sex education to their students. According to one government survey during the decade, about 45 percent of responding high schools said they offered their students some level of sex education. However, only a little more than half of high schools responded to the survey, which also did not gather fine details about the nature of sex education programs. Nonetheless, while the success of sex education programs in the 1920s remains difficult to assess, their introduction during this period provided the groundwork for future sex and health courses that would inform subsequent generations of students about human development, the mechanics of reproduction, the importance of contraception, and the dangers of sexually transmitted diseases.

Joseph F. Sanders

Further Reading

Bigelow, Maurice A. *Adolescence: Educational and Hygienic Problems.* New York: Funk & Wagnalls, 1924. An example of the many writings Bigelow produced on the topic of sex education and social hygiene.

Jensen, Robin E. *Dirty Words: The Rhetoric of Public Sex Education, 1870–1924.* Urbana: University of Illinois Press, 2010. Highlights the role of female social reformers in the early sex education movement.

Lord, Alexandra M. "The People's War, 1918–1926." In *Condom Nation: The U.S. Government's Sex Education Campaign from World War I to the Internet.* Baltimore: Johns Hopkins University Press, 2010. Describes the social climate in America after World War I and the government response to public outcry about immorality and disease.

Luker, Kristin. *When Sex Goes to School: Warring Views on Sex—and Sex Education—Since the Sixties.* New York: W. W. Norton, 2006. Contextualizes modern concerns regarding sex education in public schools, outlining its history from the early social hygiene movement through the turn of the twenty-first century.

Moran, Jeffrey P. *Teaching Sex: The Shaping of Adolescence in the Twentieth Century.* Cambridge, Mass.: Harvard University Press, 2000. Traces the history of the social and political factors that influence what and how American students learn through school-based sex education programs.

See also: Birth control; Censorship; Eugenics movement; Homosexuality and gay rights; Marriage and dating; Pornography; Psychology, psychiatry, and psychoanalysis; Sanger, Margaret

■ Sexually transmitted diseases

In addition to pain and incapacitation resulting from infection, the acquisition of sexually transmitted diseases (STDs) can result in sterility and may even be life threatening, as in the case of syphilis. STDs were a particular problem among American soldiers serving in France during World War I. The incidence of STDs in the general U.S. population rose significantly during the 1920s as a result of changes in the perception of morality.

The rise in the incidence of syphilis, gonorrhea, chancroid, and other sexually transmitted diseases (STDs), then referred to as venereal diseases, was likely the result of several factors. The end of World War I, coupled with returning soldiers who often carried such diseases, was certainly a contributing factor. In addition, much of the population was developing increasingly liberal views of sexual morality. Reduced funding of agencies such as the American Social Hygiene Association and the Public Health Service resulted in decreased education in methods of avoiding infection. Any education in birth control, particularly in the use of condoms as a means to avoid infection, was opposed not only by the Roman Catholic Church but also by much of the older American population in general. The numbers are in dispute, but the estimate was that by the end of the decade, one in ten Americans carried a form of sexually transmitted disease.

Rising Incidence

Precise numbers of cases are not available, given the unreliability of such testing and the mistaken identity with other forms of disease. Nevertheless, the number of Americans affected by STDs was probably relatively high, and some believe the number of cases of syphilis and gonorrhea may have been greater than the combined total other infectious diseases. A 1901 study suggested nearly 80 percent of men in New York City had at some point been infected with gonorrhea and as many as 20 percent with syphilis. The accuracy of these numbers is disputed, especially as the official collecting of statistics began only in 1919. By comparison, 20 percent of U.S. Army recruits during the decade prior to the 1920s were diagnosed with some form of sexually transmitted disease, suggesting that earlier numbers may not have been completely inaccurate.

The incidence of these illnesses continued to rise during the decade. Estimates are that 500,000 new

> **Reuben Leon Kahn Develops a Modified Syphilis Test**
>
> In 1923, serologist and immunologist Reuben Leon Kahn developed a modified syphilis test, the "standard Kahn test," that was simpler, faster, and more sensitive than its predecessor. This test, which is based on the reaction of serum from the tested individual with an extract of certain lipid components of beef heart, is complete after a few minutes. By 1925, Kahn's test had become the standard syphilis test used by the U.S. Navy and later was employed worldwide for the detection of the disease.

cases of syphilis appeared annually, with more than 700,000 cases of gonorrhea being diagnosed each year. As many as 25 percent of cases of infant blindness were attributed to gonorrheal infections contracted from infected mothers during birth.

Treatment, Testing, and Prevention
Since antibiotics would not become available for another decade, few treatment options were available. Salvarsan, an arsenic derivative, had been developed by immunologist Paul Ehrlich decades earlier as a treatment for syphilis, but it was often ineffective and had obvious side effects. Men were sometimes treated for gonorrhea with the insertion of a hot rod into the urethra, but the treatment did little more than to maintain an open urinary canal and involved significant discomfort.

The first accurate diagnostic test for syphilis had been developed by bacteriologist August von Wassermann in 1906. Known as the complement fixation test, the method was time consuming and often subject to error. The increasing incidence of syphilis during the 1920s required a more accurate method of diagnosis. In 1923, immunologist Reuben Kahn reported a more accurate and reliable method. The Kahn test, based on a precipitation reaction using the patient's serum, could be completed in several minutes. While it too was subject to error, the Kahn test was soon adopted by U.S. armed forces and became the standard for many decades.

While funding for public education to prevent the spread of STDs continued to decline during the 1920s and throughout the Great Depression, both the American Social Hygiene Association and the Public Health Service at least made some attempt to replace the inaccurate, and often worthless, material to which the public had access. In 1922, a survey was begun to determine the level of material addressing "social hygiene" that had been published. Lecturers were sent to educational facilities such as colleges for dissemination of proper information, and religious leaders were encouraged to address social issues contributing to the spread of the diseases.

Impact
While the impact of increased education in the late 1920s and 1930s remains uncertain, the proportion of citizens infected with either syphilis or gonorrhea was reduced to approximately 1 percent of the population by the 1930s. In addition, on the recommendation of Surgeon General Thomas Parran Jr., states began to institute premarital testing for STDs during the 1930s.

Richard Adler

Further Reading
Hager, Thomas. *The Demon Under the Microscope: From Battlefield Hospitals to Nazi Labs, One Doctor's Heroic Search for the World's First Miracle Drug.* New York: Harmony Books, 2006. Discusses the discovery of sulfa drugs, the first broad-spectrum treatment for bacterial diseases.

Hayden, Deborah. *Pox: Genius, Madness, and the Mysteries of Syphilis.* New York: Basic Books, 2003. The story of the disease and its possible impact on historical figures.

Lord, Alexandra. *Condom Nation: The U.S. Government's Sex Education Campaign from World War I to the Internet.* Baltimore: Johns Hopkins University Press, 2010. Describes the evolution of government policies in teaching sex education.

Parascandola, John. *Sex, Sin and Science: A History of Syphilis in America.* Westport, Conn.: Praeger, 2008. Describes how pre–World War I reluctance to discuss STDs contributed, along with other factors, to the increased incidence of these diseases beginning in the 1920s.

Rosebury, Theodor. *Microbes and Morals: The Strange Story of Venereal Disease.* New York: Viking Press, 1971. An early introduction to the five major forms of bacterial STDs, providing a history of these diseases in the United States, along with observations on their differentiation.

Sheik, The

Identification: A silent film about the relationship between an English woman and an Arab sheik
Director: George Melford
Date: 1921

The Sheik established the career of actor Rudolph Valentino and portrayed, through the female lead, the newly found freedom women experienced after World War I.

The Sheik was based on a popular romantic novel by Edith Maude Hill and was directed by George Melford, who later directed *Dracula* (1931). Although it was shot in Santa Barbara County, California, the film successfully capitalized on the exoticism rampant in American society at the time.

The Sheik's relatively straightforward plot combines adventure in a foreign land with romance. Independent British aristocrat Lady Diana Mayo (Agnes Ayres) is traveling alone in Arabia and wants to visit the desert. As she awaits her journey, Sheik Ahmed Ben Hassan (Valentino) takes over the local casino for the amusement of his men. Upon seeing her, Sheik Ahmed is smitten by Lady Diana, who is outraged that an Arab can commandeer the casino and exclude white Europeans. Although forewarned, Lady Diana ventures into the desert without a Western escort and is abducted by Sheik Ahmed. In desperation, she flees into the sands only to be captured by the bandit Omair (Walter Long), who she quickly learns is less restrained than the sheik. While in captivity, Lady Diana realizes that she has fallen in love with Ahmed. After the sheik rescues her from Omair, it is revealed that the sheik's father was British and his mother Spanish, which makes him Caucasian, rather than Arab, by birth. At the end of the film, Lady Diana and Sheik Ahmed express their love for each other.

Five years later, the lead actors, Valentino and Ayres, reprised their roles in the film's sequel, *The Son of the Sheik*, in which Valentino played both the father and son. The sequel was his last film, and he died eight days after its New York City premiere.

Impact

The Sheik was a box-office hit and made Valentino a star, contributing to the creation of the Latin lover image. The film also inspired the popular song "The Sheik of Araby," affected the slang of the period, and even purportedly provided the name for the mascot of Hollywood High School. Valentino's slicked-back hair, swarthy good looks, and smoldering sensuality may have contributed to the loosening of sexual norms during the Roaring Twenties.

Charles L. P. Silet

Further Reading

Dijkstra, Bram. *Evil Sisters: The Threat of Female Sexuality and the Cult of Manhood.* New York: Henry Holt, 1998.

Leider, Emily Wortis. *Dark Lover: The Life and Death of Rudolph Valentino.* New York: Farrar, Straus and Giroux, 2003.

Wintle, Sara. "The Sheik: What Can Be Made of a Daydream." *Women: A Cultural Review*, 7, no. 3 (1996): 291–302.

See also: Film; Slang; Valentino, Rudolph

Shenandoah airship disaster

The Event: The crash of the USS *Shenandoah*, the Navy's first rigid airship
Date: September 3, 1925
Place: Noble County, Ohio

The crash of the USS Shenandoah *is among the United States' most dramatic aviation disasters. The airship encountered severe winds that carried it higher into the sky than it could withstand. It ultimately broke in two and crashed in southern Ohio, killing fourteen of the men on board.*

The United States Navy received funding for its first rigid airship in 1920 and completed construction in August 1923. Based on a German dirigible that had been captured in France in 1917, the USS *Shenandoah* was 682 feet long and weighed 41 tons. It was powered by helium gas and could travel up to sixty miles per hour.

The *Shenandoah* began exercises with the Navy's Scouting Fleet on August 1, 1924. In October, it successfully flew from Lakehurst, New Jersey, to the West Coast, the first ever trans-American flight of a rigid airship. Public interest in the new ship led the Navy

The wreckage of the USS Shenandoah *airship.* (AP Photo)

to schedule a forty-city tour across the Midwest, and the USS *Shenandoah* left Lakehurst to start the tour on September 2, 1925, carrying two passengers and forty-one crew members. Commander Zachary Lansdowne was in command of the ship.

Around 6:00 A.M. on September 3, while attempting to avoid a large thunderstorm over Ohio, the *Shenandoah* encountered heavy turbulence that blew it upward and caused the crew to lose control. Its hull could not withstand the stress, and the ship broke in half. The control car, a cabin suspended below the hull, fell near a farmhouse in Noble County, Ohio, killing Lansdowne and several crew members who were inside. Others fell to their deaths from the hull.

The stern section crashed into a nearby hillside. All eighteen men inside survived the landing, as did four others who had been thrown out during the descent. Lieutenant Commander Charles Rosendahl took control of the bow section, which had risen to ten thousand feet. The crew vented helium and gasoline in order to lower it, then called for a farmer on the ground to secure one of the dangling ropes. These seven men survived as well. The crash site was heavily looted, despite the attempts of the Bureau of Investigation and the Ohio National Guard to secure the area.

Impact

The crash of the USS *Shenandoah* drew criticism from government and military officials. In response, the Navy improved the design of its new airships, making the engines and frames stronger and building the control cars into the keel instead of attaching them with cables. The military also made advances in weather-tracking technology. However, after further crashes in the 1930s, the Navy ended its airship program.

Jennifer L. Campbell

Further Reading

Althoff, William. *USS* Los Angeles: *The Navy's Venerable Airship and Aviation Technology.* Dulles, Va.: Brassey's, 2004.

Keirns, Aaron. *America's Forgotten Airship Disaster: The Crash of the USS* Shenandoah. Howard, Ohio: Little River, 2010.

Waller, Douglas. *A Question of Loyalty: General Billy Mitchell and the Court Martial that Gripped the Nation.* New York: HarperCollins, 2004.

See also: Airships; Mitchell, Billy; Science and technology

Sheppard-Towner Act

The Law: Federal law providing matching funds to the states for programs to reduce infant and maternal mortality
Also known as: Maternity Act; Sheppard-Towner Maternity and Infancy Protection Act
Date: Enacted on November 23, 1921

The Sheppard-Towner Act was the first federal law designed to promote the health and welfare of women and children and proved a relatively successful, if highly contentious, undertaking.

Although state programs for mothers and children varied widely due to differing local needs and priorities, most included some infant care education, midwife training, visiting nurses to care for pregnant women and new mothers, and the distribution of pure milk supplies. Authorizing a yearly appropriation of $1.24 million to support such programs in participating states, the Sheppard-Towner Act was administered by the newly formed U.S. Board of Maternity and Infant Hygiene and implemented by state boards of health.

The act's strongest support came from newly enfranchised women who had long fought for federal solutions to social and industrial problems. Of particular concern were the country's alarming maternal and infant death rates, some of the highest among industrialized nations. In 1920, League of Women Voters president Maud Wood Park formed the Women's Joint Congressional Committee (WJCC), an enormous lobbying clearinghouse combining the legislative efforts of ten million women representing as many as twenty-one national women's organizations. Working through the WJCC, leading female activists such as Julia Lathrop and Florence Kelley coordinated an ultimately successful campaign for the bill.

Most conspicuous among the act's opponents were members of the American Medical Association, anti-suffragists, right-wing groups, and conservative politicians, all of whom argued that the law represented socialism and a dangerous and costly federal intrusion into previously private areas of life. Conservative opposition gained momentum by the mid-1920s, as the public's fear of radicalism and growing distaste for federal solutions to social problems intensified. Despite continued lobbying efforts by the WJCC, Congress declined to renew the Sheppard-Towner Act beyond June 30, 1929.

Impact

All but three states eventually accepted the matching funds set out in the Sheppard-Towner Act. Between 1921 and 1927, maternal deaths dropped from 67.3 per 1,000 to 62.3 per 1,000; by 1929, infant deaths had dropped from 75 per 1,000 births to 64 per 1,000. Nearly three thousand prenatal care centers were established during this period.

By continuing the call for a greater federal role in human welfare, the Sheppard-Towner Act helped to ensure the survival of Progressive reform in the 1920s and to hasten what some historians describe as the transition from nineteenth-century laissez-faire liberalism to the social liberalism of the New Deal period. For one, the act presaged the provision in the Social Security Act of 1935 that extended federal grants to the states for maternal and child health programs.

Jan Doolittle Wilson

Further Reading

Felder, Deborah G. *A Century of Women: The Most Influential Events in Twentieth Century Women's History.* New York: Citadel Press, 2003.

Lemons, J. Stanley. *The Woman Citizen: Social Feminism in the 1920s.* Charlottesville: University of Virginia Press, 1990.

Lindenmeyer, Kristie. *"A Right to Childhood": The U.S. Children's Bureau and Child Welfare, 1912–1946.* Urbana: University of Illinois Press, 1997.

See also: Health care; League of Women Voters; Women's rights

Show Boat

Identification: Stage musical about the performers aboard the Mississippi riverboat *Cotton Blossom* between the years 1880 and 1927, based on the eponymous novel by Edna Ferber
Authors: Book and lyrics by Oscar Hammerstein II; music by Jerome Kern
Date: 1927

The first production to combine musical numbers with a dramatic libretto, Show Boat *pioneered the genre of the stage musical, an improvement on the comic operettas and revues that had become popular during the 1890s. The plot deals with racial prejudice, and the score features the song "Ol' Man River," which became an American classic.*

The role of the African American dockworker Joe, who performs "Ol' Man River," was written for singer Paul Robeson, who was unable to appear in the 1927 American production. The role was instead portrayed by Jules Bledsoe, in a cast including Norma Terris, Howard Marsh, Helen Morgan, Charles Winninger, Edna Mae Oliver, and Tess Gardella, a white actor who played the role of Queenie in the conventional blackface of the era.

Act I opens in Natchez, Mississippi, where Cap'n Andy Hawks presents his theatrical company to an eager crowd. When Pete, the boat's engineer, accosts Julie LaVerne, wife of leading man Steve Baker, a scuffle ensues. Meanwhile, Andy's daughter, Magnolia "Nolie" Hawks, becomes smitten with compulsive gambler Gaylord Ravenal. During a rehearsal, the sheriff arrests Steve and Julie, a mulatto, for violating an antimiscegenation law. Steve slices Julie's hand and sucks a bit of her blood, claiming that he now has mulatto blood as well. Although supported by the troupe, they depart, because African Americans were not allowed to appear on stage at that time. Andy fires Pete and hires Gaylord as leading man. Nolie and Gaylord fall in love and are married.

Act II opens in 1893. Gaylord, Nolie, and their daughter, Kim, now live in a boarding house. Gaylord abandons them, but they meet Frank and Ellie, performers from their showboat days. Nolie auditions at the Trocadero nightclub and is hired for her friend Julie's old job. Andy and Parthy visit Chicago and rally the crowd during Nolie's performance on New Year's Eve. She becomes a major star but retires in 1927, to be succeeded by Kim. Reunited with Ravenal, Nolie returns to the showboat, where Joe again sings "Ol' Man River."

Impact

Show Boat had an enormous influence on American musical theater, creating a genre replacing the comic revues and "follies" of the early twentieth century. In 1928, Paul Robeson's success in the British version forever identified him with "Ol' Man River," which he sang in stage revivals, a 1936 film adaptation, and countless concerts, and for which he rewrote the lyrics to use in his fight for civil rights. The late 1920s stage phenomenon of *Show Boat* has been revived in award-winning adaptations over the ensuing decades.

Scott Allen Nollen

Further Reading

Block, Geoffrey Holden. *Enchanted Evenings: The Broadway Musical from "Show Boat" to Sondheim.* New York: Oxford University Press, 1997.

Kreuger, Miles. *"Show Boat": The Story of a Classic American Musical.* Da Capo Press, 1990.

See also: Broadway musicals; Ferber, Edna; Hammerstein, Oscar, II; Kern, Jerome; Robeson, Paul; Theater in the United States

Shuffle Along

Identification: Musical about two grocers and their rise and subsequent fall in small-town politics
Authors: Music by Eubie Blake; lyrics by Noble Sissle
Date: 1921

Shuffle Along *stands out as the first full-length musical written, directed, and performed by African Americans to become a major hit on Broadway. Subsequent renewed interest in black musical theater ended a ten-year unofficial moratorium, broke color barriers, and set the trend for the ensuing decade on Broadway. In 1948, presidential nominee Harry S. Truman would select the production's hit song "I'm Just Wild About Harry" for his campaign.*

After desperately trying to sell songs to disinterested publishers for five years, vaudeville partners James Hubert "Eubie" Blake and Noble Sissle decided to create a musical around their unwanted wares. The resulting musical, *Shuffle Along,* contained only three newly composed songs. Blake and Sissle convinced a white theater owner, John Court, to offer them the 63rd Street Theatre in New York City, and as was the custom at the time, the show went on a road tour before opening on Broadway.

The original cast included Blake and Sissle and starred Flournoy Miller, Aubrey Lyles, and Roger Matthews. During its run, *Shuffle Along* introduced singer Paul Robeson and dancer Josephine Baker to the Broadway stage. Notably, jazz performer Adelaide Hall and composer William Grant Still performed in the thirteen-piece band. The lively jazz-infused production became an instant hit with the public and saw an astonishing 504 shows before its close on Broadway on July 15, 1922. The show continued to perform throughout the country for another year, playing to mixed-race audiences.

The plot revolves around two grocers, Sam and Steve, who both run for mayor with the agreement that the winner will appoint his opponent chief of police. Sam wins the election and appoints Steve as agreed; however, their rule deteriorates into dishonesty, and their disagreements devolve into a humorous fight scene. An opposing candidate, Harry Walton, vows to end the pair's corrupt rule, and the chorus sings, "I'm Just Wild About Harry." In the end, Sam and Steve are ousted.

Impact

The unprecedented success of *Shuffle Along* legitimized the African American musical, became an inspiration for black composers and librettists who might have otherwise been discouraged to write for Broadway, and served as a model for white artists to write for all-black casts. The musical also changed perspectives and provided opportunities for performers such as Paul Robeson and Florence Mills to take on more important roles in integrated casts and for musicians such as Eubie Blake to write for white productions throughout the 1920s.

Gary Galván

Further Reading

Kimball, Robert, and William Bolcom. *Reminiscing with Noble Sissle and Eubie Blake*. New York: Cooper Square Press, 2000.

King, Bobbi, et al. "A Legend in His Own Lifetime." *Black Perspective in Music* 1 (Fall, 1973): 151–156.

Southern, Eileen. *The Music of Black Americans: A History*. 3d ed. New York: W. W. Norton, 1997.

See also: Baker, Josephine; Broadway musicals; Robeson, Paul; Vaudeville

■ Sinclair, Upton

Identification: American writer and activist
Also known as: Upton Beall Sinclair Jr.
Born: September 20, 1878, Baltimore, Maryland
Died: December 18, 1968, Bound Brook, New Jersey

Author of the novel The Jungle, *Upton Sinclair was a major figure in the Socialist Party throughout the 1920s. He wrote many books championing socialism and exposing corruption in business and government.*

Sinclair joined the Socialist Party in 1902. In 1904, the editor of the left-wing journal *Appeal to Reason* commissioned him to investigate working conditions in Chicago's meatpacking industry. Sinclair went undercover for seven weeks, publishing his reports serially in the journal. He republished them in book form as *The Jungle*; it sold more than 150,000 copies

Upton Sinclair. (Hulton Archive/Getty Images)

worldwide in its first year and sparked the passage of the Pure Food and Drug Act and the Federal Meat Inspection Act in 1906. Sinclair continued to focus his energies on Socialist Party causes but was unsuccessful in his 1920 and 1922 campaigns for U.S. congressional office. In the late 1920s, he established California's first branch of the American Civil Liberties Union. He also ran unsuccessfully for governor of California as a Socialist in 1930 and as a Democrat in 1934.

Sinclair's 1927 novel *Oil!* exposed problems within the oil industry the way *The Jungle* had scrutinized meatpacking. He continued to write exposés of the major institutions and businesses in America, including churches, the stock market, education, and the arts. In 1928, he published the documentary novel *Boston*, about the infamous case of alleged murderers Nicola Sacco and Bartolomeo Vanzetti. Honest to a fault, Sinclair could not form a definitive conclusion, temporarily alienating him from Socialist Party members, who considered the two to be political martyrs rather than murderers.

Impact

After achieving fame with *The Jungle*, Sinclair devoted his life to campaigning against business oppression and governmental neglect and to exposing corruption and brutality in a variety of American institutions. During the course of his career, he published more than ninety books, which shone a light on the mistreatment of workers and the production of unsafe products. He was one of the most public Socialist figures in the 1920s and was a staunch supporter of unions and workers' rights. In 1943, Sinclair received a Pulitzer Prize for his novel *Dragon's Teeth* (1942).

Leslie Neilan

Further Reading

Arthur, Anthony. *Radical Innocent: Upton Sinclair*. New York: Random House, 2006.

Mitchell, Greg, and Peter Schrag. *The Campaign of the Century: Upton Sinclair's Race for Governor of California and the Birth of Media Politics*. San Francisco, Calif.: Polipoint Press, 2010.

Sinclair, Upton. *The Jungle*. Reprint. New York: Simon & Schuster, 2009.

See also: Lewis, Sinclair; Political parties; Red Scare, The; Sacco and Vanzetti case; Unionism

■ Slang

The 1920s was a decade of enormous change in almost all aspects of American life. Still reeling from the violence and carnage of World War I, Americans tended to reevaluate traditional notions of propriety and morality. These questionings, along with the growth and ultimate success of the women's suffrage movement, led to more freedom for women, a greater experimentation in clothing and hairstyles for both sexes, and a new frankness about romance and sexuality. In addition, the national ban on alcohol known as Prohibition created a number of illegal alcohol production and transportation enterprises that introduced many slang terms into American culture. For all these reasons, the 1920s represented one of the most colorful and prolific decades for slang coinage in American history.

One of the most profuse areas of 1920s slang expressions dealt with romance and sex. In response to the anxiety and austerity of the war years, many young Americans threw themselves into dating, dancing, and drinking. Furthermore, the burgeoning emancipation of women inspired many young women in their teens and twenties to be more forthright about romance and sex than previous generations. So it is not surprising that much of the slang from the 1920s relates to courtship, assessments of the opposite sex, and night life.

Words for young women were especially popular. Among the most famous of these was "flapper" to designate a young woman who embraced the trends of her generation. The origins of the word remain uncertain. Some linguists believe that it reflects a tendency in English slang to describe girls and women in avian terms, such as "bird" in British English and "chick" in both American and British colloquial speech. If so, the underlying image is that of a young bird flapping her wings as if to show off or attract a mate. Other possibilities are that it refers either to the flapping of the new, shorter skirts that young women were wearing or to the flapping of their shorter, less structured hair styles. It is also possible that the word had no specific source but reflected an ancient tradition of English semantics in which the consonant cluster of "fl-" evokes rapid, dramatic motion—for example, in words such as "fly," "flow," and "flee." A very seductive flapper was deemed a "vamp," a clipping of "vampire" first applied to screen actresses, such as Theda Bara, who frequently played appealing but dangerous women who led men to destruction.

Although the flapper had her male counterpart in young hedonistic males, no one term became as universal in identifying them, though the imitative "flipper" was common and also reflected the notion of quick, heady movement. "Flapper" may have also inspired the rhyming term "dapper," a blending of "flapper" and "dad/daddy," to indicate a flapper's father. A very attractive and possibly dangerous young man was called a "sheik," again inspired by films, especially those in which film idol Rudolph Valentino played Middle Eastern aristocrats who both attracted and intimidated women.

Dating and Drinking

The lexicon of the 1920s reflects the flippancy and cynicism of American youth, or "Bright Young Things," of the Jazz Age. For example, the lexicon of dating frequently adopted the jargon of business. Dating was sometimes referred to as "bookkeeping." A kiss was "cash," and so if a young man wished to kiss his date, he might ask her to "produce the cash." If he wished to inquire whether she wanted to kiss right away or wait until later in their date, he would ask her, "Cash or check?" If she replied, "Check," he knew that she did not feel comfortable kissing him at present but might be inclined to kiss him later. If she felt totally disinclined to kiss, she would respond, "The bank's closed." A similar attitude toward marriage was reflected in the slang referring to it, which was often based on police lingo: an engagement ring was a "handcuff," and a fiancé was a flapper's "police dog." Marriage was termed "the eye-opener," and a divorce was "the Declaration of Independence."

As alcohol became illegal under Prohibition, a lexicon of slang inevitably developed that allowed people to discuss drinking in terminology that might be unfamiliar to supporters of the ban. Illegal bars and saloons came to be known as "speakeasies," reflecting the need for one to "speak easy," or quietly, about the establishment so as not to attract unwanted attention. The distillers of the illegal beverages came to be called "bootleggers," purportedly because of their practice of concealing bottles of contraband in their boots with their trouser legs pulled down over the boots to conceal the alcohol. Bootleggers were sometimes referred to as "embalmers," and the speakeasies also came to known as "joints," as in "gin joint" or "beer joint." This latter term may reflect the original meaning of "joint" as a bend or twist in structure that establishes a separate or discrete section or entity—in this case, a wall or other concealing structure that breaks off the secret bar from the building in which it is housed. "Joint" in this sense, along with bootlegger, is one of numerous words dealing with alcohol that survived the repeal of Prohibition, another being "hooch," a term for liquor derived from the name of a Native American tribe in the Northwest, members of which became involved in bootlegging activities in the 1920s.

Approval and Opprobrium

Slang from the 1920s is replete with terms expressing like or dislike for people, places, or events. Young people of the 1920s had a plethora of such expressions, including "dud," "killjoy," "wurp," and "bozo," among many others. Adjectives describing unfavorable individuals included "sappy," "hokey," and "all wet." Approval or appreciation for people or turns of event drew such expressions of praise as "hot," "and how," "darb," "tasty," "tight," "keen," "jake," "attaboy/attagirl," "lollapalooza," and the exultant "Now you're on the trolley!" Anything that was seen as splendid or wonderful was "the nuts" or "the berries." These latter two expressions were probably more common than the animal-themed expressions of approval such as "the cat's pajamas" and "the bee's knees" that later came to be associated with the era. Nonsense exclamations included "baloney," "bunk," "piffle," "hokum," and "applesauce." "Rats," a ubiquitous cry of disappointment throughout much of the twentieth century, was first heard in the 1920s. Someone who drank too much was called a "rummy," and a young woman thought to be promiscuous was scorned as a "quiff." Older people were often disrespectfully called a "face stretcher," in reference to an older, single woman trying to appear young, or "Father Time," in reference to a man over the age of thirty. A woman who sought to date only wealthy men was contemptuously termed a "gold digger," and a man seeking wealthy women was in similar fashion dubbed a "forty-niner."

Impact

The exuberant coinage and widespread use of slang terms in the 1920s came to characterize the Jazz Age and especially the young people of the day. The phrases that became linguistically stereotypical of the period, such as "cat's pajamas, "cat's meow," and "bee's knees," survived their time of origin only as quaint historical jargon. Although a number of terms, such as "bookkeeping" for dating, fell out of popular use after the 1920s, dozens of common informal words and expressions that continued into the twenty-first century were inventions of the 1920s, including "baloney," "keen," "blind date," "live wire," "wet blanket," "baby" as a term of endearment, "hood" for hoodlum or underworld gang member, "crush" for romantic attraction, "knock up" for impregnate, and "For crying out loud!" as an expression of impatience or annoyance, among others.

Thomas Du Bose

Further Reading

American Heritage Dictionaries. *More Word Histories and Mysteries: From Aardvark to Zombie.* New York: Houghton Mifflin, 2006. Discusses American language, including notes on the survival of 1920s slang in the speech of later generations.

Ammer, Christine. *Cool Cats, Top Dogs, and Other Beastly Expressions.* New York: Houghton Mifflin, 1999. An exploration of animal imagery in slang, including a number of coinages from the 1920s.

Bryson, Bill. *Made in America: An Informal History of the English Language in the United States.* New York: W. Morrow, 1994. Analyzes many slang terms arising in the Jazz Age.

Dalzell, Tom. *Flappers 2 Rappers: American Youth Slang.* Mineola, N.Y.: Dover, 2010. A scholarly linguistics study presented for a lay audience, featuring examples of 1920s slang.

Flexner, Stuart Berg. *I Hear America Talking: An Illustrated Treasury of American Words and Phrases.* New York: Van Nostrand Reinhold, 1976. Details colloquial American English throughout U.S. history.

See also: Bara, Theda; Dances, popular; Flappers; Jazz; Roaring Twenties; Speakeasies; Valentino, Rudolph

■ Smith, Alfred E.

Identification: American politician
Born: December 30, 1873, New York, New York
Died: October 4, 1944, New York, New York

Four-time New York governor Al Smith was the first Catholic presidential candidate nominated by a major political party. As the Democratic candidate, Smith lost the 1928 election to Herbert Hoover, but the election exposed deep divides in American society, and voting patterns signaled the shift in party loyalties that would take place in subsequent elections.

Alfred E. Smith grew up on Manhattan's Lower East Side. With Irish, German, and Italian origins, Smith identified with his neighborhood's urban immigrant community and became associated with the Irish American Democratic politicians who ran Tammany Hall in New York City. As part of the New York State Assembly from 1904 to 1915, Smith established a reputation as a social and industrial reformer, an advocate of efficient administration, and a supporter of urban, immigrant, working-class populations. Smith was elected as New York's sheriff in 1915 and then president of the New York City Board of Aldermen (now City Council) in 1917. Smith won the race for governor of New York in 1918 and moved to Albany with his wife and five children.

Governor of New York

Smith lost his 1920 bid for reelection and from 1921 to 1922 worked as chairman of the New York–based United States Trucking Company. He was elected governor again in 1922, and reelected in 1924 and 1926, solidifying his record as a reformer of New York's social services, industrial conditions, and administration. Smith worked to control the state's finances and streamline its myriad committees and departments in order to achieve maximum efficiency and cost-effectiveness. Smith was known for his public speaking ability, his image as a common man, and his belief in diversity, tolerance, and the positive role of government.

The 1928 Presidential Campaign

Smith became the Democratic candidate for president in 1928. Addressing Prohibition in his presidential platform, Smith stated that fundamental changes were necessary in the national Prohibition law, which caused a break with some conservative Democratic Party members from the South and West who were against its repeal. Prohibition, however, was connected to larger issues in American society, and Smith symbolized many of the cultural conflicts of the 1920s. For Americans from small towns or rural areas dominated by native-born Protestants, Smith represented the growing threat to American values posed by urban Catholic and Jewish Americans of recent immigrant origin. For many Americans, Smith's image as a "wet" (anti-Prohibition) Irish-Catholic

> ### Alfred E. Smith's Urbanism
>
> The United States became an urban nation in the 1920s. During the decade, the Bureau of the Census reported that for the first time in the nation's history, the majority of the population resided in areas defined as urban. Major literary figures of the period took delight in emphasizing how out of touch with the realities of an increasingly urban nation the rural United States was becoming. Critics such as H. L. Mencken, editor of the *American Mercury*, assailed Puritanism and haughtily proclaimed the superiority of the city dwellers over the "hicks" and the fundamentalists. On the other side, rural voices cried out against the evil influences of the city. From rural newspapers and from conservative, fundamentalist religious leaders came warnings about the decadence of urban life. To many, the city offered a challenge to Anglo-Saxon dominance in U.S. affairs.
>
> In many ways, the 1928 presidential campaign reflected the nation's rapidly changing demographics and was permeated with these tensions between urban and rural America. Republican Herbert Hoover, who had been born in a small town in Iowa, enjoyed wide support in rural areas, while Democrat Alfred E. Smith, who had spent his entire life within the shadow of New York City's skyscrapers, was popular in urban areas of the Northeast for his anti-Prohibition stand and his Catholicism. In the eyes of his followers, Smith was the urban version of Abraham Lincoln; the son of an immigrant who aspired to the highest office in the land, he represented the fulfillment of the American Dream.

from New York City conflicted with the fundamental values of the United States; he represented the sometimes threatening diversity, urbanization, and modernization of American society.

Religion was a defining issue in the 1928 election, and as the first Catholic presidential candidate from a major party, Al Smith's religion posed a problem. Though the national power of the racist and nativist Ku Klux Klan (KKK) had begun to wane in the late 1920s, the group still exerted influence in many areas of the country. The KKK and others spread propaganda stating that with Al Smith as president, the pope would rule the United States and Protestants would be persecuted. Smith, shocked at these expressions of religious bigotry, gave a speech stating that prejudice had no place in American society and that religion should not be a factor in political campaigns. Nonetheless, Smith won only 40.9 percent of the vote, losing even his home state of New York.

Life After 1928

Al Smith retired from public life after his presidential loss. His autobiography, *Up to Now*, was published in 1929, and in August of that year, Smith announced he would be the president of Empire State, Inc., the company formed to build the Empire State Building, over whose opening Smith presided in May 1931. Smith struggled through the Depression, however, and publicly disagreed with President Franklin D. Roosevelt, a fellow Democrat, over New Deal policies, though the two later reconciled. In October 1944, Al Smith died at the age of 70 in New York City.

Impact

Historians regard Al Smith's candidacy in the 1928 presidential election as a significant event. For many Americans at the time, the religious and ethnic hatred shown during the campaign were troubling, and some felt the election highlighted the deep cultural, religious, and ethnic divides in the country. Some historians also argue that the voting patterns established during the 1928 election foreshadowed a shift in political loyalties, because for the first time, the Democratic Party won in large U.S. cities, particularly in the Northeast and Midwest. Also, the South, which had traditionally voted primarily Democratic, shifted slightly in the 1928 election, with several southern states voting Republican. The "New Deal coalition" of later years began to appear in 1928, as urban, northern, working-class Catholics and Jews, joined by organized labor advocates and many women voters, supported the Democrats. A number of black voters, who had traditionally supported Republican candidates, also voted for Al Smith, in part because of the KKK's attacks on Smith. These trends presaged the broader shift of support among minority and urban voters toward the Democratic Party and of rural conservatives toward the Republicans.

Jonathan Keljik

Further Reading

Finan, Christopher M. *Alfred E. Smith: The Happy Warrior.* New York: Hill and Wang, 2002. Presents a biography with photographs.

Neal, Donn C. *The World Beyond the Hudson: Alfred E. Smith and National Politics, 1918–1928.* New York: Garland Publishing, 1983. Focuses on Smith's politics and political career.

Silva, Ruth Caridad. *Rum, Religion, and Votes: 1928 Re-Examined.* Westport, Conn.: Greenwood Press, 1981. Examines the effect that social issues of the time may or may not have had on the 1928 election.

Slayton, Robert A. *Empire Statesman: The Rise and Redemption of Al Smith.* New York: Free Press, 2001. Biography exploring Smith's life, with sections devoted to his terms as governor, the 1928 election, and Smith's later life.

Smith, Alfred E. *Up to Now: An Autobiography.* New York: Viking, 1929. Smith reflects on his life in New York government and on his 1928 presidential campaign.

See also: Cities; Elections, U.S., of 1928; Hoover, Herbert; Immigration to the United States; Ku Klux Klan; Prohibition; Religion in the United States; Urbanization

■ Smith, Bessie

Identification: African American blues singer
Born: April 15, 1894, Chattanooga, Tennessee
Died: September 26, 1937, Clarksdale, Mississippi

Known as "Empress of the Blues," Bessie Smith was one of the most popular and influential blues singers of the 1920s and the 1930s. Her followers included singers Billie Holiday, Mahalia Jackson, and Janis Joplin.

Smith lost both of her parents as a child and was raised by her sister Viola. Her brother Clarence was influential in her early life, teaching her to sing and dance in order to make a living with street performances. Vocalist Cora Fisher also taught Smith to sing. In 1912, Clarence, who had joined the Moses Stokes Minstrel Show, arranged an audition for his sister. She started her career as a dancer and soon became a featured singer. Around this period, Smith became acquainted with noted blues singer Gertrude "Ma" Rainey, much of whose repertoire Smith later recorded. By the time Smith moved to Philadelphia in 1921, she was already a star among Southern African Americans. She played a headliner in the musical *How Come?* with pianist-composer Clarence Williams and famous saxophonist Sidney Bechet. She continued performing in theaters along the East Coast and auditioned for several record companies but was turned down because her voice was too powerful for the recording technologies of the time. In January 1923, however, Frank Walker, a Columbia Records producer, sent Williams to sign her for the label.

Recording Career

The day after an unsuccessful first recording session on February 15, 1923, Smith recorded the best-selling songs of her career: "Down Hearted Blues," written by singer Alberta Hunter, and "Gulf Coast Blues," by Williams. The record sold more than 780,000 copies in less than six months. Though she never matched this commercial success, she became the most popular female blues vocalist of the label. Initially nicknamed "Queen of the Blues," Smith soon won the title "Empress of the Blues." By 1933, she had recorded more than 160 sides for Columbia, with some alternate takes. Her classic recordings include "'Tain't Nobody's Business If I Do" (1923), "You've Been a Good Old Wagon" (1925), "Muddy Water: A Mississippi Moan" (1927), "Empty Bed Blues (Parts 1 and 2)" (1928), "Me and My Gin" (1928), "I'm Wild About That Thing" (1929), "Kitchen Man" (1929), and "Need a Little Sugar in My Bowl" (1931). While most of her materials were prepared by professional composers, she occasionally recorded her own compositions, such as "Back Water Blues" (1927) and "Poor Man's Blues" (1928). In 1929, she appeared in the short film *St. Louis Blues*, based on W. C. Handy's composition of the same name. In the same year, she recorded "Nobody Knows You When You Are Down and Out," a song that predicted the Great Depression years that would bring her career to an end. By the beginning of the 1930s, the classic blues had become less popular. In 1931, Columbia did not renew its recording contract with Smith, though she continued public performances. In 1933, producer John Hammond helped Smith make a comeback by organizing an all-star session with clarinetist Benny Goodman and others. As heard in one of the cuts from this session, "Gimmie a Pigfoot," her powerful vocal performance and lively expressions of the lyrics were still impeccable, but this was her last recording. On September 26, 1937, she was killed in a car accident while traveling near Clarksdale, Mississippi.

Impact

Bessie Smith's music contributed greatly to the legacy of 1920s and 1930s American popular culture. Thanks to the electrical recording system that Western Electric licensed to Columbia Records in 1925, most of Smith's recordings have good fidelity and vividly capture her wide vocal range and expressiveness, impeccable sense of timing and phrasing, and clear intonation and diction, all of which influenced subsequent female singers Billie Holiday, Mahalia Jackson, and Janis Joplin. Smith recorded with many top musicians of the time, such as pianists Fletcher Henderson, Irving Johns, and James P. Johnson; cornetist Louis Armstrong; saxophonists Coleman Hawkins and Don Redman; and clarinetists Buster Bailey and Benny Goodman.

During the peak of her popularity in the 1920s, Smith earned more than two thousand dollars each week. She hired her own train coach when touring, bailed friends out of jail, and bought luxury items such as a 1926 Cadillac convertible automobile as a gift for her fiancé, Jack Gee.

Smith was intolerant of racial prejudice and stood up against Ku Klux Klan members harassing her show in Concord, North Carolina, in July 1927. While she had some trusted white friends, such as producer Frank Walker and photographer Carl Van Vechten, she never tried to win the approval of white society. She was inducted to the Grammy Hall of Fame in 1973, Blues Hall of Fame in 1980, Rock and Roll Hall of Fame in 1989, and Nesuhi Ertegun Jazz Hall of Fame in 2008. She is also remembered in the Bessie Smith Cultural Center in her hometown of Chattanooga, Tennessee.

Mitsutoshi Inaba

Further Reading

Albertson, Chris. *Bessie*. Rev. ed. New Haven, Conn.: Yale University Press, 2005. A biography of Smith discussing her bisexuality and musical career.

Brooks, Edward. *The Bessie Smith Companion: A Critical and Detailed Appreciation of the Recordings*. New York: Da Capo Press, 1982. Presents insights into Smith's recordings throughout her career.

Davis, Angela Y. *Blues Legacies and Black Feminism: Gertrude "Ma" Rainey, Bessie Smith, and Billie Holiday*. New York: Pantheon Books, 1999. Explores the social, political, and sexual influence women blues singers had on their contemporary society.

Grimes, Sara. *Backwaterblues: In Search of Bessie Smith*. Amherst, Mass.: Rose Island, 2000. Offers information about Smith's life and most famous recordings in the context of 1920s and 1930s American society.

Harris, Michael A. *The Rise of Gospel Blues: The Music of Thomas Andrew Dorsey in the Urban Church*. New York: Oxford University Press, 1994. Includes information about Smith's early recordings and influence on the gospel blues genre.

See also: African Americans; Armstrong, Louis; Electrical recording; Jazz; Ku Klux Klan; Music, popular; Vaudeville

■ Soccer

Although it did not reach the same level of popularity as baseball and football, soccer drew large numbers of participants and spectators during the 1920s. The first professional league in the United States was established in this decade, with clubs attracting top talent from Europe and faring well in international play. Intercollegiate soccer also saw an expansion during this period.

By 1920, soccer was thriving in many eastern and midwestern industrial towns, where immigrant laborers took to the sport as a reprieve from their harsh working conditions. Extensive amateur leagues and clubs existed in Cleveland, Pittsburgh, and St. Louis. Ethnic and company-sponsored teams also flourished in New York and in New England cities such as Boston, New Bedford, and Pawtucket. Soccer was not simply a pastime; when the 1920s began, some players were making $3,000 to $6,000 per year, close to the average Major League Baseball salary at the time.

The American Soccer League

The expansion of soccer crystallized in the establishment of its first professional circuit, the American Soccer League (ASL), which started its first season in September 1921 and lasted until 1931. The eight teams that initially made up the ASL were semiprofessional clubs from East Coast regional leagues, including the Fall River Marksmen, Bethlehem Steel, and J&P Coats. Attendance varied, averaging eight thousand spectators per game at the New England hot spots, while games between rivals such as Fall River and the New Bedford Whalers could bring in over ten thousand fans.

The ASL's rise to international prominence began with the 1924-1925 season, when it expanded from eight teams to twelve. In addition to fielding the best U.S. and Canadian players of the time, it also imported top talent from Europe; in 1926, the league spent $100,000 to acquire around sixty foreign players. News traveled fast that players in the United States could make more money than in any other country in the world. This "American Menace" led to a conflict between ASL and European soccer associations, which, in 1927, complained to the Fédération Internationale de Football Association (FIFA), soccer's international governing body, that U.S. clubs were encouraging players to break their contracts. FIFA took up the issue, but Andrew Brown, president of the United States Football Association (soccer's governing body in the United States, later renamed the United States Soccer Federation), managed to negotiate a settlement.

Despite the success of the ASL, overspending, squabbling within the U.S. soccer community, and the stock market crash of 1929 ultimately led to its downfall. American soccer would have to wait several decades to experience success similar to that of the 1920s.

International Competition

American teams competed against international squads both at home and abroad with great success. In 1926, a combined team of U.S. players faced Austrian club Hakoah at New York City's Polo Grounds in a game that drew an audience of around forty-six thousand people, the largest crowd for a soccer match to date and a record until the glory days of the New York Cosmos in the 1970s. The Boston Wonder Workers and the Newark All-Stars beat the Uruguayan national squad in 1927; the following year, Fall River tied against Scotland's Glasgow Rangers in front of a crowd of fifteen thousand.

In 1924, the United States fielded an Olympic soccer team, which defeated Estonia by one to zero before losing three to zero to Uruguay in its second game. U.S. soccer made its second Olympic appearance in Amsterdam in 1928, where the team was soundly defeated by Argentina, with a final score of eleven to two. North American players such as Canadian-born Joe Kennaway had better luck in Europe at the club level, performing well on the high-ranking teams of the time.

Collegiate Soccer

Soccer also experienced significant expansion on college campuses around the country after World War I. In the soccer hotbeds in the East, it was common for games to draw thousands of spectators during the early 1920s. Pennsylvania State University and Princeton University monopolized the six-team Intercollegiate Association Football League (IAFL) championship through 1925. By 1926, more than twenty eastern colleges were playing soccer, and the IAFL was replaced by the Intercollegiate Soccer Football Association (ISFA), which opened the game to colleges across the country.

Impact

The popular appeal and subsequent professionalization of soccer in the 1920s are testament to the impact immigrant workers had on American sports culture during this period. For the first time, the United States made waves in the international soccer arena, attracting top players and developing local talent that would ultimately guide the U.S. national soccer team to a third-place finish in the 1930 World Cup. However, the ASL's demise prevented soccer from becoming a mainstream American pastime, dealing the sport a crucial blow from which it has not yet recovered.

Mauricio Espinoza-Quesada

Further Reading

Foulds, Sam, and Paul Harris. *America's Soccer Heritage: A History of the Game.* Manhattan Beach, Calif.: Soccer for Americans, 1979. A historical overview largely focused on players, coaches, and referees.

Hollander, Zander, ed. *The American Encyclopedia of Soccer.* New York: Everest House, 1980. A comprehensive overview of professional and collegiate soccer, with many historical photos.

Jose, Colin. *American Soccer League, 1921-1931: The Golden Years of American Soccer.* Lanham, Md.: Scarecrow Press, 1998. Provides background on the ASL, along with a wealth of league, club, and player statistics.

Markovits, Andrei S., and Steven L. Hellerman. *Offside: Soccer and American Exceptionalism.* Princeton, N.J.: Princeton University Press, 2001. Explores how professional sports such as football and baseball marginalized soccer in the American sports scene.

Wangerin, David. *Soccer in a Football World: The Story of America's Forgotten Game*. Philadelphia: Temple University Press, 2008. Provides a history of soccer in the United States and explains why the sport has come to be viewed as "un-American."

See also: Baseball; Football; Olympic Games of 1924 (Summer); Olympic Games of 1928 (Summer); Sports

■ Social sciences

Throughout the 1920s, the social sciences, which included but were not limited to the fields of sociology, economics, political science, anthropology, and psychology, were responsible for gathering data and analyses regarding human society, social institutions, social forces, and human behaviors. The founding of associations committed to social research, along with the establishment of academic social science programs in American universities, created a foundation on which studies in social sciences flourished in the twentieth century.

The 1923 formation of the Social Science Research Council (SSRC) in New York City signaled a commitment to the field of social sciences in the United States. With initial studies focusing on race relations, human migration, and Prohibition, the SSRC formed out of a concern for emerging social problems, specifically within industry. Consisting of representatives from various social science subfields and led initially by University of Chicago political scientist Charles Merriam, the SSRC would become a propelling force in the advancement of the social sciences, responsible for the formation of committees such as the 1928 Advisory Committee on Business Research and the 1929 President's Committee on Social Trends.

Sociology

According to its simplest definition, sociology is the study of society—making it perhaps the most basic social science—encompassing the study of society as a whole as well as how individuals interact within a society. Twentieth-century sociology had its roots in the work of the nineteenth-century European thinkers Emile Durkheim, Karl Marx, and Max Weber. Unlike in Europe, sociology in the United States was influenced the least by Marx, whose work was associated with radical politics. Instead, following the American philosophical tradition of pragmatism, American sociologists engaged in the study of society as it was, tending to focus on field observation and statistical methods.

In the 1920s, the University of Chicago was an important locus of American academic sociology, forming a methodology and body of work that came to be known as the Chicago school of sociology. Chicago sociologists were known for taking the city of Chicago itself as their field of research, leading to the rise of urban sociology as one of many subfields within the discipline. Another important subfield, blending sociology and psychology, was social psychology, pioneered by George Herbert Mead at Chicago, among others. Mead and another American sociologist, Charles Cooley, laid the groundwork for "symbolic interactionism," an important sociological approach later in the twentieth century that studied the way people ascribe meaning to things based on their social significance.

Founded in 1905, the American Sociological Association (ASA) was an important player in the social sciences in the 1920s. The ASA was an early supporter of the effort to create the SSRC, and in 1923, the ASA initiated the effort to create the *Encyclopedia of the Social Sciences*, whose first volume was published in 1930 with the support of other social science organizations.

Economics

An important step in the study of economics in the United States was the establishment of the National Bureau of Economic Research (NBER) in 1920. Led initially by Columbia University economist and SSRC founding member Wesley Clair Mitchell, the NBER focused its work on U.S. macroeconomics, especially the functioning of economic growth and Mitchell's own particular area of interest: business cycles. Another prominent early NBER researcher, Simon Kuznets, worked out methods of measuring the national income that laid the foundation for now-standard economic measurements such as the gross national product (GNP) and gross domestic product (GDP).

Mitchell went on to head, at various times during the decade, the American Economic Association and the President's Committee on Social Trends. He was also one of the founders of the New School for Social

> **The Hawthorne Studies**
>
> The Hawthorne studies were a series of experiments conducted between 1924 and 1932 by Harvard University professors and employees of the Hawthorne Works of the Western Electric Manufacturing Company in Cicero, Illinois. The initial purpose of the experiments was to investigate determinants of worker output. Among the results of the studies, however, were the emergence of the field of industrial sociology and recognition of the importance of social factors in worker behavior.

Research in New York City in 1919 and taught there until 1922. Founded by prominent historians, economists, and philosophers, the New School focused on progressive scholarship in politics, economics, education, and society.

Political Science

As in the other social sciences, political scientists in the 1920s strove to conceive their field as much as possible as a scientific discipline, a "science of politics." Tremendously influential in this push was yet another University of Chicago professor, Charles E. Merriam, who joined Chicago's political science department in 1900 and chaired it from 1923 to 1940. Merriam pioneered the influential "behavioralist" approach in political science, which seeks to explain individual political behavior in quantifiable ways and relate it to the functioning of the larger political system—most especially American democracy. Though no longer current, behavioralism played an important role in the field through the 1970s.

Under Merriam, political scientists at Chicago conducted groundbreaking empirical studies in voting behavior, political parties, minority politics, public opinion, and public administration. As in other social sciences, political science made use of interdisciplinary approaches, with subfields such as political psychology beginning to emerge.

Merriam was also a proponent of political scientists playing an active role as political advisers. Along with his work in the 1920s helping to found the SSRC and chairing the American Political Science Association, Merriam served as vice chair of the President's Committee on Social Trends in 1929. In the following decade, despite being a Republican, Merriam would become an important adviser in the Roosevelt administration during the Great Depression.

Anthropology

In the early twentieth century, anthropology—the study of human beings—developed in the United States under the strong influence of German American anthropologist Franz Boas, sometimes called the "father of modern anthropology." His work from the turn of the twentieth century until his death in 1942, at Columbia University and the American Anthropological Association among other institutions, helped establish academic anthropology in the form it is known today, divided into four major branches: cultural anthropology, linguistic anthropology, physical anthropology, and archaeology. Boas pioneered a progressive approach to the field that rejected labeling societies as "civilized" or "uncivilized," advocating instead studying individual cultures on their own terms and avoiding generalizations.

Some of the landmark anthropological works published in the 1920s were by students of Boas. Among these were *Language: An Introduction to the Study of Speech* (1921) by Edward Sapir, who conducted groundbreaking studies of Native American languages, and *Coming of Age in Samoa* (1928), a study of adolescent Samoan girls by Margaret Mead.

Psychology

While the theories of Austrian neurologist Sigmund Freud about the workings of the unconscious mind were taking hold in Europe, academic psychology in the United States was going the way of the other social sciences: toward an approach based in the hard sciences, focusing on measurable data. Rather than trying to investigate the depths of the unconscious, American psychological researchers turned to the overt cause-and-effect of external behavior, studying the effects of positive and negative reinforcement on behavior in both animals and humans.

"Behaviorism," as this approach was termed, became the dominant school of American psychology in the mid-twentieth century and was influenced greatly by John B. Watson's work at Johns Hopkins University during the 1910s and 1920s. Watson believed strongly that environmental influences rather than heredity were the main drivers of human behavior; he applied these ideas in his studies of child development, notably in his 1928 book *Psychological Care of Infant and Child*, as well as in the field of advertising, to which he turned during the 1920s. Along with Watson, other important behaviorists working in the 1920s included Edward C. Tolman, Clark L. Hull, and Edward Thorndike.

Rockefeller Foundation
Founded in 1913 by oil magnate John D. Rockefeller Sr., the Rockefeller Foundation was set up as a philanthropic organization aimed at expanding knowledge and improving the quality of life for people around the world, initially active in the fields of science, medicine, and public health. In 1918, John D. Rockefeller Jr. set up the Laura Spelman Rockefeller Memorial in honor of his mother to fund endeavors in the social sciences—most notably, the SSRC—before the Memorial was folded into the larger Rockefeller Foundation in 1928.

In the late nineteenth century, the elder Rockefeller had been instrumental in funding the establishment of the University of Chicago, which became a premier center of learning and innovation in the social sciences during the twentieth century, such that "Chicago school" became a term denoting distinctive approaches in a variety of disciplines, including sociology, economics, and political science. The Rockefeller Foundation continued to play an important role in supporting the University of Chicago—as well as other American institutions of higher education—in the 1920s and through the Great Depression, ensuring that U.S. scholarship in the social sciences remained vital throughout the twentieth century.

Impact
The explosive growth of the social sciences in the twentieth century was a by-product of industrialization and modernization, themselves a product of the human urge to create rational order out of the chaos of everyday life. As the population expanded along with advances in science and technology, the social systems for delivering people's basic needs—food, shelter, and security—grew larger and more complex. Efficiently organizing and managing such large social systems—whether business enterprises, cities, or educational systems—required a proportionately sophisticated understanding of human behavior within these systems, and the social sciences evolved to meet these needs.

Prominent social scientists such as Wesley Mitchell and Charles Merriam also advocated using the social sciences to inform better decision making in government, and they would be taken on board wholeheartedly in the next decade, as President Franklin D. Roosevelt worked to craft his large-scale New Deal programs to put people back to work during the Great Depression.

The American approach to the social sciences in the first half of the twentieth century was not without its critics, however. Some saw the entire development of industrial capitalism, with its drive toward quantification and standardization in every area of human life—including learning and scholarship—as being fundamentally at odds with certain basic aspects of human nature. Under the influence of Marx and Freud, alternative approaches such as the Frankfurt school of social theory would spring up in Europe and eventually migrate to the United States, where they influenced small but vocal strains of dissent that would not gain a full hearing until the social upheavals of the 1960s.

Tina Marie Forsythe

Further Reading
Bulmer, Martin. *The Chicago School of Sociology: Institutionalization, Diversity, and the Rise of Sociological Research.* Chicago: University of Chicago Press, 1986. Traces the history of sociology and its institutionalization at the University of Chicago.

Fosdick, Raymond Blaine. *The Story of the Rockefeller Foundation.* Reprint. New Brunswick, N.J.: Transaction, 1989. Discusses the foundation's inception, contributions to social sciences, and overall history.

Heaney, Michael T., and John Mark Hansen. "Building the Chicago School." *American Political Science Review* 100, no. 4 (November, 2006): 589–596. A brief overview of the formation of the Chicago school of political science in the 1920s.

Kuhn, Manford H. "Major Trends in Symbolic Interaction Theory in the Past Twenty-Five Years." *Sociological Quarterly* 5, no. 1 (January, 1964): 61–68. Briefly outlines the development of the symbolic interactionism theory in the field of sociology.

Sapir, Edward. *Language: An Introduction to the Study of Speech.* Reprint. Mineola, N.Y.: Dover, 2004. Explores the concept of language in relation to place and time, as well as the history of thought and language.

Wozniak, Robert H., ed. *The Roots of Behaviourism.* London: Routledge, 1993. An anthology of early essays by John B. Watson and others, expounding on the development of the behaviorist approach in psychology.

See also: Archaeology; *Coming of Age in Samoa;* Gross national product of the United States; Income and wages; Mead, Margaret; Migrations (within U.S.); Psychology, psychiatry, and psychoanalysis; Racial discrimination; Unemployment; Urbanization

■ Société Anonyme

Artists Katherine S. Dreier, Marcel Duchamp, and Man Ray formed the Société Anonyme, Inc. in 1920 to promote the modern art movements of Europe in the United States, where they had yet to take root. The organization sought to educate the American public about avant-garde art and provide a forum for modern artists to exchange ideas and gain recognition.

Although the United States had its unofficial introduction to modern art in the 1913 Armory Show, an international exhibition in New York City, the American art community and the wider public had not fully embraced contemporary trends by the 1920s. Société Anonyme was therefore founded to try to foster a more vibrant contemporary American art scene, striving to highlight the best of the avant-garde without regard to the status of the artist. Billing itself as an "experimental museum," the society staged many public exhibitions, lectures, and other events throughout the 1920s, advertised with taglines such as "Do you want to know what a Dada is?," referring to the Dada abstract art movement. In its first year, the society held ten exhibitions featuring modernists such as Marsden Hartley, Frank Stella, and Man Ray. Société Anonyme's largest international exhibition was held at the Brooklyn Museum from November 1926 to January 1927, and contained some three hundred works by over one hundred artists.

As the leading voice of the organization, New York artist Katherine Dreier believed that educating the public on the social significance of modern art would hasten its acceptance in the United States. In order to reach the widest audience, Dreier often brought the art to the people, toting paintings and sculptures with her to speak at high schools and women's centers. The Société Anonyme introduced artists to America not only through its educational activities but commercially as well. Dreier and French artist Marcel Duchamp frequently purchased works of American and European art to add to the society's collection, and they often served as intermediaries between artists and galleries, helping the artists to get commercial exposure and support.

Impact

The Société Anonyme paved the way for modern art's acceptance in the United States. The collection of paintings, drawings, prints, and sculpture the society amassed and eventually donated to Yale University is its greatest legacy, representing an unbiased glimpse of the international modern art scene of the early to mid-twentieth century. At its zenith, the Société Anonyme had a broad membership that included artists, critics, and patrons. After the 1920s, the society's activities waned, although Dreier still worked on building up the collection and staging exhibitions. Drier and Duchamp officially dissolved the Société Anonyme in 1950, thirty years after its founding.

Katie S. Greer

Further Reading

Altshuler, Bruce. *The Avant-Garde in Exhibition: New Art in the 20th Century.* Berkeley: University of California Press, 1998.

Corn, Wanda M. *The Great American Thing: Modern Art and National Identity, 1915–1935.* Berkeley: University of California Press, 1999.

Gross, Jennifer, and Ruth L. Bohan. *The Société Anonyme: Modernism for America.* New Haven, Conn.: Yale University Press, 2006.

See also: Art Deco; Art movements; Marin, John; Museum of Modern Art (MoMA); Stieglitz, Alfred

■ *Sound and the Fury, The*

Identification: Novel about the decline of a southern aristocratic family
Author: William Faulkner
Date: 1929

Considered by many critics to be William Faulkner's greatest novel, The Sound and the Fury *has been interpreted as a*

critique of the traditional southern planter class learning to adapt to changing times. The breakdown and eventual destruction of the novel's Compson family is said to represent the decline of the traditions of the American South during the 1920s, a theme that resonated with many southerners of the decade.

The Compson family is revealed through four distinct sections in the novel over a period of eighteen years. Through the use of flashbacks, the first three sections are told from the first-person point of view of each of the three Compson sons, while the fourth section is narrated in the third person and focuses mainly on the Compson's African American servant, Dilsey Gibson, who provides a history of the family's dysfunction. The novel employs the modernist narrative technique of stream of consciousness, revealing the characters' thoughts and psychological distress as they arise, countered only by the alternative worldview embodied in the fourth section.

Although the novel is told primarily from the Compson brothers' points of view, it is their sister, Caddy, who is central to the story. Caddy has been driven out of her family because of an out-of-wedlock pregnancy by an unknown man; critics have pointed out that her character symbolizes the South's futile efforts to retain the cultural, familial, and societal values of the past. Furthermore, Caddy's brothers are said to represent the conflicts many southerners felt during the 1920s in reconciling their past with the modern present, and that the first three sections of the novel serve as parables of the South's decline: Benjy, who is mentally disabled, waits in vain for his beloved sister's return; Quentin, a Harvard undergraduate, is distraught by Caddy's loss of virtue and commits suicide; and Jason, who supports his mother and Benjy after the death of their father, is materialistic, bigoted, and uncaring. The story is told with the rapid technological and social changes of the 1920s in the background, further illustrating the conflict between traditional southern ways and a modernizing nation and world.

Impact
The Sound and the Fury was Faulkner's fourth novel and the second set in his fictitious Yoknapatawpha County, Mississippi. It has been hailed for advancing the stream-of-consciousness technique and is commonly ranked among the greatest novels of the twentieth century. For his contributions to American fiction, Faulkner received the Nobel Prize for Literature in 1949, and he used portions of his winnings to establish a fiction writers' scholarship and a scholarship for African Americans studying education.

Kevin Eyster

Further Reading
Blotner, Joseph. *Faulkner: A Biography.* New York: Random House, 2005.
Fowler, Doreen, and Ann J. Abadie, eds. *Faulkner and the Southern Renaissance.* Jackson: University of Mississippi Press, 1982.
Singal, Daniel J. *William Faulkner: The Making of a Modernist.* Chapel Hill: University of North Carolina Press, 1997.

See also: Faulkner, William; Literature in the United States; *Sartoris;* Southern Agrarians

■ Southern Agrarians

The Southern Agrarians were a group of twelve American poets, essayists, novelists, and literary critics, many of whom were associated with Vanderbilt University in Nashville, Tennessee. Together, they published a collection of essays, I'll Take My Stand: The South and the Agrarian Tradition *(1930), which defended traditional southern values and customs in response to the nation's increasing urbanization and industrialization.*

During the 1920s, the United States experienced great technological, scientific, and medical advances. The country's population was becoming more urban as people moved from farms and rural communities to the promise of better jobs and wages in cities, and increased efficiency in agricultural technology was leading to overproduction, falling commodity prices, and diminishing demand for farm labor. While the majority of Americans seemed to embrace the decade's inventions and innovations, many southerners felt that their agrarian culture and deep-rooted traditions were being threatened by such rapid industrialization and mechanization.

The Fugitive Poets
From 1922 to 1925, a group of faculty and students at Vanderbilt University published a small, bimonthly literary magazine called *The Fugitive.* The Fugitive Poets, as they called themselves, felt the South,

especially southern writers, had been stereotyped, and they believed it important to show that a group of southern poets could produce respected, intellectual writing that was free of the romanticized language often associated with southern writing. The magazine's goal was not only to defend formal poetry techniques but also to defend the traditional southern values and southern agrarian lifestyle many felt were being lost to the dramatic changes occurring throughout the United States during the 1920s.

I'll Take My Stand

After *The Fugitive* ceased publication in 1925, the Fugitive Poets evolved into a more political, yet still literary, group of twelve who were referred to as the Southern Agrarians, the Twelve Southerners, the Vanderbilt Agrarians, or the Tennessee Agrarians. They were led by poets John Crowe Ransom, Allen Tate, and Donald Davidson, and the energies of Ransom, Tate, and Davidson in particular went into defending the customs and traditions of their native South against what they perceived to be the economic and cultural aggressions of the North against their region. The Agrarians looked to an idealized rural and simple American past to provide a template for a gentler, if not always just and equal, future. They thus reserved some of their sharpest criticism for advocates of a New South who frequently urged the willing submission of the region to the advances of manufacturing and urbanization. In addition, the ridicule directed toward the South as a result of the 1925 *Scopes* trial, in which a Tennessee schoolteacher was prosecuted for teaching Darwin's theory of evolution, further stirred the Southern Agrarians into action. Northern newspaper accounts of the trial, especially those written by H. L. Mencken for the *Baltimore Sun*, became the catalyst for the Agrarians to become more focused and earnest in their defense of southern agrarian tradition.

Beginning in 1929, Ransom, Tate, and Davidson put out a call for essays to be included in the now-landmark manifesto *I'll Take My Stand*. Twelve intellectuals, including renowned poet Robert Penn Warren, wrote on a variety of issues connected by a pro-South, pro-rural posture that rejected industrialism and secularism as dehumanizing. In *I'll Take My Stand*, the Agrarians sought to discredit the belief that the South was culturally and intellectually backward and to assert that it was in fact the southern traditions, beliefs, and agrarian lifestyle that were responsible for the region's cultural excellence. The tone of the essays advocated an agrarian focus for the United States as a whole and criticized the rapid industrial and urban growth that had occurred during the decade.

Allen Tate, one of the leaders of the Southern Agrarians. (© Corbis)

Impact

When *I'll Take My Stand* was first published, the Southern Agrarians received criticism for advocating a culture many saw as enveloped in racism and segregation. Others criticized the group for being stubborn and blind to the nation's welcomed and seemingly inevitable progress and modernization. Within the next few decades, most of the Southern Agrarians would distance themselves from agrarianism and would view its principles as worthy but ultimately unattainable. Several Southern Agrarians are believed to have initiated the New Criticism movement, which advocated an organic and holistic study of poetry apart from the poem's or the poet's cultural and historical context. John Crowe Ransom would go on to found the *Kenyon Review* in 1937, and Robert Penn Warren would win Pulitzer Prizes for fiction in 1947 and for poetry in 1958 and 1979.

Charles H. Ford

Further Reading

Beck, Charlotte H. *The Fugitive Legacy: A Critical History*. Baton Rouge: Louisiana State University Press, 2001. Analyzes the works of acclaimed writers who were protégés of the Nashville Fugitives. Explores the influence of the Fugitive Poets on future southern literature.

Conkin, Paul Keith. *The Southern Agrarians*. Knoxville, Tenn.: Vanderbilt University Press, 2001. A biography of the twelve Southern Agrarians. Examines the group's political and economic beliefs and the impact their essays had on southern literature. Explores the history behind the writing of *I'll Take My Stand*.

Havard, William C., and Walter Sullivan, eds. *A Band of Prophets: The Vanderbilt Agrarians After Fifty Years*. Baton Rouge: Louisiana State University Press, 1982. A collection of six essays written to commemorate the fiftieth anniversary of *I'll Take My Stand*.

Murphy, Paul V. *The Rebuke of History: The Southern Agrarians and American Conservative Thought*. Chapel Hill: University of North Carolina Press, 2001. Traces the Agrarian tradition and beliefs from the 1920s to modern times.

Twelve Southerners. *I'll Take My Stand: The South and the Agrarian Tradition*. New York: Harper, 1930. Reprint. Baton Rouge: Louisiana State University Press, 2006. Collects the essays written by the Southern Agrarians.

See also: Agricultural Marketing Act of 1929; Agriculture in the United States; *Fugitive, The;* Fugitive Poets; Historiography; *I'll Take My Stand;* Mencken, H. L.; New Criticism; *Scopes* trial (1925).

Soviet Union and North America

Early in the 1920s, the United States harshly condemned Russian revolutionary Vladimir Lenin's new communist government, while Canada and Mexico both temporarily normalized relations with Moscow. Lingering suspicion defined contacts between the Soviet Union and North America throughout the decade, however, creating an enduring legacy of mistrust that foreshadowed the Cold War.

After the Bolshevik Party's overthrow of the provisional Russian government in the October Revolution of 1917, Vladimir Lenin created the world's first communist government. The Russian Civil War ensued as the communist Red Army battled for power against the White Army, a coalition of anticommunists, monarchists, and ardent nationalists. Recognizing Lenin's determination to withdraw Russia from World War I, the Western Allies intervened in the conflict, sending troops to Siberia and northern Russia in hopes of reopening an eastern front with Germany. After suffering hundreds of casualties against the Red Army and achieving few of their stated aims, however, the Allies, including the United States and Canada, withdrew all troops in early 1920. Following Bolshevik victory in the civil war, the Soviet Union was officially founded in 1922.

U.S. Nonrecognition

Throughout the 1920s, the United States condemned the Soviet government and refused to recognize it as legitimate. Four successive presidential administrations—those of Woodrow Wilson, Warren G. Harding, Calvin Coolidge, and Herbert Hoover—maintained a policy of nonrecognition toward the Soviet state. Moreover, the American government refused to extend formal trade ties to Moscow, forbidding domestic companies from receiving payments in gold from the communist state. The Soviet Union, for its part, protested this policy as hostile isolation by a capitalist aggressor.

The Soviet Union, however, remained open to better relations with the United States to ameliorate difficult economic problems at home. Plagued by a deadly famine in 1921 and 1922, Moscow refused to make a direct appeal but allowed an unofficial committee to publicly request international aid. In response, the United States appropriated $20 million from Congress for the American Relief Administration, which delivered some five hundred thousand tons of food and medical supplies to the Soviet Union by 1922, aiding approximately ten million people in one way or another.

Though the United States refused to recognize the Soviet Union in the 1920s, it maintained informal economic ties with the Russian state. A few private American businesses pursued active business contacts with the new communist government; in 1924, for example, Henry Ford negotiated a deal for an annual delivery of automobiles to the Soviet Union, while General Electric supplied the Soviet government with electrical equipment for a dam-building project in 1928. Despite Moscow and Washington's diplomatic estrangement, American companies supplied more exports to the Soviet Union than any other nation, over $65 million worth in 1925.

Brief Recognition: Canada and Mexico
Canada's and Mexico's relationships with the Soviet Union remained tense throughout the 1920s. Canada, suspicious of Soviet influence in a massive 1919 labor strike in Winnipeg, remained, like the United States, fearful of the spread of communist ideology. After the emergence of positive trade relations in the early 1920s, though, Canada formally recognized the Soviet Union on March 24, 1924, following the lead of the United Kingdom. However, in the following three years, tensions heightened as Canada accused the Russian diplomatic delegation of importing Bolshevik propaganda, inciting unrest, and forging Canadian currency. After a diplomatic row erupted over suspected Russian espionage in London, Canada and England both severed relations with Moscow in 1927.

Mexico's relationship with the Soviet Union in the 1920s, while briefly amicable, ended similarly, with a mutual renunciation of relations. After the civil war, the Soviet Union eagerly sought diplomatic friends in the Western Hemisphere, in particular reaching out to Mexico in 1919 and 1922 with favorable trade overtures. Although neither attempt met with success at the time, subsequent negotiations led to Mexico formally recognizing the Soviet Union on August 4, 1924. Initially, the embassies of both states fostered warm relations and extensive contacts between Soviet and Mexican citizens. In the last years of the decade, however, the Mexican government began to accuse the Soviet Union of trying to foment political unrest through its embassy, while Moscow condemned the Mexican government as a rightist regime. Amid suspicion and animosity, both states severed diplomatic relations in 1930.

Impact
Diplomatic relations between North America and the Soviet Union in the 1920s were defined by a grave mistrust that would dramatically shape the political landscape of the coming decades. After severing diplomatic relations with the Soviet Union, neither Canada nor Mexico would restore official contacts until the midst of World War II in 1942. The United States did not recognize the Moscow regime until 1933. The Nazi threat drove the Soviets and the West into an alliance during World War II, but afterward, the ideological animosity that had originated in the 1920s quickly resurfaced as the Cold War era dawned, with all three North American states fearing Soviet espionage and the spread of communist propaganda. Under the stewardship of Joseph Stalin, the Soviet Union remained wary of any capitalist power, viewing long-term cooperation as ultimately impossible.

Brandon K. Gauthier

Further Reading
Balawyder, Aloysius. *Canadian-Soviet Relations Between the World Wars.* Toronto: University of Toronto Press, 1972. A detailed examination of tense economic relations between the two states, focusing on Canadian diplomacy independent of Britain.
Boyle, Peter G. *American-Soviet Relations: From the Russian Revolution to the Fall of Communism.* New York: Routledge, 1993. A broad yet succinct overview of this diplomatic relationship, from the Russian Revolution to the end of the Cold War.
Killen, Linda R. *The Soviet Union and the United States: A New Look at the Cold War.* Boston: Twayne, 1989. Reexamines the meaning of the American-Soviet relationship throughout the twentieth century.
Leffler, Melvyn P. *For the Soul of Mankind: The United States, the Soviet Union, and the Cold War.* New York: Hill and Wang, 2007. An authoritative history of the Cold War by an eminent historian.
Richardson, William. *Mexico Through Russian Eyes, 1806–1940.* Pittsburgh: University of Pittsburgh Press, 1988. Focuses on the Mexican-Soviet relationship in Chapters 3 and 4.
Spenser, Daniela. *The Impossible Triangle: Mexico, Soviet Russia, and the United States in the 1920s.* Durham, N.C.: Duke University Press, 1999. Examines the tangled relationship among these countries in the years after the Mexican and Russian Revolutions.

See also: Canada and Great Britain; Communism; Foreign policy, U.S.; Mexico; Palmer raids; Red Scare, The; Russian Famine Relief Act of 1921

■ Speakeasies

The proliferation of illicit nightclubs sparked bootlegging, liquor shipment hijacking, and political corruption as criminal organizations sought to provide the public with an un-

interrupted supply of alcohol. Speakeasies, which have been referred to as the first nightclubs, also provided the momentum behind the growth of organized crime enterprises that spanned the nation.

After ratification of the Eighteenth Amendment in January 1920, saloons, taverns, bars, and many restaurants were no longer able to legally sell beer, wine, and hard liquor. Speakeasies began to open across the country, offering citizens the opportunity to purchase and consume illicit alcoholic beverages.

The origin of the term "speakeasy" is under debate, as some maintain the word was first used in Pennsylvania in 1888, when the state fee for operating a saloon was dramatically increased. Others claim the word originated during Prohibition with a saloon keepers who warned customers to "speak easy," or quietly, to avoid detection by police.

Speakeasies operated throughout the United States and were managed by criminal organizations engaged in bootlegging to supply the public with alcohol. The growth of speakeasies was staggering: At least five thousand existed by 1922, and an estimated thirty thousand were in operation by the end of 1927. In New York City alone, it is estimated that five thousand speakeasies were operating by 1922.

Some speakeasies would become famous with businesses such as the Stork Club and Twenty-One reaping such enormous profits that they were able to withstand repeated closures by federal agents as customer demand made bootlegging a financially viable business.

Speakeasies were also the source of power and influence of such legendary mob bosses as Dutch Schultz, Frank Costello, Al Capone, Bugs Malone, and Dion O'Banion. Violence associated with bootlegging, protection of distilleries, and money laundering was commonplace, as were health-related incidents caused by tainted or questionable distilling practices.

Ultimately, the violence surrounding the operation of speakeasies would help the cause of anti-Prohibitionists. On February 14, 1929, in what would become known as the Saint Valentine's Day Massacre, seven gangsters were gunned down in Chicago as they waited for a shipment of hijacked whiskey.

Impact

The speakeasies of the 1920s served an important function in the cultural development of the United States as avenues for civil disobedience and financial

Sign showing the way to a speakeasy. (Hulton Archive/Getty Images)

enterprise, as well as for the growth of federal law enforcement, political corruption, and organized crime. The growth of the automobile industry was aided by bootlegging, as was the development of feminism as seen in the flapper movement that provided women increased social freedom, much of which was exercised in speakeasies. Prohibition-era speakeasies were also in the forefront of a more consumer-oriented American culture.

Wendy L. Hicks

Further Reading

Behr, Edward. *Prohibition: Thirteen Years That Changed America.* New York: Arcade Publishers, 2011.

Hirschfeld, Al, and Gordon Kahn. *The Speakeasies of 1932.* Milwaukee, Wis.: Glenn Young Books, 2006.

Walker, Stanley. *The Night Club Era.* Baltimore: John Hopkins University Press, 1999.

See also: Bathtub gin; Capone, Al; Crimes and scandals; Gambling; Nightclubs; Organized crime; Prohibition; Saint Valentine's Day Massacre; Schultz, Dutch

■ Spiritualism

The 1920s represented the last decade in which Spiritualism experienced widespread popularity and acceptance. By the end of the decade, the movement had become fragmented after most mediums had been discredited and ridiculed by scientists and stage magicians. Communicating with the dead nonetheless spread into the popular culture of the 1920s and was featured in popular literature, movies, plays, and games such as the Ouija board.

Spiritualism began near Hydesville, New York, in 1848. The Fox sisters, thirteen-year-old Maggie and eleven-year-old Kate, claimed to have heard mysterious knocking throughout their house, which they later identified as the spirit of a peddler who had been killed in the house and buried in the basement years prior. The Fox family told others of their experiences and began to travel, demonstrating the sisters' ability to communicate with the peddler's spirit. The Fox sisters became a national phenomenon, and soon others, primarily women who called themselves "mediums," claimed to be able to communicate with nonliving spirits and to act as conduits between the living and the dead.

By the 1850s, Spiritualism as a religion had increased in popularity and spread across North America and to Europe, especially to England, and mediums now entered trancelike states and acted as voices for the spirits or as scribes to write down messages from the spirits. These performances usually took place in public venues, but some were private séances, and all were for a fee. Beginning in the 1870s, mediums began to assist in the physical materialization of spirits by entering "spirit cabinets," which were hidden from spectators' view, and then helping the spirits to emerge.

In addition to spirit communication, Spiritualism was connected to social reform movements, including women's suffrage and the abolition of slavery. Initially, Spiritualists resisted formal organization, but by the end of the nineteenth century, they began to form Spiritualist communities. Many of the communities founded during this period endured into the twenty-first century.

Accusations of Fraud

Emerging out of the nineteenth century, a time when scientific authority competed with religious truth claims, Spiritualism asserted that its movement and mediums scientifically proved the existence of the afterlife. Scientists routinely took up these challenges and often found that mediums were manufacturing the noises, movements, or visual manifestations of the spirits. While spiritual investigations emerged almost as soon as mediums made claims of spirit communication, the 1920s hosted some of the most sophisticated investigations. In 1924, the magazine *Scientific American* offered a contest with a $5,000 prize for a spirit manifestation produced under scientifically controlled conditions and accompanied by an authenticated photograph. (Much like the fraudulent mediums, spirit images were regularly denounced as being produced through mechanical techniques such as multiple exposures.) Several mediums entered the contests, but no one successfully produced spirit materialization under the scrutiny of the scientists.

Stage magicians were also frequently employed to substantiate a medium's assertions because they could demonstrate the same effects without claiming supernatural ability. Harry Houdini, best known for his death-defying escapes, began exposing Spiritualist mediums during the 1920s and served as a judge in the 1924 *Scientific American* contest.

Popularity and Cultural Influence

Despite the claims of fraud, thousands of people firmly believed in the ability to communicate with the dead. After World War I, the movement experienced a brief surge in popularity as people attempted to contact loved ones lost in the war. Spiritualism's popularity was greater in Great Britain than in North America, and famous Spiritualists from England traveled to the United States and Canada to promote the religion. One such Spiritualist was the author of *Sherlock Holmes*, Sir Arthur Conan Doyle, who had converted to Spiritualism after the deaths of several close family members. He published a two-volume history of Spiritualism in 1926, which is still considered one of the most authoritative histories by a self-professed Spiritualist.

A central tenet of Spiritualism is the belief that anyone had the ability to communicate with the dead, and the Ouija board, which gained popularity during the early 1920s, claimed to allow the general public to do just that. The Ouija board became a cultural phenomenon, appearing in movies, plays, and song lyrics, and supernatural themes that emerged out of Spiritualism were common in novels, movies, and other entertainment.

Impact

From its inception, Spiritualism often brought closure and solace to thousands who had lost loved ones, and it was therefore especially popular immediately after World War I. The movement spurred the debate among religious leaders, scientists, and entertainers on the possibility of life after death. It also provided a gateway for the supernatural to reenter American popular culture. Primarily due to Houdini's debunking of the movement, the 1920s was the last decade during which Spiritualism flourished as a religion in the United States. The fascination with the spirit world, however, continues well into modern times.

John L. Crow

Further Reading

Brandon, Ruth. *The Spiritualists: The Passion for the Occult in the Nineteenth and Twentieth Centuries.* New York: A. A. Knopf, 1983. A history of the Spiritualist movement.

Braude, Ann. *Radical Spirits: Spiritualism and Women's Rights in Nineteenth Century America.* 2d ed. Bloomington: Indiana University Press, 2001. Details the connection between Spiritualism and women's rights movements.

Moore, R. Laurence. *In Search of White Crows: Spiritualism, Parapsychology, and American Culture.* New York: Oxford University Press, 1977. Examines the interaction with investigations of the Spiritualist movement by the scientific community of the time.

Weisberg, Barbara. *Talking to the Dead: Kate and Maggie Fox and the Rise of Spiritualism.* New York: HarperCollins, 2005. A biography of the Fox sisters and examination of the phenomenon they created.

Wicker, Christine. *Lily Dale: The True Story of the Town That Talks to the Dead.* New York: HarperCollins, 2003. A history of the largest Spiritualist community in America.

See also: Houdini, Harry; Ouija boards; Religion in the United States

■ Sports

The decade of the 1920s is widely considered to be the golden age of sports in the United States, when the nation's attention was drawn to the legendary performances and larger-than-life personalities of the athletes that dominated news coverage alongside the movie stars of the day. While amateurism was still the norm in sports activities, professional sports also began to gain popular attention during the 1920s, thanks to talented athletes and the growth of sports media.

The United States emerged from the shadows of World War I into an era of general prosperity and optimism. Sports and play became an obsession for many, and sportswriters were eager to celebrate individual and team accomplishments and to provide the public with images of success. In time, newspapers devoted an average of 15 percent of their space to the exploits of America's new breed of heroes, while sports newsreels contributed to the motion picture industry. Colorful sports personalities and a new emphasis on sports marketing and promotion enamored the public with record-setting performances, the expansion of spectator stadiums, and a serious challenge to the long-held ideal of the amateur athlete.

Virtually all famous athletes in the early 1920s were introduced to their sport as a leisure activity in informal play or school sports. Outside of professional baseball and boxing, sports administration organizations still clung to the notion that athletes should play for the love of the game and not seek to profit from their performance. Professional athletes were often characterized unfavorably for their lifestyle and propensity for greed; the infamous Black Sox baseball scandal, involving the manipulation of the 1919 World Series, was proof enough for many that sports should remain an amateur endeavor.

Amateur Sports

The school and college sports that were born of student interest only a generation earlier became increasingly financially important to educational institutions in the 1920s. In 1922, the National Amateur Athletic Federation was formed in an effort to uphold the amateur ideal against creeping professionalism in sports and the political dominance of the Amateur Athletic Union. The Amateur Athletic Union controlled many sports competitions and heavily influenced Olympic Team

Notre Dame's "The Four Horsemen" are shown on the field in South Bend, Indiana, in 1924. (AP Photo)

selections, especially in track-and-field events. Despite the presence of the American Olympic Association, which was essentially a loose confederation of sports groups, increasing tension emerged between the National Collegiate Athletic Association and the Amateur Athletic Union. The concern over professionalization was still present at the decade's close; a Carnegie Report on athletics at U.S. colleges released in 1929 responded to growing concerns regarding the decline of amateurism in college sports.

While the world of competitive sports was traditionally male, women made their initial mark in the Olympic Games of 1920, and many colleges fielded women's teams in basketball and individual and dual sports. The Amateur Athletic Union even sponsored the first national women's basketball championship in 1926. Interestingly, many female physical educators opposed organized competitions for women, citing their physical frailty and need for protection against the impure excesses of the male athletic model. This reluctance to support organized women's athletics was particularly evident at the secondary school level and translated into changes in national athletics as organizations like the Amateur Athletic Union adopted secondary schools' policies. By 1928, most states had organizations monitoring high school sports for boys, but fewer than ten states ran girls' basketball tournaments. Opportunities for girls' athletic participation declined somewhat during the decade and largely followed an intramural or "play day" approach. Gymnastics, a discipline that had long been a staple of schools' physical education programs for boys, quickly gave way to the growing popularity of other competitive boys' sports and became more favored for girls and women because of its health benefits. Meanwhile, track-and-field sports grew in popularity among male athletes.

College football was unquestionably the star attraction for college students and their communities, though college basketball also developed a major following, particular in the Midwest. The increasing popularity of college football in the 1920s led to the construction of massive stadiums and helped solidify intercollegiate athletics as a legitimate part of college life. National radio broadcasts for college football began in the early 1920s, bringing the sport to even larger numbers of Americans. Though the Northeast was considered the hotbed of the game, two renowned midwestern institutions, the universities of Notre Dame and Illinois, exerted their own unique influence on the game. Key Notre Dame football players known as "the Four Horsemen" lost only once during their career, which spanned from 1922 to 1924. The Illinois Fighting Illini football team's player Red Grange was arguably the best college football player of the decade, personally accounting for several instances of over two hundred yards per outing during his career of twenty games. Performances such as these contributed to the sport's growing popularity: Cumulative reported attendance at college football games topped ten million by 1930.

The Olympic Games
Interrupted by World War I, the Olympic Games were resumed in 1920 in Antwerp, Belgium. This event marked another milestone in American sports history as U.S. athletes would dominate the three Summer Games of the decade. The 1920 Summer Games were highlighted by three gold medal performances by Ethelda Bleibtrey, who won each of the women's swimming events. The 1924 Summer Games in Paris, France, were noted for the performance of swimmer Johnny Weissmuller, who won three gold medals and one bronze medal, while earlier that year, American speed skater Charles Jewtraw won the first gold medal ever given for speed skating in the initial Winter Games in Chamonix, France. U.S. teams rose to second place in the medal count at St. Moritz, Switzerland, in 1928, while that summer in Amsterdam, Weissmuller captured two more gold medals for swimming, helping launch his movie career. American athletes won more gold medals in the 1924 Summer Games than did their counterparts from the next four countries combined. However, with the offer of Olympic participation to Germany in 1928, German athletes provided a challenge to American dominance in strength sports such as weight lifting and wrestling.

Professional Sports
Baseball was firmly entrenched as the nation's pastime at the start of the 1920s. The sport's popularity only grew in response to the performance of star baseball players such as Babe Ruth and news coverage by sportswriters such as Grantland Rice. Seeing Americans' passion developing for sports, event promoters such as Charles Pyle capitalized on representing famous athletes and organizing everything from cross-country footraces and tennis tours to professional football leagues.

The public developed such a fascination with athletes that adoring crowds could not consume enough information about them. This was especially true of athletes whose skill included transformational achievements. Rice's unique style of describing exemplary athletic performance created national heroes of Ruth, tennis player William "Big Bill" Tilden, and boxer Jack Dempsey. Ruth became legendary for his powerful displays of strength and performance that captivated millions, who mostly learned of his exploits from the newspapers. In 1920, just when baseball needed a diversion from the recent Black Sox scandal, Ruth hit a staggering 54 home runs and 127 runs batted in. Such performances by Ruth and other star players set long-lasting records, changed the nature of the sport itself, and increased attendance at games. Celebrities in their own athletic disciplines, Tilden's powerful serves were more noted than his (or anyone's) ground strokes and overall court play, and a knockout punch by Dempsey upstaged the tactical boxing style employed by many skilled boxers of that day. Racecar driver Pete DePaolo became the first to exceed the 100-mile-per-hour average during the 1925 Indianapolis 500 race. Boxing and horse racing joined baseball as the sports most widely followed and easily accessible to the general public, and they were also the ones most likely to attract the attention of occasional and professional gamblers alike.

Professional football was uninspiring compared to college football, drawing a total of only seventy-five thousand spectators to all games on a typical Sunday, until Red Grange, arguably one of the top football players of all time, signed with George Halas's Chicago team, the Bears, in 1925. Bringing immediate fan interest to the new league, his reported salary of $100,000 for a nineteen-game schedule was unheard of at a time when most players only earned $100 per game.

Golf and tennis, two sports most often associated with elite clubs from the Northeast, were popularized as a venue for professional sports competition and entertainment during the 1920s. Mary Browne and Vincent "Vinnie" Richards were America's first professional tennis stars, and golf was popularized by the play of Bobby Jones, Walter Hagen, and Gene Sarazen.

African Americans and Sports

Though African American athletes participated in both amateur and professional sports during the decade, they often did so separately from their white counterparts. As most states had segregated educational systems and athletic competition at this time, opportunities for interscholastic amateur sports seldom allowed for interracial competition.

Professional sports offered few participation opportunities for African American athletes in the 1920s. Unlike the comparatively successful Negro League Baseball, where Satchel Paige debuted as a nineteen-year-old in 1926, semiprofessional or barnstorming football teams provided the only realistic avenues for continued African American competition. Even the previously integrated National Football League barred African American athletes beginning in the early 1930s. Likewise, professional basketball was segregated, with many all-black teams forming in the major cities. One such team, coach Abe Saperstein's the Big Savoy Five from New York soon became known as the Harlem Globetrotters and traveled the country, demonstrating their signature brand of sports and entertainment.

Impact

The United States was a robust and prosperous nation during the 1920s, and many Americans were eager to spend their newfound leisure time in sports venues and on the fields and courts of play. The individual athlete took precedence in many ways over team accomplishments as a fascination developed with those who could demonstrate record-breaking skill and power while winning. Many challenges to the long-held ideal of amateur sports emerged from the tension between the business and entertainment aspects of athletics. Nevertheless, recreational sports became popular and widespread at all levels, leading to the formalization of standardized rules and playing surfaces as well as the establishment of more governing bodies for various sports. Firmly entrenched in rural and urban society, the world of sports would become a refuge for many Americans as the dark days of the Great Depression took over American life in late 1929.

P. Graham Hatcher

Further Reading

Ashe, Arthur. *A Hard Road to Glory: A History of the African American Athlete, 1919–1945*. New York: Warner Books, 1988. Chronicles the achievements and challenges of African American athletes between the World Wars I and II in largely segregated competition.

Bohn, Michael K. *Heroes and Ballyhoo: How the Golden Age of the 1920s Transformed American Sports*. Washington, D.C.: Potomac Books, 2009. Chronicles ten sports heroes and their impact on the decade: Dempsey, Ruth, Tilden, Hagen, Weissmuller, Rockne, Grange, Ederle, Wills, and Jones.

Buckley, James, and John Walters. *Sports in America, 1920–1939*. 2d ed. New York: Chelsea House, 2010. Presents highlights in sports year by year for the 1920s and 1930s, written for a younger audience.

Inabinett, Mark. *Grantland Rice and His Heroes: The Sportswriter as Mythmaker in the 1920s*. Knoxville: University of Tennessee Press, 1994. Discusses the role of sportswriters in providing the nonspectator public with their only image of the great athletes of the day and fueling the American fascination with outstanding individuals' athletic performances.

Peterson, Robert. *Cages to Jump Shots: Pro Basketball's Early Years*. New York: Oxford University Press, 1990. Provides an overview of professional basketball's competition with college games for fan interest, early teams and players, and innovations in styles of play.

See also: Auto racing; Baseball; Boxing; Football; Golf; Hockey; Horse racing; Olympic Games of 1920 (Summer); Olympic Games of 1924 (Summer); Olympic Games of 1924 (Winter); Olympic Games of 1928 (Summer); Olympic Games of 1928 (Winter); Soccer; Tennis

■ Spring and All

Identification: Book of blended prose and poetry
Author: William Carlos Williams
Date: 1923

As a modernist writer, William Carlos Williams dissolved traditional genre boundaries, juxtaposing prose and poetry in a way that intensified and extended the possibilities of both forms.

Williams had published three volumes of poetry between 1909 and 1917, but his friendship with writer Ezra Pound, his evolving sense of how the English language could be utilized in a poem, and his instinctive sense of the possibilities inherent in new poetic structures led to the creation of his book *Spring and All*, a hybrid of prose and poetry that broke new ground for American literature in 1923.

Spring and All consists of twenty-seven poems with prose introductions and free verse sections. The individual poems are listed with numbers; subsequent editions feature titles mostly taken from each poem's first line. The volume is dedicated to Williams's friend, artist Charles Demuth, whose painting *I Saw the Figure Five in Gold* (1928) was inspired by Williams's poem "The Great Figure" (1921). Conversely, the *Spring and All* poem "The Pot of Flowers" is based on one of Demuth's watercolors given to Williams and his wife Flossie as a present; the poem was written in appreciation of their shared vision of the natural world in renewal, one of the central subjects of *Spring and All*. Among other prominent poems, Williams's most famous verse sections from the book include "The Red Wheelbarrow," "By the Road to the Contagious Hospital," and "To Elsie."

Williams saw the dismantling of conventional barriers between literary genres as a means of advancing modern compositional expression. Thus, the poems and prose sections in *Spring and All* are linked, although anthologies and collected volumes of the 1920s and 1930s sometimes feature them independently of one another. Williams's literary techniques in the book include the mixing of poetry and lowercase prose with little typographical intervention.

Impact

As was the case with his earlier works, Williams relied on collaboration with friends outside the mainstream publishing world to get his work into print. *Spring and All* was first published by Robert McAlmon in Dijon, France, with a run of three hundred copies. These copies were sent to the United States, but they were mostly confiscated by customs authorities as potentially dangerous foreign literature. The book essentially vanished until it was reprinted some years after Williams's death. This publication of *Spring and All* accomplished Williams's aim of resisting the influence of traditionally oriented English conceptions of poetry with his own imaginative creation of a genuine American poetic voice. Critics regard certain sections of the book as sterling examples of 1920s modernist poetry.

Leon Lewis

Further Reading

Breslin, James, E. *William Carlos Williams: An American Artist*. New York, Oxford University Press, 1970.

Williams, William Carlos. *Spring and All*. New York: New Directions, 2011.

See also: Demuth, Charles; Eliot, T. S.; Literature in the United States; Poetry; Pound, Ezra; Williams, William Carlos

■ Steamboat Willie

Identification: An animated cartoon with sound
Director: Walt Disney
Date: 1928

Steamboat Willie pushed entrepreneur Walt Disney to the forefront of famous film directors, introduced the animated character known as Mickey Mouse to the public, and used synchronized sound to accompany action for the first time in animation history. It became an instant hit with the American public.

Walt Disney produced dozens of silent 1920s cartoons, including a series known as the Alice Comedies. Rights to his popular animated character Oswald the Rabbit were lost in a dispute with a former partner. Disney and animator Ub Iwerks produced two 1928 cartoons featuring a mouse sketched by Iwerks. These cartoons, *Plane Crazy* and *The Gallopin' Gaucho*, were not shown to the public, however, because no willing distributor could be found.

Disney and Iwerks had been fascinated with *The Jazz Singer*, the first feature-length Hollywood production of a musical motion picture with spoken dialogue, released in 1927. Disney decided to use the new technique for his next cartoon, *Steamboat Willie*. Because it was difficult to perfectly synchronize pictures with sound, dialogue was kept to a minimum. Disney used his own voice for the little dialogue uttered during the cartoon's first version. Most of the sound featured in the cartoon was the timely blending of music with cartoon action.

Steamboat Willie shows Mickey Mouse merrily piloting a steamboat until Captain Pete arrives and makes Mickey leave the bridge. While picking up animals at Podunk Landing, Mickey feeds a cow hay so it will fit into the harness to hoist aboard. Mickey's girlfriend, Minnie, arrives as they depart, and Mickey hoists her onto the steamboat. When she lands, her sheet music and stringed instrument are eaten by a goat. Minnie twists its tail and the folk song "Turkey in the Straw" plays out of its mouth as Mickey dances and plays percussion with spoons, pails, and a washtub. Other animals are used as instruments, including a cat, a duck, piglets, and a cow. The fun concludes when Captain Pete arrives and forces Mickey to peel potatoes. When a parrot mocks him, Mickey knocks it into the water using a potato. The cartoon closes with Mickey enjoying a good laugh.

The cartoon premiered November 18, 1928, at New York City's Colony Theater. Disney reportedly received $1,000 for the two-week booking of *Steamboat Willie*, which aired before the movie *Gang War*, an independent film starring actor Jack Pickford. The cartoon became so popular that Disney released it a second time at the Roxy Theater in New York City.

Impact
Steamboat Willie, widely considered the birth of the Mickey Mouse character, popularized sound animation cartoons and revitalized the flagging careers of Disney and Iwerks. Copyright disputes over the cartoon continue into the twenty-first century, as some believe it to be public domain material.

Randy Hines

Further Reading
Bain, David, and Bruce S. Harris. *Mickey Mouse: Fifty Happy Years.* New York: Harmony Books, 1977.
Gabler, Neal. *Walt Disney: The Triumph of the American Imagination.* New York: Vintage Books, 2007.

See also: Disney, Walt; Film; Movie palaces; Talking motion pictures

■ St. Francis Dam disaster

The Event: The fatal collapse of a newly constructed dam
Date: March 12–13, 1928
Place: Los Angeles County, California

The failure of the St. Francis Dam destroyed the career of civil engineer William Mulholland and led to changes in civil engineering practice.

In the 1920s, the population of southern California was growing rapidly. The warm, sunny climate attracted the burgeoning movie industry, along with other businesses. Los Angeles County was an ideal place to settle, except for its lack of a reliable source of fresh water. City engineer William Mulholland had provided a partial solution by building an aqueduct from the nearby Owens Valley, as well as a number of small dams to create reservoirs on local creeks, but more water was needed to ensure a good supply for the city's growth.

Mulholland decided one solution would be to construct a reservoir in San Francisquito Canyon. The site provided a deep and narrow location that would allow for a dam about 180 feet tall. The proposed reservoir would hold approximately 30,000 acre-feet of water. Construction began in 1924 on the concrete arch-gravity dam that engineers of the time considered the safest dam design. As work progressed, Mulholland modified the dam plans several times, raising the dam to a final height of 205 feet and increasing its capacity to 38,000 acre-feet. When completed, the dam was 175 feet thick at its base and 700 feet long.

Even before the reservoir was full, reports circulated about problems with the dam. A number of cracks appeared, but Mulholland interpreted them as being a normal result of the concrete settling. Mulholland even inspected the dam the day before the disaster, responding to reports of water leaking through the dam, but he believed the seepage he observed was not unusual for a large dam.

Shortly before midnight on March 12, 1928, the dam washed out. Unbeknownst to Mulholland, the dam's eastern abutment was built not on solid rock but rather on the site of an old landslide. This ground was unstable, and the canyon wall failed. When the abutment collapsed, so did the dam. Approximately 12 billion gallons of water rushed down the canyon, destroying everything in its path. Estimates of the resulting death toll range from 450 to 600 victims.

Impact
William Mulholland had envisioned the St. Francis Dam as the crowning achievement of his life's work,

bringing water to the city of Los Angeles. Instead, he found himself suspected of shoddy engineering practices. Although Mulholland was cleared of deliberate malpractice, he was forced into retirement and obscurity. In addition to the damage done to Mulholland's career, the failure of the St. Francis Dam led to increasing scrutiny of engineering credentials and an emphasis on professionalism. The days when one engineer could both design and oversee the construction of a major dam were over.

Nancy Farm Männikkö

Further Reading

Davis, Margaret L., and Kevin Starr. *Rivers in the Desert: William Mulholland and the Inventing of Los Angeles.* 2d ed. New York: HarperCollins, 2001.

Nichols, John. *The St. Francis Dam Disaster.* Chicago: Arcadia, 2002.

See also: Castle Gate, Utah, mining disaster (1924); Los Angeles Aqueduct dynamiting; Natural disasters; Natural resources, exploitation of; West Virginia mining disaster (1924)

■ Stein, Gertrude

Identification: American writer and art collector
Born: February 3, 1874, Allegheny, Pennsylvania
Died: July 27, 1946, Neuilly-sur-Seine, France

Gertrude Stein was at the forefront of the American expatriate artistic movement in Paris in the 1920s. One of the first to embrace post-Impressionist and cubist art, Stein's avant-garde theories about art and language greatly influenced American writers and artists who frequented her salon gatherings, and her own experimental writing helped pioneer a modernist literary movement.

By 1920, Stein, a passionate devotee of modern art, had assembled piecemeal one of the finest art collections in Paris at her apartment at 27 Rue de Fleurus. Numerous painters' works, most notably those of Henri Matisse, Paul Cézanne, Pablo Picasso, Pierre-Auguste Renoir, Henri de Toulouse-Lautrec, and Henri Rousseau, adorned Stein's walls, with Picasso and Matisse, in particular, becoming personal friends of Stein's. Her weekly Saturday salon gatherings became the foremost destination for artists, writers, and intellectuals who yearned to view post-Impressionist and cubist paintings.

The Lost Generation

American writers and artists, in particular, felt they had found a home away from home in Paris with fellow American expatriates Stein and her lifelong companion, Alice B. Toklas. Salon meetings at the Stein apartment became known throughout Paris as the premier cultural haven for sparkling wit, challenging debate, and scintillating discourse about art, philosophy, literature, and psychology.

Stein became a mentor to the young writer Ernest Hemingway, becoming godmother to his son Jack, and she profoundly affected his use of language in earlier writings. Hemingway held Stein's editorial eye in high esteem and valued her insightful literary critiques. With the publication of his first novel in 1926, *The Sun Also Rises*, Hemingway credited Stein with dubbing the post–World War I generation exemplified in the novel as the "lost generation." After the horrors of trench and chemical warfare, resulting in millions of dead and wounded, the idealism, innocence, and security people had felt before World War I was irretrievably gone, and the visionaries of the age saw the chaos, disillusionment, and despair left in its wake.

Virtually all American writers who visited Paris in the 1920s were visitors of the intellectually stimulating *soirées* hosted by Stein. Particularly noteworthy participants, however, were F. Scott and Zelda Fitzgerald, Ezra Pound, Thornton Wilder, William Carlos Williams, Carl Van Vechten, Mina Loy, and Sherwood Anderson.

Literary Cubism

Anderson would later write the introduction to Stein's *Geography and Plays*, an 80,000-word collection of poems, short stories, and plays written between 1910 and 1920, published in 1922. The language employed by Stein in *Geography and Plays* was extraordinary. Stein preferred to omit punctuation, which she viewed as restrictive, as much as possible. Wishing to recreate in words the equivalent of a cubist painting or abstract musical composition, Stein's use of language in *Geography and Plays* detaches each individual word from its usual context and meaning, assigning instead an arbitrary relationship between individual words. The unexpected juxtaposition of words, and

Gertrude Stein. (Hulton Archive/Getty Images)

their prolonged repetition, in shifting rhythmical variations on the same theme, created radically new interpretations of language.

In 1925, Stein's historical and autobiographical novel, *The Making of Americans*, was published, although Stein had written the novel between 1902 and 1911. The highly experimental writing in the book intersperses a traditional Victorian novel about a heroine named Julia Dehning with a stream-of-consciousness story of an American family, the Herslands, loosely based on Stein's own family. Vacillating between poetry, fiction, meditation, soliloquy, and incantation, Stein applies her unorthodox style of literary cubism to the narrative, resulting in an extremely dense, fragmented, and abstract text. While challenging to read, *The Making of Americans* is a seminal and revolutionary departure from nineteenth-century literary style, and it marks one of the first American forays into modernist literary freedom.

In 1926, Stein lectured about her philosophy of language, art, and writing at the universities of Oxford and Cambridge. Stein's lectures were later published in 1926 as "Composition as Explanation," an essay explaining her literary and artistic theories of composition. Stein maintains that all composition is dependent upon the writer or artist creating a continuum of the present moment, uninterrupted by past or future perspectives, creating an immediate sensory immersion in the present. Stein reveals that her words are crafted to achieve a perpetual beginning of new insights, just as cubist painters use intricate brushstrokes to draw the viewer's eye to ever unfolding layers of perception.

Impact

Stein was the first modernist American feminist author whose writing posed a direct challenge to patriarchal language and precepts. Assaulting linear thought and traditional roles, Stein's rebellious, erratic writing and uncompromising intellect would come to be viewed, among other things, as the inchoate voice of the American women's movement and an important champion of literary and artistic modernism.

Mary E. Markland

Further Reading

Kostelanetz, Richard. *The Gertrude Stein Reader: The Great American Pioneer of Avant-Garde Letters.* Lanham, Md.: Cooper Square Press, 2002. Includes earlier writings with comments on the development of her writing.

Mellow, James R. *Charmed Circle: Gertrude Stein and Company.* New York: Henry Holt, 2003. An account of the renowned writers and artists of Stein's acquaintance, including Picasso, Matisse, Hemingway, and Fitzgerald.

Stein, Gertrude. *The Autobiography of Alice B. Toklas.* New York: Modern Library, 1993. Recounts Stein's and Toklas's life together over nearly thirty years.

Stein, Gertrude. *How to Write.* New York: Dover, 1975. An introduction to Stein's experimental, abstract manner of expression.

Wineapple, Brenda. *Sister Brother: Gertrude and Leo Stein.* Lincoln, Nebr.: Bison Books, 2008. Traces the strains and fractures in the relationship between Stein and her brother that led to a complete break that lasted thirty years.

See also: Art movements; Hemingway, Ernest; Homosexuality and gay rights; Literature in the United States; Lost Generation

■ Stella Dallas

Identification: A novel about a single mother's fight for her daughter's happiness
Author: Olive Higgins Prouty
Date: 1923

One of the most popular novels of the 1920s, Stella Dallas *explores a changing American society in which social class and good breeding still account for a great deal in establishing a young woman's reputation. The novel's main character fails to realize that her brash and independent ways have made her a social outcast until her daughter begins to suffer because of her mother's blithe ignorance of social standards.*

Olive Higgins Prouty's novel *Stella Dallas* resonated strongly among women readers who were keenly aware of the measures one must take to preserve one's reputation in the so-called Roaring Twenties. Stella Dallas, a young woman who marries well but does not understand her social responsibilities, is faced with challenges after her husband leaves her and she must learn to chart a new course in life for herself and her daughter.

For years, Stella gets by on mild flirtations with other men, not understanding that her husband left her because she never developed the taste or style of a society woman. Stella likes a good time and believes that her outings without her husband are harmless. She dresses vulgarly by the standards of polite society and does not take an interest in the topics of discussion and reading that a woman of the right social standing should.

That Stella has ruined her own chance to lead a respectable life only occurs to her when she sees that her beautiful and pleasing daughter, Laurel, is in danger of losing her friends and the opportunity of an excellent marriage simply because of Stella's reputation. Willing to do anything for her daughter's success, Stella marries a man her daughter despises because of his crude behavior and drinking. In so doing, Stella is able to drive away her loyal daughter, who then seeks the shelter and approval of her now remarried father. Laurel's stepmother, a woman of proper reputation, promises to provide Laurel with all of the advantages that a distinguished place in society can convey.

Impact

Commonly known as a "tearjerker," the story of Stella Dallas was made into three successful motion pictures in 1925, 1937, and 1990, as well running as a popular radio serial from 1937 to 1955. The story of this seemingly crude woman who has the nobility to sacrifice her own happiness for her daughter was irresistible because it struck at the hopes and fears of a generation of women keenly concerned with doing the socially acceptable thing while also exercising the new freedoms afforded them in the 1920s.

Carl Rollyson

Further Reading

Chandler, Karen M. "Agency and *Stella Dallas*: Audience, Melodramatic Directives, and Social Determinism in 1920s America." *Arizona Quarterly* 51, no. 4 (1995): 27–44.

Parchesky, Jennifer. "Adapting *Stella Dallas*: Class Boundaries, Consumerism, and Hierarchies of Taste." *Legacy* 23, no. 2 (2006): 178–198.

Thornton, Edie. "Fashion, Visibility, and Class Mobility in *Stella Dallas*." *American Literary History* 11, no. 3 (Fall, 1999): 426–447.

See also: Film; Literature in the United States; Marriage and dating; Roaring Twenties

■ Stieglitz, Alfred

Identification: American photographer and art promoter
Born: January 1, 1864, Hoboken, New Jersey
Died: July 13, 1946, New York, New York

In the 1920s, Alfred Stieglitz reprised his familiar dual role as innovative photographer and advocate for modern art, especially American art, roles he had been playing since the turn of the century. Although he was in his sixth decade, the quality and originality of Stieglitz's new photographic work was the basis for his continued authority as an advocate for the art of his younger contemporaries.

When the decade began, Stieglitz had been living in New York City with the painter Georgia O'Keeffe for nearly three years; they would marry in 1924, following Stieglitz's divorce from his first wife, Emmeline. Stieglitz had gained energy and artistic inspiration from his relationship with O'Keeffe following the 1917 closing of his famed Manhattan gallery, 291. Among his best-known works is what he called a "collective portrait" of O'Keeffe, which had grown to comprise more than forty photographs by the time of its first public exhibition, at New York's Anderson Galleries. The February 1921 exhibition also included an extensive selection of Stieglitz's other photographs, some dating from as early as 1886.

Among the photographs of O'Keeffe were nudes, some remarkably intimate for the era, which created considerable public interest in both Stieglitz and O'Keeffe, whose identity as the subject was widely known despite the fact that none of the pictures on display revealed her face. Apart from the arguable sensationalism of Stieglitz's gesture in publicly displaying the O'Keeffe images, the exhibition firmly established the collaborative nature of their relationship, and the publicity generated by this collective portrait helped to promote O'Keeffe's emergence in the next few years as a leading American painter.

Lake George and Photographs of Clouds

In the early 1920s, Stieglitz began a series of photographs of clouds and skies, which he took using a handheld reflex camera. Most if not all of these were taken during the months of the year that he spent at Lake George, a family gathering place in upstate New York near Saratoga Springs. Lake George was also a significant nexus for Stieglitz's extended contacts in the world of the arts and would rival Manhattan in his affections for more than four decades.

The inspiration for Stieglitz's sky photographs is uncertain, but one notion that he advanced was that they were in response to a friend, writer Waldo Frank, who felt that Stieglitz succeeded in the field of portraiture by mesmerizing his subjects. Since he could not be accused of similar influence over the atmosphere, he undertook to prove that the quality of his work transcended subject matter by aiming his camera upward. Another motivation for these photographs was Stieglitz's ambition to create a kind of abstract visual music; he cited composer Ernest Bloch's suggestion that he strive to evoke musical forms, and even specific instrumentation, by photographing clouds.

Stieglitz presented his sky images in 1922 and 1923 as two series: *Music—A Sequence of Ten Cloud Photographs* and *Songs of the Sky—Secrets of the Skies as Revealed by My Camera*. He called his later works of the same kind *Equivalents*, a term that has since come to stand for this body of work as a whole. Stieglitz's *Equivalents* are widely regarded as among the earliest examples of truly abstract photography, a genre that intentionally divorces the subject matter of the image from any literal or objective interpretation, and one whose modern expression has been largely shaped by Stieglitz's work.

Impact

Stieglitz's ongoing work with O'Keeffe and his *Equivalents* photographs both served to confirm the vitality of his creative vision. After he and O'Keeffe moved to the Shelton Hotel in 1925, he embarked on a distinguished series of photographs of New York buildings. Also in 1925, he renewed his commitment to recognizing and promoting artistic talent by creating a new exhibition space, which he called The Intimate Gallery. This was superseded in December 1929 by An American Place, where he principally showed the work of the artists who had been closest to him over the years, including O'Keeffe, John Marin, and Charles Demuth.

Clyde S. McConnell

Further Reading

Bochner, Jay. *An American Lens: Scenes from Alfred Stieglitz's New York Secession*. Cambridge, Mass.: MIT Press, 2005. Emphasizes Stieglitz's half century as a player in the development of modernism in American art.

Greenough, Sarah, and Juan Hamilton. *Alfred Stieglitz: Photographs and Writings*. Washington, D.C.: National Gallery of Art, 1983. Offers documentary materials, a selection photographs, and an essay by Greenough, senior curator of photographs at the National Gallery.

Greenough, Sarah, ed. *Modern Art and America: Alfred Stieglitz and His New York Galleries*. Washington,

D.C.: National Gallery of Art, 2000. Presents the art that Stieglitz exhibited and fostered over four decades, alongside essays on the individual artists.

Hoffman, Katherine. *Stieglitz: A Beginning Light.* New Haven, Conn.: Yale University Press, 2004. Offers perceptive, though sometimes impressionistic, connections between the earlier and later phases of Stieglitz's career.

Lowe, Sue Davidson. *Stieglitz: A Memoir/Biography.* New York: Farrar, Straus and Giroux, 1983. A comprehensive biography of Stieglitz, written by his grandniece.

Whelan, Richard. *Alfred Stieglitz: A Biography.* Boston: Little, Brown, 1995. An exceptionally detailed study of Stieglitz's life.

See also: Art movements; Demuth, Charles; Marin, John; O'Keeffe, Georgia; Photography

■ Stock market crash

Black Tuesday, October 29, 1929, saw one of the worst financial crises in U.S. history. Though there were several days of serious market declines, Black Tuesday has become infamous as being the worst single day in American brokerage history and is usually described as the start of the Great Depression.

Beginning in September of 1929 and lasting for about six weeks, various stock markets in New York and elsewhere experienced a series of corrections as the values of many stocks began to fall from their highs earlier in the decade. The most significant of these corrections came on the New York Stock Exchange and the Curb Exchange, which would later be renamed the American Stock Exchange, in October of 1929. These market adjustments were the result of many factors and occurred over a period of several days.

Causes

The activities of brokers and independent buyers and sellers of securities during the 1920s were almost totally unregulated by the U.S. government. Republican presidents Calvin Coolidge and Herbert Hoover had both personal and ideological qualms about government involvement in the operations of a free economy.

This period of apparently widespread prosperity was further reinforced by stories of investors who made fortunes in the stock market. Improvements in communication and corporate efficiency made it easier for individuals from small towns across the country to invest their money in securities. This led to an atmosphere of rampant and unrestrained speculation as more people invested in stocks. Often, stock prices rose simply by virtue of their desirability and not necessarily on the basis of sustainable and stable economic indicators for the corporation. Leaders of future trends such as U.S. Steel and General Electric, despite their high prices, could not compare to the outsized valuations of popular stocks such as RCA.

Investors and brokers soon developed questionable payment strategies in order to afford stocks at prices of $300 to $400 per share at a time when the average American was earning only $1,425 annually. Many investors cooperated in investment pools in their hometowns. More troublesome, though, was the practice of margin buying. Margin buying was a system intended to allow any person to buy stock with only a percentage of the cost paid up front. In many ways, it was a version of the increasingly popular installment buying option offered by retailers. In margin buying, an investor could purchase a block of stocks sometimes for as little as a 10 percent down

---

The Great Depression

The Great Depression is generally seen as having lasted from the stock market crash of October 1929 until the entry of the United States into World War II in December 1941. However, it is a mistake to conclude that the stock market crash itself caused the Depression. An economic depression as deep and sustained as that of the 1930s can only be attributed to a complex of causes that converge to create a business environment poised for disaster. The stock market crash did indeed contribute to the economic instability that marked the Depression, but many other factors, including agricultural overproduction and increasing levels of household debt, were responsible for the Depression, which continued for almost a decade after the stock market reached its bottom and began its slow recovery in June 1932.

payment with the expectation that the steadily rising value of the stock would provide the necessary revenue to pay off the remaining balance of the stock's initial purchase price. Throughout the 1920s, the almost unending upward trend of the markets seemed to make this practice feasible. Exacerbating this tendency was the fact that some investors got bank loans in order to pay the initial margin buy. The end result was that there was little actual money supporting the stocks' values. As investors and brokers began to recognize the fragile nature of the markets, there began a series of corrections starting in September of 1929.

The Crashes
The markets reached their peak in 1928 and early 1929. Despite a series of adjustments during the summer and fall of 1929 and warnings from a handful of commentators, there was general optimism that the upward trend of prices would continue. Many public officials, including presidents Coolidge and Hoover, had repeatedly assured the public that the nation's economic future was bright.

Thursday, October 24, 1929, however, was the worst day in the market's history up to that point. Wednesday's session had seen a late slump in stock prices, which carried over into what came to be known as Black Thursday. At times, so-called air pockets developed when the bid price was so far below the asking price that stocks could lose several dollars every few minutes. As tensions escalated toward panic, leaders of major banks and brokerages stepped onto the floor in an effort to restore confidence. The vice president of the New York Stock Exchange and a man with ties to the investment bank J. P. Morgan & Co., Richard Whitney, acted as proxy for the pooled resources of the city's financial leaders. Starting with U.S. Steel, Whitney began buying large blocks of securities at several dollars above the asking price. This helped to restore investors' faith in the market.

The exchange operated with shortened hours over the next two business days; however, many investors began planning their escape from the volatile market. After the market's close on Monday, October 28, many banks began issuing margin calls in an effort to recover their losses and limit their exposure to the plunging market. Since most investors had little or no money to pay off their margin debts, Tuesday, October 29, saw widespread sell-offs from the opening bell. By the end of Black Tuesday, the market had lost between 12 percent and 13 percent of its

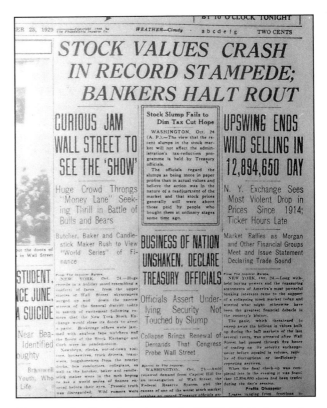

Newspaper details stock market crash of 1929. (Getty Images)

value with over sixteen million shares traded. The exchange's ticker machines could not keep up with the volume of trading, even though new systems had been installed Monday morning to avoid a repeat of the previous week's debacle. As a result, Western Union hired taxicabs to shuttle messages between the stock market and financial offices around the city. Crowds estimated at ten thousand or more gathered outside the exchanges on Wall Street, desperate to learn anything they could about the chaos inside. At the closing bell, the exchange's ticker machines were more than two hours behind, causing investors to base their decisions on inaccurate information and leading the nation to be unaware of the full scale of the damage. Ironically, the group of investors and planners responsible for the construction of the Empire State Building, unaware of the crisis on Wall Street, had met that morning at the Plaza Hotel in Midtown to finalize plans for the spire, which would make the building the tallest structure in the world.

Despite Black Tuesday's reputation as being the start of the Great Depression, the economy did not show marked signs of being in a depression until the spring of 1930. The market did not actually reach its bottom until July of 1932. In fact, on October 30, the New York Stock Exchange recovered 74 percent of its losses from the previous few days. After trading finished that Wednesday, the markets closed until Monday to allow brokers and banks to get their books in order. For the remainder of 1929, the exchanges limped along with neither substantial gains nor dramatic losses. Weak recoveries were met with additional slumps. Despite the huge crashes of October, however, most companies ended the 1920s in the black, which testifies to the strength of the bull market over the previous decade. Few businesses collapsed as a direct result of the market's decline, and most observers assumed that the crashes would remove unproductive stocks or at the very least would revalue stocks more accurately. By the spring of 1930, other indicators began to demonstrate the depth of the economic problems the country faced. Swelling inventories, shrinking credit, and the resultant unemployment combined to plunge the nation into the Great Depression.

Impact

Although many factors actually led to the Great Depression in the United States and some economists doubt that the stock market crash of 1929 was indeed a major factor, the events of September and October of 1929 have become legendary as being the cause of the Great Depression. As such, it is often pointed to as a watershed moment in U.S. history, since the social, political, and economic changes sparked by the Great Depression ostensibly would not have happened were it not for the crash of 1929.

Shawn Selby

Further Reading

Galbraith, John Kenneth. *The Great Crash, 1929.* Boston, Mass.: Houghton Mifflin, 2009. Examines the actions of investors and the government inaction in the months prior to Black Tuesday.

Klein, Maury. *Rainbow's End: The Crash of 1929.* New York: Oxford University Press, 2003. Investigates the multitude of economic, political, and social events that led to the crash of 1929.

McElvaine, Robert S. *The Great Depression: America, 1929–1941.* New York: Three Rivers Press, 2009. Provides insight into the attempts made by economists and politicians to revive the economy during the Great Depression. Relates personal stories of Americans who survived the crisis and includes descriptions of the popular culture of the time.

Parker, Selwyn. *The Great Crash: How the Stock Market Crash of 1929 Plunged the World into Depression.* London: Piatkus: 2008. A history of the stock market crash of 1929 and its ensuing worldwide effects.

Thomas, Gordon, and Max Morgan-Witts. *The Day the Bubble Burst: A Social History of the Wall Street Crash of 1929.* New York: Penguin Books, 1979. Recounts stories and experiences of average Americans, bankers, corporate officials, and Wall Street speculators from October of 1929 through the years that followed.

See also: Agricultural Marketing Act of 1929; Banking; Credit and debt; Gross national product of the United States; Installment plans; Unemployment

■ Stone, Harlan Fiske

Identification: U.S. attorney general and Supreme Court justice
Born: October 11, 1872, Chesterfield, New Hampshire
Died: April 22, 1946, Washington, D.C.

Harlan Fiske Stone's experiences as law professor and practitioner contributed to his rise to U.S. attorney general and associate justice of the United States during the 1920s. Stone's efforts as attorney general represented a move away from corruption in the Department of Justice, and his appointment to the Supreme Court marked the first time that a nominee appeared in person for a confirmation hearing.

Following years of work in private practice and as a professor at Columbia Law School, Stone entered the 1920s as dean of Columbia Law School, having been appointed to that post in 1918. Respected by his students, Stone was driven by a keen interest in the study of law and its principles. He resigned from Columbia in 1923 to pursue a partnership opportunity with Sullivan and Cromwell, a Wall Street law firm.

Attorney General

During the time that Stone was engaged as head of litigation at Sullivan and Cromwell, important

Harlan Fiske Stone. (Getty Images)

developments were occurring in the Department of Justice that would affect Stone's future. On March 28, 1924, U.S. attorney general Harry M. Daugherty resigned from his post following allegations of corrupt business dealings and scandalous practices within the Department of Justice. President Calvin Coolidge, a former college friend of Stone, appointed Stone to replace Daugherty as attorney general. Stone brought no prior government experience to the position but was committed to helping President Coolidge rid the Department of Justice of unscrupulous and improper activities.

Stone's tenure as attorney general was brief but impactful. He quickly sought to implement consistent and more effective standards for the enforcement of Prohibition and antitrust regulations, both of which were significant issues in the 1920s. Claims of corruption within the Federal Bureau of Investigation (FBI) led Stone to seek the resignation of William J. Burns, the head of the bureau. On December 19, 1924, Stone appointed J. Edgar Hoover as director of the FBI, following several months as acting director.

U.S. Supreme Court

After less than one year as attorney general, Stone was nominated to the U.S. Supreme Court by President Calvin Coolidge to fill a vacancy left by retiring Associate Justice Mahlon Pitney. Stone's nomination prompted some to question whether his efforts as attorney general or his work at a private law firm would influence his judgment on the bench. Although Supreme Court confirmations had previously been conducted through written correspondence, Stone became the first nominee in history to sit before a Senate Judiciary Committee hearing. Following Stone's testimony, the Senate voted in favor of his appointment by seventy-one to six, and he was inducted on March 2, 1925.

Stone's early years as associate justice on the Supreme Court reflected his general preference for judicial restraint, an approach with a tendency to defer to precedent and established decisions of government instead of acting in a legislative capacity. Stone also preferred plain language and a realistic interpretation of the Constitution rather than formulas and tests to be applied in analyzing the facts of a case. Stone soon found that he was in frequent agreement with Justices Oliver Wendell Holmes Jr. and Louis D. Brandeis, often on issues related to fundamental individual rights.

Impact

Stone, who was a Republican, was appointed chief justice of the Supreme Court on July 2, 1941, and remained on the Court until his death in 1946. Although he achieved the highest rank within the Supreme Court much later, Stone brought a steadfast focus on the law to each of the endeavors he undertook in the 1920s, significantly influencing academia, private practice, government office, and judicial service in the nation's highest court.

Although the early 1920s were replete with government corruption and scandal, the decade became a time of economic growth and development. Stone's appointment as attorney general contributed to the cleanup of federal law enforcement and established standards for the FBI. Despite concerns that his experience as attorney general might threaten his impartiality as a Supreme Court justice, Stone's willingness to respond to confirmation questions during a Senate Committee hearing led to his appointment and set a precedent for future Supreme Court nominees.

Heather Love Getsay

Further Reading

Konefsky, Samuel Joseph. *Chief Justice Stone and the Supreme Court.* New York: Hafner, 1971. A facsimile of the 1945 work detailing judicial review by Harlan Fiske Stone.

Mason, Alpheus Thomas. "Harlan Fiske Stone Assays Social Justice, 1912–1923." *University of Pennsylvania Law Review* 99, no. 7 (May, 1951): 887–918. A detailed scholarly article on Stone's judicial philosophies through 1923, including the time he was professor and dean at Columbia Law School.

_____. *Harlan Fiske Stone: Pillar of the Law.* New York: Viking Press, 1956. A detailed account of Stone's life and career, based on primary and secondary sources.

Renstrom, Peter G. *The Stone Court: Justices, Rulings, and Legacy.* Santa Barbara, Calif.: ABC-CLIO, 2001. A study on Stone's tenure as chief justice, with references to earlier achievements.

Smith, Young B. "Harlan Fiske Stone: Teacher, Scholar, and Dean." *Columbia Law Review* 46, no. 5 (1946): 700–709. Analyzes Stone's legal philosophies during his time as professor and dean at Columbia Law School.

Urofsky, Melvin I. *Division and Discord: The Supreme Court Under Stone and Vinson, 1941–1953.* Columbia: University of South Carolina Press, 1999. Describes important Supreme Court decisions during Stone's later career, with special focus on his leadership as chief justice.

See also: Coolidge, Calvin; Daugherty, Harry M.; Holmes, Oliver Wendell, Jr.; Hoover, J. Edgar; Prohibition; Supreme Court, U.S.

■ Strange Interlude

Identification: A nine-act play recounting the lives of five characters over the course of twenty-five years
Author: Eugene O'Neill
Date: 1928

Written in 1923, Strange Interlude *was first produced on Broadway in 1928 and ran for 426 performances. With* Strange Interlude, *dramatist Eugene O'Neill received his third Pulitzer Prize, further cementing his career as America's leading twentieth-century playwright. The play is known for its extensive use of soliloquy.*

The plot of *Strange Interlude* revolves around the life of Nina Leeds following World War I. After her fiancé is killed during the war, Nina's restless pursuit of love and happiness leads her through a series of affairs with different men. Family strife and conflicted parent-child relationships, two recurrent themes in O'Neill's plays, also feature in *Strange Interlude.* Nina is estranged from her father, Professor Leeds, because she cannot forgive him for convincing her fiancé to postpone their wedding until after the war. Although writer Charles Marsden is in love with her, Nina eventually marries a man named Sam Evans. After Nina gets pregnant, her mother-in-law reveals to her that insanity runs in the Evans family, and Nina decides to have an abortion, fearing her child will inherit the family trait. She later persuades Edmund "Ned" Darrell to get her pregnant again so she can pretend the child is Sam's. Sam and Gordon, as she names this son, remain ignorant of the child's paternity. After Sam's death, Nina marries Charles Marsden. Toward the end of the play, Nina describes their lives as "strange dark interludes," providing the inspiration for the title.

The influence of Freud's psychoanalytic theories is visible in the characterization of the cast. The play's length of four hours owes much to O'Neill's experimentation with soliloquies, through which his characters express their true opinions and point of view, often presenting a sharp contrast to their previous words. These soliloquies intend to emphasize and bridge the gap between appearances and the characters' inner thoughts.

The play takes a bold approach to themes of abortion and adultery, which were daring topics for a 1920s audience and made for a controversial reception of the play despite its critical acclaim. In 1929, the mayor of Boston even banned the production of the play in the city, making it necessary to move it to a suburban theater.

Impact

Strange Interlude became a best seller in book form. Stage revivals were produced in 1931, 1963, and 1985 in London and on Broadway. Due to its length, performances of *Strange Interlude* are often given over two consecutive days or with a dinner break.

The comedy team known as the Marx Brothers parodied *Strange Interlude* in their 1930 film *Animal Crackers.* It has been adapted for the screen twice: once in 1932, starring Clark Gable as Ned and Norma

Shearer as Nina, and again in a television miniseries in 1988, with Glenda Jackson playing Nina.

M. Carmen Gomez-Galisteo

Further Reading

Alexander, Doris. *Eugene O'Neill's Creative Struggle: The Decisive Decade, 1924–1933*. University Park: Pennsylvania State University Press, 1992.

Dubost, Thierry. *Struggle, Defeat or Rebirth: Eugene O'Neill's Vision of Humanity*. Jefferson, N.C.: McFarland, 2005.

See also: All God's Chillun Got Wings; Anna Christie; Desire Under the Elms; Emperor Jones, The; O'Neill, Eugene; Theater in the United States

■ Student Prince, The

Identification: Operetta about the romance between a prince and a barmaid in the old German city of Heidelberg
Authors: Music by Sigmund Romberg; lyrics and book by Dorothy Donnelly
Date: 1924

The Student Prince was one of the most popular American operettas of Hungarian American composer Sigmund Romberg, influenced by the works of Viennese composer Johann Strauss II, among others. It foreshadowed socially conscious American musical stage works emerging in the 1920s and 1930s.

The Student Prince was the result of a collaboration between Romberg and the librettist Dorothy Donnelly. It was based on the German play *Alt Heidelberg* by Wilhelm Meyer-Förster, which was inspired by actual events in 1863. Although Romberg's music was grounded in the past, the subject matter anticipated future plays and musicals. The sociopolitical themes explored in *The Student Prince* and Romberg's next operetta, *The Desert Song* (1926), for example, probably foreshadowed Jerome Kern's breakthrough musical *Show Boat* (1927).

Karl Franz, the prince of a fictitious German kingdom, is sent to Heidelberg University disguised as an ordinary student. While there, he makes friends with other students and falls in love with Kathie, an innkeeper's daughter. However, Karl Franz is already promised to Princess Margaret. In the end, Karl Franz becomes king and fulfills his royal duty by marrying Margaret, although he expresses his undying love for Kathie in song.

The work encompasses over twenty musical numbers divided into four acts, comprising both vocal and instrumental sections, along with ballets staged by choreographer Max Scheck in the original production. The Shubert brothers, producers with whom Romberg signed the play's first contract, objected to the old-fashioned style and unhappy ending of the operetta. It was only after serious disagreements, also involving Donnelly's book and lyrics, that the premiere of *The Student Prince* took place on December 2, 1924, at the 59th Street Theater in New York.

The Student Prince was a hit. It was first committed to silent film in 1927; other versions were filmed in the era of talking pictures. Selections from the music were originally published in New York by Harms, Inc. in 1924, and in 1932, Warner Bros. Publications released a complete score containing all of the operetta's musical numbers. Romberg's surviving manuscript sources, including orchestral scores not available in published form, are filed at the University of California at Berkeley and in the Library of Congress.

Impact

The Student Prince was one of the first American operettas to establish a culture of social realism that had been lacking from the escapist Viennese works influencing Romberg's compositional style. The blurred line between opera, operetta, and the works of the Broadway stage influenced the development of motion picture soundtracks, with Romberg's work influencing film composers from Erich Korngold to Osvaldo Golijov.

Susan M. Filler

Further Reading

Bordman, Gerald M. "The Flowering of Traditional American Operetta: Friml and Romberg." In *American Operetta From "H.M.S. Pinafore" to "Sweeney Todd."* New York: Oxford University Press, 1981.

Everett, William A. "Young Love in Old Heidelberg: *The Student Prince*." In *Sigmund Romberg*. New Haven, Conn.: Yale University Press, 2007.

Traubner, Richard. *Operetta: A Theatrical History*. Rev. ed. New York: Routledge, 2003.

Studies in Classic American Literature

Identification: Collection of critical essays on mostly nineteenth-century American authors
Author: D. H. Lawrence
Date: 1923

Written in radically informal modernist prose, Studies in Classic American Literature *was a work of interest in itself, as well as being among the first serious critical treatments of American literature as an independent field of study. It helped shape the development of modern literary criticism and contributed to a twentieth-century revival of critical interest in the works of Herman Melville.*

British author D. H. Lawrence began writing *Studies in Classic American Literature* in 1917 while under virtual house arrest in England during World War I, as he and his German wife, Frieda von Richthofen (a distant cousin of the German fighter pilot known as the Red Baron), were suspected of being spies for Germany. The early versions of the essays feature a generally positive perspective on the authors under discussion, expressing admiration for America's promise of escape from the Old World, while the 1923 versions, rewritten while living in the United States, pass harsher judgments.

Nathaniel Hawthorne, for example, was originally "a philosopher as well as an artist," and his most famous novel, *The Scarlet Letter*, was "a profound and wonderful book"; but the final version of Lawrence's critique condemns the novel's "duplicity" in exposing the "deliberate consciousness of the Americans so fair and smooth spoken, and their under-consciousness so devilish." Similarly, Edgar Allan Poe is called out for exhibiting "the inevitable falseness [and] duplicity of art, American art in particular," and James Fenimore Cooper's *Deerslayer* is dismissed as "the miserable story of the collapse of the white psyche." Lawrence's response to Walt Whitman is better, but still ambivalent: "Whitman, the great poet, has meant so much to me," he contends, and yet, "in Whitman lies the greatest of all modern humbugs." Of the authors discussed in the book, Herman Melville is unique in still receiving positive treatment after Lawrence's revisions. While reading Melville's *Moby-Dick* in 1917, Lawrence wrote to friends that he "loved" the novel, calling it a "*real* masterpiece," a view Lawrence retained to the end.

Impact

In writing *Studies in Classic American Literature*, Lawrence was a pioneer in examining American authors as subjects of serious study; approving or not, his insights into American literature as an expression of the evolution of the American psyche away from its European roots were groundbreaking. The first professorship in American literature was not established until 1919, and the Modern Language Association did not recognize scholarly interest in American literature until 1921. Literature specialists of the later twentieth century have acknowledged the significant impact of Lawrence's criticism and the role it played in shaping modern interpretations of earlier American authors.

Earl G. Ingersoll

Further Reading

Beal, Anthony, ed. *D. H. Lawrence: Selected Literary Criticism*. London: Heinemann, 1955.

Chase, Richard. *The American Novel and Its Tradition*. Baltimore: Johns Hopkins University Press, 1997.

Clarey, JoEllyn. "D. H. Lawrence's *Moby-Dick*: A Textual Note." *Modern Philology* 84, no. 2 (November, 1986): 191–195.

See also: Literature in the United States; *Main Currents of American Thought*

Sturtevant, Alfred H.

Identification: American scientist
Born: November 21, 1891, Jacksonville, Illinois
Died: April 5, 1970, Pasadena, California

Alfred Henry Sturtevant discovered several genetic principles and laid the foundation for modern genetic analysis of all organisms. Sturtevant was the first to develop chromosome-mapping techniques, find that genes are arranged in a linear order on chromosomes, and discover that the position of a gene on the chromosome influences its expression, which is each gene's contribution to the synthesis of a gene product such as a protein. He laid the foundation of modern biochemical genetics when he discovered that the effect of cell mutations can sometimes be reversed by neighboring cells.

Sturtevant made several discoveries of genetic principles in a variety of organisms, but he is best known for his development of chromosome-mapping techniques for *Drosophila melanogaster*, also known as the fruit fly. In 1911, while an undergraduate student working with genetics professor Thomas Hunt Morgan at Columbia University, he discovered that genes linked on a chromosome are arranged in a linear order and that their recombination frequency is related to the distance between them. He published the first genetic map of six X-linked genes in *Drosophila* only two years later. After receiving his doctorate from Columbia in 1914, Sturtevant remained at Columbia, where he made several seminal discoveries in the field of genetics.

Sturtevant's work contributed significantly to evolutionary thought when he found that two closely related species of *Drosophila* had similar allelic mutations, or unique forms of a gene that develop through mutation. He also discovered that mutant genes' phenotypic effect on eye color was sometimes reversible: Fruit flies' normal eye tissue produces a biochemical that can diffuse into mutant eye tissue, returning it to normal. Sturtevant further discovered that the location of a gene on a chromosome influences its expression and that the coiling of snails' shells is determined by a single pair of genes.

In 1922, Sturtevant married Phoebe Curtis Reed, with whom he had three children. His son William went on to become a noted anthropologist and ethnologist. Sturtevant eventually relocated to the California Institute of Technology (Caltech), where he taught genetics, along with Morgan.

Impact

Sturtevant was a pioneer in the field of genetics, and between 1910 and 1940, discovered several basic genetic principles in *Drosophila* and other organisms that significantly advanced the field. His work enabled geneticists to apply similar principles to more developed animals and even humans. The mapping principles and techniques he developed for *Drosophila* have been applied to numerous organisms. His work on reparable genes pioneered later work on the biochemical mechanism of gene action.

Charles L. Vigue

Further Reading

Sturtevant, A. H. *A History of Genetics*. Reprint. Cold Spring Harbor, N.Y.: Cold Spring Harbor Laboratory Press, 2001.

_____. *The North American Species of Drosophila*. Washington, D.C.: Carnegie Institution of Washington, 1921.

_____. *Genetics and Evolution: Selected Papers of A. H. Sturtevant*. Edited by E. B. Lewis. San Francisco: W. H. Freeman, 1961.

See also: California Institute of Technology (Caltech); Medicine; Morgan, Thomas Hunt; Science and technology

■ Suburbs

In the 1920s, a number of factors caused the burgeoning suburbs of many cities to experience enormous population increases. As cities grew during the late nineteenth and early twentieth centuries, they became increasingly unpleasant places to live, due to widespread economic and industrial development, waves of immigrants perceived as undesirable, and inadequate or nonexistent social services. The development of streetcar lines and the expansion of automobile ownership to the middle class supported a suburban lifestyle.

Although early-twentieth-century urban centers supported economic and cultural life, white-collar workers sought to leave cities at the end of the workday because of generally unfettered immigration, overcrowded living conditions, industrial and business expansion into residential neighborhoods, industrial pollution, and corrupt city governments. Suburbanization also benefited from the developing American idealization of rural life. The development of electrified streetcars in the late 1880s spurred the growth of neighborhoods and villages at the edges of cities, along streetcar lines.

Streetcar Suburbs to Automobile Suburbs

Streetcar lines remained critically important in the 1920s, often augmented by bus networks connecting at streetcar stops. Although automobiles had been in use since the 1890s, the 1920s was the first decade in which members of the middle class could afford cars. Private automobiles were more expensive to operate than the streetcar, limiting access and creating prestige for those who could afford suburban housing and the cost of the daily automobile commute. However, increasingly crowded streets undermined the potential speed of automobiles, spurring the development of commuter rail lines, as well as commercial and business districts, along suburban streetcar routes.

Suburban life was highly valued, with its pastoral setting, green space, low-density living, better public schools, and more direct access to private schools, country clubs, and suburban shopping enclaves. Suburbs were often initially "dry" areas, in which the prohibiting of saloons was the first official act of new communities, supporting suburban residents' belief that suburban life was better, healthier, and less sordid than life in urban centers.

Shaker Heights

Two entrepreneurial brothers, O. P. and M. J. Van Sweringen, purchased the 1,400 acres that had been the planned community of the United Society of Believers in Christ's Second Appearing, commonly known as the North Union Shakers. Since the land was on the hills that form a ridge east of Cleveland, the Van Sweringens' new development was called "Shaker Village," and after being renamed "Shaker Heights," it was officially incorporated as a city in 1931. Shaker Heights grew explosively during the 1920s, becoming known as a garden city of substantial homes with strict building codes that limited colors and building materials and allowed only colonial, English, and French architectural styles. Other residential limitations included uniform setbacks and lot sizes as well as deed restrictions.

Purchasing the Nickel Plate rail lines from the New York Central Railroad, the Van Sweringen brothers built a "rapid transit" to take commuters from Shaker Heights to the new downtown Terminal Tower and rail station. Commercial business was initially restricted to the Georgian revival-style redbrick Shaker Square, a New England–style town green with four quadrants of shops that were promptly deeded back to the city of Cleveland. Land was set aside for churches, private schools, and country clubs, though the development of a superior public school system was critical.

Although it became a multicultural community in the 1950s, Shaker Heights in the 1920s was homogeneously white and Protestant. When an African American physician and his family moved to the suburb in 1925, gunshots were fired at their house, and their garage was mysteriously burned. The

---

Shopping Centers

The development of the shopping center concept in the United States from the 1920s through the mid-twentieth century came about because of lifestyle and environmental changes taking place in the country. Increasingly widespread ownership of automobiles allowed growing numbers of city workers to live in the suburbs. As more and more Americans made their homes in the suburbs, they demanded shopping facilities that were conveniently located. Integrated shopping centers, with a variety of large and small tenants under one landlord and with affordable off-street parking, did not exist until 1922. In that year, real estate developer J. C. Nichols built the Country Club Plaza, the first planned, fully integrated shopping center in the United States. The center was located on a forty-acre site five miles south of downtown Kansas City, Missouri.

Shaker Heights Protective Association developed in the mid-1920s to keep out so-called undesirables, and it was not until the late 1950s that neighborhood associations such as the Ludlow Community Association facilitated the peaceful integration of the suburb.

Impact

The 1920s formed a pivotal decade in the migration of Americans from rural settings to the cities and suburbs. Aside from the Shaker Heights community, 1920s suburban societies included Cleveland Heights, Ohio, as well as areas of Long Island. As suburbs developed in the United States in the twentieth and twenty-first centuries, they continued to remain connected to the nearby metropolis, which provided them with access to employment and infrastructure, while generally including middle-class and upper-class residents, lower population densities, higher rates of home ownership, and communally accepted covenants and restrictions.

Richard Sax

Further Reading

Baxandall, Rosalyn F., and Elizabeth Ewen. *Picture Windows: How the Suburbs Happened.* New York: Basic Books, 2001. Examines the cultural, economic, and political contexts of suburban development in Long Island suburbs.

Marshall, Bruce T. *Shaker Heights.* Charleston, S.C.: Arcadia, 2006. Describes how the Van Sweringen brothers established and developed Shaker Heights as an elite residential community with deed restrictions, high architectural standards and style limitations, and reliance on public transportation.

Morton, Marian J. *Cleveland Heights: The Making of an Urban Suburb.* Charleston, S.C.: Arcadia, 2002. Describes the development of the Cleveland Heights suburb, including its founding in 1901, its designation as a city in 1921, and its years of rapid growth during the 1920s. Includes archival photographs.

Stilgoe, John R. *Borderland: Origins of the American Suburb, 1820–1939.* New Haven, Conn.: Yale University Press, 1990. Documents the causes of the suburban diaspora, describing the commuter residential havens that initially sought to provide a genteel lifestyle exclusively for the upper and middle classes.

Teaford, Jon C. *The American Suburb: The Basics.* London: Routledge, 2008. Examines the governance, commerce, and cultural dynamics of the American suburb, using government records and statistics, newspapers, interviews, city council and town hall meeting minutes.

See also: Architecture; Better Homes in America movement; Bungalows; Cities; Federal highway system; Housing

■ Sun Also Rises, The

Identification: A novel about a group of post–World War I expatriate Americans taking a trip to Pamplona, Spain, to experience the bullfighting festival of San Fermín
Author: Ernest Hemingway
Date: 1926

In 1926, after establishing himself as a talented journalist and author of short stories, Ernest Hemingway published his first novel, The Sun Also Rises. *This breakthrough novel was well received by both critics and the public, and it remains famous not only for epitomizing Hemingway's signature prose style of short, declarative sentences, but also for its depiction of what came to be known as the "lost generation."*

The Sun Also Rises tells the story of Jake Barnes, a World War I veteran living and working as a journalist in Paris. While in Paris, Jake finds company with other expatriates, including Robert Cohn, a rich Jewish writer and failed boxer; Bill Gorton, another war veteran; and Lady Brett Ashley, a divorced socialite who once worked as a nurse and treated Jake for a war wound he suffered in England. It is implied that this wound has rendered Jake sexually impotent.

Brett is free-spirited, independent, and manipulative; she has an emasculating effect on the men in her life. Jake is in love with Brett, as are most of the men in the novel, and while Brett claims to love Jake, she will not commit to him due to his war injury. Brett secretly spends time with all the male characters of the novel, giving each of them special attention and false hope before crushing them emotionally. The novel follows the group to Pamplona, Spain, where they experience the bullfighting festival of San Fermín while the men compete for a place in Brett's heart.

Impact

The Sun Also Rises is considered one of the seminal literary works of the lost generation, as Gertrude Stein, Hemingway's literary mentor in Paris, described the aimless young adults trying to make sense of their existence after World War I. Hemingway used Stein's quote "You are all a lost generation" as an epigraph for *The Sun Also Rises.* After the novel became a success in the Roaring Twenties, the term was widely adopted to describe the members of this generation that had lost faith in traditional values after experiencing the horrors of World War I. Hemingway went on to write many novels, but none so encompassed the posture of an entire generation as *The Sun Also Rises* had.

Timothy J. Ashton

Further Reading

Bloom, Harold. *Ernest Hemingway's "The Sun Also Rises."* New York: Chelsea House, 2007.

Dolan, Marc. *Modern Lives: A Cultural Re-Reading of the Lost Generation.* West Lafayette, Ind.: Purdue University Press, 1996.

Oliver, Charles M. *Ernest Hemingway A to Z: The Essential Reference to the Life and Work.* New York: Checkmark Books, 1999.

See also: Hemingway, Ernest; Literature in the United States; Lost Generation; Roaring Twenties; Stein, Gertrude; World War I veterans

Supreme Court, U.S.

During the 1920s, the U.S. Supreme Court decided cases about a number of issues, ranging from Prohibition to economic regulations. Under the leadership of Chief Justice William Howard Taft for the majority of the decade, the Court used the concept of due process to strike down various state and federal laws that regulated industry and infringed upon liberties.

Among the members of the U.S. Supreme Court during the 1920s were some of the Court's most historically prominent justices, including Oliver Wendell Holmes Jr., Louis Brandeis, and future chief justice Harlan Fiske Stone, as well as former U.S. president William Howard Taft. In an era of widespread economic prosperity, industrialization, and social change, the Court ruled on numerous cases related to business and industry, social concerns such as the national ban on alcohol, and civil rights and liberties.

Justices

Edward Douglass White was appointed chief justice by President William Howard Taft in 1910, having served as an associate justice since his appointment by Grover Cleveland in 1894. He had previously served in the United States Senate. White died in May 1921 and was succeeded by the very man who had appointed him to the position. The first chief justice of the United States to have also served as president, Taft was appointed by President Warren G. Harding and joined the Court on July 11, 1921. In addition to holding the presidency, Taft had also served as solicitor general, secretary of war, and governor of the Philippines. As chief justice, Taft led the Supreme Court throughout the 1920s.

A number of associate justices retired or resigned from the Supreme Court in the 1920s. John Hessin Clarke was appointed associate justice by President Woodrow Wilson in 1916, having previously served as a judge for an Ohio district court. Frustrated by the limitations of the Supreme Court, he resigned from his position in 1922. William Rufus Day joined the Court in 1903, appointed by President Theodore Roosevelt. Day, who had previously served as assistant secretary of state during the presidency of William McKinley, retired in 1922. One of several associate justices appointed by Taft during his presidency, Mahlon Pitney took the judicial oath in 1912 after nearly a decade of service in the New Jersey Supreme Court. Like Day, he retired from the position in 1922. Joseph McKenna was appointed to the Court in 1898 by McKinley, having previously served in the House of Representatives and as attorney general. He served as an associate justice until his retirement in 1925.

Due to these vacancies, four new associate justices joined the Supreme Court during the 1920s. George Sutherland was appointed to the Court by Harding in 1922, having previously served in both houses of Congress. Pierce Butler, a former president of the Minnesota State Bar Association, was appointed associate justice in 1923. The third of Harding's appointees, Tennessee district court judge Edward Terry Sanford, joined the Court less than two months after Butler. President Calvin Coolidge appointed Harlan Fiske Stone, then serving as attorney general, to the position in 1925. These associate justices served on the Supreme Court throughout the 1920s and would continue to hold their positions until leaving office due to promotion, retirement, or death.

An additional four associate justices were appointed to the Supreme Court prior to the 1920s and remained with the Court throughout the decade. Oliver Wendell Holmes Jr. was appointed by Roosevelt in 1902, having served on the Massachusetts Supreme Court for nearly two decades. Willis Van Deventer, who had previously served on the Wyoming Territorial Supreme Court and as assistant attorney general, was appointed by Taft in 1911 and became the sole remaining Taft appointee after Pitney's 1922 retirement. Serving as attorney general at the time of his appointment by Wilson, James Clark McReynolds joined the Supreme Court in 1914.

Louis Dembitz Brandeis was appointed associate justice by Wilson in 1916 after working for several decades as a prominent attorney. In addition to serving on the Supreme Court throughout the 1920s, these justices would continue to decide major cases into the next decade.

Political Stance

The Supreme Court was relatively conservative during the 1920s, reflecting an overall trend toward conservatism that followed the end of World War I. One of the most politically divisive issues that shaped the Supreme Court of the 1920s was that of due process, particularly substantive due process. This concept, which prohibits the government from denying individuals or groups such as businesses their legal rights without due process of law, served as the logic behind a number of decisions that struck down various state and federal laws. In the case of businesses, which were of particular concern during the prosperous 1920s, substantive due process typically allowed for the abolishment of state regulations on the basis that such regulations infringed upon businesses' freedom of contract or property rights.

Holmes, throughout his decades in the Court, typically argued in favor of deferring to state legislatures, particularly with regard to socioeconomic regulations. While Holmes did not necessarily approve of the laws that he voted to uphold, he believed that interfering with state legislatures was not the Court's role. Brandeis came to be Holmes's primary ally in this area, although his reasoning was very different. As a lawyer, Brandeis had perfected a style of written argument that would later come to be known as the Brandeis brief, which persuaded primarily through real-world data and reports rather than legal precedent. This approach was generally more sympathetic toward the public policies underlying legislation and thus led Brandeis to arrive at conclusions consistent with Holmes's deference to legislatures.

The remainder of the associate justices, as well as Taft, viewed government regulations and similar laws with far more skepticism and believed that the Supreme Court had the authority to rule on the legitimacy of such laws. According to these justices, the primary purpose of the Constitution was to protect liberty and property, and the right to liberty included within it the right to form contracts free from government interference. On occasion, however, justices issued an opinion or dissent that broke from their typical ideological patterns. In addition, a significant number of cases during the 1920s resulted in unanimous rulings.

Major Rulings

The Supreme Court decided a number of significant cases on a range of issues during the 1920s, some due to recent developments or changes in American society. The prohibition of alcohol was one such recent development. In 1919, the states ratified the Eighteenth Amendment to the Constitution, which banned the sale, manufacture, and distribution of alcoholic beverages. Following its ratification, opponents attempted to challenge the constitutionality of Prohibition. The Supreme Court under White's leadership ruled in 1920 that the Eighteenth Amendment was valid. In general, the Court interpreted the amendment broadly, rather than narrowly; thus, while the text of the amendment specifically addressed alcohol as a beverage and did not discuss medicinal uses, the Court nevertheless upheld federal limitations on the latter in *Lambert v. Yellowley* (1926).

The Supreme Court ruled on the constitutionality of another federal law in *Bailey v. Drexel Furniture Co.* (1922). The case involved a federal 10 percent income tax imposed upon companies that profited from child labor, which had been put in place early in 1919. Disregarding the label "tax," the Court determined that the law was really a federal attempt to regulate and discourage child labor, which the Court in an earlier case had concluded was beyond Congress's power to accomplish. The tax was ruled invalid.

Cases involving economic regulations were of particular significance, as rulings were frequently based upon the theory of substantive due process. The Court invalidated state laws setting minimum and maximum bread loaf sizes, prohibiting the use of scrap fabric for bedding filling, regulating ticket resale prices, and requiring that pharmacies be owned only by pharmacists. In each case, the court argued that the law violated the rights of the businesses by imposing regulations deemed unreasonable or arbitrary. The Supreme Court also invalidated state laws that it deemed to infringe upon personal liberty, including laws that forbade the teaching of foreign languages to young children and the operation of private schools.

The Supreme Court also ruled against federal laws, using similar lines of reasoning. One notable example was *Adkins v. Children's Hospital* (1923), in which the Court struck down a federal law mandating a minimum wage for women and children working in Washington, D.C. Again basing its decision on substantive due process, the Court ruled that the law violated the employer's freedom of contract.

As in any decade, the Supreme Court decided a number of important criminal procedure cases, including *Olmstead v. United States* (1928), which ruled that wiretapping did not violate the rights of defendants in criminal cases. In addition, the Court decided several cases based on procedural due process, which prohibits the government from depriving citizens of freedom or property without due process of law. In *Moore v. Dempsey* (1923), the Supreme Court overturned the convictions of a group of African American men on the basis that the men's trials had been influenced by an angry mob and therefore had not been conducted in a fair manner. As the trials had not followed due process of law, the men could not be deprived of their freedom. This ruling established a precedent for Supreme Court intervention into state judiciary matters in addition to legislation.

Impact

Near the end of his tenure as chief justice, Taft set in motion plans to construct the United States Supreme Court building. The building became the Court's official meeting place in 1935, and rulings made during the 1920s continued to influence the proceedings within its walls. The theory of substantive due process as used throughout the decade remained a crucial judicial tool in later years, serving as the underlying judicial principle behind a number of liberty rights, including the right to use contraception, the right to an abortion, and the generalized right to privacy.

Tung Yin

Further Reading

Ackerman, Bruce. *Transformations*. Vol. 2 in *We the People*. Reprint. Cambridge, Mass.: Belknap Press, 2000. Argues that critical events in the country's history, including the 1920s and the subsequent New Deal, by their own force changed the Constitution.

Burton, David Henry. *Taft, Holmes, and the 1920s Court: An Appraisal*. Madison, N.J.: Fairleigh Dickinson University Press, 1998. Discusses the rulings made by the Supreme Court of the 1920s, focusing on Taft and Holmes.

Currie, David P. *The Constitution in the Supreme Court: The Second Century, 1888–1986*. Chicago: University of Chicago Press, 1994. Covers the background and rulings of the major Supreme Court decisions during the 1920s.

Mason, Alpheus Thomas. *The Supreme Court from Taft to Burger*. 3d ed. Baton Rouge: Louisiana State University, 1979. Provides a historical account of the Supreme Court, with Chapter 2 focusing on Taft's tenure as chief justice.

Rehnquist, William H. *The Supreme Court*. New York: Vintage Books, 2002. Chronicles the history of the Supreme Court, with Chapter 5 focusing on Holmes and Brandeis.

Renstrom, Peter G. *The Taft Court: Justices, Rulings, and Legacy*. Santa Barbara, Calif.: ABC-CLIO, 2003. Explores the legacy of the Supreme Court under Taft's leadership.

Schwartz, Bernard. *A History of the Supreme Court*. New York: Oxford University Press, 1995. Summarizes major Supreme Court decisions in chronological order.

See also: *Adkins v. Children's Hospital; Bailey v. Drexel Furniture Co.; Gitlow v. New York* (1925); Holmes, Oliver Wendell, Jr.; *Meyer v. Nebraska; Moore v. Dempsey; Olmstead v. United States;* Stone, Harlan Fiske; Taft, William Howard

■ Swanson, Gloria

Identification: American actor
Born: March 27, 1899, Chicago, Illinois
Died: April 4, 1983, New York, New York

Gloria Swanson was a silent film icon of the 1920s known for her glamorous lifestyle and elaborate costumes. Popular with both audiences and critics, she was nominated for the first Academy Award for Best Actress in 1929. As talking motion pictures became popular, Swanson was one of the few silent actors to successfully transition to this new medium.

Gloria Swanson, born Gloria Josephine Mae Svensson, began her career as an extra in a film studio based in her hometown of Chicago, where she worked with such actors as Charlie Chaplin. Relocating to Hollywood, California, in the mid-1910s, she began to work with director Cecil B. DeMille, who cast her as a femme fatale or romantic lead in several films in the early 1920s, including *Why Change Your Wife?* (1920) and *The Affairs of Anatol* (1921).

Swanson appeared in more than twenty-five films throughout the 1920s. She became known for starring in period films and costume dramas with many different leading men, including her friend Rudolph Valentino. Though small in stature, she wore an impressive array of jewels, feathers, beads, and rich fabrics in such films, and her costumes became as popular as her performances. In 1927, Swanson turned down a studio contract that, though lucrative, would have required her to appear in films of the studio's choosing. Preferring to retain control over her career, Swanson began to produce her own films and distribute them through United Artists, a studio founded by a group of actors that included Chaplin. This proved difficult and less profitable than her earlier career, though some of her films from this period did achieve critical and popular success.

Swanson's first film as an independent actor, *The Love of Sunya*, opened in 1927. It was followed in 1928 by the controversial *Sadie Thompson*, for which Swanson was nominated for an Academy Award for Best Actress. In 1929, she starred in *Queen Kelly*, directed by Erich von Stroheim and produced by Joseph P. Kennedy (father of President John F. Kennedy), with whom she was linked romantically. Unlike many others actors of the silent era, Swanson was able to make the transition to sound films by the end of the decade. She even demonstrating her singing voice in her first talkie, *The Trespasser* (1929), for which she received her second Academy Award nomination.

Impact

Gloria Swanson continued to act for several decades, appearing in various films, television programs, and theatrical productions. She experienced a resurgence in popularity after returning to the big screen in 1950 to star in *Sunset Boulevard*—about, appropriately, an aging silent film actress. This role garnered Swanson her third Best Actress Academy Award nomination and a Golden Globe Award.

Dolores A. D'Angelo

Further Reading

Beauchamp, Cari. *Joseph P. Kennedy Presents: His Hollywood Years.* New York: Alfred A. Knopf, 2009.

Quirk, Lawrence J. *The Films of Gloria Swanson.* Seacaucus, N.J.: Citadel Press, 1984.

Swanson, Gloria. *Swanson on Swanson.* New York: Random House, 1981.

See also: Academy Awards; Chaplin, Charlie; DeMille, Cecil B.; Film; Valentino, Rudolph

T

■ Taft, William Howard

Identification: U.S. Supreme Court chief justice
Born: September 15, 1857, Cincinnati, Ohio
Died: March 8, 1930, Washington, D.C.

The first former president of the United States to serve as chief justice, William H. Taft led the Supreme Court from mid-1921 through early 1930. Serving alongside notable associate justices, some of whom he had appointed himself, he ruled on numerous cases related to major concerns of the decade, including Prohibition, economic regulation, and civil rights.

William Howard Taft rose to prominence as a judge late in the nineteenth century and served as U.S. solicitor general, governor of the Philippines, and secretary of war before being elected president in 1908. After leaving office in 1913, Taft joined the faculty of Yale University as Chancellor Kent Professor of Law and Legal History. During World War I, Taft served as president of the League to Enforce Peace, an organization that promoted international cooperation.

Supreme Court

Following the May 1921 death of Edward Douglass White, whom Taft had appointed to the position of chief justice of the United States in 1910, President Warren G. Harding nominated Taft as White's successor. Taft's anti-Prohibition views and support of the League of Nations somewhat conflicted with the "return to normalcy" heralded by Harding, but his reputation as a jurist was indisputable. On June 30, 1921, Taft was officially appointed to the Supreme Court.

At the start of his tenure as chief justice, Taft worked alongside associate justices Oliver Wendell Holmes Jr., Willis Van Deventer, James Clark McReynolds, Louis Dembitz Brandeis, John Hessin Clarke, William Rufus Day, Mahlon Pitney, and Joseph McKenna. Taft had appointed Van Deventer and Pitney to

William Howard Taft. (Hulton Archive/Getty Images)

their positions during his presidency. Following the resignation of Clarke and the respective retirements of Day, Pitney, and McKenna, Taft and his colleagues were joined by George Sutherland, Pierce Butler, Edward Terry Sanford, and Harlan Fiske Stone. The Court would not undergo any further changes in membership between Stone's appointment in 1925 and Taft's retirement in 1930. In 1929, Taft argued in favor of moving the Court from the Capitol to a new Supreme Court building. Construction would begin early in the next decade.

Rulings

Taft was a relatively conservative justice. He believed that the Supreme Court had both the authority and the responsibility to overturn state and federal laws if they violated the due process clauses included in the Fifth and Fourteenth Amendments to the U.S. Constitution, which stipulated that the government could not deprive an individual of life, liberty, or property in an arbitrary manner or without following the proper procedures. When applied to businesses rather than individuals, this interpretation frequently resulted in the abolishment of laws intended to regulate industry. In *Bailey v. Drexel Furniture Company* (1922), Taft wrote the majority opinion that struck down a federal tax on the income of businesses that employed children. Taft determined that the 10 percent tax was an unreasonable penalty against businesses engaging in legal practices, instituted as a federal attempt to discourage child labor. The Court had previously determined that the regulation of child labor was a state, rather than federal, concern.

Despite his tendency to rule against regulations that interfered with the rights of businesses to form contracts and conduct affairs without government interference, Taft argued in favor of such regulations on some occasions. Perhaps the most notable of these instances was his dissent in *Adkins v. Children's Hospital* (1923), which concerned a federal law that set a minimum wage for women and children working in Washington, D.C. Taft believed that the precedent for such regulations had already been set and that the decision upon which the majority ruling was largely based had since been overruled. In addition, Taft upheld federal mandates over states' rights in a number of cases, including *Stafford v. Wallace* (1922), which affirmed the federal government's right to regulate the meatpacking industry.

During his tenure, Taft also determined the applicability of the Fourth and Fifth Amendments to new technologies. In *Carroll v. United States* (1925), he ruled to permit authorities to search automobiles without a warrant if they had sufficient reason to believe that alcohol or other illicit items were inside. In *Olmstead v. United States* (1928), Taft ruled that wiretapping telephones without a warrant did not violate an individual's rights to freedom from unreasonable searches and seizures or freedom from self-incrimination.

Throughout the 1920s, Taft's judgments affirmed the "separate but equal" doctrine that originated in *Plessy v. Ferguson* (1896), the judicial cornerstone of legalized racial segregation. His ruling in *Lum v. Rice* (1927), in favor of Mississippi school officials who prevented a Chinese girl from attending a high school explicitly reserved for white students, was based on the precedent of *Plessy*. However, Taft opposed the codification of Jim Crow practices that applied to most public places. While he approved of segregated schooling, his political ideology led him to conclude that states should not regulate practices such as mixed seating in public spaces such as theaters.

Impact

William Howard Taft continued to serve as chief justice until February 1930, when he retired due to poor health. His work with the Court influenced law and politics in the United States throughout the following decades, and the Supreme Court building, completed in 1935, remained in use into the next century.

Charles H. Ford

Further Reading

Burton, David Henry. *Taft, Holmes, and the 1920s Court: An Appraisal*. Madison, N.J.: Fairleigh Dickinson University Press, 1998. Discusses the rulings made by the Supreme Court of the 1920s, focusing on Taft and Holmes.

Mason, Alpheus Thomas. *The Supreme Court From Taft to Burger*. Baton Rouge: Louisiana State University, 1979. Provides a historical account of the Supreme Court, with Chapter 2 focusing on Taft's tenure.

_____. *William Howard Taft, Chief Justice*. New York: Simon & Schuster, 1965. Analyzes Taft's rulings as chief justice and impact on the federal government.

Renstrom, Peter. *The Taft Court: Justices, Rulings, and Legacy*. Santa Barbara, Calif.: ABC-CLIO, 2003. Explores the legacy of the Supreme Court under Taft's leadership.

Schwartz, Bernard. *A History of the Supreme Court*. New York: Oxford University Press, 1995. Summarizes major Supreme Court decisions, organized chronologically.

See also: *Adkins v. Children's Hospital;* Jim Crow in the U.S. South; *Olmstead v. United States;* Supreme Court, U.S.

Tales of the Jazz Age

Identification: Collection of short stories about the Jazz Age
Author: F. Scott Fitzgerald
Date: 1922

Published two years after the release of his best-selling novel This Side of Paradise *(1920),* Tales of the Jazz Age *further established F. Scott Fitzgerald as one of the preeminent writers of the 1920s. Comprising various unconnected short stories, the collection sought to capture the spirit and contradictions of the Jazz Age.*

Tales of the Jazz Age collects eleven short stories by F. Scott Fitzgerald, many of which originally appeared in publications such as *Vanity Fair* and *The Smart Set.* Unlike Fitzgerald's novels, which feature relatively similar character types, *Tales of the Jazz Age* offers a wide range of characters representing various ideals of life in the 1920s. Often examining the nature of the American Dream, the stories also venture into modes of fantasy, naturalism, and allegory. Fitzgerald explores lyrical and subtly tragic topics as well as scenarios reminiscent of his later novel *The Great Gatsby* (1925). The book's table of contents includes a brief introduction to each story, and the stories themselves are divided into three sections titled "My Last Flappers," "Fantasies," and "Unclassified Masterpieces."

The four stories included in the "My Last Flappers" section reveal Fitzgerald's social conscience and portray the fallacy and failures of the American Dream. "May Day" contrasts the tumultuous events of the 1919 May Day riots with the privilege of a group of Yale alumni, while "The Camel's Back" depicts the struggle between the bourgeoisie and the proletariat and illustrates the reckless sort of wealth promoted by some during the 1920s.

The tone of Fitzgerald's introduction to each of the four stories in the "Fantasies" section is lighthearted and almost dismissive, yet each story explores the human condition, the illusion of social constructs, and the corruptive power of wealth. In "The Curious Case of Benjamin Button," Fitzgerald weaves a Kafkaesque tale of a man, born old, who grows younger as time passes. He ends the tale with a sense of loss and disillusionment that features prominently in many of his works.

"Unclassified Masterpieces," the final section, contains the remaining three stories, "The Lees of Happiness," "Mr. Icky," and "Jemina."

Impact

Tales of the Jazz Age revealed the multidimensionality of a period often remembered in later decades as an era of carefree growth and prosperity, calling attention to the fact that the wealth and success of the American Dream were not always attainable. The collection further demonstrated Fitzgerald's versatility as an author, proving that he was not limited to the themes and styles presented in the novels for which he would become most famous.

Karen E. Tatum

Further Reading

Eble, Kenneth Eugene. *F. Scott Fitzgerald*. Boston: Twayne, 1984.

Fitzgerald, F. Scott. *Before Gatsby: The First Twenty-Six Stories*. Edited by Matthew J. Bruccoli. Columbia: University of South Carolina Press, 2001.

See also: Fitzgerald, F. Scott; Fitzgerald, Zelda; *Great Gatsby, The;* Lost Generation; Roaring Twenties; *This Side of Paradise;* World War I veterans

Talking motion pictures

The advent of talking motion pictures in the 1920s transformed the film industry, effectively creating a new medium. Using a variety of sound-on-film and sound-on-disk systems, studios introduced actors' voices to audiences and popularized the musical as a film genre. This technological advance led to the abrupt decline of the silent film, ending the careers of many actors of the silent era.

Efforts to produce talking motion pictures, also known as "talkies" or sound films, began late in the nineteenth century. In the mid-1890s, inventor Thomas A. Edison and his colleagues experimented with the linking of film and the phonograph through the Kinetophone system, which displayed short films with minimally synchronized musical accompaniment. In 1913, Edison introduced a new Kinetophone that played film and sound that had been recorded simultaneously. Others also attempted to make sound films during the first two decades of the twentieth century, including French inventor Eugène

Lauste. Lauste recorded brief films using the sound-on-film recording method, in which the accompanying sound was written directly onto the film.

Synchronized Sound Technology
In the 1920s, a number of individuals and companies worked to develop practical systems for recording talking motion pictures. Lee de Forest, the inventor of the sound-amplifying audion tube, built upon the work of earlier inventors to develop the Phonofilm system, which used the sound-on-film recording method. This technology was used to produce numerous short films, mostly of musical performances by opera singers, Broadway and vaudeville stars, and other performers. De Forest was also responsible for the first recording of a president to feature sound, filming four minutes of a 1924 speech by Calvin Coolidge. Despite these innovations, the film industry remained largely uninterested in sound films.

Major companies involved in the development of talking motion pictures included Bell Laboratories, a research and development facility owned by the American Telephone and Telegraph Company (AT&T) and Western Electric. Bell Laboratories introduced a new recording system based on the sound-on-disc recording method, in which sound was recorded onto a separate disk similar to a phonograph record. In 1926, Warner Bros. purchased the rights to use the Vitaphone sound-on-disk technology developed at Bell Laboratories. While the majority of film studios did not follow suit until later in the decade, the Fox Film Corporation licensed equipment and began producing sound films with a sound-on-film system known as Movietone.

The move toward talking motion pictures not only necessitated the use of synchronized sound systems such as Vitaphone and Movietone but also the development of practical recording equipment. Cameras were particularly problematic, as they often made a great deal of noise. While this noise had little effect on the recording of silent films, it interfered with the production of sound films. Cameras were therefore placed within soundproof booths, limiting their mobility. By the end of the decade, film crews began to muffle the noise using camera covers known as "blimps."

First Sound Films
In August of 1926, Warner Bros. began releasing feature-length films with synchronized recorded music

Lee De Forest's Phonofilm sound-on-film process produced a few short films but was not a hit with audiences. (Getty Images)

and no dialogue. The first of these was *Don Juan*, starring John Barrymore. Such features were typically accompanied by a series of short sound films, some of which featured opera singers and other musical talent. A few contained straight dialogue, such as the spoken introduction to *Don Juan* given by William Hays, head of the Motion Picture Producers and Distributors of America. In October of 1927, Warner Bros. released *The Jazz Singer*, a sentimental tale starring popular vaudeville and Broadway star Al Jolson. Essentially a silent film with some interpolated songs and a few lines of ad-libbed dialogue by Jolson, *The Jazz Singer* became incredibly popular.

Following the success of *The Jazz Singer*, Warner Bros. and other studios created additional partial sound films, and in 1928, Warner Bros. produced *Lights of New York*, the first feature-length film to include synchronized dialogue throughout. Fox produced a variety of talking motion pictures, including the Academy Award–winning *In Old Arizona* (1928), in addition to numerous newsreels with synchronized sound. Despite their initial misgivings, major studios such as Metro-Goldwyn-Mayer (MGM) eventually began to produce sound films, particularly musicals. The MGM musical *The Broadway Melody* (1929) became the first talking motion picture to win the Academy Award for Outstanding Picture, later known as Best Picture.

Impact

While the development and popularization of talking motion pictures in the 1920s ushered in a new era of films, stars, and studios, it led to an abrupt decline in the popularity of silent films, which would effectively cease production in the following decade. Numerous stars of the silent era were unable to make the transition into sound films due to their unsuitable voices or acting styles, and many directors of silent films failed to flourish as well. In later decades, the sound-on-film system triumphed over sound-on-disk system, leading to further innovations in synchronized sound.

Roy Liebman

Further Reading

Eyman, Scott. *The Speed of Sound: Hollywood and the Talkie Revolution, 1926–1930.* New York: Simon & Schuster, 1997. Chronicles the transition from silent films to talking motion pictures and its effects on the film industry.

Geduld, Harry M. *The Birth of the Talkies: From Edison to Jolson.* Bloomington, Ind.: Indiana University Press, 1975. Provides a history of the development of the sound film.

Gomery, Douglas. *The Coming of Sound: A History.* New York: Routledge, 2005. Explores the role of talking motion pictures as tools of economic and social change.

Liebman, Roy. *Vitaphone Films: A Catalogue of the Features and Shorts.* Jefferson, N.C.: McFarland, 2009. Collects information on the various Vitaphone films produced in the 1920s and after.

Walker, Alexander. *The Shattered Silents: How the Talkies Came to Stay.* Reprint. London: Harrap, 1986. Describes the transition from silent films to talking motion pictures and its results.

See also: Academy Awards; Electrical recording; Film; Inventions

■ Tarkington, Booth

Identification: American novelist
Born: July 29, 1869, Indianapolis, Indiana
Died: May 19, 1946, Indianapolis, Indiana

A popular fiction writer of the 1920s, Booth Tarkington captured the public imagination with wry, perceptive narratives of the contemporary middle class. His novels about adolescent boys enjoyed an enduring popularity with teens and adults alike. Tarkington was awarded the Pulitzer Prize for fiction in 1922.

Born into an upper-middle-class midwestern family, Newton Booth Tarkington experienced firsthand the effects of the rapid growth and industrialization that featured prominently in his later novels. His writing career began in 1899 and was already well established by 1920. Several of his earlier works continued to be best sellers well into the 1920s, including *Penrod* (1914) and *Penrod and Sam* (1916), as well as the first two books of the Growth trilogy, *The Turmoil* (1915) and *The Magnificent Ambersons* (1918), the latter of which won the 1919 Pulitzer Prize for the Novel.

During the 1920s, Tarkington published numerous novels and short stories, most notably *Alice Adams* (1921), which won the 1922 Pulitzer Prize for the Novel and established Tarkington as the first author to win the award more than once. The bittersweet story of a young lower-middle-class woman and her unsuccessful attempt to marry above her station, the novel treats the subject with humor and realism and turns what another writer might view as a tragedy into a message of cautious, ambiguous optimism. Another major work, *The Midlander* (1924), concludes the Growth trilogy and critiques the rampant growth, pollution, and urban sprawl of the 1920s.

In addition to his prose, Tarkington wrote scripts for a number of plays, including *The Country Cousin* (1921), *The Intimate Strangers* (1921), and *The Wren* (1922). His 1916 novel *Seventeen* formed the basis for the musical *Hello, Lola* (1926). Several of his works were adapted into silent films, including *The Magnificent Ambersons* (as *Pampered Youth*, 1925), *Penrod* (1922), *Alice Adams* (1923), *Gentle Julia* (1923), and *Monsieur Beaucaire* (1924), a historical romance written early in Tarkington's career.

Impact

While some later critics characterized Booth Tarkington's works as lacking in social impact and perpetuating contemporary prejudicial attitudes toward women and minorities, others praised his novels as accurate depictions of 1920s society that reveal the character of the era with minimal judgment. Regardless, Tarkington's works continued to inspire stage and film adaptations, most notably writer and director Orson Welles's 1942 adaptation of *The Magnificent Ambersons*, which was nominated for several Academy Awards.

Martha A. Sherwood

Further Reading

Gray, Donald. Introduction to *Alice Adams*, by Booth Tarkington. Bloomington: Indiana University Press, 2003.

Mayberry, Susanah. *My Amiable Uncle: Recollections About Booth Tarkington*. West Lafayette, Ind.: Purdue University Press, 1986.

Woodress, James Leslie. *Booth Tarkington, Gentleman from Indiana*. Philadelphia: Lippincott, 1955.

See also: *Alice Adams;* Book publishing; Theater in the United States; Valentino, Rudolph

■ Taylor, William Desmond

Identification: American actor and director
Born: April 26, 1872, Carlow, Ireland
Died: February 1, 1922, Los Angeles, California

William Desmond Taylor was an actor who went on to become a noted director of silent films, serving as president of the Motion Picture Directors Association for several years. He was murdered in 1922, and although investigators identified several suspects, the crime was never solved. Taylor's murder and its investigation captivated the American public and drew attention to the negative aspects of the film industry.

William Desmond Taylor, born William Cunningham Deane-Tanner, immigrated to the United States in 1890 and had entered the film industry by 1913. He acted in silent films, primarily shorts, and began to direct in 1914. Taylor rose to prominence directing films for popular actors such as Mary Pickford and Mary Miles Minter. He directed more than fifty films during his career, with more than ten of them released between 1920 and mid-1922.

On February 2, 1922, Taylor was found dead of a gunshot wound. Discovered in the living room of his Hollywood home by valet Henry Peavey, Taylor was still in possession of his wallet and valuable jewelry, indicating robbery had not been the motive for his murder. The police investigation revealed that in his final hours, Taylor was visited by actor and friend Mabel Normand. As the last person to see Taylor alive, she became one of several suspects identified by the police; others included notable Hollywood figures such as Minter and her protective mother, Charlotte Shelby. Taylor had directed Minter in several films, and it had been rumored that they were in a romantic relationship.

The investigation of the crime was compromised from the beginning, as various neighbors, reporters, and possibly even studio executives had entered the bungalow prior to the arrival of the police, disturbing the crime scene and evidence. Thus, despite the numerous suspects, Taylor's murder remained unsolved.

Impact

While William Desmond Taylor's films contributed to the careers of numerous actors and the overall development of the film industry, his murder had perhaps the greatest lasting effect. Taylor's murder was one of several major Hollywood scandals of the decade, and these scandals caused various political and religious groups to call for the regulation of the seemingly immoral industry. Such pressure led to the creation of the Motion Picture Producers and Distributors of America and the Motion Picture Production Code, ushering in several decades of censorship.

Amanda J. Bahr-Evola

Further Reading

Giroux, Robert. *A Deed of Death*. New York: Knopf, 1990.

Jacobson, Laurie. *Hollywood Heartbreak: The Tragic and Mysterious Deaths of Hollywood's Most Remarkable Legends*. New York: Simon and Schuster, 1984.

Kirkpatrick, Sidney. *A Cast of Killers*. Reprint. Stony Brook, N.Y. Author, 2007.

See also: Crimes and scandals; Film; Normand, Mabel

Teapot Dome scandal

The Event: Disclosure of corrupt leasing of federal oil lands reserved for the Navy
Date: 1921 to 1931

The leasing of federal oil fields by Interior Secretary Albert B. Fall in return for bribes was the first scandal of President Warren G. Harding's administration to come to public attention. It became a symbol of the corruption and criminal activity of Harding appointees, for which many historians rate Harding among the worst American presidents.

In the early years of the twentieth century, most experts believed the world would run out of oil in a few decades. When the U.S. Navy shifted from coal to oil as a fuel source, Presidents William E. Taft in 1912 and Woodrow Wilson in 1915 dedicated two oil fields in California (Elk Hills and Buena Vista) and one in Wyoming (Teapot Dome) to serve as reserves dedicated to the U.S. Navy.

Many in the western United States were skeptical of conservation efforts and firmly believed that the nation's welfare—as well as their own—would be enhanced if all natural resources on federal land were open to exploitation. Senator Albert B. Fall of New Mexico, a mine owner and rancher, shared these views and proceeded to act on them when appointed secretary of the interior by President Warren G. Harding in 1921. Conservationists blocked his attempt to move the Forest Service into his department, where he could have opened the national forests to lumber and mining interests. However, in May 1921, two months after he took office, Fall convinced Secretary of the Navy Edwin Denby to transfer control of the naval oil reserves to Fall's department, and the transfer took place the following year.

Western oil operators were eager to drill in reserves estimated to be worth over $100 million, and Fall proceeded to secretly negotiate no-bid leases of the California reserves with Edward L. Doheny, head of Pan American Petroleum, and the Teapot Dome reserves with Harry Sinclair of Mammoth Oil. Although Fall may have acted out of sincerely held beliefs, he was not above accepting rewards for his services.

Senate Hearings

The contracts could not be kept secret, however. A neighbor complained to his senator about the drilling

Albert Fall, pictured here, was involved in the Teapot Dome scandal. (Getty Images)

at Teapot Dome, and subsequent Senate inquiries forced Fall to acknowledge the secret leases, which then led to appointment of an investigative committee headed by Democratic Senator Thomas J. Walsh of Montana. Since the questions first arose over the Teapot Dome oil field, that became the accepted title for the entire affair. The committee's request produced thousands of pages of documents, along with a letter of transmittal from President Harding asserting he knew and fully approved of what Fall had done—a document that would greatly damage Harding's reputation.

Senator Walsh spent eighteen months analyzing the information. By the time hearings opened in October 1923, Fall had retired, Harding had died, and Calvin Coolidge had become president. The hearings attracted little attention. Fall adamantly insisted everything he had done was proper and that secrecy was necessary, since it was a national defense matter. Much of the early testimony consisted of the conflicting opinions of independent geologists and oil company employees over the best way to handle the reserves. Bored reporters stopped covering the hearings.

In December, Walsh heard from Fall's neighbors in New Mexico that Fall had suddenly become wealthy in 1922, paying off long-overdue debts and buying a neighboring ranch. Interest in the hearing intensified and reporters returned. Fall denied receiving any money from the oil companies and claimed he had borrowed $100,000 from newspaper publisher Edward McLean. This assertion backfired as soon as McLean did not confirm Fall's testimony.

Called back to the hearings, Doheny apologized for neglecting to tell the committee he had lent Fall the $100,000. Newspapers gleefully reported Doheny's description of sending his son from California to a New York bank, where he received five bundles of $20,000 each, put them in a plain black satchel, and carried the money to Fall's Washington hotel suite, where Fall counted the money and signed a note for the loan. Doheny insisted the loan had nothing to do with the lease he expected Fall would shortly award him.

Sinclair refused to testify, but the committee's threat to prosecute Mahlon T. Everhart, Fall's son-in-law, forced Everhart to recount how he had collected $198,000 in government bonds from Sinclair and delivered them to Fall, and later went back for more. Fall's total take for the leases may have exceeded $400,000.

Prosecution
When Walsh asked the Senate to call on the president to cancel the leases and appoint a special prosecutor, Coolidge preempted Senate action by appointing two prosecutors in January 1924, a Republican and a Democrat, to act together on the affair. The resulting prosecutions lasted for the rest of the decade. Doheny and Sinclair fought termination of their leases all the way to the Supreme Court, which affirmed in 1927 that the leases were fraudulent.

Juries proved reluctant to convict Fall and the oil men of criminal conspiracy to defraud the United States. Doheny and Fall were tried in Washington, D.C., in October 1926. Fall did not testify, but Doheny proved an excellent witness, convincing the jury that he was just trying to help an old friend when he lent Fall $100,000. The joint trial of Sinclair and Fall did not begin until October 1927 and quickly ended in a mistrial when Sinclair was discovered trying to bribe several jurors. Sinclair went to jail for nearly seven months, but when the trial resumed in 1928, he was found not guilty.

Fall and Doheny were tried separately on bribery charges. The first jury found Fall guilty of accepting a bribe; a few months later, however, another jury acquitted Doheny of offering a bribe, Doheny again claiming the $100,000 he gave Fall was a compassionate loan. In contrast, Fall faced an insurmountable obstacle in trying to explain why he lied to the Senate committee; that he thought he needed to lie was convincing evidence he knew taking the money was wrong. Fall was sentenced to a year in prison and fined $100,000. After losing a final appeal in 1931, he was jailed for nine months, making him the first U.S. cabinet member to be imprisoned for wrongdoings in office.

Impact
Democrats optimistically hoped Teapot Dome and other scandals would assure them of victory in 1924. They were wrong: Teapot Dome had little effect. In 1924, Republicans blamed the scandal on the actions of a few rogue individuals and noted that Democratic politicians had also taken money from oil interests. Coolidge was untouched by the affair and claimed credit for appointing the prosecutors. Teapot Dome had even less impact on the 1928 campaign, when Democrats attacked Herbert Hoover because he was in the cabinet as commerce secretary when Harding approved the leases.

The greatest victim of the scandal was Fall. By the time he went to jail, he had exhausted his money and could not repay the $100,000 loan from Doheny. After Doheny died in 1935, his widow called in the loan and seized Fall's beloved ranch. Broke, aging, and ill, Fall was in and out of Veterans Administration hospitals until his death in 1944.

Although Teapot Dome was only one of the Harding-era scandals, it became the most visible public symbol of the administration's corruption, which included the head of the Veterans Bureau, Charles Forbes, embezzling funds intended for veterans hospitals; Alien Property Custodian Thoms Miller being jailed for soliciting bribes; and Attorney General Harry Daugherty only narrowly avoiding jail for selling access to his office. Because the oil reserve leases were the only scandal that Harding actually asserted in writing that he knew of and approved, it blackened his reputation more than any other.

Milton Berman

Further Reading

Davis, Margaret Leslie. *Dark Side of Fortune: Triumph and Scandal in the Life of Oil Tycoon Edward L. Doheny.* Berkeley: University of California Press, 2001. An account of Doheny's business career, with coverage of the Teapot Dome scandal.

Dean, John W. *Warren G. Harding.* New York: Times Books, 2004. Discusses the effectiveness of the Harding administration aside from the scandals and corruption.

McCartney, Laton. *The Teapot Dome Scandal: How Big Oil Bought the Harding White House and Tried to Steal the Country.* New York: Random House, 2008. Provides a detailed account of the scandal and the individuals involved.

Noggle, Burl. *Teapot Dome: Oil and Politics in the 1920s.* New York: Norton, 1965. Examines the scandal from the viewpoint of a conflict between conservationists and developers for control of public lands.

Stratton, David H. *Tempest Over Teapot Dome: The Story of Albert B. Fall.* Norman: University of Oklahoma Press, 1998. Explores Fall's political background, his role in the Harding administration in light of crime and corruption in the 1920s, and his life post–Teapot Dome.

See also: Coolidge, Calvin; Crimes and scandals; Daugherty, Harry M.; Forbes, Charles R.; Harding, Warren G.; Natural resources, exploitation of

■ Teasdale, Sara

Identification: American poet
Born: August 8, 1884, St. Louis, Missouri
Died: January 29, 1933, New York, New York

Although Sara Teasdale established her reputation as a poet before 1920, her work continued to be published and highly regarded throughout the decade. Particularly known for her lyricism, Teasdale meditated on such topics as love, death, and the spiritual legacy of World War I.

Sara Trevor Teasdale was born into a wealthy family in St. Louis, Missouri. She published her first collection of poetry, *Sonnets to Duse and Other Poems*, in 1907. This volume featured poetry inspired by Italian stage actor Eleonora Duse, who also served as a source of inspiration for poet Amy Lowell, a contemporary of Teasdale. After publishing the collections *Helen of Troy and Other Poems* (1911) and *Rivers to the Sea* (1915), Teasdale was awarded the Columbia Poetry Prize for her 1917 collection *Love Songs*; this award would later be known as the Pulitzer Prize in poetry.

Teasdale continued to publish books of poetry during the 1920s, beginning the decade with *Flame and Shadow* (1920), a collection of ninety-two poems that was met with strong sales and critical praise. Another critically acclaimed collection, *Dark of the Moon*, was published in 1926. Teasdale also edited the poetry anthology *Rainbow Gold* (1922), selecting a wide variety of poems that she believed would appeal to children.

While many of Teasdale's poems of the 1920s are deeply personal and seem removed from the issues and controversies of the decade, her recurring depression and obsession with death gave her work a thematic connection to that of many poets and writers of the era, a significant number of whom had difficulty dealing with conventional relationships and societal expectations. Teasdale was also deeply affected by World War I, and this influence is particularly evident in *Flame and Shadow*. Observing the war's devastating effect on civilization, Teasdale questions the notion of an ordered universe in poems such as "A Boy." In "There Will Come Soft Rains (War Time)," she goes so far as to prophesy a future in which the earth endures even after humankind has destroyed itself.

Impact

In a decade marked by the rejection of nineteenth-century literary conventions, Sara Teasdale echoed and modified such poetic traditions, reflecting the despair of many postwar writers while declining to adopt the new styles of free verse and terse imagism. She continued to publish poetry in this signature lyrical style into the early 1930s, with her final collection, *Strange Victory*, being published posthumously in 1933.

Carl Rollyson

Further Reading

Drake, William. *Sara Teasdale: Woman and Poet.* Knoxville: University of Tennessee Press, 1989.

Schoen, Carol. *Sara Teasdale.* Boston, Mass.: Twayne, 1986.

Showalter, Elaine. *A Jury of Her Peers: American Women Writers from Anne Bradstreet to Annie Proulx*. New York: Vintage Books, 2010.

See also: Lowell, Amy; Millay, Edna St. Vincent; Poetry; Wylie, Elinor

■ Telephone technology and service

As the 1920s began, the U.S. telephone industry remained in a disorganized state. Thousands of telephone companies competed with one another, regulated by erratic legislation, while technological developments most often addressed side issues rather than mainstream telephone operation. In these early years, the industry was still feeling its way.

Alexander Graham Bell's patents expired in 1893 and 1894, and for the next quarter century, thousands of entrepreneurs formed telephone companies. For the most part they were in competition with the Bell System and its parent company, the American Telephone and Telegraph Company (AT&T). By 1903, these independent companies provided service for more than half the telephones in operation in the United States.

After former AT&T president Theodore Vail came out of retirement in 1907 to take up his position once again, the primary goal of the Bell System became to create a single nationwide telephone company. AT&T was eager to establish a vertically integrated organization that would include design and development, manufacturing, operation of local telephone companies, and a long-distance network. Such an approach was not viewed favorably by those thousands of entrepreneurs forming their own telephone companies. Representatives of the Bell System worked to prevent the establishment of new independent telephone companies and made arrangements to purchase independents that were already in operation. The Bell System also refused to allow these independents to interconnect with its existing long-distance network.

Regulation of the Telephone Industry

In 1913, the Justice Department warned AT&T of an impending antitrust investigation. The company agreed to a settlement in order to prevent further government action. The settlement, called the Kingsbury Commitment, required AT&T to cease its takeovers of independent companies and to allow the independents to connect to Bell's long-distance network. This victory for the independents was undone several years later, in 1921, when Congress passed an amendment to the Transportation Act that gave the Interstate Commerce Commission (ICC) strong powers to rule on telephone company mergers, thereby superseding the Kingsbury Commitment. However, in 1922, AT&T vice president E. K. Hall officially stated that the company would continue to refrain from purchasing competitors, as it was in the interest of both the Bell System and the independent companies to have two strong groups in the industry. Although the Bell System would occasionally absorb independents in special circumstances, the industry entered a period of relative stability.

Technology

In the early twentieth century, the Bell System had concentrated on establishing a nationwide telephone system by building and absorbing local telephone companies and constructing a highly efficient long-distance network. Until 1920, the developed systems were manual, meaning they involved the completion of calls by operators rather than by machines. While Bell System managers saw no need to replace its staff of telephone operators, independent companies were less reluctant to adopt the machine-switching system, in which the subscriber would dial the other party's telephone number directly. The first such system, based on a design by Almon Brown Strowger and called a Strowger switch, was installed in La Porte, Indiana, in 1892. The Bell System first used the Strowger switch at a facility in Norfolk, Virginia, in November of 1919, while Western Electric, the Bell System's main equipment supplier, did not begin to manufacture the necessary equipment until sometime around 1926.

Aside from the Strowger switch, many other telephone-related technical advances and achievements made their appearance in the 1920s, including the first ever long-distance radio broadcast of a football game over telephone lines, from Chicago to the East Coast; the first transmission of pictures by telephone circuit, from Cleveland to New York to Chicago; the introduction of Bell System telephones with one-piece handsets, rather than a separate mouthpiece and earpiece; the first transatlantic telephone call, between New York and London; the development of the negative feedback amplifier, which made communication clearer; and installation of the first telephone on President Herbert Hoover's desk.

The End of an Era

On August 2, 1922, Alexander Graham Bell died at his summer home in Nova Scotia. Two days later, service on the entire telephone system of the United States and Canada was suspended for one minute just before sunset, from 6:25 to 6:26 P.M. eastern standard time, during his funeral service.

Impact

For the telephone industry, the 1920s was a decade of transition. The previous decade had witnessed cutthroat competition among struggling telephone companies, with the Bell System concentrating on expanding its network and the independent telephone companies focusing on their own individual territories; but the government's antitrust action led to a period of cooperation that continued through the 1920s. Many new telephone-related products were developed during this time, and the country's telephone exchanges moved from mostly manual to mostly automatic. However, like many businesses, the telephone industry suffered a severe blow during the first years of the Great Depression and did not rebound until well into the 1930s. In the United States, the industry's eventual recovery was due in part to increased federal regulation instituted by the Communications Act of 1934, which transferred oversight of telecommunications services from the ICC to the newly created Federal Communications Commission (FCC).

Robert E. Stoffels

Further Reading

Boettinger, H. M. *The Telephone Book: Bell, Watson, Vail, and American Life, 1876–1976*. Croton-on-Hudson, N.Y.: Riverwood, 1977. Pictures and text describing the telephone industry between 1876 and 1976.

Brooks, John. *Telephone: The First Hundred Years*. New York: Harper & Row, 1976. An important book dealing with the first hundred years of the telephone industry.

Coe, Lewis. *The Telephone and Its Several Inventors: A History*. Jefferson, N.C.: McFarland, 1995. Chronicles the invention of the telephone and the development of the telephone industry, including important advances made in the 1920s.

Mercer, David. *The Telephone: The Life Story of a Technology*. Westport, Conn.: Greenwood Press, 2006. A history of the telephone and its impact on society.

Pleasance, Charles A. *The Spirit of Independent Telephony: A Chronicle of the Accomplishments, Intrigue, and the Fight for Survival That Accompanied the Independent Telephone Movement in the United States*. Johnson City, Tenn.: Independent Telephone Books, 1989. A book dedicated to the independent telephone industry, including case histories of many of the independents.

See also: Bell Labs; Inventions; Science and technology

■ Television technology

The 1920s saw a number of important advances in television technology, as an electronic system of scanning and transmitting images proved far superior to the various mechanical systems of the previous decades. Scientists such as Philo Farnsworth and Vladimir Zworykin worked to develop practical devices using the electronic system, resulting in the successful transmission of clear images late in the decade.

Late in the nineteenth century, scientists theorized that light and images could be transmitted by electric wire over long distances, just as sound was transmitted over telephone wires. Based on the principle of "scanning," the process of converting visual images into electrical pulses that could then be transmitted, German inventor Paul Nipkow patented a mechanical system in the 1880s that used a spinning disk with holes that would permit light to pass through and onto a photoelectric cell, which converted the light to electricity. Another German, Karl Braun, later invented the cathode-ray tube, which would eventually become a key component in television sets. Scientists worked to refine Nipkow's mechanical system throughout the early twentieth century, and in 1907, the Russian scientist Boris Rosing patented a system that used a rotating scanner with mirrors to capture images and a cathode-ray tube to display them.

Mechanical Television

During the 1920s, a number of scientists labored to perfect Nipkow's mechanical television transmission

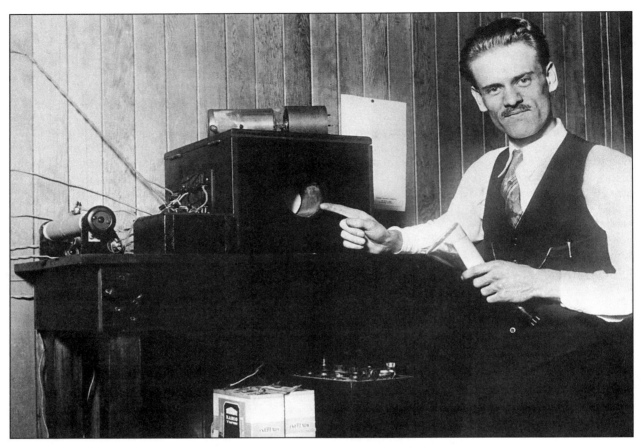
Philo T. Farnsworth invented the "electronic" transmission system. (© Bettmann/Corbis)

system. In 1925, the American inventor Charles Jenkins demonstrated a mechanical system that transmitted moving silhouettes and displayed them using a modified radio. That same year, Scottish inventor John Baird televised a human face for the first time, using a system based on a scanning disk and lenses. Herbert Ives, a scientist working for Bell Laboratories, the research and development laboratory of the American Telephone and Telegraph Company and Western Electric, transmitted moving images from Washington, D.C., to New York in 1927 using a mechanical system. These and other attempts to scan, transmit, and reassemble moving images using mechanical methods were engineering successes, but they failed to produce the clear images needed to make television a commercially viable technology rather than a novelty.

Electronic Television

One of the early pioneers of electronic television was Philo Farnsworth, a self-taught inventor from Utah. Having developed an affinity for repairing electrical equipment at an early age, Farnsworth soon became interested in radio and mechanical television technology. Early in the 1920s, the teenage Farnsworth surmised that a picture could be scanned electronically, one line at a time, just as the fields of his family's farm were plowed in rows. This scanned image could then be transmitted to a receiver. Farnsworth explained his model of television, based on the manipulation of electrons rather than a rotating mechanical device, to a teacher who took notes and copied Farnsworth's diagram illustrating the process. These records would prove vital to Farnsworth's later efforts to protect his patents.

In 1926, Farnsworth began to build and test his invention after receiving financial backing from several investors. This electronic system, which did not include the moving disks or lenses of the mechanical systems, used a glass tube that Farnsworth called an "image dissector." This tube, which contained photosensitive material, converted the light from an image into electrons. The electrical current flowed into a glass receiver, which displayed the image. Farnsworth successfully transmitted a clear image in September of 1927. Between 1927 and 1929, he successfully demonstrated this completely electronic television system to the press and public and filed a number of patents.

A Russian immigrant to the United States, Vladimir Zworykin, who had studied under Rosing, also sought to create an electronic television system during the 1920s. In 1923, while employed by Westinghouse, Zworykin applied for a patent for the iconoscope, a television camera tube that used electrons to transmit images. However, his attempts to create a working model were largely unsuccessful, and the patent would not be granted until late in the next decade. Zworykin was hired by the Radio Corporation of America (RCA) in 1929, where he became a vital contributor to the company's development of television technology.

Impact

Television technology came under intense scrutiny in the 1930s, when RCA, under the leadership of David Sarnoff, challenged Farnsworth's patents, claiming that Zworykin's 1923 patent application granted him priority of invention and established him as the true inventor of the electronic television system. A prolonged period of legal action ensued. For a number of reasons, including the fact that a working model of the device described in 1923 was not constructed until significantly after the successful testing of Farnsworth's model, the patent court ruled in favor of Farnsworth. Despite losing in court, RCA became a major force in the further development of television, displaying the latest television technology at the 1939 World's Fair in New York. The Federal Communications Commission began licensing commercial television stations in 1941, and over the next decade, early television networks began stretching across the country.

Raymond M. Weinstein

Further Reading

Godfrey, Donald G. *Philo T. Farnsworth: The Father of Television.* Salt Lake City: University of Utah Press, 2001. A biography of Farnsworth focusing on his patents and work in television.

Magoun, Alexander B. *Television: The Life Story of a Technology.* Westport, Conn.: Greenwood Press, 2007. A history of the development of television technology from the late nineteenth to the early twenty-first century.

Schatzkin, Paul. *The Boy Who Invented Television: A Story of Inspiration, Persistence and Quiet Passion.* Silver Spring, Md.: TeamCom Books, 2002. An account of Farnsworth's life from childhood, his work developing electronic television, and his struggles with financial backers.

Stashower, Daniel. *The Boy Genius and the Mogul: The Untold Story of Television.* New York: Broadway Books, 2002. A chronicle of the early lives of Farnsworth and Sarnoff and of the later legal battles between them regarding Farnsworth's and RCA's patents for electronic television.

Todorovi, Aleksandar Louis. *Television Technology Demystified: A Non-Technical Guide.* Burlington, Mass.: Focal Press, 2006. A technical history of the development of television.

See also: Electrical recording; Radio Corporation of America (RCA); Sarnoff, David; Zworykin, Vladimir

■ Ten Commandments, The

Identification: A silent film paralleling the biblical Exodus and the lives of an American family in the 1920s
Director: Cecil B. DeMille
Release Date: 1923

One of the most successful films of the silent era, The Ten Commandments *established Cecil B. DeMille's reputation as a groundbreaking director of epic films. The film's large cast, lavish sets, and innovative special effects made it one of the most expensive silent films ever produced.*

Directed by Cecil B. DeMille with a screenplay by Jeanie Macpherson, *The Ten Commandments* is essentially two films joined by an intermission. The first part of the film is the story of Moses (Theodore Roberts), an Israelite who forces Ramses (Charles de Rochefort), the Egyptian pharaoh, to free the enslaved Israelites. During their subsequent trek across the desert, Moses and his people are bestowed by God with rules by which to live their lives, known as the Ten Commandments. The second part of the film is set in the early 1920s and tells the story of two brothers, John and Dan McTavish. John (Richard Dix) is a decent man who believes God is loving and kind, while his mother, Martha (Edythe Chapman), believes God is to be feared. John's brother Dan (Rod La Rocque) rejects their mother's religious teachings and becomes an atheist. While John works as a humble carpenter, Dan makes a fortune as a contractor through dishonest business practices. When Dan uses inadequate concrete to build a new cathedral, a wall collapses and kills his mother. Dan attempts to right the wrongs he has done in his life but only manages to add to his list of sins. In the end, he breaks all ten of the commandments before dying in a boat accident.

The Ten Commandments premiered on December 4, 1923, at Grauman's Egyptian Theater in Los Angeles, California. One of the most expensive films of the decade, it also became one of the silent era's biggest hits, grossing more than $4 million at the box office. DeMille's first biblical epic, *The Ten Commandments* became especially known for its large cast and thousands of extras, elaborate sets and costumes, and creative special effects such as the use of gelatin to simulate water in the scene depicting the parting of the Red Sea. The film was one of the earliest to use a two-color Technicolor process in selected scenes and include a hand-colored segment.

Impact

Following the success of *The Ten Commandments*, DeMille went on to direct two more biblical epics, *The King of Kings* (1927) and *The Sign of the Cross* (1932). Cited by many early filmmakers as an inspiration, *The Ten Commandments* continued to influence the film industry long after the 1920s, and in 1956, it was remade by DeMille with sound and full color.

Deborah J. Wilson

Further Reading

Birchard, Robert S. *Cecil B. DeMille's Hollywood.* Lexington: University Press of Kentucky, 2004.

Higashi, Sumiko. *Cecil B. DeMille and American Culture: The Silent Era.* Berkeley: University of California Press, 1994.

See also: DeMille, Cecil B.; Film; Grauman's Chinese Theatre; Movie palaces

■ Ten Days That Shook the World

Identification: A journalist's firsthand account of the Bolshevik Revolution in Russia
Author: John Reed
Date: 1919

Ten Days That Shook the World was the most influential account of the Russian Revolution during the 1920s, both in the United States and elsewhere. The book, which celebrates the Bolshevik Revolution as the triumph of the Russian masses over the oppression of the ruling classes, met with mixed reactions due to its highly partisan character.

Ten Days That Shook the World presents American writer John Reed's personal experience of the Bolshevik Revolution in Russia. Reed, himself a socialist, believed that the revolution signified the beginning of a new era in human history, one built upon the communist ideals of radical social and economic equality. Using a plethora of materials collected during his time in Russia, Reed sought to provide his audience with an accurate firsthand account of the events surrounding the establishment of the world's first communist government.

The book is not, nor did Reed intend it to be, an unbiased account. Reed's socialist views are evident throughout the work. He argues that the revolution was the result of the miseries brought about by World War I and that the revolution represented the victory of common people over the monarchists and reactionaries who sought to maintain their power over Russia. This view contrasted significantly with prevalent attitudes toward communism in the United States in the early 1920s, when antisocialist sentiment was rampant. Due to his professed communism, Reed himself was denied entry to the United States in early 1920 and forced to return to Russia, where he died later that year.

Admirers of *Ten Days That Shook the World* included individuals as diverse as Vladimir Lenin, who wrote the foreword for the 1922 edition, and George Kennan, an American diplomat and noted anticommunist who praised the work for its raw idealism. Along with Americans who criticized the book for its communist sympathies, Joseph Stalin publicly denounced the book in 1924 for both its praise of Leon Trotsky and the absence of any substantial mention of himself.

Impact

During the 1920s and beyond, *Ten Days That Shook the World* provided Americans with an accessible firsthand account of the events of the Bolshevik Revolution. While Reed's optimism about the creation of the first communist state would later be undermined by events such as the Stalinist purges of the 1930s, the book remains an honest and detailed contemporary report on one of the most significant events of the twentieth century.

Aaron D. Horton

Further Reading

Fitzpatrick, Sheila. *The Russian Revolution.* 3d ed. Oxford: Oxford University Press, 2008.

Murray, Robert K. *Red Scare: A Study in National Hysteria, 1919–1920.* St. Paul: University of Minnesota Press, 1955.

Rosenstone, Robert A. *Romantic Revolutionary: A Biography of John Reed.* Cambridge, Mass.: Harvard University Press, 1990.

See also: Communism; Red Scare, The; Reed, John

■ Tennis

Tennis achieved a high degree of popularity during the 1920s, primarily due to the larger-than-life personalities of players such as Bill Tilden and Helen Wills Moody. Professional tennis made its appearance in the form of tours and exhibitions, but it continued to lag in popularity behind the amateur competitions of the day.

Tennis, long a leisure pursuit of the wealthy, saw its popularity expand during the prosperous 1920s as increasing numbers of people took an interest in both playing and watching the game. Lawn tennis was largely confined to the exclusive clubs of the northeastern United States, while court tennis was increasingly common in metropolitan areas and the West Coast.

Amateur Tennis

Most people familiar with tennis in the early twentieth century knew it as a recreational pastime. The game represented an opportunity to match skills as a diversion from the day's work, and the 1920s offered an increasing amount of leisure time for those working in industry, banking, or business. Tennis was easily adaptable to both men and women and lent itself well to either playing for fun or competing at the highest level, on the courts of a social club or in the emerging venues of major tournaments around the world. Within the so-called golden age of American sport, tennis was but one more example of how the individual could rise above the masses to become a local or even national hero.

Perhaps the greatest example of individual achievement in tennis throughout the 1920s was "Big" Bill Tilden, who did more than any other male player to popularize the game beyond the confines of exclusive clubs. Tilden and the French player Suzanne Lenglen captured the interest of many in both Europe and North America with their fiery brand of play, their gregarious personalities, and their flair for self-promotion.

Tilden came from a prominent Philadelphia family. After failing to make his college tennis team at the University of Pennsylvania, he dropped out of school and devoted himself to improving his playing. Although he did not rise to the top of his game until his

Bill Tilden helped popularize the game of tennis. (Hulton Archive/Getty Images)

late twenties, he eventually won seven U.S. National Championships and three British championships at Wimbledon, where he was the first American to win the men's singles championship. He played on every Davis Cup team in the 1920s, leading the United States to seven wins. Even though Tilden's reign was eventually eclipsed by France's "Four Musketeers" (Jean Borotra, Jacques Brugnon, Henri Cochet, and René Lacoste), who dominated international tennis in the latter part of the decade, he secured for himself a formidable place in the annals of American sport. In 1950, an Associated Press poll identified him as the outstanding tennis player of the first half of the twentieth century, placing him in a league with Babe Ruth (baseball), Jack Dempsey (boxing), and Bobby Jones (golf).

Lenglen had been groomed for a tennis career from an early age and thoroughly dominated the European scene. She was known for wearing low-cut dresses, arguing with linesmen, and even snubbing the British royalty at Wimbledon. Lenglen never fully captured the American audience due to defaulting in a match during her only appearance at the U.S. Nationals, but she did set the stage for the finest American woman player of the time: Helen Wills, known as Helen Wills Moody after her marriage in 1929, often called the United States' first truly international female athlete. During the decade, she won eleven of the thirteen Grand Slam events in which she played, finished in second place in the other two, and won two gold medals at the 1924 Olympic Games. She appeared on the cover of *Time* magazine twice and maintained a competitive career well into her thirties.

Professional Tennis
The amateur ideal held that the goal of sports was competition for its own sake and that true sportsmanship—and the quality of the competition itself—was demeaned by the profit motive. Although the top tennis players were at first all considered amateurs, and therefore eligible for the Grand Slam tournaments, the middle part of the 1920s saw the controversial emergence of some forms of professional tennis—that is, tennis played for profit. The better players were often sought out to teach the game to the increasing numbers of tennis hopefuls, a practice that technically made one a professional. In addition to teaching tennis, commercial ventures such as endorsements and appearance fees began to tempt those whose skills were unquestionably superior to others, offering them new opportunities to capitalize on their fame. Tilden stretched the definition of "amateur" with his career as a journalist, in which capacity he wrote and sold commentary on the game and the competitors, including discussions of some of his own matches, to feed a public hungry with fascination for the sport and its heroes. Professional baseball was the most popular American spectator sport, but the growing demand for sporting spectacles of all kinds created too much economic opportunity for amateur competition to remain the standard, in tennis or any other major sport.

Charles "C. C." Pyle is credited with being the first promoter of professional tennis competition. He sought to attract the top amateurs and succeeded in signing Lenglen and Vincent Richards, the 1924 Olympic Gold medalist in men's singles and doubles, to headline a series of exhibition matches in late 1926, beginning in New York's Madison Square Garden. Richards, the first noteworthy American player to turn professional, won three of the first four U.S. Pro Tennis Championships, the professional alternative to the U.S. National Championship.

Pyle's sponsorship soon gave way to Richards's leadership in promoting the professional game for the remainder of the decade, spurring interest in similarly professional French and British alternatives to the Grand Slam events at Roland Garros (Paris) and Wimbledon (London). Meanwhile, Tilden sought to retain his amateur status, although his journalistic writings continued to cause tension with, among others, the United States Lawn Tennis Association, which moved to suspend him from tournament and Davis Cup play in 1928. Facing diplomatic pressure from French and United States government officials, the association fully reinstated Tilden, but he eventually turned professional at the end of 1930, going on to win a professional championship in 1935 at age forty-two and playing competitively until the advent of World War II.

Impact
During the 1920s, as many sports were capturing the nation's attention following World War I, tennis evolved from a sport of the social elite to one with widespread appeal. Sportswriters, promoters, and the athletes themselves all capitalized on the public's fascination with dramatic performances and colorful personalities. This era witnessed continued

challenges to the long-held amateur ideal as professional tennis emerged in the form of worldwide tours and exhibitions, culminating in the organization of professional tournament play. However, the major world tournaments in the United States, France, and England, as well as the Olympics, fiercely maintained amateurs-only eligibility criteria. "Open" competition in tennis between amateurs and professionals would not be implemented until 1968, after which the U.S. National Championship became known as the U.S. Open.

P. Graham Hatcher

Further Reading

Baltzell, E. Digby. *Sporting Gentlemen: Men's Tennis from the Age of Honor to the Cult of the Superstar.* New York: Free Press, 1995. Examines tennis from a sociological perspective, including the sport's golden age in the 1920s.

Bohn, Michael K. *Heroes and Ballyhoo: How the Golden Age of the 1920s Transformed American Sports.* Dulles, Va.: Potomac Books, 2009. Features profiles of ten legendary athletes of the 1920s, including Tilden and Moody, and explores the beginnings of sports celebrity culture.

Deford, Frank. *Big Bill Tilden: The Triumphs and the Tragedy.* New York: Simon & Schuster, 1976. The definitive work on the tennis career and off-court tragedy of the most recognizable tennis player of the 1920s.

Voss, Arthur. *Tilden and Tennis in the Twenties.* Troy, N.Y.: Whitson, 1985. A chronicle of the game's progress and its players during the 1920s, written by a Canadian tennis champion of the era.

Williams, Paul B. *United States Lawn Tennis Association and the World War.* Charleston, S.C.: BiblioBazaar, 2009. Reprint of a 1921 work on the impact of World War I on the American tennis establishment.

See also: Moody, Helen Wills; Sports; Tilden, Bill

■ Theater in Canada

During the 1920s, francophone Canadian theaters continued to present conventional works that would not meet with disapproval from the Roman Catholic hierarchy, while anglophone Canadian theaters were often dependent on British and American professional actors presenting British and American plays. However, the little theater movement helped to expand the theatergoing public, provided training for actors, and offered opportunities to Canadian playwrights.

Historians do not consider the 1920s to be a golden age for either francophone or anglophone Canadian theater. In fact, the promising developments that had taken place during the early part of the century came to a halt with World War I, and the significance of the decade following the end of the war is evident only when viewed from a historical perspective.

Francophone Theater

Though French-language theaters had long existed in Montreal, generally presenting professional actors from France in plays by French authors, they were always threatened by the disapproval of the Roman Catholic hierarchy. A hint from the local archbishop could empty the house; a decree could close the theater. Therefore, it is hardly surprising that francophone Canada did not produce many innovative dramatists. The few French Canadian writers who were active during the 1920s turned out historical revisions of English-French strife in Canada, as well as musical revues and religious melodramas like those that had been staged in previous decades. One of these dramatists, Léopold Houlé, is remembered primarily because his play *Le Presbytère en fleurs* (1929; the parsonage in bloom) was performed two hundred times in French Canada. Another successful playwright was the Parisian Henry Deyglun, who came to Montreal in 1921. An actor as well as a playwright, Deyglun was one of the many dramatists who turned his talents to a more dependable and a much more profitable medium after French-language radio was introduced in the middle of the decade.

Another reason for the decline of francophone theater in the 1920s was that the audiences that had previously flocked to see comic sketches and monologues onstage had found a new enthusiasm: the movies. Even before World War I, some theater owners had converted their buildings to movie houses. Though sometimes vaudeville acts would be scheduled between shows, the fact remained that, for the most part, these houses were no longer staging live theater.

Anglophone Theater

Unlike francophone theater, which was largely limited to Montreal, anglophone theater had developed in communities throughout Canada. Professional companies from New York vied with British companies in scheduling tours. However, by the turn of the twentieth century, troupes advertised as being "all-Canadian" were appearing in the opera houses that had grown up in many small Canadian towns. Unfortunately, as in Montreal, the development of the film industry often caused those buildings to be converted to movie houses.

Another contributing factor to the decline of professional theater in Canada in the 1920s was the development of radio. By the middle of the decade, Canadian audiences were able to find excellent dramatic presentations on the radio, most of them written by Canadian playwrights and featuring Canadian actors. Nevertheless, even as radio seemed to be displacing the stage, it was providing a training ground for the playwrights, actors, and directors who would eventually revive Canada's anglophone theater and, indeed, make it truly Canadian.

The connection between radio and the little theater movement, in which growing numbers of smaller companies began to perform less commercial and more experimental plays, is illustrated by the rise to prominence of one of Canada's first important playwrights. An architect by training, Merrill Denison worked as a designer, actor, and playwright at the University of Toronto's Hart House Theatre, opened in 1919 and soon to be renowned as the center of the little theater movement in Canada. In 1921, Hart House presented Denison's one-act play *Brothers in Arms*, which would become one of his most popular dramas, staged fifteen hundred times over the next five decades. With his collection *The Unheroic North: Four Canadian Plays* (1923), Denison established himself as a writer primarily interested in Canada as a unique entity. He began writing radio scripts at the end of the decade and is credited with making important contributions to the development of that medium.

Another anglophone Canadian playwright who emerged during the 1920s was Herman Voaden, head of the English department at Toronto's Central High School of Commerce, who was also associated with the Hart House Theatre. His plays reflect what he called "symphonic expressionism"; inspired by the paintings of the Group of Seven, Canadian landscape painters who were active at the time, he attempted to evoke the western Ontario landscape through his use of lighting, music, dance, and poetic speech.

Impact

While few of the Canadian plays written during the 1920s have proven to be of more than historical importance, the writers and directors who emerged during the period were instrumental in eliminating Canada's long dependence on French, British, and American plays, playwrights, and professional troupes. At first it was thought that radio would displace the theater, but instead it provided many playwrights with a reliable income and enabled francophone writers to escape from the restrictions of the Roman Catholic Church. While it is true that movies made significant inroads into audience numbers, the rapid expansion of the little theater movement meant that in the decades that followed, Canadians would have more opportunities to see and participate in legitimate theater than ever before.

Rosemary M. Canfield Reisman

Further Reading

Kröller, Eva-Marie, ed. *The Cambridge Companion to Canadian Literature*. Cambridge, England: Cambridge University Press, 2006. Contains essays on drama and on francophone writing that comment briefly on developments during this period.

Londré, Felicia Hardison, and Daniel J. Watermeier. *The History of North American Theater: The United States, Canada, and Mexico—From Pre-Columbian Times to the Present*. New York: Continuum, 1998. Includes detailed discussions of dramatic writing and presentations during the 1920s.

New, William H., ed. *Encyclopedia of Literature in Canada*. Toronto: University of Toronto Press, 2002. Contains numerous essays on various genres, including radio drama.

Nischik, Reingard M., ed. *History of Literature in Canada: English-Canadian and French-Canadian*. Rochester, N.Y.: Camden House, 2008. Emphasizes issues of Canadian identity and groups within Canada.

Toye, William, ed. *The Concise Oxford Companion to Canadian Literature*. 2d ed. Don Mills, Ont.: Oxford University Press, 2011. An abridged version of the 1997 volume, with over a hundred new entries.

See also: Literature in Canada; Religion in Canada; Theater in the United States

Theater in the United States

Theater in the United States became incredibly popular during the 1920s as numerous productions opened both on Broadway and in small, noncommercial theaters. New styles of dramatic writing and performance emerged throughout the decade as various writers, directors, and actors worked to develop a truly American theater and challenge social and theatrical norms.

Theater in the United States underwent a number of important changes during the 1920s. This era of social and economic progress brought with it an interest in the development of truly American art, and folk plays and independent theaters thrived during the decade. American playwrights established successful careers, often breaking with European theatrical traditions. In addition to the elaborate musical productions and generally realistic comedies and dramas that were popular with many, the 1920s featured numerous experimental plays that challenged actors and audiences. The productions of the period also challenged the social norms of the theater industry itself, as African American actors began to star in high-profile shows such as the all-black musical *Shuffle Along* (1921).

Styles of Theater

Comedies of the 1920s tended to be in the vein of farce and satire and often featured average people triumphing over their upper-class counterparts. Two of the most successful comedy playwrights of the decade were Philip Barry and George S. Kaufman. Though Barry wrote numerous plays of various genres, his reputation was largely based on his few successful comedies, including the urbane drawing-room comedy *Holiday* (1928). Kaufman, who typically worked with a collaborator, cowrote such successful comedies as *Merton of the Movies* (1922) and *The Royal Family* (1927). Filled with snappy banter and frenzied action and often satirizing the entertainment business, Kaufman's plays showcased his skill with words.

One of the best-known dramas of the 1920s was *What Price Glory?* by Maxwell Anderson and Laurence Stallings, produced in 1924. Anderson, a pacifist, and Stallings, a combat-wounded veteran of World War I, presented a realistic depiction of soldiers responding to the stress of modern war. The play's antiwar message and rejection of romanticized theatrical depictions of war were both controversial and appealing to audiences, and the play was adapted into a film in 1926. Other dramas of the 1920s included *Anna Christie* (1922), for which playwright Eugene O'Neill was awarded the Pulitzer Prize in drama.

Musicals were extremely popular throughout the decade, with as many as fifty productions running on Broadway each season. Many of the profitable musicals of the period featured high-quality songs by such noted composers and lyricists as George and Ira Gershwin. One of the most influential musicals of the 1920s was *Show Boat* (1927), based on a novel by Edna Ferber, which featured music by Jerome Kern and lyrics by Oscar Hammerstein II. This production confronted major racial issues that were rarely depicted in theatrical works, bringing depth to the genre while also entertaining audiences with an engaging plot and well-integrated musical numbers.

The increasing popularity of the musical came at the expense of vaudeville and the operetta. While such productions continued to entertain the public in the 1920s, the popularity and profitability of the genres declined significantly. The segments of song and dance in operettas were overshadowed by the well-integrated music of the new musical productions. Vaudeville lost many of its major acts, including singer Al Jolson and the comedic Marx Brothers, to revues such as the Ziegfeld Follies as well as to other stage productions and films. Despite this decline in popularity, however, vaudeville and the operetta would continue to influence theater throughout the 1920s and the following decades.

American folk plays experienced an increase in popularity during the 1920s in conjunction with the widespread interest in developing truly American forms of art. Such plays explored the dialects and customs of people from different areas of the country, particularly the South and Midwest. Though generally presented in a realistic style, these productions often used music, dance, and other elements to evoke a dreamlike quality. Folk music often played an important role in these productions, lending them a sense of authenticity. In addition to depicting varying perspectives on life in the United States, folk plays provided further opportunities for African Americans to represent themselves before audiences, offering more nuanced characters and situations than the black musical revues of the decade, which often drew from minstrel stereotypes.

American theatrical styles that explored alternatives to realism also became popular in the 1920s.

One of the most successful playwrights of the decade was George S. Kaufman. (© Condé Nast Archive/Corbis)

Expressionist plays and related forms such as fantasy, memory, and flashback plays particularly thrived in noncommercial theaters. One of the preeminent playwrights of this movement was Eugene O'Neill, whose earlier works were largely realistic dramas. His later works, such as the Pulitzer Prize–winning *Strange Interlude* (1928), were more unconventional. Like many other playwrights, O'Neill began to experiment with theatrical styles during the 1920s, directly confronting the limitations of conventional theater. Such experimentation necessitated a change in directing and acting styles and often placed a great deal of emphasis on design and lighting. Incorporating elements such as masks, unusual poses, bizarre costumes, shafts of light, and giant set pieces such as that in Elmer Rice's *The Adding Machine* (1923), experimental theatrical productions challenged both artists and audiences.

Theater Companies

The 1920s saw the establishment and operation of a number of small theater companies that specialized in performing plays written by American dramatists. These companies fostered new artists who were encouraged to create innovative works, and several noncommercial companies emerged as the forerunners of experimental theater.

Although its period of operation was relatively short, one of the most influential independent theater companies of the 1920s was the Provincetown Players, founded in 1916 and dedicated to producing new plays by American writers. Initially producing one-act plays, the company grew in reputation and attendance and began to produce full-length plays by the 1920s. Among the playwrights in the company were Susan Glaspell, one of the founders, and O'Neill. In 1920, O'Neill's *The Emperor Jones* premiered to critical acclaim, and a national tour and international productions of the play followed later in the decade. The play, which featured African American and Caribbean characters and starred African American actor Charles Sidney Gilpin in the title role, was one of several productions by the company to challenge the racial norms of American theater.

In 1923, under the leadership of Kenneth Macgowan, Robert Edmond Jones, and O'Neill, the group was reorganized and renamed the Experimental Theatre, Inc. The company performed a mix of new plays and previously produced atypical plays at the Provincetown Playhouse and the Greenwich Village Theatre. One new play was O'Neill's *All God's Chillun Got Wings* (1924), which caused a great deal of controversy due to its depiction of an interracial relationship. In 1925, Macgowan, Jones, and O'Neill left the company but retained control of the Greenwich Village Theatre, which merged with the Actors' Theatre the following year. Experimental Theatre, Inc. continued to produce new American plays until late 1929, when the stock market crash made further productions financially unviable.

Originally founded in 1918, the Theatre Guild was established with the goal of producing works based on their value as art, even if they would have been rejected by commercial theaters. Following a steady increase in season subscriptions, the Theatre Guild moved into a larger theater in the mid-1920s, increasing its number of productions. The organization became significantly more commercial in operation over the course of the decade, but like many theaters, it encountered difficulties due to the economic downturn at the end of the decade. Nevertheless, the Theatre Guild would survive the Great Depression and continue to produce plays throughout later decades.

The Neighborhood Playhouse was founded by sisters Alice and Irene Lewisohn in 1915 and originally featured performances by residents of the Lower East Side. During the 1920–1921 season, the Lewisohns created a professional company that began holding regular performances. The company produced new plays for several years; however, economic difficulties caused the company to disband in 1927.

Eva Le Gallienne, founder of the Civic Repertory Theatre, established a permanent company that performed classic plays and some new American works starting in 1926. Attendance increased throughout the next six seasons, but due to the theater's commitment to affordable ticket prices, its revenue did not. Like many small theaters of the decade, Civic Repertory Theatre could not support itself. After various attempts to raise funds, the theater would close in 1933.

The Actors' Theatre, originally known as the Equity Players, was founded in 1922 as a completely professional company based in a Broadway theater. It differed economically from commercial theaters in that it was organized by performers, rather than producers, and supported by benefactors. The company primarily performed new American plays and supplemented its seasons with foreign works. The group's productions were critically successful, but the company was unable to succeed financially. In 1926, the Actors' Theatre merged with the company at the Greenwich Village Theatre, keeping the Actors' Theatre name. The company disbanded in 1929.

Impact

Theater in the United States underwent numerous changes in the 1920s, and the plays and musicals of the era continued to influence theater in later decades. However, while theater experienced a surge in popularity during the 1920s, the stock market crash of 1929 and the resulting Great Depression led to diminishing theater audiences, resulting in the closure of numerous theaters, particularly those featuring small, independent companies. In addition, the technological advances of the decade, including the development of radio and film, proved to have a negative effect on live theater in the long run.

Hannah K. Schauer Galli

Further Reading

Berkowitz, Gerald M. *American Drama of the Twentieth Century*. New York: Longman, 2001. A critical look at the genres of American drama through the twentieth century.

Durham, Weldon B. *American Theatre Companies, 1888–1930*. New York: Greenwood Press, 1987. An encyclopedia of American theater companies and their works and artists.

Gewirtz, Arthur, and James J. Kolb, eds. *Art, Glitter, and Glitz: Mainstream Playwrights and Popular Theatre in 1920s America*. Westport, Conn.: Praeger, 2004. A collection of essays on the predominant playwrights and popular theater styles of the 1920s.

Hewitt, Barnard. *Theatre U. S. A.: 1665–1957*. New York: McGraw-Hill, 1959. A survey of professional theater in the United States from 1665 to 1957.

Jones, John Bush. *Our Musicals, Ourselves: A Social History of the American Musical Theatre*. Lebanon, N.H.: Brandeis University Press, 2004. A history of the musical in the United States, discussing the development of the musical in the 1920s as well as the decline of vaudeville and the operetta.

Mordden, Ethan. *The American Theatre*. New York: Oxford University Press, 1981. A chronological look at the evolution of American theater through the 1970s.

Poggi, Jack. *Theater in America: The Impact of Economic Forces, 1870–1967*. Ithaca, N.Y.: Cornell University Press, 1968. An exploration of the decline of commercial and nonprofit theater in America between 1870 and 1967.

See also: *Adding Machine, The;* Broadway musicals; *Emperor Jones, The;* Hammerstein, Oscar, II; O'Neill, Eugene; *Show Boat;* Ziegfeld Follies

Thief of Bagdad, The

Identification: A silent film about an Arabian thief trying to win the love of the Caliph's daughter
Director: Raoul Walsh
Date: 1924

The Thief of Bagdad was the first Hollywood film to feature lavish special effects. The brainchild of its star, Douglas Fairbanks Sr., the movie drew on popular American notions of a magical, fantastic Arabia and a sinister Far East.

In the early 1920s, the great success of Douglas Fairbanks Sr.'s silent films such as *The Mark of Zorro* (1920), *The Three Musketeers* (1921), and *Robin Hood* (1922) made the popular actor one of Hollywood's top stars. At the height of his stardom as a swashbuckling hero, Fairbanks decided to write, produce, and star in a fantasy movie inspired by the fictional tales of the popular book *The Arabian Nights*. Fairbanks's production company selected Raoul Walsh as director and William Cameron Menzies as art director. The cast, led by Fairbanks, featured many Asian American, Native American, and African American actors, which was unusual for films at the time.

Shot on lavishly built sets reflecting the popular image of an Arabian city, the film was populated by characters in fantasy Arabian and Asian costumes. Production of *The Thief of Bagdad* ran over $2 million for United Artists studios and is said to have been the costliest film to be made to date. The special effects used in the film to represent magic and fantasy were new to American audiences.

The Thief of Bagdad tells the story of Ahmed (Fairbanks), a common thief in a medieval city. Just as the Caliph (Brandon Hurst) invites foreign princes to vie for the hand of his princess daughter (Julanne Johnston), Ahmed breaks into the Caliph's palace. There, he immediately falls in love with the sleeping princess, but he is detected by one of the princess's attendants, the Mongolian slave girl (Anna May Wong) who has been sent by one of the potential suitors, the evil Mongolian prince (Sojin Kamiyama). Ahmed escapes and poses as a foreign prince the next day, only to be denounced by the slave girl. As the suitors search for magic gifts for the princess, Ahmed escapes the city to acquire a few magic items of his own. When the Mongolian prince seizes the city and threatens the princess, Ahmed reappears to save the day and fly away with the princess on his magic carpet.

Impact

The Thief of Bagdad was extremely popular when first released, bolstering Fairbanks's stardom and launching eighteen-year-old Chinese American actor Anna May Wong to international fame. The film was remade numerous times throughout the twentieth century, and in 2008, the original 1924 film was listed as one of the top ten American fantasy movies by the American Film Institute.

R. C. Lutz

Further Reading

Chan, Anthony B. *Perpetually Cool: The Many Lives of Anna May Wong, 1905–1961.* Lanham, Md.: Scarecrow Press, 2007.

Moss, Marilyn Ann. *Raoul Walsh: The True Adventures of Hollywood's Legendary Director.* Lexington: University Press of Kentucky, 2011.

Vance, Jeffrey, Tony Maietta, and Robert Cushman. *Douglas Fairbanks.* Berkeley: University of California Press, 2008.

See also: African Americans; Asian Americans; Fairbanks, Douglas, Sr.; Film; Native Americans; Racial discrimination; United Artists

This Side of Paradise

Identification: A novel about a young man searching for his life's meaning after World War I
Author: F. Scott Fitzgerald
Date: 1920

The first novel by F. Scott Fitzgerald, This Side of Paradise *was immediately and enormously successful. Readers embraced the story of a young man's struggle after the devastation of World War I to forge his own identity apart from American ideals of faith and respectability.*

Fitzgerald's autobiographical novel *This Side of Paradise* follows Amory Blaine from childhood through his college career and into young adulthood. Blaine wants to be an important and ideal man, but he does not know what that means in terms of how to live, whom to love, or what to believe.

The novel's first section, "The Romantic Egotist," describes Blaine's boyhood relationship with his indulgent mother and his years in a Connecticut boarding school. He enters Princeton University, pleased to be part of the social elite, but becomes disillusioned when a classmate challenges Princeton's social structure. Blaine leaves Princeton to join the Army, a period covered briefly in an "Interlude" section that consists of two letters: one written to Blaine during the war and a second written from Blaine near the war's end.

In the novel's second section, "The Education of a Personage," Blaine, who equates virtue with material success, learns he is in financial straits and must join the working class. Although Blaine has lost his faith, his family fortune, and the woman of his dreams, he hopes to be a positive influence on the coming generation.

Blaine falls in love with four women, each representing a phase in his developing identity and an ideal of romantic love, intrinsic goodness, wealth, or rejection of social norms. The women in *This Side of Paradise* are shockingly willing to kiss men they do not plan to marry, reflecting a marked change in the sexual mores of young Americans in the 1920s.

Fitzgerald experimented within the novel's form, combining prose with poetry, lists, letters, and even a play with stage directions. The first printing was poorly edited and mocked for its many spelling errors and misused words. It was nonetheless the first best-selling book of the 1920s, selling out its initial printing of three thousand copies within four days of publication.

Impact

A chronicle of college life and changing values, *This Side of Paradise* beautifully captured young Americans' disenchantment following World War I. Its success and Fitzgerald's flamboyance in celebrating his newfound literary notoriety made him an iconic figure. Fitzgerald would return to the same themes in subsequent works, most notably in *The Great Gatsby* (1925).

Maureen Puffer-Rothenberg

Further Reading

Brackett, Virginia. *F. Scott Fitzgerald: Writer of the Jazz Age*. Greensboro, N.C.: Morgan Reynolds, 2002.

Fitzgerald, F. Scott. *This Side of Paradise*. New York: C. Scribner's Sons, 1920.

Pelzer, Linda C. *Student Companion to F. Scott Fitzgerald*. Westport, Conn.: Greenwood Press, 2000.

See also: Fitzgerald, F. Scott; Fitzgerald, Zelda; Flappers; *Great Gatsby, The;* Literature in the United States; *Tales of the Jazz Age*

■ Thompson machine gun

Designed during World War I to overcome the high casualties inflicted on attacking troops, the Thompson machine gun was introduced too late to see military service. Postwar sales tended to be higher among civilians and law enforcement than soldiers. The Thompson's size and firepower also made it popular with criminals, leading to widespread negative publicity.

In World War I, machine guns inflicted massive casualties. Because their recoil and size made them heavy and awkward to move, soldiers fired them from fixed positions in their trenches, slaughtering the advancing infantry in unprecedented numbers. In response, John T. Thompson, recently retired from the U.S. Army Ordnance Department, designed what he called a "trench broom," a portable automatic weapon that attacking infantry could use to suppress defensive fire by "sweeping" the enemy trench. In 1916, Thompson formed a private company, the Auto-Ordnance Corporation, to develop and manufacture his invention, but the war ended before it could be put into use.

The company coined the term "submachine gun" to reflect the weapon's smaller size and use of pistol, rather than rifle, ammunition, and soon began to market its product as the Thompson submachine gun. After failing to secure any large military orders, Auto-Ordnance had to sell wherever it could but faced tepid sales due to the Thompson's high cost, which was about half the price of a new car. One notable early purchaser was the Irish Republican Army, which used intermediaries to acquire over five hundred Thompsons. Other customers included various members of the organized crime gangs that controlled the illicit sale of alcohol during Prohibition, who often used Thompsons in public shoot-outs with police or among themselves. The most infamous of these incidents was the Saint Valentine's Day Massacre of 1929, in which gunmen used two Thompsons to execute seven members of a rival gang.

Although public perceptions linked Thompsons with gangsters, Auto-Ordnance never intended to arm criminals. Company ads described Thompsons with the slogan "A Sure Defense Against Organized Bandits and Criminals" to solicit sales to local, state, and federal law enforcement departments. In 1926, the postal service began using Thompsons to guard its deliveries. A year later, U.S. Marines in Nicaragua were the first U.S. troops to use Thompsons in active combat. It was not until World War II, however, that large numbers of Thompsons saw military service.

Impact

Although designed for use in the trenches, the Thompson machine gun was best known during the 1920s for its use in high-profile criminal activities. This notoriety, although exaggerated by popular media, was a primary impetus for the passage of the National Firearms Act in 1934, the first major gun control legislation in the United States. However, the Thompson was also used in U.S. military actions during the late 1920s and by the majority of Allied armies during World War II, where it proved sturdy and reliable in the field.

Kevin B. Reid

Further Reading

Helmer, William J. *The Gun that Made the Twenties Roar.* London: Macmillan, 1969.

Pegler, Martin. *The Thompson Submachine Gun: From Prohibition Chicago to World War II.* Oxford: Osprey, 2010.

Yenne, Bill. *Tommy Gun: How General Thompson's Submachine Gun Wrote History.* New York: Thomas Dunne Books, 2009.

See also: Capone, Al; Latin America and the Caribbean; Organized crime; Prohibition; Saint Valentine's Day Massacre; Schultz, Dutch

■ Thorpe, Jim

Identification: American athlete
Born: May 28, 1887 (sources vary), Prague, Indian Territory (now Oklahoma)
Died: March 28, 1953, Lomita, California

Jim Thorpe was an accomplished athlete in football, baseball, and track and field. Having faced controversy and the loss of his Olympic medals early in the previous decade, he further established himself as a professional athlete during the 1920s. Thorpe played football for teams such as the Canton Bulldogs and the Rock Island Independents throughout the decade and served as the first president of the American Professional Football Association.

James Francis "Jim" Thorpe began his athletic career early in the twentieth century, excelling in track and field, baseball, and football while attending the

Jim Thorpe. (Getty Images)

Carlisle Indian Industrial School in Carlisle, Pennsylvania. In 1912, Thorpe competed in the pentathlon and decathlon events at the Olympic Games in Stockholm, Sweden, winning both competitions with record scores. However, in 1913 the Amateur Athletic Union (AAU) and the International Olympic Commission (IOC) discovered that Thorpe had played semiprofessional baseball several years before. As professional and semiprofessional athletes were prohibited from competing in the Olympics, Thorpe was stripped of his Olympic titles and medals. Thorpe soon began a career in professional baseball, playing for teams such as the New York Giants, the Cincinnati Reds, and the Boston Braves throughout the remainder of the 1910s. He also began to play professional football during this period, playing for the

Pine Village Pros, based in Indiana, and joining the Ohio-based Canton Bulldogs in 1915.

American Professional Football Association

While professional football existed throughout the early twentieth century, it was not as popular with spectators or as organized as its college counterpart. No governing body existed to set or enforce consistent rules, so the sport remained fairly disorganized. Seeking to change this, representatives from four Ohio football teams, including the Canton Bulldogs, met in August of 1920 to form a professional football association initially known as the American Professional Football Conference. The founding teams were joined by six additional teams the following month, and the organization was renamed the American Professional Football Association (APFA).

Thorpe was elected the APFA's first president and held the position until April of 1921. During Thorpe's tenure as president, four additional teams joined the organization, and member teams began to play games in September. The association continued to grow in membership throughout the decade, and in 1922, it was renamed the National Football League (NFL). Although Thorpe did not return to the presidency, he went on to play for NFL teams for much of the decade.

Football Career

Thorpe played fifty-two official games for six teams throughout the 1920s, and he often coached as well as played. He began the decade as both a player and the coach of the Canton Bulldogs, having established his career with the team in the previous decade. Thorpe moved to the Cleveland Indians for the 1921 season, coaching this team as well. In 1922 and 1923, Thorpe both coached and played for the Oorang Indians, a team based in LaRue, Ohio, and composed entirely of Native American players. While Thorpe's teams were not always successful, he continued to build his reputation as a strong individual player. In 1923, various sportswriters were polled to determine their ideal lineup for an all-NFL team; Thorpe was among the players selected.

In 1924, Thorpe joined the Illinois-based Rock Island Independents, returning to the team in 1925 after a brief period with the New York Giants. After participating in a barnstorming tour, he returned to the Canton Bulldogs in 1926. However, following the 1926 season, the NFL eliminated a number of its teams, including the Bulldogs. Playing his final game for the Chicago Cardinals, Thorpe retired from professional football in 1928.

Impact

One of the United States' first sports celebrities, Jim Thorpe was voted the best football player and all-around athlete of the first half of the twentieth century by the nation's sportswriters in 1950. He was inducted into the College Football Hall of Fame in 1951, the Pro Football Hall of Fame in 1963, and the National Track and Field Hall of Fame in 1975. While Thorpe was unable to regain his Olympic titles in his lifetime, his legacy as an Olympian was restored posthumously. In 1973, the AAU restored Thorpe's status as an amateur, and the IOC followed suit in 1982 after evidence revealed that the 1913 decision had violated Olympic regulations. Thorpe's name was restored to the Olympic records, and new medals were presented to his children early in 1983.

Paul P. Sipiera

Further Reading

Buford, Kate. *Native American Son: The Life and Sporting Legend of Jim Thorpe.* New York: Alfred A. Knopf, 2010. Discusses Thorpe's life, with a particular focus on his experience as a Native American.

Cook, William A. *Jim Thorpe: A Biography.* Jefferson, N.C.: McFarland, 2011. Explores the three areas of Thorpe's sports career: track and field, baseball, and football.

Crawford, Bill. *All American: The Rise and Fall of Jim Thorpe.* Hoboken, N.J.: John Wiley & Sons, 2005. Chronicles Thorpe's career and devotes a great deal of attention to the Olympics scandal.

Peterson, Robert W. *Pigskin: The Early Years of Pro Football.* New York: Oxford University Press, 1997. Provides a history of professional football from 1920 to the 1950s and includes a chapter on Thorpe.

Wheeler, Robert L. *Jim Thorpe: World's Greatest Athlete.* Norman, Okla.: University of Oklahoma Press, 1981. Explores Thorpe's life and career and discusses the author's role in the restoration of Thorpe's Olympic honors.

See also: Baseball; Football; Grange, Red; National Football League; Native Americans; Rockne, Knute; Sports

Three Soldiers

Identification: Novel about the experiences of three U.S. soldiers in World War I
Author: John Dos Passos
Date: 1921

One of many literary works of the 1920s to focus on World War I, Three Soldiers *critiques attitudes surrounding the war, particularly the romanticized view of military service. In calling attention to the ugliness of war, novelist and veteran John Dos Passos paved the way for a generation of antiwar novelists.*

John Dos Passos served in World War I initially as an ambulance driver and then as a member of the U.S. Army Medical Corps. His wartime experiences helped inform his second novel, *Three Soldiers*. True to its title, the novel tells of three very different soldiers serving in France during World War I: Andrews, Chrisfield, and Fuselli.

Fuselli, a Californian and the son of Italian immigrants, is a member of the Medical Corps. He is eager to see combat but also frightened of the war. Fuselli is determined to become a corporal and ignores the complaints of his comrades, some of whom are budding socialists and believe that enlistment is tantamount to slavery. Like many of the Americans Dos Passos critiques, Fuselli largely ignores the dark side of the war and only focuses on the aspects that are positive for him.

Chrisfield, a young man raised on a farm in Indiana, becomes obsessed with taking vengeance against an officer named Anderson, who belittles him. When he eventually encounters a wounded Anderson after an engagement, he kills him with a grenade. Chrisfield's story calls attention to the way in which war causes people to classify some killing as permissible and justified, while other killing remains wrong.

Andrews, a Harvard graduate from Virginia, is the foremost of the novel's three main characters, the closest to representing the voice of Dos Passos himself. He is more intellectually detached than either of the other main characters, questioning the Army's motives and accomplishments. After being wounded, he eventually deserts the Army and attempts to live in France. He meets a young woman named Geneviève, works on composing a musical piece titled "The Soul and Body of John Brown," after the martyred abolitionist, and in the end is captured.

Impact

Published only a few years after the end of World War I, *Three Soldiers* was one of the first novels to challenge the prevailing attitudes of the war years. By confronting those who romanticized the war and presenting the war through multiple perspectives, Dos Passos developed a thematic and narrative template for many chroniclers of World War I and later wars.

Scott D. Yarbrough

Further Reading

Cooperman, Stanley. "John Dos Passos' *Three Soldiers*: Aesthetics and the Doom of Individualism." In *The First World War in Fiction: A Collection of Critical Essays*, edited by Holger Klein. London: Macmillan, 1976.

Stolz, Claudia Matherly. "Dos Passos's *Three Soldiers*: a Case Study." *West Virginia University Philological Papers* 51, no. 3 (Fall, 2004): 77–84.

Wagner-Martin, Linda. *Dos Passos: Artist as American*. Austin: University of Texas Press, 1979.

See also: *Farewell to Arms, A;* Literature in the United States; Lost Generation; World War I veterans

Tilden, Bill

Classification: American tennis player
Born: February 10, 1893, Philadelphia, Pennsylvania
Died: June 5, 1953, Hollywood, California

Bill Tilden dominated the sport of tennis during the early 1920s, winning two Wimbledon singles titles and six consecutive U.S. National Championships. Playing in both singles and doubles matches in the United States and abroad, Tilden was one of the world's most successful tennis players for much of the decade.

Before 1920, William Tatem "Bill" Tilden Jr., whose height and long reach earned him the nickname "Big Bill," was a formidable doubles player, but he had not yet achieved great success in singles tennis. He came in second in singles at the United States National Championship (today the U.S. Open) in both 1918 and 1919. Tilden brought a powerful serve and strong forehand stroke to the tennis court, but he became a singles champion only after improving his backhand.

Tilden won his first major singles titles at Wimbledon and the U.S. Nationals in 1920. His victory at the U.S. Nationals was the first of six consecutive U.S.

singles titles for Tilden, and he won at Wimbledon again in 1921. After 1925, younger players such as Henri Cochet and René Lacoste bested Tilden in the championships, but he rallied and won the U.S. Nationals singles title again in 1929. In addition to achieving success as a singles player, Tilden continued to excel at doubles. He was a U.S. Nationals doubles champion in 1921, 1922, 1923, and 1927 and a mixed doubles champion in 1922 and 1923. Tilden was also a mainstay on the American Davis Cup team during the 1920s, playing both singles and doubles matches and leading the team to seven consecutive championships between 1920 and 1926.

Although Tilden was a popular and successful player throughout the 1920s, he sometimes clashed with the United States Lawn Tennis Association (USLTA). In 1928, USLTA officials moved to strip Tilden of his amateur status, as he had earned money by writing about tennis, and to ban him from the Davis Cup, an amateur competition. Facing criticism from the press and tennis fans, the USLTA allowed Tilden to compete in the 1928 Davis Cup before suspending him from play for several months.

Impact
During the 1920s, Bill Tilden helped to transform tennis, initially a game followed by a small number of devotees, into an international sport followed closely by millions of fans. He continued to play and teach tennis during the following decades, achieving a final Wimbledon singles title in 1930. For his contributions to the sport, Tilden was inducted into the International Tennis Hall of Fame in 1959.

James Tackach

Further Reading
Deford, Frank. *Big Bill Tilden: The Triumphs and the Tragedy*. New York: Simon & Schuster, 1976.
Marshall, Jon Fisher. *A Terrible Splendor: Three Extraordinary Men, a World Poised for War, and the Greatest Tennis Match Ever Played*. New York: Three Rivers Press, 2009.

See also: Sports; Tennis

■ Tin Pan Alley

Sheet music publishing and sales, along with the invention of radio and the continued popularity of phonographs, created an unprecedented public demand for entertainment. The growth and development of Tin Pan Alley provided opportunities for composers, musicians, and businesses to revolutionize the music industry.

By the late nineteenth century, piano sales had radically increased. As many as 300,000 pianos were sold each year in the United States alone. As the public appetite for more piano and vocal sheet music steadily increased, entrepreneurs moved to West 28th Street between Broadway and 6th Avenues in New York City to set up their publishing businesses and begin promoting and selling music. New York City was already considered a cultural center by this point, so the location was ideal for the many emerging publishing firms that became established along Tin Pan Alley. It is generally believed that Tin Pan Alley was named by a local newspaper reporter assigned to write articles about the new publishing businesses. After hearing numerous metallic-toned pianos playing at the same time, the reporter compared it to the sound of clanging tin pans.

The ongoing daily routine of songwriting, publishing sheet music, and promotion through traveling pianists and singers, known as "song pluggers," continued from about 1885 into the 1920s. In the 1920s, jazz profoundly influenced Tin Pan Alley as new sheet music melodies were composed in a jazz style, which reflected the heightened interest in this genre of music. The 1920s also marked the beginning of a downward slide for the area as sheet music sales began to plummet because radio had replaced the piano as the primary source of at-home entertainment. Hollywood movies and Broadway musicals offered composers of popular songs an entirely new venue, adding to the decline in sheet music sales to the general public. Ultimately, the end for Tin Pan Alley came after The American Society of Composers, Authors and Publishers and Broadcast Music Incorporated waged a war that eventually prompted Hollywood companies to purchase many of the publishing companies.

Impact
Tin Pan Alley reflected the changing culture of America. It began as a sheet music empire, popularized countless songs, and kept pace with American music listeners' insatiable appetite for entertainment. In the 1920s, however, it could not sustain itself as the popularity of radio and films grew among consumers.

Douglas D. Skinner

Further Reading

Furia, Philip, and Michael L. Lasser. *America's Songs: The Stories Behind the Songs of Broadway, Hollywood, and Tin Pan Alley.* New York: Routledge, 2008.

Hischak, Thomas S. *The Tin Pan Alley Song Encyclopedia.* Westport, Conn.: Greenwood Press, 2002.

Jasen, David A. *Tin Pan Alley.* New York: Routledge, 2003.

See also: Broadway musicals; Crooners; Jazz; Music, popular; Vaudeville

■ Tomb of the Unknown Soldier

The Tomb of the Unknown Soldier was constructed in 1921 to honor the numerous unidentified soldiers killed in action during World War I. Located in Arlington National Cemetery in Virginia, the white marble tomb was designed by Lorimer Rich and sculpted by Thomas Hudson Jones.

Following World War I, several countries constructed memorials to honor the numerous soldiers killed during the war, many of whom could not be identified. Inspired by these monuments and by the suggestions of various military officials and civilians, Representative Hamilton Fish proposed the creation of the Tomb of the Unknown Soldier to Congress on December 21, 1920. In addition to being a public monument, the tomb would hold the remains of one unidentified soldier, thus symbolizing and honoring all of the soldiers whose identities remained unknown. The proposal met some resistance, as the secretary of war and the Senate Committee on Military Affairs were concerned that the rate at which remains were being identified made it likely that the Unknown Soldier would be identified as well. However, after changing the proposed date of the burial service to allow more soldiers to be identified, Congress approved Fish's resolution on March 4, 1921.

Four deceased American service members, chosen for their lack of identifying information, were disinterred from American military cemeteries in France. On October 24, U.S. Army Sergeant Edward Younger selected a soldier by placing white roses on one of the caskets. The remaining soldiers were reburied with honors in France. The casket containing the Unknown Soldier was returned to the United States and placed in the Capitol rotunda until Armistice Day, November 11, 1921, when it was interred in the newly constructed tomb.

Located within the plaza of the Memorial Amphitheater at Arlington National Cemetery in Virginia, the tomb consisted of a white marble sarcophagus designed by architect Lorimer Rich and sculpted by Thomas Hudson Jones. An inscription, "Here rests in honored glory an American soldier known but to God," would later be engraved on the western side of the tomb. The tomb was guarded by civilians until 1926, when the Army began guard duty during daylight hours.

Impact

A platoon within the Army's Third Infantry Regiment, also known as the Old Guard, began to stand constant guard over the Tomb of the Unknown Soldier in 1937. The tomb became the final resting place for unidentified service members from World War II and the Korean War in 1958. In 1984, a soldier from the Vietnam War was interred in the tomb; however, DNA testing revealed the soldier's identity in 1998, and his remains were returned to his family for burial.

Jennifer L. Campbell

Coffin on its way from the Capitol to the Tomb of the Unknown Soldier. (Getty Images)

Further Reading

Bigler, Philip. *In Honored Glory: Arlington National Cemetery, The Final Post.* 4th ed. St. Petersburg, Fla.: Vandamere Press, 2007.

Poole, Robert M. *On Hallowed Ground: The Story of Arlington National Cemetery.* New York: Walker & Co., 2009.

See also: Lincoln Memorial; World War I veterans

Tong Wars of Chinatown, San Francisco

The Event: Conflicts between Chinese criminal organizations
Date: 1920s
Place: San Francisco, California

The Tong Wars of Chinatown, San Francisco, were violent conflicts between Chinese criminal organizations known as tongs. While many tongs of the 1920s were political or charitable organizations, a number were involved in such criminal activities as extortion, prostitution, and the drug trade. By the late 1920s, various efforts by San Francisco law enforcement had largely put an end to the Tong Wars.

The tongs of San Francisco's Chinatown were organizations that offered education, protection, and social services to Chinese immigrants and Chinese Americans. Such organizations were first established in the United States in the mid-nineteenth century, following a surge in Chinese immigration due to poor economic conditions in China and the promise of job opportunities in the United States. Many of these immigrants settled in cities such as San Francisco, where they faced the typical challenges of urban life as well as racial discrimination. As the U.S. government increasingly restricted immigration from Asia, it became more difficult for Chinese immigrants living in the United States to create or reunite their families.

Tongs allowed immigrants to band together for the good of the community and exercise political and economic influence. While much of the tongs' political activity concerned Chinatowns and the cities in which they were located, some tongs became involved in Chinese politics as well, establishing ties to the Tiandihui, a secret society that sought to restore the Ming Dynasty to power in China. Over time, some tongs became involved in criminal enterprises such as gambling, prostitution, extortion, and the slave and drug trades. These illegal activities led to an ongoing series of conflicts known as the Tong Wars. While most Tong Wars occurred in the late nineteenth and early twentieth centuries, such conflicts continued to shape San Francisco's Chinatown during the 1920s.

Major Conflicts

Like many gangs of the 1920s, the criminal tongs sought to gain control over various illegal enterprises and retain control in the face of opposition from rival groups and law enforcement. Tongs were particularly known for managing the importation and sale of drugs such as opium and supervising the transportation of wives, prostitutes, and slaves from China. Competition in these areas became the focus of a number of Tong Wars. Conflicts were frequently based on property rights, with multiple tongs asserting ownership over a person or cargo, or territory disputes regarding the right to operate a brothel or gambling establishment or to extort protection money from local businesses.

The San Francisco Tong Wars of the early twentieth century featured battles between groups such as the Suey Sing tong and the Bing Kong tong. These tongs remained active during the 1920s, and other major tongs of the period included Hop Sing, Suey Dong, Sen Suey Ying, and Jun Ying. The Hop Sing and Suey Sing tongs fought a particularly brutal war in 1921, during which the Chinese homicide rate experienced a sharp increase.

The End of the Tong Wars

While the decade overall was one in which organized crime flourished, the violence and influence of the tongs declined during the 1920s, due in part to various law enforcement efforts. In addition to putting an end to prostitution and the slave and drug trades in Chinatown, law enforcement in San Francisco sought to end the violence that had resulted in numerous murders and other violent acts throughout the previous decades. A squad dedicated to policing Chinatown had been established decades before, and in 1921, Inspector Jack Manion was appointed its head. Manion used several methods to discourage tong violence, such as arresting low-level criminals and threatening leaders of the organizations with deportation. In addition, Manion encouraged mediation of disputes and used such negotiations as opportunities to gather information about tong leadership. Chinese homicide rates in San Francisco declined sharply during the 1920s, largely due to such intervention. The criminal tongs also struggled with cultural and demographic changes during the 1920s, as younger generations of Chinese Americans frequently had priorities and outlooks on life in the United States that clashed with those of older leaders. By the end of the decade, efforts to stop the slave and drug trades had diminished the power of the criminal tongs, and lesser crimes such as illegal gambling typically did not inspire major conflicts.

Impact

While conflicts between various Chinese criminal organizations continued throughout the following decades, the Tong Wars of Chinatown, San Francisco, had effectively ceased by the end of the 1920s. Many tongs of the era continued to operate as social and political organizations dedicated to helping the Chinese American and immigrant community, and a number such organizations were later renamed to included the word "association" rather than "tong," reflecting the increasing Americanization of Chinatowns.

Frank Day

Further Reading

Chen, Yong. *Chinese San Francisco, 1850–1943: A Trans-Pacific Community.* Stanford, Calif.: Stanford University Press, 2002. A history of Chinese American and immigrant life in San Francisco, including discussion of the events of the 1920s.

Chin, Ko-lin. *Chinese Subculture and Criminality: Non-Traditional Crime Groups in America.* New York: Greenwood Press, 1990. A broad survey of Chinese criminal organizations, including tongs.

Dillon, Richard H. *Hatchet Men: The Story of the Tong Wars in San Francisco's Chinatown.* Reprint. Fairfield, Calif.: James Stevenson, 2005. An account of the development of the San Francisco tongs.

Huston, Peter. *Tongs, Gangs, and Triads: Chinese Crime Groups in North America.* Reprint. San Jose, Calif.: Authors Choice Press, 2001. A summary of Chinese criminal organizations in North America.

Mullen, Kevin J. *Dangerous Strangers: Minority Newcomers and Criminal Violence in the Urban West, 1850–2000.* New York: Palgrave Macmillan, 2005. A study of immigrant criminal violence in San Francisco, featuring a chapter on Chinese immigrants that discusses the Tong Wars.

See also: Asian Americans; Crimes and scandals; Gambling; Immigration to the United States; Organized crime

■ Toomer, Jean

Identification: American writer and philosopher
Also known as: Nathan Pinchback Toomer
Born: December 26, 1894, Washington, D.C.
Died: March 30, 1967, Doylestown, Pennsylvania

Jean Toomer's 1923 novel Cane *was acclaimed as a literary masterpiece by two important movements of the 1920s, modernism and the Harlem Renaissance, although Toomer himself was reluctant to be associated with the Harlem Renaissance. He devoted much of his life to promoting the philosophical system of Georges Gurdjieff, to which he was introduced in 1924.*

Jean Toomer was born Nathan Pinchback Toomer in Washington, D.C. His father, Nathan Toomer, had been born into slavery but quickly became a wealthy planter following emancipation; his mother, Nina Pinchback, was the daughter of Pinckney Benton Stewart Pinchback, the first African American to become a U.S. state governor. P. B. S. Pinchback was a key figure in Toomer's early years, as Toomer spent much of his childhood with his grandparents in Washington, D.C., his father having left when Toomer was an infant.

Of mixed parentage on both sides of his family, Toomer was light-skinned enough to pass for white and attended both all-white and all-black schools while growing up. After high school, he enrolled in and subsequently dropped out of six different colleges, where he studied a wide range of subjects, including agriculture, fitness, biology, and sociology. He also worked at times as delivery boy, shipyard worker, and teacher, among various other jobs.

Writing Career

Toomer's life took a new direction when he began to write short stories, plays, and articles. Several newspaper articles he wrote in 1919 and 1920 regarding racial matters attracted the attention of novelist and essayist Waldo Frank, who became Toomer's mentor and introduced him into literary circles. In 1921, Toomer spent two months working as a substitute principal at the all-black Sparta Agricultural and Industrial Institute in Georgia, during which time he began to identify more closely with his African American heritage. His friendships with rural African Americans provided the inspiration for his novel, *Cane*, written upon his return to Washington.

Innovative in form and style, *Cane* is divided into three sections. The first combines stories and poetry to describe the lives and culture of African American women in the South. The second section, set in Washington and Chicago, consists of prose sketches and poems that deal with black migration to northern cities. The final section is a mixture of prose and

Jean Toomer. (© Bettmann/Corbis)

drama that brings together themes from the two earlier sections. Loosely autobiographical, it tells the story of a fair-skinned educated black man from the North who discovers his roots among rural African Americans.

 Cane was published in 1923 with an introduction by Frank, and it became a critical success despite a limited print run and modest sales. The novel was acclaimed for its innovative and experimental form by the white modernist writers whom Toomer saw as his literary influences. Its realistic presentation of black life in the South and exploration of themes such as racial mixing, racial ambiguity, and black sexuality also led Cane to be claimed as one of the first major texts of the Harlem Renaissance. Alain Locke, who considered African American folk heritage to be essential for the literature of the movement, featured extracts from Cane in his anthology The New Negro (1925) without Toomer's permission. Both Locke and W. E. B. Du Bois encouraged Toomer to write more about race, but Toomer did not want to limit himself to representing one racial perspective; conflicted about his identity, he preferred to reject racial classification in favor of membership in what he believed should be a united human race.

 The year after Cane was published, Toomer was introduced to the ideas of Russian philosopher and mystic Georges Ivanovich Gurdjieff, who was touring the United States at the time. Toomer was drawn to his system of self-development, which encouraged individuals to attempt to integrate their spiritual, intellectual, and physical consciousness. In July 1924, he went to study at Gurdjieff's Institute for the Harmonious Development of Man in Fontainebleau, France. Gurdjieff's ideas garnered a considerable American following, including many writers and artists. Upon returning to New York in September, Toomer set up a Gurdjieff group in Harlem, where his lectures attracted such African American intellectuals as writers Langston Hughes and Zora Neale Hurston and painter Aaron Douglas. He returned to France on two further occasions, in 1926 and 1927, and led workshops in Harlem and Chicago until the end of the decade.

Impact

Cane inspired many writers of the Harlem Renaissance, including Langston Hughes, Countee Cullen, and Zora Neale Hurston. Although he primarily spent the next thirty years promoting Gurdjieff's philosophy, Toomer also continued to write prolifically, but his literary style was influenced by his desire to inculcate self-awareness and spirituality in his readers, and few of his later works were published. By the 1930s, Toomer had sunk into relative obscurity and distanced himself from the literary scene. After his death in 1967, however, renewed critical and cultural interest in his writing led to the posthumous release of new editions of Cane, as well as his other, lesser-known or previously unpublished writings.

Christine Ayorinde

Further Reading

Fabre, Geneviève, and Michel Feith, eds. *Jean Toomer and the Harlem Renaissance.* New Brunswick, N.J.: Rutgers University Press, 2001. A collection of essays that offers perspectives on Cane within the context of both the Harlem Renaissance and 1920s modernism.

Kerman, Cynthia Earl, and Richard Eldridge. *The Lives of Jean Toomer: A Hunger for Wholeness.* Baton Rouge: Louisiana State University Press, 1987. Explores Toomer's attempts to transcend what he saw as the narrow definitions of race, as well as his interest in mysticism and spirituality.

McKay, Nellie Y. *Jean Toomer, Artist: A Study of His Literary Life and Work, 1894–1936.* Chapel Hill: University of North Carolina Press, 1984. A detailed evaluation of Toomer and his writing within the context of his times.

Scruggs, Charles, and Lee VanDemarr. *Jean Toomer and the Terrors of American History.* Philadelphia: University of Pennsylvania Press, 1998. Assesses how the cultural wars of the 1920s influenced the writing of *Cane* and Toomer's efforts to escape the racial definitions of American society.

Toomer, Jean. *The Uncollected Works of American Author Jean Toomer, 1894–1967.* Edited by John Chandler Griffin. Lewiston, N.Y: Edwin Mellen Press, 2003. A one-volume compilation of all of Toomer's writing.

See also: African Americans; Du Bois, W. E. B.; Harlem Renaissance; Hughes, Langston; Hurston, Zora Neale

■ Traffic signals

The invention of the traffic signal was prompted by the increase in automobile traffic in cities during the 1920s. With pedestrians, horse-drawn carriages, and automobiles often sharing the same roadways, the new technology enhanced safety and improved traffic flow while reducing congestion at busy city intersections.

From the late 1800s to the early 1900s, traffic was regulated by police officers who would manually rotate a semaphore to indicate either "stop" or "go." Because there was little warning given to motorists, collisions and accidents were common, and police officers were often injured.

By the early 1920s, automobiles began to outnumber horse-drawn wagons in many urban areas, and with this increase came an even greater increase in traffic accidents. Traffic towers were used to help regulate congested intersections, and although the police officers were safer in the towers, colored lights or flags were still operated manually, and collisions and injuries at busy intersections continued to be a problem.

African American inventor Garrett Morgan was the first to receive a patent for a mechanized traffic signal. Granted in 1923, the patent called for flags to rotate on a three-position traffic pole. The third position on the pole allowed for an all-directional stop, which meant traffic could be halted in all directions and pedestrians could cross more safely through intersections.

William L. Potts, a police officer from Detroit, Michigan, is credited with developing the first four-sided traffic signal, which was installed at a busy Detroit intersection in October of 1920. The manually operated signal was constructed from wood with a metal shell and had lights made from four-inch green, amber, and red lenses. Within a year, the city had installed the first automated light system, which Potts also designed, that accommodated traffic signals at fifteen separate intersections to be controlled from one location. Some of the signals were installed on top of manned traffic towers; others were suspended over intersections, much like modern traffic lights.

Impact

Late in the decade, traffic signals became fully automated. Until that time, signals required someone to flip a switch, pull a lever, or push a button. By 1928, however, traffic signal design had progressed to include timers or sound and pressure sensors that regulated the timing of the lights. Modern traffic signals, though fully automated, still employ the original red, amber, and green colors introduced by William Potts, and although these three colors have been standardized in the United States since 1935, the size of the lenses has increased two to three times their original diameter, making them more visible at night and in most weather conditions

Elizabeth D. Schafer

Further Reading

Barnett, LeRoy. "Michigan Gives the Green Light to Traffic Safety." *Michigan History Magazine* 86, no. 4 (July–August, 2002): 22–25.

Challoner, Jack, ed. *1001 Inventions that Changed the World.* Hauppauge, N.Y.: Barron's, 2009.

Packer, Jeremy. *Mobility Without Mayhem: Safety, Cars, and Citizenship.* Durham, N.C.: Duke University Press, 2008.

See also: Automobiles and auto manufacturing; Inventions; National Conference on Street and Highway Safety (1924, 1926); Transportation; Travel

Transportation

In the earliest days of the industrialization of the United States, waterways served as the primary means of moving goods. Later, railroads became the transportation method of choice. By the 1920s, sweeping changes were underway that included the development of trucking and air transport. Trucking eliminated the transportation industry's dependence on rivers or railroad networks, and air travel provided unprecedented speed.

The first manufacturers built their factories on the banks of rivers for easy access to the main shipping routes. During the mid-1800s, railroads dominated the transportation industry because they were economical and because payloads could be greatly expanded by adding more railcars. New factories were built with railroad sidings to ease the loading of the finished goods onto flatbed or enclosed cars for delivery to any customer located in a town with tracks. During the early 1920s, railroads were still the industry leader, but by the end of that decade the trucking field had made significant advances; long-distance truckers came to be known as the "kings of the road." The emerging aviation industry, though costly, offered a novel option in cases where speed was a top priority.

Water Transport

In the decade of the 1920s, freight-carrying barges and steamboats were still traveling the rivers, but in significantly smaller numbers than in the past. In 1916, for the first time in decades, freight shipping on the Mississippi River dropped to below one million tons annually. By the end of the 1920s, that amount had dwindled to only 750,000 tons per year, due to the continued strength of railroads and the rise of trucking. Freight trains were more efficient and could far exceed the capacity of a single barge or riverboat. More important, they had a greater geographic reach. Some of the riverboats that had formerly carried cargo therefore began to be redesigned for passenger transportation.

Barges were still in use for shipping, however, and most of the wheat and other grains shipped from the Midwest to the Gulf of Mexico moved by barge on the Mississippi River. Also, barges were still a primary method of large-scale transportation on the East Coast, West Coast, and Gulf of Mexico, moving cargo from one port city to another. In addition, ocean freighters had an impact on the country's economy, as they provided jobs and revenue for U.S. companies that exported goods made in the United States.

Ore carriers had long served the Great Lakes region and continued to be widely used. In 1920, the lake freighter *Homer D. Williams* set a seasonal cargo transportation record, moving nearly 465,000 tons of raw materials such as iron ore, stone, and coal. The Merchant Marine Act of 1920 was passed to ensure that the United States would have the safest and best-equipped freighters possible. The act regulated waterway transportation and required that goods moved between U.S. ports be carried in U.S. ships. Further stipulations included that ship owners pay all appropriate taxes and employ American workers.

Railroads

As they had for decades, railroads handled the bulk of the nation's transportation needs, for both freight and passengers. Freight trains, though slow, were relatively economical, efficient, and faster than river barge transportation. No longer bound by waterways, manufacturers expanded their scope with the ability to bring goods to new markets. Most locomotives still relied on steam engines, but during the 1920s, other means of power came into use. Diesel-powered engines were developed around 1925 in the United States, in combination with electrical traction motor technology. Though trucking was gaining a foothold, railroad shipping still prevailed, as multiple locomotives could pull dozens of cars, thus moving large amounts of freight with small numbers of employees.

The Esch-Cummins Act, also known as the Railroad Transportation Act, was passed in 1920 to regulate the railroad industry in the United States. The Interstate Commerce Commission (ICC), a regulatory organization formed in 1887, oversaw the privatization and regulation of railroads after 1920 to make sure rates remained stable and profitable. Although railroads maintained their role as a significant method of transportation in the United States into the twenty-first century, the economic downturn of the Great Depression brought about a dip in the railroad industry. The late 1920s and 1930s marked the beginning of the end of railroad dominance.

Long-Distance Trucking

Trucking became a serious player in the transportation industry in the years following World War I,

A war plane that was used by the postal service for airmail. (Gamma-Keystone via Getty Images)

during which Americans and Europeans had observed its vast potential firsthand. The first commercial trucks were used in Britain and Germany and were powered by steam or internal combustion engines. Shippers were intrigued by, and impressed with, the earliest versions of the semitrailer—a trailer without a front axle, pulled by truck—when it first appeared in the 1910s. Semis, when pulled by trucks with more efficient diesel engines, were competitive with water and rail shippers. As sizes, couplings, and power steering and brake mechanisms became standardized, they became increasingly attractive because of their versatility. With the introduction of balloon tires and closed cabs, trucks came to play a significant role in the transportation industry, as they still do.

Automobile manufacturing magnate Henry Ford, along with other car makers, made the horseless carriage the must-have item of the day during the 1920s. As increasing numbers of Americans bought vehicles, the need for more and better roads rose proportionately. As the quality of roads improved, truckers were able to move about more freely. Though some roads had weight restrictions, it was now possible to move goods without constant dependence on rivers or railroad tracks for transportation.

As early as 1921, truckers began accumulating contracts to transport perishables and dairy products, as they could move goods with greater speed than their competitors. The general prosperity of the post–World War I years in the United States made possible the first boom in the trucking industry. However, the Great Depression had a negative effect on trucking, as there was no reason to ship goods that people had no money to buy.

Air Transport

American aviator Charles Lindbergh captured the country's imagination in 1927 with his solo nonstop transatlantic flight between Long Island and Paris, France. This achievement, along with other developments in air travel, made flight seem not only possible but desirable to the ordinary citizen. Passenger air travel had an early success between 1920 and 1924 when entrepreneur Inglis Uppercu established the Aeromarine West Indies Airways to transport passengers between Florida, Cuba, and the Caribbean islands. However, when one of Uppercu's planes crashed in 1923 because of engine failure, it created bad publicity, and the company went bankrupt by 1924.

In 1918, the United States Post Office Department began experimenting with airmail deliveries, and it was only a matter of time until other goods began to be shipped by air as well. By 1920, airmail delivery had been established between New York City and San Francisco. Even the earliest aircraft could handle additional payloads, and so another viable method of transportation was established. Before he flew his *Spirit of St. Louis* plane nonstop across the Atlantic, Lindbergh flew mail from St. Louis to Chicago. But for most pilots, it was a high-risk vocation. Thirty-one of the first forty pilots on the New York to Chicago run died when their planes crashed. Before the advent of cockpit instrumentation, pilots estimated their speed by the sound of the air stream outside their open cockpits.

Henry Ford was also given an airmail route. Ford's son Edsel was keenly interested in the budding aviation industry, and the two were involved in running an air service, as well as the production of aircraft. The Fords believed the same principles of mass production that drove their automotive industry could also be used in the manufacture of aircraft. Over the next few decades, every major airline added the Ford Tri-Motor airplane, first built in 1925, to their active inventory. For his achievements in the commercial aviation industry, Ford was inducted into the National Aviation Hall of Fame in Dayton, Ohio, in 1984.

Impact

The Roaring Twenties were a time of high expectations and general euphoria. Innovations in the transportation industry, in particular in the trucking and aviation segments, contributed significantly to the continuing development of transportation methods for the rest of the century. Transportation advances during the decade also had the ripple effect of creating jobs and easing the movement of goods to market for manufacturers. Widespread prosperity ended with the stock market crash of 1929, ushering in the Great Depression; however, positive developments in transportation technology had already occurred, and it was only a matter of time before the country's economy bounced back and the demand for products, shipping, and passenger transportation returned.

Norma Lewis

Further Reading

Adams, Ronald G. *One Hundred Years of Semi Trucks.* Osceola, Wis.: MBI, 2000. A history of the trucking industry that includes valuable information on the 1920s.

Bowlus, Bruce W. *Iron Ore Transport on the Great Lakes: The Development of a Delivery System to Feed American Industry.* Jefferson, N.C.: McFarland, 2010. An in-depth account of how shipping on the Great Lakes developed over the years and became a delivery channel for the raw materials used by U.S. manufacturers.

Bryan, Ford R. *Beyond the Model T: The Other Ventures of Henry Ford.* Detroit: Wayne State University Press, 1990. Chronicles the many industries in which Ford became involved over his lifetime, including a chapter on the aircraft produced by Ford when he took over the Stout Metal Aircraft Company in the 1920s.

EuDaly, Kevin. *The Complete Book of North American Railroading.* Minneapolis: Voyageur Press, 2009. A comprehensive history of the railroad industry organized by decades, discussing trains' enormous impact on the United States' growth between the mid-1800s and the 1940s.

Evans, Harold. *They Made America: From the Steam Engine to the Search Engine: Two Centuries of Innovators.* New York: Little, Brown, 2004. Includes a detailed look at trucks and how they have affected U.S. history, economics, and society.

O'Callaghan, Timothy J. *The Aviation Legacy of Henry and Edsel Ford.* Ann Arbor, Mich.: Proctor, 2000. Contains historic images and previously unpublished anecdotes of the Fords' foray into aviation in the 1920s and during World War II.

Roland, Alex, Alexander Keyssar, and W. Jeffery Bolster. *Way of the Ship: A History of Shipping in America, 1600–2000.* Hoboken, N.J.: John Wiley & Sons, 2007. A comprehensive history of the U.S. shipping industry, its prominent ports, and some of the more famous vessels.

Sandler, Martin W. *On the Waters of the USA: Ships and Boats in American Life.* New York: Oxford University Press, 2003. An account of boating and shipping in the United States and how the waterways helped bring the country to its place of prominence in the twenty-first century.

See also: Airmail; Airships; Aviation; Cascade Tunnel; Detroit Windsor Tunnel; Federal highway system; Model A Fords; Railroads; Route 66

■ Travel

Historically limited to the very wealthy, leisure travel in the United States became more common in the 1920s, when increased industrialization brought about higher wages and more disposable income for middle-class Americans. Train travel was affordable, comfortable, and sometimes even luxurious. By 1921, there were more than ten million cars in the United States, and road trips became increasingly popular. Air travel gradually became an option as well.

At the beginning of the 1920s, many Americans still considered travel too costly and exotic for them. The affluent sailed regularly to Europe, despite the 1912 sinking of the *Titanic* off the coast of Newfoundland. Travel agencies were springing up, though they served mainly the privileged few. Families spent vacations in rented lakefront cottages or mountain cabins, usually in their home state. Only a small percentage of Americans had passports, as they were not a permanent requirement for international travel until World War II. By the end of the 1920s, more sophisticated travel patterns had emerged, and tourism was on its way to becoming a booming industry.

Road Trips
The decade of the 1920s was a time of phenomenal growth in the automotive industry. More and more Americans became proud owners of their first "horseless carriage." Lengthy road trips soon followed. Unfortunately, the roads were often made of sand, gravel, or clay and were therefore often rutted, muddy, or dusty. There were not enough roads to ensure efficient traffic patterns, making for convoluted driving routes.

Early cars were not entirely reliable. Instead of turning a key for ignition, drivers turned a crank in front of the engine and kept cranking until the engine engaged. Flat tires occurred frequently on the roads, and repairing flats meant jacking up the car, removing the inner tube, finding and patching the leak, remounting the tire, then inflating the tire with a pump. Axles broke with such regularity that many drivers carried a spare. Cars were not especially comfortable, either. Although some had windshields and back windows, there were usually no windows on the sides, making winter and rainy-day travel less than ideal. Although the lack of windows provided ventilation in the summer, heating in the winter was nonexistent. Cars without roofs were limited to use in fair weather.

Roadside hotels, restaurants, and rest areas were still on the distant horizon when the decade dawned, though a few roadhouses—inns or taverns along highways in relatively undeveloped areas—existed. Some roadhouses even provided opportunities for alcohol consumption during Prohibition. Communities and enterprising landowners reached out to the growing untapped tourist market by opening campgrounds for early motorists. Here they could buy prepared food to eat at the picnic tables provided, use the primitive restroom facilities, and pitch a tent or sleep in their cars overnight. These early campgrounds led to the first tourist cabins and motels that sprung up along all the major roads, only to be abandoned when, decades later, the Interstate Highway System siphoned traffic away from the secondary roads.

While early tourist facilities varied greatly in amenities and desirability, names like Traveler's Haven or Shady Pines conjured appealing images of rest for weary motorists. "Motor hotels" appeared on well-traveled highways; the first known use of the shortened term "motel" to describe these motor hotels occurred in 1925 in San Luis Obispo, California, when architect and developer Arthur Heineman built an establishment midway between Los Angeles and San Francisco and named it the Milestone Mo-tel.

In 1922, Yellowstone National Park celebrated its fiftieth anniversary, and the publicity it generated in major magazines and newspapers brought crowds of tourists. Many families took a cross-country drive to view the park's wildlife and geysers at first hand. Residents of both coasts made the drive in the years that followed. Other destinations included the Mississippi River, the California redwoods, and the Great Lakes. A Ford automobile and a good road atlas made one's travel options seem nearly endless.

Railway Travel
Though many travelers embraced road trips and the flexibility they afforded, trains were still the transportation method of choice in North America in the 1920s. All the most popular destinations were on railway routes. The beaches of Atlantic City, New Jersey, were a big draw, conveniently located between New York and Philadelphia. Miami was coming into its own as a popular resort destination, and the Atlantic Coast Line Railroad made it an easy trip. Once winter vacationers saw sandy beaches and swaying palms and smelled the jasmine, they were likely to return. Some did their sunbathing in Florida. For others, Miami was just the jumping-off point for short cruises to the Bahamas or Cuba.

In the summer, the same tourists who had traveled to Florida to escape the cold looked for summer getaways that promised escape from the heat. Resorts in New York's Catskill Mountains fit the bill. So did resorts in the Pocono Mountains of Pennsylvania, along with West Virginia's Greenbrier hotel and resort. People also traveled to Hot Springs, Arkansas, for the healing properties of geothermal baths. All these resorts were on railroad lines.

The completion of the transcontinental railroad network in the nineteenth century opened up the western two-thirds of the country to general travel. In the 1920s, the Union Pacific Railroad made it easy to visit the West and the Northwest from the comfort of a railcar. It was a trip of several days from the East Coast or even Chicago, but on-board sleeping accommodations made train travel an especially attractive option on trips of great length. Such accommodations varied in cost and amenities: Passengers could reserve a single berth in a car of communal berths, or more affluent travelers could reserve private sleeper compartments with beds that converted to seats during the day. One of the pleasures of train travel was the dining car. Meals were served on tablecloths set with ornate china and silver. Then there were the informal lounge cars where passengers gathered to have a drink, play cards, or smoke. The wealthiest train travelers sometimes owned their own luxurious railcars and traveled with their own cooks and servants to take care of their needs. Centrally located train stations made it easy for arriving passengers to travel by taxi from the depot to a city hotel.

Air Travel

During the 1920s, air travel became an increasingly viable means of transportation. The earliest planes were used primarily for carrying mail and other freight, but soon larger and more reliable planes appeared on the scene, and passenger transport began to emerge as a separate industry. The earliest aircraft were made of wood and canvas. Some had open cockpits, and there were no pressurized cabins.

A boon to the fledgling air travel industry was the Air Mail Act of 1925, allowing private companies to contract mail routes with commercial pilots, and also paving the way for increased passenger transport. Those early mail carriers became the nucleus of some of the largest airlines in the country, including Pan American and United Airlines. Even automobile manufacturer Henry Ford got into the act, purchasing the troubled Stout Metal Airplane Company in 1924 and renaming it the Ford Air Transport Service, which offered flights from Detroit to Chicago and Cleveland. During the time Ford ran the company, he produced the Ford Tri-Motor, a metal plane also known as the Tin Goose. Two of the first passenger airport terminals, complete with seating, restrooms, and a counter where passengers could purchase tickets, opened between 1925 and 1927 in Detroit and Dearborn, Michigan.

Despite advances in air and automobile travel, it was still faster to get across the country by rail. For one thing, flying at night was not yet possible. For another, early planes had small gas tanks and required frequent refueling stops. During this time aviators also explored the use of airships as a means of passenger transport. The first transatlantic airship crossing took place in 1919. The airship industry seemed promising, because these aircraft were larger and could carry more passengers and cargo; the popularity of airship travel dropped off precipitously in the later 1930s, however, after a number of spectacular crashes.

The 1920s were a time of great excitement in the aviation field. Pilots like Charles A. Lindbergh and James Doolittle were the heroes of the day. Lindbergh made his historic nonstop solo transatlantic flight to Paris in 1927, and Doolittle, in 1929, became the first pilot to complete a flight relying solely on dashboard instruments. Commercial aviation continued to grow in popularity thereafter.

Impact

Rail travel was the most popular mode of travel in the 1920s, but it was quickly superseded by the automobile in the years that followed. Advances in aviation eventually made commercial airlines the method of choice for longer distances, such that trains are now in last place behind cars and airplanes among Americans' preferred modes of transportation. The 1920s unquestionably ushered in the age of the automobile, setting off a pattern of improvements in vehicular comfort and efficiency—and in the transportation infrastructure that supports them—that continues into the twenty-first century, although the long-term effects of the rising cost of oil are yet to be known.

Norma Lewis

Further Reading

Bilstein, Roger E. *Flight in America 1900–1983: From the Wrights to the Astronauts.* Baltimore: Johns Hopkins University Press, 1994. Covers more than eight decades of American aviation, including much detailed information about advances made in the 1920s.

Jakle, John A., and Keith A. Sculle. *America's Main Street Hotels: Transiency and Community in the Early Auto Age.* Knoxville: University of Tennessee Press, 2009. A look back at the early hotels that came into existence to serve the growing number of automobile travelers.

Johnson, Lyn, and Michael O'Leary. *All Aboard! Images from the Golden Age of Rail Travel.* San Francisco: Chronicle Books, 1999. A collection of photography and text telling the history of rail travel during the early decades of the twentieth century.

Welsh, Joe, Jim Boyd, and William F. Howes. *The American Railroad*. Minneapolis: Motorbooks International, 1999. A history of the American railroad industry from its beginnings.

White, John H. *The American Railroad Passenger Car*. Baltimore: The Johns Hopkins University Press, 1985. An authoritative look at the rise of the passenger car and rail travel in general.

See also: Airships; Automobiles and auto manufacturing; Aviation; Federal highway system; Hobbies and recreation; Model A Fords; Railroads; Transportation

Tunney, Gene

Identification: American boxer
Also known as: James Joseph Tunney
Born: May 25, 1897, New York, New York
Died: November 7, 1978, Greenwich, Connecticut

One of the most underrated of all boxing champions, Gene Tunney established a new prototype for heavyweight fighters and twice defeated the legendary heavyweight champion Jack Dempsey.

One of seven children born to Irish immigrants, James Joseph "Gene" Tunney grew up loving learning and boxing. His boxing career started in 1915 when he defeated the more experienced Bobby Dawson in six rounds. While serving in the U.S. Marines during World War I, Tunney became the U.S. Expeditionary Forces boxing champion. He continued to compete locally after the war ended, although he spent the winter of 1921 working as a lumberjack for the J. R. Booth Company in northern Ontario, Canada.

After returning from Canada, Tunney concentrated on professional boxing and maintained his winning streak, capturing the American light heavyweight championship by defeating reigning champion Battling Levinsky in early 1922. Later that year, Tunney suffered his only loss as a professional when Henry "the Human Windmill" Greb took the light heavyweight belt from him. In a rematch in 1923, Tunney avenged the loss by defeating Greb and regaining the belt.

After moving up to the heavyweight division, Tunney defeated heavyweight challengers Bartley Madden, Jack Martin, and Dan O'Dowd in 1925, gaining a shot at the heavyweight world championship the following year. His fleet feet, left jab, and relentless power helped him defeat champion Jack Dempsey and win the title by a unanimous decision. In the rematch a year later, Dempsey knocked Tunney down in the seventh round, the only time Tunney was ever knocked down in a professional fight. For a few seconds after the knockdown, Dempsey failed to retreat to a neutral corner so that the count on Tunney could begin. That extra time allowed Tunney to regain his composure, and he went on to defeat Dempsey for the second time. After defending his title in 1928 against New Zealander Tom Heeney, Tunney retired from boxing with an overall record of one loss, three draws, and eighty-one wins, forty-eight of which ended in a knockout.

Impact

Known as a thinking fighter, Gene Tunney was among the first boxers to use both brains and brawn in the ring. He constantly moved and boxed behind a stiff, accurate left jab, providing a model for later heavyweights such as Muhammad Ali and Larry Holmes. As recognition for his prowess in the ring, Tunney earned the distinction of being named *Ring Magazine*'s first ever Fighter of the Year in 1928. In 1980, he was inducted into the World Boxing Hall of Fame. Ten years later, he was inducted into the International Boxing Hall of Fame.

Alvin K. Benson

Further Reading

Cavanaugh, Jack. *Tunney: Boxing's Brainiest Champ and His Upset of the Great Jack Dempsey*. New York: Ballantine Books, 2007.

Jarrett, John. *Gene Tunney: The Golden Guy Who Licked Jack Dempsey Twice*. London: Robson Books, 2003.

Tunney, Jay R. *The Prizefighter and the Playwright: Gene Tunney and George Bernard Shaw*. Willowdale, Ont.: Firefly Books, 2010.

See also: Boxing; Dempsey, Jack; Johnson, Jack; Sports

U

Unemployment

Although unemployment as a public issue has not been associated with the 1920s nearly as much as with the decade that followed, it was a matter of official concern during the 1920–1921 recession and again in the closing months of 1929, following the stock market crash that ushered in the Great Depression of the 1930s. During the 1920s, business, government, and labor played various roles in the development of programs designed to relieve unemployment.

Scholars and government officials have often studied and debated the causes and consequences of unemployment, as well as what should be considered an acceptable level of unemployment in the U.S. economy. Although unemployment in the United States has not generally been associated with the 1920s nearly as much as with the 1930s, it became enough of a problem, particularly during the post–World War I recession of 1920–1921 and again after the stock market crash of 1929, that its causes and cures became a subject of public concern.

The 1920–1921 Recession

The recession of 1920–1921, sometimes referred to as "the forgotten depression," was an economic downturn at the beginning of the 1920s that lasted only a few months, attributable largely to the country's economic and industrial readjustment following the end of World War I. This early minidepression forced unprecedented discussion of the roles that businesses, unions, and the government should play in relieving unemployment. Although exact figures are not available, the total number of unemployed is believed to have reached as many as four million in 1920.

Newly elected president Warren G. Harding's initial response to the economic crisis was to cut spending and discourage government intervention. As the recession continued into 1921, Harding, at the urging of Commerce Secretary Herbert Hoover, assembled a President's Conference on Unemployment. Hoover promoted a more ambitious set of solutions to the crisis that emphasized the role of local governments in coordinating unemployment relief and that allowed the federal government an advisory and educational role. Harding, by contrast, stuck to his view that the federal government should intervene as little as possible. The conference's findings included a call for local governmental relief efforts, improved industrial efficiency to reduce unemployment, and, as a last resort, federal public works projects as a source of work relief. Following the conference, over two hundred cities mounted local efforts that proved inadequate to the crisis, and Congress passed none of the proposed federal measures to address unemployment.

By the end of 1921, the economic crisis had passed, influenced less by official economic policies than by a high level of technological innovation that resulted in new growth in American industry. The feeling of general prosperity was sustained throughout the 1920s, in spite of reports of continued unemployment among Americans based on factors that fell beyond the control of the affected workers. During this time, there were active efforts within American industries to reduce unemployment, ranging from job shifting to unemployment compensation. These innovations also built on the already established union-based unemployment insurance systems pioneered by the clothing trades unions, which had long experience with the seasonal employment characteristic of the industry.

However, these efforts to reduce unemployment mainly benefited the white male workers who formed the majority of the workforce. Although African American unemployment was reduced in part by the postwar curtailment of immigration, black workers still suffered from lingering discrimination in American industries. Similarly, numerous women who had held wartime industrial jobs lost their jobs when soldiers returned home, and gender discrimination, especially against married women, remained legal and widely accepted during this period. Race- and gender-based unemployment, however, were not subjects of widespread public concern amid the general prosperity that inspired Hoover, when he campaigned for president in 1928, to famously proclaim that "we in America today are nearer to the final triumph over poverty than ever before in the history of any land."

The Crash of 1929

A little more than a year after Hoover uttered these words, the stock market crash of October 1929 triggered a chain reaction of bank and business failures that created a larger and more widespread unemployment crisis than had ever been experienced by Americans. Although no official statistics were available, the number of jobless Americans is believed to have soared into the millions as the depression continued and deepened. African Americans were disproportionately affected by job losses, and black activists began what became the "don't buy where you can't work" campaign to boycott businesses that refused to hire African Americans.

Many of the early government unemployment policies supported the notion of the man as the primary household breadwinner. Several laws were passed barring married women from teaching and other public service jobs on the basis of the primary importance of helping unemployed men. These laws in turn created additional hardship for the many American women who provided the primary or even sole support for their families.

From late 1929 until the end of his presidency in 1933, Hoover was very reluctant, despite mounting public criticism, to push for direct public relief, out of concern that it would undermine the self-reliance of American workers. Instead, he backed legislation that helped to support banks and business. Hoover was also reluctant to authorize public works relief programs. Hoover's unwillingness to address the unemployment crisis more forcefully contributed to a sharp drop in his approval rating and his electoral defeat by Franklin Delano Roosevelt in the 1932 presidential election.

A few states began their own unemployment relief programs, most notably New York under the leadership of then-Governor Roosevelt, some of whose state-level programs would become models for the federal programs that became cornerstones of the New Deal. In addition, the stock market crash of 1929, which contributed to unprecedented widespread unemployment, forced a reevaluation of unemployment and its causes that would in turn affect views concerning the proper role of government in the prevention and relief of unemployment.

Impact

The relatively quick resolution of the recession of 1920–1921 caused it to fade quickly in the public memory. By contrast, the stock market crash of 1929 and the economic depression that followed would challenge President Hoover's belief in a laissez-faire approach to unemployment. The lessons of 1920–1921, however, inspired concerted efforts by President Harry S. Truman immediately after World War II to promote the Full Employment Bill in 1946. The bill promoted maximum employment and prescribed an advisory role for the government in addressing unemployment. On the whole, the appropriate role that the federal government should play in preventing and relieving unemployment has remained controversial up to the present. The development of private and union unemployment compensation systems during the 1920s had some success in moderating or reducing employment in major American industries, but it would prove inadequate to reduce the more widespread unemployment experienced during future economic downturns.

Susan Roth Breitzer

Further Reading

Calkins, Clinch, Helen Hall. *Some Folks Won't Work.* New York: Harcourt, Brace, 1930. An exposé written following the stock market crash of 1929 of the continued unemployment during the presumed prosperity of the 1920s.

Folsom, Franklin. *Impatient Armies of the Poor: The Story of Collective Action of the Unemployed, 1808–1942.* Niwot: University Presses of Colorado, 1991. A history of efforts to organize the unemployed to demand governmental solutions to unemployment. Explores the role of antilabor repression in contributing to the 1920–1921 recession.

Leuchtenburg, William E. *Herbert Hoover.* New York: Times Books, 2009. A biography of President Herbert Hoover that looks at his views on the role of government in regulating employment and the economy.

Sinclair, Andrew. *The Available Man: The Life Behind the Masks of Warren Gamaliel Harding.* New York: MacMillan, 1965. A biography of Warren G. Harding that examines the effect of his political background and small-town heritage on his presidency that began with the recession of 1920–1921.

Stewart, Bryce M. *Unemployment Benefits in the United States: The Plans and Their Setting.* New York: Industrial Relations Counselors, 1930. A study of the public, business, and union unemployment benefit systems operating in the United States by the late 1920s.

Wilson, Joan Hoff. *Herbert Hoover: Forgotten Progressive.* Prospect Heights, Ill.: Waveland Press, 1992. A biography of President Herbert Hoover that examines the development and application of his philosophy of public economic and social responsibility throughout his career in politics beginning in the 1920s.

See also: Agricultural Marketing Act of 1929; American Federation of Labor (AFL); Harding, Warren G.; Hoover, Herbert; Income and wages; Recession of 1920–1921; Stock market crash (1929)

■ Unionism

Unionism declined during the 1920s as unions faced significant challenges from businesses and the United States government. The overall prosperity of the period, along with widespread suspicion of leftist political groups and labor organizers, led to a significant decrease in union membership and influence. Nevertheless, unions such as the United Mine Workers of America continued to organize workers and engage in strikes throughout the decade.

Throughout the late nineteenth and early twentieth centuries, influential unions developed in the mining, railroad, and textile industries, among others. These organizations promoted labor reforms such as shorter workdays, higher wages, and safer working conditions and led workers in strikes when bargaining attempts failed. However, while unions made some significant achievements in earlier decades, unionism as a whole faced numerous challenges and setbacks in the 1920s. Direct opposition by businesses as well as the federal government hindered further progress, while changing public attitudes toward unions contributed to a decrease in membership over the course of the decade. Despite these factors, a number of unions continued to play a major role in the labor movement during the period.

John L. Lewis, the head of the United Mine Workers, was the most influential union leader of the 1920s. (AP Photo)

Major Unions

Founded in the nineteenth century, the American Federation of Labor (AFL) was an organization that worked to unite a number of craft unions. These member unions organized workers who performed a specific craft, rather than all those working in a particular industry. The AFL remained under the leadership of longtime president Samuel Gompers until his death in 1924, when he was succeeded by William Green. In comparison to some unions of the period, the AFL was relatively conservative. The organization's efforts typically focused on areas such as wages, rather than on broad social reforms. In addition, the AFL opposed the various socialist and communist parties, although the organization did support the unsuccessful Progressive Party candidate, Robert M. La Follette, in the 1924 presidential election.

Like the AFL, the United Mine Workers of America (UMWA) was founded late in the nineteenth century and continued to operate throughout the 1920s.

John L. Lewis was elected president of the union in 1920 and remained in the position throughout the decade. Wages and the length of the workday were major concerns of the union, and many of its efforts focused on the areas of health and safety, calling for the installation of proper safety measures within the mines, including ventilation systems to prevent respiratory diseases, and the banning of child labor. The UMWA was involved in several major strikes during the 1920s, including a nationwide 1922 strike that resulted in numerous violent conflicts.

The Industrial Workers of the World (IWW), much like unionism as a whole, declined in influence during the 1920s, largely due to the loss of leaders and union members to government efforts to suppress union and antiwar activity. Despite these difficulties and various internal conflicts, the union continued to organize workers and lead membership drives and strikes throughout the decade.

A number of unions active during the 1920s were affiliated with the communist organizations of the period, which took on various names throughout the decade. In 1929, the Communist Party USA founded the Trade Union Unity League, which comprised a number of trade unions, including the National Textile Workers Union. This union was responsible for organizing the Loray Mill strike, which began in April of 1929 at a textile mill in Gastonia, North Carolina. This controversial strike resulted in numerous arrests as well as several deaths, and while it failed to make an immediate impact on wages or working conditions, it succeeded in attracting public attention to the cause of the textile workers.

Despite their commitment to improving the lives of workers in various industries, many major labor unions neglected the concerns of and were often hostile toward women, African Americans, and immigrants, who collectively made up a substantial portion of the nation's industrial workforce by the 1920s. Nevertheless, female workers continued to play a significant role in labor organizing, particularly in textile industry unions such as the International Ladies' Garment Workers' Union, which had been founded in 1900. Organized in 1925, the Brotherhood of Sleeping Car Porters was an all-black union representing African American porters working for the Pullman Company. Particularly in the Southwest, Latino workers organized *mutualistas*, or mutual aid societies, some of which evolved into unions such as the Imperial Valley Workers Union, founded in 1928. In addition, some major unions accepted members regardless of race or national origin; UMWA, in particular, banned racial or ethnic discrimination in its constitution.

Challenges from Government and Business

Unions faced numerous challenges during the 1920s, some due to the events of the previous decade. The end of World War I began a period of prosperity for many in the United States, and workers who were satisfied with their wages and buying power often did not feel the need to join unions. In addition, following the 1917 revolution in Russia and the successful establishment of a communist regime there, the U.S. government and many American citizens became increasingly suspicious of leftist political groups and philosophies. Many unions included members with ties to socialist, communist, or anarchist groups, and the prevalence of foreign-born union members exacerbated fears of foreign interference in U.S. politics and industry. During a period at the beginning of the decade known as the Red Scare, numerous foreign-born union members and political activists were deported, and many of their native-born counterparts were jailed following government efforts such as the Palmer raids of 1919 and 1920.

Businesses were particularly hostile to unions in the 1920s, typically considering union goals such as increased wages and improved working conditions detrimental to their financial success. During World War I, the coal and textile industries, among others, had increased production dramatically in support of the war effort. After the war, the demand for these products decreased. In an attempt to increase revenue, some businesses, particularly textile mills, instituted a strategy known as the "stretch-out." This strategy, which increased the workers' responsibilities but often lowered their wages, became the cause of many strikes and other conflicts throughout the decade. Facing attempts by unions to organize dissatisfied workers, businesses worked to suppress union activity through coercion and violence, at times employing private police forces tasked with subduing strikers. Companies also made a number of successful appeals to business-friendly government bodies.

In addition to carrying out antileftist raids and prosecuting activists who had spoken out against the United States' entry into World War I, the federal and state governments directly opposed unions on a number of occasions. The Harding, Coolidge, and

Hoover administrations were all relatively business-friendly, and the Supreme Court of the 1920s, led by Chief Justice William H. Taft, regularly took action against unions. The Court often issued opinions that characterized union activities as illegal efforts to restrict trade and regularly invoked the Sherman Antitrust Act against unions. In *American Steel Foundries v. Tri-City Trades Council* (1921), the Court limited picketing to only one picketer per mill gate, effectively eliminating picketing as a viable protest strategy. The Court also continued to uphold the legality of "yellow-dog contracts," documents prohibiting workers from joining unions under penalty of dismissal. In *Lewis v. Red Jacket* (1927), the Supreme Court refused to grant a writ of certiorari, or a writ of judicial review, thus upholding the previous court's decision to charge UMWA leadership with violating the Sherman Antitrust Act through the union's attempts to organize the employees of Red Jacket Consolidated Coal and Coke.

Unions even faced military action, as in the 1921 West Virginia conflict known as the Battle of Blair Mountain. During this event, miners associated with the UMWA marched in solidarity with nonunionized miners, engaging in a violent conflict with local and federal troops that lasted for several days and resulted in deaths on both sides. In other states, government officials regularly used the National Guard and police to protect strikebreakers, arrest union leaders, and attack strikers.

Internal Conflict
While many of the challenges faced by unions during the 1920s came from businesses or the government, many unions also experienced internal conflicts during the decade. Ideological schisms within unions, including the split into multiple socialist and communist factions that greatly divided the Left during the decade, caused conflicts regarding the missions and goals of the organizations. Additional challenges stemmed from the rejection of female, African American, and immigrant workers by some unions, which thereby reduced the unions' potential membership and influence. Such neglected groups of workers were often used as strikebreakers during the decade, further undermining union activities.

Another significant challenge facing the unions of the period was that of leadership. The authoritarian management styles of some earlier union heads, such as Samuel Gompers of the AFL, left their organizations with members ill prepared to assume leadership during the 1920s. In addition, a number of prominent union leaders of earlier decades had been jailed for their activist work, particularly those who had actively opposed the United States' participation in World War I. These included such prominent activists as Eugene V. Debs, former organizer of the American Railway Union and the IWW and five-time Socialist Party presidential candidate, who was imprisoned for violating the Espionage Act of 1917. Other union leaders, such as IWW cofounder Big Bill Haywood, fled to the newly established Soviet Union to avoid imprisonment. Such arrests and emigrations contributed greatly to the problems faced by unions during the decade.

Impact
Unionism experienced a resurgence of popular support during the 1930s, as the harsh effects of the Great Depression on workers in the United States prompted many to seek labor reforms. In later decades, many unions joined under the banner of federations such as the AFL and the Congress of Industrial Organizations (CIO), which merged in 1955 to form the AFL-CIO. While the membership of individual unions declined throughout the latter half of the twentieth century, such federations allowed unionized workers to exert political and economic pressure into the twenty-first century.

John M. Theilmann

Further Reading
Bernstein, Irving. *The Lean Years: A History of the American Worker, 1920–1933*. Reprint. Chicago: Haymarket Books, 2010. A discussion of the American worker and the impact of unions in the 1920s.

Cohen, Lizabeth. *Making a New Deal: Industrial Workers in Chicago, 1919–1939*. 2d ed. New York: Cambridge University Press, 2008. A case study of workers and unions in Chicago.

Dubofsky, Melvyn, and Warren R. Van Tine. *John L. Lewis: A Biography*. Urbana: University of Illinois Press, 1986. A biography of the influential leader of the UMWA.

Phelan, Craig. *William Green: Biography of a Labor Leader*. Albany: State University of New York Press, 1989. A biography of the leader of the AFL.

Salmond, John A. *Gastonia, 1929: The Story of the Loray Mill Strike*. Chapel Hill: University of North Carolina Press, 2009. An account of the strike at the Loray textile mill in North Carolina and the role of the National Textile Workers' Union.

Shogan, Robert. *The Battle of Blair Mountain: The Story of America's Largest Labor Uprising.* Boulder, Colo.: Westview Press, 2004. An exploration of the massive 1921 strike in the West Virginia coal fields that places the strike within the context of union politics and attitudes toward unions.

Zieger, Robert H., and Gilbert J. Gall. *American Workers, American Unions: The Twentieth Century.* 3d ed. Baltimore: Johns Hopkins University Press, 2002. A history of American organized labor containing a chapter on unions in the 1920s.

See also: American Federation of Labor (AFL); Gompers, Samuel; Haywood, Big Bill; Income and wages; Labor strikes; Lewis, John L.; Randolph, A. Philip; Taft, William Howard

■ United Artists

Identification: Independent Hollywood motion picture distributor
Also known as: UA
Date: Established on February 5, 1919

United Artists (UA) was first formed in response to the rampant exploitation of top talent by the major film studios. As the motion picture industry's first independent distribution company, it allowed Hollywood stars to produce their own films, maintain creative control, and retain a larger share of the profits.

In 1918, acting luminaries Douglas Fairbanks Sr., Mary Pickford, Charlie Chaplin, and William S. Hart began to discuss the idea of breaking away from the studios to form their own distribution company. On February 5, 1919, United Artists was incorporated, with the understanding that each star would produce five pictures per year. By this time, Hart had dropped out, but the company gained greater prestige when pioneer director D. W. Griffith took his place. Ownership of the company was evenly divided among the four filmmakers and attorney William Gibbs McAdoo, former secretary of the treasury under President Woodrow Wilson.

As more expensive and lavishly produced feature films became the norm, the UA members were unable to meet their yearly quotas, and Griffith left in 1924. When producer Joseph Schenck became president, he brought with him the rights to films starring his wife, Norma Talmadge, and sister-in-law, Constance Talmadge. He also brought his brother-in-law, the great comic genius Buster Keaton, whose Civil War comedy *The General*, released by UA in 1926, is considered one of the greatest films ever made.

During the late 1920s, the industry's transition to talking motion pictures ended the careers of Fairbanks and Pickford, while the independently wealthy Chaplin, refusing to abandon the silent format, began making ambitious feature films on a very sporadic basis. His masterpiece *The Gold Rush* (1925) was followed by his final film of the decade, *The Circus* (1928). Keaton's brand of physical, deadpan comedy suffered with the coming of sound, and he eventually signed a contract with Metro-Goldwyn-Mayer (MGM), finishing out his career with a series of mediocre films costarring Jimmy Durante. After many leadership changes, UA was sold by the two remaining founders, Chaplin and Pickford, to attorneys Arthur Krim and Robert Benjamin during the early 1950s.

Impact

The example set by United Artists encouraged other ambitious filmmakers to produce their own films outside the studio system, eventually leading to the formation of the Society of Independent Motion Picture Producers in 1941. In 1948, when a U.S. Supreme Court antitrust ruling broke up the studio system, these once-monolithic Hollywood companies essentially became distributors in the mold of United Artists. Eventually, after decades of dizzying changes in ownership, mergers, and financial fiascoes, UA became a division of MGM, where it mostly continued to exist in name only.

Scott Allen Nollen

Further Reading

Nowell-Smith, Geoffrey, ed. *The Oxford History of World Cinema.* Oxford, England: Oxford University Press, 1999.

Schatz, Thomas. *The Genius of the System: Hollywood Filmmaking in the Studio Era.* Minneapolis: University of Minnesota Press, 2010.

See also: Chaplin, Charlie; Circus, The; Fairbanks, Douglas, Sr.; Film; *General, The*; *Gold Rush, The*; Griffith, D. W.; Keaton, Buster; Pickford, Mary

United States v. Ninety-Five Barrels Alleged Apple Cider Vinegar

The Case: U.S. Supreme Court ruling on what constituted misbranding under the Pure Food and Drug Act of 1906

Date: Decided on June 2, 1924

The Supreme Court held that food items with misleading or deceptive statements on their labels violated the Pure Food and Drug Act, affirming the government's power to regulate the safety and accuracy of food labeling.

By the 1920s, food labeling was a well-established practice, with manufacturers using the labels to attract consumers to their products. Food labeling in the 1920s was regulated by the Pure Food and Drug Act of 1906, which banned "misbranded" food items from interstate commerce. Although the government developed enforcement procedures, disputes over misbranded food items were ultimately resolved by the courts.

In a landmark case, the government seized ninety-five barrels of apple cider vinegar produced by the Douglas Packing Company in upstate New York. The label on each barrel stated that the product was "Excelsior Brand Apple Cider Vinegar Made from Selected Apples." The company's manufacturing process was explained at the trial: When apples were in season, the company used fresh apples to make cider and vinegar; during the off-season, the company used dried apples, from which it had removed about eighty percent of the moisture content, later reintroducing about the same amount of fresh water. The government argued that because the confiscated vinegar was made from dried rather than fresh apples, the labeling was false and misleading, therefore amounting to misbranding. While not denying that dried apples were used, the company asserted that the resulting product was nonetheless pure apple cider vinegar.

Citing Section 8 of the act, the Supreme Court held that "every statement, design, and device which could mislead or deceive" was prohibited, even if a statement was not technically false or could literally be true. Although the Court determined that the vinegar made from the dried apples was similar to that derived from fresh apples, it concluded that the products were not identical because the water content of the dried apples was not the same as the fresh juice. The Court also found that the phrase "made from selected apples" implied that the apples were chosen for their fitness to make apple cider vinegar and "gave no hint that the vinegar was made from dried apples." Accordingly, the Court held that the label violated the act's prohibition against misbranding, regardless of whether the vinegar made from dried apples was inferior to that made from fresh apples.

Impact

The Supreme Court's decision made it clear that manufacturers were required to use labeling statements that accurately reflected the contents of food items. Urged on by consumers, Congress enacted more food labeling requirements after the 1920s: The 1938 Federal Food, Drug, and Cosmetic Act largely superseded the 1906 law, expanding the power of the U.S. Food and Drug Administration to oversee food and drug safety.

Diane S. Carter

Further Reading

Hilts, Philip J. *Protecting America's Health: The FDA, Business, and One Hundred Years of Regulation.* New York: Alfred A. Knopf, 2003.

Nestle, Marion. *Food Politics: How the Industry Influences Nutrition and Health.* Rev. ed. Berkeley: University of California Press, 2007.

See also: Food trends; Food, Drug, and Insecticide Administration, U.S.; Frozen foods; Supreme Court, U.S.

United States v. United States Steel Corp

The Case: U.S. Supreme Court ruling on what constitutes a monopoly and violation of the Sherman Antitrust Act

Date: Decided on March 1, 1920

The Supreme Court ruled that a monopoly is not implicated by the mere size of a corporation. Instead, the Court directed the focus on a corporation's overt acts, specifically acts committed after a lawsuit has been filed or acts that are in danger of being resumed once suspended. This ruling effectively and temporarily weakened the monopoly ban of the Sherman Antitrust Act of 1890.

In 1901, four businessmen—Andrew Carnegie, Elbert Gary, Charles M. Schwab, and J. P. Morgan—consolidated ten steel companies into one corporate giant, U.S. Steel Corporation. Ten years later, the Department of Justice brought a federal lawsuit against the corporation, claiming it was a monopoly and thus in violation of the Sherman Antitrust Act. The government's primary argument focused on the immense size of the company. When the corporation was first established, it maintained about 90 percent of the domestic share of steel production. By the time the suit began in district court, however, U.S. Steel's share of the market had fallen to 50 percent, which became a central issue in the Supreme Court's decision.

By a vote of four to three (with Justices McReynolds and Brandeis not participating), the Supreme Court ruled in favor of U.S. Steel. Writing for the majority, Justice McKenna stated that abusive acts by a corporation must be present to constitute an antitrust violation. The size of a company, he stated, or even its ability to exert influence over competitors was deemed not indicative of a monopoly. Furthermore, the Court stated that a corporation could only be in violation of antitrust laws if overt acts had not ceased by the time of the lawsuit or if there was reason to believe that the corporation would resume those acts at a later time. The Court found that any monopolistic acts perpetrated by U.S. Steel had been discontinued due to their ineffectiveness and not because of fear of an impending lawsuit. The Court also found no evidence of intention to resume illegal acts. Consequently, U.S. Steel won the case and was not forced to dissolve.

Impact

United States v. United States Steel Corp characterized the shift from an increase in federal antitrust enforcement at the turn of the twentieth century to President Calvin Coolidge's hands-off approach to business during much of the 1920s. At the time of the Court's ruling in favor of U.S. Steel, many believed the effectiveness of the Sherman Antitrust Act was weakened. The 1930s, however, saw a return to strict federal enforcement of antitrust legislation under the administration of President Franklin D. Roosevelt.

Ramses Jalalpour

Further Reading

Armentano, Dominick T. *Antitrust and Monopoly: Anatomy of a Policy Failure.* 2d ed. Oakland, Calif.: Independent Institute, 1996.

Hylton, Keith N. *Antitrust Law: Economic Theory and Common Law Evolution.* New York: Cambridge University Press, 2003.

Sullivan, E. Thomas. *The Political Economy of the Sherman Act: The First One Hundred Years.* New York: Oxford University Press, 1991.

See also: Business and the economy; Coolidge, Calvin; Roosevelt, Franklin D.; Supreme Court, U.S.

Universal Negro Improvement Association (UNIA)

Identification: African American political and social organization

Also known as: Universal Negro Improvement Association and African Communities (Imperial) League; UNIA-ACL

Date: Established in July 1914

The Universal Negro Improvement Association (UNIA) served as one of the most important political and social organizations in African American history.

Founded in Kingston, Jamaica, in 1914 by writer and businessman Marcus Garvey, the UNIA began as a fraternal, philanthropic organization. In 1918, Garvey organized a UNIA chapter in New York City, which he had visited two years earlier. With its motto of One God, One Aim, One Destiny, the UNIA gave voice to the rising discontent felt among many African Americans. The organization's emphasis on racial consciousness and pride resonated with African Americans who had endured years of racial discrimination and coincided with their migration from the South to cities in the North, where it was believed that social conditions were better.

In keeping with its broad message of political, social, and economic independence, the UNIA established numerous auxiliary divisions, including the Negro Factories Corporation, the Black Star Line steamship company, and the African Black Cross Nurses. In August 1918, the organization established the weekly newspaper *The Negro World* as its official conduit for disseminating information.

In August 1920, the UNIA held its first international convention, an assembly of some twenty-five

> **From "The Principles of the Universal Negro Improvement Association"**
>
> *On November 25, 1922, UNIA leader Marcus Garvey delivered his address, "The Principles of the Universal Negro Improvement Association," to an audience at Liberty Hall in New York in an effort to boost the spirits and determination of the UNIA. Here is an excerpt from the speech:*
>
> We represent peace, harmony, love, human sympathy, human rights and human justice, and that is why we fight so much. Wheresoever human rights are denied to any group, wheresoever justice is denied to any group, there the UNIA finds a cause. And at this time among all the peoples of the world, the group that suffers most from injustice, the group that is denied most of those rights that belong to all humanity, is the black group of 400,000,000. Because of that injustice, because of that denial of our rights, we go forth under the leadership of the One who is always on the side of right to fight the common cause of humanity....

thousand supporters. An important outcome from this gathering was the creation of The Declaration of Rights of the Negro Peoples of the World, which called for an immediate end to the colonial control of Africa. Between 1918 and 1924, the UNIA experienced rapid growth in its membership, making the organization a powerful advocate for black self-determination.

Garvey's ambition to establish material and economic success through the UNIA ran into problems. The Black Star Line, founded in 1919, began as a very successful promotional endeavor, but the enterprise failed, damaging both Garvey's reputation and the UNIA's financial standing. In 1923, Garvey was convicted on charges of mail fraud, and beginning in February 1925, he served a prison sentence in the federal penitentiary in Atlanta, Georgia. Upon release in November 1927, Garvey was deported to Jamaica, which negatively affected the UNIA's American operations. In 1929, he established a new base of operations, the "UNIA-ACL August 1929 of the World," to compete with the New York UNIA chapter. Fragmentation among UNIA leaders, combined with the stock market crash, contributed to a rapid decline in the organization's membership and financial support. Although the organization continued operations, its heyday had passed by the 1930s.

Impact

At its peak, the UNIA established hundreds of chapters as one of the largest organized movements in black history. UNIA and African Americans' growing dissatisfaction with the slow pace of positive social change following World War I played a pivotal role in the spread of Black Nationalism.

Kelly R. McBride

Further Reading

Goldberg, David J. *Discontented America: The United States in the 1920s.* Baltimore: Johns Hopkins University Press, 1999.

Grant, Colin. *Negro with a Hat: The Rise and Fall of Marcus Garvey.* New York: Oxford University Press, 2008.

Vincent, Theodore G. *Black Power and the Garvey Movement.* Reprint. Baltimore: Black Classic Press, 2006.

See also: African Americans; Civil rights and liberties; Garvey, Marcus; Great Migration; Racial discrimination

■ Urbanization

The 1920s continued earlier trends of growth in the number, size, and importance of cities in American life. Cities solidified their position as emerging cultural and intellectual centers, even as they sprouted satellite residential developments and suburbs. Southern and western cities developed alongside older eastern and midwestern centers.

The 1920 census showed that, for the first time, more than half of the U.S. population (51.4 percent) lived in an urban area with over 2,500 residents, while one-quarter lived in cities with over 100,000 residents. The 1910s had witnessed industrialization and economic concentration that drew millions into the cities, a trend that was accelerated by U.S. participation in World War I. Hundreds of thousands of men and women were cycled through the military and demobilized at war's end, just as factories manufacturing war provisions were downsizing and shifting to a peacetime footing; after a brief recession in the first years of the 1920s, however, business once again began to boom. While Progressive social engineers tried to manage urban growth, cultural habits, and politics, social tensions and the geographically emancipating automobile proved to be insuperable and unpredictable agents of change. Urban centers felt the early pangs of decentralization as they increasingly evolved into racial and ethnic enclaves, while growing numbers of well-heeled Caucasians decamped to suburbs and planned communities.

Over the course of the 1920s, the U.S. population grew from around 106 million to around 123 million, or by just over 15.6 percent, while the percentage of the population living in urban areas increased from 51.4 percent in 1920 to 56.1 percent in 1930. Among the fastest-growing cities were Miami, Los Angeles, and those cities whose major industries were associated with automobiles: Detroit, Michigan (manufacturing); Akron, Ohio (tires); and Houston, Texas, and Tulsa, Oklahoma (oil). Land values in cities with over thirty thousand residents doubled between 1920 and 1926, from $25 billion to $50 billion.

Mobility and Movement
The automobile made huge inroads into American society during the 1920s, profoundly affecting the patterns of urbanization. In 1920, Americans owned around 9 million cars and trucks; that number more than doubled by 1925, reaching almost 20 million, and had nearly tripled by 1930, at 26.5 million. Annual automobile sales doubled from 2.3 million units in 1922 to 4.5 million in 1929. Chicago in 1920 had one car for every thirty residents; in 1925, one for every eleven; and in 1930, one for every eight. By mid-decade, sprawling Los Angeles boasted one car for every third resident, about twice the national average. This radical increase in car ownership translated into growth in every aspect of automobile sales and service, as well as increased availability of parking both at home and at distant destinations, from factories to schools to stores.

Suburban commuters drove into the cities for work, creating traffic jams, parking problems, and pollution. Ridership on railways and streetcars steadily dropped, undermining the economic viability of mass transit. Urban streetcars in the United States carried 13.7 billion passengers in 1920, 12.9 billion in 1925, and only 10.5 billion in 1930. The decline was greater in middling cities that tended to have less well-developed mass transit and where the automobile might be more easily accommodated. Thus cities began employing traffic planners and traffic engineers to plan and build streets, overpasses, and other auto-friendly infrastructures using new inventions such as the traffic light to rationalize the flow of cars and to protect pedestrians.

While the older forms of line transportation drew people from nearby outer rings into city centers, automobiles had the opposite effect, shifting not only people but also economic activities away from the urban core into newly developing residential areas. The United States' postwar prosperity led to upper- and middle-class Caucasian families leaving the increasingly troubled urban cores for the new, well-organized suburbs. With the automobile obviating the need for walking-distance local stores and services in this newly decentralized world, the first suburban shopping center appeared in Kansas City, Missouri, in 1922. Over the decade, the suburb of Beverly Hills grew by 2,485 percent, while Elmwood Park, near Chicago, grew by 700 percent, and the Cleveland suburb of Shaker Heights grew by 1,000 percent. Still, many people continued to move into the cities; in Los Angeles, apartment buildings constituted only 8 percent of all new construction in 1920, a proportion that increased to 53 percent by 1928.

Changes in urban demographics aggravated ethnic and racial tensions. In border areas, the Mexican presence expanded as industrial and agricultural opportunities abounded. By 1930, Los Angeles had 167,000 Mexican and Mexican American residents, while San Antonio's population was fully one-third Latino. Most lived in poor conditions and earned only minimal pay. Meanwhile, European American ethnic groups fought to maintain their communal identities

---

The Great Northern Migration

From roughly 1910 to 1930, more than one million African Americans moved from the rural South to industrial cities of the Midwest and the North, leading to the establishment of vibrant African American communities within those cities. During the Great Northern Migration, the industrial northern and midwestern states of New York, Illinois, Pennsylvania, Ohio, and Michigan experienced the greatest positive net migration of African Americans.

in Little Italy and Greek Town neighborhoods, Catholic Polish parishes and schools, and Czech newspapers. As African Americans and other minorities settled in northern cities, due in part to the Great Migration, members of white ethnic minorities felt pressured or threatened. As long as jobs were plentiful, tensions were minimized but not eliminated. During the 1920s, over 118,000 white residents left Harlem, while more than 87,000 black residents moved into the New York City neighborhood. Overall, New York City's black population increased by 115 percent during the decade, rising from over 152,000 to nearly 328,000. This population shift spawned the Harlem Renaissance artistic and literary movement, spurred the political radicalization of many New York City African Americans, and contributed to the decay of housing and other infrastructure as construction slowed toward the end of 1920s.

City Governance and Urban Planning
Despite the growth of commuter towns (urban communities that were primarily residential), urban centers retained much of their wealth, as well as their longstanding corruption and crime. Prohibition went into effect in January 1920, outlawing the manufacture, transportation, and sale of alcohol; by 1929, over thirty-two thousand speakeasies were selling alcohol in New York City. Illegal alcohol fueled criminal activity and competition, which left some five hundred Chicago gang members dead between 1924 and 1929. Its proceeds induced corrupt officials, including the mayors of Chicago, New York City, and Boston, to tolerate the violence and criminality. Cities such as Detroit, Philadelphia, San Francisco, Kansas City, and Cleveland were also shaken by crime and corruption. This prompted experiments in governance with Progressive-style city managers who were thought to be incorruptible. Though the experiment failed in Cleveland, Ohio, and Kansas City, Missouri, it proved successful in Cincinnati, and by decade's end, 430 towns, mostly small and midsize ones, had city managers.

Growth of the new, decay of the old, social tensions, and the realities of the automobile prompted the development of urban planning. Proponents were convinced that the market was incapable of operating efficiently, that urban ethnic and racial minorities were little better than children at problem solving, and that professional, rational ordering, whether influenced by communist or fascist models, was the answer for a better tomorrow. Progressive social scientists at urban universities such as Columbia and Chicago studied urban histories and current conditions to uncover the reasons for social and physical problems.

Meanwhile, city planners and engineers organized planning boards and commissions made up of experts and wealthy stakeholders. By 1930, there were 735 of these, up from 17 in 1914. Originally advisory, these boards and commissions' power to effect change grew as confidence in unfettered growth dwindled. One of their major tools for controlling growth and change was zoning legislation, usually seen as illegal interference with the value and use of one's private property. In 1920, the court case *Town of Windsor v. Whitney* upheld the legality of planning on the basis of community "health and safety." In 1923, 183 communities had zoning ordinances, increasing to 981 by 1930. In the Supreme Court case *Village of Euclid, Ohio v. Ambler Realty Co.* (1926), the Court upheld the right of the Cleveland suburb of Euclid—and, by extension, all local governments—to institute zoning laws if there is a preexisting plan and no damage ensues to the region. Planning had to be fair and reasonable. Despite the trend toward greater planning, a split remained between urban planning processes and regional or metropolitan planning, as those outside of the urban core did not want to be responsible for the burgeoning social, economic, and political problems of the big city.

Planning for urban housing remained problematic as African Americans and other ethnic minorities replaced working- and middle-class Caucasians in increasingly aging housing units. One potential solution was the 1926 State Housing Law of New York State, which offered government funding for companies to construct housing units that would rent for a maximum of $12.50 per month, in an effort to provide housing for those who otherwise could not afford it. Within ten years, around six thousand units had been built under this program. Despite all efforts, however, the postwar housing boom had peaked around 1924, and as a harbinger of things to come, foreclosures steadily increased from 68,100 in 1926 to over 150,000 by the end of the decade. Between 1928 and 1933, the number of new housing units under construction fell by 95 percent, while expenditures on necessary repairs fell from $55 million to $500,000.

Impact

The economic boom of the 1920s translated into optimism as speculation soared, people relocated to find better jobs, and local planners and politicians sought to make the best of urban centers. Typical American values began to shift from those of rural farmers and small-town neighbors to those of city dwellers. Life in the cities was characterized by competition for scarce resources and by high levels of crime, while speculation and credit replaced individual initiative and delayed gratification for consumers faced with a growing range of choices. By the end of the decade, the United States had become an urban society and culture. The automobile, now firmly ensconced in that culture, provided escape from the farm as well as from the urban center, though the heyday of the suburbs was still yet to come.

Joseph P. Byrne

Further Reading

Abbott, Carl. *Urban America in the Modern Age: 1920 to the Present.* 2d ed. Wheeling, Ill.: Harlan Davidson, 2007. A broad overview of the dynamic nature of American urbanization.

Goldberg, David Joseph. *Discontented America: The United States in the 1920s.* Baltimore: Johns Hopkins University Press, 1999. Focuses on the postwar failures of Progressivism and issues of urban labor and race relations.

Kyvig, David E. *Daily Life in the United States, 1920–1940: How Americans Lived Through the Roaring Twenties and Great Depression.* Chicago: Ivan R. Dee, 2004. Treats many aspects of urbanization from the perspective of the ordinary citizen.

Light, Jennifer S. *The Nature of Cities: Ecological Visions and the American Urban Professions, 1920–1960.* Baltimore: Johns Hopkins University Press, 2009. Focuses on how academic social scientists, real estate professionals, and urban planners came to treat the ecology of American cities in the 1920s.

Miller, Nathan. *New World Coming: The 1920s and the Making of Modern America.* Cambridge, Mass.: Da Capo Press, 2004. Emphasizes the famous people and events of the 1920s and their effects on American urban life and culture.

Teaford, Jon C. *The Twentieth Century American City: Problem, Promise, and Reality.* 2d ed. Baltimore: Johns Hopkins University Press, 1993. Discusses the major problems and tensions of the 1920s in the context of twentieth-century urban history.

Watson, Steven. *The Harlem Renaissance: Hub of African American Culture, 1920–1930.* New York: Pantheon Books, 1996. Discusses black Harlem as a unique place in the United States as well as a case study in urban race relations, urban creativity, and the effects of the stock market crash on the community.

See also: African Americans; Automobiles and auto manufacturing; Chain stores; Cities; Demographics; Great Migration; Housing; Immigration to the United States; Migrations (within U.S.); Suburbs

V

■ Valentino, Rudolph

Identification: American film star
Also known as: Rodolfo Alfonso Raffaello Piero Filiberto Guglielmi di Valentina d'Antonguolla; the Latin Lover
Born: May 6, 1895, Castellaneta, Italy
Died: August 23, 1926, New York, New York

Charismatic film star Rudolph Valentino made a distinct impression on the silent film industry in the 1920s, earning recognition as one of the decade's acting icons in films such as The Four Horsemen of the Apocalypse *(1921),* The Sheik *(1921),* Blood and Sand *(1922), and* The Son of the Sheik *(1926).*

In a life of just over three decades, Rudolph Valentino developed from an impoverished Italian immigrant to a New York dancer to a silent film star to a tragic legend killed by a fatal illness. Born in 1895 to an Italian veterinarian father and a French mother, Valentino came to the United States as a teenager and supported himself with odd jobs. Leaving New York City, Valentino was involved in a few stage productions before landing in Hollywood, where he used dancing contacts to secure bit acting parts, soon moving up to performing dark male roles because of his foreign look.

Rudolph Valentino. (Moviepix/Getty Images)

Silent Film Career

Valentino's breakthrough came when the motion picture studio Metro Pictures Corporation cast him as the lead in *The Four Horsemen of the Apocalypse* (1921), about an Argentine youth in the French army during World War I whose extended family is split between the German and French sides. The film was a tremendous success with both critics and audiences, becoming one of the top-grossing silent films and one of the first to earn over $1 million. Valentino did not immediately reap the rewards of this success, however, with Metro declining to increase his pay. Valentino did three more films for Metro in 1921, and the success of the third, *The Conquering Power*, motivated Valentino to leave Metro for the Famous Players-Lasky Corporation run by producer Jesse Lasky.

In the Famous Players-Lasky production *The Sheik* (1921), Valentino sealed his reputation as a major performer and won legions of female fans with his sultry good looks. Famous Players-Lasky knew the value of its leading actor and featured Valentino in four more lucrative films, including the lavish *Beyond the Rocks* (1922).

Although Valentino's pay increased greatly during his time with Famous Players-Lasky, he felt it was not on par with that of other leading actors, and a two-year legal battle ensued, during which Valentino made no films. At the end of the dispute, Valentino received a huge pay increase, to $7,500 per week, and increased artistic control over his films. However, the next two, *Monsieur Beaucaire* (1924) and *The Sainted Devil* (1924), were not successful, and Valentino soon left Famous Players and moved to United Artists, for whom he made *The Eagle* (1925) and *The Son of the Sheik* (1926), the latter of which was a blockbuster success for all involved. During production, however, Valentino became ill; he later collapsed in New York City, had emergency surgery for appendicitis, and died of complications a little more than a week later.

Personal Life

After his arrival in Hollywood, Valentino married actress Jean Acker, but the marriage was unsuccessful and the couple soon separated. While working with Metro, he met and fell in love with the costume designer and sometime actress Natacha Rambova. They married in 1923, overcoming charges of bigamy while Valentino's divorce from Acker became finalized under California law. Rambova was very influential in Valentino's career, encouraging his challenge to Famous Players-Lasky and negotiating film deals on his behalf. She alienated many of his personal and professional contacts though, and United Artists insisted she be sidelined, leading to marital strain and then divorce in 1925.

Women crammed theaters to see Valentino, his flowing costumes, and his romantic screen presence. Reactions to his image were mixed, however: While many women found him exotically handsome, his appearance did not fit the rugged American mold, and he chafed repeatedly at public commentary suggesting he was effeminate. The hysterical outpouring of grief at his early death, however, testified to his popularity, as thousands thronged the streets of New York for his funeral. His body was transported to Los Angeles, where it rests in Hollywood Forever Cemetery.

Impact

During the first half of the 1920s, Valentino was seen by many as the personification of forces demolishing conservative cultural barriers that had existed prior to that time. Audiences responded strongly to his performances, and his unique attractiveness contributed to the shifts in gender expectations and aesthetics that occurred in the 1920s and 1930s.

Joseph Edward Lee

Further Reading

Basinger, Jeanine. *Silent Stars*. New York: Knopf, 1999. Examines the lives of silent film stars, with information on Valentino's life, career, and impact on the film industry.

Ellenberger, Allan R. *The Valentino Mystique: The Death and Afterlife of the Silent Film Idol*. Jefferson, N.C.: McFarland, 2005. Presents a detailed report on Valentino's death, estate transactions, and filmography, including excerpts from newspapers discussing his life and death.

Hill, Donna L. *Rudolph Valentino, The Silent Idol: His Life in Photographs*. San Francisco: Blurbs, 2010. Features a collection of photographs depicting Valentino, some of which have never been published.

Leider, Emily W. *Dark Lover: The Life and Death of Rudolph Valentino*. New York: Farrar, Strauss and Giroux, 2003. Explores Valentino's ascent from immigrant to film star, noting his contributions to the shaping of American masculinity.

Menefee, David W. *The First Male Stars: Men of the Silent Era*. Albany: Bear Manor Media, 2007. Discusses the careers of early-twentieth-century male movie stars, including a section on the life and work of Valentino.

See also: Film; Lasky, Jesse L.; Metro-Goldwyn-Mayer (MGM); *Sheik, The*

■ Vallée, Rudy

Identification: American singer, bandleader, and entertainer
Also known as: Hubert Prior Vallée
Born: July 28, 1901, Island Pond, Vermont
Died: July 3, 1986, North Hollywood, California

Originally a saxophonist, Rudy Vallée became a singing bandleader and sex symbol of the late 1920s. Thanks to the invention of the electric microphone, Vallée's thin, nasal voice could be easily recorded and broadcast, and he quickly became known as a soft-voiced "crooner," a title given to many singers of the next decade, such as Bing Crosby.

Vallée grew up in Maine, where he learned to play the saxophone and drums. After serving briefly in World War I, Vallée was discharged for being underage and began working in a motion picture theater in Maine. The saxophone became his trademark instrument. He attended the University of Maine and then Yale University until 1927, taking a break to play with the Savoy Hotel's house orchestra in London, England. He received a contract to record with Columbia Records in 1928, along with his newly formed band, the Connecticut Yankees. They produced several up-tempo ballads, and the following year Vallée and his group had their first smash hit, "I'm Just a Vagabond Lover." Vallée's popularity skyrocketed in the last two years of the 1920s, when he became a major figure in a variety of mass media: He was heard on radio and records and could be seen in magazines and movies.

He made his first short film in the mid-1920s, but his first cameo appearance in a major film was in Florenz Ziegfeld's massive production *Glorifying the American Girl* (1929), in which Vallée sang through a megaphone, as he was known to do in live appearances where there was no microphone. Quickly realizing the power of motion pictures, Vallée went on to star in *The Vagabond Lover* in 1929. In the same year, he hosted his first radio program, *The Fleischmann Hour*. Among his many hits were "The Whiffenpoof Song" (1927), "Maine Stein Song" (1930), and "Life Is Just a Bowl of Cherries" (1931). By the end of the 1920s, Vallée was one of the most recognizable stars in America.

Impact
Vallée's career continued to build throughout the 1930s, with numerous song hits both as a performer and a composer, many more radio and movie appearances, and even several stage performances, including in the revue *George White's Scandals*. During the early 1940s, however, his popularity began to fade, and one of his last major hits, "As Time Goes By," was recorded in 1943. He maintained a career as an entertainer and stand-up comedian during the 1950s. One of his most notable appearances later in life was in the stage and screen productions of the musical *How to Succeed in Business Without Really Trying* (1961), and he made intermittent appearances on television and films up to the time of his death in 1986.

Jonas Westover

Further Reading
Johnson, Richard J., and Bernard H. Shirley. *American Dance Bands on Record and Film, 1915–1942*. Fairplay, Colo.: Rustbooks, 2010.

Vallée, Eleanor. *My Vagabond Lover: An Intimate Biography of Rudy Vallée*. Dallas: Taylor, 1996.

See also: Crosby, Bing; Loudspeakers; Music, popular

■ Van Der Zee, James

Identification: African American photographer
Born: June 29, 1886, Lenox, Massachusetts
Died: May 15, 1983, Washington, D.C.

James Van Der Zee was a portrait photographer best known for his work from the 1920s and 1930s. From his Harlem studio, he captured the energy, aspirations, and prosperity of the local African American community and documented the flourishing local artistic, literary, and cultural scene known as the Harlem Renaissance. Rediscovered in the 1960s, his work from the 1920s is both socially and artistically significant.

Although he had long aspired to open a studio, Van Der Zee did not meet this goal until the years after 1915, during which he opened the Guarantee Photo Studio in Harlem with Gaynella Greenlee, his second wife. The studio was established at an auspicious moment. Buoyed by the burgeoning African American community in Harlem that sought out the services of the young and talented photographer, the studio also profited from a growing demand for portrait photographs by families of young servicemen setting out for military service in World War I. With the end of the war, Van Der Zee found particular success in the booming New York City economy of the 1920s. His work has come to be identified most specifically with the flourishing art and culture of the Harlem Renaissance.

Portraiture
Van Der Zee's best-known work of the 1920s is his portrait photography. Some of his portrait photographs document renowned figures of Harlem's most culturally productive years, such as writer Countee Cullen or social reformer Marcus Garvey, while many others record local community events including weddings and funerals. Even in routine photographs, Van Der Zee attempted to attain a high degree of aesthetic caliber, and he retouched his work by hand both on the prints and on the negatives. The resulting images represent their sitters in a complimentary light and depict an exceptionally confident and prosperous African American community. These

photographs testify to the prosperity of the decade and represent key characteristics of life in the African American urban community.

Also significant among Van Der Zee's portrait photographs are his mortuary images that document dead friends, family, and other significant figures. Often, as in his ambitious studio photographs, Van Der Zee spliced together photographs or inserted painted backdrops into these mortuary studies in order to create particular aesthetic effects.

Studio Work

Van Der Zee's work was by no means limited to portraiture. Among his more interesting works of the 1920s are the pieces that he created as ambitious photographic projects, many of which were probably intended for calendars or other promotional imagery. One example of this type of imagery was *Daydreams* (1925), in which Van Der Zee posed a young woman with a photograph and bouquet on her lap. As she stares dreamily into the distance, she is embraced by a ghost-like male partner in front of a seaside backdrop. Another such image, *Nude* (1923), features a naked young woman seated in front of a fireplace in a foyer. Although her face seems to be lit by the fire, a painted backdrop of curling flames is set inside the hearth instead of a real fire. Such images create fictional scenes by utilizing complex photographic processes.

Subsequent Career

With the decline of the Harlem economy after the stock market crash of 1929, Van Der Zee's business suffered. The aging photographer did not update his studio practice to coincide with the photographic trends of the 1940s and 1950s, so his work came to be unfashionable and his popularity faded. Following the inclusion of Van Der Zee's work in the Metropolitan Museum of Art's 1969 exhibition "Harlem on My Mind," however, the photographer attained widespread acclaim that lasted throughout the final years of his life.

Impact

Because Van Der Zee's popularity was initially limited to the Harlem community, his artistic prominence came to an end with the decline of the Harlem Renaissance. His studio practice of the 1920s and 1930s had little connection to the modernist photographic work being created in other New York City art circles.

Despite the size and popularity of his work, Van Der Zee did not have an immediate or direct impact on subsequent photographers. Since the 1960s, however, Van Der Zee's work has been widely exhibited. His photographs of the 1920s and 1930s have given a vibrant voice to African American history of the early twentieth century, capturing the strength and excitement of the Harlem community of that time.

Julia A. Sienkewicz

Further Reading

Haskell, Barbara. *The American Century: Art and Culture, 1900–1950*. New York: Whitney Museum of Art, 1999. Situates Van Der Zee's work in the larger context of the Harlem Renaissance and in the ambitious New York City art scene of the years discussed.

Mercer, Kobena. *James Van Der Zee*. London: Phaidon, 2003. Offers a selection of photographs by Van Der Zee.

Thaggert, Miriam. *Images of Black Modernism: Verbal and Visual Strategies of the Harlem Renaissance*. Amherst: University of Massachusetts Press, 2010. Provides a broader context for Van Der Zee's work with respect to modernism and twentieth-century African American photography.

Willis, Deborah. *Black Photographers, 1840–1940: An Illustrated Bio-Bibliography*. New York: Garland, 1985. Discusses Van Der Zee's life and work, placing Van Der Zee within the context of the African American photographic tradition. Features a thorough bibliography.

Willis, Deborah, and Rodger C. Birt. *Van Der Zee: Photographer, 1886–1983*. New York: Harry N. Abrams, 1998. Features two significant essays analyzing Van Der Zee's oeuvre and biography. Includes reproductions of a large number of Van Der Zee's photographs, especially significant works from the 1920s.

See also: African Americans; Harlem Renaissance; Photography

■ Vaudeville

Less risqué than burlesque, vaudeville provided a form of engaging yet family-friendly entertainment that appealed to people of different social classes. Although vaudeville's popularity had eroded by the end of the 1920s, it served as a crucial bridge to new forms of entertainment, and it introduced many early stars and styles that helped fuel American entertainment's transition to radio, film, and ultimately to television.

Modeled on earlier forms of French theater bearing the same name, American vaudeville—variety shows featuring song, dance, comedy acts, performing animals, and other entertainments—was the successor to minstrelsy as the nation's most popular form of entertainment from the late eighteenth century through the 1920s. The French term was used to evoke a sense of European respectability and to distinguish vaudeville as a more high-class and less lascivious form of popular entertainment. Its performers came primarily from working-class backgrounds, many from emerging immigrant communities of Irish, Italian, Polish, and eastern European Jewish extraction. Vaudeville also featured many African American performers and served as a crucial medium for the folk entertainment traditions of various cultural groups to reach a broad national audience.

The Early 1920s

By the start of the 1920s, vaudeville was the most prominent theatrical genre in the United States and Canada, with theaters featuring performances from coast to coast and performers traveling across the continent on vaudeville theater circuits. During this time, vaudeville was dominated by two theater networks: the Keith-Albee theaters in the East and the Orpheum Circuit theaters in the West. However, the 1920s saw the emergence of new competitors for Keith-Albee, most notably Marcus Loew and his chain of Loews Theatres. Loew became successful by featuring less well-known and therefore less expensive performers and by charging significantly less for tickets. The dominant chains were forced to respond by lowering prices and featuring cheaper performers. This led to a decline in wages for many vaudeville performers as promoters became more willing to sacrifice show quality in the name of lower prices and bigger audiences. While the "big time" theaters continued to cater to America's middle and upper classes, the emergent "small time" theaters drew the rapidly growing working- and lower-middle-class communities in New York and other major cities into the vaudeville theater.

Accommodating their diverse audiences, vaudeville performers drew from a wide array of folk and popular traditions, though these borrowings often took the form of crude stereotypes. Nevertheless,

Marcus Loew, the founder of Loews Theatres. (Gamma-Keystone via Getty Images)

such portrayals still managed to universalize the experiences of specific communities. For example, Sophie Tucker's 1925 hit "My Yiddish Mama" spoke to the struggle other immigrant groups were having with assimilation into American culture. The 1920s also saw a shift away from the allusions to Victorian morality that had defined vaudeville in earlier decades as performers began to embrace a rowdier and arguably more subversive style that lampooned traditional social roles and restrictions.

Although vaudeville acts, like any good theater, tended to draw attention to universal aspects of the human condition, racial segregation had a strong impact on the tradition, and many shows, including those with African American performers, were performed for white-only audiences. While black vaudeville performers had their own theater circuits that catered to black audiences, many performed in the mainstream theaters as well. Though black artists often performed in blackface (further darkening their own skin), acting out crude minstrel stereotypes, they were crucial contributors to the vaudeville tradition. Many significant black musicians, comedians, and dancers, including Eubie Blake, Bert Williams, and Bill "Bojangles" Robinson, were active vaudeville performers during the 1920s. Their work formed the core of a wave of successful Broadway musicals, often referred to as "Black Broadway" throughout the decade. Black performers also played a crucial role in the infusion of jazz music into vaudeville performances.

Rapid Decline

Vaudeville's popularity suffered a sharp decline in the latter half of the 1920s for a number of reasons, most prominently the introduction and popularization of sound film. This development led many popular vaudeville entertainers to abandon the live stage in favor of roles in the new "talkies." Though motion pictures had long been combined with vaudeville shows in penny arcades across the country, they began to eclipse vaudeville's headlining acts in popularity during the latter half of the decade. Additionally, the formation of the National Broadcasting Company (NBC) in 1926 and the Columbia Broadcasting System (CBS) in 1928 expanded the scope of radio and created more opportunities for top vaudeville stars such as George Burns, Jack Benny, and Bing Crosby. Stars also left vaudeville for the emerging genre of the Broadway musical, which absorbed many vaudeville conventions yet featured a coherent narrative story. At the same time, the top motion picture companies, including RKO and Paramount, put together their own stage shows to pair with film showings. Featuring less famous talent, these shows were significantly cheaper to put on but still drew audiences because of the popularity of motion pictures.

The decline in vaudeville's popularity was hastened by the business decisions of the industry's top promoters, who saw that the future lay in sound film. The Keith-Albee and Orpheum circuits merged in 1927 to form Keith-Albee-Orpheum, a controlling stake in which was then sold to Joseph Kennedy and his Film Booking Offices of America in 1928; Keith-Albee-Orpheum and Film Booking Offices were in turn taken over by the Radio Corporation of America (RCA) to form Radio-Keith-Orpheum, or RKO, which became a major Hollywood film studio. By the decade's end, many vaudeville theaters had been converted into full-time movie houses. Vaudeville, however, did not die out completely, continuing to thrive through the 1940s within the African American community as the black vaudeville circuits came to occupy many theaters formerly patronized by white audiences.

Impact

Vaudeville played a crucial role in the development of twentieth-century American popular entertainment. Due to the size and breadth of its audience, as well as the diverse ethnic backgrounds of its performers, vaudeville helped create a coherent and unified national culture out of the folk traditions of different immigrant populations. It spoke to America's transition into a more urban nation with a coherent national identity forged from the experiences of citizens with widely diverse backgrounds and experiences. As such, vaudeville produced many of the theatrical, musical, and comedic styles and conventions that continue to shape various entertainment genres. Vaudeville's impact may be felt most strongly through its significant influence on early film and television programming, as many of the first film and television performers were veterans of the vaudeville stage.

Christopher J. Wells

Further Reading

Gottschild, Brenda Dixon. *Waltzing in the Dark: African American Vaudeville and Race Politics in the Swing Era.* New York: St. Martin's Press, 2000. Surveys African American vaudeville performance from the late 1920s through the 1940s, with a focus on the dance team of Norton and Margot.

Kibler, M. Alison. *Rank Ladies: Gender and Cultural Hierarchy in American Vaudeville.* Chapel Hill: University of North Carolina Press, 1999. An account of vaudeville through the lens of American gender politics, with a focus on significant female performers; concluding chapters discuss vaudeville's decline in the late 1920s.

Snyder, Robert W. *The Voice of the City: Vaudeville and Popular Culture in New York.* Chicago: Ivan R. Dee, 2000. A social history of vaudeville in New York City. Presents the various types of theaters throughout New York neighborhoods and their appeal to different social classes and ethnic groups.

Stein, Charles W. *American Vaudeville as Seen by Its Contemporaries.* New York: Da Capo Press, 1985. Presents a collection of original documents, letters, and newspaper reviews from the vaudeville era, as well as the author's commentary on a variety of topics, including vaudeville's decline.

Wertheim, Arthur Frank. *Vaudeville Wars: How the Keith-*

Albee and Orpheum Circuits Controlled the Big-Time and Its Performers. New York: Palgrave MacMillan, 2009. Chronicles the rise and fall of the dominant vaudeville circuits of the 1920s; provides an account of their ascendency and decline during the decade as well as the emergence of Loews Theatres.

See also: Broadway musicals; Crosby, Bing; Marx Brothers; Talking motion pictures; Theater in the United States

■ Vidor, King

Identification: American film director
Also known as: King Wallis Vidor
Born: February 8, 1894, Galveston, Texas
Died: November 1, 1982, Paso Robles, California

King Vidor was one of the most prolific Hollywood directors of the 1920s, making films in a variety of genres. His best-known and most groundbreaking films from this period addressed social concerns and the human condition.

King Vidor moved to Hollywood in 1915 and worked at various jobs in the film industry before directing his first film in 1919. He directed twenty-three films in the 1920s, the majority of which were produced by Metro-Goldwyn-Mayer (MGM) studios. Vidor's silent films generally focused more on the storyline than on acting, and he vowed early in his career to produce films based on human realism that did not "portray fright, suggest fear, or glorify evil."

As the silent film era reached its peak in the mid-1920s, Vidor decided to make a film that would have great impact, and in 1925, the antiwar drama *The Big Parade* (1925) starring John Gilbert was released. Realistically depicting the horrors of trench warfare during World War I, *The Big Parade* was at the time the highest-grossing silent film and was the director's first major hit. Vidor made two more films starring Gilbert. The first, costarring Lillian Gish, was the very profitable *La Bohème* (1926), which implemented a new film technique, the flashback. Later that same year, the costume drama *Bardelys the Magnificent*, costarring Vidor's wife Eleanor Boardman, was released. *The Crowd* followed in 1928 and is considered a silent film masterpiece. Boardman and James Murray starred in the social commentary, which was unlike any other film of the era in its treatment of the realistic problems of an ordinary married couple who are emotionally lost.

Vidor's final two silent films, *The Patsy* (1928) and *Show People* (1928), were comedies and starred Marion Davies. In 1929, Vidor transitioned to sound with *Hallelujah!*, starring Daniel L. Haynes and Nina Mae McKinney. It was the director's only musical and the first film from a major studio featuring an all-black cast. MGM considered the venture so risky that Vidor contributed his salary to cover the cost of producing the film.

Impact
Vidor led a successful directing career through the 1950s, and his breadth of work included Westerns, comedies, historical subjects, and epic dramas that strove to be entertaining yet socially conscious and highly cinematic. Over the course of his career, Vidor was nominated five times for the Academy Award for Best Director and was presented with an Honorary Award in 1979 for his lifetime achievements.

Michael Adams

Further Reading
Crafton, Donald. *The Talkies: American Cinema's Tradition to Sound, 1926–1931.* Berkeley: University of California Press, 1999.

Dowd, Nancy, and David Shepard. *King Vidor.* Hollywood, Calif.: Directors Guild of America, 1988.

Kobel, Peter. *Silent Movies: The Birth of Film and the Triumph of Movie Culture.* New York: Bulfinch Press, 2006.

See also: Academy Awards; African Americans; Film; Gilbert, John; Gish, Lillian; *Hallelujah!;* Metro-Goldwyn-Mayer (MGM); Talking motion pictures

■ Vitamin D discovery

The 1920s was a decade of numerous scientific advances related to food and medicine, including the discovery of antibacterial medicines, vaccines to help wipe out disease, and vitamins to improve health. The identification of vitamin D and its role in bone formation and bone health led the way to the prevention and cure of certain bone diseases.

The mid-seventeenth century witnessed an epidemic rise among children of the potentially fatal bone disease known as rickets. Observers of the epidemic

> **Vitamin D and Rickets**
>
> Rickets (or rachitis) is a disease that causes abnormal bone formation, particularly in the long bones and the ribs. First described in the second century C.E. by Galen of Pergamum and Soranus of Ephesus, rickets was a widespread health problem until the discovery and dissemination of the antirachitic factor, vitamin D. Elmer Verner McCollum and coworkers pioneered this effort in 1922, showing that the antirachitic factor was a distinctive substance. They named this substance vitamin D because it was the fourth vitamin to be discovered. The occurrence of rachitis is now rare—except in developing countries—due to the vitamin D fortification of food (especially milk) in the industrialized nations of the world.

noticed an association between a lack of sunlight and an increased prevalence of rickets. By the early 1800s, cod liver oil was recommended as a treatment, and by the early part of the twentieth century, scientists discovered the curative powers of a then-unknown substance and its role in the prevention and cure of rickets.

In 1919, German researcher Kurt Huldschinsky found that infants exposed to ultraviolet light rays were cured of rickets and that a substance in the skin was the means of the cure. In 1922, American scientist Elmer McCollum proved that when cod liver oil was heated, the beneficial effects of vitamin A in the oil were diminished; however, the oil remained effective in curing rickets. McCollum soon deduced that a nutrient different from vitamin A must be present in the oil, and he named it vitamin D, the fourth vitamin to be discovered and named.

Harry Steenbock of the University of Wisconsin demonstrated in 1924 that foods exposed to ultraviolet radiation promoted growth in rats, and in 1925 he was granted a patent for his food irradiation process. The Wisconsin Alumni Research Foundation was founded in 1925 to administer the patents, with the first license being granted in 1927 to Quaker Oats for vitamin D–fortified cereal. Soon a nationwide public health campaign was launched promoting increased sun exposure and food fortified with vitamin D.

Impact

The irradiation of food and the synthesis of vitamin D supplements led to a dramatic decline in the incidence of rickets in the 1920s and prevented epidemic recurrences of the disease for future generations. Subsequent research in the 1930s established that vitamin D is not a true vitamin: Activation by light converts it, through a process involving the liver and kidneys, into a hormone. In the following decades, scientists discovered a multifaceted role for vitamin D in the body, and new applications of this hormone continue to be developed.

Paul J. Chara

Further Reading

Carlson, Laurie Winn. *The Sunlight Solution: Why More Sun Exposure and Vitamin D Are Essential to Your Health.* Amherst, N.Y.: Prometheus Books, 2009.

Frankenburg, Frances Rachel. *Vitamin Discoveries and Disasters: History, Science, and Controversies.* Santa Barbara, Calif.: ABC-CLIO, 2009.

Holick, Michael, F., ed. *Vitamin D: Physiology, Molecular Biology, and Clinical Applications.* 2d ed. Totowa, N.J.: Humana, 2010.

See also: Chemistry; Health care; Science and technology

■ Voting rights

The history of voting rights in the United States is one of hard-fought campaigns to make elections more representative and democratic. Political action and legal challenges to denials of voting rights in the 1920s illustrate well this struggle to expand the electorate.

Government in the United States is based upon the doctrine of popular consent, meaning a legitimate government derives its just powers from the consent of its citizens through their vote in elections. The U.S. Constitution, however, did not originally contain any explicit guarantee of a right to vote. Instead, each state determined voter qualifications, and those qualifications differed widely from state to state. Many states denied voting privileges on the basis of sex, race, or age, and some states required voters to own property or pay taxes. Most states limited the right to vote to free, white, male citizens, although a few states permitted free blacks to vote. Beginning in

A suffragette urging women to use their right to vote. (Hulton Archive/Getty Images)

the nineteenth century, however, voting rights were gradually extended, and by 1860, all states had abolished property or significant taxpaying requirements for voting. Additionally, the Fifteenth Amendment, ratified in 1870, forbade using race as a criterion for voting. The twentieth century witnessed even greater inclusion by extending voting privileges to women and young adults and prohibiting polls taxes as a prerequisite to voting. Amendments to the Constitution address voting rights more than any other single subject matter: Five of the seventeen post–Bill of Rights amendments expanded the electorate.

Voting Rights and Gender

During the nineteenth century, for a variety of reasons, most states prohibited women from voting. The formal movement for female suffrage began in the 1840s at the first Women's Rights Convention, which was held in Seneca Falls, New York, in 1848. In 1869, the Wyoming Territory became the first jurisdiction to permit women to vote. But when the Supreme Court, in *Minor v. Happersett* (1875), rejected a Fourteenth Amendment challenge to a Missouri law that limited the franchise to men, it became clear that female suffrage was a law-based privilege and not a constitutional right. By the end of the nineteenth century, only five states—Wyoming (1869), Montana (1887), Colorado (1893), Utah (1896), and Idaho (1896)—had embraced full female suffrage.

The strategy of women's rights organizations was twofold: lobby individual states to confer voting rights upon women and push for a suffrage amendment to the Constitution. Congress rejected amendment proposals in 1914 and 1915. By 1917, however, more members of Congress were elected from states that permitted women to vote than from states that did not, and the following year, President Woodrow Wilson articulated his support for a constitutional amendment. On May 21, 1919, the House of Representatives passed a proposed constitutional amendment that read in part, "The right of citizens of the United States to vote shall not be denied or abridged by the United States or by any State on account of sex." The Senate voted favorably on June 4, 1919. The proposed amendment was then sent to the states for ratification. On August 18, 1920, Tennessee became the thirty-sixth state to ratify the proposed amendment, thus reaching the constitutionally required three-fourths support from the states. Eight days later, the Nineteenth Amendment went in effect.

Voting Rights and Race

Although the Fifteenth Amendment barred racial discrimination in voting, many states found ways to deny blacks the vote anyway. For decades following the Civil War, some states required poll taxes, literacy tests, or residency requirements to vote. Though seemingly racially neutral, these restrictions, often selectively applied against blacks, depressed black turnout. Additionally, the Supreme Court ruled in *Newberry v. United States* (1921), which involved allegations of electoral fraud in a Republican primary, that the Fifteenth Amendment did not apply to primary elections. Primaries were "in no real sense" part of the manner of holding an election, said the Court. As such, primaries were exempt from the Fifteenth Amendment's prohibition on racial discrimination in voting. Southern states thus discriminated against blacks by embracing "whites only" primaries. Given that many of these states were "one party" operations—where the winner in the Democratic primary was virtually guaranteed victory in the general election—white primaries effectively kept blacks from meaningful participation in electoral politics.

In 1923, the Texas legislature forbade blacks from participating in any Democratic Party primary held in the state. L. A. Nixon, a black physician from El Paso, challenged the state law as a violation of the Equal Protection Clause of the Fourteenth Amendment—"No state shall . . . deny to any person within its jurisdiction the equal protection of the laws"—and the Fifteenth Amendment. In *Nixon v. Herndon* (1927), a unanimous Supreme Court struck down the white primary in Texas as a denial of the Equal Protection Clause, which Justice Oliver Wendell Holmes said was intended to protect blacks from discrimination. The Court did not consider the Fifteenth Amendment claim, perhaps because doing so would have required the justices to equate primaries with elections, a contention they had rejected in *Newberry*.

Impact
For several decades after ratification of the Nineteenth Amendment, women voted at lower rates than men. By the end of the 1980s, however, that gap had closed. Recent data from academic and government sources confirm that women vote at a higher rate than men. In the 2008 presidential election, for example, 65.7 percent of eligible women cast ballots, whereas only 61.5 percent of eligible men did so.

Nixon v. Herndon did not mark the end of the white primary. The Texas legislature responded by enacting legislation that authorized each political party in the state to determine who was qualified to vote in its primaries. The Texas Democratic Party then declared that only white Democrats were so qualified. In *Nixon v. Condon* (1932), the Court struck down the rule, tracing the party's decision to the power conferred upon it by the state legislature. Subsequently, in the absence of any state legislation, the Texas Democratic Party limited participation in its primaries to "white citizens." In *Grovey v. Townsend* (1935), a unanimous Court upheld this resolution on the grounds that the Fourteenth and Fifteenth Amendments restricted state action only; private organizations were entirely free to engage in discriminatory practices.

Newberry was overturned by the justices in 1941, when *United States v. Classic* asserted that primaries were an integral part of the election process and that participating in primaries was therefore protected against interference by individual and state action. Finally, in *Smith v. Allwright* (1944), the Court ruled that the Texas Democratic Party could not restrict membership to whites and bar blacks from voting in its primaries, as the Fifteenth Amendment prevented racial discrimination in primaries just as it did in general elections.

Richard A. Glenn

Further Reading
Bardolph, Richard, ed. *The Civil Rights Record: Black Americans and the Law, 1849–1970.* New York: Crowell, 1970. A collection of statutes, cases, and other documents on civil rights, many of which relate to voting rights.

Elliott, Ward E. Y. *The Rise of Guardian Democracy: The Supreme Court's Role in Voting Rights Disputes, 1845–1969.* Cambridge, Mass.: Harvard University Press, 1974. An examination of voting reforms both before and after the Supreme Court's intervention in voting rights issues.

Keyssar, Alexander. *The Right to Vote: The Contested History of Democracy in the United States.* New York: Basic Books, 2001. A comprehensive analysis of voting rights that explores the conditions under which voting rights have expanded and contracted, and the effects of war and class conflict on voting rights.

Rogers, Donald W., ed. *Voting and the Spirit of American Democracy: Essays on the History of Voting and Voting Rights in America.* Urbana: University of Illinois Press, 1992. A collection of essays on various aspect of voting rights.

Stephenson, Donald Grier, Jr. *The Right to Vote: Rights and Liberties Under the Law.* Santa Barbara, Calif.: ABC-CLIO Press, 2004. An examination of how various elements, forces, factors, and individuals have guided the development of the right to vote in the United States.

See also: African Americans; Civil rights and liberties; Holmes, Oliver Wendell, Jr.; *Newberry v. United States;* Nineteenth Amendment; *Nixon v. Herndon;* Racial discrimination; Supreme Court, U.S.; Women's rights

W

■ Walker, Jimmy

Identification: American politician
Also known as: Beau James; James John Walker
Born: June 19, 1881, New York, New York
Died: November 18, 1946, New York, New York

Jimmy Walker was the Democratic mayor of New York City between 1926 and 1932. Successful and popular in his first term, he was forced to resign in his second term because of questionable personal financial dealings and possible business corruption. However, no charges were definitively proven against him.

Walker was elected New York's mayor in 1925 and again in 1929. A fashionable dresser and witty conversationalist, he gained many friends, some of whom may have contributed to his political downfall as the 1930s began. Walker's political career began when he won a seat in the New York state assembly in Albany in the election of 1909. In the 1914 election, he was elected state senator. Very intelligent, personable, and a persuasive speaker, he served as floor leader for the Democratic Party from 1921 to 1925 and worked closely with Governor Alfred E. Smith Jr. The bills that Walker proposed and passed permitted major-league baseball games to be played on Sundays and formally legalized professional boxing in New York.

In the summer of 1925, Walker's friends urged Tammany Hall members, who were powerful Democratic leaders in New York, to endorse Walker as a candidate for mayor. In a September primary that year, he defeated incumbent mayor John F. Hylan. Walker went on to win the November election and became the one hundredth mayor of the city.

Despite taking long vacations and displaying a noticeable lack of interest in the mundane details of city governance, Walker accomplished much during his mayoral terms. In his first term, he unified the city's public hospitals, created the vital Department of Sanitation, and kept the subway fare at five cents.

In his second run for mayor, he faced a well-prepared and strong opponent in Republican Fiorello La Guardia; however, Walker bested him by a two-to-one margin in the 1929 election. Walker's questionable financial dealings with some prominent citizens such as publisher Paul Block, with whom he shared a joint brokerage account, came to the public's attention shortly after his 1929 election. Then-governor Franklin D. Roosevelt was pressured to begin a formal investigation into Walker's administration. The early 1930s marked Walker's political decline, and his resignation from office took place on September 1, 1932.

Impact
Walker personified the New York City lifestyle of the Roaring Twenties with his elegance, wit, and notoriety. However, he also faced political turmoil in the early 1930s, due in part to accusations of corrupt financial arrangements with business executives, as well as an extramarital relationship with Betty Compton, a stage actress.

Patricia E. Sweeney

Further Reading
Mitgang, Herbert. *Once Upon a Time in New York: Jimmy Walker, Franklin Roosevelt, and the Last Great Battle of the Jazz Age.* New York: Free Press, 2000.
Walsh, George. *Gentleman Jimmy Walker: Mayor of the Jazz Age.* New York: Praeger, 1974.

See also: Crimes and scandals; Roosevelt, Franklin D.; Smith, Alfred E.

■ Wallace, DeWitt

Identification: American magazine editor and publisher
Also known as: William Roy DeWitt Wallace
Born: November 12, 1889, St. Paul, Minnesota
Died: March 30, 1981, Mt. Kisco, New York

With the help of his wife, Lila Bell Acheson, DeWitt Wallace began publishing the Reader's Digest *periodical in the early 1920s. It soon became one of the best-selling magazines in the United States and remained so until the final decade of the twentieth century. Wallace served as editor of the* Digest *from its inception until the early 1970s.*

After dropping out of college, Wallace went on to found and oversee one of the most popular and influential magazines in the history of American journalism. Although the publication did not reach its greatest sales peak for several more decades, it was definitely a product of the Roaring Twenties, born out of the growing desire for speed and modern convenience that characterized the 1920s.

Wallace began selling self-published pamphlets as a college student, but the inspiration for *Reader's Digest* came only after he was severely wounded while fighting in the Meuse-Argonne offensive in World War I. While recovering, he began to write summaries of the many magazine articles he read. He tried shopping a prototype edition of the magazine to various publishers in the early 1920s, but no one showed interest.

When he married Lila Acheson in 1921, the couple settled in New York. Having failed to interest established publishing firms in the *Digest*, they decided to try selling subscriptions through the mail. This approach proved successful: Soon, over a thousand people had sent in three dollars each for a year's subscription. The first issue appeared in 1922, and by the end of the decade, nearly 300,000 Americans were subscribing to the *Digest*. The Wallaces found themselves with an annual income of well over $600,000.

Impact
The success and longevity of the Wallaces' *Reader's Digest* is a legend within the history of American journalism: A young couple working out of their basement forged a publishing empire that brought them wealth and prestige. For over fifty years, the *Digest* was a best-selling magazine in the United States, offering readers a monthly compendium of pithy, concise articles on diverse subjects gleaned from a wide array of publications. In 1972, the Wallaces received the American civilian's highest honor, the Medal of Freedom, in recognition of their service to the nation. His philanthropic activities continued beyond his death with the Wallace Foundation that supports various charities and causes.

Thomas Du Bose

Further Reading
Canning, Peter. *American Dreamers: The Wallaces and "Reader's Digest," An Insider's Story*. New York: Simon & Schuster, 1996.
Drowne, Kathleen Morgan, and Patrick Huber. *American Popular Culture Through History: The 1920s*. Westport, Conn.: Greenwood Press, 2004.
Heidenry, John. *Theirs Was the Kingdom: Lila and DeWitt Wallace and the Story of "Reader's Digest."* New York: Norton, 1993.

See also: *American Mercury, The;* Magazines; *New Yorker, The*

■ Waller, Fats

Identification: American jazz pianist and composer
Also known as: Thomas Wright Waller
Born: May 21, 1904, New York, New York
Died: December 15, 1943, Kansas City, Missouri

Fats Waller was an accomplished African American stride pianist, a prolific and popular composer of jazz standards, and an inimitable comic showman.

Thomas Wright "Fats" Waller started playing piano and organ at an early age and learned jazz as a house musician in movie theaters and nightclubs. He studied with pianist James P. Johnson. As a party entertainer in Harlem, he learned to intersperse his playing with humorous asides and physical mannerisms that became a trademark of his performing style.

Waller perfected the style of stride piano, a difficult form in which the left hand outlines rhythm and chord progressions while the right hand plays melodies and embellishments. In 1922, Waller made his first player piano roll, "Got to Cool My Doggies Now." That same year, he made his first recordings for Okeh Records, "Muscle Shoals Blues" and "Birmingham Blues." His music was broadcast on radio stations in New York and New Jersey, and he played as an accompanist to leading blues singers Alberta Hunter, Sara Martin, and Bessie Smith. In 1926, he began recording for Victor Records; he would go on to make over four hundred recordings for Victor over the course of his life.

As a composer, Waller scored his first hit with "Squeeze Me" in 1924. In the following years he wrote a steady succession of hits with lyricist Andy Razaf, including "Honeysuckle Rose" (1928), "(What Did I Do to Be So) Black and Blue" (1929), "I've Got a Feeling I'm Falling" (1929), and "A Handful of Keys" (1929). His biggest hit was "Ain't Misbehavin'," written for the 1929 revue *Hot Chocolates* at the Harlem nightclub Connie's Inn. It was popularized by jazz trumpeter Louis Armstrong's nightly performances in the show, as well as Armstrong's recording of it on July 19, 1929.

In 1921, Waller married Edith Hatchett and they had one child, Thomas Jr., before divorcing. He married Anita Rutherford in 1927. They had two sons, Ronald and Maurice. Waller's compositions and recordings brought him a steady stream of royalties that he spent on indulgent living and alimony payments.

Impact

Waller became a recording star in the 1930s with his six-piece band Fats Waller and His Rhythm. He died of pneumonia at age thirty-nine. Although he was best known for his novelty songs and comedic mannerisms, he was a master pianist and organist. His jazz compositions have stood the test of time. His performances recorded on albums and in film reflected both the absurdity of race relations in the United States and the surrealist ethos of the lost generation.

Howard Bromberg

Further Reading

Shipton, Alyn. *Fats Waller: The Cheerful Little Earful.* New York: Continuum, 2002.

Vance, Joel. *Fats Waller: His Life and Times.* New York: Berkley, 1979.

Waller, Maurice, and Anthony Calabrese. *Fats Waller.* New York: Schirmer Books, 1977.

See also: Armstrong, Louis; Jazz; Music, popular; Smith, Bessie

■ Warner, Harry

Identification: Jewish American film entrepreneur
Born: December 12, 1881, Krasnosielc, Poland
Died: July 27, 1958, Los Angeles, California

Along with his brothers, Harry Warner founded the major American film studio Warner Bros. It is best known for producing The Jazz Singer *(1927), the first full-length feature film with sound.*

Harry Warner. (Getty Images)

Harry Morris Warner was born into a Jewish family that gradually made its way from Poland to North America. Benjamin, the father, moved to Baltimore in the early 1880s, and the rest of the family followed some years later. The family changed its name to Warner and moved several times in the United States and Canada, finally settling in Youngstown, Ohio. Warner worked with his father in the shoe repair business until he opened a bicycle shop with his brother Albert. In 1907, Warner married Rea Levinson, with whom he had three children.

Warner's brothers Albert and Sam began exhibiting movies in Pennsylvania and Ohio. In 1905, Warner sold his bicycle shop and joined them in purchasing real estate in New Castle, Pennsylvania, where they established their first movie theater. The three brothers bought other theaters and were joined by their brother Jack. After some years they decided to begin making films themselves, instead of just showing and distributing them. They established the Warner Bros. motion picture studio and bought the Vitagraph film studios in 1925. However, other studios hampered their distribution rights.

After consulting with Western Electric and Bell Telephone Laboratories, the brothers decided to introduce music into their pictures. In 1926, they released the film *Don Juan*, starring John Barrymore, with synchronized sound effects and a musical sound track. In 1927, they put voice in the landmark film *The Jazz Singer*, starring Al Jolson, even though Harry was initially skeptical about talking motion pictures. Harry and Albert moved to New York to run the business end of the studios, while Jack remained in California in charge of production. Harry became chief executive officer after Sam died in 1927. In the following decades, the studio had successes and failures, but it survived as a major studio. Harry Warner died on July 27, 1958, from a cerebral occlusion.

Impact
Harry Warner and his brothers were a major force in the developing American film industry. Their studio challenged the monopoly of early film production companies and was able to break through with the development of sound pictures. Although he quarreled with his brothers over their vision for the studio, Harry Warner was an important part of the enterprise.

Frederick B. Chary

Further Reading
Schickel, Richard, and George C. Perry. *You Must Remember This: The Warner Bros. Story*. Philadelphia: Running Press, 2008.

Sperling, Cass Warner, Cork Millner, and Jack Warner Jr. *Hollywood Be Thy Name: The Warner Brothers Story*. Lexington: University Press of Kentucky, 1998.

See also: Barrymore, John; Film; *Jazz Singer, The*; Jolson, Al; Metro-Goldwyn-Mayer (MGM); Movie palaces; Talking motion pictures; Warner Bros.; Warner, Sam

---

■ Warner, Sam

Identification: American film producer and pioneer of sound films
Also known as: Samuel Louis Warner
Born: August 10, 1887, Baltimore, Maryland
Died: October 5, 1927, Los Angeles, California

Many have referred to Sam Warner as the "father of talking pictures." At his insistence, Warner Bros. Studios partnered with Western Electric to incorporate the Vitaphone sound-on-disk technology into films and, in 1927, soon produced the first commercially successful feature-length film with synchronized sound, The Jazz Singer.

Brothers Sam, Jack, Albert, and Harry formed Warner Bros. Studios in 1918 and incorporated it in 1923. The studio remained small for much of the early 1920s and depended on the talents and popularity of actor John Barrymore and dog actor Rin Tin Tin for many film productions in its early years.

In the mid-1920s, Sam Warner became fascinated by the use of sound in films. Despite other production company heads scoffing at the idea, Warner believed it to be a cost saver. Warner did not initially envision actors speaking in films. Instead, he believed that if music were added, theaters would no longer need to pay for musicians and orchestras to provide the musical accompaniment to silent films. Although the other brothers were skeptical, Warner eventually persuaded them to begin producing films with music and songs. Warner Bros. Studios first released a few unprofitable sound shorts. Not until the 1927 release of *The Jazz Singer* starring well-known singer Al Jolson would the impact of sound in films be realized.

Initially, *The Jazz Singer* was only to incorporate sound in the musical sequences; however, when Sam Warner heard Al Jolson's ad-libbed lines between songs, he insisted these remain in the final cut of the film. Audiences loved hearing Jolson speak, and the spoken sequences helped make the film a success, grossing an unprecedented $100,000 per week. It became the first example of the successful use of synchronized sound in a full-length film.

Impact
Because of Sam Warner's persistence and perseverance, *The Jazz Singer* helped revolutionize the film industry. While the sound-on-disk technology used in *The Jazz Singer* became obsolete rather quickly, it was the catalyst for innovations in less cumbersome methods of incorporating sound into films. However, Sam Warner never saw the impact that his vision and hard work had on the industry; he died of a cerebral hemorrhage the day before *The Jazz Singer* premiered.

Kimberly Miller

Further Reading

Fleeger, Jennifer. "How to Say Things with Songs: Al Jolson, Vitaphone Technology, and the Rhetoric of Warner Bros. in 1929." *Quarterly Review of Film and Video* 27, no. 1 (2009): 27–43.

Spadoni, Robert. "The Uncanny Body of Early Sound Film." *Velvet Light Trap*, no. 51 (Spring, 2003): 4–16.

Sperling, Cass Warner, Cork Millner, and Jack Warner Jr. *Hollywood Be Thy Name: The Warner Brothers Story.* Lexington: University Press of Kentucky, 1998.

See also: Film; *Jazz Singer, The;* Jolson, Al; Talking motion pictures; Warner, Harry

■ Warner Bros.

Identification: American film studio
Date: Incorporated on April 4, 1923

Throughout the 1920s, Warner Bros. Studio produced feature films ranging from popular adventures starring the dog actor Rin Tin Tin to dramatic adaptations of serious literature. The studio pioneered the use of the Vitaphone sound system, becoming one of the first studios to produce talking motion pictures. With films such as The Jazz Singer *(1927), Warner Bros. helped usher in a new era in filmmaking.*

One of several film studios to rise to prominence during the 1920s, Warner Bros. was founded by brothers Harry, Albert, Sam, and Jack Warner. The brothers had first entered the film industry early in the twentieth century, traveling and exhibiting short films as early as 1903. In the following years, they opened several permanent theaters in New Castle, Pennsylvania. The brothers established the Duquesne Film Exchange, a film distribution company with a catalog of more than two hundred titles, by 1908. The Warners soon relocated to Culver City, California, where they began producing motion pictures such as the financially successful *My Four Years in Germany*, released in 1918. The brothers purchased property for a studio in Hollywood later that year.

Warner Bros. Studio was incorporated on April 4, 1923. Although the studio faced significant competition from larger, more established studios such as Paramount Pictures and Metro-Goldwyn-Mayer (MGM), it released a number of films during the early 1920s and focused on acquiring popular talent such as John Barrymore. In addition to the four Warner brothers, the studio employed such notable industry professionals as publicity director and later producer Hal B. Wallis and writer and producer Darryl F. Zanuck.

Vitaphone

In 1925, Sam Warner began to investigate the possibility of producing sound films. While short films with synchronized sound had already been produced by various independent inventors and companies, this technology had yet to capture the interest of the mainstream film industry. One of the major contributors to the development of talking motion pictures was Bell Laboratories, the research and development branch of Western Electric and the American Telephone and Telegraph Company (AT&T), which developed a sound-on-disk system known as the Vitaphone. In this system, sound was recorded onto a disk resembling a phonograph record, which was then played at the same time as the film. Recognizing the possibilities of this technology, Warner Bros. acquired the rights to produce films using the Vitaphone system.

Warner Bros. began producing films with synchronized music and sound effects in 1926 and speech the following year. By 1928, the studio was a leader in the production of sound films. This success led Warner Bros. to purchase First National Pictures, a Burbank, California, studio with newer production facilities and an extensive distribution operation.

An aerial view of Warner Bros. Studio in Burbank, California. (Hulton Archive/Getty Images)

Films

Warner Bros. produced hundreds of films during the 1920s, releasing as many as eighty films per year by the end of the decade. The studio produced many of its most notable films following the acquisition of Vitaphone technology, entertaining audiences with synchronized background music, dialogue, and even elaborate musical numbers. *Don Juan* (1926), starring John Barrymore, became the first feature film to use this new technology and included a synchronized score and sound effects. It was accompanied by a number of short sound films, some with synchronized speech. Released the following year, the full-length film *The Jazz Singer* featured synchronized songs performed by singer Al Jolson as well as several lines of synchronized dialogue. Talking motion pictures proved popular with 1920s audiences, and Warner Bros. further distinguished itself as a leader in the medium with the release of *Lights of New York* (1928), the first "all-talking" feature-length film, and *On With the Show!* (1929), the first all-talking feature film with full color.

Other Warner Bros. films of the 1920s included a number of features starring the dog actor Rin Tin Tin, among them *Clash of the Wolves* (1925) and *Land of the Silver Fox* (1928). The studio also produced various film adaptations of popular books; these included *The Beautiful and Damned* (1922), based on the novel by F. Scott Fitzgerald, and *Main Street* (1923), based on the novel by Sinclair Lewis.

Impact

Despite the effects of the Great Depression, Warner Bros. continued to prosper during the 1930s, producing popular adventure films and musicals similar to those of the late 1920s as well as serious films dealing with gang violence, prison life, and other social concerns. The success of these films and those of later decades, many of which came to be considered classics of the medium, made Warner Bros. one of the most influential film studios in the United States.

Scott Allen Nollen

Further Reading

Eyman, Scott. *The Speed of Sound: Hollywood and the Talkie Revolution, 1926–1930.* New York: Simon & Schuster, 1997. A discussion of the development of the talking motion picture, including the role of Warner Bros. in popularizing the medium.

Hirschhorn, Clive. *The Warner Bros. Story.* New York: Crown, 1987. A history of the studio, including descriptions of its films.

Schatz, Thomas. *The Genius of the System: Hollywood Filmmaking in the Studio Era.* Minneapolis: University of Minnesota Press, 2010. A comprehensive study of the "film factory" mentality that drove the major Hollywood companies, including Warner Bros., during the 1920s and afterward.

Schickel, Richard, and George C. Perry. *You Must Remember This: The Warner Bros. Story.* Philadelphia: Running Press, 2008. A heavily illustrated history of the studio from its origins through its many changes in corporate ownership.

Sperling, Cass Warner, Cork Millner, and Jack Warner Jr. *Hollywood Be Thy Name: The Warner Brothers Story.* Lexington: University Press of Kentucky, 1998. A biography of the four Warner brothers.

See also: Barrymore, John; Film; *Jazz Singer, The;* Jolson, Al; Rin Tin Tin films; Talking motion pictures; Warner, Harry; Warner, Sam

■ Washington Naval Conference

The Event: International arms control conference
Date: November 12, 1921 to February 6, 1922
Place: Washington, D.C.

With delegations from nine nations, the Washington Naval Conference was convened for the purpose of limiting naval armaments and peacefully alleviating tensions in the Pacific. The conference was a success—at least in the short term—resulting in a number of accords, including the Nine-Power Treaty and the Five-Power Treaty.

The Washington Naval Conference was an international arms limitation conference convened with the aim of reducing naval armaments, specifically capital ships, or major warships. In the years following the conclusion of World War I, a naval rivalry over interests in the western Pacific began to develop among Great Britain, the United States, and Japan. Concerned that this competition could lead to another war, members of Congress, led by Republican Senator William E. Borah, proposed an international conference focused on disarmament. In addition to naval arms control, the conference's organizers sought to alleviate tensions among the various nations with colonial and commercial interests in the western Pacific and East Asia. The U.S. government extended invitations to eight European and Asian powers in the summer of 1921, and the conference formally opened on Armistice Day, November 11, of the same year.

Proceedings

The conference occurred between November 12, 1921, and February 6, 1922. The major naval powers participating in disarmament talks were the United States, France, Great Britain, Italy, and Japan. The other attending nations with interests in the region were Belgium, the Netherlands, Portugal, and China.

Secretary of State Charles Evans Hughes led a U.S. delegation that also included former secretary of state Elihu Root and Senators Oscar Underwood and Henry Cabot Lodge. Hughes opened the sessions by proposing a concrete agenda for the drastic reduction of naval armaments, calling upon the major participants to scrap a large number of their capital ships and to refrain from building new ships for a ten-year period. Extensive negotiations culminated in a series of agreements that established a basis for both peaceful interaction in the Pacific and drastic reductions in naval construction.

Accords

By the conclusion of the Washington Naval Conference, the participating nations had reached a number of significant agreements. These included the Four-Power Treaty, the Five-Power Treaty, the Nine-Power Treaty, the Yap Island Agreement, and the Shandong Treaty.

The major arms control agreement to come out of the conference was the Five-Power or Washington Naval Treaty, which set specific limits on the tonnage of capital ships in the navies of the five nations and instituted guidelines regarding the future construction of ships. The total tonnage of capital ships was capped at 525,000 tons standard displacement for both the United States and Great Britain; 315,000 tons for Japan; and 175,000 tons for both France and Italy. In addition, no individual ship could be larger than 35,000 tons. It also limited the caliber and number of guns allowed on individual ships. Separate provisions within the agreement froze the construction of additional naval facilities and fortifications in the western Pacific.

The Four-Power Treaty, signed by the United States, Great Britain, France, and Japan, stipulated that the member countries would respect the territorial status quo in East Asia and the Pacific and consult with one another before taking any military action in response to international disputes in the region. This agreement superseded an earlier accord between Great Britain and Japan.

The Nine-Power Treaty, signed by all the conference attendees, was aimed at formalizing the long-standing Open Door Policy, specifying that China would remain independent and that all treaty signatories would have equal rights to trade with and do business in China. The signatories agreed to consult with one another to mediate any disputes that might arise.

Additional, bilateral treaties regarded territories in the Pacific. Signed by the United States and Japan, the Yap Island Agreement gave the United States the right to access and use communications technology based on the Pacific island of Yap, a former German territory granted to Japan at the end of World War I. The Shandong Treaty, an agreement between China and Japan, restored Chinese control of Shandong Province, which had also been controlled by Germany and then transferred to Japan after the war.

Impact

The Washington Naval Conference and the resulting accords served to reduce tensions in the western Pacific and halt the burgeoning naval race developing among the United States, Great Britain, and Japan. However, the treaties did not solve the underlying causes of international tension, nor did the treaty provisions include adequate enforcement mechanisms. Thus, while the conference prevented large-scale conflicts throughout the 1920s and much of the following decade, it was unable to prevent the Japanese military expansionism of the late 1930s and the onset of the Pacific War.

James R. McIntyre

Further Reading:

Fanning, Richard. *Peace and Disarmament.* Lexington: University Press of Kentucky, 1994. Focuses on the efforts of the international disarmament movement in the late 1920s.

Goldman, Emily O. *Sunken Treaties: Naval Arms Control Between the Wars.* University Park: Pennsylvania State University Press, 1994. Discusses the various attempts at naval arms control made between World Wars I and II.

Goldstein, Erik, and John Maurer, eds. *The Washington Conference, 1921–22: Naval Rivalry, East Asian Stability and the Road to Pearl Harbor.* London: Frank Cass, 1994. Outlines the political positions of the participants in the Washington Naval Conference.

Kaufman, Robert G. *Arms Control During the Pre-Nuclear Era: The United States and Naval Limitation Between the Two World Wars.* New York: Columbia University Press, 1990. Details the movement toward naval arms control in the interwar period, including the Washington Naval Conference.

Willmott, H. P. *The Last Century of Sea Power.* Vol. 2. Bloomington: Indiana University Press, 2010. Explores the effects of the conference between the 1920s and the end of World War II.

See also: Europe; Foreign policy, U.S.; Harding, Warren G.; Hughes, Charles Evans; Lodge, Henry Cabot

---

■ Waste Land, The

Identification: A poem expressing the disillusionment of the postwar years
Author: T. S. Eliot
Date: 1922

One of the best-known works by American expatriate poet T. S. Eliot, The Waste Land *incorporated numerous literary allusions and changes in structure and language, serving as a key example of Eliot's modernist style. Although critical responses to* The Waste Land *were mixed, it became one of the decade's most influential works of poetry.*

The Waste Land was written over a period of several years, beginning in 1919. T. S. Eliot gave the manuscript to the poet and literary critic Ezra Pound for editing prior to its publication. Pound, who had previously aided in the publication of Eliot's long poem "The Love-Song of J. Alfred Prufrock" (1915), made significant changes to the poem, and Eliot dedicated later editions of the work to him. The poem was first published in Great Britain in October 1922, appearing in Eliot's literary magazine, *The Criterion*. The work was next published in the November 1922 issue of the American magazine *The Dial*, and an annotated edition of the poem was published in book form by Boni and Liveright in December.

Comprising 434 lines, *The Waste Land* is divided into five sections: "The Burial of the Dead," "A Game of Chess," "The Fire Sermon," "Death by Water," and "What the Thunder Said." The poem incorporates allusions to a wide range of classical Western literature, including works by Ovid and Homer; canonical poems such as the works of Geoffrey Chaucer, John Milton, and Walt Whitman; and Western and Eastern religious traditions. The work also includes direct quotations from source texts, reproducing words or phrases in such languages as Italian and Sanskrit.

Noted for its dissonant style and sense of despair, the poem was frequently interpreted as an expression of the disillusionment experienced by many following World War I. However, as a dramatic monologue featuring a number of distinct voices and lacking a cohesive narrative, *The Waste Land* is a complex work open to multiple interpretations. The work's meaning is both clarified and further complicated by the explanatory notes included in the Boni and Liveright publication and subsequent editions.

Impact

In the decades following its publication, *The Waste Land* became one of the signature pieces of modernist poetry, influencing later writers ranging from the Nobel Prize–winning Irish poet Seamus Heaney to American writer Stephen King. Eliot, in turn, came to be recognized as a member of the disillusioned "lost generation" that shaped the literature of the 1920s and afterward. In recognition of his contributions to poetry, including *The Waste Land*, Eliot was awarded the Nobel Prize in Literature in 1948.

Tyrone Williams

Further Reading

Menand, Louis. *Discovering Modernism: T. S. Eliot and His Context.* 2d ed. New York: Oxford University Press, 2007.

Moody, Anthony David, ed. *The Cambridge Companion to T. S. Eliot.* Cambridge, England: Cambridge University Press, 2006.

Rainey, Lawrence S. *Revisiting "The Waste Land."* New Haven, Conn.: Yale University Press, 2007.

See also: *Dial, The;* Literature in the United States; Poetry; Pound, Ezra

Weissmuller, Johnny

Identification: American athlete and actor
Also known as: Peter János Weissmüller; Peter Johann Weissmüller
Born: June 2, 1904, Freidorf, Austro-Hungarian Empire (now Timişoara, Romania)
Died: January 20, 1984, Acapulco, Mexico

Johnny Weissmuller was an internationally known swimmer in the 1920s, widely regarded in his day as the greatest swimmer of all time. After retiring from amateur competition following the 1928 Olympics, Weissmuller went on to play the lead in twelve Tarzan films in the 1930s and 1940s, becoming the most enduring and popular actor to portray the character. Weissmuller also created the role of Jungle Jim for television and film.

Johnny Weissmuller was raised in Chicago, Illinois, and as a child suffered from polio, a viral disease that affects the spinal cord and causes muscle weakness and sometimes paralysis. As part of his recovery, Weissmuller, like many polio victims, took up swimming to regain lost strength and muscle tone.

As a teenager, Weissmuller began to compete in U.S. swimming events, and in 1921, he won the U.S. Amateur Athletic Outdoor swimming championships. He began to break world records soon thereafter, and in 1922 shattered Hawaiian swimmer and surfing pioneer Duke Kahanamoku's record in the 100-meter freestyle race, becoming the first person to swim that length in under one minute. Weissmuller set over sixty world records by the time of his retirement from amateur competition in 1928. His 1927 world record for the 100-yard freestyle remained intact for seventeen years.

Weissmuller's Olympic career began at the 1924 Games in Paris, where he won three gold medals in freestyle events and a bronze medal as a member of the U.S. water polo team. At the 1928 Amsterdam Olympics, Weissmuller won two additional gold medals in freestyle events and broke the record in each race. From 1921 to 1929, Weissmuller won every freestyle race he entered.

When Weissmuller announced his retirement in December 1928, he was one of the most famous athletes in America, having dominated both long- and short-distance swimming. His marriage in 1931 to Broadway and nightclub performer Bobby Arnst was front-page news, as was his selection by MGM Studios

Johnny Weissmuller. (Hulton Archive/Getty Images)

to portray the lead in the first Tarzan "talkie," *Tarzan the Ape Man* (1932).

Impact
Weissmuller's acting career ended in 1956 following the *Jungle Jim* television series. After a series of failed entrepreneurial ventures, Weissmuller retired to Florida in 1965, where he became founding chairman of the International Swimming Hall of Fame. He moved to Acapulco, Mexico, in 1973, where he died eleven years later. Weissmuller was inducted into the Body Building Hall of Fame in 1976 and the U.S. Olympic Hall of Fame in 1983.

Patricia King Hanson

Further Reading
Fury, David A. *Johnny Weissmuller: Twice the Hero.* Minneapolis, Minn.: Artist's Press, 2000.
Onyx, Narda. *Water, World & Weissmuller: A Biography.* Los Angeles, Calif.: Vion Publishing Company, 1964.

West, Mae

Identification: American actor, playwright, and cultural icon
Born: August 17, 1893, Brooklyn, New York
Died: November 22, 1980, Los Angeles, California

Iconic actor Mae West developed an inimitable style that combined a sultry sexuality with her signature ironic wit. Constantly transgressing social boundaries of gender, race, age, and class, she is a controversial figure, viewed by some as a powerful woman who dared challenge stifling middle-class mores and by others merely as a symbol of immorality and vulgarity.

Mae West was among those of the 1920s who used the arts to challenge artistic conventions and bourgeois morality. Strict conventions defined what was permissible in the representation of sexuality in burlesque, vaudeville, and mainstream theater in the early twentieth century, and West deliberately flouted those conventions. Her "shimmy" in *The Mimic World of 1921* (1921) shocked theater audiences, partly because of its unabashed celebration of sexuality in mainstream theater, but even more because it was a move normally performed by African American dancers.

West's other plays of the 1920s pushed even harder against the boundaries of acceptability. She played a spirited prostitute in the first play she helped author, *Sex* (1926), which ran successfully for almost a year before it was closed for indecency. West was convicted of corrupting public morals and served eight days in a workhouse. Two other plays she wrote and produced, *The Drag* (1927) and *The Pleasure Man* (1928), were closed because of their frank and comedic treatment of homosexuality.

West's popularity in part reflects the political and societal strides achieved by women in the 1920s, beginning with women's suffrage in the ratification of the Nineteenth Amendment in 1920. West's play *Diamond Lil* (1928) celebrates 1920s women's newfound power even as it reflects the era's nostalgia for the glamour and revelry of the 1890s. The part of Lil established the mold for future West roles: the sexy, powerful, independent woman who is desired by all but refuses permanent ties, including marriage or children. Her sardonic attitude toward men and sex would inform almost all of West's future parts. Lil wears the long, clinging gowns, tight corsets, and elaborate headpieces typical of the 1890s, and West's popularity in the role helped shift 1920s fashion away from the minimalist androgynous flapper style and toward styles for more full-figured women.

Impact

Mae West created an original sexual type that is often imitated. Her prodigious, stylized sexuality called attention to the social constructions of masculinity and femininity and has since made her a celebrity in the gay community. West's comic timing and sexual innuendos are even more striking; film censors frowned on the flagrant sexuality of her 1920s plays, inspiring her to resort to more witty and subtle wordplay and double entendres in her films and later works.

Laura Cowan

Further Reading

Chandler, Charlotte. *She Always Knew How: Mae West, a Personal Biography*. New York: Simon & Schuster, 2009.

West, Mae. *Goodness Had Nothing to Do with It: The Autobiography of Mae West*. Reprint. New York: Belvedere, 1981.

See also: Censorship; Crimes and scandals; Dances, popular; Homosexuality and gay rights; Sex and sex education; Theater in the United States; Vaudeville

West Virginia mining disaster

The Event: A coal mine explosion that killed 119 miners
Date: April 28, 1924
Place: Benwood, West Virginia

Coal mining in the 1920s was considered one of the most dangerous but necessary occupations in the United States. The Benwood accident brought increased attention to mining safety and the need for additional mining precautions.

Coal mines have always been understood as dangerous places to work, with explosions from the buildup of methane and coal dust a constant danger. Nonetheless, in the early twentieth century, rural workers with few other employment options, including large numbers of immigrants from eastern and southern Europe, were willing to take their chances.

On the morning of April 28, 1924, at the coal mine operated by Wheeling Steel Corporation outside Benwood, West Virginia, two fire bosses—inspectors who tested gas levels to determine whether miners could safely use open lights, which could ignite flammable gases and dust—conducted routine inspections of methane and coal dust and pronounced the Benwood mine safe for working. Only a few minutes after the miners entered the mine, however, a huge explosion blew though the mine. Hearing the blast, women and children dashed from the mining company houses and gathered at the main entrance of the mine to wait for word about their husbands and fathers. In a few hours, the officials announced that all of the miners had been killed in the explosion. Getting an exact body count took some time, because the explosion released toxic gases, making it necessary for rescue workers to rely on oxygen masks to enter the mine and retrieve the miners' bodies. Additionally, the explosion had weakened portions of the mine's roof, requiring extreme caution from the rescue team.

Impact

Coal mining accidents have been numerous in the United States and worldwide since the industry began, with companies slow to adopt and enforce safety regulations because of their cost in both time and money. Accidents like the one in Benwood—the third worst in the state's history—have decreased significantly, however, because of better regulations and improvements in coal mining safety and technology. During the search and rescue initiatives after the Benwood mine disaster, it was determined that some of the miners might have survived had they had access to a certain type of gas mask.

Wilton Eckley

Further Reading

Dillon, Lacy. *They Died in the Darkness*. Parsons, W.Va.: McClain Printing, 1976.

Williams, John Alexander. *West Virginia: A History*. Morgantown: West Virginia University Press, 2001.

See also: Science and technology

Wharton, Edith

Identification: American writer
Born: January 24, 1862, New York, New York
Died: August 11, 1937, Saint-Brice-sous-Forêt, France

As a commentator on the elite Old New York in which she grew up, most notably in the novel The Age of Innocence, *Edith Wharton exposed the city's formality, conformity, and hypocrisy while demonstrating nostalgia for what superficially seemed a gentler time, particularly in the post–World War I decade.*

Wharton's novels, novellas, poems, travel writing, essays, and short stories from the 1920s show her remarkable productivity during this time. The decade was also her most lucrative, as she became a bestselling author whose work, though receiving mixed critical reviews, was in high popular demand, with her novels featured in book-of-the-month clubs and serialized in magazines.

Wharton had traveled to Europe throughout her life, starting when she was a child, and preferred it to the United States. By the 1920s, she had already settled permanently in France, where she would live for the rest of her life. She acquired two homes there, complete with gardens that she avidly cultivated, and only returned to the United States to visit friends, attend funerals, or receive honors. She financed her two homes, active social life, and full travel schedule with both her earnings as a writer and her trust fund income.

Literary Life

During the 1920s, when writers such as F. Scott Fitzgerald, Ernest Hemingway, William Faulkner, Virginia Woolf, and James Joyce were employing techniques that would come to be associated with modern writing, such as stream of consciousness, symbolism, and minimalism, Wharton, too, was experimenting. This was largely in response to her displeasure with much modern literature, apart from the works of novelists such as Sinclair Lewis and Theodore Dreiser, which showed Wharton's influence in their realistic portrayals of conventional society and the yearnings of unconventional characters to escape it.

Although Wharton disliked the dissoluteness and the lack of depth and character she perceived in stories of the Jazz Age, with their emphasis on instant

Edith Wharton. (Time & Life Pictures/Getty Images)

gratification rather than the discipline that she admired and practiced herself, she portrayed similar qualities in *The Age of Innocence* (1920). In it, she depicts the marriage between Newland Archer, a young but worldly gentleman lawyer from a well-respected New York family, and May Welland, his naïve, conformist new wife from a similarly well-respected New York family. While the attraction that develops between Newland and the divorced Countess Ellen Olenska is never consummated in an actual affair, the novel chronicles their frustrated meetings with each other and the subtle and successful attempts of others to keep them apart. Through Newland's relationships, Wharton exposes the shallowness of a society in which deviating from the rules of decorum consigns one to the outer fringes of society, even as those in the inner circle pretend as if the outsider belongs. *The Age of Innocence* became Wharton's most critically acclaimed novel of the time and received the 1921 Pulitzer Prize in fiction.

Wharton published a number of other novels during the 1920s. Some of her most notable works from this era include *The Glimpses of the Moon* (1922), which features an itinerant couple living off of wedding presents and the generosity of wealthy friends, similar to the young, opportunistic couples in the works of Fitzgerald and Hemingway; *A Son at the Front* (1923), the story of a soldier's parents and their struggle during World War I; *The Mother's Recompense* (1925), a tale of modern New York; and *Hudson River Bracketed* (1929), the story of an unsophisticated man and an upper-class woman who bond over literature. Several works address family dysfunction: *Twilight Sleep* (1927) tells the story of a multitasking woman so dedicated to self-improvement and discipline that her own children must schedule appointments with her, and *The Children* (1928) portrays rich friends who are all divorced and remarried and give their children everything that money can buy but not what they truly need. In contrast to *The Age of Innocence*, which both nostalgically and satirically recalls the social rigidity and strict codes of conduct of Wharton's youth, her other novels of the 1920s explore the relative anarchy of contemporary society and the ramifications of its "anything goes" ethos.

Impact

One of the most honored and best-selling authors of her time, Edith Wharton influenced a generation of modern writers with her meticulous attention to detail in plot, character, and setting, as well as her portrayal of the thwarted hopes and dreams of those caught in a society with no patience with, or appreciation for, deviation from convention. She published more than forty books during her lifetime.

Holly L. Norton

Further Reading

Dwight, Eleanor. *Edith Wharton: An Extraordinary Life*. New York: Harry N. Abrams, 1999. An illustrated biography that chronicles Wharton's coming of age in New York, her career as a writer, and her travels through Europe.

Lee, Hermione. *Edith Wharton*. New York: Vintage Books, 2008. A comprehensive and thoroughly researched biography.

Lewis, R. W. B. *Edith Wharton: A Biography*. London: Vintage Books, 1993. Portrays Wharton as a major American writer in her own right, independent of fellow writer Henry James's much-discussed influence on her.

Wharton, Edith. *A Backward Glance: An Autobiography*. Reprint. New York: Simon & Schuster, 1998. Wharton's detailed account of growing up in a wealthy New York family, addressing both the privileges it afforded her and the challenges that it created in her personal and professional life.

Wooldridge, Connie Nordhielm. *The Brave Escape of Edith Wharton: A Biography*. Boston, Mass.: Clarion Books, 2010. A portrayal of Wharton as a woman who defied the conventions of the society in which she grew up, written for young adults.

See also: Age of Innocence, The; Faulkner, William; Fitzgerald, F. Scott; Hemingway, Ernest; Lewis, Sinclair; Literature in the United States

■ What's O'Clock

Identification: A book of poetry
Author: Amy Lowell
Date: 1925

Published posthumously and awarded the Pulitzer Prize, this collection of poetry includes some of Amy Lowell's most notable poems, including "The On-looker," "Lilacs," "The Sisters," "Nuit Blanche," and "Eleonora Duse." These poems and others reflect the poet's wide-ranging concerns with Western history, the theater, and the role of women in literary life at a time when women writers such as Willa Cather, Edna St. Vincent Millay, and Elinor Wylie were reshaping the figure of the female writer in response to the changing literary and cultural currents of the 1920s.

In "The Sisters," Lowell presents herself as a modern woman assessing her place in the ranks of women poets from the ancient Greek poet Sappho to nineteenth-century poets Elizabeth Barrett Browning and Emily Dickinson. Like many of the other poems in *What's O'Clock*, "The Sisters" reflects the sensibility of a writer willing to bring her poetry into the public arena and to measure it against the achievements of her illustrious predecessors as well as her contemporaries. Although not a feminist in political terms, Lowell was outspoken in her desire to engage with history, taking to public platforms throughout the 1920s to debate the proper subjects and styles of modern poetry.

Lowell greatly admired Italian stage actor Eleonora Duse and acknowledged her devotion to the self-directed Duse as one of the primary reasons she became a poet. Indeed, critics consider "Lilacs" to be Lowell's own quest to fuse her poet-self to the spirit of the 1920s and, more particularly, to her native New England. At the same time, the poem also recalls Walt Whitman's "When Lilacs Last in the Dooryard Bloom'd," his elegy for President Abraham Lincoln. Linking herself to Whitman, Lowell presents a reflective view of her own life and career, thus making her consciousness the subject of the poem itself—as did many modernist writers of the 1920s, including T. S. Eliot and William Carlos Williams.

Impact

What's O'Clock remains one of the highest achievements of Lowell's career. Many feel that the book's title—an allusion to a scene in Shakespeare's historical play *Richard III*—suggests the scope of her ambition and the impact she hoped to have on her contemporaries and on posterity. Although her reputation declined after her death, respect for Lowell's work revived in the 1970s when feminist critics began reevaluating the canon of American literature and rediscovering the works of women writers and poets. Later poets such as Sylvia Plath regarded Lowell as an important literary predecessor in much the same way Lowell contemplated hers in "The Sisters."

Carl Rollyson

Further Reading

Benvenuto, Richard. *Amy Lowell*. Boston: Twayne, 1985.

Munich, Adrienne, and Melissa Bradshaw. *Amy Lowell: American Modern*. New Brunswick, N.J.: Rutgers University Press, 2004.

See also: Cather, Willa; Eliot, T. S.; Millay, Edna St. Vincent; Poetry; Teasdale, Sara; Williams, William Carlos; Wylie, Elinor

■ Whiteman, Paul

Identification: American musician, composer, and bandleader
Born: March 28, 1890, Denver, Colorado
Died: December 29, 1967, Doylestown, Pennsylvania

As the leader of some of the most popular musical ensembles of the 1920s, Paul Whiteman played a major role in establishing jazz as part of American popular music. He became

known as the "King of Jazz," although some critics dispute this title, as his orchestral performances largely did away with the improvisational element of the genre.

Paul Whiteman began his career in classical music with the San Francisco Symphony before becoming the leader of a jazz-inspired orchestra at San Francisco's Fairmont Hotel. In 1920, he moved to New York City, where he began recording for Victor Records. Whiteman and his orchestra benefited from the exponential rise in the popularity of recorded music and musical radio programs on the newly created national radio networks during the 1920s. A formidable negotiator, Whiteman made sure that ballrooms, hotels, record companies, and radio sponsors all compensated his band handsomely for their efforts.

Whiteman was a composer and bandleader of modest skill whose real gift lay in assembling a lineup of world-class musical talent. Superb instrumentalists such as Charlie Teagarden, Bix Beiderbecke, Joe Venuti, and Eddie Lang all played in the Paul Whiteman Orchestra, while Bing Crosby, Johnny Mercer, and Mildred Bailey were among those who contributed their vocal talents. Whiteman released thirty-two number-one records over the course of his career, twenty-eight of them during the 1920s.

Whiteman also achieved some success in Hollywood. Between 1924 and 1947, he appeared in a number of films, often portraying himself or appearing with his band. His most memorable film was *King of Jazz* (1930), which included the first ever animated sequence to be produced in Technicolor. The film achieved fame for its lavish production of *Rhapsody in Blue*, composed by George Gershwin for Whiteman's orchestra in 1924.

The popularity of Whiteman's band faded with the arrival of swing bands in the 1930s. In the 1940s, he became the musical director of the Blue Network radio station, later the American Broadcasting Company (ABC), where he remained long enough to give young television personality Dick Clark his first big break.

Impact

Some jazz purists choose to dismiss Paul Whiteman as a popularizer of jazz who diluted its edgy origins in favor of saccharine dance music. Despite this, Whiteman, along with renowned jazz trumpeter Louis Armstrong, deserves credit for transforming jazz in the 1920s and ensuring its enduring appeal within American culture.

Michael Polley

Further Reading

Berrett, Joshua. *Louis Armstrong and Paul Whiteman: Two Kings of Jazz.* New Haven, Conn.: Yale University Press, 2005.

Simon, George Thomas. *The Big Bands.* 4th ed. New York: Collier Macmillan, 1981.

Whiteman, Paul. *Jazz.* New York: J. H. Sears, 1926.

See also: Armstrong, Louis; Gershwin, George; Jazz; Lang, Eddie; Radio; *Rhapsody in Blue*

Wilder, Thornton

Identification: American novelist and playwright
Born: April 17, 1897, Madison, Wisconsin
Died: December 7, 1975, Hamden, Connecticut

Thornton Wilder's 1927 novel The Bridge of San Luis Rey *catapulted him to fame as a serious writer of philosophical literature. His fable about a disaster in Peru encouraged readers to focus on moral and cosmological issues and prefigured the emphasis of his later writings.*

Thornton Niven Wilder once remarked that he was the only American writer in the 1920s who did not go to Paris. This was not literally true, for he visited there several times, but he never joined the American expatriate community there, known as the "lost generation," whose members included novelists Ernest Hemingway and F. Scott Fitzgerald.

Many commentators see Wilder as out of step with his contemporaries: not indulging in Hemingway's cynicism, nor making himself a regional representative like William Faulkner, nor producing works of naturalistic detail in the manner of Theodore Dreiser or Sinclair Lewis. Others have described Wilder as a humanist, as a Christian writer, and as an optimist. Critics have also seen Wilder's writings as reflections on Zen Buddhism or Hinduism. There is general agreement, however, that his works explore serious philosophical issues and sometimes take on the appearance of parables in which he pushes readers to ponder issues such as love and suffering, faith and reason, and the question of whether there is design in the universe.

Thornton Wilder. (AP Photo)

Early Writings

When the 1920s began, Wilder was just completing his studies at Yale University, where he wrote stories, plays, and reviews. One of these plays, *The Trumpet Shall Sound*, was produced in New York in 1926. In it, Wilder, whose family heritage was one of New England Puritanism, constructed an allegory about a master and servants, with clear biblical overtones. Wilder also wrote several "three-minute plays" at Yale and after, which were published in the collection *The Angel That Troubled the Waters and Other Plays* in 1928. These, too, dealt with biblical themes and explored the notions of faith and suffering. They also introduced experimental techniques that Wilder was to develop more fully in his later dramatic works, most notably in the play *Our Town* (1938).

After graduating from Yale, Wilder spent a year studying in Rome and then returned to teach French at Lawrenceville School in New Jersey. In 1924, he took a leave of absence from teaching to complete a master's degree at Princeton University, during which time he also worked on his first novel, *The Cabala*, which he published in 1926. In this work, Wilder drew in part on his experiences in Rome, producing a series of episodes about a young American who encounters various members of the decaying Roman aristocracy. The novel, which mixes fantasy with realism, portrays a series of disasters but ends with the American returning home full of hope for the New World.

Later Career

The Cabala received favorable reviews, but nothing like Wilder's next novel, *The Bridge of San Luis Rey* (1927). This novel is the story of five people who perish when a bridge collapses in eighteenth-century Peru. It was hailed as a masterpiece as soon as it appeared and became a huge best seller; some accounts say as many as two million copies were sold over the next thirty years. In 1928, it was awarded the Pulitzer Prize and was made into a movie in 1929, 1944, and 2004.

Framed by two chapters about Brother Juniper, the monk who tries to determine why these particular five people died in the disaster, the book raises the issues of design and chance. The first chapter is entitled "Perhaps an Accident"; the last is called "Perhaps an Intention." Some commentators see Wilder as saying there was a clear intention for the deaths; others say the key word in both chapter titles is "perhaps." Wilder himself noted that both atheists and religious fundamentalists thought the book expressed their point of view, and in the book itself, Brother Juniper is put to death for trying to solve the mystery.

After the success of *The Bridge of San Luis Rey*, Wilder resigned from his teaching position, though within two years he was to become a lecturer at the University of Chicago. Before that, however, he went on a lecture tour and traveled in Europe.

Impact

In the last years of the 1920s, Wilder worked on his third novel, *The Woman of Andros*, set in ancient Greece. When it was published in 1930 at the beginning of the Great Depression, he found himself under attack for not setting his works in modern-day America and for ignoring the crises around him. Perhaps in response to these charges, Wilder first produced *Heaven's My Destination* (1935), a novel set in the United States, and in 1938, published the play *Our Town*, which is what many consider his tribute to traditional American values. However, most commentators agree that Wilder did not change his approach to his art during this period; whether setting his novels and plays in the present-day United States or Europe or in eighteenth-century Peru, Wilder's focus always remained on larger, universal issues.

Sheldon Goldfarb

Further Reading

Bloom, Harold. *Thornton Wilder.* Philadelphia: Chelsea House, 2003. Provides critical analysis of Wilder's works.

Burbank, Rex J. *Thornton Wilder.* 2d ed. Boston: Twayne, 1978. Provides overview of Wilder's works and situates him in the New Humanist tradition of the 1920s.

Konkle, Lincoln. *Thornton Wilder and the Puritan Narrative Tradition.* Columbia: University of Missouri Press, 2006. Reviews Wilder's work as stemming from a Puritan ideal.

Wilder, Thornton. *Conversations with Thornton Wilder.* Edited by Jackson R. Bryer. Jackson: University Press of Mississippi, 1992. Provides transcripts of American, foreign, and radio interviews from 1928 through the 1970s.

_____. *The Selected Letters of Thornton Wilder.* Edited by Robin G. Wilder and Jackson R. Bryer. New York: Harper Perennial, 2009. Includes letters written between 1909 and 1960 and photographs of Thornton with family and dignitaries.

See also: *Bridge of San Luis Rey, The;* Literature in the United States; Religion in the United States; Theater in the United States

■ Williams, William Carlos

Identification: American writer and physician
Born: September 17, 1883, Rutherford, New Jersey
Died: March 4, 1963, Rutherford, New Jersey

William Carlos Williams developed a unique literary voice that embraced innovation in form and expression. He proved a major influence on twentieth-century modernist poetry, both through his own work and as a contemporary critic of poets Ezra Pound and T. S. Eliot, although he was less renowned in his time than either of them.

The son of an English father and Puerto Rican mother, William Carlos Williams was raised in Rutherford, New Jersey. He attended local schools, as well as schools outside Geneva, Switzerland, and in Paris, France. Upon graduation from Horace Mann High School in New York City, Williams entered the University of Pennsylvania to study medicine. There he met poet Ezra Pound, who would become a lifelong supporter. Following an internship in New York City and some time in private practice, Williams studied pediatrics in Leipzig, Germany, for one year. Before returning home, he visited Pound in London. In 1912, he married Florence "Floss" Hermann, and they settled into their lifelong home in Rutherford, where Williams would practice medicine and write forty-five books over the next fifty years.

Early Influences

Williams developed an understanding of image creation through his proximity to New York City artists and the influence of his mother, who had once been a promising art student in Europe. This, together with the experiences of his clinical practice, strongly influenced his concrete, nonmetaphorical writing style. His early poetry was associated with Imagists such as Pound and H. D. (Hilda Doolittle), and, later, modernists such as Wallace Stevens and Marianne Moore. On sabbatical from medical practice in 1924, he toured western Europe with Floss. There he met the writers James Joyce and Ernest Hemingway, who were part of a flourishing literary and artistic expatriate community; however, Williams formed a conviction that the United States was the only place he could call home. He began to write to rediscover the American voice in literature.

Major Works of the 1920s

Contemporary art, literature, and European travels were particular influences on Williams's early writing. With his publisher friend Robert McAlmon, he released five issues of *Contact*, a literary magazine that featured his work along with that of other American modernists. In 1920, Williams published *Kora in Hell: Improvisations*, a diary of exploratory prose interspersed with commentary. The lengthy prologue to *Kora*, derived from Williams's interests in the avant-garde and Dadaism, represents his break from and challenge to popular conceptions of art.

Two collections of Williams's verse appeared in the early 1920s. *Sour Grapes* (1921) is seen by some critics a melancholic reaction to disappointments in his personal life. *Spring and All* (1923), published by McAlmon, is one of Williams's most significant early collections, consisting of both free verse and prose passages. It contains two of his best-known poems, "Spring and All" and "The Red Wheelbarrow."

Pound invited Williams to contribute prose to the next installment in a series by publisher William Bird's Three Mountain Press. William's contribution was *The Great American Novel* (1923), a work challenging what he viewed as the complacency of American writing. *In the American Grain* appeared in 1925, a collection of twenty-one impressionistic essays on important figures and events in American history, with a focus on the essence of American culture and literature. The experiences of his 1924 European trip inspired Williams's second novel, *A Voyage to Pagany* (1928), the story of an American doctor traveling as an innocent in Europe.

Impact

Williams's experiences in the 1920s began his struggle to find and define the American literary voice as separate from European ideas and poetic forms. His medical education and practice instilled an observational, concrete point of view that he later summarized in the statement "No ideas but in things." Although in later years Williams wrote novels, short stories, essays, and criticism, he was best known as an American poet. He directly influenced subsequent generations of poets, including 1950s literary movements such as the Beat generation, the Black Mountain school, the San Francisco Renaissance, and the New York School. He received major awards for poetry in the 1950s, including the Bollingen Prize and the first National Book Award for poetry. Williams's major books of poetry appearing in later decades include the five-volume *Paterson* (1956–1958), an in-depth treatment of modernization in Paterson, New Jersey, and *Pictures from Brueghel and Other Poems* (1962), for which Williams posthumously received the Pulitzer Prize.

John P. Doucet

Further Reading

Boone, April. "William Carlos Williams's *The Great American Novel*: Flamboyance and the Beginning of Art." *William Carlos Williams Review* 26, no. 1 (2006): 1–25. Offers twenty-first-century appreciation for Williams's innovative prose work.

Leibowitz, Herbert. *"Something Urgent I Have to Say to You": The Life and Works of William Carlos Williams.* New York: Farrar, Straus, and Giroux, 2011. A biography focusing on Williams's personality, influence as a writer, and position in the avant-garde literary movement of the 1920s.

Mariani, Paul. *William Carlos Williams: A New World Naked.* New York: McGraw-Hill, 1981. A biography addressing both the writer's life and use of language.

Williams, William Carlos. *The Autobiography of William Carlos Williams.* New York: New Directions, 1967. A key to understanding Williams's personal motivations regarding medicine and writing.

_____. *Selected Poems.* Edited by Robert Pinsky. New York: Library of America, 2004. A collection of Williams's poems as part of the American Poets Project, presenting a helpful introduction to his work.

See also: Eliot, T. S.; *In the American Grain;* Literature in the United States; Poetry; Pound, Ezra; *Spring and All*

Wilson, Edith

Identification: First Lady of the United States
Also known as: Edith Bolling; Edith Bolling Galt; the Secret President
Born: October 15, 1872, Wytheville, Virginia
Died: December 28, 1961, Washington, D.C.

Edith Wilson actively participated in the national and international political activities of President Woodrow Wilson from their wedding in late 1915 until his term of office ended in March 1921. For the last seventeen months of Wilson's term, she served as intermediary between him and the rest of the world.

Edith Wilson was President Woodrow Wilson's second wife. The president became a widower in 1914 while in office, and fourteen months later, he and Edith married. On October 2, 1919, President Wilson suffered a stroke and spent the remainder of his term in almost total seclusion. During that time, Edith Wilson decided who would have access to the president, and she allowed very few people to be in his presence. She also decided what information would be brought before him. Edith Wilson later stated in her memoirs that she did not make presidential decisions and that all the decisions she reported as the president's were indeed his. Regardless of the truth of this claim, her control of presidential access and her secrecy about the true state of his health gave her unprecedented political power, and many have felt that the White House was adrift during this time because many decisions were left unhandled except when Cabinet members insisted on action.

Despite her extensive participation in political matters, both before and after her husband's stroke,

Edith Wilson was mostly silent concerning the political rights of women, only speaking out against suffragists because she felt they had mistreated her husband. After the death of President Wilson, she was considered a potential Democratic candidate for vice president in 1927, and the following year she was invited to speak at the Democratic National Convention.

Impact

After her husband's death, Edith Wilson made it her life's work to control the narrative of his presidency. She chose the author of his official biography, and she is reported to have jealously guarded his papers. She also wrote to and publicly chastised authors who she felt were mistaken or malicious in their reporting of events. In 1967, six years after Edith Wilson's death, the Twenty-Fifth Amendment was passed; this amendment outlined official procedures for transfer of power in the event of the president becoming incapacitated or dying in office, thereby preventing future repetitions of the chaos that followed President Wilson's stroke.

Judy E. Gaughan

Further Reading

Black, Allida M. "The Modern First Lady and Public Policy: From Edith Wilson Through Hillary Rodham Clinton." *Organization of American Historians Magazine of History* 15, no. 3 (Spring, 2001): 15–20.

Slagell, Amy R., and Susan Zaeske. "Edith Bolling Galt Wilson: Actions Speak Louder than Words." In *Inventing a Voice: The Rhetoric of American First Ladies of the Twentieth Century*, edited by Molly Meijer Wertheimer. Lanham, Md.: Rowman & Littlefield, 2004.

Wilson, Edith Bolling. *My Memoir*. Reprint. New York: Arno Press, 1980.

See also: Elections, U.S., of 1928; Wilson, Woodrow

■ Wilson, Edmund

Identification: American literary critic and writer
Born: May 8, 1895, Red Bank, New Jersey
Died: June 12, 1972, Talcottville, New York

Considered America's most influential literary critic, Edmund Wilson's career began in the 1920s and continued until his death. Although he produced novels, plays, short stories, and poetry, Wilson is best known as a critic and social commentator, credited with introducing a wider public to important literary trends and ideas such as European modernism and Freudian influence in literature.

Edmund Wilson graduated from Princeton University in 1916, worked briefly as a reporter for the *New York Evening Sun*, and served in the U.S. Army Intelligence Corps during World War I. He launched his career as a literary journalist in 1920 by becoming managing editor of *Vanity Fair*, the culture magazine whose famous contributors included Robert Benchley, Dorothy Parker, and Robert E. Sherwood.

Wilson left *Vanity Fair* in 1921 to become managing editor of *The New Republic*. Throughout the decade he began establishing his reputation as an especially astute literary journalist. In addition to book reviews and essays, he served as drama critic for the literary magazine *The Dial*.

During the 1920s, Wilson continued his friendships with Princeton classmates such as novelist F. Scott Fitzgerald and poet John Peale Bishop, collaborating with the latter on his first book, *The Undertaker's Garland* (1922). He knew most of the leading cultural figures of the time, including Eugene O'Neill, spending the summer of 1927 at the playwright's home in Provincetown, Massachusetts.

While Wilson's professional endeavors flourished, his personal life was less successful. His 1923 marriage to actress Mary Blair was short-lived, and in 1929 he suffered a nervous breakdown and was admitted to a sanatorium. Such experiences influenced Wilson's three novels, the first of which, *I Thought of Daisy* (1929), is a colorful depiction of bohemian life in Greenwich Village, with a protagonist based on poet Edna St. Vincent Millay, to whom Wilson had once proposed.

Wilson became increasingly concerned with political and social issues during the 1920s and published extensively about these matters beginning in the 1930s. In 1927, he started work on *Axel's Castle* (1931), widely considered a masterpiece of literary criticism. Its chapters on T. S. Eliot, James Joyce, and Gertrude Stein offer insight into major literary movements of the 1920s.

Impact

At the time of his death, Wilson was assembling an autobiographical portrait of the 1920s from his notebooks and diaries, and literary biographer Leon Edel completed the project in 1975. *The Twenties: From Notebooks and Diaries of the Period* describes American cultural life during the decade, from the effects of increasing industrialization to the rise of Hollywood, while providing vivid portraits of such literary figures as E. E. Cummings, John Dos Passos, Fitzgerald, Millay, and O'Neill. It is considered a valuable and insightful account of the 1920s.

Michael Adams

Further Reading
Castronovo, David. *Edmund Wilson Revisited.* New York: Twayne, 1998.
Dabney, Lewis M. *Edmund Wilson: A Life in Literature.* New York: Farrar, Straus, and Giroux, 2005.

See also: Cummings, E. E.; *Dial, The;* Eliot, T. S.; Fitzgerald, F. Scott; Literature in the United States; Millay, Edna St. Vincent; O'Neill, Eugene

■ Wilson, Woodrow

Identification: Twenty-eighth president of the United States
Born: December 28, 1856, Staunton, Virginia
Died: February 3, 1924, Washington, D.C.

Woodrow Wilson was a domestic reformer and a promoter of transparency in foreign affairs and international relations. Although his idea of the United States as an active force for good on the world stage was rejected by the voters in 1920, it became the cornerstone of American foreign policy in 1940 and has remained so ever since.

During the 1920s, Woodrow Wilson largely served as a foil for isolationists who saw him as an example of how the United States had overreached by meddling in European affairs. The decade did not begin well for the president; in 1920, he was incapacitated by a stroke, Prohibition went into effect despite his veto of the Volstead Act, and the Senate voted against ratification of the Treaty of Versailles, which ended World War I and which Wilson had staked his political life on seeing passed. The year before, he had been meeting with Allied leaders in preparation for the Paris Peace Conference, and hopes had been high that Wilson could act as an honest broker and secure a balanced settlement. Instead, he was pressured by

Woodrow Wilson. (Getty Images)

the French, British, and, to a lesser extent, the Italians to agree to terms that punished Germany. After returning home in July of 1919, Wilson began an unsuccessful campaign to sell the Treaty of Versailles to politicians and the American people. He collapsed on the presidential train on September 26, 1919, and was rushed back to Washington, D.C., where he suffered a massive stroke six days later.

For the next four months, the American government ran virtually unsupervised. Vice President Thomas Marshall refused to take over without either Wilson's approval or a joint congressional resolution. Rumors abounded that the first lady, Edith Bolling Wilson, was running the government, but in truth, departments and agencies were left to regulate themselves. In the resulting power vacuum, the federal government did little to nothing to stem the tide of lynchings that was sweeping through the South and the Midwest. Instead, Attorney General A. Mitchell Palmer used a series of bombings by anarchists to help foster the first Red Scare.

On the political front, American opposition to the Versailles treaty centered on several issues. Some felt that it was not harsh enough, while many believed that it was not fair to blame Germany for the entire war or force the German government to pay such high reparations. Massachusetts senator Henry Cabot Lodge led Republican opposition to the treaty, based on fears of allowing Wilson's international peacekeeping organization, the League of Nations, to dictate American foreign and military policy. By March of 1920, Wilson had recovered enough to answer his critics. The stroke had made him inflexible, however, and the president refused to compromise, thus dooming the Treaty of Versailles to defeat in the Senate.

Later Life

The 1920 election became a referendum on Wilson's international policies. The Democratic candidates, James M. Cox and Franklin D. Roosevelt, supported Wilson and American entry into the League of Nations and lost. The American people instead embraced Republican candidate Warren G. Harding's call for a "return to normalcy." There were only two positive outcomes for Wilson in 1920: In August, Tennessee ratified the Nineteenth Amendment, thus guaranteeing its passage and giving all American women the right to vote, a cause he had embraced during the war, and in December, he won the Noble Peace Prize for his work in creating the League of Nations.

After Harding's inauguration, Wilson only acted as a public figure three more times in his life. He attended the funeral of the Unknown Soldier on Armistice Day, November 11, 1921; he attended Harding's funeral in August of 1923; and on November 10, 1923, he gave a radio address in commemoration of Armistice Day, in which he called on the American people to accept their role as leaders in world affairs or suffer the consequences. The former president hoped that the speech might mark his return to politics, but this was not to be the case; his heart was weak, and many Americans, including members of his own party, had moved beyond Wilson's crusading style of leadership. Wilson died at his home on S Street in Washington, D.C., on February 3, 1924, and was buried in the then-unfinished Washington National Cathedral.

Impact

Much of Wilson's impact stems from the decade prior to the 1920s, in which he set a domestic reform agenda and sought unsuccessfully to "make the world safe for democracy" at the end of World War I. Unfortunately, his Federal Reserve system, created out of compromise, lacked the strength or understanding to react effectively to the stock market crash of 1929. In the 1930s, as unrest grew in Europe, Wilson's wife Edith reminded all who would listen of her late husband's unfulfilled desire for the United States to take a leading role in world affairs. Both Wilsons were somewhat vindicated when Franklin D. Roosevelt, one of Woodrow Wilson's protégés, succeeded Herbert Hoover as president in 1932. Roosevelt's New Deal was built on the foundations of Wilson's domestic reforms; after World War II, Roosevelt's United Nations was an improved version of Wilson's League of Nations, with the United States not only participating but serving as its leader.

Edmund D. Potter

Further Reading

Cooper, John Milton. *Woodrow Wilson: A Biography*. New York: Alfred A. Knopf, 2009. An authoritative account, covering Wilson's faults as well as his virtues and accomplishments.

Knock, Thomas J. *To End All Wars: Woodrow Wilson and the Quest for a New World Order*. Princeton, N.J.: Princeton University Press, 1995. Focuses on Wilson's role in establishing the League of Nations.

Link, Arthur Stanley. *Woodrow Wilson: Revolution, War, and Peace*. Arlington Heights, Ill.: Harlan Davidson, 1986. A reexamination of Wilson's foreign policies.

_____, ed. *The Papers of Woodrow Wilson*. Princeton, N.J.: Princeton University Press, 1991–1993. Volumes covering the period from Wilson's stroke in 1919 to his death in 1924.

Pietrusza, David. *1920: The Year of the Six Presidents*. New York: Basic Books, 2008. Chronicles the 1920 presidential election.

See also: Elections, U.S., of 1920; Foreign policy, U.S.; Harding, Warren G.; Isolationism; League of Nations; Nineteenth Amendment; Red Scare, The; Roosevelt, Franklin D.; Tomb of the Unknown Soldier; Wilson, Edith

■ *Wings*

Identification: Film about fighter pilots in World War I
Director: William A. Wellman
Date: 1927

Directed by former pilot William A. Wellman, Wings *captured the imagination of 1920s audiences with its realistic depictions of aerial battles, capitalizing on the public's newfound interest in aviation. The film, which featured such popular actors as Charles "Buddy" Rogers and Clara Bow, was met with critical and popular acclaim and won two Academy Awards.*

Known primarily as a director of action films, William A. Wellman drew on his own experience as a pilot during World War I to direct *Wings.* A Paramount production, the film premiered at the New York's Criterion Theatre on August 12, 1927.

The film follows Jack Powell (Rogers) and David Armstrong (Richard Arlen), young men who join the U.S. Army Air Service following the United States' entry into World War I. Both are attracted to Sylvia Lewis (Jobyna Ralston), who, in turn, is in love with David. The heroine, Mary Preston (Bow), loves and remains loyal to Jack, although he remains oblivious to her feelings. After completing their training, Jack and David are stationed in France. Mary joins the war effort as well, but she is forced to return to the United States after an embarrassing misunderstanding. In September of 1918, the fighter pilots participate in the Battle of Saint-Mihiel. David is shot down, but he survives and steals a German plane in an attempt to rejoin the other Americans. Mistaking David for an enemy, Jack shoots down the stolen plane, killing his friend. Upon returning to the United States after the end of the war, Jack recognizes and returns Mary's affections.

Wings was immediately successful with audiences, in large part because it starred Bow, the popular "It girl" of the period. In addition, the film's focus on aviation appealed to many in the wake of Charles Lindbergh's transatlantic solo flight, which occurred several months before the film's release. Although *Wings* was a silent film, it was rereleased early in 1929 with a synchronized score and sound effects, taking advantage of the newly popular sound-on-film technology.

Impact

At the first Academy Awards ceremony, held in May of 1929, *Wings* won the Academy Award for Most Outstanding Production, later deemed equivalent to the award for Best Picture, as well as the award for Best Engineering Effects. In addition to furthering the careers of the main cast, all of whom continued to act into the 1930s, the film became particularly notable in later decades for the appearance of Gary Cooper in one of his first credited roles.

Carl Rollyson

Further Reading

Thompson, Frank T. *William A. Wellman.* Metuchen, N.J.: Scarecrow Press, 1983.

Wellman, William. *A Short Time for Insanity.* New York: Hawthorn Books, 1974.

Wellman, William, Jr. *The Man and His Wings: William A. Wellman and the Making of the First Best Picture.* New York: Praeger Publishers, 2006.

See also: Aviation; Bow, Clara; Film

■ Women in college

Spurred by several societal changes during the 1920s, including ratification of the Nineteenth Amendment in 1920 granting women the right to vote, American women began attending college in increasing numbers. The overall economic prosperity of the period further contributed to this growth in college attendance. Overall, women's college enrollment increased from less than 4 percent in 1910 to over 10 percent by the end of the 1920s. For the majority of women, however, college was vocational, and they primarily attended teacher-training programs or majored in home economics or domestic science.

The mid-nineteenth century brought with it the first wave of the feminist movement. At the Women's Rights Convention in Seneca Falls, New York, in 1848, early feminists recognized that a college education was pivotal for women in achieving equality with men, and they denounced colleges who refused to admit women. Although the 1862 Morrill Land Grant College Act prompted several newly established colleges and universities to open their doors to women on a limited basis, two-thirds of American colleges and universities in 1870 still did not admit women. By 1889, seven women's colleges had been founded, including Smith College in Massachusetts and Vassar College in New York, which dramatically increased educational opportunities for women. Despite this, college was primarily for the very wealthy.

Women's newly acquired right to vote accompanied by the economic prosperity of the 1920s made it more feasible for middle-class families to send their

> **Eleanor Roosevelt on Women and College**
>
> *Responding to the persistent political and social inequality of women at the time, Eleanor Roosevelt published the article "Women Must Learn to Play the Game as Men Do" in* Red Book *magazine in 1928. Here is an excerpt from her essay:*
>
> An old politician once objected, "Don't you think these women lose their allure, that the bloom is just a little gone? Men are no longer interested?" Frankly, I don't know. I imagine the answer is individual. It was once said that men did not marry women who showed too much intelligence. In my youth I knew women who hid their college degrees as if they were one of the seven deadly sins. But all that is passing, and so will pass many other prejudices that have their origin in the ancient tradition that women are a by-product of creation.

daughters to college, and women on college campuses enjoyed new freedoms in dress and behavior. Many college women bobbed their hair and wore more modern and less modest fashion. Drinking alcohol on campus was common (though illegal during Prohibition), and many women took up smoking cigarettes, which added to their sense of newfound liberation. Women also played a number of sports, including tennis, swimming, and basketball.

Obstacles and Limitations

In 1921, Vice President Calvin Coolidge denounced women's colleges as hotbeds of radicalism. Others argued against college education for women, contending that it rendered them unfit for marriage and motherhood. These concerns led to vocation-based curricula. Many women enrolled in two-year teacher-training colleges, while others pursued a course of study called home economics or domestic science, which proliferated through the 1920s and was primarily designed to help women become better wives and mothers. However, several colleges, such as the Michigan State Agricultural College (later renamed Michigan State University), incorporated coursework into home economics programs that provided opportunities for women to train for work outside the home. Food majors, for instance, were trained to work as dieticians in hospitals or schools, clothing majors went on to become clothes designers or interior decorators, and textile students found jobs in advertising or teaching.

"Marriage bars" became more common in the 1920s and extended well into the 1950s. A marriage bar was a policy set in place by school boards and businesses that would not hire a married woman. A "retention bar," on the other hand, was a policy that allowed a female employee who married to be fired. Such bars made college degrees less desirable for women who were married or intended to marry, so attendance by women at many colleges declined substantially in the late 1920s through the 1930s.

African American women seeking a college education in the 1920s faced racial discrimination in addition to gender discrimination. Many did attend college but were often excluded by whites from joining sororities and other social and political organizations. In the South, where racial discrimination was particularly pronounced, African American women primarily attended coeducational all-black colleges, and the majority of them enrolled in teacher-training programs.

Impact

Women's enrollment in colleges dropped dramatically with the stock market crash of 1929 and the Great Depression of the 1930s. As of 1940, only 40 percent of college students were women, since economic hard times meant fewer families had the money to send their daughters to college. Marriage and retention bars became prevalent as school districts and other businesses saved their limited job openings for the male breadwinner of a family. Men's enrollment in college increased, fueled in part by the passage of the G.I. Bill after World War II, which gave tuition assistance to veterans. By the latter part of the 1940s, more than twice as many men attended college than women.

With the second-wave feminism of the late 1960s and early 1970s, however, marriage and retention bars disappeared, and as women gained more reproductive freedom and greater career opportunities, they began attending colleges in greater numbers. By 1980, men and women were attending college in equal numbers.

Kimberlee Candela

Further Reading

Brown, Dorothy M. *Setting a Course: American Women in the 1920s*. Boston, Mass.: Twayne, 1987. Addresses women's changing role during the 1920s.

Goldin, Claudia. "The Quiet Revolution That Transformed Women's Employment, Education, and Family." *American Economic Review* 96, no. 2 (May, 2006): 1–21. Examines women's participation in the labor force over the past century.

Goldin, Claudia, Lawrence F. Katz, and Ilyana Kuziemko. "The Homecoming of American College Women: The Reversal of the College Gender Gap." *Journal of Economic Perspectives* 20, no. 4 (Fall, 2006): 133–156. Traces women's college enrollment over the course of the twentieth century.

Solomon, Barbara Miller. *In the Company of Educated Women: A History of Women and Higher Education in America*. New Haven, Conn.: Yale University Press, 1985. An examination of women in college from 1800 through the 1940s.

Thelin, John R. *A History of American Higher Education*. 2d ed. Baltimore, Md.: Johns Hopkins University Press, 2011. Provides a history of the evolution of American colleges and universities and includes several sections pertaining to the history of women in college.

See also: African Americans; Marriage and dating; Nineteenth Amendment; Roaring Twenties; Women in the workforce; Women's rights

■ Women in the workforce

During the 1920s, unprecedented numbers of American women worked in a greater variety of professions than ever before. However, the increased presence of women in the workforce had a limited impact on gender inequality, instead contributing to the divide between individualist and social justice feminists.

Prior to the 1920s, the role of women in the American workforce had traditionally been limited. The increased separation of work and home that began in the nineteenth century made the idea of women working for pay socially unacceptable, especially for married women who were not working class or poor. Even the expansion of women's public roles in the late nineteenth century did not lead to a general acceptance of working women. It was the exigencies of World War I that brought large numbers of women into the workforce, including into traditionally male occupations. Although this wartime employment of women did not have as dramatic an impact as it later would in World War II, and although most female wartime workers were not able to continue their jobs following demobilization, the phenomenon nevertheless paved the way for a greater acceptance of middle-class, single—and, to a lesser extent, married (but childless)—women working for pay.

In the postwar era, the occupational choices of working American women of all backgrounds began to change. Although these changes primarily affected white middle-class women, and it was mainly white middle-class women who had opportunities to pursue clerical or professional work, working-class women from immigrant backgrounds increasingly moved up from industrial to office jobs, and African American women, previously limited to domestic labor, enjoyed unprecedented opportunities in industrial work. These new developments also affected precollege and vocational education and began to legitimize the idea of women seeking paid employment for reasons other than strict economic necessity.

Class, Work, and the Limitations of Change

Contrary to the expectations that followed passage of the Nineteenth Amendment, the achievement of women's suffrage had a limited impact on gender balance in the workforce. If anything, it contributed to a split between individualist feminists, who supported the movement for an Equal Rights Amendment (ERA), and social justice feminists, who opposed the ERA on the basis that it could negatively affect the passage of protective workforce legislation for women. Both stances were affected by considerations of class and education. During this period, individualist feminists—including one of the most famous career women of the 1920s, Amelia Earhart—promoted the ERA as an essential step, not only toward equal legal rights for women, but also toward equal opportunities to pursue educations and careers. Social justice feminists, by contrast, were primarily concerned with the needs of working-class women, who had jobs rather than careers and were still dealing with poor working conditions, long hours, unequal pay, and less unionization and union protection than male workers. Notably, the Women's Trade Union League (WTUL), founded in 1903 to promote trade unionism among female

> **Muller v. Oregon**
>
> Although the passage of the Nineteenth Amendment to the U.S. Constitution in 1920, granting women the right to vote, was a significant milestone in women's rights, women still faced many obstacles to real freedom. Among other things, they did not have the same educational opportunities as men or economic independence. Still in effect at the time was the U.S. Supreme Court's finding in *Muller v. Oregon* (1908):
>
>> The two sexes differ in structure of body, in the functions to be performed by each, in the amount of physical strength, in the capacity for long-continued labor, particularly when done standing. . . . This difference justifies a difference in legislation, and upholds that which is designed to compensate for some of the burdens which rest upon her.
>
> Although this decision protected some women, it proved discriminatory in many cases. Because of the assumption that women were weaker and more vulnerable than men, women were prohibited from practicing certain professions, such as law, even when they were fully qualified to do so. They were forbidden to lift weights, even those no heavier than an eighteen-month-old child. Women were forbidden to serve in bars at night, although they were able to work as cleaners or entertainers at the same hour.

workers, had, by the 1920s, shifted its emphasis to protective legislation.

Regardless of class, the increasingly anti-regulation political climate of the 1920s blocked the passage of protective legislation for women, in some cases on the basis of women's greater equality following the achievement of universal suffrage. The most famous example of this came to public attention in the 1923 Supreme Court case *Adkins v. Children's Hospital*, in which the Court struck down a minimum-wage law for women on the basis that it interfered with a female worker's freedom to contract and was therefore unconstitutional. At the same time, women's advancement into various service and clerical professions contributed to the characterization of those jobs as "feminine" and thus deserving of lower status and pay. Progress varied among fields, and in the case of medicine and dentistry, the number of women in these professions decreased from the end of the nineteenth century. Finally, although an unprecedented number of middle-class married women worked during the 1920s, their acceptance in the workforce was limited enough that in the early years of the Great Depression, married women were pushed out of many jobs in order to create more employment for men, the presumed breadwinners.

Impact

The advances of women in the workforce during the 1920s proved tenuous and limited in the short term. Although middle-class women, including married women, held jobs in greater numbers than ever before, this did not lead to their full acceptance as working women. The optimistic environment of the 1920s, however, did lead to brand new possibilities for women, contributing to their subsequent advancement in the American workforce.

Susan Roth Breitzer

Further Reading

Blackwelder, Julia Kirk. *Now Hiring: The Feminization of Work in the United States, 1900–1995*. College Station: Texas A&M University Press, 1997. Studies the long history of women's migration into the American workforce and the social and economic forces affecting this migration.

Brown, Dorothy M. *Setting a Course: American Women in the 1920s*. Boston: Twayne, 1987. A monograph on the history of women in the United States following the passage of the Nineteenth Amendment that examines the expectations and the realities of change during this period.

Hesse-Biber, Sharlene Nagy, and Gregg Lee Carter. *Working Women in America: Split Dreams*. New York: Oxford University Press, 2005. A history of women in the American workforce that emphasizes the dilemma of work versus family.

Kessler-Harris, Alice. *Out to Work: A History of Wage-Earning Women in the United States*. New York: Oxford University Press, 1982. A study of women's gainful employment in American history from the colonial era to the present.

Milkman, Ruth, ed. *Women, Work, and Protest: A Century of U.S. Women's Labor History*. Boston: Routledge & Kegan Paul, 1985. A collection of essays on women and the twentieth-century American labor movement, some of which address their changing roles in the 1920s.

See also: *Adkins v. Children's Hospital*; Earhart, Amelia; Equal Rights Amendment; Women in college; Women's rights

■ Women's rights

The women's rights movement seemed to flounder following the achievement of the right to vote in 1920, accomplishing little else of lasting substance, though it was hardly inactive during the 1920s. Throughout the decade, the movement remained divided between individualist feminists who promoted the Equal Rights Amendment and social feminists who worked for social and workplace legislation.

Characterized by significant political conservatism and a retreat from the activism of the Progressive Era, the ideological shift of the 1920s had a profound effect on the women's rights movement in the United States. In the post–World War I "return to normalcy" heralded by President Warren G. Harding, Americans retreated from political participation and activism as personal fulfillment was emphasized and consumerism and entertainment became increasingly important parts of the public culture. Additionally, anticommunist sentiment and the social culture of the 1920s, with its emphasis on individualism and personal freedom, created a popular distaste for the earlier feminist activism. This cultural shift, combined with the achievement of women's suffrage early in the decade, contributed to the perception that feminism had been rendered irrelevant. As a result, the women's movement appeared to disintegrate, and relatively few advances in women's rights were made during the remainder of the decade.

Yet, this image of the women's movement in the 1920s oversimplifies what was in fact a much more complex picture for American women following the passage of the Nineteenth Amendment. The movement remained active and relevant throughout the decade, although a divide formed between the individualist feminist movement, which emphasized equal rights with men and promoted the passage of the Equal Rights Amendment (ERA), and the social feminist movement, which focused its efforts on protecting poor and working-class women. Women's rights activists of the 1920s sought to determine the extent of women's political participation following the achievement of the vote and identify which issues were most important to address in a postsuffrage United States. Against a backdrop of increased political conservatism and a social climate that emphasized individualism, the women's movement would, in fact, make significant progress throughout the decade.

The Women's Suffrage Movement

By the 1920s, the decades-old women's suffrage movement had shifted the case for women's suffrage from one based on women's equality with men to one based on women's difference from men, arguing that the latter could better American society by bringing an increased morality to politics and government. The women's rights movement that had emerged in the late nineteenth century was very much shaped by this ideology of "separate spheres" even as it worked to transcend it, and women's activism took the form of social betterment efforts that became known as "social housekeeping." These efforts at times successfully transcended barriers of class and ethnicity, but unifying women's rights activists of different races was frequently difficult. As a result, African American women were largely left to create their own women's movement, one at least partially devoted to addressing racial as well as gender discrimination. This effective segregation remained in place throughout the 1920s and beyond.

The shift from an emphasis on equality to an emphasis on difference continued during the 1890 reunification of the American Woman Suffrage Association and the National Woman Suffrage Association, which had split in 1869. The reunited organization, named the North American Woman Suffrage Association (NAWSA), emphasized women's purifying roles in society, while the equality argument for women's suffrage was taken up in 1913 by the radical Congressional Union for Woman Suffrage, founded by Alice Paul and other dissident members of NAWSA. During the war years, Paul and other Congressional Union activists picketed the White House and endured arrest and force-feeding in prison to draw public attention to the issue.

A number of states granted full or limited suffrage to women throughout the nineteenth and

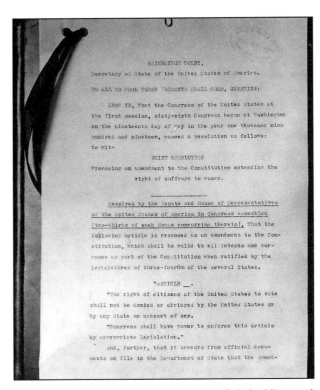
A copy of the original document that ratified the Nineteenth Amendment. (Hulton Archive/Getty Images)

early twentieth centuries, particularly in the western half of the country, but women's rights activists sought to achieve nationwide suffrage. When efforts to pass an equal suffrage law failed in Congress, suffragists lobbied individual states for support in adding a suffrage amendment to the Constitution. The United States' entrance into World War I allowed activists to promote women's suffrage as a democratic cause, drawing a connection between the war for democracy abroad and the domestic struggle for women's suffrage.

The House of Representatives passed a women's suffrage amendment in 1918, but the Senate did not support it. Both houses of Congress went on to pass the amendment the following year, and suffragists urged state governments to ratify the amendment before the 1920 presidential election. On August 18, 1920, the necessary number of states ratified the Nineteenth Amendment to the United States Constitution, and it was certified six days later. This amendment made it illegal to deny a citizen the right to vote based on sex, thus granting all female U.S. citizens the right to vote.

At the outset, the achievement of women's suffrage appeared to have little effect on the political culture of the 1920s. A "women's bloc" of voters, something that was both hoped for and feared, largely failed to materialize; women typically voted along the same lines as men, rather than as a cohesive group. In addition, after an initial increase in the number of voters following suffrage, American voting levels declined in the next presidential election, even with women's participation. More significant and troubling for women's suffrage activists, women's suffrage only briefly translated into greater political power for women, and it did not enhance the effectiveness of further women's activism. Groups such as NAWSA and the Congressional Union remained at odds following the passage of the Nineteenth Amendment, and this ideological divide affected the later efforts to introduce and pass the ERA.

Women and Politics
With women's suffrage achieved, women's rights activists sought to educate women for public citizenship and against a lingering reluctance to vote. They also sought to determine whether women would and should vote as women or along party lines. The latter became increasingly of interest as the Democratic and Republican political candidates courted women's votes, each party emphasizing its support for women's suffrage. Left largely unaddressed by women's suffrage organizations were the voting rights of African American women, who now increasingly shared the civil rights concerns of African American men. Even for white women, however, significant political and legal challenges remained following the achievement of suffrage. On the one hand, the major political parties wanted the votes and loyalties of the newly enfranchised American women. On the other hand, these male-dominated political parties were initially reluctant to grant women more than a limited amount of power and influence within the parties, whether in terms of political office or party leadership. The latter issue led to the creation of women's divisions within the two major parties. These divisions, along with independent women's political organizations, gave women valuable experience in party politics as well as opportunities for leadership and influence. However, these separate organizations ultimately limited women's influence within the larger party structures. Even with these limitations, the women's partisan organizations played a vital role in

educating idealistic female voters and activists about the realities of party politics. They also educated activists about the expectations of party loyalty at a time in which the major parties maintained significant influence over the American political process.

The postsuffrage women's movement also led to the creation of nonpartisan voter education efforts, which sought to address such issues. Founded by NAWSA leadership in 1920, the League of Women Voters worked alongside women's political organizations to educate and encourage women to exercise their newly won right to vote. Although the League of Women Voters maintained a firm nonpartisan stance, it encouraged women to vote within the two-party system rather than solely on the basis of women's issues. The Congressional Union, which had represented the more radical and individualist wing of the women's suffrage movement, likewise transformed itself into the National Woman's Party, maintaining a militant stance toward women's political participation and emphasizing women's issues. The National Woman's Party also devoted itself to the promotion of the ERA, beginning another long struggle to introduce women's legal equality into the United States Constitution.

The Equal Rights Amendment and Social Feminism
The ERA, which stipulated that women and men nationwide be granted equal rights, was first introduced in Congress in 1923. Following the introduction of the ERA, its passage became the primary goal of the radical and individualist wing of the 1920s women's movement, and its celebrity supporters included aviator Amelia Earhart. However, despite the amendment's repeated introduction in Congress throughout the decade, it was not passed and consequently was not ratified by any states.

From the beginning, the ERA faced significant opposition from both feminists and antifeminists, in part due to the broad and open-ended nature of the proposed amendment. In fact, some of the strongest opponents of the ERA were social feminist activists who feared that legislating complete legal equality would have a negative impact on protective workplace legislation for women, which had become the principal concern of social feminist organizations such as the Women's Trade Union League. Although social feminists did not oppose full equality as an ideal, they maintained an awareness of the effects of class and other considerations on women's equality, and they did not want working-class women in particular to lose the right to legal protections in the workplace and elsewhere.

The Women's Trade Union League remained a major player in the social feminist movement of the 1920s, having by this time shifted its focus from organizing working women into unions to lobbying for protective workplace legislation, in recognition of both the limited success of their earlier efforts and the overall decline of the American labor movement in the 1920s. Their struggle to address inequalities at work continued throughout the decade and was especially stymied by the 1923 Supreme Court decision in *Adkins v. Children's Hospital*, which struck down minimum wage legislation for women on the basis that a legislated minimum wage restricted the right of workers and employers to form contracts without government interference. In his majority opinion, Associate Justice George Sutherland further wrote that the achievement of women's suffrage had eliminated the political and social differences between men and women and put an end to the need for protective legislation. Beyond the workplace, the social feminist movement still enjoyed successes in promoting the concerns of poor and working-class women. One of the most significant achievements was the passage of the Sheppard-Towner Maternity and Infancy Protection Act in 1921, which appropriated federal funding for maternal and infant health care, particularly for poor women, and included provisions for health clinics and visiting nurse programs.

Legal and Social Change
Even with the continued efforts of the varied feminist movements of the 1920s, women's rights and obligations of citizenship remained limited compared to those of men. For example, in many states and localities, women's jury service was either prohibited or made optional, and in some cases, the ability to hold political office was restricted to men. Women's legal rights and status, including the right to citizenship itself, also continued to be affected by marriage. When a woman married, she assumed the citizenship of her husband, causing a multitude of problems for American women who married foreign citizens and consequently lost all of their rights as U.S. citizens, including, when it became applicable, the right to vote. This forced change of status caused additional problems during World War I, as American women married to citizens of Germany or its allies

were declared enemy aliens and threatened with deportation. To address this problem, Congress passed the Cable Act of 1922, named for its sponsor, Ohio representative John Cable. The act made it possible for a woman who married a foreign citizen to retain her U.S. citizenship, provided she lived in the United States and not her husband's country of citizenship. However, reflecting the prejudices of the period, the act only benefited women who married men deemed eligible for naturalization under U.S. law, which did not include those of Asian descent; women who married Asian men continued to assume the citizenship status of their husbands.

These continued limitations on women's rights during the 1920s became largely obscured in the public imagination by the greater social freedom that became a well-known hallmark of the period. The changes that largely affected dress, personal behavior, and relationships also shaped the perception that women's rights had ceased to be a relevant issue. Race and class significantly limited this kind of personal freedom, but even for middle-class white women, the personal and social freedom of the stereotypical flapper translated into little substantive change. Marriage was still expected for women, although the controversial idea of the "companionate marriage," a model that emphasized the necessity of spouses being both lovers and friends, began to spread during the decade. Although the companionate marriage concept affected some relationships, married women's lives were more profoundly affected by the new availability of labor-saving technology and consumer goods such as refrigerators. Women also benefited from the increased availability of birth control and educational material regarding reproductive health, accessible due in large part to the efforts of birth control activists such as Margaret Sanger. Nevertheless, the expectation remained that middle-class women would cease work following marriage, and even when women combined marriage with a career, women's opportunities for professional advancement remained limited.

Impact

Having lost its unifying goal of suffrage with the passage of the Nineteenth Amendment, the women's rights movement would remain largely fragmented for several decades. However, the advances of the 1920s continued to influence women's rights efforts during later periods. The ERA remained a major goal of the women's movement, passing in Congress in 1972. While the amendment failed to be ratified by the required number of states, it continued to be reintroduced in Congress into the twenty-first century. Social feminism reaped lasting benefits, improving workplaces for both women and men and working to differentiate between legal protection and legal discrimination. Although the scope of women's public roles was shaped over time by the changing political climate, women continued to play a key role in electoral politics in the decades following the ratification of the Nineteenth Amendment, paving the way for the eventual diversity of women's political involvement.

Susan Roth Breitzer

Further Reading

Baer, Judith A., and Leslie Friedman Goldstein. *The Constitutional and Legal Rights of Women: Cases in Law and Social Change.* Rev. ed. New York: Oxford University Press, 2006. Explains key Supreme Court cases concerning women's rights throughout American history.

Banner, Lois W. *Women in Modern America: A Brief History.* 3d ed. New York: Harcourt Brace Jovanovich, 1995. Provides a background to the political and social climate of the 1920s and explores how this climate affected the advancement of women's rights.

Becker, Susan. D. *The Origins of the Equal Rights Amendment: American Feminism Between The Wars.* Westport, Conn.: Greenwood Press, 1985. Chronicles the early history of the effort to introduce the Equal Rights Amendment, as well as the essentially conservative political climate faced by its chief sponsor, the National Woman's Party.

Chafe, William Henry. *The American Woman: Her Changing Social, Economic, and Political Roles, 1920–1970.* Reprint. London: Oxford University Press, 1979. Demonstrates the impact of lingering social and economic pressures on the achievement of political and legal equality.

Gustafson, Melanie Susan. *Women and the Republican Party, 1854–1924.* Urbana: University of Illinois Press, 2001. Examines the changing relationship between the Republican Party and women's rights activists, from the Republican Party's original role as a major supporter of women's suffrage to its more ambivalent relationship with women voters in the 1920s.

Kerber, Linda K. *No Constitutional Right to Be Ladies: Women and the Obligations of Citizenship.* New York:

Hill and Wang, 1999. Studies the changes in women's legal status throughout American history and emphasizes the importance of the development of women's equal obligations as citizens.

Matthews, Donald, and Jane Sherron De Hart. *Sex, Gender, and the Politics of ERA: A State and a Nation.* New York: Oxford University Press, 1992. Uses North Carolina as a case study of the history of the Equal Rights Amendment to demonstrate how an essentially conservative political culture affected the attempts to pass the ERA from the beginning.

See also: *Adkins v. Children's Hospital;* Birth control; Cable Act of 1922; Equal Rights Amendment; League of Women Voters; Marriage and dating; Sheppard-Towner Act of 1921; Voting rights; Women in college; Women in the workforce

■ Workers' education

U.S. labor activists in the 1920s founded a number of experimental "labor colleges," intended to train better-informed labor organizers and build a stronger labor movement that could effect greater social change. Most, however, did not survive beyond the interwar period.

Labor colleges, which were not accredited by state educational departments and offered no degrees, fell into three basic categories: residential facilities in a campus-like setting, such as Brookwood in Katonah, New York; summer-school programs for women, such as the Bryn Mawr Summer School for Women Workers, near Philadelphia; and urban, nonresidential colleges with evening and weekend classes, such as the Boston Trade Union College. All three types of educational training offered similar courses, which included traditional coursework combined with instruction in union organization and the history of the American labor movement.

Early Workers' Education
Serious challenges to organized labor in the United States following World War I, including the Red Scare of 1919, led progressive unionists and pro-labor intellectuals and educators such as John Dewey, Sinclair Lewis, Upton Sinclair, and W. E. B. Du Bois to promote a more deeply rooted unionization of workers grounded in theories of economic and social justice, taught in the classroom. Subsequent plans for workers' education programs focused not only on training unionists to become effective organizers but also to create a reform-minded working class able to reach out to unorganized industrial workers. The curriculum balanced radical content with practical objectives as a means of maintaining organized labor's support, and the programs themselves were able to call attention to needs for social and economic reform during a decade considered hostile to labor. They also provided an educational environment in which instructors and students could exchange expertise, insight, and experience in the area of labor reform.

Notable Labor Colleges
Labor colleges were established across the United States and included Workers' University in New York City, which was founded by the International Ladies Garment Workers Union; Seattle Labor College, which catered to dock workers; Boston Trade Union College, which elicited support from sympathetic members of the Harvard University faculty; and Milwaukee Workers' College, which also operated satellite campuses in twelve industrial cities throughout Wisconsin. The most popular workers' colleges appealed to women factory workers, including the Bryn Mawr Summer School for Women Workers, the Southern Summer School for Women Workers in Industry (held in various locations in the South), the Barnard Summer School for Women Workers in Industry (in New York City), and the Wisconsin School for Workers in Industry. These were especially important because they acknowledged the growing social and political importance of women in the workforce and helped to put women labor organizers on a more equal footing with men.

Residential labor colleges were popular among sympathetic labor intellectuals and progressive unionists anxious to move the American Federation of Labor (AFL) beyond its focus on workers' wages and hours (business unionism) to more emphasis on reform of the capitalist system (social unionism). Many wanted these labor colleges to become the vanguard for social and economic change in the United States, where Republican leadership was perceived as hostile to labor interests. Work People's College in Duluth, Minnesota, focused its program on educating ethnic minorities, especially Finns and Swedes, while drawing connections with labor-farmer politics. Commonwealth College was founded originally in Louisiana in 1923. The school was eventually relocated to Mena,

Arkansas, in 1925, where a program was developed based on class-consciousness and communist principles. The program was shut down by local authorities and state officials before the end of the decade when Commonwealth's teachings were perceived as anarchistic and anti-American.

The most famous of all the residential labor colleges was Brookwood Labor College in Katonah, New York, north of New York City. Founded in 1921, the college was led by pacifist minister A. J. Muste and a faculty of progressive-minded educators. During the 1920s, Brookwood's two-year residential program not only encouraged organizing southern textile workers but also challenged the AFL's traditional goals of organizing only craft workers. Its drama program, featuring the Brookwood Labor Players, traveled thousands of miles each year performing labor skits throughout the nation. However, Brookwood fell out of favor with the AFL, whose leadership saw the school and its faculty as too radical. In 1928, the AFL asked its local chapters to suspend financial support and not send student workers to Brookwood; with declining support, the school closed in 1937.

Impact

Most workers' education programs went out of existence because of lack of support and a lack of union funds during the Great Depression. What replaced this novel educational experiment was the establishment of union education departments and university-based extension centers such as Cornell University's School of Industrial and Labor Relations. The focus thus became less on social and economic change through unionism and more on educating labor leaders to be skilled in the art of collective bargaining. Nonetheless, the labor colleges founded after World War I formed a significant chapter in the history of the American labor movement. Several Brookwood students, for example, played instrumental roles in the mid-1930s in the creation of the Congress of Industrial Organizations (CIO), which merged with the AFL in 1955.

Charles F. Howlett

Further Reading

Altenbaugh, Richard J. *Education for Struggle: The American Labor Colleges of the 1920s and 1930s.* Philadelphia: Temple University Press, 1990. Focuses on the establishment and evolution of three major labor colleges: Work People's College in Minnesota; Brookwood Labor College in New York; and Commonwealth College in Arkansas.

Dray, Philip. *There Is Power in a Union: The Epic Story of Labor in America.* New York: Doubleday, 2010. Explores the history of American labor from the early 1900s to modern times.

Foner, Philip Sheldon. *Women and the American Labor Movement.* New York: Free Press, 1980. Presents a history through documentation and contemporary writings of women's struggles to gain union recognition and equality with male workers.

Howlett, Charles F. *Brookwood Labor College and the Struggle for Peace and Social Justice in America.* Lewiston, N.Y.: Mellen Press, 1993. Provides historical information on Brookwood and its contributions to social reform.

Howlett, Charles F., Robbie Lieberman, and Harriet Hyman Alonso. *A History of the American Peace Movement: From Colonial Times to the Present.* Lewiston: N.Y.: Mellen Press, 2008. Provides a history of U.S. antiwar movements and covers Brookwood Labor College's peace and justice curriculum.

See also: American Federation of Labor (AFL); Dewey, John; Du Bois, W. E. B.; Labor strikes; Lewis, Sinclair; Women in the workforce

---

American Management Review

The American Management Associations journal, the *American Management Review,* energetically promoted human relations as an essential ingredient in industrial success. First published in April, 1923, the journal gained increasing popularity by featuring individual and industry opinions on the issues affecting employee relations. It raised important topics ranging from declining productivity to the fragility of the work ethic. The *American Management Review* also furthered the debate on educational training of workers to improve their productivity and ensure their loyalty to their companies.

World War I veterans

The experience of World War I veterans in the United States during the 1920s varied widely as they dealt with the sometimes tumultuous aspects of a recovering society and their own physical and psychological recovery. Throughout the

decade, veterans worked, raised families, and became an integral part of the rapid social and economic changes occurring in the United States. Until the stock market crash of 1929 and the ensuing Great Depression, American veterans benefited from the post–World War I economic boom.

Going into World War I, Congress had set in motion a series of benefits to be claimed by that war's veterans, such as financial support, insurance options, and vocational guidance for veterans with disabilities. By the 1920s, three federal agencies—the Veterans Bureau, the Bureau of Pensions of the Interior Department, and the National Home for Disabled Volunteer Soldiers—had been established to manage the distribution of veterans' benefits.

Economic Opportunities for Veterans

In spite of minor recessions and political scandals, the early and mid-1920s offered a reasonable number of economic opportunities for returning soldiers. Some veterans were able to find jobs in factories and in the construction industry. Many other former service members joined the automobile and machine manufacturing industry, which was growing rapidly thanks to technological advances and increases in the use of assembly lines.

Well-paying jobs also allowed veterans to buy homes and raise families during the 1920s, which was an era of ongoing construction. Affordable housing options, such as bungalows and housing cooperatives, appeared throughout the country. A high point of the affordable housing endeavor was New York governor Al Smith's leadership in achieving the passing of the New York State Limited Dividend Housing Companies Act in 1927. Through this act, government aid was given to support the founding and maintenance of housing cooperatives. Affordable housing options were also created specifically for World War I veterans, setting a pattern for veteran support lasting into the twenty-first century.

Lasting Effects of War

World War I affected many Americans' perspectives on international relationships, approaches to medicine, and even popular culture and entertainment. Many Americans shared World War I veterans' disillusionment with global politics, and the United States adopted a generally isolationist policy as the country tried to return to life the way it had been before World War I.

For veterans significantly changed by their service, advances in medicine benefited those struggling with disfiguring or debilitating physical injuries incurred during the war. Prostheses became more common for war survivors who had lost limbs, and physical therapy became more widespread, leading to improved rehabilitation for veterans but also for anyone injured in manufacturing accidents in the United States. Noted public figure Helen Keller encouraged veterans to learn to live with their new realities, using her own struggle with blindness and deafness as a model.

Many World War I veterans also suffered from mental and emotional trauma long after the end of the war. Americans called this type of disturbance "shell shock," although it later became known as post-traumatic stress disorder (PTSD) or post-traumatic stress syndrome. Some veterans found support from developments in the growing fields of psychiatry and psychoanalysis, but the majority had no alternative but to cope with their lingering trauma symptoms without help.

While navigating their transformation from military service back into civilian life, World War I veterans found resonance with characters and issues in literature by noted authors such as Ernest Hemingway, including his 1929 work *A Farewell to Arms*. The burgeoning cinema industry also capitalized on memories from World War I with movies such as *Wings* (1927), a film that centered on two World War I pilots who shared a common love interest, portrayed by popular actors Buddy Rogers, Richard Arlen, and Clara Bow.

Men were not the only ones who returned from the life-altering events of World War I. Women had also served extensively as nurses, ambulance drivers, and in other support positions, some of which placed them in the line of fire. While they were not allowed to fight in the trenches or participate in other combat action with the male soldiers, female service members returned to the United States deeply affected by their experiences. Government and military pension funds frequently considered their war efforts to be civilian, not military, service and therefore ineligible for veterans' benefits, leaving these women with fewer resources and less formal recognition than male veterans.

Impact

During the 1920s, World War I veterans benefited from developments in physical and vocational rehabilitation, a real estate boom that created inexpensive housing opportunities, and increased research into the nature of PTSD. Government support for World War I veterans continued to evolve, and in 1930, the existing benefits were combined under the authority of a single federal agency, the Veterans Administration. A further step in the evolution of veterans' services was the founding of the Department of Veterans Affairs (VA) in 1989 under President George H. W. Bush.

Bonnye Busbice Good

Further Reading

Gavin, Lettie. *American Women in World War I: They Also Served.* Boulder: University Press of Colorado, 2006. Recounts details of service from some of the thousands of women who served during World War I as nurses and in other occupations.

Kennedy, David M. *Over Here: The First World War and American Society.* New York: Oxford University Press, 2004. Describes the difficulties the United States faced as a result of World War I, also noting how the country's reactions laid the foundation for twentieth-century politics, economics, and society.

Schneider, Dorothy, and Carl J. Schneider. *Into the Breach: American Women Overseas in World War I.* New York: Viking, 1991. Discusses women's military service in World War I and their attempts to gain pensions and recognition equal to that of male veterans during the 1920s.

Winter, Jay, Geoffrey Parker, and Mary R. Habeck, eds. *The Great War and the Twentieth Century.* New Haven, Conn.: Yale University Press, 2000. Explains how World War I shaped society, politics, and culture.

Wynn, Neil A. *From Progressivism to Prosperity: World War I and American Society.* New York: Holmes & Meier, 1986. Examines the political issues and popular movements that spurred Progressive ideals and explores the impact of government aid and private industry on post–World War I prosperity in the United States.

See also: *Farewell to Arms, A;* Foreign policy, U.S.; Housing; Unemployment

■ Wright, Frank Lloyd

Identification: American architect
Born: June 8, 1867, Richland Center, Wisconsin
Died: April 9, 1959, Phoenix, Arizona

Though Frank Lloyd Wright built few buildings in the 1920s, his structural achievements, new construction techniques, integration of design with natural setting, and voice in the architectural discourse of the day propelled him from a local residential Chicago architect to one of international renown.

Frank Lloyd Wright's architectural career thrived at the turn of the century, with the success of his Prairie School houses and his determination to create a distinctly American architecture that did not rely on European precedents. Although his practice waned due to a decline in his personal reputation, he continued to explore structure and materials in both his writings and his buildings.

In 1921, Wright completed the Aline Barnsdall Hollyhock House in Los Angeles, a flat-roofed, rectangular structure surrounding a central courtyard. The house had a wood frame finished with stucco, creating a massive appearance that concealed a lightweight structure. Wishing for more congruity between appearance and structure, Wright turned toward heavier materials for his next houses.

Textile-Block Construction

In 1923 and 1924, Wright built four "textile-block" houses in the Los Angeles area, utilizing a construction technique developed with his son Lloyd. Concrete blocks were cast on site in decorative molds, then stacked and reinforced with horizontal and vertical bars inserted into notches at the block edges. Concrete poured into the cavities served to grout the structure together. This system comprised both the exterior and interior walls, which were separated with an air space for insulation. The Alice Millard House, or La Miniatura, was the first of the textile-block houses, followed chronologically by the John Storer House, the Samuel and Harriet Freeman House, and the Mabel and Charles Ennis House.

Also in 1923, Wright began to plan the Doheny Ranch Resort for Edward Doheny. The pre-Columbian-inspired textile-block complex would consist of twenty-five houses, terraces, and hanging gardens designed to nestle among natural waterfalls in the canyon hillside of Beverly Hills. The project ended, however, with the discovery of Doheny's involvement in the Teapot Dome Scandal.

The Imperial Hotel

In September of 1923, an earthquake struck the region surrounding Tokyo, Japan, the site of Wright's

Frank Lloyd Wright. (Time & Life Pictures/Getty Images)

Imperial Hotel, which he had completed earlier that year. The hotel structure was intended to withstand such a natural disaster, employing the principle of a waiter balancing a tray on his fingers: Independent of the exterior walls, the floor slabs cantilevered off interior supports resting on concrete pins, which in turn extended down through the hard upper soil to the mud underneath. Though the disaster leveled much of the city, the Imperial Hotel remained intact, gaining worldwide attention.

End of the Decade
Wright's Wisconsin home, called Taliesin ("shining brow" in Welsh), was constructed of limestone, wood, and plaster against the bank of the Wisconsin River. First built in 1911, a fire badly damaged it in 1914. Taliesin burned for a second time in 1925, prompting Wright to rebuild the living quarters and expand them westward. He would continue to experiment with the structure throughout his life. Later, in 1926, Wright began work on the Isabel Martin Residence in Derby, New York, a cliffside stone-and-plaster building at Lake Erie. He would complete the residence, also known as Graycliff, in 1931.

In 1927, former associate Albert McArthur asked Wright to help design the Arizona Biltmore Hotel in Phoenix, a textile-block building completed in 1928. While Wright was working in Phoenix, he met Alexander Chandler, who commissioned him for a mountainside resort called San Marcos-in-the-Desert. Wright decided to move to Arizona with his apprentices to work. There he built the Ocatillo Desert Camp, a collection of canvas-covered structures arranged around a hill and linked by a board and batten wall. Though San Marcos-in-the-Desert ended with the stock market crash of 1929, Wright's fascination with the desert would remain with him, evident in Taliesin West, the winter home he later built in Scottsdale.

In 1929, Wright completed his final built work of the decade: the textile-block-and-glass home of his cousin, Richard Lloyd Jones, in Tulsa, Oklahoma.

Writings
In 1926, with his practice virtually stagnant, Wright began writing his autobiography, which he completed in 1932. He was also commissioned for a series of articles for the *Architectural Record* under the title "In the Cause of Architecture," published in 1927 and 1928. In them, he responded to the industrial world of the machine as it related to imagination and explored the aesthetic nature of materials.

In September of 1928, Wright wrote a review of Le Corbusier's *Toward an Architecture*, also known as *Towards a New Architecture*, in which he criticized the Swiss architect's buildings as severe and lacking depth. Although Wright's work helped establish what was later known as the International Style, an architectural movement that rejected ornament and emphasized industrialized mass production, he was also one of its harshest critics, describing modernist buildings of this style as "cardboard" structures seemingly "glued" together to look like lifeless machines. To Wright, architecture was about texture, material weight, depth, and a connection with the natural setting.

Impact
Frank Lloyd Wright's marriage of structure and material, combined with a deep emphasis on the relationship of architecture with nature, secured his status as an influential American architect. Though he critiqued the International Style for relying solely on the machine, he did not abandon modern architecture altogether, instead seeing the machine as useful only in the hands of an artist. It was this theory

that later impelled him to create his most famous works, among them Fallingwater and the Johnson Wax Building.

Leslie D. S. Book

Further Reading

Gill, Brendan. *Many Masks: A Life of Frank Lloyd Wright.* New York: Da Capo Press, 1998. Detailed bibliographic account of Frank Lloyd Wright's life and architecture.

McCarter, Robert. *Frank Lloyd Wright.* London: Reaktion Books, 2006. Concise bibliographic account of Frank Lloyd Wright's life and works, organized by decade.

Smith, Kathryn, and Alan Weintraub. *Frank Lloyd Wright: American Master.* New York: Rizzoli, 2009. Photographic collection of Wright's works, with a chronological discussion of his theories and architecture.

Storrer, William Allin. *The Architecture of Frank Lloyd Wright: A Complete Catalog.* 3d ed. Chicago: University of Chicago Press, 2002. Chronological catalog of Wright's architectural works, including photos and short descriptions.

Tafel, Edgar. *Apprentice to Genius: Years with Frank Lloyd Wright.* New York: McGraw-Hill, 1979. An apprentice's personal account of working under Wright that gives insight into his design process.

See also: Architecture

■ Wylie, Elinor

Identification: American poet and novelist
Born: September 7, 1885, Somerville, New Jersey
Died: December 16, 1928, New York, New York

Elinor Wylie was a poet and novelist who rose to prominence at the start of the 1920s and published numerous books of poetry or prose during the decade, several appearing posthumously. A traditionalist poet in a decade typically known as one of experimentation and modernism, she favored sonnets and other short forms and was known for her concise but evocative language.

Elinor Wylie anonymously published her first book of poetry in 1912 and began her public career as a poet in 1920, publishing several poems in the magazine *Poetry.* One such poem, "Velvet Shoes," garnered a great deal of praise among contemporaries, establishing Wylie as a significant talent of the era. The poem, which describes a walk in the snow, showcases Wylie's skill with language as she establishes a subtle rhythm that evokes both the tactile feel and the visual appeal of the snow. The first collection of poems to bear her name, *Nets to Catch the Wind*, was published the following year and included "Velvet Shoes." She followed this book with the poetry collection *Black Armor* and the novel *Jennifer Lorn,* both published in 1923.

A prolific writer, Wylie published another two novels, *The Venetian Glass Nephew* (1925) and *The Orphan Angel* (1926), before releasing another collection of poetry, *Trivial Breath*, in 1928. The novel *Mr. Hodge and Mr. Hazard* was published the same year. In addition to writing, Wylie worked as an editor for several publications during the 1920s, including *Vanity Fair* and the *New Republic.*

Impact

Several works by Elinor Wylie were published following her death in 1928, including the poetry collections *Angels and Earthly Creatures* (1929), based on an earlier, privately published work. Edited collections of her poetry and prose were released in the following decade. Although Wylie established a reputation as a talented writer during the 1920s, garnering praise from contemporaries such as Carl Van Vechten and Edna St. Vincent Millay, her traditionalism fell out of favor with critics influenced by the modernist ethos of T. S. Eliot and Ezra Pound. However, Wylie's work experienced a resurgence in popularity in later decades, inspiring a variety of biographies and works of critical analysis, particularly from a feminist perspective.

Carl Rollyson

Further Reading

Hively, Evelyn. *Private Madness: The Genius of Elinor Wylie.* Kent, Ohio: Kent State University Press, 2003.

Olson, Stanley. *Elinor Wylie: A Biography.* New York: Dial Press, 1979.

Showalter, Elaine. *A Jury of Her Peers: American Women Writers from Anne Bradstreet to Annie Proulx.* New York: Knopf, 2009.

See also: Lowell, Amy; Millay, Edna St. Vincent; Poetry; Teasdale, Sara

Y

■ Yo-yos

The yo-yo existed in ancient Greece and China, was a common diversion in France during the eighteenth century, and is thought to have been used as a Filipino hunting weapon for several hundred years before it was popularized in the United States as a children's toy in the late 1920s. Yo-yo manufacturers' successful marketing schemes quickly made it one of the more enduring fads of the era.

Although an earlier version was patented in 1866, the modern yo-yo was first introduced to American popular culture in the late 1920s by Filipino immigrant Pedro Flores. In 1923, Flores began hand carving the wooden toys, which were common in his homeland, and selling them locally. Originally, the yo-yo was carved out of a single piece of wood with the string affixed directly to the axle, which allowed the yo-yo to go up and down only. Flores reworked the toy so the string looped around the axle, allowing the yo-yo to spin, or "sleep," among other advanced yo-yo tricks.

In 1928, Flores established the Flores Yo-Yo Company in Santa Barbara, California, to mass-produce the toy, which swiftly gained popularity. Contests were held to promote sales of the yo-yo and became

The yo-yo was popularized as a children's toy in the late 1920s, becoming one of the more enduring fads of the era. (Gamma-Keystone via Getty Images)

so popular that they inspired a widespread yo-yo fad lasting several decades.

In 1930, Flores trademarked the name "yo-yo," preventing potential competitors from using the same term for their products. An entrepreneur and inventor, Donald F. Duncan, discovered the toy in southern California and bought the company and product name from Flores that summer for an estimated $250,000, a remarkable sum during the Great Depression.

To advertise his new product, Duncan and newspaper magnate William Randolph Hearst successfully collaborated to create joint advertising campaigns in which prospective yo-yo contestants sold newspaper subscriptions. Duncan also hired Flores and other demonstrators to travel across North and South America and western Europe teaching and demonstrating yo-yo tricks.

Impact

As a result of trademark disputes, Duncan's business went bankrupt and was bought out in the late 1960s by Flambeau Products Corporation, a contractor that had previously made plastic versions of the Duncan yo-yo. The trademark on the term "yo-yo" expired in the 1960s, and since then other companies have been able to use it. Though the toy's popularity has waned, Flambeau still produces Duncan brand yo-yos, and several competing brands are available as well.

Macey M. Freudensprung

Further Reading

Hirahara, Naomi. *Distinguished Asian American Business Leaders*. Westport, Conn.: Greenwood Press, 2003.

Long, Mark A. *Bad Fads*. Toronto: ECW Press, 2002.

Sobey, Ed, and Woody Sobey. *The Way Toys Work: The Science Behind the Magic Eight Ball, Etch a Sketch, Boomerang, and More*. Chicago: Chicago Review Press, 2008.

See also: Advertising in the United States; Fads; Hobbies and recreation

Z

Ziegfeld, Florenz

Identification: American theatrical manager and producer
Born: March 15, 1867, Chicago, Illinois
Died: July 22, 1932, New York, New York

Florenz Ziegfeld was a theater impresario best known for his series of theatrical revues, the Ziegfeld Follies. Quickly becoming a model for other revues, Ziegfeld's shows reached their peak of opulence and popularity during the 1920s. Ziegfeld is also credited with launching the careers of such performers as Fanny Brice, Bert Williams, and Mary Eaton.

Florenz Ziegfeld Jr. was born into a show business family. His father operated the Trocadero Club in Chicago and sent him to Europe to secure entertainment acts to support the venue. While abroad, he absorbed aspects of European arts and culture and was especially impressed with the Parisian music hall Folies Bergère.

Ziegfeld married stage performer Anna Held in 1897 and began managing theatrical productions. Some of his early shows included *Papa's Wife* (1899), *The Red Feather* (1903), and the revue *Higgledy-Piggledy* (1904). Coinciding with the slow development of the musical revue, a genre that began making inroads in the mid-1890s, Ziegfeld decided to develop a theatrical vehicle for his wife's acting, and so he created the Follies. The revue series began in 1907 and went annually until 1925, with less regular productions appearing until 1957.

When the 1920s began, the Follies were already considered a New York institution. Ziegfeld's lavish sets, high-fashion costuming, and large musical numbers surpassed those of his competitors in the theatrical revue industry. The Follies became the primary trendsetter for large-scale Broadway revues. One of Ziegfeld's skills as a producer was his ability to choose talented entertainers such as W. C. Fields, Eddie Cantor, and Marilyn Miller to perform in his shows. He also engaged the services of architect and theatrical designer Joseph Urban, who designed the sets for Follies productions, beginning in 1915. Urban was also responsible for designing the Ziegfeld Theatre, built in 1927.

Ziegfeld produced several successful plot-driven shows during the 1920s. Perhaps the most significant of these was *Show Boat* (1927), which was written by lyricist Oscar Hammerstein II and composer Jerome Kern based on the eponymous novel by Edna Ferber. Ziegfeld's productions *Sally* (1920) and *Sunny* (1925) were vehicles for Miller, along with the operetta *Rosalie* (1928). Toward the late 1920s, Ziegfeld developed an interest in sound films. His first motion picture, *Glorifying the American Girl*, starred Mary Eaton, one of his former chorus girls. Filmed versions of several Follies shows came out around the end of the 1920s and into the 1930s.

Impact

Ziegfeld's Follies and other productions were some of the most popular and influential shows of the 1920s. Although Ziegfeld's legacy continued well into the 1950s, his shows in the 1920s particularly exhibited the opulence and exuberance that characterized the Roaring Twenties.

Jonas Westover

Further Reading

Cantor, Eddie, and David Freedman: *Ziegfeld: The Great Glorifier*. New York: A. H. King, 1934.

Van der Merwe, Ann Ommen. *The Ziegfeld Follies: A History in Song*. Lanham, Md.: Scarecrow Press, 2009.

Ziegfeld, Richard, and Paulette Ziegfeld. *The Ziegfeld Touch: The Life and Times of Florenz Ziegfeld Jr.* New York: H. N. Abrams, 1993.

See also: Broadway musicals; Fields, W. C.; Hammerstein, Oscar, II; Kern, Jerome; Theater in the United States; Ziegfeld Follies

Ziegfeld Follies

The theatrical productions known as the Ziegfeld Follies were first seen at the Jardin de Paris theater in New York City in 1907 and flourished there until 1931. The Ziegfeld Follies became the model for large-scale musical revues from the first show until the mid-1950s, when televised revues became more popular than stage revues.

American theater manager Florenz Ziegfeld Jr. took command of the theatrical revue form with his annual Follies productions. These shows combined comedic scenes, chorus and solo songs, and dancing, performed by a wide array of star entertainers. In their early years, the Follies productions were arranged around a script, but most critics agreed that the plot was the least important part of the show. One of the most important elements of Follies productions was the large number of chorus girls featured in the show; these "Ziegfeld Girls" were expected to dance, sing, and look beautiful for audiences. Their costumes became increasingly revealing as the revues continued into the 1920s. The Ziegfeld Follies were at their height during that decade, costing thousands of dollars to produce and epitomizing the extravagant and exuberant quality of life in 1920s America.

By the 1920s, the Ziegfeld Follies were being held every year at the New Amsterdam Theater in New York City. Although the Follies did not immediately experience major competition, similar revues began to emerge in the 1910s and 1920s. The theatrical producers known as the Shubert Brothers owned a significant portion of the American theater industry, and in the early 1920s, a slew of revue series appeared—including the Greenwich Village Follies, Earl Carroll's Vanities, Music Box Revues, and George White's Scandals—all vying for space on the Broadway stage.

Notable Cast and Crew

Ziegfeld's lavish shows rose above the rest of the competition. His broad spectrum of performers often included stars that not every producer would feature. One of these was Fanny Brice, a Jewish comedian who made her Follies debut the same year as African American comedian Bert Williams. The two were highly successful in the format that the Follies offered, allowing them the possibility of working with large groups or in solo numbers, both of which were acceptable revue performance types. Brice continued

Ziegfeld Follies performer in costume. (Getty Images)

appearing in the Ziegfeld Follies into the early 1920s, as did some others from the 1910s Follies productions. For example, comedian W. C. Fields was first a part of the show in 1915 but continued to appear on the Ziegfeld Follies stage intermittently until 1925. Another important star was Will Rogers, who performed songs, demonstrated rope tricks, and told jokes in the Ziegfeld Follies well into the middle of the decade. A major draw for much of the 1920s was performer Eddie Cantor, who was famous for his interpretations of songs such as "If You Knew Susie Like I Know Susie" (1925), as well as his comedic skills in entertaining skits. Other regulars included the duo Van and Schenck, known for their comedic songs, and singers Vivienne Segal, Ann Pennington, and Billie Burke, who became Ziegfeld's wife in 1914 after his divorce from stage performer Anna Held. Some of the other Follies stars, including the Eaton sisters (Mary, Pearl, and Doris), rose from the ranks of chorus girls to become major celebrities.

Lyricist Gene Buck and composer Dave Stamper wrote much of the material for the Ziegfeld Follies.

Additional composers included Victor Herbert, Irving Berlin, Rudolf Friml, Louis Hirsch, and Raymond Hubbell. Some of the songs to emerge from these shows include "Second Hand Rose," "My Man," and "Weaving (My Dreams)." The large orchestra played music for tableaux vivants and huge chorus and dance numbers.

The visual elements of the revues were also important; the sumptuous scenery and players' costumes, created by top New York designers, became legendary. Women were draped in costumes that mimicked dollar bills, animals, and even the city skylines. Elaborate choreography gave performances another layer of visual splendor.

The secondary title for the show eventually became *Glorifying the American Girl*, and Ziegfeld made this the name of his motion picture revue, released in 1929. This film presents a huge theatrical number at the end, featuring entertainers Helen Morgan, Rudy Vallée, Mary Eaton, and Eddie Cantor.

Impact

Ziegfeld died in 1932, but his Follies productions continued to appear on stage, on the ice, and in motion pictures. Films relating to Ziegfeld's life and the history of the Ziegfeld Follies continued to be made in subsequent decades, including *The Great Ziegfeld* (1936), *Ziegfeld Follies* (1945), and *Funny Girl* (1968).

Jonas Westover

Further Reading

Cohen-Stratyner, Barbara Naomi. *Ned Wayburn and the Dance Routine: From Vaudeville to the Ziegfeld Follies*. Madison: University of Wisconsin Press, 1996. Focuses on the career of choreographer Ned Wayburn, noting his invention of a walking style that displayed the costumes of Ziegfeld Follies performers.

Davis, Lee. *Scandals and Follies: The Rise and Fall of the Great Broadway Revue*. New York: Limelight Editions, 2000. Provides a history of the musical revue form on American stages, including the development of the Ziegfeld Follies.

Rogers, Will, and Arthur Frank Wertheim. *Will Rogers at the Ziegfeld Follies*. Norman: University of Oklahoma Press, 1992. Features the entertainer's reflections on American politics and society during the 1920s and his experiences performing in the Ziegfeld Follies.

Van der Merwe, Ann Ommen. *The Ziegfeld Follies: A History in Song*. Lanham, Md.: Scarecrow Press, 2009. Offers an overview of the musical numbers performed throughout the history of the Ziegfeld Follies.

Ziegfeld, Richard E., and Paulette Ziegfeld. *The Ziegfeld Touch: The Life and Times of Florenz Ziegfeld Jr*. New York: H. N. Abrams, 1993. A biography written by Ziegfeld's relatives, presenting information on his personal life, career as a theatrical manager, and impact on the history of American theater.

See also: Berlin, Irving; Broadway musicals; Rogers, Will; Theater in the United States; Ziegfeld, Florenz

■ Zworykin, Vladimir

Identification: Russian American physicist and engineer
Born: July 30, 1889, Murom, Russia
Died: July 29, 1982, Princeton, New Jersey

Considered by many to be the father of television technology, Vladimir Zworykin's pioneering ideas during the 1920s made significant contributions to the advancement and development of television.

By the time he was nine years old, Vladimir Kozmich Zworykin was repairing electrical equipment on boats in his father's boatyard. While attending the St. Petersburg Institute of Technology in 1910, Zworykin studied electrical engineering with professor and television researcher Boris Rosing and experimented with transmitting pictures using cathode ray tubes and a mechanical transmitter.

In 1919, Zworykin immigrated to the United States and joined Westinghouse Electric in Pittsburgh, Pennsylvania, to work on the development of radio tubes. The development of electronic television remained his passion, however, and in 1923, he applied for a patent for the first all-electronic camera tube, later known as the iconoscope, which produced pictures by scanning images. The next year, Zworykin applied for a patent for a sophisticated cathode-ray picture tube known as the kinescope, which reproduced the iconoscope's scanned images onto a picture tube. After showing his designs to Westinghouse executives, however, he was told to spend his time on more practical pursuits than television.

Zworykin continued working on television technology on his own time, and in November of 1929, he demonstrated the iconoscope and a television receiver that contained his kinescope to a convention of radio engineers. When an executive from the Radio Corporation of America (RCA) learned that Zworykin needed $100,000 in funding and eighteen months to produce a marketable television, Zworykin was hired as director of RCA's Electronic Research Laboratory in Camden, New Jersey, where he concentrated on refining his inventions. Zworykin's work would eventually evolve into the tubes used in RCA's first commercial television, which was unveiled at the 1939 World's Fair in New York City.

Impact

Zworykin's inventions of the iconoscope, the kinescope, and his use of the charge storage principle were important developments in early television technology. In the 1930s, Zworykin developed infrared ray technology, which led to the development of night-vision devices, and his work in television technology led to the development in RCA's electron microscope. Zworykin's work also led to the development of garage door openers and electronically controlled missiles. Among his many honors, Zworykin was awarded the Institute of Radio Engineers' Morris Liebmann Memorial Prize in 1934, the Edison Medal in 1952, and the National Medal of Science in 1967. Zworykin was inducted into the United States National Inventors Hall of Fame in 1977.

Alvin K. Benson

Further Reading

Abramson, Albert. *Zworykin, Pioneer of Television.* Urbana: University of Illinois Press, 1995.

Webb, Richard C. *Tele-visionaries: The People Behind the Invention of Television.* Hoboken, N.J.: Wiley-Interscience, 2005.

See also: Inventions; National Broadcasting Company (NBC); Physics; Radio Corporation of America (RCA); Science and technology; Television technology

Appendixes

Entertainment: Major Broadway Plays and Awards

This list includes all Broadway plays that ran for at least one full month between January 1, 1920, and December 31, 1929, and had total runs of at least 220 performances. The list includes plays that opened before 1920 and ran for at least one month into the 1920s. It also includes plays with shorter runs that received major awards. Plays are listed in order of their opening dates, which are given within parentheses after the titles.

Shows Opening Before 1920

John Ferguson (May 13, 1919), 354 performances
The Greenwich Village Follies [1919] (July 15, 1919), 232 performances
Happy Days (August 23, 1919), 452 performances
Scandal (September 12, 1919), 318 performances
Adam and Eva (September 13, 1919), 312 performances
Clarence (September 20, 1919), 300 performances
The Gold Diggers (September 30, 1919), 282 performances
Declassee (October 6, 1919), 257 performances
Apple Blossoms (October 7, 1919), 256 performances
The Storm (October 2, 1919), 282 performances
The Passing Show of 1919 (October 23, 1919), 280 performances
Buddies (October 27, 1919), 259 performances
Irene (November 18, 1919), 675 performances
The Son-Daughter (November 19, 1919), 223 performances

Shows Opening in 1920

Beyond the Horizon (February 2, 1920), 190 performances
 —1920 Pulitzer Prize for Drama: Eugene O'Neill
The Night Boat (February 2, 1920), 313 performances
Good Times (August 9, 1920), 456 performances
Ladies' Night (August 9, 1920), 360 performances
Enter Madame (August 16, 1920), 350 performances
Spanish Love (August 17, 1920), 308 performances
The Bat (August 23, 1920), 867 performances
The Bad Man (August 30, 1920), 342 performances
Honeydew (September 6, 1920), 249 performances
The Woman of Bronze (September 7, 1920), 252 performances
Little Old New York (September 8, 1920), 308 performances
Welcome Stranger (September 13, 1920), 309 performances
The Tavern (September 27, 1920), 252 performances
Three Live Ghosts (September 29, 1920), 250 performances
Tip Top (October 5, 1920), 246 performances
Mary (October 18, 1920), 220 performances
The First Year (October 20, 1920), 760 performances
Rollo's Wild Oat (November 23, 1920), 228 performances
Sally (December 21, 1920), 561 performances
Miss Lulu Bett (December 27, 1920), 198 performances
 —1921 Pulitzer Prize for Drama: Zona Gale

Shows Opening in 1921

Peg o' My Heart (February 14, 1921), 692 performances
Shuffle Along (May 23, 1921), 484 performances
Tangerine (August 9, 1921), 361 performances
Dulcy (August 13, 1921), 241 performances
Six-Cylinder Love (August 25, 1921), 344 performances
Get Together (September 3, 1921), 397 performances
Music Box Revue (September 22, 1921), 440 performances
Blossom Time (September 29, 1921), 516 performances
Thank You (October 3, 1921), 257 performances
The Demi-Virgin (October 18, 1921), 268 performances
Good Morning Dearie (November 1, 1921), 347 performances
Anna Christie (November 2, 1921), 177 performances
 —1922 Pulitzer Prize for Drama: Eugene O'Neill
The Perfect Fool (November 7, 1921), 275 performances
Kiki (November 29, 1921), 233 performances

Shows Opening in 1922

Abie's Irish Rose (May 23, 1922), 2327 performances
Ziegfeld Follies of 1922 (June 5, 1922), 424 performances
Whispering Wires (August 7, 1922), 352 performances

The Old Soak (August 22, 1922), 423 performances
The Gingham Girl (August 28, 1922), 322 performances
So This Is London (August 30, 1922), 343 performances
Better Times (September 2, 1922), 405 performances
Sally, Irene, and Mary (September 4, 1922), 313 performances
Loyalties (September 27, 1922), 220 performances
The Lady in Ermine (October 2, 1922), 238 performances
The Fool (October 23, 1922), 272 performances
Music Box Review [1922–23] (October 23, 1922), 330 performances
The Last Warning (October 24, 1922), 238 performances
Seventh Heaven (October 30, 1922), 704 performances
Up She Goes (November 6, 1922), 256 performances
Rain (November 7, 1922), 256 performances
Little Nellie Kelly (November 13, 1922), 276 performances
Merton of the Movies (November 13, 1922), 392 performances

Shows Opening in 1923

Wildflower (February 7, 1923), 477 performances
Icebound (February 10, 1923), 145 performances
 –1923 Pulitzer Prize for Drama: Owen Davis
Adrienne (May 28, 1923), 235 performances
Little Jessie James (August 15, 1923), 385 performances
Artists and Models [1923] (August 20, 1923), 312 performances
Poppy (September 3, 1923), 346 performances
Music Box Revue [1923] (September 22, 1923), 273 performances
Tarnish (October 1, 1923), 248 performances
Battling Buttler (October 8, 1923), 313 performances
The Nervous Wreck (October 9, 1923), 279 performances
The Shame Woman (October 16, 1923), 278 performances
Ziegfeld Follies of 1923 (October 20, 1923), 233 performances
The Swan (October 23, 1923), 255 performances
Runnin' Wild (October 29, 1923), 228 performances
Cyrano de Bergerac (November 1, 1923), 232 performances
White Cargo (November 5, 1923), 257 performances
Stepping Stones (November 6, 1923), 281 performances
Spring Cleaning (November 9, 1923), 251 performances
Meet the Wife (November 26, 1923), 232 performances
Kid Boots (December 31, 1923), 489 performances

Shows Opening in 1924

Hell-Bent fer Heaven (January 4, 1924), 122 performances
 –1924 Pulitzer Prize for Drama: Hatcher Hughes
André Charlot's Revue of 1924 (January 9, 1924), 298 performances
The Show Off (February 5, 1924), 571 performances
Beggar on Horseback (February 12, 1924), 223 performances
I'll Say She Is (May 19, 1924), 313 performances
Ziegfeld Follies of 1924 (June 24, 1924), 295 performances
Dancing Mothers (August 11, 1924), 312 performances
Pigs (September 1, 1924), 312 performances
Rose-Marie (September 2, 1924), 557 performances
What Price Glory (September 5, 1924), 435 performances
My Son (September 17, 1924), 278 performances
The Guardsman (October 13, 1924), 248 performances
Artists and Models [1924] (October 15, 1924), 519 performances
The Firebrand (October 15, 1924), 261 performances
Desire Under the Elms (November 11, 1924), 420 performances
My Girl (November 24, 1924), 291 performances
They Knew What They Wanted (November 24, 1924), 192 performances
 –1925 Pulitzer Prize for Drama: Sidney Howard
Lady, Be Good (December 1, 1924), 330 performances
The Student Prince (December 2, 1924), 608 performances

Shows Opening in 1925

Is Zat So? (January 5, 1925), 618 performances
Louie the 14th (March 3, 1925), 319 performances
Artists and Models [1925] (June 24, 1925), 416 performances
Cradle Snatchers (September 7, 1925), 332 performances

The Jazz Singer (September 14, 1925), 303 performances
The Green Hat (September 15, 1925), 231 performances
No, No, Nanette (September 16, 1925), 321 performances
Dearest Enemy (September 18, 1925), 286 performances
The Vagabond King (September 21, 1925), 511 performances
Sunny (September 22, 1925), 517 performances
The Butter and Egg Man (September 23, 1925), 243 performances
Craig's Wife (October 12, 1925), 360 performances
— 1926 Pulitzer Prize for Drama: George Kelly
Laff That Off (November 2, 1925), 263 performances
Young Woodley (November 2, 1925), 260 performances
The Last of Mrs. Cheyney (November 9, 1925), 385 performances
Alias the Deacon (November 24, 1925), 277 performances
The Cocoanuts (December 8, 1925), 276 performances
One of the Family (December 21, 1925), 238 performances
The Patsy (December 22, 1925), 245 performances

Shows Opening in 1926

The Great God Brown (January 23, 1926), 271 performances
Lulu Belle (February 9, 1926), 461 performances
The Girl Friend (March 17, 1926), 301 performances
What Every Woman Knows (April 13, 1926), 268 performances
Iolanthe (April 19, 1926), 255 performances
At Mrs. Beam's (April 26, 1926), 222 performances
Sex (April 26, 1926), 375 performances
The Great Temptations (May 18, 1926), 223 performances
George White's Scandals (June 14, 1926), 432 performances
Americana (July 26, 1926), 224 performances
Earl Carroll's Vanities [1926] (August 24, 1926), 303 performances
Queen High (September 8, 1926), 367 performances
Two Girls Wanted (September 9, 1926), 324 performances
Broadway (September 16, 1926), 603 performances
Countess Maritza (September 18, 1926), 321 performances
Honeymoon Lane (September 20, 1926), 353 performances
The Ramblers (September 20, 1926), 289 performances
The Ladder (October 22, 1926), 640 performances
Caponsacchi (October 26, 1926), 269 performances
The Play's the Thing (November 3, 1926), 326 performances
Oh, Kay! (November 8, 1926), 256 performances
The Squall (November 11, 1926), 444 performances
Gertie (November 15, 1926), 248 performances
The Constant Wife (November 29, 1926), 296 performances
The Desert Song (November 30, 1926), 471 performances
Peggy-Ann (December 27, 1926), 333 performances
In Abraham's Bosom (December 30, 1926), 200 performances
— 1927 Pulitzer Prize for Drama: Paul Green

Shows Opening in 1927

Tommy (January 10, 1927), 232 performances
The Barker (January 18, 1927), 221 performances
Saturday's Children (January 26, 1927), 326 performances
The Road to Rome (January 31, 1927), 392 performances
Rio Rita (February 2, 1927), 494 performances
The Spider (March 22, 1927), 319 performances
Hit the Deck (April 25, 1927), 352 performances
Burlesque (September 1, 1927), 372 performances
Good News (September 6, 1927), 557 performances
My Maryland (September 12, 1927), 312 performances
The Trial of Mary Dugan (September 19, 1927), 437 performances
The Command to Love (September 20, 1927), 247 performances
Manhattan Mary (September 26, 1927), 264 performances
The Shannons of Broadway (September 26, 1927), 288 performances
Dracula (October 5, 1927), 261 performances
The Five O'Clock Girl (October 10, 1927), 280 performances
Porgy (October 10, 1927), 367 performances
Interference (October 18, 1927), 224 performances
The Ivory Door (October 18, 1927), 310 performances
A Connecticut Yankee (November 3, 1927), 421 performances

Coquette (November 8, 1927), 366 performances
Funny Face (November 22, 1927), 244 performances
Paris Bound (December 27, 1927), 234 performances
Show Boat (December 27, 1927), 572 performances
The Royal Family (December 28, 1927), 345 performances

Shows Opening in 1928
Rosalie (January 10, 1928), 335 performances
Strange Interlude (January 30, 1928), 426 performances
 −1928 Pulitzer Prize for Drama: Eugene O'Neill
The Silent House (February 7, 1928), 277 performances
Rain or Shine (February 9, 1928), 356 performances
The Bachelor Father (February 28, 1928), 263 performances
The Three Musketeers (March 13, 1928), 318 performances
Blackbirds of 1928 (May 9, 1928), 518 performances
Skidding (May 21, 1928), 472 performances
George White's Scandals [1928] (July 2, 1928), 240 performances
The Front Page (August 14, 1928), 276 performances
Good Boy (September 5, 1928), 253 performances
The New Moon (September 19, 1928), 509 performances
Courage (October 8, 1928), 280 performances
Little Accident (October 9, 1928), 303 performances
Hold Everything (October 10, 1928), 409 performances
Holiday (November 26, 1928), 229 performances
The Perfect Alibi (November 27, 1928), 255 performances
Whoopee! (December 4, 1928), 407 performances
Brothers (December 25, 1928), 255 performances

Shows Opening in 1929
Follow Thru (January 9, 1929), 401 performances
Street Scene (January 10, 1929), 601 performances
 −1929 Pulitzer Prize for Drama: Elmer Rice
My Girl Friday (February 12, 1929), 253 performances
Let Us Be Gay (February 19, 1929), 353 performances
Journey's End (March 22, 1929), 485 performances
Bird in Hand (April 4, 1929), 500 performances
The Little Show (April 30, 1929), 321 performances
Earl Carroll's Sketch Book [1929] (July 1, 1929), 392 performances
It's a Wise Child (August 6, 1929), 378 performances
Sweet Adeline (September 3, 1929), 234 performances
Strictly Dishonorable (September 18, 1929), 557 performances
Subway Express (September 24, 1929), 271 performances
June Moon (October 9, 1929), 273 performances
Berkeley Square (November 4, 1929), 229 performances
Sons o' Guns (November 26, 1929), 295 performances
Fifty Million Frenchmen (November 27, 1929), 254 performances
Young Sinners (November 28, 1929), 289 performances

Entertainment: Major Films

The seventy films from the 1920s listed here are a representative sampling of films regarded as significant because of their box-office success, their Academy Award honors, or their critical reputations. All references to best-acting and other awards refer to the Oscars awarded annually (beginning in 1928) by the Academy of Motion Picture Arts and Sciences. Titles followed by an asterisk (*) are films inducted (as of 2010) into the National Film Registry, which is the United States National Film Board's selection of films to be preserved in the Library of Congress.

1920

*The Last of the Mohicans** (Maurice Tourneur Productions; dir. Clarence Brown and Maurice Tourneur) Set during the French and Indian War, this adaptation of James Fenimore Cooper's popular 1826 novel follows the exploits of sisters Alice (Lillian Hall) and Cora (Barbara Bedford) as they search for their father. The last of his tribe, the brave Uncas (Alan Roscoe) joins with Caucasian ally Natty Bumppo/Hawkeye (Harry Lorraine) to liberate the sisters from the Huron tribe. A romance between Cora and Uncas is not to be; both die tragically.

The Mark of Zorro (Douglas Fairbanks Pictures; dir. Fred Niblo) Setting the tone for other adventure films, this story of a Spanish nobleman who defends Mexican peasants as the mysterious, masked Zorro is set during the Mexican War of Independence. The film is energized by Douglas Fairbanks's gymnastic feats, charming wit, and striking costumes.

Treasure Island (Maurice Tourneur Productions; dir. Maurice Tourneur) One of many versions of Robert Louis Stevenson's classic adventure story, this adaptation is notable for its casting of a nineteen-year-old actor (Shirley Mason) as young Jim Hawkins. The sumptuous production of the hunt for buried treasure features Charles Ogle as the flamboyant pirate Long John Silver and Lon Chaney as Blind Pew.

Way Down East (D. W. Griffith Productions; dir. D. W. Griffith) Based on a popular play, this was one of Griffith's most expensive films. Lillian Gish delivers a memorable performance in a sentimental story of innocence betrayed, contrasting country life with its decent values to the deceit and decadence of the city. Gish and costar Richard Barthelmess performed their own stunts in the climactic rescue sequence on the ice.

*Within Our Gates** (Micheaux Book & Film Company; dir. Oscar Micheaux) The first feature film produced by and for African Americans, this melodrama charts the difficulties of southern schoolteacher Sylvia Landry (Evelyn Preer), who goes North to raise funds for a school for needy youth. The complicated plot includes provocative topics such as racism and shocking events such as rape and lynching, but it ends happily with Sylvia coupled with a good man, Dr. V. Vivian (Charles D. Lucas).

1921

*The Four Horsemen of the Apocalypse** (Metro Pictures Corporation; dir. Rex Ingram) June Mathis wrote the sophisticated scenario and was also responsible for casting the then-unknown actor Rudolph Valentino in the tango-dancing role that made him an instant star. Argentinean sisters, one married to a German, the other to a Frenchman, move to Europe on the eve of World War I; their families are separated by the war's horrors. With cinematography by John F. Seitz, this antiwar epic was a tremendous hit.

The Kid (Charles Chaplin Productions; dir. Charlie Chaplin) In his first feature-length film, Chaplin develops the balance between comedy and drama that had been impossible to sustain in his quickly produced two-reelers. *The Kid* tenderly tracks the relationship between an abandoned child (Jackie Coogan) and the man (Chaplin) who fights to keep the boy out of the state orphanage and workhouse.

The Sheik (Paramount Pictures; dir. George Melford) Rudolph Valentino plays an Arab chieftain who, after kidnapping English socialite Lady Diane Mayo (Agnes Ayers), reveals himself to be a Western European aristocrat. Lady Diane Mayo is also involved in masquerade, posing as a Bedouin dancer when they first meet. The film made such an impact that the term "sheik" entered American slang as the male equivalent of "vamp."

The Three Musketeers (Douglas Fairbanks Pictures; dir. Fred Niblo) The dashing D'Artagnan (Douglas Fairbanks) joins celebrated royal swordsmen Athos (Léon Bary), Porthos (George Siegmann), and Aramis (Eugene Pallette) to fight for France and stymie the intrigues of evil Cardinal Richelieu (Nigel de Brulier). The musketeers pledge "all for one and one for all" in everything but D'Artagnan's romance with Constance (Marguerite De La Motte).

Tol'able David* (Inspiration Pictures; dir. Henry King) Filmed in rural Virginia and set at the turn of the century, this poignant melodrama is a coming-of-age story about David (Richard Barthelmess), a mild-tempered teenager who must become a man of action to revenge his sharecropper father's death. Gladys Hulette plays David's sweetheart Esther Hatburn, while Ernest Torrence plays the most violent of the three bad relatives who invade the Hatburn home and wreak havoc in the town.

1922

Blood and Sand (Paramount Pictures and Famous Players-Lasky Corporation; dir. Fred Niblo) Rudolph Valentino plays a poor Spanish boy who rises to fame as a matador but struggles with the competing demands of three women: his wife, a society vamp, and his devoted mother. The climactic bullfight in which Juan is gored is brilliantly edited by Dorothy Arzner, who intercut close-ups of Valentino with stock footage of actual bullfights.

Dr. Jack (Hal Roach Studios; dir. Fred C. Newmeyer) Energetic and well-meaning, Dr. Jack (Harold Lloyd) is good to children, the elderly, and puppies. In contrast to the isolation and drugs prescribed to the Sick-Little-Well-Girl (Mildred Davis) by Dr. Ludwig von Saulsbourg (Eric Mayne), Dr. Jack's positive thinking and kindly treatment work wonders. A chase activated by an escaped mental patient provides a manic finale to the comedy.

Foolish Wives* (Universal Pictures; dir. Erich von Stroheim) Written and directed by and starring Eric von Stroheim, the film was billed by Universal as the first million-dollar movie. Amidst the decadence of Monte Carlo high society, Count Karanzim (von Stroheim) lives off rich women; the plot turns on his attempts to seduce the naïve wife (Miss DuPont) of the new U.S. Special Envoy to Monaco (Rudolph Christians).

Nanook of the North* (Les Frères Revillon and Pathé Exchange; dir. Robert J. Flaherty) Flaherty's remarkable photographic record of a year in the life of the intrepid Inuk Nanook fascinated audiences and, together with Flaherty's later film *Moana*, led cinematographer John Grierson to create a new term to describe this type of film: documentary. The struggles of Nanook and his family against a hostile environment provide realistic drama, along with some moments of comedy—for example, when Nanook confronts modern technology.

Oliver Twist (Jackie Coogan Productions; dir. Frank Lloyd) One of many adaptations of Charles Dickens's classic novel, this film showcases Jackie Coogan as the orphaned boy who escapes a workhouse, becomes apprenticed to an undertaker, and is embraced by a band of thieves. Lon Chaney plays a memorable Fagin, and Gladys Brockwell shines as Nancy. Stephen Goosson managed the film's art direction.

Orphans of the Storm (D. W. Griffith Productions; dir. D. W. Griffith) The last collaboration of the seminal director and his favorite leading lady, Lillian Gish, is set during the French Revolution and features an emotionally powerful sequence in which Gish hears the voice of her long-lost blind sister, played by her actual sister, Dorothy Gish.

Robin Hood (Douglas Fairbanks Pictures; dir. Allan Dwan) Financed by its handsome star, the lavish production topped the box office for the year. Fairbanks turns the familiar and much-loved tale of knights, bravery, and justice set in the Middle Ages into rousing entertainment as he displays his acrobatic skill and charm. The film also features Wallace Beery as King Richard I.

Tess of the Storm Country (Mary Pickford Company; dir. John S. Robertson) Mary Pickford plays Tess, the sweet but spunky daughter of a fisherman. Tess lives with other squatters on the bottom of the hill owned by wealthy, hypocritical Elias Graves (David Torrence); she cares for the illegitimate child of Elias's daughter (Gloria Hope) and secretly loves his son (Lloyd Hughes). A heart-wrenching, audience-pleasing melodrama, the film glorifies the goodness and resilience of the working poor.

1923

The Covered Wagon (Famous Players-Lasky Corporation and Paramount Pictures; dir. James Cruz) The first Western movie taken seriously by historians and hugely popular with audiences, *The Cov-*

ered Wagon revitalized interest in the genre. Mostly shot on location in the Snake River Valley, the film pits the gold-seekers against the settlers. Within this division, a romantic triangle emerges as the heroic settler (Jack Warren Kerrigan) competes with a prospector (Alan Hale) for the heart and hand of "the girl" (Lois Wilson).

The Gold Diggers (Warner Bros. Pictures; dir. Harry Beaumont) Adapted from a Broadway play and the stimulus for several sequels, this breezy comedy turns on the efforts of Stephen Lee (Wyndham Standing) to prevent the marriage of his nephew (John Harron) to chorus girl Violet Dayne (Anne Cornwall). Violet's friend Jerry (Hope Hampton) goes after Uncle Stephen to prove that Violet is not a gold digger, but she ends up falling for him.

The Hunchback of Notre Dame (Universal Pictures; dir. Wallace Worsley) Adapted from Victor Hugo's first novel, *Notre Dame de Paris* (1831), this expensive costume spectacle was a hit for Universal. Lon Chaney plays the deaf, half-blind bell ringer who courageously saves the dancer Esmeralda (Patsy Ruth Miller) from the gallows, only to be mortally wounded himself.

Safety Last* (Hal Roach Studios; dir. Fred C. Newmeyer and Sam Taylor) Lloyd spoofs the dedication to achievement that characterized the 1920s in this parody of American ambition. The still of Lloyd, the aspiring young businessman in his suit and straw hat, hanging on the minute hand of a gigantic outdoor clock high above a city street, is one of the most famous images in silent cinema.

The Ten Commandments (Paramount Pictures; dir. Cecil B. DeMille) This extravagant blockbuster tells two stories. A biblical prologue pits the cruel pharaoh Ramses (Charles de Rochefort) against Moses (Theodore Roberts) and ends with the successful exodus of the Israelites and Moses's reception of the Ten Commandments. The melodramatic modern version of the story contrasts two brothers: an honest carpenter (Richard Dix) who follows the Bible and a greedy architect (Rod La Rocque), both of whom love the same woman (Leatrice Joy).

The White Sister (Inspiration Pictures; dir. Henry King) Set in modern Italy and partially filmed in Italian locations, this expensively produced sentimental drama stars Lillian Gish and British actor Ronald Colman as Italian sweethearts. Captain Severini (Colman) is captured by Arabs while in Africa. Thinking him dead, Angela (Gish) becomes a nun. Severini's surprising return was filmed against the dramatic background of Mount Vesuvius erupting.

1924

Greed* (Metro-Goldwyn Pictures; dir. Erich von Stroheim) Famously slashed to one-quarter of its original length of nine hours, this adaptation of Frank Norris's novel *McTeague* (1899) is a story of degradation. Rich in detail and filled with complex characterizations, *Greed* charts the dissolution of the relationship between husband (Gibson Gowland) and wife (Zasu Pitts).

The Iron Horse (Fox Film Corporation; dir. John Ford) This epic Western established John Ford as a master of the genre and made actor George O'Brien a star. The plot turns on the building of the transcontinental railroad during the Civil War. Despite striking workers and Indian raids, the building continues to the film's climax: the intersection of the Union Pacific and Central Pacific railways in 1869, forming a transcontinental railroad.

Peter Pan* (Famous Players-Lasky Corporation; dir. Herbert Brenon) J. M. Barrie's 1904 play is beautifully shot by James Wong Howe in this first of many film versions. The boy who refused to grow up is played by eighteen-year-old Betty Bronson, with Ernest Torrence as Captain Hook. The tinted film features special effects, with a highlight being the portrayal of Tinkerbell's home.

The Sea Hawk (Frank Lloyd Productions; dir. Frank Lloyd) This popular, fast-paced adventure film stars Milton Sills as Oliver Tressilian, an English nobleman who is made a galley slave on a ship controlled by kidnapper Jasper Leigh (Wallace Berry). As "Sakr-el Bahr," Tressilian captains a Moorish fighting ship and finally regains his love, Lady Rosamund (Enid Bennett).

Sherlock, Jr.* (Buster Keaton Productions; dir. Buster Keaton) Keaton plays a projectionist who falls asleep and dreams himself into various movie narratives, transporting himself from shy suitor to dashing hero. Later considered a masterpiece, the film was not a great success when released.

The Thief of Bagdad* (Douglas Fairbanks Pictures; dir. Raoul Walsh) In elaborate sets designed by William Cameron Menzies, Fairbanks gracefully moves from one adventure to another. This lavish production, like Fairbanks's other films, was carefully researched and planned by its star and delivers the action, romance, and spectacle that thrilled audiences. Anna May Wong also stars.

1925

The Big Parade* (Metro-Goldwyn-Mayer (MGM); dir. King Vidor) John Gilbert became a star due to his poignant portrayal of a young World War I soldier in this sobering film. The horror of war is alleviated by light moments, such as Jim's introduction of chewing gum to his French girlfriend (Renée Adorée). *The Big Parade* was one of the year's most popular films.

Body and Soul (Micheaux Film; dir. Oscar Micheaux) Written and directed by African American producer Oscar Micheaux and filmed in the Bronx on a low budget, this melodrama introduced twenty-seven-year-old entertainer Paul Robeson to movie audiences. Robeson is electrifying in the dual roles of an escaped prisoner and his honest twin brother. Posing as a minister, the ex-con exploits his congregation and betrays his brother's sweetheart, Isabella (Julia Theresa Russell).

Don Q, Son of Zorro (Elton Corporation; dir. Donald Crisp) Douglas Fairbanks plays both father (Zorro) and son (Don Cesar) in this rousing sequel to *The Mark of Zorro* that finds Don Cesar studying in Spain. When the young Mexican is framed for murder, he turns into the whip-wielding outlaw Don Q. Director Donald Crisp portrays the evil Don Sebastian, Don Q's rival for the beautiful Dolores de Muro (Mary Astor).

The Freshman* (Harold Lloyd Corporation; dir. Fred C. Newmeyer and Sam Taylor) Lloyd uses his fresh face and eternally optimistic, energetic persona to spoof the importance of football in collegiate life in this box-office hit. Among the eager student's challenges are how to deal with a suit that is coming apart at a college dance.

The Gold Rush* (Charles Chaplin Productions; dir. Charlie Chaplin) Out of place in the Klondike region of Canada among huge, violent men, including Chaplin's frequent nemesis Mack Swain, the gallant little Tramp (Chaplin) nevertheless manages to win the dance-hall girl (Georgia Hale) and the gold. Scenes in which a starving Chaplin eats his shoelaces like spaghetti and makes his rolls dance on the dinner table are especially memorable.

The Lost World* (First National Pictures; dir. Harry O. Holt) A great success, this first film adaptation of Arthur Conan Doyle's 1912 adventure novel about a hidden world where dinosaurs rule features pioneering special effects designed by Willis H. O'Brien utilizing stop-motion animation. Wallace Beery plays the scientist Professor Challenger, Lloyd Hughes is the cowardly journalist, and Bessie Love portrays the lost explorer's daughter.

The Merry Widow (MGM; dir. Erich von Stroheim) Loosely based on the popular operetta by Franz Lehár, this film stars John Gilbert as Prince Danilo and Mae Murray as an American dancer who becomes "the merry widow" when her aged husband dies on their wedding night. The surface of the film glitters with romance, but von Stroheim's common theme of degradation is also apparent.

Phantom of the Opera* (Universal Pictures; dir. Rupert Julian) Lon Chaney plays a mysterious organist who resides beneath the opulent Paris Opera House. The moment when a young singer (Mary Philbin) removes the Phantom's mask to reveal a horrifying skeleton face (with makeup created and applied by the star) shocked and thrilled audiences. The film became the first in a long list of classic horror films made at Universal.

Stella Dallas (Samuel Goldwyn Company; dir. Henry King) Belle Bennett plays the lower-class mother Stella Dallas. Based on an emotional best seller, this popular tear-jerker features Lois Moran as Stella's daughter, Laurel. Douglas Fairbanks Jr. plays Laurel's sweetheart, and Ronald Coleman plays Laurel's father. The heart-wrenching ending places Stella in the rain, watching her daughter's wedding through a window.

1926

Beau Geste (Paramount Pictures; dir. Herbert Brenon) Ronald Colman is dashing as a valiant foreign legionnaire dealing with Arab attacks, prison floggings, and various crises. This adaptation of the Percival C. Wren novel was a tremendous hit with audiences; new versions of the courageous legionnaire's exploits were later produced in 1939 and 1966.

Ben-Hur: A Tale of the Christ* (MGM; dir. Fred Niblo) After a disastrous beginning in Italy, this remake moved to California to produce an extravagant recounting of the story of Jewish prince Ben-Hur (Ramon Navarro) and his childhood friend and adult rival, Messala (Francis X. Bushman). Photographed by forty-two cameras, the chariot race in the Roman Circus Maximus is one of the most thrilling action sequences in silent film.

The Black Pirate* (Douglas Fairbanks Pictures; dir. Albert Parker) Douglas Fairbanks is at his swashbuckling best in this fast-paced motion picture filmed in an early Technicolor process. Donald Crisp plays a good-hearted pirate, and Sam de Grasse is the villain from whom Fairbanks must protect the lovely damsel in distress (Billie Dove).

Don Juan (Warner Bros. Pictures; dir. Alan Crosland) Warner Bros. established its reputation as a pioneer in sound development when it released this adventure romance starring John Barrymore and Mary Astor with an all-synchronized soundtrack using the Vitaphone process. Popular with audiences, the film was not considered a "talkie," since there was no synchronized dialogue.

For Heaven's Sake (Harold Lloyd Corporation; dir. Sam Taylor) Millionaire playboy Lloyd finds himself the benefactor of a mission to the urban poor. Lloyd falls for the downtown girl (Jobyna Ralston) who helps her father (Paul Weigel) run the mission. Two remarkable chases energize this comic film: In one, Lloyd accumulates a motley crowd for the mission, and in another, he races to his own wedding.

The General* (Buster Keaton Productions and Joseph M. Schenck Productions; dir. Clyde Bruckman and Buster Keaton) A parody of the Civil War, this film is actor-director Keaton's most ambitious production. As in most of his films, Keaton performs his own stunts and plays a pragmatic, simple man who heroically struggles to achieve some order in a chaotic universe that seems governed by chance.

Son of the Sheik* (Feature Productions; dir. George Fitzmaurice) One of the first feature-length sequels, the picture stars Rudolph Valentino as Ahmed, the son of Diana and Sheik Ahmed Ben Hassan from *The Sheik* (1921). Once again, an exotic tale of forbidden love revolves around masquerade when Ahmed falls in love with a dancing girl (Vilma Bánky). Valentino unexpectedly died at age thirty-one shortly before the film was released.

What Price Glory? (Fox Film Corporation; dir. Raoul Walsh) Friends and romantic rivals, U.S. Marine sergeants Flagg (Victor McLaglen) and Quirt (Edmund Lowe) travel from peacetime China and the Philippines to war-torn France. Although there are two World War I battle sequences, most of the film is a light hearted, comedic romance in which the two Marines compete for the attentions of the beautiful Charmaine (Dolores del Rio), a French innkeeper's daughter.

1927

Flesh and the Devil* (MGM; dir. Clarence Brown) Greta Garbo's stardom was launched with her seductive performance in this melodrama in which the Swedish actor plays an independent, sexually liberated German woman, Felicitas. John Gilbert plays her lover who kills her husband in a duel. After several years in Africa, Leo returns to find Felicitas married to his best friend (Lars Hanson), creating another dramatic triangle.

The Gaucho (Elton Corporation; dir. F. Richard Jones) As the Gaucho, a charismatic leader of outlaws from the Argentine Andes, Douglas Fairbanks rescues a city terrorized by the ruthless Ruiz (Gustav von Seyffertitz) and romances a defiant mountain girl (Lupe Velez). Fairbanks's typical athleticism is on display, alongside a portrayal of religious mysticism. Two scenes of apparitions of the Virgin Mary (Mary Pickford) were shot in two-strip Technicolor.

The Jazz Singer* (Warner Bros. Pictures; dir. Alan Crosland) This is the sentimental story of Jakie Rabinowitz (Al Jolson), the son of an immigrant Jewish cantor. Jakie changes his name to Jack Robin, enters vaudeville, dons blackface makeup as a circuit performer, and becomes a Broadway success. Still employing title cards, the hybrid sound and silent film delighted audiences when they heard Jolson's voice delivering the signature line from his stage act: "You ain't heard nothin' yet."

The Kid Brother (Harold Lloyd Corporation; dir. Ted Wilde and J. A. Howe) Although his films usually involve urban settings, this motion picture is set on a ranch. Harold Lloyd plays the timid kid brother to two manly sons of the tough Sheriff Jim (Walter James). Lloyd is characteristically resourceful when he must fight a villain to win the respect of his father and the love of the beautiful Mary (Jobyna Ralston).

The King of Kings (DeMille Pictures; dir. Cecil B. DeMille) DeMille magnifies both righteousness and lewdness within a biblical setting with this motion picture based on the life of Jesus Christ. Beginning with the conversion of Mary Magdalene (Jacqueline Logan) and ending with a stunning

Resurrection of Christ (H. B. Warren) shot in two-color Technicolor, the film was a popular success.

Seventh Heaven* (Fox Film Corporation; dir. Frank Borzage) Janet Gaynor won the Best Actress in a Leading Role Oscar for her portrayal of a prostitute whose life is saved by a sewer worker (Charles Farrell) who must then pretend to be her husband to save them both from jail. Oscars also went to director Frank Borzage and to writer Benjamin Glazer for Best Adaptation. Gaynor and Farrell became a beloved screen couple and went on to make over ten more films together.

Sunrise: A Song of Two Humans* (Fox Film Corporation; dir. F. W. Murnau) Fox brought German director F. W. Murnau to Hollywood to direct the studio's first sound film. The result is a cautionary tale about a man (George O'Brien), his wife (Janet Gaynor), and a woman from the city (Margaret Livingston). This fable of sin and forgiveness won three of the newly introduced Academy Awards.

Uncle Tom's Cabin (Universal Pictures; dir. Harry A Pollard) James B. Lowe, portraying Uncle Tom, is the only African American actor in this story of an African American family torn apart by slavery in antebellum Kentucky; white actors Margarita Fischer and Mona Ray play Eliza and Topsy. The uplifting ending in which the slaves on Simon Legree's (George Siegmann) plantation are freed by the Union army is a striking departure from Harriet Beecher Stowe's influential novel. Expensively produced, the film lost money for Universal.

Wings (Paramount Famous Lasky Corporation; dir. William A. Wellman) One of the most popular pictures of the year and winner of the first Oscar for Best Production, *Wings* is a crowd-pleasing war epic and romantic comedy. Filled with remarkable cinematography and stunning special effects, the combat sequences celebrate the skill and bravery of American airmen (and cinematographers). Charles "Buddy" Rogers and Clara Bow shine as sweethearts.

1928

The Circus (Charles Chaplin Productions; dir. Charlie Chaplin) Chaplin's Tramp finds himself inadvertently becoming a circus act sensation as he enters the circus tent while running from the police. He stays at the circus as a janitor and falls for the owner's beautiful acrobatic stepdaughter (Merna Kennedy). Chaplin was determined that the Tramp should not speak, which confined the memorable figure to silent cinema.

The Crowd* (MGM; dir. King Vidor) Director King Vidor chose two unknown actors to star in this critique of the American dream of financial success. As John and Mary, James Murray and Eleanor Boardman bring a tender freshness to their roles, enacting happy moments of early courtship through married difficulties. Largely filmed on location in New York City, sometimes with hidden cameras, *The Crowd* dramatizes the disappointments and anonymity of ordinary life.

The Docks of New York* (Paramount Pictures; dir. Josef von Sternberg) Beautifully photographed by Harold Rosson and featuring the intense atmosphere that would make von Sternberg famous, this drama won Oscar nominations for the riveting performances of George Bancroft and Betty Compson. Bill (Bancroft), a stoker on a waterfront ship, rescues the prostitute Mae (Compson) from suicide. They spend the night together in a local tavern during Bill's last hours of leave.

The Last Command* (Paramount Pictures; dir. Josef von Sternberg) This drama finds an aristocratic former Imperial Russian general (Emil Jannings) reenacting the Russian Revolution in a Hollywood movie directed by a former political adversary (William Powell). Swiss-born Jannings won a Best Actor in a Leading Role Oscar for his performance in this film.

The Singing Fool (Warner Bros. Pictures; dir. Lloyd Bacon) A successor to *The Jazz Singer* and even more financially successful, this part-talkie film also starred Al Jolson. Playing nightclub performer Al Stone, Jolson delivers a series of songs such as "Sonny Boy," which he sings to his character's son (Davey Lee). The Jolson songs and the film's resulting popularity helped move Warner Bros. from a weak position to the front ranks of the film industry.

Steamboat Bill, Jr. (Buster Keaton Productions and Joseph M. Schenck Productions; dir. Charles Reisner) As the small, meek "junior" to his burly steamboat captain father (Ernest Torrence), Keaton moves adroitly from one misadventure to another. In a memorable sequence, Keaton tries on a series of hats, adapting his personality to match each hat.

The Wedding March* (Paramount Famous Lasky Corporation; dir. Erich von Stroheim) Impoverished aristocrat Prince Nikki (von Stroheim) falls in love with innkeeper's daughter Mitzi (Fay Wray), but they are pressured by their families to marry others. Mitzi is forced to help with preparations for Nikki's wedding to a wealthy industrialist's daughter (Zasu Pitts). Set in 1914 Vienna, this beautifully filmed drama about class rigidity was edited by the studio, creating its sequel, *The Honeymoon*.

The Wind* (MGM; dir. Victor Sjöström) In her last major role, Lillian Gish plays a desperate prairie woman driven to murder. Mostly shot on location in the Mojave Desert, this silent film is an extraordinary contribution to cinematic naturalism. However, it was not a box-office success, probably due to the diminishing popularity of silent films and Gish's acting.

1929

Applause* (Paramount Pictures; dir. Rouben Mamoulian) Although only twenty-seven, Helen Morgan gives a moving performance as Kitty Darling, a burlesque dancer nearing the end of her career. Kitty's convent-educated daughter April (Joan Peers) returns at seventeen to the grim reality of life on the burlesque stage. Filmed in Paramount's Astoria Studios, with much shooting at additional locations, this melodrama presents a story of private and professional humiliation.

Broadway Melody (MGM; dir. Harry Beaumont) A crowd-pleasing musical that won the Oscar for Best Picture, *Broadway Melody* tells the story of two sisters (Anita Page and Bessie Love) from small-town vaudeville who go to the big city, where their hearts are broken. "You Were Meant for Me" is one of the many featured songs that became hits. Several parts of the film were shot in early Technicolor.

The Cocoanuts (Paramount Pictures; dir. Robert Florey and Joseph Santley) Filmed at Paramount's Astoria Studios on Long Island and based on the Marx Brothers' Broadway hit (written by George S. Kaufman and Morrie Rysking, with music and lyrics by Irving Berlin), this film adaptation about the Florida land boom is set in a hotel. The film is energized by the Marx Brothers' wit and reworked music from the opera *Carmen*.

Coquette (Pickford Corporation; dir. Sam Taylor) At thirty-seven, Mary Pickford won the Best Actress Oscar for her portrayal of a young, flirtatious socialite named Norma Besant. Adapted from a Broadway hit, this popular melodrama is a tale of class boundaries, passion, and the father-daughter relationship. Norma's father, a proud southern doctor (John St. Polis) kills Norma's boyfriend (Johnny Mack Brown). In the midst of an emotional trial, Dr. Besant commits suicide.

The Divine Lady (First National Pictures; dir. Frank Lloyd) Lloyd won an Oscar for directing this big-budget historical romance that follows the life of the willful Emma Hart (Corinne Griffith). Wife of the ambassador to Naples, Emma meets the dashing (and married) Admiral Horatio Nelson and becomes involved in a passionate affair with the British war hero. Brief comic turns by Marie Dressler (as Emma's mother) and a spectacularly staged sea battle are memorable.

The Gold Diggers of Broadway (Warner Bros. Pictures; dir. Roy Del Ruth) This full-length musical comedy filmed in color and sound portrays gold-digging showgirls searching for wealthy lovers. Only two reels of the exuberant backstage musical remain, but they include a kaleidoscopic finale and Nick Lucas's rendition of the song "Tip Toe Through the Tulips."

Hallelujah!* (MGM; dir. King Vidor) One of the first major studio films with an all–African American cast, this musical drama features spirituals, traditional tunes, work songs, jazz, and several Irving Berlin songs. The story follows the misadventures and redemption of a poor sharecropper (Daniel L. Haynes), who is led astray by a female dancer (Nina McKinney). *Hallelujah!* won critical praise, but MGM encountered some obstacles to distributing it, especially in the South.

In Old Arizona (Fox Film Corporation; dir. Irving Cummings and Raoul Walsh) Warner Baxter won an Oscar for his portrayal of the charming bandit known as the Cisco Kid. This sprightly Western was the first talkie shot outdoors. With the help of the duplicitous Tonia Maria (Dorothy Burgess), Sergeant Mickey Dunn (Edmund Lowe) attempts to capture the elusive Kid.

The Iron Mask (Elton Corporation; dir. Allan Dwan) Billed as Douglas Fairbanks's final swashbuckling silent film, this lavish production showcases the star reprising his role of D'Artagnan. He reunites the Musketeers to come to the king's aid when the villainous Count De Rochefort (Ullrich Haupt) confines Louis XIV (William Bakewell) in an iron mask and puts his secret twin (also played by Bakewell) on the throne. Although he was forty-six during production, Fairbanks performed breathtaking swordfights in this film.

The Kiss (MGM; dir. Jacques Feyder) Greta Garbo plays a married French woman who moves from one affair to another. Audacious in its moral stance, yet a box-office hit, *The Kiss* presents Garbo as a woman who literally gets away with murder when her husband's death is ruled a suicide and she is free to resume her affair with her former lover (Conrad Nagel) who defended her in court.

Carolyn Anderson

■ Entertainment: Radio Programs, Personalities, and Firsts

This list includes top radio personalities and shows of the 1920s, along with some historic firsts in the radio industry.

Some Radio Firsts

1920

May 20: Singer Dorothy Lutton broadcasts on station XWA in Montreal, Quebec, and is heard at a meeting of the Royal Society of Canada in Ottawa, Ontario, in what is arguably North America's first scheduled radio broadcast.

November 2: On its first scheduled commercial broadcast, the Pittsburgh radio station KDKA reports on President Warren G. Harding's election.

1921

April 11: KDKA broadcasts a boxing match between lightweights Johnny Ray and Johnny Dundee. Sports announcer Florent Gibson telephones the action to the KDKA station, where another announcer relays it to listeners.

July 2: Andrew White delivers ringside commentary on the world heavyweight boxing match between Jack Dempsey and Georges Carpentier to sports reporter J. O. Smith, who repeats White's descriptions of the match from a WJZ transmitting shed in Newark, New Jersey.

August 5: Harold Arlin gives a play-by-play KDKA broadcast of a baseball game between the Philadelphia Phillies and the Pittsburgh Pirates.

October 5–13: WJZ broadcasts the World Series game between the New York Yankees and the New York Giants. Reporter Sandy Hunt at the Polo Grounds in Manhattan telephones events to announcer Tommy Cowan, who broadcasts them on the air.

1922

February 18: Norm Albert announces the first Canadian play-by-play hockey broadcast, a game between North Toronto and a Midland, Ontario, team.

February 19: Vaudeville comedian Ed Wynn airs much of his Broadway revue, *The Perfect Fool*, on WJZ. It is considered to be the first musical revue broadcast in front of a studio audience.

May 9: Bertha Brainard begins presenting the show *Broadcasting Broadway* on WJZ, the first program of drama criticism with interviews and show highlights. By 1928, she is the NBC commercial program manager; Brainard goes on to introduce such popular radio programs as Rudy Vallée's variety show and *The Goldbergs*.

August 28: WEAF (New York, New York) becomes the first-known major station to air a commercial. A variety show is named after American author Nathaniel Hawthorne, which is also the name of the apartment development the Queensboro real estate company is advertising.

August 22–September: WGY (Schenectady, New York) begins a live drama broadcast with an abridged version of Eugene Walter's play *The Wolf* (1908), launching a series of radio plays that begin to develop sound effects.

November: The Boston Radio Exposition features African American entertainers Eubie Blake and Noble Sissle in a broadcast of highlights from *Shuffle Along*, the first hit musical to be created, directed, and acted exclusively by African Americans.

1923

September 20: KFKB (Milford, Kansas) is licensed. Owner John R. Brinkley promotes his hospital, his theories on male rejuvenation, and various remedies. He pioneers distance education when, to provide full days of live programs for his station (named most popular station in North America in a 1929 *Radio Digest* poll), he allows professors at Kansas State Agricultural College to broadcast their lectures by telephone hook-up. Response is positive; in 1924, the college establishes its own station.

1924

January 5: The first major North American radio network is launched when a Canadian National Railways (CNR) train leaves Montreal for Vancouver, equipped with radios that will eventually receive broadcasts from CNR stations in various Canadian locations.

1925

March 4: Graham McNamee announces the inauguration speech of President Calvin Coolidge over WEAF and its affiliates. This may be the first such speech to be directly broadcast, rather than being recorded and then broadcast.

July 10–21: WGN (Chicago, Illinois) announcer Quin Ryan broadcasts from Dayton, Tennessee, where high school teacher John T. Scopes has been charged with violating Tennessee law banning the teaching of evolution. Microphones in the courtroom broadcast speeches by trial attorneys William Jennings Bryan and Clarence Darrow over landlines to a transmitter on top of Chicago's Drake Hotel.

1926
September 26: NBC's first broadcast is a four-hour gala program from New York's Waldorf-Astoria Hotel. Walter Damrosch conducts the New York Symphony, and opera star Mary Garden and humorist Will Rogers perform.

1927
June: The National Broadcasting Company (NBC) broadcasts the return to the United States of aviator Charles Lindbergh after his solo transatlantic flight. Graham McNamee is the primary announcer, but the event marks the first use of multiple announcers placed at different locations to cover a single event.

July 1: CNR temporarily expands its radio network through telephone and telegraph companies to provide an audience for the celebration of Canada's Diamond Jubilee of Confederation. Morning, afternoon, and evening programs include speeches, poetry, and music, the latter featuring a choir of ten thousand children.

1929
December 31: WEAF and WJZ broadcast "Pursuing Time Around the World." Starting after the midnight chimes of London's Big Ben at 7 p.m. eastern standard time, the program becomes "Pursuing Time Across the Country," with live music from various locations around the United States. At midnight in New York, Rudy Vallée and his Connecticut Yankees perform to greet the New Year.

Radio Personalities

De Leath, Vaughn
Dates: 1920–1929, 1931–1939
Networks: Various stations, 1920–1926; NBC, 1926–1929; CBS, 1931–1933; NBC, 1934–1936; Blue, 1937–1939; Mutual, 1939

Among radio's earliest performers, De Leath is said to have made her formal singing radio debut on a 1920 experimental broadcast for inventor Lee DeForest. She came to be known as the "Original Radio Girl" and "The First Lady of Radio." High or loud voices were incompatible with early microphones, so De Leath lowered her soprano voice and developed a soft, intimate, singing style, becoming one of the first radio crooners. She sang on many stations and on the stage, recording with such musicians as Paul Whiteman. In 1923, she became manager of WDT. When transatlantic broadcasting began, hers was one of the first American voices heard in Europe.

Kaltenborn, H. V.
Dates: 1921–1925, 1927–1939, 1940–1955
Networks: Various stations including WJZ, Newark (later, New York), and WVP, New York, 1921–1923; WEAF, New York, 1923–1925; WOR, New York, irregularly, 1925–1927; CBS, 1927–1939; NBC, 1940–1955

One of the best-known early radio news reporters, Milwaukee-born Hans Von Kaltenborn was a *Brooklyn Eagle* reporter who had covered World War I. He was among the most trusted radio voices from the 1920s through the 1950s, although his outspoken commentary often led to censorship conflicts. Kaltenborn gained his greatest prominence during the 1930s and 1940s when his fluency in foreign languages allowed him to react quickly, without a translator, to speeches by world leaders.

Lopez, Vincent
Dates: 1921–1928; 1933–1934, 1941–1946, 1949–1956
Networks: WJZ, Newark (later New York), 1921–1928; CBS, 1928; Blue, 1933; CBS, 1934; Blue, 1941–1943; Mutual, 1943–1946, 1949–1956; NBC, 1950–1951; ABC, 1951–1956

Rivaling the Kansas City Coon-Sanders Nighthawks (WDAF) as radio's first dance band, Lopez began broadcasting nightly jazz shows from New York's Hotel Pennsylvania; by 1924, his group was known as the Hotel Pennsylvania Orchestra. The commercial possibilities of radio became obvious when the broadcasts brought large audiences to the hotel and Lopez's theme song, "Nola," became popular. Of the early 1920s radio bandleaders, Lopez maintained the most lasting popularity. His principal radio rivals were George Olsen and Paul Whiteman, but neither began regular broadcasts until the decade's end.

McNamee, Graham

Dates: 1923–1939

Networks: WEAF, New York, 1923–1926; NBC, 1926–1939

Generally described as the outstanding radio personality of the 1920s, McNamee is credited with inventing modern sports broadcasting. In 1923, he was assigned to enliven sports broadcasting with his flair for description; he worked as a play-by-play announcer as well as a color commentator, offering analysis and variety during pauses in sports events. In August 1923, he announced a middleweight boxing championship between Harry Greb and Johnny Wilson. That summer, he also broadcast his first of many World Series games, assisting Grantland Rice until the fourth inning of the third game, when McNamee took over. With Andrew White, he covered the 1926 boxing match between Jack Dempsey and Gene Tunney, and, assisted by Philips Carlin, broadcast their 1927 rematch. In 1927, he covered the first Rose Bowl game to be broadcast all over the United States.

McNamee was also an important general announcer, covering political conventions starting in 1924, and the inauguration of President Calvin Coolidge in 1925, the year he also broadcast from the airship *Los Angeles*. On November 15, 1926, he hosted the four-hour celebration marking NBC's first broadcast and was the principal broadcaster for aviator Charles Lindbergh's return to New York in June 1927. He announced many regularly scheduled programs, including *The Atwater-Kent Hour* and *The Cities Service Orchestra*, also making appearances on Ed Wynn's radio show *Fire Chief* and Rudy Vallée's *The Fleischmann's Yeast Hour* in the late 1930s. His book *You're On the Air* (1926), written with Robert G. Anderson, describes his early career.

Vallée, Rudy

Dates: 1928–1947, 1950–1951, 1955

Networks: WABC, New York, 1928 (segments of shows also broadcast on WOR and WMCA); NBC, 1929–1947; WOR, New York, 1950–1951; CBS, 1955

Best known as host of *The Fleischmann's Yeast Hour* (1929–1939; also *The Rudy Vallée Show, The Sunshine Hour, The Royal Gelatin Hour, Vallée Varieties, Sealtest Village Store,* and *Villa Vallée*), singing host Vallée first performed on radio while touring in London from 1924 through 1925. He also made a radio appearance on WABC in 1928 from the small Heigh-Ho Club in Manhattan. His variety show became one of the most important showcases for new talent. His guests in the 1920s and 1930s included such future stars as singer Kate Smith, ventriloquist Edgar Bergen (with Charlie McCarthy), and comedian Milton Berle. The Aldrich Family, a comedic group, premiered as a skit on the *Rudy Vallée Hour* before becoming its own series. Vallée also conducted serious interviews, such as one with deaf and blind writer and activist Helen Keller.

Radio Shows

The A&P Gypsies

Dates: 1923–1936

Networks: WEAF, New York, 1923–1926; NBC, 1927–1936

Harry Horlick's band began as a house orchestra for WEAF and was soon carried on six stations. Its theme, "Two Guitars," became a hit. In 1924, it gained sponsorship from The Great Atlantic and Pacific Tea Company (A&P) and took the company's name to acknowledge its sponsorship without commercials. The original six-piece orchestra was expanded to more than twenty musicians. The program became one of radio's top musical shows, featuring traditional gypsy, folk, classical, and semiclassical music, some written by Russian-born Horlick.

The Adventures of Helen and Mary
1929–1954

Network: CBS

This first major network show for children featured Estelle Levy and Patricia Ryan playing Helen and Mary, telling children's stories. By 1934, it evolved into the popular *Let's Pretend* radio show under the leadership of Nila Mack. Child actors told children's stories, with an emphasis on traditional fairy tales.

Amos 'n' Andy

Dates: 1926–1960

Networks: WGN, Chicago, 1926–1927; WMAQ, Chicago, 1928–1929; NBC, 1929–1939; CBS, 1939–1943; NBC, 1943–1948; CBS, 1948–1960

After briefly broadcasting on Chicago's WEBH, Charles Correll and Freeman Gosden created the radio show *Sam 'n' Henry* for WGN. They portrayed two African American men from Alabama who came to Chicago seeking work. The comedy was enormously popular, but WGN refused to allow them to record the show for sale to other stations. The station claimed ownership of the show and characters. Gosden and Correll moved to WMAQ and renamed the show as *Amos 'n' Andy*. Set in New York's Harlem area, the show depicts the frustrations of the three main characters (Andrew H. Brown, Amos Jones, and George "Kingfish" Stevens) as they seek to improve their lives. The broadcasts began March 19, 1928, and the show's recordings quickly sold to thirty other stations. It was soon became radio's most popular show. Until the mid-1930s, Correll and Gosden wrote all their own material and played all roles, male and female.

The Atwater-Kent Hour
Dates: 1925–31, 1934
Networks: WEAF, New York, 1925; NBC, 1926–1933; CBS, 1934

Taking its name from a radio manufacturer, this was arguably the most important early concert series, featuring a large symphony orchestra and major Metropolitan Opera stars as guests. In 1927, a spin-off called *The Atwater-Kent Auditions* was briefly aired; it was radio's first talent scout program. Ten finalists competed for a $5,000 grand prize.

Cities Service Orchestra
Dates: 1925–1956
Networks: Trial broadcasts in New York, 1925–1926; NBC, 1927–1935; Red, 1935–1941; NBC, 1941–1944

Also known as *The Cities Services Concerts, Highways in Melody*, and *The Cities Services Band of America*, this was among radio's earliest popular music programs and one of the longest-running shows in radio history. It began by featuring brass music. In 1927, conductor Rosario Bourdon introduced a more symphonic style and various soloists, performing selections from classical to popular music.

The Clicquot Club Eskimos Orchestra
Dates: 1923–1933, 1935–1936
Networks: WEAF, New York, 1923–1926; NBC, 1926–1933; CBS, 1935–1936; NBC, 1936

Musician Harry Reser led a banjo ensemble in this early musical program. The show took its name from the sponsor; at that time, no products could be named on the show for advertisement, so commercial brands named and sponsored radio shows for marketing purposes. As time passed and the program's success grew, the band became a full orchestra.

The Collier Hour
Dates: 1927–1933
Networks: Blue, 1927–1932; CBS, 1932–1933

The first important dramatic show, this program publicized *Collier's* magazine through radio adaptations of its stories. Most popular was a *Fu Manchu* series, based on stories by Sax Rohmer, with host/actor Arthur Hughes playing the Chinese master criminal. *Fu Manchu* became a separate series on CBS. In 1929, *The Collier Hour* became a variety show, on which actor/composer George M. Cohan made his first radio appearance.

The Eveready Hour
Dates: 1923–1924, 1926–1930
Networks: WEAF, New York, linked 1924 with WRG, Buffalo, and WJAR, Providence; NBC, 1926–1930

Enormously popular, this was radio's first fully sponsored variety show, combining music, drama, news, and comedy, created to advertise National Carbon Company products, such as Eveready batteries. Guests included humorist Will Rogers, comedian Eddie Cantor, and composer George Gershwin. Entertainment ranged from the vaudeville comedy of Joe Weber and Lew Fields to readings from William Shakespeare. The program also featured stars who toured to perform on local stations, of whom one of the most prominent was singer and ukulele-player Wendell Hall. His song "It Ain't Gonna Rain No Mo'" became a hit. True stories were also included, such as the experiences of New York cabdriver Martin "Red" Christianson, who recounted his adventures to radio audiences.

The Goldbergs
Dates: 1929–1934, 1936–1946
Networks: NBC, 1929–1934; CBS, 1936; NBC, 1937; CBS, 1938–1946

Gertrude Berg created and performed in this early Jewish comedy. She wrote scripts, played Molly Goldberg, and directed the program. Originally called *The Rise of the Goldbergs*, it followed the lives of European-born Jake, his wife Molly, and their two American-born children. The family lived in a fictional ghetto in the Bronx; episodes in the early years focused on the problems of everyday life and assimilation into U.S. culture.

The Grand Ole Opry
Dates: 1925–
Networks: WSM, Nashville, 1925–; NBC, 1939–1957; WSM, 1957–

George D. Hay had helped create Chicago's radio show *National Barn Dance* before moving to Nashville to direct WSM programming. Harmonica-playing physician Humphrey Bate and his Possum Hunters were already broadcasting on what was originally billed as *The WSM Barn Dance* with early southern vaudeville star Uncle Dave Macon. Hay and Bate recruited Civil War veteran and champion fiddler Uncle Jimmy Thompson and African American harmonica player DeFord Bailey. With Hay portraying an old judge, they attracted people with country roots to the studio, where they played their own musical instruments and shared songs handed down orally from previous generations. The show was renamed *The Grand Ole Opry* in 1927.

The Happiness Boys
Dates: 1921, 1923, 1926–1940
Networks: WJZ, Newark, 1921; WEAF, New York, 1923; NBC, 1926–1929; Blue, 1929–1931; NBC, 1931–1938; WMCA, New York, 1939–1940

Tenor William Reese "Billy" Jones and baritone Thomas Ernest "Ernie" Hare aired talk segments, songs, and comedy. They took their title from their sponsors, the Happiness Candy Company, performing as the Happiness Boys, the Interwoven Pair, the Best Food Boys, the Taystee Loafers, and the Flit Soldiers.

Music Appreciation Hour
Dates: 1928–1942
Network: NBC

New York Symphony conductor Walter Damrosch developed this program as a classroom tool, first called *The RCA Educational Hour*. He lectured about the recorded music he broadcast and provided different music for use in elementary and high schools, eventually reaching an estimated audience of seven million.

National Barn Dance
Dates: 1924–1940, 1949–1970
Networks: WLS, Chicago, 1924–1933; NBC, 1933–1946; ABC, 1948–1950; WLW, Cincinnati, 1950–1960; WGN, Chicago, 1960–1970

Begun under the sponsorship of Sears, Roebuck (the station's call letters stood for "World's Largest Store") and later under the *Prairie Farmer* magazine, this program became so popular that when an hour of it was broadcast from Chicago's Eighth Street Theater, studio audiences paid admission to watch the show. Luther Ossenbrink, as Arkansas Woodchopper Arkie, called square dances. Early performers included Gene Autry, who went on to become a film star. Program manager George Hay, who had helped create the show, moved to Nashville's WSM in 1925 and established *The Grand Ole Opry*.

National Farm and Home Hour
Dates: 1928–1959
Networks: KDKA, Pittsburgh, 1928–1929; Blue/ABC, 1929–1945; NBC, 1945–1959

Offering farming tips, news, political discussions, and music for rural audiences, the program was broadcast from livestock shows, harvest festivals, and other rural events. The Chicago-based show was produced in cooperation with the U.S. Department of Agriculture and involved the 4-H Club, the American Farm Bureau, the National Grange, and the Future Farmers of America, among others.

Roxy and His Gang
Dates: 1923–1925, 1927–1931, 1934–1935
Networks: WEAF, New York, 1923–1925; Blue, 1927–1931; CBS, 1934–1935

Briefly aired first as *The Capitol Theatre Gang* and *Capitol Family Broadcasts*, this show and its successor, *Major Bowes' Capitol Family*, were broadcast from New York's Capitol Theater, then the world's largest movie palace. The partnership responsible for the theater included both Samuel L. "Roxy" Rothafel and Edward Bowes. It featured serious music performed by distinguished soloists, a large orchestra and chorus, and young talent. In 1925, Rothafel, the original master of ceremonies, left the broadcast to Bowes so that he would be free to participate in the construction of the Roxy Theatre, later called the Radio City Music Hall. Bowes became known in the 1930s for his *Amateur Hour* radio program.

The Voice of Firestone
Dates: 1928–1950s
Networks: NBC, 1928–1954; ABC, 1954–1950s

Sponsor Harvey S. Firestone Sr. and his wife Idabelle, who wrote the show's theme music, were deeply involved in ensuring the quality of the show, along with their son, Harvey S. Firestone. *The Voice of Firestone* was also known as *The Firestone Hour* and *The Firestone Concert*. Hugo Marini originally conducted the show's orchestra. In the 1920s, the program offered popular music with soloists Vaughn De Leath and Franklyn Baur, along with presentations of more serious music.

Betty Richardson

Legislation: Major U.S. Legislation

1920

Death on the High Seas Act
Allowed the family members and dependents of a person who dies at sea outside U.S. waters to file a wrongful death lawsuit seeking monetary damages from the shipowner; since expanded to cover airlines flying over the ocean.

Federal Power Act
Created the Federal Power Commission (FPC) to grant licenses for hydroelectric projects on interstate waterways; the FPC's mandate expanded in 1935 to include regulation of all interstate electricity transmission; the FPC was superseded in 1977 by the Federal Energy Regulatory Commission.

Merchant Marine Act
Supported the U.S. merchant marine by requiring (in a section known as the Jones Act) that goods shipped between U.S. ports be carried aboard U.S. ships crewed by U.S. seamen; also required ships operating between ports in U.S. waters to follow U.S. laws and labor regulations.

Mineral Leasing Act
Authorized the leasing of public lands for the extraction of minerals such as petroleum, coal, and phosphates; leases issued by competitive bidding for terms of ten or twenty years, with royalties divided between state and federal governments.

Nineteenth Amendment
Constitutional amendment giving all U.S. citizens the right to vote regardless of sex.

Railroad Transportation Act (Esch-Cummins Act)
Restored railroads to private control following their nationalization during World War I; authorized railways to be compensated for wartime losses and reestablished regulation of the industry by the Interstate Commerce Commission (ICC); set up the Railroad Labor Board to settle railroad labor disputes.

Sterling-Lehlbach Act
The first law establishing retirement pensions for federal workers; affected some 300,000 federal workers.

1921

Emergency Tariff of 1921
Raised tariff rates on imported agricultural products to stem the effects of sharply falling agricultural prices after the end of World War I; superseded by the Fordney-McCumber Tariff of 1922.

Federal Aid Highway Act (Phipps Act)
Responded to increasing automobile traffic by providing federal funds for highway construction, to be matched by state dollars and overseen by the Bureau of Public Roads (later the Federal Highway Administration).

General Accounting Act (Budget and Accounting Act)
Established the practice of the president presenting an annual federal budget to Congress for approval; consolidated the budget agencies of the executive and legislative branches into the Bureau of the Budget (later the Office of Management and Budget) and the General Accounting Office (later the Government Accountability Office), respectively.

Immigration Act of 1921 (Emergency Quota Act)
Established the first numerical limits on immigration to the United States, as well as the first immigration quotas based on country of origin; under the law, the number of immigrants admitted each year from a given country was limited to 3 percent of the number of people from that country already residing in the United States according to the 1910 census; superseded by the Immigration Act of 1924.

Packers and Stockyards Act
Subjected the stockyard, meatpacking, dairy, poultry, and related industries to federal regulation intended to prevent anticompetitive practices such as price fixing, deception, and monopoly formation.

Revenue Act of 1921
Lowered income tax rates on individuals and instituted a capital gains tax rate much lower than that on ordinary income; part of a larger, decade-long Republican push to lower taxes.

Russian Famine Relief Act

Authorized funds for the newly privatized American Relief Administration to send food to Russia to help fight the devastating famine of 1921, brought about by drought combined with civil war; overseen by U.S. secretary of commerce Herbert Hoover; aid program ended in 192

Sheppard-Towner Act (Maternity and Infancy Protection Act)

Provided federal funding for maternal and child health care, in part through matching state funds for the construction of health care centers; ended in 1929 under conservative political pressure from the American Medical Association.

1922

Cable Act (Married Women's Citizenship Act)

Partially reversed laws making an American woman's citizenship entirely dependent on being married to a U.S. citizen; allowed American women to keep their U.S. citizenship if they married noncitizens who were eligible for U.S. citizenship and if they continued to reside in the United States; repealed in 1936.

Capper-Volstead Act

Exempted agricultural producers from certain antitrust laws; intended to allow agricultural cooperatives to form during a time of sagging agricultural prices.

Equal Rights Amendment (Lucretia Mott Amendment)

Proposed constitutional amendment granting equal rights and protections to men and women under the law; resubmitted every session for more than forty years; passed in Congress in 1972 but never ratified by a sufficient number of states.

Five Power Treaty (Washington Naval Treaty)

An agreement signed by the United States, Great Britain, Japan, France, and Italy to limit the size of naval forces; intended to halt a costly naval arms race in the wake of World War I.

Fordney-McCumber Tariff

Raised average tariff rates on dutiable imports to 38.5 percent; emblematic of U.S. protectionism and isolationism in the postwar era.

General Land Exchange Act

Allowed the federal government to acquire privately held land within or near national forests by exchange for land elsewhere in the same state.

World War Foreign Debts Commission Act

Created a commission to determine how much the U.S. allies in Europe owed the United States for debts incurred during World War I and to establish a repayment schedule; the initial total principal of some $11 billion was later reduced, as were the interest rates; most affected the largest debtors: Great Britain, France, Italy, and Belgium.

1923

Agricultural Credits Act

Created twelve Federal Intermediate Credit Banks authorized to lend money to farm cooperatives, which in turn were supposed to lend to farmers; one of many largely unsuccessful efforts to address the agricultural crisis of the 1920s.

1924

Bonus Act (World War Adjusted Compensation Act)

Provided compensation to veterans of World War I in the form of certificates redeemable starting in 1945 and valid in the meantime as collateral on bank loans. This promised bonus was what prompted the Bonus Army that marched on the District of Columbia in 1932.

Child Labor Amendment

Proposed constitutional amendment giving Congress the power to regulate the labor of people under age eighteen; passed in Congress but never ratified by a sufficient number of states.

Clarke-McNary Act

Made land acquisition easier for the National Forest Service, along with the General Exchange Act; included provisions for federal and state cooperation on fire prevention, water resources management, and reforestation.

Immigration Act of 1924 (Johnson-Reed Act, National Origins Act)

Further tightened the restrictions of the Immigration Act of 1921, limiting the number of immigrants admitted from a given country to 2 percent of the number already residing in the United States as of the 1890 census; after three years, a fixed limit of 150,000 immigrants per year from outside the Western Hemisphere came into effect; also effectively banned immigration from Asia entirely.

Indian Citizenship Act

Granted full U.S. citizenship to all Native Americans born in the United States, allowing them to retain tribal citizenship as well.

Oil Pollution Act

Outlawed the dumping of oil in coastal waterways and established fines and other penalties for violators; one of the first federal laws to address the effects of pollution on the environment.

Revenue Act of 1924

Lowered the top income tax rate from 58 percent to 46 percent and lowered other rates as well.

Rogers Act (Foreign Service Act)

Established the U.S. Foreign Service by combining the diplomatic service, which carries out U.S. foreign policy through embassies in other countries, with the consular service, which serves the needs of U.S. citizens and business interests in other countries; also established a merit-based system of hiring and promotion.

1925

Air Mail Act (Kelly Act)

Allowed the U.S. Post Office to contract with private air carriers for mail delivery, thus replacing government-run airmail and fostering innovation in commercial aviation.

Corrupt Practices Act

Amended the 1910 Federal Corrupt Practices Act, which set campaign spending limits for political parties; the 1925 amendment prohibited bribery and direct corporate campaign contributions and mandated quarterly campaign finance reports listing every contribution and expenditure above one hundred dollars; weakened by a lack of enforcement mechanisms.

Judges Act

Gave the Supreme Court greater ability to choose the cases it would hear by removing almost all right of direct appeal and requiring appellants to instead petition for a writ of certiorari from the Court; promoted by Chief Justice William Howard Taft as a way to reduce the Court's caseload.

Mount Rushmore National Memorial Act

Authorized and partially funded the carving of the Mount Rushmore National Memorial in South Dakota; construction began in 1927 and ended in 1941 after funding ran out.

1926

Air Commerce Act

Established the first federal aviation regulations, enforced by the Aeronautics Branch of the Department of Commerce (forerunner of the Federal Aviation Administration in the Department of Transportation); provided for the licensing of pilots, safety inspections of aircraft, and basic air traffic controls.

Cooperative Marketing Act

Augmented the provisions of the Capper-Volstead Act, increasing the amount of information that could be shared by members of agricultural cooperatives to improve their businesses; also created a new division the U.S. Department of Agriculture to assist in this area.

Public Buildings Act

Provided funds for the construction of new federal buildings both in the District of Columbia and across the country; funded construction of the Supreme Court building and federal buildings in Alabama, Indiana, and Kentucky, among others.

Railway Labor Act

Granted railroad workers the right to organize labor unions and to bargain collectively with employers; also established a labor mediation board; later extended to cover airline workers as well.

Revenue Act of 1926
Further reduced the top income tax rate to 25 percent and increased the tax on corporate income to 13.5 percent.

1927

McFadden Act
Allowed nationally chartered banks to open multiple branches within one state, subject to state banking laws, in order to better compete with state banks; did not allow interstate branching.

McNary-Haugen Farm Relief Bill
Failed legislation that aimed to support farmers by having the government buy agricultural surpluses and either store them for use in lean years or export them; passed by Congress in 1927 and 1928 and vetoed both times by President Calvin Coolidge.

Radio Act
Created the Federal Radio Commission (FRC), which was empowered to grant or revoke radio broadcasting licenses and assign frequencies; replaced in 1934 by the Federal Communications Commission (FCC), which regulated television as well as radio broadcasting.

1928

Boulder Canyon Project Act
Authorized and provided funds for construction of the Boulder Dam, later renamed the Hoover Dam, on the Colorado River along the border between Nevada and Arizona; also formally ratified the Colorado River compact, the interstate agreement governing water rights and use of the river.

Capper-Ketchum Act
Provided additional funding for the cooperative extension service for agricultural education; also supported the agricultural youth organizations 4-H and Future Farmers of America.

Flood Control Act
Authorized the U.S. Army Corps of Engineers to undertake flood control projects along the Mississippi and Sacramento rivers, largely in response to the devastating Great Mississippi Flood of 1927.

Kellogg-Briand Pact
International agreement renouncing war as an instrument of foreign policy; crafted primarily by U.S. secretary of state Frank Kellogg and French foreign minister Aristide Briand; lacked enforcement mechanisms.

Revenue Act of 1928
Lowered the corporate income tax rate from 13.5 to 12 percent; maintained the top individual income tax rate at 25 percent on incomes of $100,000 or more.

1929

Agricultural Marketing Act
Authorized money for a revolving loan fund for agricultural cooperatives amid ongoing overproduction and falling prices in the farm sector; also created the Federal Farm Board to facilitate the formation of additional marketing cooperatives and pursue additional price stabilization measures.

Cruiser Act
Authorized the building of twenty new ships for the U.S. Navy, construction of which was undertaken in the 1930s; only about ten cruisers were ultimately built, largely due to financial constraints during the Great Depression.

Migratory Bird Conservation Act
Created a commission to oversee the acquisition of land for a nationwide system of wildlife refuges for migratory birds.

Reapportionment Act
Set the number of seats in the U.S. House of Representatives at 435, where it has remained ever since; previously, the number of seats had increased with each decennial census; districting methods were left to the states.

Scott A. Merriman

Legislation: Major U.S. Supreme Court Decisions

Legislation	Significance
1920	
Missouri v. Holland	Upheld the Migratory Bird Treaty Act of 1918 against a states' rights challenge because that law was enacted pursuant to a treaty with Great Britain, and under the Supremacy Clause, treaties are "the supreme law of the land," and thus any laws enacted pursuant to a treaty supersede states' rights under the Tenth Amendment. This case led to concerns that treaties could be used to abrogate constitutional rights, a proposition ultimately rejected in 1957 in *Reid v. Covert*.
National Prohibition Cases	Upheld the Eighteenth Amendment against challenges that Prohibition was not a proper subject for constitutional amendment and that it required joint action by the federal and state governments to enact appropriate laws.
Silverthorne Lumber Co. v. United States	Ruled that not only illegally seized evidence, but also any "fruits" of such evidence (e.g., evidence from a lockbox, the key to which was obtained illegally) would be excluded in federal trials so as to enforce the Fourth Amendment's protection against unreasonable searches and seizures; known as the "fruit of the poisonous tree" doctrine.
United States v. Wheeler	Reinforced and emphasized that there is a constitutional right to travel; also held that only the states, not the federal government, may punish kidnapping (until a federal law against kidnapping was passed in the 1930s).
1921	
Dillon v. Gloss	Held that Congress may include an explicit deadline by which proposed constitutional amendments fail if they have not been ratified.
Gouled v. United States	Confirmed the "mere evidence rule," which held that, under the Fourth Amendment, the government could not lawfully seize a criminal defendant's property unless it was used in or derived from the commission of a crime; abandoned later in the twentieth century.
Newberry v. United States	Held that Congress's constitutional authority to regulate the time, place, and manner of federal elections did not give it the power to regulate political primaries or other such nomination procedures.
Smith v. Kansas City Title & Trust Co.	Upheld the constitutionality of the 1916 Federal Farm Loan Act, which created land banks that could lend to farmers; also affirmed the jurisdiction of federal courts in cases involving state law claims, where the construction or application of federal law is relevant.
Truax v. Corrigan	Struck down an Arizona law that prohibited courts from ordering workers not to strike or picket a business, on the ground that the law deprived businesses of their right to equal protection of the laws; an example of the Court's increasing willingness to invalidate government efforts to regulate economic affairs, a trend that largely continued until the 1930s.
1922	
Bailey v. Drexel Furniture Co.	Struck down a federal tax on products made with child labor on the grounds that the tax was an attempt to regulate child labor rather than raise revenue and that child labor was a matter for the states to address.

Legislation	Significance
1922 (Cont.)	
Balzac v. Porto Rico	Held that not all parts of the Constitution applied in U.S. territories, only those guaranteeing fundamental rights; applied to a libel case in Puerto Rico.
Fairchild v. Hughes	Held that a private citizen did not have standing to challenge the validity of a constitutional amendment—in this case, the Nineteenth Amendment, giving women the right to vote. The plaintiff, the Court noted, was not an elected official and lived in New York, where women already had the right to vote.
Federal Baseball Club v. National League	Ruled that Major League Baseball was not subject to federal antitrust laws because the league's games were exhibition games and did not qualify as interstate commerce.
Leser v. Garnett	Upheld the constitutionality of the Nineteenth Amendment (granting women the right to vote) against claims that, among other objections, the ratifications by states whose own constitutions barred women's suffrage were invalid.
Ng Fung Ho v. White	Held that an alien ordered deported by an administrative agency had the right to judicial review of that order. The decision thus established a significant difference in the due process available to aliens depending on whether they are inside the United States and fighting deportation or are outside the United States and fighting exclusion (in which case they have no rights).
Ozawa v. United States	Ruled that Japanese people were not "Caucasian" and therefore could not become naturalized U.S. citizens under the Naturalization Act of 1906.
Pennsylvania Coal Co. v. Mahon	Established the doctrine of "regulatory taking," according to which government regulation that diminishes the value of private property beyond a certain point qualifies as a taking and therefore requires fair compensation under the Fifth Amendment, even though no physical taking occurred; opened the door to property owners challenging various property regulations.
United States v. Lanza	Held that a person could be prosecuted for violating federal Prohibition laws even after having been prosecuted for the same act in state court, notwithstanding the double-jeopardy clause of the Fifth Amendment, because the state and federal courts represented separate sovereigns.
Vigliotti v. Pennsylvania	Decided that a state Prohibition law remained valid even after the Eighteenth Amendment was ratified; in other words, the states could continue to legislate their own alcohol bans.
1923	
Adkins v. Children's Hospital	Struck down a minimum wage law in Washington, D.C., as violating the freedom of contract rights of both employees and employers. Earlier cases upholding maximum hour laws still permitted workers and owners to bargain about wages, which this law did not.
Frothingham v. Mellon	Rejected a taxpayer lawsuit challenging government spending, thus establishing the doctrine of "standing," according to which a plaintiff must demonstrate suffering specific harm from an act in order to challenge it in court.

Legislation	Significance
1923 (Cont.)	
Meyer v. Nebraska	Struck down a Nebraska law that forbade the teaching of foreign languages to children below ninth grade, as infringing on the freedom of, in this case, teachers and parents protected by the due process clause of the Fourteenth Amendment.
Moore v. Dempsey	Held that African Americans tried in the wake of the 1919 race riot in Elaine, Arkansas, had been denied their right to due process by armed white mobs demanding guilty verdicts; represented the first step toward a broad use of federal habeas corpus power as a means for federal courts to review convictions in state courts.
Pennsylvania v. West Virginia	Held that a state cannot force companies to discriminate against out-of-state customers in selling natural resources because of the "dormant" commerce clause, the constitutional doctrine under which the Supreme Court presumes that Congress would block states from discriminating against interstate commerce.
Rindge Co. v. County of Los Angeles	Upheld a local government's use of the power of eminent domain to take private property in order to build a public scenic road.
Rooker v. Fidelity Trust Co.	Held that federal district courts (i.e., federal trial courts) do not have the power to review decisions by state supreme courts; apart from the special situation of federal habeas corpus petitions to review the convictions of state prisoners, the only federal court with the authority to review state supreme court decisions is the U.S. Supreme Court.
United States v. Bhagat Singh Thind	Like *Ozawa*, held that an Asian person was not "white" and therefore could not become a naturalized citizen, notwithstanding the fact that some scientific authorities would have classified the Indian-born plaintiff as "Caucasian." The result was not reversed until 1946, when Congress enacted the Luce-Celler Act.
1924	
Hester v. United States	Established the "open fields doctrine," according to which the Fourth Amendment's protection against unreasonable searches and seizures did not apply to open fields on private property. This doctrine was later replaced by the assumption that the Fourth Amendment applies anywhere a person has a "reasonable expectation" of privacy.
James Everard's Breweries v. Day	Upheld a federal ban on the sale of malt liquors for medical uses under the Eighteenth Amendment, which empowered Congress to enact legislation to enforce the terms of the amendment.
Jay Burns Baking Co. v. Bryan	Struck down a state law mandating the size of bread loaves as violating substantive due process; another example of the Supreme Court's aggressive review of economic regulations.
Radice v. New York	Upheld a state law that barred women from working in restaurants at night; unlike the minimum wage law struck down in *Adkins*, this law survived because it was seen as a protective health and safety measure.
1925	
Agnello v. United States	Held that a warrantless search of a private home was per se unreasonable and thus prohibited by the Fourth Amendment, a proposition that had been assumed but never before decided explicitly.

Legislation	Significance
1925 (Cont.)	
Brooks v. United States	Upheld a federal statute barring interstate transportation of stolen cars, despite the apparent tension with earlier cases that struck down similar laws barring interstate transportation of products made from child labor.
Carroll v. United States	Established the "automobile exception" to the Fourth Amendment's prohibition on unreasonable searches and seizures, thus permitting police to search a motor vehicle without a warrant when there is probable cause to believe it contains evidence or contraband and there is concern that the vehicle could be moved before a warrant could be obtained.
George W. Bush & Sons Co. v. Maloy	Held that the commerce clause of the U.S. Constitution blocked a state from requiring a transportation company to obtain a certificate allowing it to transport people and goods through the state.
Gitlow v. New York	Upheld the appellant's conviction under a New York law that made it a crime to argue for overthrowing the United States government. More significant, the Court also asserted that the First Amendment protections of freedom of speech and the press do apply to the states as well as the federal government; this case started the process of "incorporating" many other provisions in the Bill of Rights, or extending them to apply to state governments.
Pierce v. Society of Sisters	Struck down an Oregon law requiring most eight- to sixteen-year-old children to attend a public (as opposed to private or parochial) school; further expanded the application of the Fourteenth Amendment's due process clause.
1926	
Corrigan v. Buckley	Upheld the legality of racially restrictive covenants in private land deeds.
Myers v. United States	Struck down a federal law requiring the president to obtain the consent of the Senate before removing an executive branch official (in this case, a federal postmaster); such a restriction was found invalid because the Constitution provides for the advice and consent of the Senate only with regard to the appointment, not removal, of executive branch officials.
Village of Euclid v. Ambler Realty Co.	Upheld a local city's power to enact reasonable zoning ordinances because cities have a valid interest in maintaining neighborhood character; an early case upholding the constitutionality of zoning.
Weaver v. Palmer Brothers Co.	Struck down a law that barred the use of shoddy (recycled wool), on the grounds that the ostensible health concerns underlying the statute could be addressed by sterilization.
1927	
Buck v. Bell	Upheld a Virginia law calling for mandatory sterilization of persons with mental disabilities, opening the door to further eugenics laws in the pre–World War II period.
Farrington v. Tokushige	Struck down a law in the Territory of Hawaii requiring foreign-language schools to obtain a permit from the territory.
Fiske v. Kansas	Reversed the conviction of a defendant in Kansas charged with criminal syndicalism, finding no evidence in the record that the defendant had called for violent or forceful overthrow of the government.

Legislation	Significance
1927 (Cont.)	
Lum v. Rice	Upheld a Mississippi school board's decision to block an American citizen of Chinese ancestry from attending a whites-only school; at the time, segregated schools were considered constitutional under the separate-but-equal doctrine established by *Plessy v. Ferguson*.
McGrain v. Daugherty	Held that Congress could hold hearings and investigate issues relevant to legislation.
Nixon v. Herndon	Held that the Texas Democratic Party's whites-only primary violated the Fourteenth Amendment's equal protection clause, effectively disenfranchising African Americans on the basis of their race.
United States v. Lee	Extended the warrant exception for automobiles, established in *Carroll v. United States* (1925), to boats; also held that the use of a searchlight was not a "search" for Fourth Amendment purposes.
Whitney v. California	Upheld a conviction for violating a California law prohibiting the teaching or advocating of the violent overthrow of the government, on the basis that the speech presented a "clear and present danger."
1928	
J. W. Hampton, Jr. & Co. v. United States	Held that the president's power to raise the tariff rate was not an unconstitutional delegation of legislative power because the president is executing the law according to broad principles.
Louis K. Liggett Co. v. Baldridge	Struck down a state law requiring that pharmacies be owned by licensed pharmacists.
Miller v. Schoene	Held that a state could use its eminent domain power to require a homeowner to remove a tree that posed a risk of infecting other trees with a disease.
Olmstead v. United States	Held that the police could wiretap telephone lines and record private conversations without a warrant because there was no physical intrusion onto the defendant's property and thus no search or seizure occurred.
Quaker City Cab Co. v. Pennsylvania	Struck down a law that taxed corporate owners, but not individual owners, of taxicabs.
1929	
Pocket Veto Case	Held that a bill had not become a law where Congress adjourned nine days after presenting it to the president because the "pocket veto" provision of the Constitution requires that the president have ten days in which to consider the bill.
Wisconsin v. Illinois	Held that the federal government has the authority to intervene in a dispute between two states and to take action against one state so as to protect the interests of other states.
United States v. Schwimmer	Upheld the denial of naturalization to a Hungarian pacifist who refused to take the Oath of Allegiance because of its statement of willingness to "take up arms personally" to defend the United States.

Tung Yin

Literature: Best-Selling Books in the United States

1920 Fiction
1. *The Man of the Forest*, Zane Grey
2. *Kindred of the Dust*, Peter B. Kyne
3. *The Re-creation of Brian Kent*, Harold Bell Wright
4. *The River's End*, James Oliver Curwood
5. *A Man for the Ages*, Irving Bacheller
6. *Mary-Marie*, Eleanor H. Porter
7. *The Portygee*, Joseph C. Lincoln
8. *The Great Impersonation*, E. Phillips Oppenheim
9. *The Lamp in the Desert*, Ethel M. Dell
10. *Harriet and the Piper*, Kathleen Norris

1920 Nonfiction
1. *Now It Can Be Told*, Philip Gibbs
2. *The Economic Consequences of the Peace*, John Maynard Keynes
3. *Theodore Roosevelt's Letters to His Children*, Theodore Roosevelt, edited by Joseph B. Bishop
4. *Theodore Roosevelt*, William Roscoe Thayer
5. *White Shadows in the South Seas*, Frederick O'Brien
6. *An American Idyll*, Cornelia Stratton Parker

1921 Fiction
1. *Main Street*, Sinclair Lewis
2. *The Brimming Cup*, Dorothy Canfield
3. *The Mysterious Rider*, Zane Grey
4. *The Age of Innocence*, Edith Wharton
5. *The Valley of Silent Men*, James Oliver Curwood
6. *The Sheik*, Edith M. Hull
7. *A Poor Wise Man*, Mary Roberts Rinehart
8. *Her Father's Daughter*, Gene Stratton Porter
9. *The Sisters-in-Law*, Gertrude Atherton
10. *The Kingdom Round the Corner*, Coningsby Dawson

1921 Nonfiction
1. *The Outline of History*, H. G. Wells
2. *White Shadows in the South Seas*, Frederick O'Brien
3. *The Mirrors of Downing Street*, Harold Begbie
4. *The Autobiography of Margot Asquith*, Margot Asquith
5. *Peace Negotiations*, Robert Lansing

1922 Fiction
1. *If Winter Comes*, A. S. M. Hutchinson
2. *The Sheik*, Edith M. Hull
3. *Gentle Julia*, Booth Tarkington
4. *The Head of the House of Coombe*, Frances Hodgson Burnett
5. *Simon Called Peter*, Robert Keable
6. *The Breaking Point*, Mary Roberts Rinehart
7. *This Freedom*, A. S. M. Hutchinson
8. *Maria Chapdelaine*, Louis Hemon
9. *To the Last Man*, Zane Grey
10. *Babbitt*, Sinclair Lewis (tie)
11. *Helen of the Old House*, Harold Bell Wright (tie)

1922 Nonfiction
1. *The Outline of History*, H. G. Wells
2. *The Story of Mankind*, Hendrik Willem Van Loon
3. *The Americanization of Edward Bok*, Edward Bok
4. *Diet and Health*, Lulu Hunt Peters
5. *The Mind in the Making*, James Harvey Robinson
6. *The Outline of Science*, J. Arthur Thomson
7. *Outwitting Our Nerves*, Josephine A. Jackson and Helen M. Salisbury
8. *Queen Victoria*, Lytton Strachey
9. *Mirrors of Washington*, Anonymous (Clinton W. Gilbert)
10. *Painted Windows*, Harold Begbie

1923 Fiction
1. *Black Oxen*, Gertrude Atherton
2. *His Children's Children*, Arthur Train
3. *The Enchanted April*, Elizabeth von Arnim
4. *Babbitt*, Sinclair Lewis
5. *The Dim Lantern*, Temple Bailey
6. *This Freedom*, A. S. M. Hutchinson
7. *The Mine with the Iron Door*, Harold Bell Wright
8. *The Wanderer of the Wasteland*, Zane Grey
9. *The Sea-Hawk*, Rafael Sabatini
10. *The Breaking Point*, Mary Roberts Rinehart

1923 Nonfiction
1. *Etiquette*, Emily Post
2. *The Life of Christ*, Giovanni Papini
3. *The Life and Letters of Walter H. Page*, Burton J. Hendrick, editor

4. *The Mind in the Making*, James Harvey Robinson
5. *The Outline of History*, H. G. Wells
6. *Diet and Health*, Lulu Hunt Peters
7. *Self-Mastery Through Conscious Auto-Suggestion*, Emile Coue
8. *The Americanization of Edward Bok*, Edward Bok
9. *The Story of Mankind*, Hendrik Willem Van Loon
10. *A Man from Maine*, Edward Bok

1924 Fiction
1. *So Big*, Edna Ferber
2. *The Plastic Age*, Percy Marks
3. *The Little French Girl*, Anne Douglas Sedgwick
4. *The Heirs Apparent*, Philip Gibbs
5. *A Gentleman of Courage*, James Oliver Curwood
6. *The Call of the Canyon*, Zane Grey
7. *The Midlander*, Booth Tarkington
8. *The Coast of Folly*, Coningsby Dawson
9. *Mistress Wilding*, Rafael Sabatini
10. *The Homemaker*, Dorothy Canfield Fisher

1924 Nonfiction
1. *Diet and Health*, Lulu Hunt Peters
2. *The Life of Christ*, Giovanni Papini
3. *The Boston Cooking-School Cook Book*, Fannie Farmer
4. *Etiquette*, Emily Post
5. *Ariel*, André Maurois
6. *The Cross Word Puzzle Books*, Prosper Buranelli, et al.
7. *Mark Twain's Autobiography*, Mark Twain
8. *Saint Joan*, George Bernard Shaw
9. *The New Decalogue of Science*, Albert E. Wiggam
10. *The Americanization of Edward Bok*, Edward Bok

1925 Fiction
1. *Soundings*, A. Hamilton Gibbs
2. *The Constant Nymph*, Margaret Kennedy
3. *The Keeper of the Bees*, Gene Stratton Porter
4. *Glorious Apollo*, E. Barrington (Elizabeth Louisa Moresby)
5. *The Green Hat*, Michael Arlen
6. *The Little French Girl*, Anne Douglas Sedgwick
7. *Arrowsmith*, Sinclair Lewis
8. *The Perennial Bachelor*, Anne Parrish
9. *The Carolinian*, Rafael Sabatini
10. *One Increasing Purpose*, A. S. M. Hutchinson

1925 Nonfiction
1. *Diet and Health*, Lulu Hunt Peters
2. *The Boston Cooking-School Cook Book*, Fannie Farmer
3. *When We Were Very Young*, A. A. Milne
4. *The Man Nobody Knows*, Bruce Barton
5. *The Life of Christ*, Giovanni Papini
6. *Ariel*, André Maurois
7. *Twice Thirty*, Edward Bok
8. *Twenty-Five Years: 1892–1916*, Viscount Grey of Fallodon (Sir Edward Grey)
9. *Anatole France Himself*, J. J. Brousson
10. *The Cross Word Puzzle Books*, Prosper Buranelli, et al.

1926 Fiction
1. *The Private Life of Helen of Troy*, John Erskine
2. *Gentlemen Prefer Blondes*, Anita Loos
3. *Sorrell and Son*, Warwick Deeping
4. *The Hounds of Spring*, Sylvia Thompson
5. *Beau Sabreur*, P. C. Wren
6. *The Silver Spoon*, John Galsworthy
7. *Beau Geste*, P. C. Wren
8. *Show Boat*, Edna Ferber
9. *After Noon*, Susan Ertz
10. *The Blue Window*, Temple Bailey

1926 Nonfiction
1. *The Man Nobody Knows*, Bruce Barton
2. *Why We Behave Like Human Beings*, George A. Dorsey
3. *Diet and Health*, Lulu Hunt Peters
4. *Our Times, Volume 1*, Mark Sullivan
5. *The Boston Cooking-School Cook Book*, Fannie Farmer
6. *Auction Bridge Complete*, Milton C. Work
7. *The Book Nobody Knows*, Bruce Barton
8. *The Story of Philosophy*, Will Durant
9. *The Light of Faith*, Edgar A. Guest
10. *Jefferson and Hamilton*, Claude G. Bowers

1927 Fiction
1. *Elmer Gantry*, Sinclair Lewis
2. *The Plutocrat*, Booth Tarkington
3. *Doomsday*, Warwick Deeping
4. *Sorrell and Son*, Warwick Deeping
5. *Jalna*, Mazo de la Roche
6. *Lost Ecstasy*, Mary Roberts Rinehart
7. *Twilight Sleep*, Edith Wharton

8. *Tomorrow Morning*, Anne Parrish
9. *The Old Countess*, Anne Douglas Sedgwick
10. *A Good Woman*, Louis Bromfield

1927 Nonfiction
1. *The Story of Philosophy*, Will Durant
2. *Napoleon*, Emil Ludwig
3. *Revolt in the Desert*, T. E. Lawrence
4. *Trader Horn*, Alfred A. Horn and Ethelreda Lewis
5. *We*, Charles A. Lindbergh
6. *Ask Me Another*, Julian Spafford
7. *The Royal Road to Romance*, Richard Halliburton
8. *The Glorious Adventure*, Richard Halliburton
9. *Why We Behave Like Human Beings*, George A. Dorsey
10. *Mother India*, Katherine Mayo

1928 Fiction
1. *The Bridge of San Luis Rey*, Thornton Wilder
2. *Wintersmoon*, Hugh Walpole
3. *Swan Song*, John Galsworthy
4. *The Greene Murder Case*, S. S. Van Dine
5. *Bad Girl*, Vina Delmar
6. *Claire Ambler*, Booth Tarkington
7. *Old Pybus*, Warwick Deeping
8. *All Kneeling*, Anne Parrish
9. *Jalna*, Mazo de la Roche
10. *The Strange Case of Miss Annie Spragg*, Louis Bromfield

1928 Nonfiction
1. *Disraeli*, André Maurois
2. *Mother India*, Katherine Mayo
3. *Trader Horn*, Alfred A. Horn and Ethelreda Lewis
4. *Napoleon*, Emil Ludwig
5. *Strange Interlude*, Eugene O'Neill
6. *We*, Charles A. Lindbergh
7. *Count Luckner: The Sea Devil*, Lowell Thomas
8. *Goethe*, Emil Ludwig
9. *Skyward*, Richard E. Byrd
10. *The Intelligent Woman's Guide to Socialism and Capitalism*, George Bernard Shaw

1929 Fiction
1. *All Quiet on the Western Front*, Erich Maria Remarque
2. *Dodsworth*, Sinclair Lewis
3. *Dark Hester*, Anne Douglas Sedgwick
4. *The Bishop Murder Case*, S. S. Van Dine
5. *Roper's Row*, Warwick Deeping
6. *Peder Victorious*, O. E. Rølvaag
7. *Mamba's Daughters*, DuBose Heyward
8. *The Galaxy*, Susan Ertz
9. *Scarlet Sister Mary*, Julia Peterkin
10. *Joseph and His Brethren*, H. W. Freeman

1929 Nonfiction
1. *The Art of Thinking*, Ernest Dimnet
2. *Henry the Eighth*, Francis Hackett
3. *The Cradle of the Deep*, Joan Lowell
4. *Elizabeth and Essex*, Lytton Strachey
5. *The Specialist*, Chic Sale
6. *A Preface for Morals*, Walter Lippmann
7. *Believe It or Not*, Robert L. Ripley
8. *John Brown's Body*, Stephen Vincent Benét
9. *The Tragic Era*, Claude G. Bowers
10. *The Mansions of Philosophy*, Will Durant

Laurence W. Mazzeno

■ Music: Popular Musicians

Louis Armstrong
"Basin Street Blues," "Heebie Jeebies," "Knockin' a Jug" (with Eddie Lang and Jack Teagarden), "Muggles" (with Earl "Fatha" Hines), "Muskrat Ramble," "St. Louis Blues" (with Bessie Smith), "Tight like This" (with Earl "Fatha" Hines), "Weather Bird" (with Earl "Fatha" Hines), "West End Blues" (with Earl "Fatha" Hines)

A Dixieland cornetist, trumpeter, and singer, one of the best-known jazz musicians of all time.

Gus Arnheim
"I Cried for You"

Early popular songwriter and bandleader who would later work with such crooners as Bing Crosby and Russ Columbo.

Gene Austin
"The Lonesome Road" (with Nat Shilkret), "My Blue Heaven," "Ramona," "Tonight You Belong to Me," "When My Sugar Walks down the Street," "Yes Sir, That's My Baby"

Lyricist and early crooner who worked with composer Nat Shilkret.

Bix Beiderbecke
"Davenport Blues," "For No Reason at All in C" (with Eddie Lang and Frankie Trumbauer), "From Monday on" (with Bing Crosby), "I'm Coming, Virginia," "Mississippi Mud" (with Bing Crosby and Irene Taylor), "Ol' Man River" (with Bing Crosby), "Ramona," "Singin' the Blues" (with Eddie Lang and Frankie Trumbauer), "Together"

Dixieland cornetist, pianist, and composer who worked with Louis Armstrong, Jean Goldkette, Frankie Trumbauer, Jack Teagarden, and Paul Whiteman and influenced Hoagy Carmichael and Bing Crosby.

Irving Berlin
"All by Myself," "Always," "Blue Skies," "Marie," "Waiting at the End of the Road," "What'll I Do?"

Song composer and lyricist of popular and Broadway standards. Also published sheet music.

Ben Bernie
"Ain't She Sweet," "Sweet Georgia Brown" (with Maceo Pinkard), "Tea for Two"

Jazz violinist with his orchestra, sometimes called Ben Bernie and All the Lads. Best known as cocomposer of "Sweet Georgia Brown."

Earl Burtnett
"If I Should Lose You," "Leave Me with a Smile," "Mandalay," "Sleep"

Songwriter, bandleader, and pianist who took over Art Hickman's band in 1929.

Eddie Cantor
"Charley, My Boy," "I Love Her, She Loves Me," "If You Knew Susie," "I've Got the Yes! We Have No Bananas Blues," "Makin' Whoopee," "Margie," "No, No, Nora," "You'd Be Surprised"

Singer, songwriter, comedian, performing artist, actor, and radio personality.

Hoagy Carmichael
"Rockin' Chair," "Star Dust," "Washboard Blues" (with Paul Whiteman)

Composer, singer, and pianist, best known for his popular standards. Also composed "Georgia on My Mind," which he recorded with Bix Beiderbecke in 1930.

Fiddlin' John Carson
"The Little Old Log Cabin in the Lane," "The Old Hen Cackled and the Rooster's Going to Crow"

Old-time fiddler and early country-music recording artist who made close to 150 recordings between 1923 and 1931.

The Carter Family
"Can the Circle Be Unbroken," "Engine 143," "Keep on the Sunny Side," "River of Jordan," "Wildwood Flower," "Will You Miss Me when I'm Gone"

Family of American folk singers who performed spirituals, traditional songs, bluegrass, and country music.

Enrico Caruso
"A Dream"
Popular Italian-born tenor with the Metropolitan Opera who recorded many long-playing records in the 1910s and throughout 1920 before retiring in 1921.

Maurice Chevalier
"Louise," "Valentine"
French film actor and singer whose popularity grew in the United States in the 1920s.

"Crying" Sam Collins
"Hesitation Blues," "The Jailhouse Blues," "Midnight Special Blues," "The Worried Man Blues," "Yellow Dog Blues"
Blues guitarist and singer whose sound recordings helped popularize the blues in mainstream culture.

Bing Crosby
"From Monday on" (with Bix Beiderbecke), "Mississippi Mud" (with Bix Beiderbecke and Irene Taylor), "Ol' Man River" (with Bix Beiderbecke), "That's Grandma"
Crooner and songwriter whose career was launched in the 1920s.

Vaughn De Leath
"Are You Lonesome Tonight?," "Ukulele Lady"
Popular radio singer and recording artist who was called the "First Lady of Radio" in her day.

Cliff "Ukulele Ike" Edwards
"I Can't Give You Anything but Love," "Singin' in the Rain"
Popular singer, entertainer, and ukulele player who helped popularize the ukulele during the 1920s.

Duke Ellington
"Black and Tan Fantasy," "Creole Love Call"
Musical arranger, bandleader, jazz pianist, and one of the most prolific and influential composers of jazz and swing music.

Seger Ellis
"Prairie Blues," "Sentimental Blues," "Sunday"
Jazz pianist, singer, and bandleader who worked on Houston radio and in vaudeville. Later married singer Irene Taylor.

Ruth Etting
"'Deed I Do," "Love Me or Leave Me," "Shaking the Blues Away"
Popular singer with many hits in the 1920s and 1930s. Also acted in films and worked in theater and radio.

Jan Garber
"Baby Face," "Sonny Boy," "Was It a Dream?"
Popular dance bandleader during the 1920s.

George Gershwin
An American in Paris, "Fascinating Rhythm," "Oh, Lady Be Good!," *Rhapsody in Blue*
Legendary composer and pianist who often worked with his brother Ira Gershwin, particularly on musicals. Later began to compose film scores as well.

Jean Goldkette
"Painting the Clouds with Sunshine," "Slow River," "Sunny Disposish," "Tiptoe Through the Tulips"
Jazz pianist and bandleader who worked with such musicians as Bix Beiderbecke, Hoagy Carmichael, Eddie Lang, Tommy and Jimmy Dorsey, and Frankie Trumbauer during the 1920s.

Benny Goodman
"Clarinetitis," "Room 1411"
Clarinetist and recording artist who would become one of the best-known and most successful jazz ensemble leaders in the 1930s.

Otto Gray and His Oklahoma Cowboys
"Bury Me on the Lone Prairie," "Midnight Special," "Pistol Pete's Midnight Special"
The first commercially successful Western string band in the United States, composed of genuine cowboys from Oklahoma.

Annette Hanshaw
"Ain't Cha?," "Ain't He Sweet?," "Black Bottom," "Carolina Moon," "Do, Do, Do," "Forget-Me-Not," "I Can't Give You Anything but Love," "I Get the Blues when It Rains," "What Wouldn't I Do for That Man"
Jazz singer with a flapper persona who recorded under several pseudonyms in addition to her own name, best known for adding "That's all" at the end of her songs.

Bob Haring
"Dardanella," "Go Wash an Elephant," "Some Sweet Day"

Popular bandleader and arranger in the 1920s and 1930s.

Marion Harris
"Beale Street Blues," "Did You Mean It?," "Left All Alone Again Blues," "Look for the Silver Lining," "St. Louis Blues," "Somebody Loves Me," "Who's Sorry Now?"

One of the first white singers to record blues and jazz.

Fletcher Henderson
"Have It Ready," "Shake Your Feet," "The Stampede," "Swamp Blues"

Hot jazz composer, arranger, bandleader, and pianist who was influenced by Paul Whiteman, influenced Duke Ellington, and worked with such musicians as Louis Armstrong, Don Redman, Charlie Dixon, and Coleman Hawkins, among others.

Earl "Fatha" Hines
"Muggles" (with Louis Armstrong), "Tight like This" (with Louis Armstrong), "Weather Bird" (with Louis Armstrong), "West End Blues" (with Louis Armstrong)

Jazz pianist who worked with Louis Armstrong's Hot Five and collaborated with Armstrong on several important jazz recordings. Became the leader of a Chicago-based jazz band at the end of the 1920s.

Lonnie Johnson
"6/88 Glide"

Songwriter, twelve-string guitarist, and singer of jazz and the blues who recorded for Okeh Records in the 1920s. Worked with numerous other musicians, including Louis Armstrong, Bessie Smith, Eddie Lang, and Duke Ellington. Famous for his single-string guitar solos.

Al Jolson
"Avalon," "California, Here I Come," "I'm Sitting on Top of the World," "My Buddy," "My Mammy," "Sonny Boy," "Swanee," "Toot, Toot, Tootsie," "When the Red, Red Robin Comes Bob, Bob, Bobbin' Along"

Popular singer and actor who starred in *The Jazz Singer* (1927), the movie that marked the advent of talking motion pictures.

Isham Jones
"I'll See You in My Dreams," "It Had to Be You," "Not a Cloud in the Sky"

Composer and popular dance bandleader who worked with such musicians as Gordon Jenkins, Gus Kahn, Bing Crosby, and Benny Goodman.

Roger Wolfe Kahn
"Anything You Say," "Crazy Rhythm," "Imagination"

Musician and songwriter who became leader of a jazz orchestra at age sixteen. An especially animated conductor whose compositions include Broadway musicals.

Helen Kane
"Button up Your Overcoat," "I Wanna Be Loved by You," "Is There Anything Wrong with That?," "That's My Weakness Now"

Popular singer whose voice and appearance allegedly helped inspire the character Betty Boop, created by animator Max Fleischer.

Irving Kaufman
"Five Foot Two, Eyes of Blue," "Roam On, My Little Gypsy Sweetheart"

Popular singer and vaudeville entertainer who worked with a number of jazz musicians, including Bix Beiderbecke, Eddie Lang, and Frankie Trumbauer.

Eddie Lang
"April Kisses," "Doin' Things," "For No Reason at All in C" (with Bix Beiderbecke and Frankie Trumbauer), "Knockin' a Jug" (with Louis Armstrong and Jack Teagarden), "Singin' the Blues" (with Bix Beiderbecke and Frankie Trumbauer), "Sunshine"

Prolific composer and highly influential jazz guitarist who worked with many prominent bandleaders of the 1920s.

Sam Lanin
"My Ohio Home," "St. Louis Blues," "You Took Advantage of Me"

Bandleader and arranger who recorded many popular standards with numerous ensembles during the 1920s.

Ted Lewis
"Bee's Knees," "Clarinet Marmalade," "A Good Man Is Hard to Find," "Hi-Diddle-Diddle," "I'm the

Medicine Man for the Blues," "When My Baby Smiles at Me"

Entertainer, comedian, singer, and leader of a hot jazz band that rivaled the Paul Whiteman Orchestra.

Vincent Lopez
"Nola"

Jazz ensemble leader, radio personality, and early Latin influence on American jazz.

Abe Lyman
"Bugle Call Rag," "California Blues," "Honey Babe"

Popular bandleader of Abe Lyman's California Ambassador Hotel Orchestra who often worked with Gus Arnheim.

Glenn Miller
"Hello, Lola," "If I Could Be with You One Hour Tonight," "Room 1411"

Composer and trombonist who worked with Benny Goodman, Nat Shilkret, and Tommy Dorsey.

Jelly Roll Morton
"Black Bottom Stomp," "Kansas City Stomp," "Someday Sweetheart," "Wolverine Blues"

Creole ragtime and jazz pianist, bandleader, and composer, often credited as being the first to successfully arrange jazz music while still allowing for improvisation.

Red Nichols
"Five Pennies," "Ida, Sweet as Apple Cider"

Jazz cornetist, composer, and bandleader whose ensembles included musicians such as Jack Teagarden, Benny Goodman, Glenn Miller, and Eddie Lang.

Joe "King" Oliver
"Dippermouth Blues," "Doctor Jazz," "Snag It"

Dixieland bandleader and cornetist who mentored Louis Armstrong.

George Olsen
"A Precious Little Thing Called Love," "Who?"

Dance bandleader of the 1920s who worked on Broadway and in the *Ziegfeld Follies* of 1924.

Edward "Kid" Ory
"Ory's Creole Trombone," "Society Blues"

Creole jazz trombonist and bandleader who worked with such musicians as Joe "King" Oliver, Jelly Roll Morton, and Louis Armstrong during the 1920s.

Maceo Pinkard
"Here Comes the Show Boat," "Sugar," "Sweet Georgia Brown" (with Ben Bernie)

Composer, lyricist, Broadway producer, and publisher, best known for cowriting "Sweet Georgia Brown."

Ben Pollack
"'Deed I Do," "Memphis Blues," "Singapore Sorrows," "Sweet Sue—Just You"

Chicago-born drummer and bandleader who worked with Jack Teagarden, Benny Goodman, and Glenn Miller, among others.

Cole Porter
"Let's Do It, Let's Fall in Love," "What Is This Thing Called Love?," "You Do Something to Me"

Composer and songwriter whose musical numbers achieved mainstream success.

Ma Rainey
"Bad Luck Blues," "Black Bottom," "Bo-Weevil Blues," "Moonshine Blues," "See See Rider Blues," "Soon This Morning"

Early blues singer who became known as the "Mother of the Blues."

Leo Reisman
"Happy Days Are Here Again," "The Wedding of the Painted Doll"

Popular dance and hot jazz ensemble leader and violinist.

Harry Reser
"Adorable," "Avalon Town," "Chinky Butterfly," "Clicquot," "The Two of Us," "You've Got That Thing"

Hot jazz ensemble leader and banjo player who worked as director of the Clicquot Club Eskimos banjo orchestra on the NBC radio show of the same name.

The Rhythm Boys
"From Monday on," "Mississippi Mud"

Singing trio of Bing Crosby, Harry Barris, and Al Rinker that joined the Paul Whiteman Orchestra in 1926.

Jimmie Rodgers
"Blue Yodel," "In the Jailhouse Now," "Sleep, Baby, Sleep"

An early country-music singer and songwriter who popularized honky-tonk and was known for his yodeling style.

Ben Selvin
"Dardanella," "Margie," "The Original Charleston"

Dance bandleader, violinist, and innovator of recorded music, said to have made more than nine thousand recordings during his career.

Nat Shilkret
An American in Paris (as conductor), "The Lonesome Road" (with Gene Austin)

Composer, arranger, conductor, clarinetist, pianist, radio producer, and Victor Records music director. Worked with Louis Armstrong, Bing Crosby, and many other popular musicians of the 1920s.

Bessie Smith
"Cemetery Blues," "Downhearted Blues," "Gulf Coast Blues," "St. Louis Blues" (with Louis Armstrong)

Blues singer contemporary with Mamie Smith who became known as "The Empress of the Blues." Appeared in the film *St. Louis Blues* in 1929.

Mamie Smith
"Crazy Blues"

A vaudeville singer who was the first black vocalist to make a blues recording, establishing the market for recorded African American music.

"Whispering" Jack Smith
"Gimme Me a Little Kiss, Will Ya, Huh?," "Me and My Shadow"

Baritone novelty singer known for his intimate, "crooning" style of singing, which he adopted due to lung injuries sustained in World War I.

Irene Taylor
"I Ain't Thinkin' 'Bout You," "I Must Have That Man," "Mississippi Mud" (with Bing Crosby and Bix Beiderbecke), "My Castle in the Clouds"

Popular singer who recorded and performed with Paul Whiteman and His Orchestra. Later married pianist Seger Ellis.

Jack Teagarden
"Knockin' a Jug" (with Louis Armstrong and Eddie Lang), "She's a Great, Great Girl" (with Roger Wolfe Kahn), "That's a Serious Thing" (with Eddie Condon)

Jazz trombonist, bandleader, composer, and singer who worked with Louis Armstrong, Bix Beiderbecke, Roger Wolfe Kahn, and other prominent musicians of the 1920s.

Frankie Trumbauer
"For No Reason at All in C" (with Eddie Lang and Bix Beiderbecke), "Krazy Kat," "Singin' the Blues" (with Eddie Lang and Bix Beiderbecke)

Dixieland and hot jazz saxophonist and composer who often collaborated with Bix Beiderbecke.

Sophie Tucker
"My Yiddishe Momme," "Some of These Days"

Singer and actor also known as "The Last of the Red Hot Mamas." Received singing lessons from vocalists such as Mamie Smith and Ethel Waters.

Rudy Vallée
"Honey"

Popular singer, actor, and bandleader known for being one of the first crooners. Rivaled Bing Crosby and Russ Columbo for a short while in the 1920s and 1930s.

Fats Waller
"Ain't Misbehavin'," "Honey Suckle Rose," "I've Got a Feeling I'm Falling," "Squeeze Me"

Composer, singer, and jazz pianist especially known for his stride piano playing style.

Fred Waring
"Laugh, Clown, Laugh," "Memory Lane," "Sleep"

Singer, arranger, and leader of the Dixieland band Waring's Pennsylvanians.

Ethel Waters
"Am I Blue?," "Dinah," "Sweet Georgia Brown"

Singer of blues, spirituals, popular music, and Broadway musicals who began to appear in films in the late 1920s.

Ted Weems
"Piccolo Pete," "Somebody Stole My Gal"

Popular dance bandleader whose All-American Band played at President Warren G. Harding's inaugural ball.

Paul Whiteman
"Among My Souvenirs," "Linger Awhile," "Mississippi Mud" (with Bing Crosby, Bix Beiderbecke, and Irene Taylor), "My Mammy," *Rhapsody in Blue* (composed by George Gershwin), "Say It with Music," "Somebody Loves Me," "Song of India," "Valencia," "Washboard Blues" (with Hoagy Carmichael), "Whispering"

Popular jazz bandleader called the "King of Jazz," whose orchestra appeared frequently on radio and in film. One of the greatest positive influences on the success of African American bandleaders and musicians in the 1920s.

Bert Williams
"The Moon Shines on the Moonshine"

Popular entertainer, comedian, and singer who was the first African American to become a Broadway star.

Clarence Williams
"Baby, Won't You Please Come Home," "'Tain't Nobody's Business if I Do"

Jazz pianist, singer, and composer who was one of the foremost African American music publishers in the country. Recorded with Louis Armstrong, Sidney Bechet, Joe "King" Oliver, and Bessie Smith, among others.

Margaret Young
"Hard-Hearted Hannah," "Lovin' Sam, the Sheik of Alabam'," "Somebody's Wrong," "Ukulele Lady," "Way down Yonder in New Orleans"

Popular singer and comedian known for her novelty songs.

Melissa Ursula Dawn Goldsmith

Music: Top-Selling U.S. Recordings

"Ain't Misbehavin'"
Fats Waller
1929

Recorded for Victor Records, featuring Waller playing stride piano. Won a posthumous Grammy Hall of Fame Award in 1984.

"Ain't She Sweet"
Ben Bernie and His Orchestra; Gene Austin; Johnny Marvin
1927

Recorded in three versions in 1927, which together made the song a hit. Repopularized by the Beatles in the 1960s and variety shows such as *The Lawrence Welk Show* in the 1970s.

"Ain't We Got Fun?"
Gus Van and Joe Schenck
1921

Brought great financial success to popular musical comedy duo Van and Schenck. Mentioned in F. Scott Fitzgerald's novel *The Great Gatsby* (1925) as the epitome of the "Roaring Twenties."

"Alabamy Bound"
Al Jolson
1924

A top-selling Tin Pan Alley song originally meant for the vaudeville stage. Rerecorded by Paul Whiteman and His Orchestra (1924) and Isham Jones and His Orchestra (1925) with less success.

"All Alone"
John McCormack
1925

The famous Irish tenor's last top-selling sound recording.

"All by Myself"
Ted Lewis and His Band
1921

A jazz version that became a best seller for Lewis's band. Originally written by Irving Berlin for a musical revue.

"Always"
George Olsen and His Music
1926

A 1925 Irving Berlin song popularized by Olsen's orchestra. Originally intended for the stage musical *The Cocoanuts* (1925) but later cut from the work.

"April Showers"
Al Jolson
1921

First performed by Jolson in the 1921 musical *Bombo*.

"Are You Lonesome Tonight?"
Vaughn De Leath
1927

A top-selling recording performed by the "First Lady of Radio," later remade by Elvis Presley in 1960.

"Avalon"
Al Jolson
1920

A highly successful song subsequently inserted into the musicals *Sinbad* (1918) and *Bombo* (1921). Later became a jazz standard.

"Black and Tan Fantasy"
Duke Ellington
1927

A top-selling jazz recording that epitomized the Harlem Renaissance. Later covered by Thelonious Monk.

"Blue Skies"
Ben Selvin and His Orchestra
1927

A popular version of the Irving Berlin song that reached number one in the charts.

"Blue Yodel"
Jimmie Rodgers
1928

A top-selling song that helped popularize folk and blues in the United States, featuring a twelve-bar blues structure with yodeling in the refrain.

"Bye Bye Blackbird"
Gene Austin
1926

Composed by Ray Henderson with lyrics by Mort Dixon. Later became a popular music standard.

"California, Here I Come"
Al Jolson; Georgie Price
1924

A best-selling recording by Jolson and a hit for vaudeville singer Price, both in the same year.

"Charleston"
Arthur Gibbs and His Gang
1924

The best-selling recording that created the dance craze of the same name.

"Crazy Blues"
Mamie Smith and Her Jazz Hounds
1920

A best-selling blues recording that paved the way for female blues singers such as Bessie Smith.

"Dardanella"
Ben Selvin and His Orchestra
1920

Allegedly sold over five million copies in the 1920s.

"Dippermouth Blues"
King Oliver's Creole Jazz Band
1923

A Dixieland favorite featuring a young Louis Armstrong, then nicknamed "Dipper."

"Downhearted Blues"
Bessie Smith
1923

A top-selling blues recording of the 1920s, composed by singer Alberta Hunter and bandleader Lovie Austin.

"Handful of Keys"
Fats Waller
1929

One of Waller's best-selling recordings and original compositions in stride piano style.

"Hard-Hearted Hannah"
Dolly Kay
1924

A popular Tin Pan Alley standard about a femme fatale.

"I Can't Give You Anything but Love, Baby"
Cliff "Ukulele Ike" Edwards
1928

Originally featured in the 1928 Broadway musical *Blackbird Revue*.

"If You Knew Susie"
Eddie Cantor
1925

Cantor's best-known success of the 1920s, still popularly associated with him.

"I'll See You in My Dreams"
Isham Jones with the Ray Miller Orchestra
1924

Remained at number one in popular music charts for seven weeks.

"It Had to Be You"
Isham Jones and His Orchestra
1924

A popular standard written by Jones and Gus Kahn, often classified as a torch song.

"Keep on the Sunny Side"
The Carter Family
1928

Originally a nineteenth-century inspirational song, later the theme song of the Carter Family's radio show.

"King Porter Stomp"
Jelly Roll Morton
1923

Composed by Morton in 1905 but not recorded until 1923.

"The Little Old Log Cabin in the Lane"
Fiddlin' John Carson
1923

Originally composed in the late nineteenth century for minstrel shows. Subsequently became a bluegrass standard.

"Makin' Whoopee"
Eddie Cantor
1928

A popular standard with blues inflections, performed by Cantor in the 1928 Broadway musical *Whoopee!*

"Manhattan"
Ben Selvin and His Orchestra
1925

The first major hit from songwriting team Richard Rodgers and Lorenz Hart.

"The Man I Love"
Marion Harris
1927

Originally written as "The Girl I Love" for the musical *Lady, Be Good!* (1924) but cut from the final production.

"Margie"
Eddie Cantor
1921

Ranked number one on the popular music charts for five weeks. Named after Cantor's daughter Marjorie.

"Me and My Shadow"
"Whispering" Jack Smith
1927

The recording that first popularized this well-known standard by Dave Dreyer and Billy Rose.

"Muskrat Ramble"
Louis Armstrong and His Hot Five
1926

The original version of what would become the Hot Five's most frequently recorded song.

"My Man"
Fanny Brice
1922

Became Brice's signature song in the *Ziegfeld Follies of 1921*.

"The Prisoner's Song"
Vernon Dalhart
1924

A top-selling recording of the decade, charting at number one for twelve weeks. Was then the biggest vocal hit in recording history.

Rhapsody in Blue
George Gershwin with Paul Whiteman and His Orchestra
1924

Features Gershwin on piano. The song that established him as a serious composer.

"See See Rider Blues"
Ma Rainey
1924

The recording that popularized this blues standard, featuring Louis Armstrong on cornet.

"Singin' the Blues"
Frankie Trumbauer and His Orchestra
1927

Features Eddie Lang on guitar and a famous cornet solo by Bix Beiderbecke.

"Some of These Days"
Sophie Tucker with Ted Lewis and His Band
1926

Tucker's signature song, first recorded by her in 1911.

"Sonny Boy"
Al Jolson
1928

Allegedly sold more than a million copies in the 1920s.

"Star Dust"
Hoagy Carmichael and His Pals
1927

The original version of what would become one of the most recorded songs in American history.

"St. Louis Blues"
Marion Harris; Louis Armstrong with Bessie Smith
1920; 1925

A top-selling hit in 1920 and even more popular in 1925, best known from the Armstrong and Smith recording.

"Swanee"
Al Jolson
1920

Sold nearly two million records and remained at number one in the charts for nine weeks.

"Sweet Georgia Brown"
Ben Bernie and His Hotel Roosevelt Orchestra
1925
  Held steady at number one for five weeks.

"West End Blues"
Louis Armstrong
1928
  Armstrong's best-selling single, composed by Joe "King" Oliver, and the best-known recording of the song.

"When My Baby Smiles at Me"
Ted Lewis
1920
  Lewis's first big hit, which later became his theme song.

"Who?"
George Olsen and His Music
1925
  A fox-trot recording of a Jerome Kern song that sold over one million copies. Originally featured in the musical *Sunny* (1925).

"Wildwood Flower"
The Carter Family
1928
  A nineteenth-century parlor song, revived as a folk song to huge acclaim.

"The Wreck of the Old 97"
Vernon Dalhart
1924
  Based on the 1903 Southern Railway mail train crash, allegedly written by an eyewitness.

"Yes! We Have No Bananas"
Ben Selvin and His Orchestra with Irving Kaufman; Billy Jones
1923
  A novelty song featured in the Broadway revue *Make It Snappy* (1922), originally performed onstage by Eddie Cantor.

Melissa Ursula Dawn Goldsmith

Sports: Winners of Major Events

MAJOR LEAGUE BASEBALL

World Series
Year Result
1920 Cleveland Indians (American League) 5, Brooklyn Robins (National League) 2[1]
1921 New York Giants (NL) 5, New York Yankees (AL) 3
1922 New York Giants (NL) 4, New York Yankees (AL) 0 (tie 1)[2]
1923 New York Yankees (AL) 4, New York Giants (NL) 2
1924 Washington Senators (AL) 4, New York Giants (NL) 3
1925 Pittsburgh Pirates (NL) 4, Washington Senators (AL) 3
1926 St. Louis Cardinals (NL) 4, New York Yankees (AL) 3
1927 New York Yankees (AL) 4, Pittsburgh Pirates (NL) 0
1928 New York Yankees (AL) 4, St. Louis Cardinals (NL) 0
1929 Philadelphia Athletics (AL) 4, Chicago Cubs (NL) 1

American League Most Valuable Players
Year Player
1920 none
1921 none
1922 George Sisler, St. Louis Browns
1923 Babe Ruth, New York Yankees
1924 Walter Johnson, Washington Senators
1925 Roger Peckinpaugh, Washington Senators
1926 George Burns, Cleveland Indians
1927 Lou Gehrig, New York Yankees
1928 Mickey Cochran, Philadelphia Athletics
1929 none

National League Most Valuable Players
Year Player
1920 none
1921 none
1922 none
1923 none
1924 Dazzy Vance, Brooklyn Robins
1925 Rogers Hornsby, St. Louis Cardinals
1926 Bob O'Farrell, St. Louis Cardinals
1927 Paul Waner, Pittsburgh Pirates
1928 Jim Bottomley, St. Louis Cardinals
1929 Rodgers Hornsby, Chicago Cubs

1. The Brooklyn Robins officially changed names to become the Dodgers in 1932.
2. World Series games of the era permitted tie games. The 1907, 1912, and 1922 World Series each had a tied game. The 1922 World Series established the familiar best-of-seven-games format.

NEGRO LEAGUE BASEBALL

World Series
Year Result
1920 none
1921 none
1922 none
1923 none
1924 Kansas City Monarchs (Negro National League) 5, Philadelphia Hilldales (Eastern Colored League) 4
1925 Philadelphia Hilldales (ECL) 5, Kansas City Monarchs (NNL) 1
1926 Chicago American Giants (NNL) 5, Atlantic City Bacharachs (ECL) 3
1927 Chicago American Giants (NNL) 5, Atlantic City Bacharachs (ECL) 3
1928 none
1929 none

PROFESSIONAL FOOTBALL

National Football League Championship
Year Result
1920 Akron Pros 8–0–3[3]
1921 Chicago Stanleys 9–1–1
1922 Canton Bulldogs 10–0–2
1923 Canton Bulldogs 11–0–1
1924 Cleveland Bulldogs 7–1–1
1925 Chicago Cardinals 11–2–1
1926 Frankford Yellow Jackets 14–1–2
1927 New York Giants 11–1–1
1928 Providence Steam Roller 8–1–2
1929 Green Bay Packers 12–0–1

Canadian Football League Championship (Grey Cup)
Year Result
1920 Toronto Varsity Blues 16, Toronto Argonauts 3
1921 Toronto Argonauts 23, Edmonton Eskimos 0
1922 Queen's University 13, Edmonton Elks 1
1923 Queen's University 54, Regina Rugby Club 0
1924 Queen's University 11, Toronto Balmy Beach 2
1925 Ottawa Senators 24, Winnipeg Tammany Tigers 1
1926 Ottawa Senators 10, Toronto Varsity Blues 7
1927 Toronto Balmy Beach 9, Hamilton Tigers 6
1928 Hamilton Tigers 30, Regina Roughriders 0
1929 Hamilton Tigers 14, Regina Roughriders 3

3. There were no playoffs in the National Football League at this time. The league declared the team with the best record at the end of the season the champion. Wins, losses, and ties are listed.

COLLEGE FOOTBALL

National Collegiate Athletic Association (NCAA) Champions
Year Champions (based on multiple title-granting entities)
1920 California, Harvard, Notre Dame, and Princeton
1921 California, Cornell, Iowa, Lafayette, and Washington & Jefferson
1922 California, Cornell, and Princeton
1923 California, Cornell, Illinois, and Michigan
1924 Notre Dame and Pennsylvania
1925 Alabama, Dartmouth, and Michigan
1926 Alabama, Lafayette, Michigan, Navy, and Stanford
1927 Georgia, Illinois, Notre Dame, Texas A&M, and Yale
1928 Detroit, Georgia Tech, and Southern California
1929 Notre Dame, Pittsburgh, and Southern California

Rose Bowl Winners
Year Result
1920 Harvard 7, Oregon 6
1921 California 28, Ohio State 0
1922 California 0, Washington & Jefferson 0
1923 Southern California 14, Pennsylvania State 3
1924 Navy 14, Washington 14
1925 Notre Dame 27, Stanford 10
1926 Alabama 20, Washington 19
1927 Alabama 7, Stanford 7
1928 Stanford 7, Pittsburgh 6
1929 Georgia Tech 8, California 7

PROFESSIONAL HOCKEY

National Hockey League Championship (Stanley Cup)
Year Result
1920 Ottawa Senators 3, Seattle Metropolitans 2
1921 Ottawa Senators 3, Vancouver Millionaires 2
1922 Toronto St. Pats 3, Vancouver Millionaires 2
1923 Ottawa Senators 2, Edmonton Eskimos 0
1924 Montreal Canadiens 2, Calgary Tigers 0
1925 Victoria Cougars 3, Montreal Canadiens 1
1926 Montreal Maroons 3, Victoria Cougars 1
1927 Ottawa Senators 2, Boston Bruins 0 (ties 2)
1928 New York Rangers 3, Montreal Maroons 2
1929 Boston Bruins 2, New York Rangers 0

National Hockey League Most Valuable Players (Hart Memorial Trophy)
Year Player
1920 none
1921 none
1922 none
1923 Frank Nighbor, Ottawa Senators
1924 Billy Burch, Hamilton Tigers
1925 Nels Stewart, Montreal Maroons
1926 Herb Gardiner, Montreal Canadiens
1927 Howie Morenz, Montreal Canadiens
1928 Roy Worters, New York Americans
1929 Nels Stewart, Montreal Maroons

AUTOMOBILE RACING

Indianapolis 500 Winners
Year Winner Average Speed
1920 Gaston Chevrolet (89 miles per hour)
1921 Tommy Milton (90 mph)
1922 Jimmy Murphy (94 mph)
1923 Tommy Milton (91 mph)
1924 Lora L. Corum; Joe Boyer[4] (98 mph)
1925 Peter DePaolo (101 mph)
1926 Frank Lockhart (96 mph)
1927 George Souders (98 mph)
1928 Louis Mayer (99 mph)
1929 Ray Keech (98 mph)

4. Corum began the race, but Boyer completed the race in Corum's car.

BOXING

Heavyweight Champion of the World
Year Champion
1919–1926 Jack Dempsey
1926–1928 Gene Tunney[5]
1929 none

5. Tunney retired as champion in 1928, leaving the heavyweight championship vacant until 1930.

RUNNING

Boston Marathon Winners
Year Winner
1920 Peter Trivoulides
1921 Frank Zuna
1922 Clarence DeMar
1923 Clarence DeMar
1924 Clarence DeMar
1925 Charles Mellor
1926 John C. Miles
1927 Clarence DeMar
1928 Clarence DeMar
1929 John C. Miles

YACHTING

America's Cup
Year Result
1920 *Resolute* (United States) 3, *Shamrock IV* (Northern Ireland) 2

PROFESSIONAL TENNIS

Men's Singles

Year	Australian Open	French Open	Wimbledon	U.S. Open
1920	Pat O'Hara Wood	André Gobert	Bill Tilden	Bill Tilden
1921	Rhys Gemmell	Jean Samazeuilh	Bill Tilden	Bill Tilden
1922	James Anderson	Henri Cochet	Gerald Patterson	Bill Tilden
1923	Pat O'Hara Wood	François Blanchy	William Johnston	Bill Tilden
1924	James Anderson	Jean Borotra	Jean Borotra	Bill Tilden
1925	James Anderson	René Lacoste	René Lacoste	Bill Tilden
1926	John Hawkes	Henri Cochet	Jean Borotra	René Lacoste
1927	Gerald Patterson	René Lacoste	Henri Cochet	René Lacoste
1928	Jean Borotra	Henri Cochet	René Lacoste	Henri Cochet
1929	John Conlin Gregory	René Lacoste	Henri Cochet	Bill Tilden

Women's Singles

Year	Australian Open	French Open	Wimbledon	U.S. Open
1920	not established	Suzanne Lenglen	Suzanne Lenglen	Molla Bjurstedt Mallory
1921	not established	Suzanne Lenglen	Suzanne Lenglen	Molla Bjurstedt Mallory
1922	Margaret Molesworth	Suzanne Lenglen	Suzanne Lenglen	Molla Bjurstedt Mallory
1923	Margaret Molesworth	Suzanne Lenglen	Suzanne Lenglen	Helen Wills Moody
1924	Sylvia Lance Harper	Julie "Diddie" Vlasto	Kitty McKane Godfree	Helen Wills Moody
1925	Daphne Akhurst	Suzanne Lenglen	Suzanne Lenglen	Helen Wills Moody
1926	Daphne Akhurst	Suzanne Lenglen	Kitty McKane Godfree	Molla Bjurstedt Mallory
1927	Esna Boyd	Kornelia "Kea" Bouman	Helen Wills Moody	Helen Wills Moody
1928	Daphne Akhurst	Helen Wills Moody	Helen Wills Moody	Helen Wills Moody
1929	Daphne Akhurst	Helen Wills Moody	Helen Wills Moody	Helen Wills Moody

Davis Cup

Year	Winner	Runner-up	Final Score
1920	United States	Australia	5–0
1921	United States	Japan	5–0
1922	United States	Australia	4–1
1923	United States	Australia	4–1
1924	United States	Australia	5–0
1925	United States	France	5–0
1926	United States	France	4–1
1927	France	United States	3–2
1928	France	United States	4–1
1929	France	United States	3–2

PROFESSIONAL GOLF

Men

Year	U.S. Open	British Open	PGA Championship
1920	Ted Ray	George Duncan	Jock Hutchinson
1921	Jim Barnes	Jock Hutchison	Walter Hagen
1922	Gene Sarazen	Walter Hagen	Gene Sarazen
1923	Bobby Jones	Arthur Havers	Gene Sarazen
1924	Cyril Walker	Walter Hagen	Walter Hagen
1925	Willie Macfarlane	Jim Barnes	Walter Hagen
1926	Bobby Jones	Bobby Jones	Walter Hagen
1927	Tommy Armour	Bobby Jones	Walter Hagen
1928	Johnny Farrell	Walter Hagen	Leo Diegel
1929	Bobby Jones	Walter Hagen	Leo Diegel

HORSE RACING

Year	Kentucky Derby	Preakness Stakes	Belmont Stakes
1920	Paul Jones	Man o' War	Man o' War
1921	Behave Yourself	Broomspun	Grey Lag
1922	Morvich	Pillory	Pillory
1923	Zev	Vigil	Zev
1924	Black Gold	Nellie Morse	Mad Play
1925	Flying Ebony	Coventry	American Flag
1926	Bubbling Over	Display	Crusader
1927	Whiskery	Bostonian	Chance Shot
1928	Reigh Count	Victorian	Vito
1929	Clyde Van Dusen	Dr. Freeland	Blue Larkspur

OLYMPIC GAMES

Summer Games

Year	Location	Medal Count Winner	Number of Medals
1920	Antwerp, Belgium	United States	95
1924	Paris, France	United States	99
1928	Amsterdam, Netherlands	United States	56

Winter Games

Year	Location	Medal Count Winner	Number of Medals
1924	Chamonix, France	Norway	17
1928	St. Moritz, Switzerland	Norway	15

■ Time Line

Additional dates relating to major U.S. legislation, Supreme Court cases, films, plays, radio shows, literature, popular music, and sports can be found in other appendixes.

1920

International: (Jan. 16) The League of Nations holds its first council meeting in Paris six days after the Treaty of Versailles went into effect. (Feb. 24) The German Workers' Party adds National Socialist to its name, becoming the NSDAP or Nazi Party. (Apr. 23) The Grand National Assembly of Turkey forms a new government and denounces the rule of Sultan Mehmed VI. (Aug. 10) The Treaty of Sèvres is signed between the Ottoman Empire and the Allied Powers of World War I.

Government and politics: (Jan. 2) J. Edgar Hoover assists Attorney General A. Mitchell Palmer in carrying out the second Palmer Raid. (Jan. 16) The Eighteenth Amendment to the Constitution goes into effect, prohibiting the manufacture, sale, or transportation of alcohol. (Feb. 14) Carrie Chapman Catt founds the League of Women Voters in Chicago. (Mar. 19) The U.S. Senate votes against joining the League of Nations. (Aug. 18) Tennessee becomes the thirty-sixth state to ratify the Nineteenth Amendment to the Constitution, prohibiting any state from denying women the right to vote.

Military: (June 4) Amendments to the National Defense Act of 1916 reorganize the United States Army into three major components: a standing Regular Army, the National Guard, and the Organized Reserves. The maximum number of enlisted men in the Regular Army is set at 280,000, and two new branches are officially added: the Chemical Warfare Service and the Air Service.

Society: The U.S. Census records a population of more than 106 million. For the first time in history, more Americans live in cities than in rural areas. (Apr. 3) Novelist F. Scott Fitzgerald marries Zelda Sayre. (May 10) The silent film *The Flapper* is released, popularizing the so-called flapper lifestyle.

Business and labor: The U.S. gross national product (GNP) rises to an estimated $91.5 billion, up from an estimated $35.4 billion nominal GNP in 1910.

Transportation and communications: (May 20) Radio station XWA in Montreal, Quebec, begins broadcasting the first regularly scheduled radio programs in North America. (Aug. 31) The first radio news program is broadcast by station 8MK in Detroit, Michigan.

Science and technology: (Apr. 26) Astronomers Harlow Shapley and Heber Curtis hold a public debate about the size of the universe.

Environment: (Mar. 28) The Palm Sunday tornado outbreak spawns at least thirty-eight major tornadoes across the South and Midwest. Nearly four hundred people are killed and more than twelve hundred injured. (July 29) Work begins on the Link River Dam, a project intended to supply irrigation water and hydroelectric power to southern Oregon and northern California.

Arts and literature: Ezra Pound publishes the long poem *Hugh Selwyn Mauberley*. Eugene O'Neill is awarded the Pulitzer Prize in drama. (May 7) The Group of Seven opens its first exhibition of paintings at the Art Gallery of Toronto. Fiction: *The Age of Innocence* (Edith Wharton), *Main Street* (Sinclair Lewis), *This Side of Paradise* (F. Scott Fitzgerald). Plays: *Beyond the Horizon* (Eugene O'Neill), *The Emperor Jones* (Eugene O'Neill).

Popular culture: The ukulele becomes a popular musical instrument, and sheet music begins to include ukulele chords. Movies: *Dr. Jekyll and Mr. Hyde*, *Silk Hosiery*, *Way Down East*. Music: "Dardanella," "The Japanese Sandman," "Swanee." Products: Handheld hair dryers, Mah-Jongg sets.

Sports: Babe Ruth plays his first season with the New York Yankees, hitting fifty-four home runs with a batting average of .376. (Feb. 13) The Negro National League (NNL) is formed, the first African American baseball league to achieve some financial stability and last more than one season. (Apr. 20–Sept. 12) The 1920 Olympic Games are held in Antwerp, Belgium. American athletes take home ninety-five medals. (July) Bill Tilden becomes the first American to win the men's singles tennis championship at Wimbledon. (Aug. 17) Major-league baseball player Ray Chapman of the Cleveland Indians dies as the result of a head injury from a pitched ball. (Sept. 26) The American Professional Football Association (APFA) opens its inaugural season. (Oct. 12) The Cleveland Indians beat the Brooklyn Dodgers to win the World Series. (Nov. 12) Kenesaw Mountain Landis becomes commissioner of baseball.

Crime: (May 5) Nicola Sacco and Bartolomeo Vanzetti are arrested for the April killing of a paymaster and a security guard during an armed robbery in South Braintree, Massachusetts. (May 11) Chicago crime boss Jim Colosimo is gunned down outside a café, possibly by Al Capone. (June 15) Three black circus workers are lynched in Duluth, Minnesota, after being accused of raping a white teenager. (Sept. 16) A bomb explodes in the financial district of New York City, killing thirty-eight and injuring hundreds. The unsolved crime is attributed to Italian anarchists.

1921

International: Weimar Germany begins to experience a period of hyperinflation of its currency that will last through 1923. (Mar. 8) The prime minister of Spain, Eduardo Dato e Iradier, is assassinated by three anarchists in Madrid. (Jul. 1) The Communist Party of China is formed. (July 11) The Irish war of independence ends in a truce, followed by a formal treaty in December. (Nov. 12) The Washington Naval Conference begins.

Government and politics: (Mar. 4) Warren G. Harding is inaugurated as the twenty-ninth president of the United States. (May 3) West Virginia becomes the first state to implement a sales tax. (May 19) The Emergency Quota Act is passed, limiting immigration to the United States based on a quota system. (June 30) Harding nominates former president William Howard Taft for chief justice of the Supreme Court; Taft is approved the same day.

Military: (July 1) John J. Pershing becomes U.S. Army chief of staff. (Nov. 11) Harding dedicates the Tomb of the Unknown Soldier at Arlington National Cemetery.

Society: (Sept. 3) Novelist Louise Rosine is arrested in Atlantic City for wearing a one-piece swimsuit on the beach with her stockings rolled to below her knees. (Sept. 7) Margaret Gorman wins the first Miss America pageant. (Nov. 10) Margaret Sanger founds the American Birth Control League.

Business and labor: The Florida land boom begins, becoming the state's first real estate bubble. (Aug.-Sept.) The Battle of Blair Mountain, a violent confrontation between coal miners, police, and strikebreakers in Logan County, West Virginia, results in scores of deaths and hundreds of arrests.

Transportation and communications: (Oct. 5–13) The 1921 World Series is the first baseball postseason championship to be broadcast over the radio.

Science and technology: (Dec.) Thomas Midgley Jr. discovers that the addition of tetraethyl lead (TEL) to gasoline prevents knocking, a destructive form of improper combustion that occurs in internal combustion engines.

Environment: (Mar. 4) Hot Springs, Arkansas, is designated a national park.

Arts and literature: Edith Wharton is the first woman to be awarded the Pulitzer Prize in the novel. H. L. Mencken publishes the second edition of *The American Language*. Fiction: *Alice Adams* (Booth Tarkington), *The Black Moth* (Georgette Heyer), *The Blind Spot* (Austin Hall and Homer Eon Flint), *Three Soldiers* (John Dos Passos). Plays: *Anna Christie* (Eugene O'Neill), *The Green Goddess* (William Archer), *The Hairy Ape* (Eugene O'Neill).

Popular culture: Listerine mouthwash is first advertised as a preventive for halitosis, transforming bad breath into a major social failing. Americans smoke more than fifty billion cigarettes annually. (Oct. 26) The landmark Chicago Theatre opens. Movies: *The Four Horsemen of the Apocalypse*, *The Kid*, *Orphans of the Storm*, *The Sheik*. Music: "Ain't We Got Fun?," "Look for the Silver Lining," "Margie." Radio: *The Happiness Boys*. Products: Baby Ruth candy bars, Chanel No. 5 perfume, Parker Duofold fountain pens, Wonder Bread.

Sports: (Apr. 30) The 1920 APFA championship is awarded to the Akron Pros. (Jul. 2) Jack Dempsey defends his heavyweight boxing title against the French challenger Georges Carpentier at a match in Jersey City. (Oct. 13) The New York Giants defeat the New York Yankees in the World Series. (Oct. 29) Kentucky's Centre College football team defeats Harvard University by six to zero in a major upset. (Dec.) The Chicago Staleys win the 1921 APFA championship.

Crime: (May 31–June 1) A two-day race riot occurs in Tulsa, Oklahoma, leading to deaths, severe injuries, and the destruction of homes and businesses.

1922

International: (Feb. 6) The Washington Naval Treaty (Five-Power Treaty) is signed in Washington, D.C., limiting the naval armaments of Great Britain, Japan, France, Italy, and the United States to prevent a naval arms race. (Feb. 6) Achille Ratti, archbishop of Milan, is elected to the papacy and takes the name of Pius XI. (Feb. 28) The United Kingdom grants Egypt nominal independence. (Mar. 15) Fuad I, already the sultan of Egypt, takes the title of king. (June 28) The Irish Civil War begins. (Oct. 30) Benito Mussolini is appointed prime minister of Italy. (Nov. 4) A team of archaeologists led by Howard Carter discover the entrance to Tutankhamun's tomb in Egypt's Valley of the Kings. (Dec. 6) The Irish Free State comes into formal existence as a dominion under British sovereignty.

Government and politics: (Feb. 27) The Supreme Court rules in *Leser v. Garnett* that the Nineteenth Amendment is constitutional. (Apr. 14) The *Wall Street Journal* publishes the first investigative report on what will become known as the Teapot Dome scandal. (May 30) The Lincoln Memorial is dedicated in Washington, D.C.

Military: (Feb. 21) The *Roma*, an Italian airship acquired by the United States in 1921, explodes and crashes, killing more than thirty passengers and calling attention to the dangers of hydrogen-filled airships. (Mar. 20) The USS *Langley* is commissioned as the United States' first aircraft carrier. (Sept. 30) The North Carolina training site Camp Bragg is renamed Fort Bragg and becomes a permanent Army post.

Society: Emily Post publishes the first edition of *Etiquette in Society, in Business, in Politics, and at Home*.

Business and labor: (June 21–22) Union workers and strikebreakers are killed during a coal mine strike and subsequent massacre in Herrin, Illinois.

Transportation and communications: (Feb. 8) Harding installs the first radio in the White House.

Science and technology: Herbert McLean Evans and Katharine Scott Bishop discover vitamin E. (Jan. 11) A diabetic teenager is the first human patient to be successfully treated with insulin.

Environment: (Jan. 27–29) A blizzard buries Washington, D.C., under 28 inches of snow, causing the roof of the Knickerbocker Theatre to collapse and kill nearly one hundred patrons.

Arts and literature: (Dec.) Boni and Liveright publishes T. S. Eliot's modernist poem *The Waste Land* in book form. Fiction: *Babbitt* (Sinclair Lewis), *One of Ours* (Willa Cather). Plays: *Abie's Irish Rose* (Anne Nichols), *The Cat and the Canary* (John Willard).

Popular culture: Americans smoke about forty-three billion cigarettes annually. (Jan.) The Motion Picture Producers and Distributors of America (MPPDA) forms under the leadership of William Hays. (Mar. 10) *Variety* notes that one million radio sets are in use across the United States. (Apr. 18) The MPPDA effectively bans Roscoe "Fatty" Arbuckle from working in the U.S. film industry. (July 11) The Hollywood Bowl is officially opened. Movies: *Blood and Sand, Nanook of the North, Robin Hood*. Music: "Hot Lips," "Three O'Clock in the Morning."

Sports: (June 24) APFA is renamed the National Football League (NFL). (Oct. 8) The New York Giants defeat the New York Yankees to win the World Series. (Dec.) The Canton Bulldogs win the NFL championship.

Crime: (Feb. 1) William Desmond Taylor, an actor and film director, is shot in the back in his Los Angeles home by an unknown killer. (Sept. 16) The bodies and love letters of the Reverend Edward Hall and Eleanor Mills are discovered near New Brunswick, New Jersey, prompting nationwide media interest in their murders. (Dec. 18) Five men hijack a Federal Reserve truck transporting $200,000 from the U.S. Mint in Denver, Colorado.

1923

International: (Jan. 11) French and Belgian troops invade and occupy the German region of the Ruhr to ensure the payment of reparations for World War I. (Mar. 2) Canada and the United States sign the Halibut Treaty, an agreement regarding fishing rights in northern Pacific waters. (July 24) The Treaty of Lausanne is signed, partitioning the defunct Ottoman Empire and leading to the recognition of the Republic of Turkey as the successor state. (Sept. 1) An earthquake measuring an estimated 7.9 on the Richter scale devastates the Kantō region of Japan, killing more than 100,000 people. (Sept. 29) The British Mandate for Palestine goes into effect. (Nov. 8–9) Adolf Hitler leads the Beer Hall Putsch, an unsuccessful attempt to overthrow the Bavarian government.

Government and politics: (July) Harding visits Alaska, becoming the first U.S. president to do so. (Aug. 2) Harding dies suddenly in San Francisco, possibly of congestive heart failure. (Aug. 3) Vice President Calvin Coolidge is sworn in as president by his father, a notary public.

Military: (Sept. 8) Seven U.S. Navy destroyers run aground near Honda Point on the California coast, leading to the deaths of twenty-three sailors.

Society: (Jan. 1) Aimee Semple McPherson dedicates Angelus Temple in Los Angeles, California.

Business and labor: (Apr. 5) The Firestone Tire and Rubber Company begins production of low-pressure balloon tires. (Dec. 8) National Dairy Products, the precursor to the Kraft Cheese Company, is incorporated.

Transportation and communications: The New York Symphony Orchestra begins radio broadcasts of live performances. (Feb. 8) The first live hockey game is broadcast over the radio.

Science and technology: (Jan. 13) The Bridging the Golden Gate Association is formed to promote the construction of the Golden Gate Bridge. (Apr.–Aug.) Scientists aboard the USS *Tanager* conduct biological surveys of the northwestern Hawaiian islands. (Dec. 10) Robert Millikan receives the Nobel Prize in Physics for his work on photoelectricity.

Environment: (Jan. 24) The Aztec Ruins National Monument is established in New Mexico. (Mar. 2) Hovenweep National Monument is established in Colorado and Utah.

Arts and literature: Edna St. Vincent Millay wins the Pulitzer Prize in poetry for *The Ballad of the Harp-Weaver*. Frank Lloyd Wright designs several homes in Hollywood using the innovative "textile-block" technique. The Arts Club of Chicago hosts the first American museum exhibition of drawings by Pablo Picasso. Fiction: *Many Marriages* (Sherwood Anderson), *The Prophet* (Kahlil Gibran). Plays: *The Adding Machine* (Elmer Rice), *Icebound* (Owen Davis).

Popular culture: (Jan. 18) Silent film actor Wallace Reid dies while being treated for morphine addiction. (Mar. 3) The first issue of *Time* magazine is published. (Apr. 4) The Warner Bros. film studio is incorporated. (Oct. 16) The Disney Brothers Cartoon Studio is founded. Movies: *The Covered Wagon, The Daring Years, The Hunchback of Notre Dame, Safety Last, The Ten Commandments, A Woman of Paris.* Music: "Charleston," "That Old Gang of Mine," "Yes! We Have No Bananas." Radio: *The Clicquot Club Eskimos, The Eveready Hour, The Ipana Troubadors.* Comic Strips: *Felix.* Products: Drano drain cleaner.

Sports: Golf player Bobby Jones wins his first U.S. Open. (Apr. 18) Yankee Stadium hosts its first game, which the Yankees win. (Oct. 15) The New York Yankees defeat the New York Giants to win the World Series. (Dec.) The Canton Bulldogs win the NFL championship.

Crime: (Jan.) A race riot destroys the town of Rosewood, Florida.

1924

International: (Mar. 24) Greece becomes a republic. (Apr. 1) Hitler is sentenced to five years in prison for his role in the Beer Hall Putsch. (June 8) George Mallory and Andrew Irvine disappear while attempting to reach the summit of Mount Everest. (Sept. 1) The Dawes Plan goes into effect, ending the French and Belgian occupation of the Ruhr. (Dec. 20) Hitler is released from prison.

Government and politics: (Feb. 3) Former president Woodrow Wilson dies in Washington, D.C. (May 10) J. Edgar Hoover is appointed director of the Federal Bureau of Investigation (FBI). (May 26) The Immigration Act of 1924 (Johnson-Reed Act) is enacted, superseding the Emergency Quota Act of 1921 and restricting immigration from Asia and southern and eastern Europe. (June 2) Coolidge signs the Indian Citizenship Act, which confers U.S. citizenship on all Native Americans born within U.S. territories. (July 7) Calvin Coolidge Jr., the president's son, dies of sepsis. (Nov. 4) Coolidge wins the presidential election, defeating the Democratic candidate, John Davis, and the Progressive Party leader, Robert La Follette.

Military: (May 19): The World War Adjusted Compensation Act (also known as the Bonus Act) is enacted, awarding financial benefits to veterans of World War I.

Society: (Apr. 15) Rand McNally publishes its first road atlas, reflecting the increasing popularity of automobile travel. (Oct. 22) Ralph Smedley founds the first official Toastmasters public speaking club in Santa Ana, California.

Business and labor: (Sept. 9) Sixteen sugar plantation workers and several police officers are killed in a labor dispute in Hanapepe, Hawaii.

Transportation and communications: (Feb. 22) Calvin Coolidge becomes the first president to deliver an address from the White House on the radio.

Science and technology: Thomas Hunt Morgan receives the Darwin Medal for his work in genetics.

Environment: (Mar. 8) A series of explosions at Castle Gate Mine No. 2 near Castle Gate, Utah, kills 172 miners.

Arts and literature: (Feb. 12) George Gershwin's jazz-influenced orchestral work *Rhapsody in Blue* is performed for the first time. Fiction: *The Call of the Canyon* (Zane Grey), *So Big* (Edna Ferber), *Tarzan and the Ant Men* (Edgar Rice Burroughs). Plays: *Beggar on Horseback* (George S. Kaufman and Marc Connelly), *Desire Under the Elms* (Eugene O'Neill), *Hell-Bent fer Heaven* (Hatcher Hughes), *They Knew What They Wanted* (Sidney Howard).

Popular culture: Hollywood stuntman Alvin "Shipwreck" Kelly is hired by a theater owner to sit atop a flagpole as a publicity stunt, beginning a nationwide fad. Simon and Schuster publishes the first crossword puzzle book. (Apr.) Metro-Goldwyn-Mayer Pictures Corporation (MGM) is formed from the merger of three smaller companies. (Nov. 27) Macy's holds its first Christmas parade, later known as the Thanksgiving Day parade, in New York City. Movies: *Girl Shy*, *The Iron Horse*, *Monsieur Beaucaire*, *Peter Pan*, *The Thief of Bagdad*. Music: "California, Here I Come," "It Had to Be You," "Somebody Loves Me." Radio: *The National Barn Dance*. Comic Strips: *Little Orphan Annie*. Products: Wheaties cereal, Lux soap, Rayon.

Sports: (Jan. 25–Feb. 5) The first Winter Olympic Games are held in Chamonix in the French Alps. Athletes from the United States win a total of four medals. (May 4–July 27) The Summer Olympic Games are held in Paris, France. Athletes from the United States win a total of ninety-nine medals. (Oct. 10) The Washington Senators win the World Series, defeating the New York Giants. (Nov.) The Cleveland Bulldogs win the NFL championship.

Crime: (Feb. 8) The first execution by means of the gas chamber takes place in Carson City, Nevada. (Sept. 19) Nathan Leopold and Richard Loeb are sentenced to life imprisonment plus ninety-nine years for the May 21 murder of fourteen-year-old Bobbie Franks. (Nov. 19) Thomas Ince, a film producer and director, dies after taking ill aboard newspaper magnate William Randolph Hearst's yacht, fueling rumors that Ince was actually murdered by Hearst.

1925

International: (Apr. 26) Paul von Hindenburg is elected president of the Weimar Republic. (July 18) Hitler publishes the first volume of *Mein Kampf*. (Oct. 16) The Locarno Pact is signed by representatives from Germany, Italy, the United Kingdom, France, and Belgium, normalizing relations and securing postwar territorial boundaries.

Government and politics: (Jan. 5) Nellie Tayloe Ross of Wyoming becomes the first female state governor in the United States.

Military: (Sept. 3) The USS *Shenandoah*, the first American-built rigid airship and the first in the world to be inflated with helium, crashes in Ohio due to a thunderstorm, killing fourteen on board.

Society: (Jul. 21) John Scopes is found guilty of violating the Butler Act, which bans the teaching of evolution in Tennessee schools.

Business and labor: The Florida land bubble begins to burst. (June 6) Walter Chrysler founds the Chrysler Corporation.

Transportation and communications: (Mar. 4) Coolidge becomes the first president to have his inauguration broadcast on the radio. (Dec. 12) Arthur Heineman opens the first motel, known as the Milestone Mo-Tel, near San Luis Obispo, California.

Science and technology: (Jan. 1) The astronomer Edwin Hubble's paper proving the existence of galaxies outside the Milky Way is presented at a conference in Washington, D.C.

Environment: (Feb. 28) The Charlevoix-Kamouraska earthquake strikes eastern Canada and parts of the northeastern United States, measuring an estimated 6.7 on the Richter scale. (Mar. 18) The Tri-State tornado kills at least 695 people in Missouri, Indiana, and Illinois.

Arts and literature: Alain Locke edits and publishes *The New Negro*, an anthology of short stories, poetry, and essays relating to art, literature, and the African American experience. (Feb. 21) *The New Yorker* publishes its first issue. Fiction: *An American Tragedy* (Theodore Dreiser), *Arrowsmith* (Sinclair Lewis), *Dark Laughter* (Sherwood Anderson), *The Great Gatsby* (F. Scott Fitzgerald), *Manhattan Transfer* (John Dos Passos), *The Professor's House* (Willa Cather). Plays: *Color Struck* (Zora Neale Hurston), *Craig's Wife* (George Kelly), *Easy Virtue* (Noël Coward), *The Gorilla* (Ralph Spence), *Hell Bells* (Barry Conners).

Popular culture: The population of Hollywood, California, reaches 130,000, up from 35,000 in 1919. Movies: *Ben-Hur*, *The Big Parade*, *The Freshman*, *The Gold Rush*, *The Lost World*, *The Phantom of the Opera*, *Street of Forgotten Men*. Music: "Collegiate," "If You

Knew Susie," "Sweet Georgia Brown," "Yes, Sir! That's My Baby." Radio: *Cities Service Concerts, Grand Ole Opry*. Products: Burma-Shave, D-Zerta artificially sweetened gelatin, Green Giant canned peas, Shalimar perfume.

Sports: (Oct. 15) The Pittsburgh Pirates win the World Series, defeating the Washington Senators.

Crime: (Mar. 27) Madge Oberholtzer, an Indianapolis schoolteacher, is kidnapped and raped by the leader of the Indiana Ku Klux Klan (KKK), leading to her death on April 14.

1926

International: (Nov. 18) The Balfour Declaration of 1926 defines Canada and the other British dominions as autonomous and equal within the British Empire. (Dec. 25) Hirohito becomes the 124th emperor of Japan.

Government and politics: (May 20) The Railway Labor Act is enacted, granting railroad workers the right to join unions and work toward labor reforms. (Dec. 10) Vice President Charles Dawes receives the 1925 Nobel Peace Prize for his work on the Dawes Plan.

Military: (July 2) The U.S. Army Air Service is renamed the U.S. Army Air Corps.

Society: (June 23) The College Board administers the first multiple-choice Scholastic Aptitude Test (SAT) examination.

Business and labor: (Nov. 15) David Sarnoff of the Radio Corporation of America launches the National Broadcasting Company (NBC), the first nationwide radio broadcasting network.

Transportation and communications: (Feb. 15) The U.S. Postal Service begins to contract out its airmail service to the private sector. (Mar. 7) The first successful transatlantic telephone call is placed between London and New York City. (Apr. 6) Varney Air Lines of Boise, Idaho, begins service as an airmail carrier.

Science and technology: Louis Sauer, a pediatrician in Evanston, Illinois, develops a vaccine against pertussis (whooping cough). (Mar. 16) Robert Goddard successfully launches the first liquid-fueled rocket, which rises 41 feet in its 2.5-second flight. (May 9) Richard E. Byrd and Floyd Bennett attempt to fly to the North Pole; controversy remains regarding whether they actually accomplished their goal.

Environment: (Apr.-May) Congress authorizes the creation of three national parks, Great Smoky Mountains in North Carolina and Tennessee, Shenandoah in Virginia, and Mammoth Cave in Kentucky. (Sept. 18) A category 4 hurricane makes landfall south of Miami, Florida, killing more than 240 people, causing $100 million in damage, and largely ending the Florida land boom. (Nov. 25) A Thanksgiving Day outbreak of tornadoes devastates the Midwest, causing numerous deaths.

Arts and literature: S. S. Van Dine (pseudonym of Willard Wright) publishes *The Benson Murder Case*, the first of a series of detective novels featuring an amateur sleuth named Philo Vance. Dorothy Parker publishes her first volume of poetry, *Enough Rope*. Langston Hughes publishes *The Weary Blues*. Fiction: *Show Boat* (Edna Ferber), *The Sun Also Rises* (Ernest Hemingway). Plays: *Chicago* (Maurine Dallas Watkins), *The Great God Brown* (Eugene O'Neill), *In Abraham's Bosom* (Paul Green), *The Noose* (Willard Mack), *Sex* (Mae West).

Popular culture: Greta Garbo makes her first American film, *The Torrent*. (Aug. 5) Harry Houdini completes one of his greatest feats, remaining in a sealed casket submerged in a New York hotel pool for ninety-one minutes before escaping. (Aug. 23) Rudolph Valentino's sudden death at the age of thirty-one triggers hysterics among his fans. (Oct. 31) Houdini dies of complications from a ruptured appendix. Movies: *Flesh and the Devil, House without a Key, Mantrap, The Son of the Sheik, What Price Glory?* Music: "Black Bottom," "Bye Bye Blackbird," "Muskrat Ramble," "Valencia." Radio: *Champion Spark Plug Hour, House of Myths, The Vikings*. Products: Camay soap, Prince Matchabelli perfumes.

Sports: (Feb. 6) The 1925 NFL championship is awarded to the Chicago Cardinals following a dispute regarding the eligibility of the Pottsville Maroons. (Aug. 6) Gertrude Ederle becomes the first woman to swim across the English Channel. (Oct. 10) The St. Louis Cardinals defeat the New York Yankees in the World Series. (Dec.) The Frankford Yellow Jackets win the NFL championship.

Crime: (Nov.–Dec.) The Hall-Mills murder case is reopened and a trial held, but all defendants are acquitted.

1927

International: (Apr.) The Chinese Civil War begins. (June 1) The Peace Bridge over the Niagara River between Canada and the United States is opened to the public. (Aug. 1) The People's Liberation Army is founded in China.

Government and politics: Residents of the U.S. Virgin Islands are granted U.S. citizenship.

Military: (Dec. 17) The USS *S-4*, a Navy submarine, sinks after colliding with a Coast Guard ship, killing all on board.

Society: (Feb. 21) Mae West's play *Sex* is raided by police, who arrest West and several cast members for obscenity.

Business and labor: (May) The last Ford Model T is produced. (Dec. 2) The new Ford Model A is introduced to the public. (Nov. 21) Six striking coal miners are killed and dozens injured by police and guards at the Columbine Mine in Serene, Colorado.

Transportation and communications: (Feb. 23) The Federal Radio Act is passed, creating the Federal Radio Commission (the forerunner of the Federal Communications Commission) for the purpose of regulating radio stations and frequencies in the United States. (Apr. 7) The first long-distance television broadcast is made from Washington, D.C., to New York City. (May 20–21) Charles Lindbergh makes the first successful nonstop solo transatlantic flight, flying the *Spirit of St. Louis* from Roosevelt Field on Long Island to Le Bourget Field outside Paris. (July 4) The Lockheed Vega, a plane later favored by Amelia Earhart and other record-breaking aviators, is flown for the first time. (Nov. 13) The Holland Tunnel beneath the Hudson River is officially opened.

Science and technology: (Dec. 10) Arthur Holly Compton wins the Nobel Prize in Physics for his discovery of the Compton effect.

Environment: (Apr.) The Great Mississippi Flood spreads throughout eleven states, killing more than two hundred people and displacing thousands.

Arts and literature: (Sept. 14) Isadora Duncan dies in an accident in Nice, France. (Oct. 4) Gutzon Borglum begins sculpting the monument at Mount Rushmore. Fiction: *Death Comes for the Archbishop* (Willa Cather), *Elmer Gantry* (Sinclair Lewis). Plays: *Dracula* (John Balderston and Hamilton Deane), *Loud Speaker* (John Howard Lawson), *Paris Bound* (Philip Barry), *The Royal Family* (George S. Kaufman and Edna Ferber), *The Trial of Mary Dugan* (Bayard Veiller).

Popular culture: Crooner Rudy Vallée becomes a mass-media pop star. (Mar. 11) Samuel "Roxy" Rothafel opens the 5,920-seat Roxy Theatre in New York City. (May 18) Grauman's Chinese Theatre opens in Hollywood. Movies: *The Cat and the Canary*, *Duck Soup*, *The Jazz Singer*, *The Kid Brother*, *The King of Kings*, *The Love of Sunya*, *Rolled Stockings*, *Seventh Heaven*, *Wings*. Music: "Ain't She Sweet," "Lucky Lindy," "Me and My Shadow," "My Blue Heaven," "The Varsity Drag." Radio: *The Collier Hour*, *Great Moments in History*, *The Palmolive Hour*, *The Voice of Firestone*. Products: Arpège perfume, Hardy Boys mystery novels, Kool-Aid drink mix.

Sports: Babe Ruth becomes the first baseball player to hit sixty home runs in one season, a record that will stand until 1961. (July) Helen Wills Moody wins the first of four consecutive ladies' singles tennis championships at Wimbledon. (Oct. 8) The New York Yankees defeat the Pittsburgh Pirates to win the World Series. (19) The New York Giants win the NFL championship.

Crime: (Apr. 30) The first federal prison for women in the United States opens in Alderson, West Virginia. (May 18) Andrew Kehoe murders his wife and detonates a dynamite bomb in the Bath School in Michigan, killing more than forty children and adults. (Aug. 23) Sacco and Vanzetti are executed at Charlestown State Prison. (Dec. 23) Several men rob a bank in Cisco, Texas, one dressed as Santa Claus.

1928

International: (Aug. 27) The Kellogg-Briand Pact, a multilateral agreement renouncing aggressive war coauthored by Secretary of State Frank B. Kellogg and French foreign minister Aristide Briand, is signed in Paris. (Oct. 1) The Soviet Union announces its first Five-Year Plan to increase industrial and agricultural production. (Oct.) Chiang Kai-shek becomes leader of the Republic of China.

Government and politics: (Nov. 6) Republican nominee Herbert Hoover defeats Democratic candidate Al Smith in the presidential election.

Military: (July) At the request of Secretary of War Dwight Davis, the Army forms the Experimental Mechanized Force, which uses tanks, armored cars, and additional mechanized equipment.

Society: Margaret Sanger forms the National Committee on Federal Legislation for Birth Control.

Business and labor: (Sept.) Construction begins on the Chrysler Building in New York.

Transportation and communications: (Feb. 25) Charles Jenkins Laboratories in Washington, D.C., obtains the first television broadcasting license from the Federal Radio Commission. (Aug. 24) A New York City subway train crashes at the Times Square station, killing sixteen people.

Science and technology: (Sept. 28) Alexander Fleming discovers penicillin. (Oct. 12) At the Children's Hospital in Boston, an iron lung respirator is first used to treat a patient with polio.

Environment: (Mar. 12–13) The St. Francis Dam near Los Angeles fails catastrophically, releasing 12 billion gallons of water and killing more than four hundred people. (Sept. 15) Bryce Canyon in Utah becomes a national park. (Sept.) The Okeechobee hurricane hits a number of islands in the Atlantic before striking southern Florida as a category 4 storm, killing an estimated twenty-five hundred people.

Arts and literature: Fiction: *Home to Harlem* (Claude McKay), *Rockbound* (Frank Parker Day), *Tarzan, Lord of the Jungle* (Edgar Rice Burroughs). Plays: *Diamond Lil* (Mae West), *The Front Page* (Ben Hecht and Charles MacArthur), *Holiday* (Philip Barry), *The International* (John Howard Lawson), *Strange Interlude* (Eugene O'Neill).

Popular culture: (Nov. 18) Walt Disney releases *Steamboat Willie*, an animated sound cartoon introducing Mickey Mouse. Movies: *The Circus, The Crowd, Four Sons, Ladies of the Mob*. Music: "Among My Souvenirs," "Let's Misbehave," "Mack the Knife," "My Melancholy Baby," "Ol' Man River." Radio: *Amos 'n' Andy, The National Farm and Home Hour, Uncle Don*. Products: Peter Pan peanut butter, sliced bread.

Sports: (Feb. 11–19) The second Winter Olympic Games are held in St. Moritz, Switzerland. The United States wins six medals. (May 17–Aug. 12) The 1928 Summer Olympics are held in Amsterdam, Netherlands. American athletes win a total of fifty-six medals. The games are the first to be sponsored by Coca-Cola. (Oct. 9) The New York Yankees defeat the St. Louis Cardinals to win the 1928 World Series. (Dec.) The Providence Steam Roller becomes the first New England team to win the NFL championship.

Crime: (Oct. 10) Gangster Salvatore "Toto" D'Aquila is killed as part of rival gangster Joe Masseria's attempt to gain control of the New York mafia. (Dec. 4) Daniel "Dapper Dan" Hogan, boss of the Irish mob of St. Paul, Minnesota, is killed by a car bomb.

1929

International: (Jan. 31) The Soviet Union exiles Leon Trotsky. (Feb. 11) The Lateran Treaty, in which the Italian government recognizes the independence and sovereignty of Vatican City, is signed. (Aug. 23–24) An Arab mob kills sixty-seven Jews in Hebron, Palestine.

Government and politics: (Mar. 4) Herbert Hoover is inaugurated as the thirty-first President of the United States; his vice president, Charles Curtis, is the first person of Native American ancestry to be elected to this office.

Military: (Nov. 29) Admiral Richard Byrd and pilot Bernt Balchen embark on an attempt to fly over the South Pole.

Society: *Reader's Digest*, first published in 1922, reaches a paid circulation of 290,000.

Business and labor: Clarence Birdseye sells his frozen food company and patents to Goldman Sachs and the Postum Company. (Sept. 3) Stock prices reach their peak. (Oct. 24–29) The stock market crashes over a period of several days, signaling the beginning of the Great Depression.

Transportation and communications: Nearly 27 million cars are registered in the United States, up from 6.8 million in 1919. (Jan. 18) William S. Paley purchases a radio network and renames it the Columbia Broadcasting Company (CBS). (July 5) The Curtiss-Wright Aviation Corporation is founded.

Science and technology: (July 17) Robert Goddard tests a rocket that carries a camera and a barometer on board. (Sept. 24) Jimmy Doolittle becomes the first aviator to complete a blind flight, proving that it is possible to take off, fly, and land an airplane using instruments alone.

Environment: (Feb. 26) Congress authorizes the creation of Grand Teton National Park in Wyoming. (Nov. 18) The 7.2-magnitude Grand Banks earthquake off the coast of Newfoundland, Canada, breaks underwater telegraph cables and causes a tsunami that kills nearly thirty people.

Arts and literature: (Feb. 23) The Arizona Biltmore Hotel in Phoenix, designed by Frank Lloyd Wright, opens. (Nov. 7) The Museum of Modern Art in New York City is opened to the public. Fiction: *A Farewell to Arms* (Ernest Hemingway), *Is Sex Necessary?* (James Thurber and E. B. White), *Red Harvest* (Dashiell Hammett), *The Sound and the Fury* (William Faulkner). Plays: *Dynamo* (Eugene O'Neill), *The Guinea Pig* (Preston Sturges), *June Moon*

(George S. Kaufman and Ring Lardner), *Street Scene* (Elmer Rice), *Strictly Dishonorable* (Preston Sturges).

Popular culture: (Jan. 17) Popeye the Sailor Man first appears in the comic strip *Thimble Theatre*. (May 16) The American Academy of Motion Picture Arts and Sciences presents the first Academy Awards. Movies: *Broadway Melody, The Cocoanuts, The Godless Girl, In Old Arizona, The Iron Mask, The Jazz Age, The Mysterious Dr. Fu Manchu, The Vagabond Lover.* Music: "Makin' Whoopee," "Singin' in the Rain," "Sweethearts on Parade," "When You're Smiling." Radio: *The Chase and Sanborn Choral Orchestra, The Cuckoo Hour, General Motors Concerts, The Goldbergs, Music and the Spoken Word.* Comic strips: *Buck Rogers, Tarzan of the Apes.* Products: Avon cosmetics, Oscar Mayer wieners.

Sports: (Oct. 14) The Philadelphia Athletics defeat the Chicago Cubs to win the World Series. (Dec.) The Green Bay Packers win the NFL championship.

Crime: (Feb. 14) Seven men are murdered in Chicago in a gang-related event known as the Saint Valentine's Day Massacre.

Rebecca J. Frey

■ Bibliography

This bibliography lists books containing substantial material about a wide variety of basic topics pertaining to the 1920s. Many additional works, and especially works on narrower subjects, can be found in the Further Readings notes at the end of each essay in *The Twenties in America*.

1. General Works on the 1920s
2. Art and Architecture
3. Biographies
4. Business and Economics
5. Crime and Scandal
6. Entertainment
7. Fads, Fashions, and Popular Culture
8. Gender and Sexuality
9. Great Migration
10. Harlem Renaissance
11. International Relations
12. Judicial System
13. Literature and Theater
14. Music and Dance
15. Politics and Government
16. Prohibition
17. Race and Ethnicity
18. Science, Medicine, and Technology
19. Social Issues
20. Sports
21. Transportation and Communications

General Works on the 1920s

Allen, Frederick Lewis. *Only Yesterday: An Informal History of the 1920s.* New York: Harper, 1931. Provides a social history of life in the United States during the 1920s.

Goldberg, David J. *Discontented America: The United States in the 1920s.* Baltimore: Johns Hopkins University Press, 1999. Challenges the myth of the so-called Roaring Twenties and the idea that all of the United States was a happy and harmonious place.

Kyvig, David E. *Daily Life in the United States, 1920–1940: How Americans Lived Through the Roaring Twenties and the Great Depression.* Chicago: Ivan R. Dee, 2004. An overview of society and popular culture, with a section on books and book clubs.

Miller, Nathan. *New World Coming: The 1920s and the Making of Modern America.* New York: Scribner, 2003. An overview of the social and economic trends of the decade.

Moore, Lucy. *Anything Goes: A Biography of the Roaring Twenties.* New York: Overlook Press, 2010. Addresses social, political, and economic changes occurring during the 1920s, with information about notable historical figures, jazz music, and flapper culture.

Palmer, Niall. *The Twenties in America: Politics and History.* Edinburgh: Edinburgh University Press, 2006. Examines American politics and society during the 1920s.

Perrett, Geoffrey. *America in the Twenties: A History.* New York: Simon & Schuster, 1982. A popularized account of the decade that covers major social issues, politics, popular culture, and the varied crimes and scandals.

Shannon, David A. *Between the Wars: America, 1919–1941.* 2d ed. Boston: Houghton Mifflin, 1979. A general overview of the social, political, cultural, and economic history of the period.

Art and Architecture

Fiell, Charlotte, and Peter Fiell. *Decorative Art, 1920s.* New York: Taschen, 2000. Describes the decade's design trends and styles in architecture, furniture, interiors, glassware, lighting, ceramics, textiles, and metalware, with illustrations and an index.

Greenough, Sarah, ed. *Modern Art and America: Alfred Stieglitz and His New York Galleries.* Washington, D.C.: National Gallery of Art, 2000. Presents the art that Stieglitz exhibited and fostered over four decades, alongside essays on the individual artists.

Haskell, Barbara. *The American Century: Art and Culture, 1900–1950.* New York: Whitney Museum of American Art, 1999. An overview of American art written by a curator of early American art at the Whitney Museum of American Art in New York.

———. *Charles Demuth.* New York: Whitney Museum of American Art, 1987. Considered a defining work on Demuth's career; includes the influence of cubism, the development of Demuth's poster portraits and precisionism, and a helpful commentary on Demuth's early watercolor phase.

Weber, Eva. *American Art Deco*. East Bridgewater, Mass.: J. G. Press, 2003. A general overview for the nonspecialist with an emphasis on illustrations.

Biographies

Bergreen, Laurence. *Capone: The Man and the Era*. New York: Simon & Schuster, 1994. Captures the contradictions and complexities of this enigmatic 1920s crime lord through a detailed biography.

Breuer, William B. *J. Edgar Hoover and His G-Men*. Westport, Conn.: Praeger, 1995. A laudatory biography that focuses on the 1920s and 1930s.

Bruccoli, Matthew J., and Scottie Fitzgerald Smith. *Some Sort of Epic Grandeur: The Life of F. Scott Fitzgerald*. Columbia: University of South Carolina Press, 2002. Revised edition of the definitive biography by a leading Fitzgerald scholar; describes his wild life as one of the most celebrated writers of the 1920s.

Clements, Kendrick A. *The Life of Herbert Hoover: Imperfect Visionary, 1918–1928*. New York: Palgrave Macmillan, 2010. Covers Hoover's time as the secretary of commerce and the public philosophy he developed for dealing with the problems of the United States.

Cooper, John Milton. *Woodrow Wilson: A Biography*. New York: Alfred A. Knopf, 2009. An authoritative account, covering Wilson's faults as well as his virtues and accomplishments.

Drohojowska-Philp, Hunter. *Full Bloom: The Art and Life of Georgia O'Keeffe*. New York: W. W. Norton, 2006. A comprehensive biography of O'Keeffe, discussing her artistic career, relationship with photographer Alfred Stieglitz, and her later years.

Fuess, Claude M. *Calvin Coolidge: The Man from Vermont*. Boston: Little, Brown, 1940. A highly regarded biography of Coolidge based partly on interviews with Coolidge and his family.

Sinclair, Andrew. *The Available Man: The Life Behind the Masks of Warren Gamaliel Harding*. New York: MacMillan, 1965. A biography of Warren G. Harding that examines the effect of his political background and small-town heritage on his presidency that began with the recession of 1920–21.

Wilson, Joan Hoff. *Herbert Hoover: Forgotten Progressive*. Prospect Heights, Ill.: Waveland Press, 1992: A biography of President Herbert Hoover that examines the development and application of his philosophy of public economic and social responsibility throughout his career in politics beginning in the 1920s.

Business and Economics

Bak, Richard. *Henry and Edsel: The Creation of the Ford Empire*. Hoboken, N.J.: Wiley, 2003. Describes the development of the Model A, listing its many innovations and discussing its impact on the car-buying market.

Ewen, Stuart. *Captains of Consciousness: Advertising and the Social Roots of Consumer Culture*. Toronto, ON: McGraw-Hill Book Company, 1977. A sociological examination of the origins of the advertising and consumerism.

Feinstein, Charles H., Peter Temin, and Gianni Toniolo. *The World Economy Between the Wars*. New York: Oxford University Press, 2008. A comprehensive and detailed study that provides valuable information and insights on the reparations issue that dominated the 1920s.

Friedman, Milton, and Anna J. Schwartz. *A Monetary History of the United States, 1867–1960*. Princeton, N.J.: Princeton University Press, 1963. Includes several chapters devoted to the changing structure of the banking system and 1920s U.S. Federal Reserve policy.

Galbraith, John Kenneth. *The Great Crash, 1929*. Boston, Mass.: Houghton Mifflin, 2009. Examines the actions of investors and the government inaction in the months prior to Black Tuesday.

Hyde, Charles K. *Riding the Roller Coaster: A History of the Chrysler Corporation*. Detroit: Wayne State University Press, 2003. A history of Chrysler Corporation outlining Walter Chrysler's philosophy for building cars that would compete with larger rivals in the industry; recounts his early successes during the 1920s.

Klein, Maury. *Rainbow's End: The Crash of 1929*. New York: Oxford University Press, 2003. Investigates the multitude of economic, political, and social events that led to the crash of 1929.

Crime and Scandal

Anthony, Carl Sferrazza. *Florence Harding: The First Lady, the Jazz Age, and the Death of America's Most Scandalous President*. New York: William Morrow, 1998. Provides painstaking details of the Harding scandals, largely exonerating Florence Harding from blame for her husband's death.

Dillon, Richard H. *Hatchet Men: The Story of the Tong Wars in San Francisco's Chinatown*. Reprint. Fairfield, Calif.: James Stevenson, 2005. An account of the development of the San Francisco tongs.

Edmonds, Andy. *Frame Up: The Untold Story of Roscoe "Fatty" Arbuckle.* New York: Morrow, 1991. An examination of the scandal and its consequences.

Eig, Jonathan. *Get Capone: The Secret Plot that Captured America's Most Wanted Gangster.* New York: Simon & Schuster, 2010. Ascribes Capone's downfall to hitherto unsung individuals and cites hubris as Capone's major shortcoming.

Helmer, William, and Arthur Bilek. *The St. Valentine's Day Massacre: The Untold Story of the Gangland Bloodbath That Brought Down Al Capone.* Nashville: Cumberland House Publishing, 2006. Suggests that a group of gangsters from St. Louis were responsible for the massacre and that law enforcement ignored evidence that pointed to anyone except Capone.

Levin, Meyer. *Compulsion.* New York: Simon & Schuster, 1956. Although framed as a novel, the book is fact-based and is one of the best studies of the Leopold-Loeb murder case.

McCartney, Laton. *The Teapot Dome Scandal: How Big Oil Bought the Harding White House and Tried to Steal the Country.* New York: Random House, 2008. Provides a detailed account of the scandal and the individuals involved.

Topp, Michael M. *The Sacco and Vanzetti Case: A Brief History with Documents.* New York: Bedford/St. Martin's, 2004. An introduction to the case accompanied by key case documents.

Zuckoff, Mitchell. *Ponzi's Scheme: The True Story of a Financial Legend.* New York: Random House, 2005. An appraisal of the man who created the quintessential American financial scam, with an analysis of the scheme's repercussions.

Entertainment

Everson, William K. *American Silent Film.* New York: Da Capo Press, 1998. A detailed overview of the silent film era and the transition to sound films.

Fischer, Lucy, ed. *American Cinema of the 1920s: Themes and Variations.* New Brunswick, N.J.: Rutgers University Press, 2009. Analyzes the evolution of the industry in terms of the decade's cultural and technological changes.

Schatz, Thomas. *The Genius of the System: Hollywood Filmmaking in the Studio Era.* Minneapolis: University of Minnesota Press, 2010. A comprehensive study of the "film factory" mentality that drove the major Hollywood companies, including Warner Bros., during the 1920s and afterward.

Wertheim, Arthur Frank. *Vaudeville Wars: How the Keith-Albee and Orpheum Circuits Controlled the Big-Time and Its Performers.* New York: Palgrave MacMillan, 2009. Chronicles the rise and fall of the dominant vaudeville circuits of the 1920s; provides an account of their ascendency and decline during the decade as well as the emergence of Loew's Theatres.

Fads, Fashions, and Popular Culture

Blum, Stella, ed. *Everyday Fashions of the Twenties: As Pictured in Sears and Other Catalogs.* New York: Dover, 1981. A pictorial review of clothing from mail-order catalogs in the 1920s.

Calabria, Frank M. *Dance of the Sleepwalkers: The Dance Marathon Fad.* Bowling Green, Ohio: Bowling Green State University Popular Press, 1993. A comprehensive study of this commercially successful fad, which drew over twenty thousand contestants and millions of spectators during the 1920s and 1930s.

Drowne, Kathleen Morgan, and Patrick Huber. *The 1920s.* Westport, Conn.: Greenwood Press, 2004. Covers all aspects of popular culture in the 1920s, including fashion, food and drink, leisure activities, music, and travel and recreation.

Giordano, Ralph G. *Satan in the Dance Hall: Rev. John Roach Straton, Social Dancing, and Morality in 1920s New York City.* Lanham, Md.: Scarecrow Press, 2008. Focuses on the social debate surrounding the morality of social dancing and jazz music in the 1920s, with dance halls in New York City highlighted.

Zeitz, Joshua. *Flapper: A Madcap Story of Sex, Style, Celebrity, and the Women Who Made America Modern.* New York: Crown, 2006. A history of the fashion that redefined American womanhood.

Gender and Sexuality

Andersen, Kristi. *After Suffrage: Women in Partisan and Electoral Politics Before the New Deal.* Chicago: University of Chicago Press, 1996. Recounts the victories and struggles of women in politics after the passing of women's suffrage.

Becker, Susan. D. *The Origins of the Equal Rights Amendment: American Feminism Between The Wars.* Westport, Conn.: Greenwood Press, 1985. Chronicles the early history of the effort to introduce the Equal Rights Amendment, as well as the essentially conservative political climate faced by its chief sponsor, the National Woman's Party.

Brown, Dorothy M. *Setting a Course: American Women in the 1920s*. Boston, Mass.: Twayne, 1987. Addresses women's changing role during the 1920s.

Chauncey, George. *Gay New York: Gender, Urban Culture, and the Making of the Gay Male World, 1890–1940*. New York: BasicBooks, 1996. Examines the gay world in turn-of-the-century New York City.

Eaklor, Vicki Lynn. *Queer America: A GLBT History of the 20th Century*. Westport, Conn.: Greenwood Press, 2008. An extensive chronicle of the movements, people, and events that contributed to the gay, lesbian, bisexual, and transsexual history of the twentieth century.

Great Migration

Gregory, James N. *The Southern Diaspora: How the Great Migrations of Black and White Southerners Transformed America*. Chapel Hill: University of North Carolina Press, 2005. A history of migration out of the South, describing socioeconomic developments that can be traced to the decade of the 1920s.

Harrison, Alferdteen. *Black Exodus: The Great Migration from the American South*. Jackson: University of Mississippi Press, 1992. Focuses on the cultural and socioeconomic effects on both the areas of origin and destination.

Trotter, Joe William Jr., ed. *The Great Migration in Historical Perspective: New Dimensions of Race, Class, and Gender*. Bloomington: Indiana University Press, 1991. A collection of essays examining the role of black social networks in spurring the exodus from the South.

Wilkerson, Isabel. *The Warmth of Other Suns: The Epic Story of America's Great Migration*. New York: Random, 2010. Discusses the history of the Great Migration through the stories of a number of individual African Americans who made the trek.

Harlem Renaissance

Chambers, Veronica. *The Harlem Renaissance*. Philadelphia: Chelsea House, 1998. A general overview written for teens.

Lewis, David Levering. *When Harlem Was in Vogue*. New York: Penguin Books, 1997. A detailed account of Harlem Renaissance participants and includes an examination of nightclubs, cabarets, and speakeasies of the 1920s.

Locke, Alain L., ed. *The New Negro*. New York: Touchstone, 1997. A compendium of contributions to the ideas and goals of the Harlem Renaissance, edited by one of the movement's most prominent representatives.

Watson, Steven. *The Harlem Renaissance: Hub of African-American Culture, 1920–1930*. New York: Pantheon Books, 1995. Summarizes the intellectual and cultural life and contributions of the Harlem Renaissance.

Wintz, Cary. *Harlem Speaks: A Living History of the Harlem Renaissance*. Naperville, Ill.: Sourcebooks MediaFusion, 2007. Features essays on people and themes involved in the Harlem Renaissance, including historical audio material and photographs.

International Relations

Davis, Kathryn W. *The Soviets at Geneva: The U.S.S.R. and the League of Nations, 1919–1933*. Westport, Conn.: Hyperion Press, 1977. Details the Soviet involvement in League issues, such as prisoner exchanges, medical work, and labor issues, until the Soviet Union joined the League of Nations in 1933.

Fanning, Richard. *Peace and Disarmament*. Lexington: University Press of Kentucky, 1994. Focuses on the efforts of the international disarmament movement in the late 1920s.

Ferrell, Robert H. *Peace in Their Time: The Origins of the Kellogg-Briand Pact*. New Haven, Conn.: Yale University Press, 1952. Written by an esteemed historian of U.S. foreign policy in the twentieth century.

Louria, Margo. *Triumph and Downfall: America's Pursuit of Peace and Prosperity, 1921–1933*. Westport, Conn.: Greenwood Press, 2000. An analysis of U.S. foreign policy in the 1920s and early 1930s challenging the traditional interpretation of American isolationism. Contains a chapter on Kellogg and his foreign policy.

Rhodes, Benjamin. *United States Foreign Policy and the Interwar Period, 1918–1941: The Golden Age of American Diplomatic and Military Complacency*. Westport, Conn.: Praeger, 2001. Examines U.S. foreign policy between the world wars.

Spenser, Daniela. *The Impossible Triangle: Mexico, Soviet Russia, and the United States in the 1920s*. Durham, N.C.: Duke University Press, 1999. Examines the tangled relationship between these states in the years after the Mexican and Russian revolutions.

Judicial System

Benjamin, Louise. *Freedom of the Air and the Public Interest: First Amendment Rights in Broadcasting to 1935*. Carbondale: Southern Illinois University Press,

2006. Provides an examination of the fine line between freedom of speech and censorship in the infancy of the radio industry.

Bloomfield, Maxwell H. *Peaceful Revolution: Constitutional Change and American Culture from Progressivism to the New Deal.* Cambridge, Mass.: Harvard University Press, 2000. An analysis of the cultural climate that produced changes in constitutional law, expanding both the power of the federal government and the rights of citizens.

Burton, David Henry. *Taft, Holmes, and the 1920s Court: An Appraisal.* Madison, N.J.: Fairleigh Dickinson University Press, 1998. Discusses the rulings made by the Supreme Court of the 1920s, focusing on Taft and Holmes.

Johnson, Anne Janette. *The Scopes Monkey Trial.* Detroit: Omnigraphics, 2007. A readable account of the trial including biographies of key participants and a selection of primary-source materials.

Lombardo, Paul A. *Three Generations, No Imbeciles: Eugenics, the Supreme Court, and* Buck v. Bell. Baltimore: Johns Hopkins University Press, 2010. An examination of one of the most important Supreme Court cases pertaining to eugenics and compulsory sterilization laws.

Literature and Theater

Baym, Nina. *Between the Wars 1914–1945.* Vol. D in *The Norton Anthology of American Literature.* 6th ed. New York: Norton, 2003. A critically acclaimed anthology of major works representing American literature between the world wars.

Carpenter, Humphrey. *Geniuses Together: American Writers in Paris in the 1920s.* Boston: Houghton Mifflin, 1987. An account of Hemingway, Anderson, Pound, Kay Boyle, Djuna Barnes, and other expatriates in Paris.

Cowley, Malcolm. *Exile's Return: A Literary Odyssey of the 1920s.* New York: Viking Press, 1951. A firsthand account of the expatriate experience and the literary movements of the time.

Davis, Lee. *Scandals and Follies: The Rise and Fall of the Great Broadway Revue.* New York: Limelight Editions, 2000. Provides a history of the musical revue form on American stages, including the development of the Ziegfeld Follies.

French, Warren, ed. *The Twenties: Fiction, Poetry, Drama.* Deland, Fla.: Everett/Edwards, 1975. Thirty essays on significant writers of the 1920s, both famous and obscure.

Gaines, James R. *Wit's End: Days and Nights of the Algonquin Round Table.* New York: Harcourt, 1977. A more contemporary look at the stories about the Round Table, including photos and illustrations.

Gewirtz, Arthur, and James J. Kolb, eds. *Art, Glitter, and Glitz: Mainstream Playwrights and Popular Theatre in 1920s America.* Westport, Conn.: Praeger, 2004. A collection of essays on the predominant playwrights and popular theater styles of the 1920s.

Twelve Southerners. *I'll Take My Stand: The South and the Agrarian Tradition.* New York: Harper, 1930. Reprint. Baton Rouge: Louisiana State University Press, 2006. Collects the essays written by the Southern Agrarians.

Music and Dance

Hadlock, Richard. *Jazz Masters of the 1920s.* New York: Macmillan, 1965. A general overview of jazz styles from the 1920s, organized by significant individuals and groups.

Harrison, Daphne Duval. *Black Pearls: Blues Queens of the 1920s.* Reprint. New Brunswick, N.J.: Rutgers University Press, 2000. Describes the influence of the blues, as sung by African American women, on the music and society of the 1920s.

Malnig, Julie, ed. *Ballroom, Boogie, Shimmy Sham, Shake: A Social and Popular Dance Reader.* Chicago: University of Illinois Press, 2009. Focuses on the history and social aspects of popular and choreographed dances; covers influences and overlapping contexts in the 1920s.

Oja, Carol J. *Making Music Modern: New York in the 1920s.* New York: Oxford University Press, 2003. Explores the significance of modernist composers in shaping the decade's music.

Shaw, Arnold. *The Jazz Age: Popular Music in the 1920s.* New York: Oxford University Press, 1989. Chronicles the musical developments of the 1920s, including sections on specific songs and performers.

Simon, George Thomas. *The Big Bands.* 4th ed. New York: Collier Macmillan, 1981.

Politics and Government

Ferrell, Robert H. *The Presidency of Calvin Coolidge.* Lawrence: University Press of Kansas, 1998. An analysis of the policies of the Coolidge administration.

Freeberg, Ernest. *Democracy's Prisoner: Eugene V. Debs, the Great War, and the Right to Dissent.* Cambridge, Mass.: Harvard University Press, 2008. An account of Debs's sedition trial and incarceration, including a chapter discussing the 1920 presidential election.

Leuchtenburg, William E. *The Perils of Prosperity, 1914–1932*. Chicago: University of Chicago Press, 1993. Illustrates the transition from the Progressive Era to the Republican ascendancy in the 1920s and the New Deal consensus in the 1930s.

Murray, Robert K. *Red Scare: A Study in National Hysteria, 1919–1920*. 1955. Reprint. Westport, Conn.: Greenwood Press, 1980. A landmark scholarly study of the event.

Trani, Eugene P., and David L. Wilson. *The Presidency of Warren G. Harding*. Lawrence: Regents Press of Kansas, 1989. A critical analysis of the Harding presidency.

Wynn, Neil A. *From Progressivism to Prosperity: World War I and American Society*. New York: Holmes & Meier, 1986. Examines the political issues and popular movements that spurred Progressive ideals and explores the impact of government aid and private industry on post–World War I prosperity in the United States.

Prohibition

Clark, Norman H. *Deliver Us from Evil: An Interpretation of American Prohibition*. New York: Norton, 1976. An overview of the historical developments resulting in Prohibition, from the nineteenth century through the 1920s to its repeal.

Okrent, David. *Last Call: The Rise and Fall of Prohibition*. New York: Scribner, 2010. Describes the tenor of the age in which Capone operated and his role in the overall picture.

Sinclair, Andrew. *Era of Excess: A Social History of the Prohibition Movement*. New York: Harper Colophon Books, 1962. A general history of Prohibition in the United States.

Race and Ethnicity

Alexander, Michael. *Jazz Age Jews*. Princeton, N.J.: Princeton University Press, 2001. A portrait of Jewish life in the United States during the 1920s, specifically using the figures Al Rothstein, Felix Frankfurter, and Al Jolson.

Hoxie, Frederick E. *Talking Back to Civilization: Indian Voices From the Progressive Era*. Boston, Mass.: Bedford/St. Martins, 2001. Discusses the experiences of Native Americans in the early twentieth century, including a selection of primary historical sources, illustrations, and a chronology of significant dates.

Jonas, Gilbert. *Freedom's Sword: The NAACP and the Struggle Against Racism in America, 1909–1969*. New York: Routledge, 2007. Presents a discussion on the first sixty years of the NAACP, discussing the activities of NAACP leaders Du Bois, Thurgood Marshall, and James Weldon Johnson.

Madigan, Tim. *The Burning: Massacre, Destruction, and the Tulsa Race Riot of 1921*. New York: St. Martin's Press, 2001. Recounts the Tulsa, Oklahoma, race riot of 1921, using taped interviews with survivors and witnesses.

Takaki, Ronald. *Strangers from a Different Shore: A History of Asian Americans*. Rev. ed. Boston: Back Bay, 1998. Third section covers the 1920s.

Science, Medicine, and Technology

Best, Gary Dean. *The Dollar Decade: Mammon and the Machine in 1920s America*. Santa Barbara, Calif.: Praeger, 2003. Explores the multitude of innovations introduced during the 1920s and their impact on American culture.

Bliss, Michael. *The Discovery of Insulin*. Reprint. Chicago: University of Chicago Press, 2007. Contains many details of Banting's experiments and analyzes the conflict that developed among Macleod, Banting, Best, and Collip over credit for the discovery of insulin.

Crease, Robert P., and Charles C. Mann. *The Second Creation: Makers of the Revolution in Twentieth-Century Physics*. Rev. ed. New Brunswick, N.J.: Rutgers University Press, 1996. A history of particle physics, containing a chapter on the cosmic ray research of Millikan and others.

Nussbaumer, Harry, and Lydia Bieri. *Discovering the Expanding Universe*. New York: Cambridge University Press, 2009. Puts the discovery of the expanding universe in context with the work of several other astronomers and argues that Hubble should not receive sole credit.

Nye, David E. *Electrifying America: Social Meanings of a New Technology, 1880–1940*. Cambridge, Mass.: MIT Press, 1992. Explores the effects of the introduction of electricity and related technology, including refrigerators, into American homes.

Rogers, Naomi. *Dirt and Disease: Polio before FDR*. New Brunswick, N.J.: Rutgers University Press, 1992. A history of polio and societal responses to it in the early decades of the twentieth century.

Starr, Paul. *The Social Transformation of American Medicine: The Rise of a Sovereign Profession and the Making of a Vast Industry.* New York, Basic Books, 1982. A detailed history of medicine, with several chapters covering topics relevant to the 1920s.

Winter, Frank H. *Rockets into Space.* Cambridge, Mass.: Harvard University Press, 1993. Describes the evolution of space launch vehicles.

Social Issues

Bernstein, Irving. *The Lean Years: A History of the American Worker, 1920–1933.* Reprint. Chicago: Haymarket Books, 2010. A discussion of the American worker and the impact of unions in the 1920s.

Engelman, Peter C. *A History of the Birth Control Movement in America.* Santa Barbara, Calif.: ABC-CLIO, 2011. Provides context for the attitudes of and developments in 1920s birth control efforts.

King, Desmond S *Making Americans: Immigration, Race, and the Origins of the Diverse Democracy.* Cambridge, Mass.: Harvard University Press, 2002. An analysis of U.S. immigration policy in the twentieth century, with a focus on the legislative debates of the 1920s and the role of eugenics.

Klarman, Michael J. *From Jim Crow to Civil Rights: The Supreme Court and the Struggle for Racial Equality.* New York: Oxford University Press, 2006. An overview of the topic that relates the events of the 1920s to the evolution of the twentieth-century civil rights movement.

Lienesch, Michael. *In the Beginning: Fundamentalism, the Scopes Trial, and the Making of the Antievolution Movement.* Chapel Hill: University of North Carolina Press, 2007. Discusses the trial as a significant event in the history of two antagonistic social movements.

Maclean, Nancy K. *Behind the Mask of Chivalry: The Making of the Second Ku Klux Klan.* New York: Oxford University Press, 1995. Stresses the 1920s Klan connection to the larger social forces operating in the United States.

Pickens, Donald K. *Eugenics and the Progressives.* Nashville, Tenn.: Vanderbilt University Press, 1968. The most complete study of how the eugenics movement fit within the reform tradition of the Progressive era.

Sports

Bohn, Michael K. *Heroes and Ballyhoo: How the Golden Age of the 1920s Transformed American Sports.* Washington, D.C.: Potomac Books, 2009. Features profiles of ten legendary athletes of the 1920s, including Tilden and Moody, and explores the beginnings of sports celebrity culture.

Borgeson, Griffith. *The Golden Age of the American Racing Car.* Warrendale, Pa.: SAE International, 1997. An important work on historical auto racing, originally published in 1966.

Jose, Colin. *American Soccer League, 1921–1931: The Golden Years of American Soccer.* Lanham, Md.: Scarecrow Press, 1998. Provides background on the ASL along with a wealth of league, club, and player statistics.

Lefcourt, Blossom, and Eric Rachlis, eds. *Horse Racing: The Golden Age of the Track.* San Francisco: Chronicle Books, 2001. Photographic coverage of thoroughbred racing, which is represented as a sport enjoyed by all social classes.

Peterson, Robert W. *Pigskin: The Early Years of Pro Football.* New York: Oxford University Press, 1997. Details the rise of professional football from the 1920s to the memorable championship game of 1958.

_____. *Cages to Jump Shots: Pro Basketball's Early Years.* New York: Oxford University Press, 1990. Provides an overview of professional basketball's competition with college games for fan interest, early teams and players, and innovations in styles of play.

Seymour, Harold. *Baseball: The Golden Age.* New York: Oxford University Press, 1989. A history of baseball focusing on the early twentieth century through the 1920s.

Voss, Arthur. *Tilden and Tennis in the Twenties.* Troy, N.Y.: Whitson, 1985. A chronicle of the game's progress and its players during the 1920s, written by a Canadian tennis champion of the era.

Transportation and Communications

Bak, Richard. *The Big Jump: Lindbergh and the Great Atlantic Air Race.* Hoboken, N.J.: John Wiley & Sons, 2011. Explores the technological advances in aviation at the time of Lindberg's transatlantic flight and provides information on the other pilots who attempted the trip.

Douglas, George H. *The Early Days of Radio Broadcasting.* Jefferson, N.C.: McFarland, 2002. Explores the rapid development of radio from infancy to its venture into politics, sports, and entertainment.

Goddard, Stephen B. *Getting There: The Epic Struggle*

Between Road and Rail in the American Century. New York: Basic Books, 1994. Includes good information on the 1920s, the decade in which the automobile began to offer significant competition to the railroads for passenger travel and the long-distance freight-trucking industry saw significant growth.

Kaszynski, William. *The American Highway: The History and Culture of Roads in the United States.* Jefferson, N.C.: McFarland, 2000. Provides historical context for the road development that occurred in the 1920s.

Lewis, David L., and Laurence Goldstein, eds. *The Automobile and American Culture.* Reprint. Ann Arbor: University of Michigan Press, 1993. Offers cultural context for the role of automobiles and roads during the 1920s.

Glossary

This list is a representative collection of words and phrases that were either first used or gained prominence during the 1920s in the United States. (n. = noun; adj. = adjective; adv. = adverb; v. = verb; exp. = expression)

Academy Awards, n. Annual prizes given to members of the film industry.
ace, n. A dollar bill.
Airedale, n. A naval aviator; a plain-looking man.
alarm clock, n. A chaperone.
all wet, exp. Wrong.
ankle, v. To walk.
aptitude test, n. A standardized test that measures a person's ability to learn particular skills.
Attaboy!/Attagirl!, exp. An exclamation of approbation or support.
ax, v. To dismiss someone from his or her job.
babe, n. An attractive girl or woman.
baby, n. A sweetheart.
balled up, adj. Confused.
baloney, n. Nonsense.
banana split, n. A dessert that combines scoops of ice cream atop banana halves and may be topped with fruit, nuts, candies, or syrups.
Band-Aid, n. A trademarked product that consists of an adhesive strip with a gauze pad, used to cover small scrapes or cuts.
bangtail, n. A racehorse.
bank's closed, exp. No kissing or petting.
bathtub gin, n. Homemade liquor containing juniper oil and other flavorings to imitate gin.
barnstormer, n. An aviator who puts on stunt shows around the country.
bean-shooter, n. A Bostonian.
beat one's gums, v. To chat.
beaucoup, adj. A lot, much.
beef, n. A problem or disagreement.
bee's knees, n. A wonderful person, object, or idea.
beeswax, n. Business.
behind the eight ball, exp. To be in a difficult situation
bell-bottom, n. A sailor.
bent, adj. Stolen; corrupt.
Bible Belt, n. Parts of the United States where Protestant Fundamentalism flourishes, particularly areas of the South.
big cheese, n. An influential or important person.
big house n. Prison.
Black Bottom, n. A popular dance of African American origin, named for a neighborhood of Detroit, Michigan.
blind date, n. A date between two people who have never met before.
blow, v. To leave hurriedly.
bluenose, n. Someone who is prudish or stringently moral.
bob, n. A short hairstyle worn by many women during the 1920s.
booger, n. A piece of nasal mucus, often dry.
bootlegger, n. A smuggler of illicit alcohol during Prohibition.
bozo, n. Someone who is silly or ignorant.
breeze, n. Something that is very easily accomplished.
Bronx cheer, n. A crude sound made by blowing air through closed lips to express displeasure or derision.
bull session, n. A casual group conversation.
bump off, v. To murder.
bungalow, n. A small house, usually with one story, that became popular during the 1920s.
buzz, n. A telephone call.
buzz, v. To call by telephone
caper, n. A crime, especially a theft.
carry a torch, v. To love someone without reciprocation.
cash, n. A kiss.
cat's meow, n. Something that is desirable or in high demand.
Charleston, n. A popular dance of African American origin that may have originated near Charleston, South Carolina.
Charlie, n. A man with a mustache.
chassis, n. A woman's body.
check, n. An agreement to kiss at a later time.
chick, n. A woman; attributed to Sinclair Lewis's novel *Elmer Gantry*.
chopper, n. A Thompson submachine gun.
chopper squad, n. A group armed with submachine guns.
ciggy, n. A cigarette.
clam, n. A dollar.
conk, v. To hit.
copacetic, adj. Satisfactory.

crackers, adj. Crazy.
crate, n. An old or run-down car.
croaker, n. A physician working in a prison.
crossword, n. A type of word puzzle invented in the 1910s and popularized during the 1920s.
cruiser, n. A police car used to patrol the streets.
crush, n. An infatuation; the object of one's infatuation.
cutie, n. An attractive person, particularly a desirable young woman.
daddy, n. A wealthy, often older man who takes care of a younger lover's financial needs.
dame, n. A woman.
dapper, n. A flapper's father.
date, n. A romantic meeting; a person with whom one meets for a romantic encounter.
dick, n. A private detective.
dish-down, n. Something disappointing.
dish the dirt, v. To share gossip.
dive, n. A run-down bar or nightclub.
dogs, n. Feet.
doll, n. An attractive woman.
don't take any wooden nickels, exp. Refrain from doing anything foolish.
doozy, n. Something extraordinary.
dope, n. Illegal drugs, particularly narcotics and cocaine.
dough, n. Money.
ducky, adj. Wonderful.
dumb Dora, n. An ignorant woman.
earful, n. A complaint or diatribe.
egg, n. A prosperous person.
embalmed, adj. Drunk.
embalmer, n. A smuggler of illicit alcohol during Prohibition.
Eskimo Pie, n. A trademarked dessert consisting of chocolate-covered ice cream on a stick.
eye-opener, n. Marriage.
face stretcher, n. An older woman who tries to appear young.
fag, n. A cigarette; a pejorative term for a male homosexual.
fall guy, n. A person who becomes a scapegoat.
Father Time, n. A pejorative term for a man over age thirty.
fin, n. A five-dollar bill.
fire alarm, n. A woman who is divorced.
fire bell, n. A woman who is married.
fire extinguisher, n. A chaperone.
fix, v. To bribe or pay off.

flapper, n. A young woman who wore her hair short, dressed in short skirts, and flouted traditional social conventions by dancing, smoking, and drinking illicit alcohol.
flipper, n. A male flapper.
fly boy, n. A pilot.
forty-niner, n. A man who seduces wealthy women for their money.
Freon, n. A trademarked synthetic coolant used in refrigerators.
fried, adj. Drunk.
fuzz, n. The police.
gam, n. A leg, particularly a woman's leg.
gay, n. Cheerful and spirited.
gigolo, n. A man who is financially supported by a woman in exchange for sexual favors.
gimp, n. A person who is disabled or has a limp.
gin mill, n. An establishment that sells hard liquor, particularly a bar or speakeasy.
glad rags, n. Dressy or fancy clothes.
gold digger, n. A woman who seduces wealthy men for their money.
goofy, adj. Crazy or silly.
grand, n. One thousand dollars.
gravy train, n. An easy source for money.
Great Migration, n. The movement of a large percentage of African Americans from the rural South to cities in the industrial North during the first decades of the twentieth century.
grilled cheese, n. A sandwich made by toasting bread and cheese that became more prevalent after the advent of sliced bread in the 1920s.
guy, n. A man.
hack, n. A prison guard.
hair of the dog, n. An alcoholic drink employed as a remedy for a hangover.
handcuff, n. An engagement ring.
hard-boiled, adj. Strictly obedient to the laws or rules.
Harlem Renaissance, n. An influential black literary and artistic movement that started in the Harlem section of New York City.
heater, n. A gun.
heebie-jeebies, n. A feeling of anxiety or apprehension.
heist, v. To rob.
hick, adj. Describing or related to an unsophisticated person from a rural area or the area itself.
hijack, v. To steal a vehicle carrying illegal alcohol.
hit on all sixes, v. To do something in a perfect manner.

hit the road, v. To leave.
hooch, n. Alcoholic beverages.
hood, n. A gangster.
hooey, n. Nonsense.
hoofer, n. A dancer.
hook, v. To addict.
hoopty-doo!, exp. An exclamation of joy.
horn, n. A trumpet.
horse around, v. To play around, especially in a rough, noisy way.
hot seat, n. The electric chair.
hotsy-totsy, adj. Something that is wonderful.
house dick, n. A hotel detective.
ice, n. Diamonds.
in hot water, exp. To be in trouble.
installment plan, n. A payment schedule allowing someone to buy something over time; became more prevalent during the 1920s.
intelligence quotient (IQ), n. A test score that represents a person's intelligence as compared to others of the same age.
iron, n. A motorcycle.
it, n. Sex appeal.
jalopy, n. An old car that does not run very well.
java, n. Coffee.
jazz, n. A type of syncopated music that became very popular during the 1920s.
Jazz Age, n. The 1920s, with particular reference to the growing popularity of jazz and its attendant cultural phenomena; the term is attributed to American novelist F. Scott Fitzgerald.
jive, n. Fast-paced jazz music of the 1920s; a meaningless statement.
jive, v. To play 1920s-style jazz music.
joe, n. Coffee.
john, n. A man who hires a prostitute.
joint, n. An establishment where illegal alcohol was sold during Prohibition. Often used in combination with terms for alcohol, as in "beer joint" or "gin joint."
juice joint, n. An establishment where illegal alcohol was sold during Prohibition.
jump in the lake!, exp. Leave me alone.
junkie, n. A person who is addicted to or sells drugs, especially narcotics.
kid stuff, n. Something that is more appropriate for children than adults.
killjoy, n. Someone who spoils others' fun.
kisser, n. The mouth.
knock sideways, v. To amaze or dumbfound.

Kool-Ade, n. A trademarked soft drink made by mixing a dried powder with water; spelling later changed to "Kool-Aid."
kosher, adj. Fair or honest; satisfactory.
lettuce, n. Cash.
level, adj. Truthful.
lie detector, n. A machine that uses physiological data to help determine whether a person is telling the truth.
live wire, n. A person who is full of energy.
lollygagger, n. A lazy person; someone who enjoys hugging, kissing, and caressing.
look down one's nose, exp. To show contempt for someone or something.
lost generation, n. Group of expatriate American writers in Europe who found much of life to be meaningless; attributed to writer Gertrude Stein.
make whoopee, v. To engage in amorous or sexual activities such as kissing and fondling.
manacle, n. A wedding ring.
map, n. A face.
marble orchard, n. A cemetery.
marbles, n. Mental capabilities.
mass production, n. A large quantity of products being manufactured.
meat wagon, n. An ambulance.
milquetoast, n. An unassertive person; derived from the 1924 comics character Caspar Milquetoast.
mob, n. An organized crime gang.
mojo, n. A magic spell or object; an inner strength or mystical power.
moll, n. A woman who dates a gangster.
moonshine, n. Homemade liquor, usually made with distilled corn to imitate whiskey.
motel, n. A lodging establishment usually located near a highway that has rooms accessible directly from the road.
mouthpiece, n. A lawyer.
Mrs. Grundy, n. A woman who is prudish or stringently moral.
neck, v. To kiss and caress with great passion.
newshound, n. A reporter.
nifty, adj. Something fantastic.
nightclub, n. An establishment that served illegal alcohol during Prohibition, also usually offering live music and dancing.
nobody home, exp. A clueless, unintelligent, or ignorant person.
noodle, n. Head.
noodle juice, n. Tea.

nookie, n. Sex.
nose candy, n. A drug that is inhaled through the nostrils, such as cocaine.
nose dive, n. A abrupt, sharp drop.
off the deep end, exp. Losing control or going crazy.
oil-burner, n. A person who chews tobacco.
Oliver Twist, n. An expert dancer.
on the lam, exp. Running from the police or authorities.
on the level, exp. Being honest.
on the make, exp. Attempting to seduce someone.
on the up and up, exp. Being honest.
out on parole, n. A divorced person.
over the edge, exp. Crazy.
overpass, n. A section of road that has been raised in order for it to pass over another road below; may also refer to a similar intersection between a railroad and a road or a pedestrian walkway and a road.
owl, n. A flapper who only appears at social events.
pack a rod, v. To carry a firearm.
pack heat, v. To carry a firearm.
palooka, n. An average or inept boxer; any clumsy, unintelligent person.
peanut butter and jelly sandwich, n. A sandwich consisting of a ground-peanut spread, fruit preserves, and bread that became more prevalent after the advent of sliced bread in the 1920s.
pecker, n. A penis.
peepers, n. Eyes.
pet, v. To kiss, hug, and caress.
petting pantry, n. A movie theater.
pick up, v. To persuade a stranger to accompany you home to engage in sexual activity.
pill, n. A disagreeable or boring person.
pinch, v. To arrest or catch a criminal.
piped, adj. Drunk.
pipe down, v. Be silent.
plastered, adj. Drunk.
police dog, n. A flapper's fiancé.
pop, v. To punch or hit.
potted, adj. Drunk.
primed, adj. Drunk.
Prohibition, n. The ban on the manufacture, sale, and transportation of liquor in the United States following the passage of the Eighteenth Amendment to the Constitution.
pull rank, v. To use one's authority to compel another person to do something.
punk, n. A small-time thug.
pusher, n. A prostitute.
pushover, n. A person who easily can be convinced to do something.
put on the Ritz, v. To do something with a remarkable sense of style.
Q-tip, n. A trademarked cotton swab attached at both ends of a stick designed for cleaning ears, faces, infants' bodies, or minor wounds.
queen, n. A pejorative term for a male homosexual.
rag, n. A newspaper.
razz, v. To tease.
real McCoy, n. Something that is authentic or genuine.
Red Scare, n. Anxiety in the United States about the possibility of a communist takeover, resulting in a yearlong panic and police actions from 1919 to 1920.
ritzy, adj. Fancy or luxurious.
sap, n. Someone who is very studious.
sap, v. To study.
scofflaw, n. Someone who drank alcohol during Prohibition.
Scopes **trial**, n. The trial of a Tennessee biology teacher who violated a state law making teaching evolution illegal; also called the Scopes monkey trial.
scram, v. To leave immediately.
shack up, v. To have sex with or temporarily live with someone who is not one's spouse.
shamus, n. A private detective or police officer.
sheik, n. An attractive man; derives from the 1921 film *The Sheik*, starring Rudolph Valentino.
shiv, n. A knife.
sing, v. To confess or offer information to the authorities.
skirt, n. An attractive woman.
sleep around, v. To have several lovers.
slum, v. To visit the poor section of town.
smoke, v. To murder someone.
snozzle, v. To drink.
speakeasy, n. An establishment that sold illegal alcohol during Prohibition.
stiff, n. A murder target.
stilts, n. Legs.
swanky, adj. Luxurious or fashionable.
sweetie, n. A sarcastic term referring to someone who is disagreeable.
T-shirt, n. A man's undershirt that is usually short-sleeved, has no buttons or collar, and is made of cotton.

talkies, n. Movies featuring synchronized sound tracks that allowed the audience to hear actors' dialogue.
tasty, adj. Enjoyable.
tearjerker, n. A sentimental film or story.
tin, n. A police officer's badge; a police officer.
Tin Pan Alley, n. The popular music industry; the district of New York City where composers and music publishers were located.
tomato, n. A voluptuous woman.
Tommy gun, n. A Thompson submachine gun.
torpedo, n. A killer for hire.
twerp, n. A disagreeable or silly person.
two-bit, adj. Tasteless, gaudy.
upchuck, v. To vomit.
vamp, n. A woman who charms and seduces men; derives from the 1911 film *The Vampire*, starring Theda Bara.
washed up, adj. Finished.
weed, n. Marijuana.
wetback, n. A pejorative term for an illegal Mexican immigrant, derived from the practice of crossing into the United States from Mexico by swimming across the Rio Grande.
wet blanket, n. Someone who spoils others' fun.
wooden kimono, n. A coffin.
workweek, n. The specific hours or days that an employee will work during a calendar week.
yahoo, n. A socially awkward or unsophisticated person.
zozzled, adj. Drunk.

Jeffry Jensen

List of Entries by Category

African Americans
African Americans
Ali, Noble Drew
All God's Chillun Got Wings
Anderson, Marian
Armstrong, Louis
Baker, Josephine
Bell, James "Cool Papa"
Black-and-tan clubs
Black Swan Records
Brotherhood of Sleeping Car Porters
Cities
Civil rights and liberties
Coleman, Bessie
Corrigan v. Buckley
Cotton Club
Cox, Ida
Demographics
Du Bois, W. E. B.
Dyer antilynching bill
Emperor Jones, The
Garvey, Marcus
Great Migration
Harlem Renaissance
Hughes, Langston
Hurston, Zora Neale
Immigration to Canada
Jim Crow in the U.S. South
Johnson, Jack
Johnson, James Weldon
Johnson, Judy
Lynching
Micheaux, Oscar
Migrations
Moore v. Dempsey
National Association for the Advancement of Colored People (NAACP)
Negro History Week
Negro League Baseball
Nixon v. Herndon
Racial discrimination
Randolph, A. Philip
Robeson, Paul
Shuffle Along
Smith, Bessie
Universal Negro Improvement Association (UNIA)
Van Der Zee, James
Voting rights
Waller, Fats

Agriculture
Agricultural Marketing Act of 1929
Agriculture in Canada
Agriculture in the United States
Air pollution
Business and the economy
Farm subsidies
Frozen foods

Architecture & Engineering
Architecture
Bungalows
Cascade Tunnel
Chrysler Building
Detroit-Windsor Tunnel
Hearst Castle
Holland Tunnel
Lincoln Memorial
Mount Rushmore
Saarinen, Eliel
Schindler, Rudolph
Tomb of the Unknown Soldier
Wright, Frank Lloyd

Art & Photography
Art Deco
Art movements
Comic strips
Demuth, Charles
Felix the Cat
Group of Seven
Hopper, Edward
Marin, John
Museum of Modern Art (MoMA)
O'Keeffe, Georgia
Parrish, Maxfield
Phillips, C. Coles
Photography
Rockwell, Norman
Stein, Gertrude
Stieglitz, Alfred
Van Der Zee, James

Asia & Asian Americans
Asia
Asian Americans
Bose, Sudhindra
Immigration to Canada
Immigration to the United States
Racial discrimination

Automobiles & Automotive Manufacturing
Auto racing
Automobiles and auto manufacturing
Business and the economy
Chrysler, Walter P.
Hood ornaments
Model A Fords
National Conference on Street and Highway Safety
Traffic signals
Transportation
Travel

Business & Economics
A. C. Nielsen Company
Advertising in Canada
Advertising in the United States
Agricultural Marketing Act of 1929
Agriculture in Canada
Agriculture in the United States
Air Commerce Act of 1926
Airmail
Air Mail Act of 1925
Automobiles and auto manufacturing
Banking
Baylor Plan
Black Swan Records
Bonus Act of 1924
Book publishing
Business and the economy
Chain stores

Credit and debt
Currency and coinage
Douglas Aircraft Company
Electrification
Farm subsidies
Gross national product of the United States
Housing
Income and wages
Installment plans
International Business Machines (IBM)
International trade
Labor strikes
McFadden Act of 1927
National Broadcasting Company (NBC)
National debt, U.S.
Radio Corporation of America (RCA)
Recession of 1920–1921
Rural Life
Sears, Roebuck and Co.
Stock market crash
Unemployment
Unionism
United States v. United States Steel Corp
Warner Bros.

Business & Economics: People
Chandler, Harry
Chanel, Coco
Chrysler, Walter P.
Cox, James M.
Dawes, Charles G.
Disney, Walt
Eastman, George
Fokker, Anthony
Fox, William
Hearst, William Randolph
Hughes, Howard
Landis, Kenesaw Mountain
McKinsey, James Oscar
Mellon, Andrew
Sarnoff, David

Canada
Advertising in Canada
Agriculture in Canada

Alberta Sexual Sterilization Act
Canada and Great Britain
Canadian minority communities
Canadian nationalism
Chinese Immigration Act of 1923
Elections, Canadian
Group of Seven
Halibut Treaty of 1924
Immigration to Canada
Jews in Canada
King, William Lyon Mackenzie
Literature in Canada
Meighen, Arthur
Religion in Canada
Rosenfeld, Fanny "Bobbie"
Royal Canadian Air Force
Theater in Canada

Civil Rights & Liberties
Alberta Sexual Sterilization Act
American Civil Liberties Union (ACLU)
Asian Americans
Birth control
Bose, Sudhindra
Cable Act of 1922
Censorship
Chinese Immigration Act of 1923
Civil rights and liberties
Corrigan v. Buckley
Darrow, Clarence
Du Bois, W. E. B.
Equal Rights Amendment
Eugenics movement
Garvey, Marcus
Gitlow v. New York
Hester v. United States
Homosexuality and gay rights
Indian Citizenship Act of 1924
Japanese American Citizens League
Johnson, James Weldon
Keller, Helen
Latinos
League of United Latin American Citizens
League of Women Voters
Moore v. Dempsey
National Association for the Advancement of Colored People (NAACP)

Native Americans
Negro History Week
Nineteenth Amendment
Nixon v. Herndon
Olmstead v. United States
Ozawa v. United States
Palmer raids
Paul, Alice
Racial discrimination
Randolph, A. Philip
Red Scare, The
Robeson, Paul
Voting rights
Women's rights

Communications
Advertising in Canada
Advertising in the United States
American Mercury, The
Bookman, The
Book publishing
Dial, The
Federal Radio Commission (FRC)
Fugitive, The
Loudspeakers
Newspapers, U.S.
Public Opinion
Radio
Radio Act of 1927
Telephone technology and service
Television technology

Courts & Court Cases
Adkins v. Children's Hospital
Bailey v. Drexel Furniture Co.
Buck v. Bell
Gitlow v. New York
Hester v. United States
Holmes, Oliver Wendell Jr.
Hughes, Charles Evans
Meyer v. Nebraska
Moore v. Dempsey
Newberry v. United States
Nixon v. Herndon
Olmstead v. United States
Ozawa v. United States
Pierce v. Society of Sisters
Sacco and Vanzetti case
Scopes trial
Stone, Harlan Fiske

Supreme Court, U.S.
United States v. United States Steel Corp

Crime & Scandal
Arbuckle, Fatty
Capone, Al
Crimes and scandals
Denby, Edwin
Gambling
Hall-Mills murder case
Leopold-Loeb murder case
Lynching
Organized crime
Polygraph
President's Daughter, The
Prohibition
Saint Valentine's Day Massacre
Schultz, Dutch
Teapot Dome scandal
Thompson machine gun
Tong Wars of Chinatown, San Francisco

Dance
Broadway musicals
Brooks, Louise
Charleston, The
Dance and choreography
Dances, popular
Denishawn School of Dancing and Related Arts
Duncan, Isadora
Graham, Martha
Lindy Hop

Demographics
African Americans
Asian Americans
Canadian minority communities
Cities
City, The
Coney Island
Demographics
Great Migration
Housing
Immigration Act of 1921
Immigration Act of 1924
Immigration to Canada
Immigration to the United States
Jews in Canada
Jews in the United States
Latinos
Migrations
Native Americans
Rural Life
Suburbs
Urbanization

Diplomacy & International Relations
Asia
Canada and Great Britain
Chinese Immigration Act of 1923
Dawes Plan
Europe
Foreign policy, U.S.
Halibut Treaty of 1924
Isolationism
Kellogg-Briand Pact of 1928
Latin America and the Caribbean
League of Nations
Mexico
Nobel Prizes
Russian Famine Relief Act of 1921
Soviet Union and North America
Washington Naval Conference

Disasters
Castle Gate, Utah, mining disaster
Great Mississippi Flood of 1927
Knickerbocker Storm
Natural disasters
Okeechobee Hurricane of 1928
Shenandoah airship disaster
St. Francis Dam disaster
West Virginia mining disaster

Education & Scholarship
Archaeology
Astronomy
Bose, Sudhindra
California Institute of Technology (Caltech)
Chemistry
City, The
Coming of Age in Samoa
Denishawn School of Dancing and Related Arts
Dewey, John
Du Bois, W. E. B.
Durant, Will
Education
Einstein, Albert
Eugenics movement
Frontier in American History, The
Historiography
I'll Take My Stand
In the American Grain
John Keats
Little Blue Books
Main Currents in American Thought
Mead, Margaret
Meyer v. Nebraska
Montessori method
Negro History Week
New Criticism
Philosophy and philosophers
Pierce v. Society of Sisters
Psychology, psychiatry, and psychoanalysis
Scholastic Aptitude Test (SAT)
Scopes trial
Sex and sex education
Social sciences
Société Anonyme
Studies in Classic American Literature
Toomer, Jean
Women in college
Workers' education

Environmental Issues
Air pollution
Appalachian Trail
Byrd, Richard E.
Cancer
Federal Power Act of 1920
Gila Wilderness Area
Halibut Treaty of 1924
Izaak Walton League of America
National Parks, U.S.
Natural resources, exploitation of
Oil Pollution Act of 1924
Sinclair, Upton

Events
Better Homes in America movement
Castle Gate, Utah, mining disaster
Great Migration
Los Angeles Aqueduct dynamiting

Macy's Thanksgiving Day Parade
National Conference on Street and Highway Safety
Palmer raids
President's Conference on Unemployment
Recession of 1920-1921
Saint Valentine's Day Massacre
Scopes trial
Sesquicentennial Exposition
Tong Wars of Chinatown, San Francisco
Washington Naval Conference

Fads & Fashions
Art Deco
Bathing suits
Bobbed hair
Bubble Gum
Chanel, Coco
Cloche hats
Comic strips
Crossword puzzles
Dance and choreography
Dances, popular
Eskimo Pie
Fads
Fashions and clothing
Felix the Cat
Flagpole sitting
Flappers
Food trends
Hairstyles
Home furnishings
Hood ornaments
Mah-Jongg
Marathon dancing
Ouija boards
Player pianos
Postage stamps
Rayon stockings
Schiaparelli, Elsa
Yo-yos

Family Issues
Better Homes in America movement
Birth control
Chain stores
Demographics
Electrification
Eugenics movement
Food trends
Marriage and dating
Psychology, psychiatry, and psychoanalysis
Sex and sex education

Film
Academy Awards
Ben-Hur
Burns and Allen
Censorship
Circus, The
Cocoanut Grove
Cocoanuts, The
Felix the Cat
Film
Flesh and the Devil
General, The
Gold Diggers of Broadway
Gold Rush, The
Grauman's Chinese Theatre
Greed
Hallelujah
Hearst Castle
Hollywood sign
Jazz Singer, The
King of Kings, The
Koko the Clown
Laurel and Hardy
Marx Brothers
Merry Widow, The
Metro-Goldwyn-Mayer (MGM)
Movie palaces
Nanook of the North
Orphans of the Storm
Our Gang comedies
Rin Tin Tin films
Safety Last
Sheik, The
Steamboat Willie
Talking motion pictures
Ten Commandments, The
Thief of Bagdad
United Artists
Warner Bros.
Wings

Film: People
Arbuckle, Fatty
Baker, Josephine
Bánky, Vilma
Bara, Theda
Barrymore, John
Bow, Clara
Brooks, Louise
Bushman, Francis X.
Carr, Mary
Chaney, Lon
Chaplin, Charlie
Colman, Ronald
Coogan, Jackie
Crosby, Bing
DeMille, Cecil B.
Disney, Walt
Fairbanks, Douglas, Sr.
Fields, W. C.
Fox, William
Garbo, Greta
Gilbert, John
Gish, Dorothy
Gish, Lillian
Goldwyn, Samuel
Griffith, D. W.
Houdini, Harry
Hughes, Howard
Ince, Thomas H.
Jannings, Emil
Jolson, Al
Keaton, Buster
Langdon, Harry
Lasky, Jesse L.
Lloyd, Harold
Micheaux, Oscar
Mix, Tom
Normand, Mabel
Novarro, Ramón
Pickford, Mary
Reid, Wallace
Roach, Hal, Sr.
Rogers, Will
Sennett, Mack
Swanson, Gloria
Taylor, William Desmond
Valentino, Rudolph
Vidor, King
Warner, Harry

Warner, Sam
Weissmuller, Johnny
West, Mae

Government & Politics
Canadian nationalism
Communism
Congress, U.S.
Corrupt Practices Act of 1925
Dawes Plan
Elections, Canadian
Elections, midterm, U.S.
Elections of 1920, U.S.
Elections of 1924, U.S.
Elections of 1928, U.S.
Farm subsidies
Federal highway system
Foreign policy, U.S.
Newberry v. United States
Nineteenth Amendment
Olmstead v. United States
Political parties
President's Conference on Unemployment
Progressive Party of 1924
Recession of 1920–1921
"Return to Normalcy"
Unionism
Universal Negro Improvement Association (UNIA)

Government & Politics: People
Bryan, William Jennings
Cline, Genevieve R.
Coolidge, Calvin
Coolidge, Grace
Cox, James M.
Curtis, Charles
Daugherty, Harry M.
Davis, John W.
Dawes, Charles G.
Debs, Eugene V.
Denby, Edwin
Forbes, Charles R.
Garvey, Marcus
Gompers, Samuel
Harding, Warren G.
Haywood, Big Bill
Holmes, Oliver Wendell, Jr.
Hoover, Herbert
Hoover, J. Edgar
Hughes, Charles Evans
Kellogg, Frank B.
King, William Lyon Mackenzie
La Follette, Robert M.
Langley, John W.
Lodge, Henry Cabot
Meighen, Arthur
Mellon, Andrew
Roosevelt, Franklin D.
Ross, Nellie Tayloe
Smith, Alfred E.
Taft, William Howard
Walker, Jimmy
Wilson, Edith
Wilson, Woodrow

Government Agencies, Branches & Programs
Border Patrol, U.S.
Bureau of Chemistry and Soils, U.S.
Congress, U.S.
Federal Radio Commission (FRC)
Food, Drug, and Insecticide Administration, U.S.
National Parks, U.S.
Supreme Court, U.S.

Great Depression
Installment plans
National debt, U.S.
Stock market crash

Health & Medicine
Alberta Sexual Sterilization Act
Band-Aids
Banting, Frederick Grant
Baylor Plan
Birth control
Cancer
Cotton swabs
Food trends
Frozen foods
Health care
Insulin
Iron lung
Medicine
Polio
Sanger, Margaret
Sexually transmitted diseases
Vitamin D discovery

Jewish Americans
Jews in Canada
Jews in the United States
Immigration to Canada
Racial discrimination

Journalism & Publishing
Adams, Franklin P.
American Mercury, The
Book clubs
Bookman, The
Book publishing
Censorship
Chandler, Harry
Comic strips
Cox, James M.
Dial, The
Durant, Will
Ferber, Edna
Fugitive, The
Hearst, William Randolph
Historiography
I'll Take My Stand
In the American Grain
John Keats
Kirby, Rollin
Lardner, Ring
Lippmann, Walter
Little Blue Books
Luce, Henry R.
Magazines
Main Currents in American Thought
Mencken, H. L.
Micheaux, Oscar
Newspapers, U.S.
New Yorker, The
Post, Emily
Reed, John
Ross, Harold
Science fiction
Ten Days That Shook the World
Wallace, DeWitt
Wilson, Edmund

Labor
Adkins v. Children's Hospital
American Federation of Labor (AFL)
Bailey v. Drexel Furniture Co.
Brotherhood of Sleeping Car Porters
Business and the economy
Communism
Darrow, Clarence
Debs, Eugene V.
Electrification
Gompers, Samuel
Haywood, Big Bill
Income and wages
Labor strikes
Lewis, John L.
Railway Labor Act of 1926
Randolph, A. Philip
Unemployment
Unionism
Women in the workforce
Workers' education

Latin America & Latinos
Immigration to the United States
Latin America and the Caribbean
Latinos
League of United Latin American Citizens
Mexico
Novarro, Ramón
Racial discrimination
Valentino, Rudolph

Laws & Treaties
Agricultural Marketing Act of 1929
Air Commerce Act of 1926
Air Mail Act of 1925
Alberta Sexual Sterilization Act
Bonus Act of 1924
Cable Act of 1922
Chinese Immigration Act of 1923
Corrigan v. Buckley
Corrupt Practices Act of 1925
Dyer antilynching bill
Equal Rights Amendment
Federal Aid Highway Act of 1921
Federal Power Act of 1920
Halibut Treaty of 1924
Immigration Act of 1921
Immigration Act of 1924
Indian Citizenship Act of 1924
Kellogg-Briand Pact of 1928
McFadden Act of 1927
Nineteenth Amendment
Oil Pollution Act of 1924
Prohibition
Radio Act of 1927
Railway Labor Act of 1926
Revenue Acts of 1924, 1926, and 1928
Russian Famine Relief Act of 1921
Sheppard-Towner Act
United States v. Ninety-Five Barrels Alleged Apple Cider Vinegar

Literature
Age of Innocence, The
Algonquin Round Table
Alice Adams
Babbitt
Bridge of San Luis Rey, The
Death Comes for the Archbishop
Elmer Gantry
Farewell to Arms, A
Gentlemen Prefer Blondes
Great Gatsby, The
Harlem Renaissance
Harp Weaver and Other Poems, The
John Brown's Body
John Keats
Literature in Canada
Literature in the United States
Lost generation
Lowell, Amy
Main Street
New Criticism
Nobel Prizes
O'Neill, Eugene
Poetry
Prophet, The
Sartoris
Science fiction
Sound and the Fury, The
Southern Agrarians
Spring and All
Stella Dallas
Strange Interlude
Studies in Classic American Literature
Sun Also Rises, The
Tales of the Jazz Age
This Side of Paradise
Three Soldiers
Toomer, Jean
Waste Land, The
What's O'Clock

Literature: People
Aiken, Conrad
Anderson, Sherwood
Cabell, James Branch
Cather, Willa
Cummings, E. E.
Doolittle, Hilda
Eliot, T. S.
Faulkner, William
Faust, Frederick
Ferber, Edna
Fitzgerald, F. Scott
Fitzgerald, Zelda
Frost, Robert
Fugitive Poets
Hammett, Dashiell
Hemingway, Ernest
Hughes, Langston
Hurston, Zora Neale
Johnson, James Weldon
Kirby, Rollin
Lardner, Ring
Lewis, Sinclair
Lindsay, Vachel
Look Homeward, Angel
MacLeish, Archibald
Millay, Edna St. Vincent
Parker, Dorothy
Pound, Ezra
Robinson, Edwin Arlington
Sandburg, Carl
Sinclair, Upton
Stein, Gertrude
Tarkington, Booth
Teasdale, Sara
Wharton, Edith
Wilder, Thornton
Williams, William Carlos
Wylie, Elinor

Military & War
Airships
Bonus Act of 1924
Europe
Farewell to Arms, A
Kellogg-Briand Pact of 1928
Mitchell, Billy
Royal Canadian Air Force
Thompson machine gun
Three Soldiers
Tomb of the Unknown Soldier
Washington Naval Conference
Wings
World War I veterans

Music
Black-and-tan clubs
Black Swan Records
Broadway musicals
Charleston, The
Classical music
Cotton Club
Crooners
Dance and choreography
Dances, popular
Electrical recording
Grand Ole Opry, The
Harlem Renaissance
Jazz
Lindy Hop
Music, popular
Rhapsody in Blue
Show Boat
Shuffle Along
Student Prince, The
Tin Pan Alley

Music: People
Anderson, Marian
Armstrong, Louis
Baker, Josephine
Beiderbecke, Bix
Berlin, Irving
Carmichael, Hoagy
Carter Family
Cohan, George M.
Copland, Aaron
Cox, Ida
Crosby, Bing
Ellington, Duke
Gershwin, George
Hammerstein, Oscar, II
Hardin, Lillian
Hart, Lorenz
Jolson, Al
Kane, Helen
Kern, Jerome
Lang, Eddie
Menuhin, Yehudi
Morton, Jelly Roll
Oliver, Joe King
Piston, Walter
Rodgers, Jimmie
Romberg, Sigmund
Smith, Bessie
Vallée, Rudy
Waller, Fats
Whiteman, Paul

Native Americans
Archaeology
Civil rights and liberties
Indian Citizenship Act of 1924
Native Americans

Organizations
American Civil Liberties Union (ACLU)
American Federation of Labor (AFL)
Book clubs
Brotherhood of Sleeping Car Porters
Izaak Walton League of America
Japanese American Citizens League
Ku Klux Klan
League of Nations
League of United Latin American Citizens
League of Women Voters
National Association for the Advancement of Colored People (NAACP)
Société Anonyme
Universal Negro Improvement Association (UNIA)

Products & Inventions
Airships
Automobiles and auto manufacturing
Band-Aids
Birdseye, Clarence
Bread slicer
Bubble Gum
Bulldozer
Cellophane
Cotton swabs
Differential analyzer
Eskimo Pie
Freon
Frozen foods
Girl Scout Cookies
Hair dryers
Inventions
Kool-Aid
Loudspeakers
Peanut butter and jelly sandwiches
Player pianos
Polygraph
Refrigerators
Telephone technology and service
Television technology
Thompson machine gun

Prohibition
Bathtub gin
Black-and-tan clubs
Cotton Club
Gambling
Organized crime
Prohibition
Roaring Twenties
Saint Valentine's Day Massacre
Speakeasies

Radio
Advertising in Canada
Advertising in the United States
Burns and Allen
Classical music
Evangelism
Federal Radio Commission (FRC)
Grand Ole Opry, The
National Broadcasting Company (NBC)
Radio
Radio Act of 1927
Vaudeville

Recreation & Entertainment

Appalachian Trail
Auto racing
Aviation
Baseball
Boxing
Cocoanut Grove
Coney Island
Crossword puzzles
Dance and choreography
Dances, popular
Fads
Film
Golf
Hobbies and recreation
Hollywood Bowl
Horse racing
Mah-Jongg
Marathon dancing
Miss America pageants
Movie palaces
Nightclubs
Ouija boards
Ringling Bros. and Barnum & Bailey Circus
Rogers, Will
Sports
Steamboat Willie
Talking motion pictures
Tennis
Travel
Vaudeville
Ziegfeld Follies

Religion & Theology

Ali, Noble Drew
Elmer Gantry
Evangelism
McPherson, Aimee Semple
Pierce v. Society of Sisters
Religion in Canada
Religion in the United States
Scopes trial
Spiritualism

Science & Technology

Andrews, Roy Chapman
Archaeology
Astronomy
Aviation
Banting, Frederick Grant
Bell Labs
Birdseye, Clarence
Bulldozer
Byrd, Richard E.
Cellophane
Chemistry
Compton, Arthur Holly
Differential analyzer
Einstein, Albert
Electrical recording
Electrification
Freon
Frozen foods
Goddard, Robert
Hubble, Edwin Powell
Loudspeakers
Millikan, Robert Andrews
Morgan, Thomas Hunt
Nobel Prizes
Physics
Rocketry
Science and technology
Sturtevant, Alfred H.
Telephone technology and service
Television technology
Zworykin, Vladimir

Social Issues

Anti-Semitism
Better Homes in America movement
Black-and-tan clubs
Canadian minority communities
Cities
City, The
Coleman, Bessie
Coming of Age in Samoa
Corrigan v. Buckley
Cotton Club
Du Bois, W. E. B.
Eugenics movement
Harlem Renaissance
Homosexuality and gay rights
Jim Crow in the U.S. South
Marriage and dating
Migrations
Photography
Pornography
Prohibition
Psychology, psychiatry, and psychoanalysis
Red Scare, The
Roaring Twenties
Rural Life
Sex and sex education
Slang
Speakeasies
Suburbs
Urbanization
Women in college
World War I veterans

Sports

Alexander, Grover Cleveland
Auto racing
Baseball
Bell, James "Cool Papa"
Boxing
Bunion Derby
Capablanca, José Raúl
Cobb, Ty
Dempsey, Jack
Ederle, Gertrude
Flagpole sitting
Football
Four Horsemen of Notre Dame
Foxx, Jimmie
Gehrig, Lou
Gipp, George
Golf
Grange, Red
Grove, Lefty
Hockey
Hornsby, Rogers
Horse racing
Johnson, Jack
Johnson, Judy
Jones, Bobby
Kahanamoku, Duke
Landis, Kenesaw Mountain
Los Angeles Memorial Coliseum
Man o' War
Moody, Helen Wills
National Football League
Negro League Baseball
New York Yankees
Olympic Games of 1920 (Summer)
Olympic Games of 1924 (Summer)

Olympic Games of 1924 (Winter)
Olympic Games of 1928 (Summer)
Olympic Games of 1928 (Winter)
Ott, Mel
Paddock, Charles
Robeson, Paul
Rockne, Knute
Rosenfeld, Fanny "Bobbie"
Ruth, Babe
Scholz, Jackson
Soccer
Sports
Tennis
Thorpe, Jim
Tilden, Bill
Tunney, Gene
Weissmuller, Johnny

Theater
Adding Machine, The
All God's Chillun Got Wings
Anna Christie
Broadway musicals
Burns and Allen
Cohan, George M.
Desire Under the Elms
Emperor Jones, The
Show Boat
Shuffle Along
Strange Interlude
Student Prince, The
Theater in Canada
Theater in the United States
Vaudeville
Wilder, Thornton
Ziegfeld, Florenz
Ziegfeld Follies

Transportation & Travel
Air Commerce Act of 1926
Airmail
Air Mail Act of 1925
Airships
Appalachian Trail
Automobiles and auto manufacturing
Aviation
Cascade Tunnel
Cities
Earhart, Amelia
Federal Aid Highway Act of 1921
Federal highway system
Fokker, Anthony
Lindbergh, Charles
Motels
Pershing Map
Railroads
Railway Labor Act of 1926
Route 66
Traffic signals
Transportation

Women's Issues
Adkins v. Children's Hospital
Birth control
Cline, Genevieve R.
Coolidge, Grace
Doolittle, Hilda
Earhart, Amelia
Equal Rights Amendment
Fads
Fashions and clothing
Fitzgerald, Zelda
Flappers
League of Women Voters
Miss America pageants
Nineteenth Amendment
Paul, Alice
Sanger, Margaret
Sheppard-Towner Act
Voting rights
Women in college
Women in the workforce
Women's rights

Indexes

Photo Index

Adams, Franklin P., 3
advertisement for chewing gum, 9
African Americans: Cotton Club, 200; family, 11; Negro League Baseball, 618
agriculture, farmer in wheat field, 19
airmail plane, 876
air pollution, 24
Alexander, Grover Cleveland, 29
Allen, Gracie, 121
Anderson, Marian, 39
Andrews, Roy Chapman, 41
Arbuckle, Roscoe "Fatty," 46
Armstrong, Louis, 52
Art Deco, Chrysler Building, 163
Astaire, Adele, 402
Astaire, Fred, 402
automobiles: air pollution from, 24; Model T Ford, 64
aviation, airmail, 876

Baker, Josephine, 75
Banting, Frederick Grant, 449
Bara, Theda, 82
baseball, Negro League, 618
Beiderbecke, Bix, 89
Ben-Hur (film, 1959), 91
Berlin, Irving, 92
Best, Charles, 449
Birdseye, Clarence, 319
bobbed hair, 98
Book-of-the-Month Club, 100
Bow, Clara, 107
Brooks, Louise, 98
Bryan, William Jennings, 115
bungalows, 118
Burns, George, 121
Burns and Allen, 121

California Institute of Technology (Caltech), 129
Capone, Al, 141
Carter family, 144
Cather, Willa, 146
Chandler, Harry, 152

Chaplin, Charles, 156
Charleston, The (dance), 218
chewing gum advertising, 9
Chicago American Giants (Negro League Baseball), 618
Chicago Bears (football), 322
Chrysler Building, 163
cigarettes, 138
Clemenceau, Georges, 281
Cobb, Ty, 177
Coleman, Bessie, 181
Coney Island, 188
Coolidge, Calvin, 193, 226, 268, 737
Copeland, Aaron, 197
Cotton Club, 200
Cox, James M., 202, 265
Crash of 1929, 830
Creole Jazz Band, 641
Crosby, Bing, 211
Cummings, E. E., 213

dance, The Charleston, 218
Darrow, Clarence, 221
Dawes, Charles G., 226
Debs, Eugene V., 228
De Forest, Lee, 846
Dempsey, Jack "Manassa Mauler," 235
Denby, Edwin, 238
Dewey, John, 241
dinosaur eggs, fossil, 41
Disney, Walt, 244
Duncan, Isadora, 249

Earhart, Amelia, 253
Eliot, T. S., 273
Ellington, Duke, 464

factory production, 124
Fairbanks, Douglas, Sr., 288
Fall, Albert, 849
farmer in wheat field, 19
Farnsworth, Philo T., 854
Faulkner, William, 295
Fauset, Jessie Redmon, 384

Federal Aid Highway Act of 1921, 299
federal highway system, 299
Ferber, Edna, 303
film actresses, 634
Finland, 645
Fitzgerald, F. Scott, 311, 531
Fitzgerald, Zelda, 311
flappers, 313
football: Four Horsemen of Notre Dame, 820; Los Angeles Memorial Coliseum, 539
Ford, Henry, 64
Ford Model T, 64, 455
Four Horsemen of Notre Dame, 820
Fox, William, 328
Freud, Sigmund, 704
Frost, Robert, 332

gambling, 338
Garbo, Greta, 339
Gehrig, Lou, 85, 342
George, David Lloyd, 281
Gershwin, George, 173, 345, 596
Gershwin, Ira, 596
Gipp, George, 347
Gish, Lillian, 349
Goddard, Robert H., 352
golf, 356
Grange, Red, 361
Great Mississippi Flood of 1927, 366
Griffith, D. W., 367
Grove, Lefty, 371

Hadden, Briton, 550
Hagen, Walter, 356
Hammerstein, Oscar II, 378
Harding, Warren G., 207, 265
Haywood, Big Bill, 389
Hearst, William Randolph, 392
Hemingway, Ernest, 395
Hollywood Bowl, 406
Hooker Telescope, Mount Wilson Observatory, 62

Hoover, Herbert, 414
Hopper, Edward, 55
Houdini, Harry, 421
housing, bungalows, 118
Hubble, Edwin Powell, 425
Hughes, Howard R., Jr., 428

Immigration Act of 1921
   (cartoon), 434
Ince, Thomas H., 443

Jannings, Emil, 461
Jazz Singer, The (film poster), 467
Johnson, Jack, 474
Jones, Bobby, 478

Kaufman, George S., 862
Keaton, Buster, 481
Kellogg, Frank B., 483
Kern, Jerome, 112
King, William Lyon Mackenzie, 488
Knickerbocker Storm damage, 492

La Follette, Robert M., 500
Langdon, Harry, 503
Lardner, Ring, 505
Laurel and Hardy, 512
League of Women Voters poster, 517
Lewis, John L., 883
Lewis, Sinclair, 520
Lippmann, Walter, 526
Lodge, Henry Cabot, 536
Loew, Marcus, 897
Luce, Henry R., 544

Mah-Jongg, 402
Man o' War (race horse), 554
Marx Brothers, 558
McKinney, Nina Mae, 376
McPherson, Aimee Semple, 561
Mellon, Andrew (cartoon), 737
Mencken, H. L., 569
MGM studio postcard, 573
Millay, Edna St. Vincent, 580
Mississippi River Flood of 1927, 366

Mitchell, Billy, 585
Model T Ford, 64, 455
Moody, Helen Wills, 589
Morgan, Thomas Hunt, 591
Mount Rushmore, 593
Mount Wilson Observatory, 62

NBC control room, 602
Negro League Baseball, 618
newspapers: *New York Daily News*
   front page, 622; stock market
   crash headline, 830
Nineteenth Amendment
   document, 928
Normand, Mabel, 634
Notre Dame University, Four
   Horsemen of Notre Dame, 820
Nurmi, Paavo, 645

O'Keeffe, Georgia, 639
Oliver, Joe "King," 641
Olympic Games of 1924
   (Summer), 645
Olympic Games of 1928
   (Summer), 649
O'Neill, Eugene, 653
Ott, Mel, 658
Our Gang comedies, 660

Paddock, Charles, 663
Paul, Alice, 666
Phonofilm, 846
Pickford, Mary, 678
political cartoons, 207, 434, 737
Post, Emily, 692
Pound, Ezra, 694
Prohibition, 700

Randolph, Asa Philip, 720
Reid, Wallace, 729
Revenue Act pf 1924 (cartoon), 737
Roach, Hal, Sr., 740
road construction and safety, 299
Robeson, Paul, 276
rocketry, 352

Rockne, Knute, 747
Rogers, Will, 750
Roosevelt, Franklin Delano, 202, 753
Ross, Harold, 624
Ross, Nellie Tayloe, 756
Ruth, Babe, 85, 763

Sandburg, Carl, 770
Schiaparelli, Elsa, 775
Schultz, Dutch, 778
Scopes, John, 787
Sennett, Mack, 790
Sennett comedy, 313
USS *Shenandoah* airship disaster, 27, 798
Shenandoah National Park, 607
Sinclair, Upton, 801
skyscraper, Chrysler Building, 163
smoking, 138
speakeasies, 817
Stein, Gertrude, 826
stock market crash, 830
Stone, Harlan Fiske, 832

Taft, William Howard, 843
Tarkington, Booth, 32
Tate, Allen, 814
Teapot Dome scandal (cartoon), 207
telescope, Mount Wilson
   Observatory, 62
television, Farnsworth's
   transmission system, 854
Thorpe, Jim, 866
Tilden, "Big" Bill, 857
Tomb of the Unknown Soldier, 870
Toomer, Jean, 873
tornadoes, 612
track and field, Olympic Games, 645, 649
Tri-State tornadoes, 612

Valentino, Rudolph, 893
voting rights (U.S.), women, 901

Waner, Lloyd, 85
Waner, Paul, 85
Warner, Harry, 905
Warner Bros. studio aerial view, 907
Weissmuller, Johnny, 911

Wharton, Edith, 914
Whitehead, Alfred North, 671
Wilder, Thornton, 917
Williams, William Carlos, 683
Wilson, Woodrow, 281, 921
women smoking cigarettes, 138

women's voting rights, 901
Wright, Frank Lloyd, 935

yo-yos, 937

Ziegfeld Follies, 940

■ Personages Index

Note: Page numbers in **bold** indicate main discussion.

Abel, John Jacob, 449–450
Adams, Franklin P., **3–4**
Aiken, Conrad, **21**
Albright, Horace M., 607–608
Alekhine, Alexander, 140
Alexander, Beatrice, 403
Alexander, Grover Cleveland, **29–30**
Ali, Noble Drew, **31–32**
Anderson, Marian, **38–39**
Anderson, Maxwell, 861
Anderson, Sherwood, **39–41**, 530
Andrews, Roy Chapman, **41–42**
Antheil, George, 174
Arbuckle, Roscoe "Fatty," **45–47**, 207, 481, **634**
Armstrong, Louis, **52–53**; jazz bands and recordings, 464–465; and Lillian Hardin, 380; nightclubs, 627; Joe "King" Oliver, 641
Astaire, Adele, 402
Astaire, Fred, 402

Babcock, Joseph Park, 402, 551
Baker, George Pierce, 530
Baker, Josephine, **74–76**, 801
Baldwin, Roger, 34
Bánky, Vilma, **80–81**
Banting, Frederick Grant, **81**, 449, 450, 566, 632–633
Bara, Theda, **82**
Barnes, Harry Elmer, 398
Barney, Natalie, 540
Barnsdall, Aline, 776, 934
Barry, Philip, 861
Barrymore, John, **82–83**, 906, 908
Baum, L. Frank, 666
Beard, Charles A., 398–399
Beauchemin, Nérée, 528
Beiderbecke, Bix, **88–89**
Bell, Alexander Graham, 541, 852, 853
Bell, James "Cool Papa," **89–90, 619**
Benét, Stephen Vincent, 472, 530
Berlin, Irving, **91–93**, 111–112
Best, Charles, 449, 450, 566, 632
Bethune, Mary McLeod, 257
Bigelow, Maurice, 792
Binet, Alfred, 704
Birdseye, Clarence, **94–95**, 319, 333–334
Blake, Eubie, **800–801**
Bliss, Lillie P., 594
Blizzard, William, 499
Blumgart, Hermann, 566
Boas, Franz, 431, 810
Bohr, Niels, 675
Boothe, Clare, 544
Borglum, Gutzon, 593
Bose, Sudhindra, **105–106**
Bourke-White, Margaret, 674
Bow, Clara, **106–107**, 923
Brand, Max. See Faust, Frederick
Brandeis, Louis D., 832, 839, 840
Brandenberger, Jacques E., 147–148
Brawne, Fanny, 473, 543
Breasted, James Henry, 399
Breuer, Marcel, 409
Briand, Aristide, 484
Brice, Fanny, 940
Brigham, Carl, 776
Britton, Nan, **696**
Brooks, Louise, 98, **113–114**
Brown, Wade Hampton, 564
Bryan, William Jennings, **115–116**; religion in the U.S., 734, 782; *Scopes* trial, 786, 787, 923
Buck, Gene, 940–941
Bugnet, Georges-Charles-Jules (Henri Doutremont), 528–529
Burgess, Ernest W., 169–170
Burns, George, **120–121**
Burns, William J., 416
Bush, Vannevar, 243
Bushman, Francis X, **121–122**
Butler, Pierce, 839
Byng, Lord (Governor-General of Canada), 567
Byrd, Richard E., 71, **125–126**

Cabell, James Branch, **127–128**, 690
Cable, John, 128, 930
Cady, Walter G., 676
Calder, Alexander, 56
Callaghan, Morley, 527–528
Calles, Plutarco Elías, 575
Campbell, Walter, 317
Cantor, Eddie, 940
Capablanca, José Raúl, **140**
Capone, Al, **140–142**, 654, 768–769
Capra, Frank, 504
Carman, Bliss, 528
Carmichael, Franklin, 370–371
Carmichael, Hoagy, **142–143**
Carr, Joe F., 322–323
Carr, Mary, **143**
Carter, Alvin Pleasant, 143–144
Carter, Howard, 48
Carter family, **143–144**
Castle, Irene, 98, 554
Castle, Vernon, 554
Cather, Willa, **146–147, 227–228**
Catt, Carrie Chapman, 516, 517, 629
Chandler, Harry, **151–152**, 407
Chanel, Coco, **152–154**, 176
Chaney, Lon, **154–155**
Chaplin, Charles, **155–157**; *Circus, The,* 157, **164–165**; *Gold Rush, The,* 353–354; Thomas H. Ince scandal, 207–208; Keystone Kops films, 790; *Kid, The,* 155–156, 192; Harold Lloyd's character *vs.*, 534; notable acquaintances, 355, 443, 841–842; scandals, 634; Tramp character, 157, 164–165; United Artists, 678, 886
Chase, Frank J., 570

Choquette, Robert, 528
Chrysler, Walter P., 65, **162–163**
Clarke, John Hessin, 839
Clemenceau, Georges, 281
Cline, Genevieve R., **175–176**
Cobb, Ty, 84, **177–178**
Cohan, George M., 112, **180–181**
Coleman, Bessie, 69, **181–182**
Collier, John, 609–610
Collip, James, 449, 450
Colman, Ronald, 80–81, **182–183**, 355
Compton, Arthur Holly, **187–188**, 633, 675–676
Conant, James Bryant, 159
Conrad, Frank, 710
Constantin-Weyer, Maurice, 529
Coogan, Jackie, 155, **192–193**
Cook, George Cram, 530
Coolidge, Calvin, **193–196**; Charles G. Dawes, 224, 226; elections of 1924, 223, **266–269**; Oil Pollution Act, 615, **637–638**; railroad, 719; Revenue Act of 1924 cartoon, 737; Sesquicentennial Exposition, 791; Harlan Fiske Stone, 832; support of Better Homes in America movement, 93; Teapot Dome scandal, 849; on women's colleges, 924
Coolidge, Grace, **196**
Cooper, Gary, 355
Copeland, Aaron, 173–174, **197**
Cowell, Henry, 173
Cox, Ida, **201**
Cox, James M., **202**, 265
Crane, Hart, 682–683
Crosby, Bing, **210–211**
Cukor, George, 349
Cullen, Countée, 683–684
Cummings, E. E., **212–214**
Cummings, James D., 118, 454
Cummins, Albert, 716
Cunningham, Imogen, 673
Curtis, Charles, **215–216**
Curtis, Edward, 675

Darrow, Clarence, **220–222**, 518, 623, 786–788

Darwin, Charles, 671
Daugherty, Harry M., **222–223**
Davies, Marion, 392
Davis, John W., **223–224**
Davis, Stuart, 55
Davisson, Clinton J., 676, 677
Dawes, Charles G., **224–225**, 226, 560, 632, 633
Day, William Rufus, 839
de Broglie, Louis, 676
Debs, Eugene V., **228–229**, 687, 885
de Coubertin, Pierre, 643, 645, 649, 651
de la Roche, Mazo, 527
DeMille, Cecil B., **229–230**; *King of Kings* (film), 490, 506–507; *Ten Commandments, The* (film, 1923), 230, 507, **855–856**
Dempsey, Jack "Manassa Mauler," 108–109, **234–236**, 821, 880
Demuth, Charles, 55, **236–237**
Denby, Edwin, **237–238**
Denison, Merrill, 860
Desrochers, Alfred, 528
Dewey, John, **241–242**, 588, 668–669
Dickson, Earle, 76–77
Diemer, Walter, 116
Dilg, Will H., 460
Dillingham, William, 435
Disney, Walt, **244–245**, 401, **823–824**
Doheny, Edward L., 849, 850
Doolittle, Hilda (H. D.), **245–246**
Doolittle, James, 879
Dos Passos, John, 868
Douglas, Andrew, 48
Douglas, Donald, 246–247
Doyle, Arthur Conan, 818
Dreier, Katherine, **812**
Drinker, Cecil, 457
Drinker, Philip, 457, 566
Du Bois, W. E. B., **247–248**; on history, 399; influence on Harlem Renaissance, 383; Fayette McKenzie, 471; political activism, 13, 600
Duchamp, Marcel, **812**
Dumont, Margaret, 559

Dunbar-Nelson, Alice Moore, 630
Duncan, F. Duncan, 938
Duncan, Isadora, **249–250**
Dunning, William A., 399
Durant, Will, **250–251**, 400
Durant, William (GM founder), 65
Dyer, Leonidas C., 251, 546, 600–601

Earhart, Amelia, 70, **253–254**
Eastman, George, **254–255**
Eaton, Fred, 537
Eckholm, H. Conrad, 583
Edel, Leon, 921
Ederle, Gertrude, **255–256**, 646
Edison, Thomas A., 845
Ehrlich, Paul, 564
Einstein, Albert, **259–260**, 425, 671
Eisenhower, Dwight D., 668
Eliot, T. S., **273–274**, 530, **910**
Ellington, Duke, **274–275**, 384, 465, 596, 627
Evans, Hiram Wesley, 495
Evans, Walker, 674
Everhart, Mahlon T., 850

Fairbanks, Douglas, Sr., **288–289**, 578, 678, **864**, 886
Fall, Albert, 849–850, 849
Farnsworth, Philo T., 854–855
Farrar, John, 101, 102
Faulkner, William, **294–296**, 531, **774**
Fauset, Jessie Redmon, 383, 384, 385
Faust, Frederick, **296–298**
Fay, Sidney B., 398
Ferber, Edna, **303–304**
Fields, W. C., **305**, 940
Fitzgerald, F. Scott, **308–310**, 531; bobbed hair, 98, 374; *Great Gatsby, The,* 362, 531; Earnest Hemingway, 396; Ring Lardner, 505–506; marriage to Zelda, 310–312; in Paris, 103; Arnold Rothstein, 337; *Tales of the Jazz Age,* **845**; *This Side of Paradise,* **864–865**

Fitzgerald, Zelda, 309, **310–312**, 374
Fleischer, Dave, 493
Fleischer, Max, 493
Fleming, Alexander, 391, 565
Flint, Charles R., 450
Flores, Pedro, 937
Flowers, Theodore "Tiger," 108–109
Fokker, Anthony, **315–316**
Forbes, Charles R., **323–324**
Ford, Edsel, 586, 587, 876–877
Ford, Henry: airmail, 876–877, 879; Anti-Semitism, 709; automobile industry, 43, 64, 586; automobiles to the Soviet Union, 815–816; with Model T, 64; trucking, 876
Fosdick, Harry Emerson, 734
Foster, Andrew "Rube," 617–618
Foster, William Z., 36, 498
Fox, William, **327–329**
Foxx, Jimmie, **329–330**
Frankfurter, Felix, 5
Franklin, Benjamin, 692, 693
Franks, Bobbie, 518
Freeman, Milton H., 405
Freud, Sigmund, 702–703, 704, 810
Friml, Rudolf, 112
Frost, Robert, **332–333**, 683
Fuld, William, 658–659
Fuller, R. Buckminster, 50, 423

Garbo, Greta, **314–315, 338–340**
Garvey, Marcus, **340–341**; Harlem Renaissance, 385; Pan-Africanism, 247–248; political activism, 13, 888
Gehrig, Lou, 85, **342**, 626, 627, 763, 764
George, David Lloyd, 281
Gerber, Henry, 412
Gernsback, Hugo, 785
Gershwin, George, **344–345**; classical music, 172–173; musical theater in the U.S., 861; operettas, 112, 751–752; recorded sound, 596; *Rhapsody in Blue*, 344, 464, 596, **737–738**, 916

Gershwin, Ira, 344, 596, 861
Gilbert, John, **314–315**, 332, **346**
Gipp, George, **347–348**
Gish, Dorothy, **348–349**, 657
Gish, Lillian, 348, **349–350**, 657
Gitlow, Benjamin, 350
Goddard, Henry, 704, 776
Goddard, Robert H., **351–352**, 745
Godefoy, Alexander F., 373
Goldwyn, Samuel, 80, 81, **354–355**, 572–573
Gompers, Samuel, 35–37, **357–358**, 699–700, 885
Graham, Martha, 217–218, **358–359**
Grange, Red, 119, **360–361**, 606, 821
Grant, Madison, 440
Grauman, Sid, 361–362
Greb, Harry, 108, 109
Greenlee, Gus, 618
Griffith, D. W., **367–368**; actors, 348, 349, 678, 789; film techniques of, 657; United Artists, 678, 886
Grove, Frederick Philip, 527
Grove, Lefty, **371–372**
Guilledo, Filipino Francisco (Pancho Villa), 109
Gurdjieff, Georges Ivanovich, 873

Hadden, Briton, 544, 549, 550
Hagen, Walter, 356
Haldeman-Julius, Emanuel, **533–534**
Hale, George Ellery, 582
Hall, Edward, 377
Hall, Frances, 377
Hall, Radclyffe, 412
Hammerstein, Oscar II, **378–379**, 800, 861, 939
Hammett, Dashiell, **379**
Hanson, Howard, 173
Hardin, Lillian "Lil Hot Miss," **379–380**
Harding, Warren G., **380–383**; Charles Curtis, 215–216; Harry M. Daugherty, 222; death of, 267; elections of 1920, **264–266**; front porch campaign, 266; Charles Evans Hughes, 426; President's Conference on Unemployment, **695–696**; radio, 712; railroads, 716–717; recession of 1920–1921, 381–382, 881; religion in the U.S., 732; "return to normalcy," 687, **735–736**, 922, 927; Roaring Twenties, 741; scandals involving Ohio gang, 207, 208; Shopmen's Strike, 716–717, 719; William Howard Taft as Supreme Court chief justice, 839, 843; Teapot Dome scandal, 207, 849; U.S. foreign policy, 324
Hardy, Oliver, 511–513, 740
Harris, Lawren, 370–371
Hart, Lorenz, **387–388**
Hatfield, Sid, 499
Hawthorne, Nathanial, 835
Hayes, Carlton, 398
Haynes, Daniel L., 376
Haywood, Big Bill, **388–389**
Hearst, William Randolph, **392–393**; Hearst Castle, 50, **393–395**; Thomas H. Ince scandal, 207–208, 443; newspapers, 621–623; yo-yos, 938
Heidelberger, Michael, 564
Hemingway, Ernest, **395–397**; *Farewell to Arms, A*, **289–290**; lost generation in Paris, 103, 532, 540; Gertrude Stein, 825; *Torrents of Spring, The*, 40. *See also Sun Also Rises, The* (in subject index)
Henderson, Fletcher, 98, 464
Hess, Victor Francis, 676
Hirsch, Sidney M., 335
Hitchcock, Alfred, 418
Holland, Clifford Milburn, 405
Hollerith, Herman, 450
Holmes, Oliver Wendell, Jr., **407–408**; birth control, 117; *Moore v. Dempsey*, 590; as Supreme Court justice, 832, 839, 840; voting rights, 631

Hoover, Herbert, **414–416**; Better Homes in America movement, 93; as Commerce Secretary, 195; Charles Curtis, 216; elections of 1928, **269–271**, 712; gang violence, 141; Great Mississippi Flood, 365; laissez-faire response to unemployment, 881, 882; National Conference on Street and Highway Safety, 604; pacifism, 733; President's Conference on Unemployment, 695; Prohibition, 700; radio, 713
Hoover, J. Edgar, **416–417**; FBI, 416–417, 832; Palmer raids, 185, 664, 724, 725–726; Red Scare, 724
Hopper, Edward, 55, 56, **417–419**
Hopwood, Avery, 353
Hornsby, Rogers, 85, **419**
Houdini, Harry, **421–422**, 818–819
Hubbard, William Dehart, 645
Hubble, Edwin Powell, 61–62, **424–426**
Hughes, Charles Evans, **426–427**, 459, 909
Hughes, Howard R., Jr., **427–429**
Hughes, Howard R., Sr., 428
Hughes, Langston, 385, **429–431**, 683
Huld, Anna, 939
Hunt, Myron, 406
Hurston, Zora Neale, **431–432**

Ince, Thomas H., **442–443**
Ingle, Gladys, 69
Ives, Charles, 173

Jackson, A. Y., 370–371
Jacobs, Walter, 564
James, William, 610
Jannings, Emil, **461–462**
Jewett, Frank B., 90
Johnson, Charles, 11, 384
Johnson, Jack, **473–474**
Johnson, James Weldon, **474–475**
Johnson, Judy, **476**
Johnston, Franz, 370–371

Jolson, Al, 466–467, **476–477**, 906, 908
Jones, Bobby, 402, **477–478**
Just, Ernest E., 780

Kahanamoku, Duke, **479**, 644, 646
Kahn, Reuben Leon, 796
Kane, Helen, **479–480**
Kaufman, George S., 304, 861, 862
Keaton, Buster, 343, **480–482**, 886
Keats, John, **472–473**, 543
Keeler, Leonarde, 689
Keller, Helen, **482–483**, 933
Kellogg, Edward W., 541
Kellogg, Frank B., 263, 326, 459, **483–484**, 632
Kelly, Alvin, 312
Kern, Jerome, **486–487**; Broadway musicals, 93, 111, 112; *Show Boat*, 486–487, 800, 861, 939
Keyes, Asa, 562
Kimball, Justin Ford, 87–88, 566
King, William Lyon Mackenzie, **487–490**; Canadian elections, 260–262; Canadian independence and nationalism, 131, 132, 136; Halibut Treaty (1924), 375; Arthur Meighen, 567
Kirby, Rollin, **490–491**
Knister, Raymond, 527

La Follette, Robert M., 267–268, **500–501**, 688, 696–697
La Guardia, Fiorella, 903
Lamontagne-Beauregard, Blanche, 528
Landis, Kenesaw Mountain, **501–502**, 764
Lang, Eddie, **502–503**
Langdon, Harry, **503–504**
Langley, John W., **504–505**
Langmuir, Irving, 158
Lardner, Ring, **505–506**
Larson, John, 689
Lasky, Jesse L., 354, **506–507**, 893
Laurel, Stan, 511–513, 740
Laurier, Sir Wilfred, 487
Lawrence, D. H., **835**

Le Corbusier (Charles-Édouard Jeanneret), 935
Le Gallienne, Eva, 863
Leginska, Ethel, 174
Lenglen, Suzanne, 857, 858
Lenin, Vladimir, 724, 815, 856
Leonard, Benny, 108
Leopold, Aldo, 345
Leopold, Nathan Freudenthal, Jr., 518, 519
Lewis, Gilbert Newton, 158–159
Lewis, John L., 499, **519–520**, 883, 884, 885
Lewis, Sinclair, **73**, 276–277, **520–521**, 532–533
Lindbergh, Charles, **522–524**; aviation, 69–70, 71, 126, 876; Robert Goddard, 352, 746; Red Scare, 623
Lindsay, Vachel, **524–525**
Lippmann, Walter, **525–526, 705–706**
Lismer, Arthur, 370–371
Little, Arthur D., 160
Livesay, Dorothy, 528
Lloyd, Harold, **534–535**
Lloyd George, David, 130, 131
Locke, Alain, 383, 384, 684, 873
Lodge, Henry Cabot, **535–536**, 922
Loeb, Richard, 518
Loew, Marcus, 572, 897
Long Lance, Buffalo Child, 306
Loos, Anita, 343–344
Loos, H. Clifford, 390
Lowell, Amy, 472–473, **542–543, 915**
Lubitsch, Ernst, 461
Luce, Clare Boothe, 544
Luce, Henry R., **543–545**, 549
Luhan, Mabel Dodge, 556
Lynch, Charles, 545
Lynd, Robert and Helen, 257

MacDonald, J. E. H., 370–371
Machen, J. Gresham, 734
Mackay, Ellin, 92
MacLeish, Archibald, **547–548**
Macleod, John, 81, 118, 449, 450, 632–633

Macy, Anne Sullivan, 482
Marin, John, 56, **555–556**
Marston, William, 689
Mart, Stam, 409
Marx, Adolph, 557–559
Marx, Chico, 558
Marx, Groucho, 179–180
Marx, Harpo, 558
Marx, Herbert Manfred, 557–559
Marx, Julius Henry, 557–559
Marx, Leonard, 557–559
Marx, Milton, 557
Marx Brothers, **179–180, 557–559,** 833
Mather, Stephen, 607–608
Mayer, Louis B., **1–2,** 339, 346, 572
McAdoo, William Gibbs, 267, 715
McAlmon, Robert, 918
McCollum, Elmer, 899
McFadden, Louis Thomas, 559
McKay, Claude, 384, 385, 684
McKaye, Benton, 45
McKenna, Joseph, 839
McKenzie, Fayette, 471
McKenzie, Roderick D., 169–170
McKinney, Nina Mae, 376–377
McKinsey, James Oscar, **560–561**
McLeod, John, 454, 566
McPherson, Aimee Semple, 208–209, **561–563,** 733
McReynolds, James, 576
Mead, Margaret, **184–185, 563–564**
Meighen, Arthur, 487–489, **567–568**
Mellon, Andrew, **568–569,** 736–737, 780
Mencken, H. L., 37, 549, **569–571,** 671, 786, 814
Menuhin, Yehudi, 174, **571**
Meredith, Edwin T., 549
Merriam, Charles E., 810, 811
Meyer, Adolph, 703
Meyer, Robert T., 576
Micheaux, Oscar, **577–578**
Mickey Mouse, 244, **823–824**
Milestone, Lewis, 428
Millay, Edna St. Vincent, 386–387, **580–581**

Miller, Marilyn, 486
Millikan, Robert Andrews, **581–583,** 633, 675, 676
Mills, Eleanor, 377
Mills, James, 377
Mims, Edward, 336
Minkowski, Oskar, 449
Mitchell, Billy, **584–585**
Mitchell, Wesley Clair, 809, 811
Mix, Tom, **585–586**
Montessori, Maria, 588
Montgomery, Lucy Maud, 527
Moody, Helen Wills, **588–589,** 858
Moran, George "Bugs," 654, 655, 768–769
Morgan, Garrett, 874
Morgan, Julia, 393
Morgan, Thomas Hunt, **590–591**
Morrow, Dwight Whitney, 575
Morton, Jelly Roll, 380, **591–592,** 641
Mott, Lucretia, 629
Mulholland, William, 537, **824–825**

Nathan, George Jean, 549
Neil, Florence E., 348
Nelles, Walter, 350
Nelson, Christian Kent, 278
Nielson, Arthur C., 2–3
Nipkow, Paul, 853
Nivison, Josephine Verstille, 418
Normand, Mabel, **633–635**
Norris, Frank, 366
Novarro, Ramón, **635–636**
Noyes, Arthur A., 582
Nurmi, Paavo, 644–646, 650

Obregón, Alvaro, 574, 575
O'Keeffe, Georgia, **639–640;** art movements, 55, 56; marriage to Alfred Stieglitz, 639–640, 672, 828
Oliver, Joe "King," 52, **640–642**
O'Neill, Eugene, **652–654;** *All God's Chillun Got Wings,* **33–34,** 862–863; *Anna Christie,* **42–43,** 653, 861; *Desire Under the Elms,* **239–240;** *Emperor Jones, The,* **276–277,** 653, 862; impact on

theater, 530, 862; *Strange Interlude,* 653, **833–834,** 862
Ostenso, Martha, 527
Ott, Mel, **657–658**
Owen, Chandler, 720
Owen, Robert Latham, 398

Pace, Harry, 98
Paige, Satchel, 822
Palmer, A. Mitchell, 416, 724–725
Pancho Villa, 109
Papendick, Gustav, 110
Park, Robert E., 169–170
Parker, Dorothy, **665**
Parkinson, Donald, 539
Parkinson, John, 539
Parrington, Vernon Louis, 399, 552
Parrish, Maxfield, **665–666**
Paul, Alice, 629–630, **666–667,** 927
Pauling, Linus C., 159, 676, 677
Pearce, Louis, 564–565
Peer, Ralph S., 760
Perkins, Edwin, 494
Pershing, John, 668
Persinger, Louis, 571
Phillips, C. Coles, **669**
Phillips, Ulrich B., 399
Pickford, Mary, 348, 349, **678–679,** 886
Pinchback, P. B. S., 872
Piper, Watty, 103
Piston, Walter, **680–681**
Pitney, Mahlon, 839
Planck, Max, 675
Poe, Edgar Allan, 835
Pollak, Walter, 350
Ponzi, Charles, 204, 207
Pooler, Frank, 345
Post, Emily, **691–692**
Potts, William L., 874
Pound, Ezra, **694–695;** T. S. Eliot, 273, 910; poetry, 682; William Carlos Williams, 823, 918–919
Pratt, E. J., 528
Prouty, Olive Higgins, **827**
Pyle, Charles C. C., 119, 606, 858

Randolph, Asa Philip, 13, 114–115, **720–721**
Ransom, John Crowe, 814
Raphaelson, Samson, 466
Razaf, Andy, 904–905
Reagan, Ronald, 347
Redman, Don, 465
Reed, John, **726–727, 856–857**
Rehn, Frank K. M., 418
Reid, Wallace, **728–729**
Reis, Johann Philipp, 541
Rice, Chester W., 541
Rice, Elmer, **4–5,** 862
Richards, Vincent, 858
Richardson, Willis, 384–385
Rickard, George "Tex," 108, 109
Riddle, Sam, 420, 553
Ringling, John, 739
Roach, Hal, Sr., 511–512, 659–661, **739–741,** 768
Roberts, Charles G. D., 528
Robeson, Paul, 276, **742–743,** 800, 801
Robinson, Doane, 593
Robinson, Edwin Arlington, 530, **743–745**
Robinson, James Harvey, 398
Robscheit-Robbins, Frieda S., 565
Rockefeller, Abby Aldrich, 594
Rockefeller, John D., 811
Rockne, Knute, 347, **746–748**
Rockwell, Norman, **748**
Rodgers, Jimmie, **749**
Roebuck, Alvah C., 788
Rogers, Richards, 378, 387–388
Rogers, Will, **749–751,** 940
Rogers, Will, Jr., 750
Rohwedder, Otto, 110, 668
Romberg, Sigmund, 112, **751–752, 834–835**
Roosevelt, Eleanor, 752, 924
Roosevelt, Franklin Delano, **752–754;** James M. Cox, 202; defeat of Herbert Hoover, 882; polio, 685; and polio, 565; social science impact on the New Deal, 811; unemployment relief program, 881–882; Jimmy Walker, 903; Woodrow Wilson, 922
Rosenfeld, Fanny "Bobbie," **754–755**
Rosenfield, Joseph, 667–668
Ross, Donald E., 390
Ross, Harold, 549, 624, **755**
Ross, Nellie Tayloe, **755–757**
Ross, William Bradford, 756
Rothafel, Samuel, 594
Rothstein, Arnold, 337
Ruth, Babe, 84, 85, 626–627, **762–764**

Saarinen, Eliel, **765**
Sabin, Florence, 780
Sacco, Nicola, 709, **766–767**
St. Denis, Ruth, 238–239
Salk, Jonas, 685
Sandburg, Carl, **770–771**
Sandino, Augusto, 509
Sanford, Edward Terry, 350, 839
Sanger, Margaret, 95–96, **771–773,** 793
Sarnoff, David, 601, **773–774**
Scherman, Harry, 100
Schiaparelli, Elsa, **774–775**
Schindler, Rudolph, 51, **775–776**
Schlesinger, Arthur, 400
Schmitt, Bernadotte, 398
Scholz, Jackson, **777–778**
Schultz, Dutch, **778–779**
Scopes, John, 115–116, 257, 623, **786–788**
Scott, Duncan Campbell, 528
Sears, Richard W., 788
Sennett, Mack, 313, 407, 503, 634, **789–791**
Shaw, Louis Agassiz, 457
Shawn, Ted, 238–239
Sheeler, Charles, 673
Sheppard, John Morris, 22
Shotwell, James T., 484
Shubert Brothers, 940
Simmons, William Joseph, 495
Sinclair, Upton, 317, **801–802**
Singstad, Ole, 405–406
Sissle, Noble, 800–801
Skinner, B. F., 705
Sloan, Alfred P., 65
Smith, Bessie, 464, **806–807**
Smith, Oswald J., 731
Snowden, George, 525
Snyder, Homer, **447–448**
Stallings, Laurence, 861
Stamper, Dave, 940–941
Stanton, Elizabeth Cady, 629
Stead, Robert J. C., 527
Steenbock, Harry, 780, 899
Steichen, Edward, 555, 672–673, 690
Stein, Gertrude, 540, **825–827**
Stephenson, David C., 495
Stevens, Henry, 377
Stevens, Wallace, 683
Stevens, William "Willie," 377
Stieglitz, Alfred, **827–829;** art movements, 56; John Marin, 555–556; marriage to Georgia O'Keeffe, 639–640, 672, 828; nudes, 690; photography, 672, 827–828
Stone, Harlan Fiske, **831–833,** 839
Stover, Russell C., 278
Strand, Paul, 673
Strauss, Herbert, 548
Sturtevant, Alfred H., **835–836**
Sullivan, Anne, 482
Sullivan, Mary Quinn, 594
Sutherland, George, 839
Swanson, Gloria, **841–842**
Sweetser, Jesse, 356
Szent-Györgyi, Albert, 159

Taft, William Howard, **843–844;** child labor laws, 74; postal savings bank, 78; as Supreme Court chief justice, 381, 839, 840, 841, **843–844**
Tarkington, Booth, **32–33, 847–848**
Tate, Allen, 335–336, 814
Taylor, Frederick Winslow, 716
Taylor, William Desmond, 634, **848**
Teasdale, Sara, **851–852**
Thalberg, Irving, 367, 572

Thayer, Scofield, 242–243
Thompson, John T., 865
Thorpe, Jim, **866–867**
Tilden, "Big" Bill, 821, 857–858, **868–869**
Toklas, Alice B., 825
Toomer, Jean, **872–874**
Truman, Harry S., 882
Trumbull, Edward, 164
Trumpler, Robert J., 62–63
Tunney, Gene, 108, 234–235, **880**
Turner, Frederick Jackson, 331

Ulmann, Doris, 673
Urban, Joseph, 939

Valasek, Joseph, 676
Valentino, Rudolph, **893–894**; actor transition to talkies, 80; John Gilbert's career, 346; as sex symbol, 306; *Sheik, The,* 306, **797**, 893
Van Alen, William, 163
Van Der Zee, James, 674, **895–896**
Van Deventer, Willis, 839
Van Vechten, Carl, 385–386
Vanzetti, Bartolemeo, 709, **766–767**
Varley, Frederick, 370–371
Vidor, King, 376, **899**
Voaden, Herman, 860
von Stroheim, Erich, 366, 367, 572

Wadsworth, James W., Jr., 700, 701
Walker, Jimmy, **903**
Wallace, DeWitt, 549, **903–904**
Wallace, Lew, 91
Wallace, Lila, 549
Waller, Fats, **904–905**
Walsh, Thomas J., 849, 850
Walton, Izaak, 460
Waner, Lloyd, 85
Waner, Paul, 85
Warner, Albert, 905, 906, 907
Warner, Harry, **905–906**, 907
Warner, Jack, 905, 907
Warner, Sam, 905, **906–907**
Warren, Robert Penn, 814
Washington, George, 693
Watson, James Sibley, Jr., 242–243
Watson, John, 703–705, 810–811
Watson, Thomas J., 450
Weissmuller, Johnny, 646, 650, **911–912**
Wellman, William A., 922–923
West, Mae, **912**
Weston, Edward, 673
Wharton, Edith, **14–15, 913–915**
Wheeler, Burton K., 697
Whipple, George Hoyt, 565
White, Edward Douglass, 839, 843
Whitehead, Alfred North, 671–672
Whiteman, Paul, 463, 464, 596, **915–916**

Whitman, Walt, 835
Wilder, Thornton, **110–111, 916–918**
Williams, Michael, 549
Williams, William Carlos, **918–919**; Ezra Pound, 823, 918–919; works, **442**, 683, **822–823**
Wilson, Charles T. R., 633
Wilson, Edith Bolling, **919–920**, 921, 922
Wilson, Edmund, **920–921**
Wilson, Woodrow, **921–922**; League of Nations, 513; Henry Cabot Lodge, 535; railroads, 715; Treaty of Versailles, 281, 458
Wolfe, Thomas, **536–537**
Woodson, Carter G., 399, 616–617
Woollcott, Alexander, 30, 558
Work, Hubert, 610
Wright, Frank Lloyd, 50, 776, **934–936**
Wylie, Elinor, **936**

Yeats, William Butler, 682
Yens, Otto, 566
Yerkes, Robert, 704

Ziegfeld, Florenz, Jr., 92, 93, 113, 486, **939**
Zukor, Adolph, 506–507, 678
Zworykin, Vladimir, 855, **941–942**

■ Subject Index

Note: Page numbers in **bold** indicate main discussion.

ABC (American Broadcasting Company) radio, 714
Abel, John Jacob, 449–450
aboriginal peoples. *See* Native Americans
Abraham Lincoln: The Prairie Years (Sandburg), 770
abstract expressionism, 371, **555–556**
Academy Awards, **1–2**; Douglas Fairbanks, 288–289; Grauman's Chinese Theatre, 362; *Wings*, 923. *See also* silent film; talking motion pictures ("talkies")
accessories and jewelry, 293, 294
ACLU (American Civil Liberties Union), **34–35**; founding of, 483; Palmer raids, 664; *Scopes* trial, 34–35, 786–787; Upton Sinclair, 802
A. C. Nielsen Company, **2–3**, 232
Actor's Theatre, 863
Adams, Franklin P., **3–4**
addiction of Wallace Reid, 728–729
Adding Machine, The (Rice), **4–5**, 862
adhesives, cellophane, **147–148**
Adkins v. Children's Hospital (1923), **5–6**, 840, 844, 926, 929
adventure books, 103, 104
advertising: behaviorism, 811; for boxing, 108; broadcast marketing (commercials), 456; in Canada, **6–7**; *New Yorker, The*, 625; radio, 6, 8–9, 10, 456, 711; in the United States, **7–11**, 138, 456
advertising agencies, Canadian, 6–7
AFL. *See* American Federation of Labor (AFL); American Football League (AFL)
African Americans, **11–14**; *All God's Chillun Got Wings* (O'Neill),

33–34, 862–863; American Federation of Labor (AFL), 36–37; athletic achievements, 645; authors, 104; aviation, 69; baseball, 83–84, 402, 476; black-and-tan clubs, **96–97**, 628; Black Swan Records, **97–98**; blues, 463–464, **806–807**; book publishing, 104; boxing, 108–109; Brotherhood of Sleeping Car Porters (BSCP), 13, **114–115**, 600, 720, 884; in Canada, 134; Canadian restrictions on immigration, 438; *Cane* (Toomer), **872–874**; Charleston, The, **157**; civil rights and liberties, 171; Cotton Club, **199–200**; Dyer anti-lynching bill, **251–252**; eugenics, 279; family photo, 11; in film, 376–377, 660; golf, 356; historical perspectives, 399; housing issue in urban North, 422–423; Islam, 31–32; Jim Crow in the U.S. South, 363, 399, **471–472**; labor unions, 114–115; musical shows, 113; Negro History Week, 616–617; Negro League Baseball, 89–90, 402, **617–619**, 822; photography of, 674, 895–896; poetry, 683–684; population in North America, 231–233; professional sports, 822; racial discrimination, 707–708; radio, 711, 712; restrictive covenants and, 198; rural life, 761; scientific and technical field, 160, 780; Shaker Heights, OH, suburbs, 837; theater, 800–801, 861, 862–863, 897–898; urban development, 166–167, 232; urbanization, 891; vaudeville, 897–898; voting rights, 12, 631, 927, 928; women

in college, 924; women's rights, 928. *See also* Great Migration; Harlem Renaissance; *List of Entries by Categories;* NAACP
African sleeping sickness, 564
Age of Innocence, The (Wharton), **14–15**, 914
Agrarians, 814
Agrarians, Southern, 531–532, **620–621**, 683, **813–815**
Agricultural Marketing Act of 1929, **15–16**, 19, 291
agriculture in Canada, **16–18**
agriculture in the United States, **18–21**; advertising in the United States, 8; Agricultural Marketing Act of 1929, **15–16**; bulldozers, 117–118; business and economy, 123; downturn of 1920–1921, 451; employment, 124; exports, 452; farm policy, 191, 262–263, 290–291; farm subsidies, **290–291**; and international trade, 453; natural resources, exploitation of, 614–616; rural life, **759–761**; sharecroppers, 12, 13, 363, 365, 366; transportation, 123–124; U.S. Bureau of Chemistry and Soils, 120. *See also List of Entries by Categories*
Aiken, Conrad, **21**
Air Commerce Act of 1926, **21–22**
aircraft carriers, 71
airmail, **22–23**, 24, 26, 876, 879
Air Mail Act of 1925, **23–24**, 26, 879
air pollution, **24–26**
air races, 253–254
airships, **26–28**, 71, **797–799**
air transportation. *See* aviation
Alberta Sexual Sterilization Act (Canada), **28–29**, 95–96, 133, 709
Albright, Horace M., 607–608

1037

alcohol: bathtub gin, **87,** 627; bootlegging, 699, 778, 803, 817; drinking habits and establishments, 698–699; popular culture, 285; slang, 802; speakeasies, 655. *See also* Prohibition; speakeasies

Alekhine, Alexander, 140

Alexander, Beatrice, 403

Alexander, Grover Cleveland, **29–30**

Alexander Doll Company, 403

Algonquin Round Table, 4, **30–31,** 624, 665, 755

Ali, Noble Drew, **31–32**

Alice Adams (Tarkington), **32–33,** 847

Allen, Gracie, **120–121**

All God's Chillun Got Wings (O'Neill), **33–34,** 862–863

All Indian Pueblo Council (AIPC), 609–610

ALS (amyotrophic lateral sclerosis), 342

alternatives to realism, in theater, 861–862

Amalgamated Clothing Workers of America, 497

Amateur Athletic Union (AAU), 819–820, 866

amateur sports: collegiate, 819–821; football, 321–322, 347–348, 360–361, 820–821; soccer, 807–808; swimming, 255, 479, 911; tennis, 857–858. *See also* college sports

Amazing Stories (magazine), 785

Ambassador Hotel, Cocoanut Grove nightclub, **178–179**

amendments to the U.S. Constitution. *See* Constitution, U.S.

American Association for the Advancement of Science (AAAS), 779, 780, 781, 782, 783

American Birth Control League, 95–96, 772

American Farm Bureau Federation, 18

American Federation of Labor (AFL), **35–37**; attacks on IWW, 497; generally, 883; Samuel Gompers, **357–358**; John L. Lewis, **519–520**; Prohibition, 699–700; A. Philip Randolph, 721; workers' education, 931, 932

American Football League (AFL), 360–361, 606

American Foundation for the Blind (AFB), 482–483

American in Paris, An (Gershwin), 344

American Institute of Sacred Literature (AISL), 782–783

American League (baseball), 83–84, 626

American Management Associations, 932

American Management Review (journal), 932

American Mercury, The (magazine), **37–38,** 549, 570

American Negro League (ANL), 618

American Professional Football Association (APFA). *See* National Football League (NFL)

American Relief Administration (ARA), 415, 762, 815

American Rhapsody. See Rhapsody in Blue (G. Gershwin)

American Soccer League (ASL), 807–808

American Social Hygiene Association, 792, 796

American Sociological Association (ASA), 809

American Songbag, The (Sandburg), 770

American Steel Foundries v. Tri-City Trades Council, 885

American Stock Exchange, stock market crash, 829

American Transcendentalism, 610

American Woman Suffrage Association (AWSA), 629, 927

Amos 'n' Andy radio show, 711, 712

amusement parks, 401

Anarchist Exclusion Act (1918), 416

anarchists: Red Scare, 724; Sacco and Vanzetti case, 709, **766–767**

Anderson, Marian, **38–39**

Anderson, Maxwell, 861

Anderson, Sherwood, **39–41,** 530

Andrews, Roy Chapman, **41–42**

anemia, 565

Angelus Temple, 561

Anglophone theater in Canada, 859–860

Animal Crackers (film), 833

Animal Crackers (play), 559

animation: Koko the Clown, **493**; *Steamboat Willie,* **823–824**

Anna Christie (film), 340

Anna Christie (O'Neill), **42–43,** 653, 861

Anne of Green Gables (Montgomery), 527

Antheil, George, 174

anthropology, **184–185,** 810

antibiotics, development of, 391, 564–565

anticlericalism in Mexico, 574, 575

anti-immigrant sentiment. *See* immigration

antilynching bill, Dyer, **251–252,** 546, 600–601

Anti-Semitism, **43–44**; in Canada, 468–469; Ezra Pound, 695; racial discrimination, 709; in U.S., 469–470

antitrust and chain stores, 151

apartments, increase in, 422

Apollo Theater, 384

Appalachian Forest Act of 1911, 615

Appalachian Trail, **45**

Appeal to Reason (Sinclair), 801

appliances: developments in, 409–410, 455–456; home cooking, 318; refrigerators, **727–728**; residential electrification, 272

applied physics, 676–677

approval, as expressed as slang, 803

Arbuckle, Roscoe "Fatty," **45–47**, 207, 481, **634**
archaeology, **47–49**
architecture, **49–52**; Art Deco, 49, 50, 51, 53–54, 423; bungalows, 118–119; Chrysler Building, 51, 54, 162, **163–164**; Finnish National Romantic Style, 765; International Style, 935–936; modernism, 50, 51, 409, 775–776; Prairie School, 934–936. *See also List of Entries by Categories*
Arctic, archeology in, 49
Arizona structures, Wright's, 935
Arlington National Cemetery, Tomb of the Unknown Soldier, **870**
arms control, Washington Naval Conference, **908–910**
Armstrong, Louis, **52–53**; jazz bands and recordings, 464–465; and Lillian Hardin, 380; nightclubs, 627; Joe "King" Oliver, 641
Army Alpha test, 776–777
Army Appropriations Act, 715
Arrowsmith (Lewis), 521
"Ars Poetica" (MacLeish), 547
Art Deco, **53–54**; architecture, 49, 50, 51, 53–54, 423; Chrysler Building, 51, 54, 162, **163–164**; illustrators, 665–666, 669; interior design, 409; Native Americans, 53–54
Art Hickman's Orchestra, 463
art movements, **54–57**; nudity and pornography, 690; Société Anonyme, **812**; Gertrude Stein, 825–826
Art Nouveau style, 409
Arts and Crafts movement, 119, 765
Asia, **57–59**; naturalist exploration of, 41–42; Washington Naval Conference, **908–910**. *See also specific countries*
Asian Americans, **59–61**; Sudhindra Bose, **105–106**; immigration, 57–58, 462–463, 661–662;

Washington Naval Conference, **908–910**. *See also List of Entries by Categories*
Asian immigrants: in Canada, 134–135; Canadian restrictions on, 438; racial discrimination, 708; U.S. restrictions on, 440–441
Association Against the Prohibition Amendment (AAPA), 699
Association for the Study of Negro Life and History (ASNLH), 616
Astaire, Adele, 402
Astaire, Fred, 402
astronomy, **61–63**
atoms, in physics, 676–677
AT&T (American Telephone & Telegraph): Bell Labs, **90**; radio, 601–602, 710, 711, 713; synchronized-sound technology, 846; telephone technology, **852–853**
attacks on the U.S. and Red Scare, 724
Augusta National Golf Club, 477, 478
authors, book publishing, 102–104. *See also specific authors; specific works*
auto insurance, development of, 391
automobiles and auto manufacturing, **63–67**; advertising in the United States, 9–10; bulldozer, **117–118**, 454; hood ornaments, **413–414**; as major innovation of the period, 454–455; National Conference on Street and Highway Safety, 603–604; Pershing Map, **668–669**; railroad impact, 717; Route 66, **757–758**; rural life, 760; safety problems, 390–391; science and technology, 123–124; to the Soviet Union, 815–816; suburbs, 836–837; tourism, 401, 455, 592, 878; traffic signals, **874**; transportation, 603–604; trucking, 717, 875–876; urbanization, 890. *See also specific manufacturers*

auto racing, **67–68**, 821
avant-garde composers, 173
aviation, **68–72**; airmail, 22–24, 26, 876, 879; airships, **26–28**, 71, **797–799**; Canada, **758–759**; Billy Mitchell's crusade for air power, 584–585; passenger, 876, 879; shipping and freight, 876–877; transportation, 125–126. *See also List of Entries by Categories*
Axel's Castle (Edmund Wilson), 920

Babbitt (Lewis), **73**, 520
Babcock, Joseph Park, 402, 551
back-to-Africa movement, 340–341
Bailey v. Drexel Furniture Co. (1922), **73–74**, 840, 844
Baker, George Pierce, 530
Baker, Josephine, **74–76**, 801
Baldwin, Roger, 34
Baldwin-Felts Detective Agency, 499
ballet, 217–218
Baltimore Orioles, 371
Baltimore Talking Board Co. Inc. v. Miles, Collector of Internal Revenue, 659
Band-Aids, **76–77**
bank failures, 77, 78, 79, 80, 123
banking, **77–80**; McFadden Act, **559–560**; national debt of the U.S., **604–605**. *See also consumer credit; Federal Reserve System*
Bánky, Vilma, **80–81**
Banting, Frederick Grant, **81**, 449, 450, 566, 632–633
Bara, Theda, **82**
barges, water transport, 875
Barnes, Harry Elmer, 398
Barney, Natalie, 540
Barnsdall, Aline, 776, 934
barnstormers, 68–69
Barry, Philip, 861
Barrymore, John, **82–83**, 906, 908
baseball, **83–86**; American League, 83–84, 626; Black Sox scandal, 206–207, 501, 502; National League, 83–84, 658; Negro League Baseball, 89–90,

baseball (continued)
617–619, 822; popular culture, 85; as professional sport, 821; radio, 711–712; World Series, 84, 337, 342, 712. *See also specific athletes and teams*
basketball, 822
bathing suits, **86–87**
bathtub gin, **87**, 627
Battle of Blair Mountain, 499, 885
Baum, L. Frank, 666
Baylor Hospital, Dallas, 87–88
Baylor Plan, **87–88**
Beard, Charles A., 398–399
Beauchemin, Nérée, 528
behaviorism, 703–704, 810–811
Beiderbecke, Bix, **88–89**
Bell, Alexander Graham, 541, 852, 853
Bell, James "Cool Papa," **89–90, 619**
Bell Labs, **90**; physics, 676, 677; sound in film, 906, 907; synchronized-sound technology, 846; telephone technology, 852–853; television technology, 854
Benét, Stephen Vincent, 472, 530
Ben-Hur (film, 1924), **91**, 122, 573, 635
Ben-Hur (film, 1959), 91
Ben-Hur (Wallace), 91
Berlin, Irving, **91–93**, 111–112
Best, Charles, 449, 450, 566, 632
Bethune, Mary McLeod, 257
Better Homes and Gardens, The (magazine), 549
Better Homes in America movement, **93–94**, 410
Betty Boop cartoon character, 480
Bigelow, Maurice, 792
Big Parade, The (film), 346, 899
Binet, Alfred, 704
Bingham-Parker-Merritt Bill. *See* Air Commerce Act of 1926
Birdseye, Clarence, **94–95**, 319, 333–334
birth control, **95–96**; Catholic opposition to, 795; Margaret Sanger, 95–96, **771–773**;

women's rights, 117, 374, 930. *See also* sterilization
Birth of a Nation, The (film), 349, 367, 494
birthrate, decrease in, 233
black-and-tan clubs, **96–97**, 628
blackball, 617
blackface, 476–477, 897
black hole theory, 260
Black Pirate, The (1926), 288
blacks. *See* African Americans
Black Sox scandal (baseball), 206–207, 501, 502
Black Star Line, 340, 341, 888, 889
Black Swan Records, **97–98**
Black Thursday (1929), 830
Black Tuesday (1929), 829, 830–831
Blake, Eubie, **800–801**
blimps, 26
Bliss, Lillie P., 594
Blizzard, William, 499
blizzards, 613
Blue Angel, The (Der Blaue Engel) (film), 461
Blue Cross health insurance system, 390, 566–567
blues, 463–464, **806–807**
Blumgart, Hermann, 566
Boas, Franz, 431, 810
bobbed hair, **98–99**, 113, 373–374, 924
Bohr, Niels, 675
Bolshevik Revolution, Russia, 724, 726, 815, 856–857
Bonus Act of 1924, **99–100**
book clubs, **100–101**
Bookman, The (periodical), **101–102**
Book of American Negro Poetry (J. W. Johnson, ed.), 475
Book-of-the-Month Club, 100, 103
book publishing, **102–105**; authors, 102–104; children's books, 103–104, 748, 770–771; illustrators, 665–666, 669. *See also List of Entries by Categories;* literature
boom and bust cycles, Federal Reserve role in, 79
Booth, George, 765

Boothe, Clare, 544
bootlegging, 699, 778, 803, 817
Border Patrol, U.S., **105**, 440, 441
Borglum, Gutzon, 593
Bose, Sudhindra, **105–106**
Boston Red Sox, 84
Boston Symphony Orchestra, 174
Bourke-White, Margaret, 674
Bow, Clara, **106–107**, 923
boxing, **107–109**; champions, 108–109, **234–236, 880**; as professional sport, 821; radio, 711
Boyce Motometer Company, 413
Brand, Max. *See* Faust, Frederick
Brandeis, Louis D., 832, 839, 840
Brandenberger, Jacques E., 147–148
Brandenburg v. Ohio (1969), 351
brands, food, 319
Brawne, Fanny, 473, 543
bread: bread slicer, **109–110**, 668; peanut butter and jelly sandwiches, 667–668
Breasted, James Henry, 399
Breuer, Marcel, 409
Briand, Aristide, 484
Brice, Fanny, 940
Bridge, The (Crane), 682–683
Bridge of San Luis Rey, The (Wilder), **110–111**, 917
Brief History of the Great War, A (Hayes), 398
Brigham, Carl, 776
Britton, Nan, **696**
broadcast clubs, 101
broadcast marketing (commercials), 456
Broadway: dances on, 219; musicals on, 92–93, **111–113**; vaudeville on, 898; Ziegfeld Follies, 92, 111, 113, 114, 939
Broadway Melody, The (film), 573, 847
Broken Blossoms (film), 349
Brooks, Louise, 98, **113–114**
Brookwood Labor College, NY, 932

Brotherhood of Sleeping Car Porters (BSCP), 13, **114–115,** 600, 720, 884
Brown, Wade Hampton, 564
Bryan, William Jennings, **115–116;** religion in the U.S., 734, 782; *Scopes* trial, 786, 787, 923
bubble gum, **116**
Buck, Gene, 940–941
Buck v. Bell, **116–117,** 704
Bugnet, Georges-Charles-Jules (Henri Doutremont), 528–529
bulldozer, **117–118,** 454
bungalows, **118–119,** 409, 423–424
Bunion Derby (1928), **119–120**
bureaucratic organization of schools, 257
Bureau of Chemistry, U.S., 316–317
Bureau of Chemistry and Soils, U.S. (BCS), **120,** 317
Bureau of Indian Affairs (BIA), 609
Bureau of Investigation (BOI), 416–417. *See also* FBI (Federal Bureau of Investigation)
Burgess, Ernest W., 169–170
Burns, George, **120–121**
Burns, William J., 416
Burns and Allen, **120–121**
Bursum bill (1921), 609
Bush, Vannevar, 243
Bushman, Francis X, **121–122**
business and economics, **122–125;** *Babbitt* (Lewis), **73;** business cycle during the period, 368–369; unionism, **883–886;** World War I veterans, 933. *See also List of Entries by Categories*
Butler, Pierce, 839
Butler Act, 786, 787, 788
Byng, Lord (Governor-General of Canada), 567
Byrd, Richard E., 71, **125–126**

Cabell, James Branch, **127–128,** 690
Cable, John, 128, 930
Cable Act of 1922, 60, **128–129,** 930
Cady, Walter G., 676
Calder, Alexander, 56

California Institute of Technology (Caltech), **129–130;** Robert Millikan, 582; Nobel Prize for Physics, 633; physical chemistry, 159; physics, 675, 677
California Water Wars. *See* Los Angeles Aqueduct dynamiting
Callaghan, Morley, 527–528
Calles, Plutarco Elías, 575
Campbell, Walter, 317
Canada: advertising, **6–7;** agriculture, **16–18;** archeology, 49; aviation, **758–759;** banking, **77–80;** Canadian nationalism, **136–137;** census, 16, 133, 232; economic history, 205; education, 256–257; elections, **260–262;** electricity, 410; employment and wages, 445; federal *vs.* provincial government, 136–137; foreign policy, 489; GNP, 444; Great Britain relationship, **130–132,** 136, 489; Halibut Treaty of 1924, 375–376; insulin research, 81; international trade, 451, 452–453; landscape painting, 370–371; minority communities, **28–29, 132–136;** nationalism, **136–137;** Olympic achievements, 648, 650, 651; population growth, 231; railroads, 718; recognition of Soviet Union, 816; religion, **729–732;** science and technology, 780–781; sports, 404, **754–755;** sterilization laws, **28–29,** 95–96, 133, 709; theater, **859–860.** *See also* immigration to Canada; *List of Entries by Categories*
Canadian Air Force (CAF), 758
Canadian National Railroad, 718
Canadian Short Stories (Knister, ed.), 527
cancer, **137–140**
candies, 319
Cane (Toomer), **872–874**
canned foods, 319
cantilever chair, 409

Cantor, Eddie, 940
Capablanca, José Raúl, **140**
Capone, Al, **140–142,** 654, 768–769
Capra, Frank, 504
cardiovascular disease (CVD), 566
Carman, Bliss, 528
Carmichael, Franklin, 370–371
Carmichael, Hoagy, **142–143**
Carr, Joe F., 322–323
Carr, Mary, **143**
Carroll v. United States, 844
Carter, Alvin Pleasant, 143–144
Carter, Howard, 48
Carter family, **143–144**
Cascade Tunnel, **144–145,** 718
"Case for Birth Control, The" (Sanger), 793
Castle, Irene, 98, 554
Castle, Vernon, 554
Castle Gate, Utah, mining disaster (1924), **145–146,** 614
catalogs, mail-order, 294
Caterpillar Tractor Company, 118
Cather, Willa, **146–147, 227–228**
Catholics and the Catholic Church: birth control opposition, 795; church influence in Mexico, 574, 575; religion in Canada, **729–732;** religion in the United States, **732–735**
Catt, Carrie Chapman, 516, 517, 629
CBS (Columbia Broadcasting System), 456, 711, 714
cellophane, **147–148**
censorship, **148–150**
Census, Canadian, 16, 133, 232
Census, U.S.: Asian Americans, 59, 60, 661–662; home ownership, 93; IBM tabulation, 450; immigration reform, 191, 435, 436, 440, 441; Latinos, 509–510; racial and ethnic composition, 233; radio ownership, 603; rural life, 760–761; school enrollment, 256; urbanization, 232, 622, 890–891
Central Experimental Farm (CEF), Canada, 17

chain stores, **150–151**
Chandler, Harry, **151–152,** 407
Chanel, Coco, **152–154,** 176
Chanel No. 5, 153
Chanel suit, 153, 293
Chaney, Lon, **154–155**
Chaplin, Charlie, **155–157**; *Circus, The,* 157, **164–165**; *Gold Rush, The,* 353–354; Thomas H. Ince scandal, 207–208; Keystone Kops films, 790; *Kid, The,* 155–156, 192; notable acquaintances, 355, 443, 841–842; scandals, 634; Tramp character, 157, 164–165; United Artists, 678, 886; *vs.* Harold Lloyd's character, 534
Charleston, The (dance), **157–158,** 218, 219, 403
Chase, Frank J., 570
checking accounts, banking, 78–79
chemical engineering and industry, 160
chemistry, **158–161**
chess, Cuban champion, 140
chewing gum advertising, 9
Chicago American Giants (Negro League Baseball), 618
Chicago Bears (football), 322, 360, 361, 821
Chicago Daily News (newspaper), 770
Chicago Outfit gang, 140–142
Chicago Symphony Orchestra, 174
Chicago Tribune Tower, 50, 765
Chicago White Sox (baseball), 84, 206–207
Child Actors Bill, 193
child labor, 73–74, 124–125
Child Labor Tax Law, 74
children: child labor, 73–74, 124–125; children's books, 103–104, 748, 770–771; masturbation, sex development theories, 792
China and U.S. foreign policy, 58, 326, 483, 909
Chinatown, 60, **871–872**

Chinese Americans. *See* Asian Americans
Chinese Exclusion Act of 1923 (Canada), **161–162**
Chinese immigrants, **161–162,** 434, 438
Chinese Immigration Act of 1923 (Canada), **161–162**
Chip Woman's Fortune (play), 384
chlorofluorocarbons (CFCs), 330
Choquette, Robert, 528
choreography. *See* dance and choreography
Christianity. *See* religion
Christianity and Liberalism (Machen), 734
Chrysler, Walter P., 65, **162–163**
Chrysler Building, 51, 54, 162, **163–164**
Chrysler Corporation, 65–66, 162–163
cigarettes, 138–139
Cincinnati Redlegs (baseball), 206–207
Circus, Ringling Bros. and Barnum & Bailey, 401, **738–739**
Circus, The (film), 157, **164–165**
circuses, traveling, 401
cities, **165–169**
citizenship: Japanese-Americans, 661–662; married women, 60, **128–129,** 929–930; Native American, 171, **447–448,** 609
City, The (Park, Burgess, and McKenzie), **169–170**
City Lights (film), 157
city planning, growth of, 422
Civic Repertory Theatre, 863
civil rights and liberties, **170–172**; African American, 171, 631, 720–721; due process, 576, 589; Dyer antilynching bill, **251–252,** 546, 600–601; free speech, 350–351; Japanese American Citizens League, **462–463**; Latinos, 510–511, 515; voting, 631. *See also* ACLU (American Civil Liberties Union); *List of Entries by Categories;* NAACP

(National Association for the Advancement of Colored People)
Civil War: *General, The* (film), 343; *John Brown's Body* (Benét), **472**
Clarke, John Hessin, 839
Clarke-McNary Act, 615
class and women, 923–926
classical ballet, 217
classical music, 38–39, **172–175.** *See also specific composers and works*
Clemenceau, Georges, 281
Cline, Genevieve R., **175–176**
cloche hats, **176**
clothing. *See* fashion and clothing
clouds, Stieglitz photographs of, 828
Coal Glen disaster, 614
coal industry: Castle Gate, UT, mining disaster, **145–146**; labor strike, 498–499; mining accidents, 614, **912–913**; smoke from burning, as air pollution, 24–26; unionism, 884
Cobb, Ty, 84, **177–178**
Cocoanut Grove, **178–179,** 627
Cocoanuts, The (film), **179–180,** 559
Cocoanuts, The (play), 92–93, 558–559
Cohan, George M., 112, **180–181**
coins, commemorative, 214, 791
Coleman, Bessie, 69, **181–182**
college: science and technology, 780–781; social sciences, **809–812**; women in, **923–925.** *See also specific colleges*
college sports: amateur, 819–821; football, 321–322, 347–348, 360–361, 820–821; soccer, 808. *See also* Notre Dame University
Collier, John, 609–610
Collip, James, 449, 450
Colman, Ronald, 80–81, **182–183,** 355
Colored Hockey League (CHL), 404
color films, 307
comedy: in jazz performance, 904–905; on radio, 120–121,

711, 712; in silent film, 155–157, 164–165, 480–482; in talking film, 179, 511–513, 659–661; theater, 861. *See also* vaudeville
comic strips, **183–184**
Coming of Age in Samoa (Mead), **184–185,** 563, 564
Coming of the War, 1914, The (Schmitt), 398
commemorative coins, 214, 791
commercials on radio, 456
Committee of One Hundred, 610
Commonweal (magazine), 549
communications: English-language theater in Canada, 859–860; French-language theater in Canada, 859; slang, **802–804**; telephone technology and service, 601–602, 642–643, **852–853.** *See also List of Entries by Categories*
communism, **185–187**; Bolshevik Revolution, Russia, 724, 726, 815, 856–857; Isadora Duncan, 249–250; John Reed, **726–727, 856–857**; unionism, 884
Communist Labor Party of American, 416, 726. *See also* Red Scare
Communist Party USA, 687–688
companionate marriage, 930
Compton, Arthur Holly, **187–188,** 633, 675–676
Compton effect, 187–88, 582, 583, 675–676
Compulsory Education Act "School Bill," 679
computing machines. *See* differential analyzer
Computing-Tabulating-Recording Company (CTR). *See* International Business Machines (IBM)
Comstock Act (1873), 95, 771
Conant, James Bryant, 159
Coney Island, **188–189**
Confederation Poets, 528
Conference for Progressive Political Action (CPPA), 697
Congress, U.S., **189–192.** *See also*

elections, U.S.; *specific legislation; specific legislators*
Congressional Union, 929
Conning Tower, The (*New York Tribune* column), 4
Conquistador (MacLeish), 547
Conrad, Frank, 710
Conservative Party (Canada), 260–262, 487–488, **567–568**
conservative religion: in Canada, 730–731; in the U.S., 733–734
Constantin-Weyer, Maurice, 529
Constitution, Mexican of 1917, 574
Constitution, U.S.: First Amendment, 350, 408, 713; Fourth Amendment, 397; Fifth Amendment, **5–6,** 699, 844, 926, 929; Fourteenth Amendment, 34, 170–171, 844, 902; Fifteenth Amendment, 901–902; Eighteenth Amendment, 337, 688, **698–701,** 733, 817, 839; Twenty-First Amendment, 733; Equal Rights Amendment (ERA), **277–278,** 667, 925, 927, 929, 930. *See also* Nineteenth Amendment; Supreme Court, U.S.
construction industry, 124
consumer credit: automobile production, 123, 455; banking, 78; development of, 203; installment plans, 10, **448–449,** 454
consumerism, 93–94, 369, 760
Contract Air Mail Act. *See* Air Mail Act of 1925
Coogan, Jackie, 155, **192–193**
Cook, George Cram, 530
cookbooks, 320
Coolidge, Calvin, **193–196**; Charles G. Dawes, 224, 226; elections of 1924, 223, **266–269**; Oil Pollution Act, 615, **637–638**; railroad, 719; Revenue Act of 1924 cartoon, 737; Sesquicentennial Exposition, 791; Harlan Fiske Stone, 832; support of Better Homes in America movement,

93; Teapot Dome scandal, 849; on women's colleges, 924
Coolidge, Grace, **196**
Cooper, Gary, 355
cooperatives, agricultural: in Canada, 16–17; in the U.S., 18–19
Copeland, Aaron, 173–174, **197**
Cops (film), 481
Coquette (film), 679
Corrigan v. Buckley, **198**
corruption: Harlan Fiske Stone, **831–833**; Tammany Hall, 753, 804, 903; Teapot Dome, 207, 238, 416, **849–851**
Corrupt Practices Act of 1925, **198–199,** 620
cosmetics and fragrance, 137–138, 153, 154, 293
cosmic ray research, Millikan's, 582, 583
Cotton Club, **199–200**; Duke Ellington, 465; Harlem Renaissance role of, 384, 596; nightclubs, 627, 628; origins of, 474; radio, 711
cotton swabs, **200–201**
country music, **143–144,** 359–360, **749**
courts and court cases. *See List of Entries by Categories*
Cowell, Henry, 173
Cox, Ida, **201**
Cox, James M., **202,** 265
Craftsman style in homes, 409
craft *vs.* industrial unionism, 357–358, 446, 497, 498
Cranbrook Educational Community, 765
Crane, Hart, 682–683
Crash of 1929, **829–831,** 882
credit and debt, **203–206, 604–605.** *See also* consumer credit
Creole Jazz Band, 641
crime and scandals, **206–209**; Fatty Arbuckle, 46–47; bootlegged and smuggled alcohol, 699; Chicago White Sox (baseball), 84, 206–207; Thomas H. Ince

crime and scandals (continued)
scandal, 207-208; organized crime, 654-656; pornography, **690-691**; Wallace Reid, 728-729; William Desmond Taylor, 634, **848**; Teapot Dome, 207, 238, 416, **849-851**; Tong Wars of Chinatown, **871-872**; urbanization, 891. *See also List of Entries by Categories;* organized crime

crimes and scandal: Black Sox (baseball), 206-207, 501, 502

Crisis, The (magazine), 384-385

Cristero Rebellion, 575

crooners, **209-211, 894-895**

Crosby, Bing, **210-211**

crossword puzzles, **211-212,** 285-286, 403

Cuba, U.S. activity and influence, 507, 508

cubism, 55

Cukor, George, 349

Cullen, Countée, 683-684

cultural identity, advertising in Canada, 6-7

culture. *See* popular culture

Cummings, E. E., **212-214**

Cummings, James D., 118, 454

Cummins, Albert, 716

Cunningham, Imogen, 673

currency and coinage, **214-215**; banking, 77-79; commemorative coins, 214, 791; consumer credit, 203; gold standard, 79, 453

Curtis, Charles, **215-216**

Curtis, Edward, 675

Curtis aircraft engines, 70-71

C vitamin discovery, 159

dadaism, Société Anonyme, **812**

Daily Mirror, 622

dance and choreography, **217-220**; Charleston, **157-158,** 218, 219, 403; dance bands, 463; dance contests, 287; dance marathons, 287, **554-555**; Lindy Hop, **525**; modern dance, 217-218, 359; popular, **219-220,** 285, 403;

Ziegfeld Follies, **940-941**. *See also List of Entries by Categories*

"dapper" as slang, 803

Dark Laughter (S. Anderson), 39, 40

Darrow, Clarence, **220-222,** 518, 623, 786-788

Darwin, Charles, 671

dating and courtship, 556-557

Daugherty, Harry M., **222-223**

Davies, Marion, 392

Davis, John W., **223-224**

Davis, Stuart, 55

Davisson, Clinton J., 676, 677

Dawes, Charles G., **224-225,** 226, 560, 632, 633

Dawes Plan, 224, **225-227,** 325-326, 459

Day, William Rufus, 839

Daybreak (Parrish), 666

daylight savings time, 402

Death Comes for the Archbishop (Cather), 147, **227-228**

de Broglie, Louis, 676

Debs, Eugene V., **228-229,** 687, 885

debt. *See* credit and debt

debt securities, 204

de Coubertin, Pierre, 643, 645, 649, 651

deflation, post-WWI, 444, 722-723

De Forest, Lee, 846

de la Roche, Mazo, 527

The Delineator (magazine), 93

DeMille, Cecil B., **229-230**; *King of Kings,* 490, 506-507; *Ten Commandments, The,* 230, 507, **855-856**

Democratic Party: elections of 1920, **264-266,** 710; elections of 1922 (midterm), **262-264**; elections of 1924, **266-269,** 267, 268; elections of 1926 (midterm), **262-264**; elections of 1928, **269-271,** 712, 804-805; founding, 686; political parties, **686-689**; Tammany Hall, 903; women's rights, 928

demographics, **231-234**; agriculture in the United States, 19-20; Asian Americans, 59, 60;

Japanese Americans, 661-662; organized crime, 654, 656; rural life, 760-761; urbanization, 232, 622, 890-891. *See also List of Entries by Categories*

Dempsey, Jack "Manassa Mauler," 108-109, **234-236,** 821, 880

Demuth, Charles, 55, **236-237**

Denby, Edwin, **237-238**

dendochronology, 48

Denishawn School of Dancing and Related Arts, 217, **238-239**

Denison, Merrill, 860

department stores, 294, **788-789**

deposits, banking, 77-78

Desert Song, The (operetta), 751

Desire Under the Elms (O'Neill), **239-240,** 653

Desrochers, Alfred, 528

detective fiction, 379

Detroit-Windsor Tunnel, **240-241**

Dewey, John, **241-242,** 588, 668-669

diabetes, 81, 390, 566

Dial, The (magazine), **242-243,** 682, 694

Dial Award, 242-243

Diamond Lil (film), 912

Dickson, Earle, 76-77

Diemer, Walter, 116

differential analyzer, **243-244**

Dilg, Will H., 460

Dillingham, William, 435

dime novels, 103

diners, 320

dinosaur eggs, fossil, 41-42

diplomacy and international relations. *See List of Entries by Categories*

disabled persons, Helen Keller's work for, 482

disapproval or dislike, as expressed as slang, 803

disasters. *See List of Entries by Categories*

discrimination and prejudice: Anti-Semitism, 43-44; anti-urban, 168-169; ethnic differences, 168; homosexuality and

gay rights, **411–413**; immigration, 134–135, 161–162. *See also* racial discrimination
Disney, Walt, **244–245**, 401, **823–824**
disposable income for households, 369
divorce, 557
Dixieland jazz in Chicago, 596
Dixie Syncopators, 641–642
dock strike, 497, 723
documentary filmmaking, 599
Dodsworth (Lewis), 521
dogs, Rin Tin Tin films, **739**, 906
Doheny, Edward L., 849, 850
dolls and dollhouses, 403
Don Juan (film), 906, 908, 946
Doolittle, Hilda (H. D.), **245–246**
Doolittle, James, 879
Dos Passos, John, 868
Douglas, Andrew, 48
Douglas, Donald, 246–247
Douglas Aircraft Company, 71, **246–247**
Doyle, Arthur Conan, 818
drama, radio, 712
Dreier, Katherine, **812**
Drinker, Cecil, 457
Drinker, Philip, 457, 566
drinking. *See* alcohol; Prohibition
Drosophila melanogaster (fruit fly) genetics research, 836
drugs. *See* pharmaceuticals
Du Bois, W. E. B., **247–248**; on history, 399; influence on Harlem Renaissance, 383; Fayette McKenzie, 471; political activism, 13, 600
Duchamp, Marcel, **812**
Dumont, Margaret, 559
Dunbar-Nelson, Alice Moore, 630
Duncan, F. Duncan, 938
Duncan, Isadora, **249–250**
Dunning, William A., 399
Du Pont Company, 148, 781–782
Durant, Will, **250–251**, 400
Durant, William (GM founder), 65
D vitamin discovery, **899–900**

Dyer, Leonidas C., 251, 546, 600–601
Dyer antilynching bill, **251–252**, 546, 600–601
Dymaxion House, 423

Earhart, Amelia, 70, **253–254**
earnings, increase in annual, 370
Eastern Colored League (ECL), 402, 617–619
Eastman, George, **254–255**
Eastman Kodak Company, 673
Eastman School of Music, 359
Eaton, Fred, 537
Eckholm, H. Conrad, 583
economic issues: boom and bust cycles, Federal Reserve role in, 79; business cycle during the period, 368–369; deflation, 444, 722–723; GDP (gross domestic product) of the U.S., 722, 809; GNP (gross national product) of the U.S., **368–370**, 444, 809; national debt of the U.S., **604–605**; natural resources, exploitation of, 614–616; rural life, 759; social sciences focus on, 809–810; structure of, 123; unionism, **883–886**; World War I veterans, 933. *See also* business and economics
Edel, Leon, 921
Ederle, Gertrude, **255–256**, 646
Edison, Thomas A., 845
education and scholarship, **256–259**; in Canada, 256–257; John Dewey's philosophy of, 241–242; film studies, 289; Montessori method, **587–588**; *Pierce v. Society of Sisters*, **679–680**; schools of dance, 217, 238–239; sex education, **792–795**; in the U.S, 115–116, **256–259**; workers', **931–932**. *See also* List of Entries by Categories
Ego and the Id, The (Freud), 702–703
Ehrlich, Paul, 564
Eighteenth Amendment, 337, 688,

698–701, 733, 817, 839. *See also* Prohibition
Einstein, Albert, **259–260**, 425, 671
Eisenhower, Dwight D., 668
Elaine Massacre, 12
elderly, pensions for, 445
elections, Canadian, **260–262**
elections, U.S.: of 1918 (midterm), 264–265; of 1920, 228, **264–266**, 710; of 1922 (midterm), **262–264**; of 1924, 223, **266–269**, **696–698**; of 1926 (midterm), **262–264**; of 1928, **269–271**, 712, 804–805; campaign spending, 619–620; pioneering of primary, 500, 631
electrical recording, **271–272**
electrification, **272–273**; advertising, 8; agriculture, 20; expansion, 124, 408–409, 455–456; hydroelectricity, 300–301. *See also* appliances
electromagnetic waves, 676
electronic television, 854–855
Eliot, T. S., **273–274**, 530, **910**
Ellington, Duke, **274–275**, 384, 465, 596, 627
Elmer Gantry (Lewis), **275–276**
Emergency Quota Act. *See* Immigration Act of 1921
Emperor Jones, The (O'Neill), **276–277**, 653, 862
Empire State Building, 50, 51, 54, 805
employment: business and economics, **122–125**; unemployment, 124–125, **695–696**, **881–883**; worker output and Hawthorn Studies, 810. *See also* income and wages; unemployment
endurance fads, 286, 287
energy policy, in Congress, 190–191
engineering and construction: chemical engineering, 160; construction industry, 124; differential analyzer, **243–244**. *See also* List of Entries by Categories; specific buildings

English-language theater in Canada, 859–860
Enlightenment, 610
entertainment. *See specific types of entertainment*
environmental issues: Appalachian Trail, **45**; Gila Wilderness Area, **345–346**; Izaak Walton League of America, **459–460**; Robert La Follette's leadership, 500; National Parks of the United States, 403, **607–608**, 878. *See also List of Entries by Categories*
Equal Rights Amendment (ERA), **277–278**, 667, 925, 927, 929, 930
Equivalents photographs (Stieglitz), 828
Esch-Cummins Act, 715–716, 875
Eskimo Pie, **278**, 319
ethnic composition of North America, 233
Etiquette (Post), 691–692
eugenics movement, **278–280**; Alberta Sexual Sterilization Act, **28–29**, 95–96, 133, 709; birth control, 95–96; *Buck v. Bell*, 116–117; immigration, 279, 440, 709; IQ testing, 704–705; racial discrimination, 709
Europe, **280–283**; economy, 123; film, 307; post-war trade challenges, 451–452; Paul Robeson, 742; spiritualism, 818–819; sterilization, 117; U.S. isolationism, 459
European immigrants: in Canada, 133–134; restrictions on welcome for, 433–437, 440
evangelism, **283–284**
Evans, Hiram Wesley, 495
Evans, Walker, 674
Evening Graphic, 622
events. *See List of Entries by Categories*
Everhart, Mahlon T., 850
evolution: eugenics movement, 279; religion in the U.S., 733–734; science and religion, 782; star cluster studies, 62–63; theory of, 115–116. *See also Scopes* trial; *Scopes* trial (1925)
expatriate writers, American, 532, **539–541**
Experimental Theatre, Inc., 862–863
explorers, 125–126
Exterminator (race horse), 420

fads and fashion, **285–287**. *See also* fashion and clothing; *List of Entries by Categories*
Fairbanks, Douglas, Sr., **288–289**, 578, 678, **864**, 886
Fall, Albert, 849–850, 849*f*
family issues. *See List of Entries by Categories*
Famous Players-Lasky, 506–507, 678, 893
Farewell to Arms, A (Hemingway), **289–290**, 395, 396
farmland and forests, 615
farm subsidies, **290–291**. *See also* agriculture in the United States
farm system, baseball, 84
Farnsworth, Philo T., 854–855
Farrar, John, 101, 102
fascism, 282
fashion and clothing, **292–294**; bathing suits, **86–87**; bobbed hair, **98–99**, 113, 373–374, 924; dresses, 292–293, 314, 374; flappers, 314, 374; hats, **176**, 293, 294; knitwear, 774–775; "little black dress," 153; for men, 293–294; raccoon coats, 286–287; rayon stockings, **721–722**; Elsa Schiaparelli, **774–775**; Ziegfeld Follies costumes, 940–941. *See also* hairstyles
fast-food franchises, 320
Faulkner, William, **294–296**, 531, **774**
Fauset, Jessie Redmon, 383, 384, 385
Faust, Frederick, **296–298**
Fay, Sidney B., 398
FBI (Federal Bureau of Investigation): Marcus Garvey, 341; J. Edgar Hoover, 416–417, 832; organized crime, 654
FCC (Federal Communication Commission), 714
Federal Aid Highway Act of 1921, 66, **298**, 299, 454, 757
Federal Bureau of Investigation. *See* FBI
Federal Communication Commission (FCC), 714
Federal Corrupt Practices Act. *See* Corrupt Practices Act of 1925
Federal Farm Board, 15, 16, 19, 123, 291
federal highway system, **298–300**; development of, 401; motels, **592–593**, 878; in national parks, 607–608; Pershing Map, **668–669**; as response to automobile ownership, 454; road trips, 878; Route 66, **757–758**
Federal Meat Inspection Act, 802
Federal Oil Pollution Act. *See* Oil Pollution Act of 1924
Federal Power Act of 1920, **300–301**, 608, 614
Federal Power Commission (FPC), 301
Federal Radio Commission (FRC), **301–302**, 712
Federal Railway Labor Act. *See* Railway Labor Act of 1926
Federal Reserve Act of 1913, 79
Federal Reserve System: banking, 77, 79, 560; bonds, 204–205; business and economy, **122–125**; credit and debt, 204–205; international trade, 453; national debt of the U.S., **604–605**; recession of 1920-1921, 722–723
Federal Water Power Act. *See* Federal Power Act of 1920
fedoras, 294
Felix the Cat, **302–303**
feminism: bobbed hair, 373–374, 924; Isadora Duncan, 249; Equal Rights Amendment (ERA),

277–278, 667, 925, 927, 929, 930; flappers, 313–314, 930; Margaret Mead's, 563; political progress, 517; second-wave, 924; women in the workforce, 925–926
Ferber, Edna, **303–304**
ferroelectrics, 676
Fields, W. C., **305**, 940
Fiery Cross news weekly, 708
FIFA (Federation Internationale de Football Association), 808
Fifteenth Amendment, 901–902
Fifteen Years in America (Bose), 106
Fifth Amendment, **5–6**, 699, 844, 926, 929
Fighting Irish, 322
Filled Milk Act, 516
film, **305–308**; Academy Awards, **1–2**; actresses, 633–635; censorship, 149; comedy, 659–661; documentary filmmaking, 599; movie palaces, **594**; as recreation activity, 400–401; sex symbols in, 106–107, 635–636; stag films, 690; swashbuckling, 288; vaudeville *vs.*, 898; World War I, 933. *See also* silent film; talking motion pictures ("talkies"); *specific actors, films, and studios*
film: people. *See List of Entries by Categories*
film studies, 289
Finland, 644–648, 650, 651
First Amendment, 350, 408, 713
First World War. *See* World War I
fishing, 403
Fisk University, 471
fitness fads, 287
Fitzgerald, F. Scott, **308–310**; bobbed hair, 98, 374; *Great Gatsby, The,* 362, 531; Earnest Hemingway, 396; Ring Lardner, 505–506; marriage to Zelda, 310–312; in Paris, 103; Arnold Rothstein, 337; *Tales of the Jazz Age,* **845**; *This Side of Paradise,* **864–865**
Fitzgerald, Zelda, 309, **310–312**, 374

Five-Power Treaty, 909
flagpole sitting, **312–313**
Flags in the Dust (Faulkner), 295
Flame and Shadow (Teasdale), 851
flappers, **313–314**; as fad, 286; feminism, 313–314, 930; influence on fashion, 314, 374; influence on interior design, 409; in silent film, 106–107, 113–114; slang, 802–803
flash-frozen foods. *See* frozen foods
Fleer Chewing Gum Company, 116
Fleischer, Dave, 493
Fleischer, Max, 493
Fleming, Alexander, 391, 565
Flesh and the Devil (film), **314–315**, 339
Flint, Charles R., 450
floods, 364–366, 415, 613, 638
Flores, Pedro, 937
Flowers, Theodore "Tiger," 108–109
flying circus, 68–69
Fokker, Anthony, **315–316**
folk music, Carter family, **143–144**
folk plays, 861
Food, Drug, and Insecticide Administration, U.S. (FDIA), **316–318**
food trends, **318–321**; bread slicer, **109–110**, 668; bubble gum, 116; Eskimo Pie, **278**, 319; frozen foods, 94–95, **278**, 319, **333–334**; Girl Scout Cookies, **348**; grocery stores, 318–319; home cooking and preparation, 286, 318; meatpacking industry working conditions, 317, 801–802; peanut butter and jelly sandwiches, **667–668**; Pure Food and Drug Act, 316, 317, 802, 887; quick-freezing method, 94–95; refrigerators, **727–728**; regulation, 316–317; vitamin D-fortified, 899
football, **321–323**; amateur sports, 321–322, 347–348, 360–361, 820–821; American Football League (AFL), 360–361, 606;

Los Angeles Memorial Coliseum, 539; National Football League (NFL), 360–361, **605–607**, 822, 867; as professional sport, 322–323, 360–361, 821; radio, 821. *See also* Notre Dame University; *specific athletes and teams*
Forbes, Charles R., **323–324**
Ford, Edsel, 586, 587, 876–877
Ford, Henry: airmail, 876–877, 879; Anti-Semitism, 709; automobile industry, 43, 64, 586, 815–816; trucking, 876
Ford Motor Company: advertising, 9; automobiles to the Soviet Union, 815–816; founding, 64–65; Model A, 65, **586–587**; Model T, 9, 64–65, 454–455
Fordney-McCumber Tariff, 451–452
foreign policy: in Canada, 489; in the U.S., **324–327**, 574–575
forests and farmland, 615
Fortune (magazine), 544
Fosdick, Harry Emerson, 734
Foster, Andrew "Rube," 617–618
Foster, William Z., 36, 498
Four Horsemen of Notre Dame, 322, **327**, 747, 820
Four Horsemen of the Apocalypse, The (film), 893
Four-Power Treaty, 909
"Foursquare Gospel" of Aimee Semple McPherson, 562
Fourteenth Amendment, 34, 170–171, 844, 902
Fourth Amendment, 397
Fox, William, **327–329**
Fox Film Corporation, 328–329
Fox sisters, 818
Foxx, Jimmie, **329–330**
fragrance and cosmetics, 137–138, 153, 154, 293
France: Kellogg-Briand Pact, 484–485; Paris as center for lost generation of writers, 103, 532, 539–540; post–World War I, 280–282; religion in Canada, 729; Rurh occupation, 226–227

Francophone theater in Canada, 859
Frankfurter, Felix, 5
Franklin, Benjamin, 692, 693
Franks, Bobbie, 518
Freeman, Milton H., 405
freight transport. *See* shipping and freight industry
French Symbolists, poetry, 682
Freon, **330–331**
Freud, Sigmund, 702–703, 704, 810
Friml, Rudolf, 112
Frontier in American History, The (Turner), **331–332**
Frost, Robert, **332–333**, 683
frozen foods, 94–95, **278**, 319, **333–334**
Fry v. United States, 689
FTC (Federal Trade Commission), 151, 710
fuel: leaded gasoline, 781–782; rocketry, 351–352
Fugitive, The (magazine), **334–335**, 683
Fugitive Poets, **335–336**, 620, 683, 813–814
Fuld, William, 658–659
Full Employment Bill, 882
Fuller, R. Buckminster, 50, 423
fundamentalist Christians (Protestants): in Canada, 731–732; evangelism, **283–284**; in the U.S., 733–734, 779, 782–783. *See also Scopes* trial

gambling, **337–338**, 501
games, 285–286. *See also* hobbies and recreation
Garbo, Greta, **314–315, 338–340**
Garvey, Marcus, **340–341**; Harlem Renaissance, 385; Pan-Africanism, 247–248; political activism, 13, 888
gasoline, leaded, as public health risk, 781–782
gay rights movement, **411–413**
GDP (gross domestic product) of the United States, 722, 809

Gehrig, Lou, 85, **342**, 626, 627, 763, 764
gender discrimination, 516, 627–628, 667, 882. *See also* women's rights
General, The (film), 886
General Electric (GE), 710, 711, 727, 815–816
General Foods Corporation, 94
General Motors (GM), 9–10, 65, 727, 781–782
General Seafoods Company, 94
General, The (1926), **343**
genetics research, 590–591, **835–836**
Gentlemen Prefer Blondes (Loos), **343–344**
Geography and Plays (Stein), 825–826
George, David Lloyd, 281
Gerber, Henry, 412
Germany: film, 307; hyperinflation in, 453; lynching immigrants from, 724; post–World War I, 280–282; reparations for World War I, 226–227, 280, 281, 325–326
Gernsback, Hugo, 785
Gershwin, George, **344–345**; classical music, 172–173; musical theater in the U.S., 861; operettas, 112, 751–752; recorded sound, 596; *Rhapsody in Blue*, 344, 464, 596, **737–738**, 916
Gershwin, Ira, 344, 596, 861
Gila Wilderness Area, **345–346**
Gilbert, John, **314–315**, 332, **346**
Gipp, George, **347–348**
Girl Scout Cookies, **348**
Gish, Dorothy, **348–349**, 657
Gish, Lillian, 348, **349–350**, 657
Gitlow, Benjamin, 350
Gitlow v. New York, 34, 170–171, **350–351**
Glorifying the American Girl (theatrical revue and film), 895, 941
GM (General Motors), 9–10, 65, 727, 781–782

GNP (gross national product) of the United States, **368–370**, 444, 809
Goddard, Henry, 704, 776
Goddard, Robert H., **351–352**, 745
Godefoy, Alexander F., 373
Gold Diggers, The (Hopwood), 353
Gold Diggers of Broadway (film), **353**
Gold Rush, The (film), 156, **353–354**, 886
gold standard, 79, 453
Goldwyn, Samuel, 80, 81, **354–355**, 572–573
Goldwyn Pictures Corporation, 91, 354, 367
golf, **355–357**, 821–822
Gompers, Samuel, 35–37, **357–358**, 699–700, 885
Goodyear Tire and Rubber Company, 26
Gothic architecture, Hearst Castle, 394
government agencies, branches and programs. *See List of Entries by Categories*
government and politics: political parties, **686–689**. *See* elections; *List of Entries by Categories*; political activism
government and politics: people. *See List of Entries by Categories*
Graham, Martha, 217–218, **358–359**
Grand Ole Opry, The (radio show), **359–360**, 711
Grange, Red, 119, **360–361**, 606, 821
Grant, Madison, 440
Grauman, Sid, 361–362
Grauman's Chinese Theatre, **361–362**, 856
Great Britain: athletic achievements, 644, 646, 650; banking in, 77; book publishing, 102–103, 104; Canadian independence from, **130–132**, 136, 489; gold standard, 453; religion in Canada, 729; spiritualism, 818; stability after

World War I, 282; Washington Naval Conference, **908–910**
Great Depression: Agricultural Marketing Act of 1929, **15–16**; consumer credit role in, 448; and Herbert Hoover, 415; steel production, 614; stock market crash, **829–831,** 882; women in college, 924; workers' education impact, 932. *See also List of Entries by Categories*
Great Gatsby, The (Fitzgerald), 103, 309–310, 337, **362–363,** 531
Great Kanto earthquake, Japan, 58
Great Lakes water transport, 875
Great Miami Hurricane of 1926, 612
Great Migration, **363–364**; civil rights and liberties, 171; Harlem Renaissance, 363, 383; income and wages, 12, 13; as Jim Crow escape, 471; lynching reduction in South, 545–546; racial discrimination, 707; urbanization, 166–167, 232, 890
Great Mississippi Flood of 1927, **364–366,** 415, 613
Great Northern Migration. *See* Great Migration
Great Steel Strike (1919-20), 36, 498, 723–724
Great Steel Strike and Its Lessons, The (Foster), 498
Greb, Harry, 108, 109
Greed (film), 355, **366–367,** 573
Green Bay Packers (football), 605–606
Greenlee, Gus, 618
Greenwich Village Theatre, 862–863
Griffith, D. W., **367–368**; actors, 348, 349, 678, 789; film techniques of, 657; United Artists, 678, 886
grocery stores, 318–319
gross domestic product (GDP) of the United States, 722, 809
gross national product (GNP) of the United States, **368–370,** 444, 809
Group of Seven, **370–371**
Grove, Frederick Philip, 527

Grove, Lefty, **371–372**
Grovey v. Townsend, 902
Guatemala, U.S. influence in, 508
Guilledo, Filipino Francisco (Pancho Villa), 109
guitar method, 502–503
Gurdjieff, Georges Ivanovich, 873

Hadden, Briton, 544, 549, 550
Hagen, Walter, 356
hair dryers, **373**
hairstyles, **373–375**; bobbed hair, **98–99,** 113, 373–374, 924
Haiti, U.S. occupation of, 507, 508
Haldeman-Julius, Emanuel, **533–534**
Hale, George Ellery, 582
Halibut Treaty of 1924, **375–376**
Hall, Edward, 377
Hall, Frances, 377
Hall, Radclyffe, 412
Hallelujah (film), **376–377,** 899
Hall-Mills murder case, **377**
Halsey v. New York Society for the Suppression of Vice, 690, 691
Hammerstein, Oscar II, **378–379,** 800, 861, 939
Hammett, Dashiell, **379**
hanging. *See* lynching
Hanson, Howard, 173
Hardin, Lillian "Lil Hot Miss," **379–380**
Harding, Warren G., **380–383**; Charles Curtis, 215–216; Harry M. Daugherty, 222; death of, 267; elections of 1920, **264–266**; front porch campaign, 266; Charles Evans Hughes, 426; Ohio gang scandals, 207, 208; President's Conference on Unemployment, **695–696**; radio, 712; railroads, 716–717; recession of 1920-1921, 381–382, 881; religion in the U.S., 732; "return to normalcy," 687, **735–736,** 922, 927; Roaring Twenties, 741; Shopmen's Strike, 716–717, 719; William Howard Taft as Supreme Court chief justice, 839,

843; Teapot Dome scandal, 207, 849; U.S. foreign policy, 324
Hardy, Oliver, 511–513, 740
Harlem Renaissance, **383–386**; African American art, 56; African American life, 11–13; Black Swan Records, **97–98**; book publishing, 104; *Cane* (Toomer), 872–873; city development, 167; gay and lesbian culture, 411–412; Great Migration, 363, 383; jazz's role, 596; literature, 532, 550; music and dance styles, 219; notable artists, **379–380, 474–475, 895–896, 904–905**; poetry, 683–684; urbanization, 891
Harlem Shadows (McKay), 384, 684
Harmonium (W. Stevens), 683
Harp Weaver and Other Poems, The (Millay), **386–387**
Harris, Lawren, 370–371
Hart, Lorenz, **387–388**
Hart House Theatre, Toronto, 860
Hatfield, Sid, 499
hats, **176,** 293, 294
Hawthorne, Nathanial, 835
Hawthorn Studies, 810
Hayes, Carlton, 398
Haynes, Daniel L., 376
Hays code, 308
Haywood, Big Bill, **388–389**
health and medicine: air pollution, **24–26**; antibiotics, development of, 391, 564–565; cancer, **137–140**; food trends, 319–320; innovations, 456; medicine, **564–567**; Physiology or Medicine Prize (Nobel), 632–633; psychiatry, 703; public health, 781–782; radiation exposure among health care workers, 138, 139; science and technology, 781–782; Sheppard-Towner Maternity and Infancy Protection Act, 516, 630, **799,** 929; vitamin D, **898–899**; World War I veterans, 933. *See also List of Entries by Categories*

health care, **389–392**
health insurance, **87–88,** 390, 566–567
Hearst, William Randolph, **392–393**; Hearst Castle, 50, **393–395**; Thomas H. Ince scandal, 207–208, 443; newspapers, 621–623; yo-yos, 938
Hearst Castle, 50, **393–395**
Heidelberger, Michael, 564
Hell's Angels (film), 428–429
Hemingway, Ernest, **395–397**; *Farewell to Arms, A,* **289–290**; lost generation in Paris, 103, 532, 540; Gertrude Stein, 825; *Torrents of Spring, The,* 40. *See also Sun Also Rises, The*
Henderson, Fletcher, 98, 464
Heretic (dance production, 1929), 359
Hess, Victor Francis, 676
Hester v. United States, **397**
higher education, 258–259
high schools, 256
highway system. *See* federal highway system
hiking, 403
Hindenburg (airship), 27
Hirsch, Sidney M., 335
Hispanics. *See* Latinos
historiography, **397–400**
Hitchcock, Alfred, 418
hitchhiking, 579
HMOs (health maintenance organizations), 390
hobbies and recreation, **400–404**; comic strips, **183–184**; crossword puzzles, **211–212,** 285–286, 403; fads, 285–286; gambling, **337–338,** 501; games, 285–286; Mah-Jongg, 285, 402–403, **551–552**; National Parks of the United States, 403, **607–608,** 878; stamp collecting, 693; yo-yos, **937–938.** *See also* dance and choreography; racing; silent film; sports; talking motion pictures ("talkies"); tourism
hockey, **404–405**

Holland, Clifford Milburn, 405
Holland Tunnel, **405–406**
Hollerith, Herman, 450
Hollow Men, The (Eliot), 274
Hollyhock House, Los Angeles, 776, 934
Hollywood Bowl, **406–407**
Hollywood scandals, 207–208
Hollywood sign, **407**
Hollywood songs, 93
Holmes, Oliver Wendell, Jr., **407–408**; birth control, 117; *Moore v. Dempsey,* 590; as Supreme Court justice, 832, 839, 840; voting rights, 631
home cooking, 286, 318
home furnishings, **408–411**
Homesteader, The (film), 577
homosexuality and gay rights, 149, **411–413**
hood ornaments, **413–414**
Hooker Telescope, Mount Wilson Observatory, 61, 62, 63
Hoover, Herbert, **414–416**; Better Homes in America movement, 93; as Commerce Secretary, 195; Charles Curtis, 216; elections of 1928, **269–271,** 712; gang violence, 141; Great Mississippi Flood, 365; laissez-faire response to unemployment, 881, 882; National Conference on Street and Highway Safety, 604; pacifism, 733; President's Conference on Unemployment, 695; Prohibition, 700; radio, 713
Hoover, J. Edgar, **416–417**; FBI, 416–417, 832; Palmer raids, 185, 664, 724, 725–726; Red Scare, 724
Hoover Commission, 415
Hoppé, E. O., 674
Hopper, Edward, 55, 56, **417–419**
Hopwood, Avery, 353
Hornsby, Rogers, 85, **419**
horse racing, **419–421, 553–554**
Hot Five, 465
Houdini, Harry, **421–422,** 818–819
House by the Railroad (Hopper), 418

housing, **422–424**; Better Homes in America movement, 93–94; bungalows, **118–119,** 409, 423–424; home furnishings, **408–411**; urban planning, 891; World War I veterans, 933
Hubbard, William Dehart, 645
Hubble, Edwin Powell, 61–62, **424–426**
Hughes, Charles Evans, **426–427,** 459, 909
Hughes, Howard R., Jr., **427–429**
Hughes, Howard R., Sr., 428
Hughes, Langston, 385, **429–431,** 683
Hugh Selwyn Mauberley (Pound), 694
Huld, Anna, 939
human flies, *Safety Last* (film), 534, **767–768**
humor. *See* comedy
Hunchback of Notre Dame, The (film), 154
Hunt, Myron, 406
hurricanes, 611–613, 638–639
Hurston, Zora Neale, **431–432**
hydroelectricity, 300–301

IBM (International Business Machines), **450–451**
ice hockey, **404–405**
I'll Say She Is! (musical play), 558
I'll Take My Stand (Southern Agrarians), **433,** 814
imagism, 245, **542–543**
"I'm Just Wild About Harry" (Blake and Sissle), 800, 801
immigration: anti-immigrant sentiment and immigration restrictions, 434–435, 439–442; Cable Act of 1922, 60, **128–129**; Chinese, **161–162**; city development, 167–168; eugenics movement, 279, 440, 709; passports, 878; racial inferiority, 708; Sacco and Vanzetti case, 709, **766–767**; social science focus, 809. *See also* Palmer raids
Immigration Act of 1917, 434

Immigration Act of 1918, 664
Immigration Act of 1919, Canada, 134
Immigration Act of 1921, **433–435**; anti-immigration sentiment, 440, 708–709; Anti-Semitism, 44; Asians, 60, 662; Congress, 191; democraphics, 232; eugenics movement, 279; Great Migration, 363; racial discrimination, 57, 708; religion in the U.S., 732
Immigration Act of 1924, **435–437**; anti-immigration sentiment, 440, 708–709; Anti-Semitism, 44; Asians, 57, 60, 708; Congress, 191; demographics, 232–233; eugenics movement, 279; Great Migration, 363; IQ testing, 704; racial discrimination, 57; religion in the U.S., 732
Immigration Restriction Act of 1921, 191, 279
immigration to Canada, 131–134, 231–233, **437–439**. *See also* Jews in Canada
immigration to United States, **439–442**; African Americans, 231–233; birth control, 95–96; Border Patrol, U.S., 105; Sudhindra Bose, 105–106; German, and Red Scare, 724; IQ testing, 704–705; Italians, 439–440; Japanese, **462–463**, 661–662; Jews, **43–44**, 468–470, 469–470; KKK's opposition to, 434, 440, 708; Latinos, 441, 510, 515, 574; racial discrimination, 708–709; reforms in, 191; union opposition to, 446; urbanization, 890–891. *See also* List of Entries by Categories
Imperial Conferences, Great Britain, 130–131, 136
Imperial Hotel, Japan, 934–935
Ince, Thomas H., **442–443**
income and wages, **443–447**; *Adkins v. Children's Hospital*, **5–6**, 926, 929; advertising in the United States, 9–10; Canada, 445;
changes and patterns in, 369, 444–445; Great Migration, 12, 13; jobs, 124–125; minimum wage, 5–6; unionism, 124
income tax, 446, 569, 736–737
Independent, 709
Indianapolis "Indy" 500 auto race, 67, 821
Indian Citizen Act of 1924, 171, **447–448**, 609
Indian Reorganization Act, 171
Indian Rights Association (IRA), 609
indigenous peoples. *See* Native Americans
industrialization: industrial education, 258–259; post–World War I, 281–282; urban development, 165–166. *See also* automobiles and auto manufacturing; aviation
Industrial Workers of the World (IWW), 357, 388–389, 497, 884
infectious disease: antibiotic development, 391, 564–565; vaccines, 391, 456, 685
inflation, 122–125, 444
Ingle, Gladys, 69
installment plans, 10, **448–449**, 454
instrumentation: aviation, 70; rocketry, 745–746
insulin, 81, 390, **449–450**
intelligence testing: eugenics movement, 279; IQ testing, 258, 704–705; Progressive Era education, 258; Scholastic Aptitude Test (SAT), **776–777**
Interchurch World Movement (IWM), 732
International Business Machines (IBM), **450–451**
International Olympic Commission (IOC), 866
international relations. *See* diplomacy and international relations
International Style architecture, 49, 50, 51, 935–936
international trade, **451–454**; Canada, 131–132, 451, 452–453; tariffs, 451–452, 453; World War I effects, 451, 452
International Transcontinental Foot Race, 119
International Treaty for the Renunciation of War. *See* Kellogg-Briand Pact of 1928
Interstate Commerce Commission (ICC), 716, 852, 875
interstate highway system. *See* federal highway system
interventionism, Democratic Party, 686
In the American Grain (Williams), **442**
Inuit religion in Canada, 731
inventions, **454–457**
investment. *See* business and economics
iodine, nutritive qualities of, 391
IQ (intelligence quotient) testing, 258, 704–705
iron (nutrient), 565
iron lung, 390, **457–458**
Islam, 31–32
isolationism, 57, **458–459**, 535–536, 921
Italian immigration to U.S., 439–440, 709
Ives, Charles, 173
Izaak Walton League of America, **459–460**

Jacbos Cavern, Missouri, bones, 47
Jackson, A. Y., 370–371
Jacobs, Walter, 564
Jalna (de la Roche), 527
James, William, 610
Jannings, Emil, **461–462**
Jannings Vehicle, 461
Japan: immigration to U.S., 57–58, 462–463, 661–662; Japanese-American citizenship, 661–662; Washington Naval Conference, **908–910**
Japanese American Citizens League (JACL), **462–463**

jazz, **463–466**. *See also specific artists and works*

Jazz Age in Europe, 75

Jazz Age in the United States: African American influence, 52–53; art movements, 54; black-and-tan clubs, 96–97; Black Swan Records, **97–98**; cool jazz predecessor, 88–89; dance, 158, 218; as fad, 285; nightclubs, 627–628; *Rhapsody in Blue* (Gershwin), **737–738**; Roaring Twenties, **741–742**; slang, 803–804; social role of popular music, 595–596; Tin Pan Alley, 344, 463, 486, **869–870**; Edith Wharton, 913–914

Jazz Singer, The (film), **466–467**; Academy Awards, 1; as Disney inspiration, 823; as first "talkie," 1, 846; Al Jolson, 466–467, 906, 908; Paul Robeson, 742; Mack Sennett, 789; Warner Bros., 846, 906, 908

jelly and peanut butter, **667–668**

Jewett, Frank B., 90

Jews in Canada, **468–469**; Anti-Semitism, **43–44**; communities, 730, 731; immigration restrictions, 134, 438

Jews in the United States, **469–471**; American Reformed Judaism, 734–735; Anti-Semitism, **43–44**; in entertainment, 469, 905–907; immigration, 439, 440; musicians, 91–93. *See also List of Entries by Categories*

Jim Crow in the U.S. South, 363, 399, **471–472**

jobs and wages, 124–125

John Brown's Body (Benét), **472**, 530

John Keats (Lowell), **472–473**

Johnson, Charles, 11, 384

Johnson, Jack, **473–474**

Johnson, James Weldon, **474–475**

Johnson, Judy, **476**

Johnson & Johnson, 76–77

Johnson Quota Act. *See* Immigration Act of 1921

Johnson-Reed Act [***note*** this is Reid on page 232 and Reed on page 435]. *See* Immigration Act of 1924

Johnston, Franz, 370–371

"joint" as slang, 803

Jolson, Al, 466–467, **476–477**, 906, 908

Jones, Bobby, 402, **477–478**

journalism: Algonquin Round Table, 4, **30–31**, 624, 665, 755; as American writer influence, 103; Native Americans in, 306; *New Yorker, The*, **624–626**; women in, 303–304, 665. *See also List of Entries by Categories;* publishing industry

Judaism. *See* Jews

Jungle, The (Sinclair), 317, 801–802

Jungle Jim (TV program), 911

"Jungle Style," 465

Jurgen: A Comedy of Justice (Cabell), 127, 690

Just, Ernest E., 780

Kahanamoku, Duke, **479**, 644, 646

Kahn, Reuben Leon, 796

Kane, Helen, **479–480**

Kaufman, George S., 304, 861, 862

Keaton, Buster, 343, **480–482**, 886

Keats, John, **472–473**, 543

Keeler, Leonarde, 689

Keith-Albee theaters, 897, 898

Keller, Helen, **482–483**, 933

Kellogg, Edward W., 541

Kellogg, Frank B., 263, 326, 459, **483–484**, 632

Kellogg-Briand Pact of 1928, 58, 195, 326, 459, **484–486**

Kelly, Alvin, 312

Kelly Act. *See* Air Mail Act of 1925

Kern, Jerome, **486–487**; Broadway musicals, 93, 111, 112; *Show Boat*, 486–487, 800, 861, 939

Keyes, Asa, 562

Keystone Kops films, 790

Kid, The (film), 155–156, 192

Kid Blackie. *See* Dempsey, Jack "Manassa Mauler"

Kimball, Justin Ford, 87–88, 566

Kinetophone system, 846

King, William Lyon Mackenzie, **487–490**; Canadian elections, 260–262; Canadian independence and nationalism, 131, 132, 136; Halibut Treaty, 375; Arthur Meighen, 567

King of Jazz (film), 916

King of Kings, The (film), 230, **490**

Kirby, Rollin, **490–491**

KKK (Ku Klux Klan), **494–496**; anti-immigration sentiment, 434, 440; Anti-Semitism, 43–44, 470; birth control support, 96; Marcus Garvey, 341; immigration, 133–134, 708; lynching, 545; power of, 208; racial discrimination, 707–708; religion in the U.S., 732; Al Smith, Jr., 805

Knickerbocker Storm, **491–493**, 613

Knickerbocker Theatre, 491–492

Knister, Raymond, 527

knitwear designed by Elsa Schiaparelli, **774–775**

Knute Rockne, All American (film), 747

Koko the Clown, **493**

Kona in Hell: Improvisations (W. C. Williams), 918

Kool-Aid, **494**

Korea, 58–59

Korean Americans. *See* Asian Americans

Ku Klux Klan. *See* KKK (Ku Klux Klan)

labor: auto workers, 66; child labor, 73–74, 124–125; Hawthorn Studies, 810; meatpacking industry working conditions, 317, 801–802; railroads, 716–717; religion in Canada, 730; workers', **931–932**; World War I veterans, 933. *See also* income and wages; *List of Entries*

by Categories; women in the workforce
Labor Appropriation Act of 1924, 105
labor colleges for workers' education, **931–932**
labor strikes, **497–500**; coal industry, 498–499; Great Steel Strike, 36, 498, 723–724; Red Scare, 723–724; religion in Canada, 730; seaman's strike, 497, 723; Shopmen's Strike, 716–717, 719; textile industry, 497–498, 884
Labour Party, Canada, 261
La Follette, Robert M., 267–268, **500–501,** 688, 696–697
La Guardia, Fiorella, 903
Lake George, Stieglitz photographs of, 828
Lamontagne-Beauregard, Blanche, 528
Landis, Kenesaw Mountain, **501–502,** 764
landscape painting, Group of Seven, 370–371
Lang, Eddie, **502–503**
Langdon, Harry, **503–504**
Langley, John W., **504–505**
Langmuir, Irving, 158
Lardner, Ring, **505–506**
Larson, John, 689
Lasky, Jesse L., 354, **506–507,** 893
Las Vegas gambling, 337–338
Latin America and the Caribbean, **507–509**; immigration from, 441; U.S. foreign policy in, 326, 427, 459, 483. *See also List of Entries by Categories*
Latinos, **509–511**; city development, 168; immigration of, 441, 510, 515, 574; LULAC, 511, **515**; unionism, 884; urbanization, 890–891
Laurel, Stan, 511–513, 740
Laurel and Hardy, **511–513,** 740
Laurier, Sir Wilfred, 487
Lawrence, D. H., **835**

laws and treaties. *See List of Entries by Categories*
leaded gasoline public health risks, 781–782
League of Nations, **513–514**; Canadian seat, 130; post–World War I, 281–282; U.S. congressional rejection of, 458, 535; U.S. elections of 1920, 265–266; Woodrow Wilson, 921, 922
League of United Latin American Citizens (LULAC), 511, **515**
League of Women Voters, **515–517,** 929
Le Corbusier (Charles-Édouard Jeanneret), 935
Le Gallienne, Eva, 863
Leginska, Ethel, 174
leisure time, increase in, 370. *See also* hobbies and recreation
lending by banks, 77–78, 79
Lenglen, Suzanne, 857, 858
Lenin, Vladimir, 724, 815, 856
Leonard, Benny, 108
Leopold, Aldo, 345
Leopold, Nathan Freudenthal, Jr., 518, 519
Leopold-Loeb murder case, 220–221, **518–519**
lesbian and gay rights, 411–413
Le Terroir (magazine), 528
levee system, failure of Mississippi, 364–366
Lewis, Gilbert Newton, 158–159
Lewis, John L., 499, **519–520,** 883, 884, 885
Lewis, Sinclair, **73,** 276–277, **520–521,** 532–533
Lewis-Langmuir theory, 158–159
Lewis v. Red Jacket, 885
USS *Lexington*, 71
Liberal Party, Canada, 260–262, 487–488, 489
liberal religion in Canada, 730–731
Liberia, Marcus Garvey's back-to-Africa movement, 340–341
Life and Labor in the Old South (Phillips), 399
life insurance reserves, 203

Lights of New York (film), 846–847
Lincoln Memorial, 39, 50, **521–522**
Lindbergh, Charles, **522–524**; aviation, 69–70, 71, 126, 876; Robert Goddard, 352, 746; Red Scare, 623
Lindsay, Vachel, **524–525**
Lindy Hop (dance), **525**
Lippmann, Walter, **525–526, 705–706**
liquid-fueled rockets, 351–352
Lismer, Arthur, 370–371
literacy and advertising, 10
literary criticism: Algonquin Round Table, 4, **30–31,** 624, 665, 755; New Criticism, **620–621,** 683; Edmund Wilson, **920–921**
literary cubism, 825
Literary Guild, 100, 103
literature: in Canada, **526–529**; in the United States, **529–533,** 825, 933. *See also List of Entries by Categories; specific authors and works*
literature: people. *See List of Entries by Categories*
Little, Arthur D., 160
"little black dress," 153
Little Blue Books, **533–534**
Little Engine That Could (Piper), 103, 104
Little Rascals in Our Gang comedies, **659–661,** 740
Little Review, The (magazine), 529–530, 540
Livesay, Dorothy, 528
Lloyd, Harold, 534–535
Lloyd George, David, 130, 131
loans on securities, 203–204
Locke, Alain, 383, 384, 684, 873
Lodge, Henry Cabot, **535–536,** 922
Loeb, Richard, 518
Loew, Marcus, 572, 897
Loew's Theatres, 329, 572, 897
London After Midnight (film), 154–155
Long Lance, Buffalo Child, 306
Lonsdale Belt (boxing), 108

Look Homeward, Angel (Wolfe), **536–537**
Loos, Anita, 343–344
Loos, H. Clifford, 390
Loray Mill strike, 497–498, 884
USS *Los Angeles* (airship), 27
Los Angeles Aqueduct dynamiting, **537–538**
Los Angeles Memorial Coliseum, **538–539**
Lost Generation, 103, 532, **539–541**
loudspeakers, **541–542**
Love Me Tonight (film), 387
"Love-Song of J. Alfred Prufrock, The" (Eliot), 273, 682, 910
Lowell, Amy, 472–473, **542–543, 915**
Lubitsch, Ernst, 461
Luce, Clare Boothe, 544
Luce, Henry R., **543–545**, 549
Lucretia Mott Amendment. *See* Equal Rights Amendment (ERA)
Luhan, Mabel Dodge, 556
LULAC (League of United Latin American Citizens), 511, **515**
Lynch, Charles, 545
lynching, **251–252, 545–546,** 600–601, 724
Lynd, Robert and Helen, 257

MacDonald, J. E. H., 370–371
Machen, J. Gresham, 734
machine-switching system, telephone, 852
Mackay, Ellin, 92
MacLeish, Archibald, **547–548**
Macleod, John, 81, 118, 449, 450, 632–633
Macy, Anne Sullivan, 482
Macy's Thanksgiving Day Parade, **548–549**
Madame Dubarry (film), 461
Mad Hatter (race horse), 420
Mad Play (race horse), 420
magazines, 320, **549–551**
magic, Harry Houdini, **421–422**
Mah-Jongg, 285, 402–403, **551–552**
mail: airmail, **22–23,** 24, 26, 876,

879; mail-order catalogs, 294; postage stamps, **692–694**
Main Currents in American Thought (Parrington), 399, **552–553**
Main Street (Lewis), 520, **553**
major league baseball, **83–86**
makeup and fragrance, 137–138, 153, 154, 293
Making of Americas, The (Stein), 826
Maltese Falcon (Hammett), 379
Mann Act, 473
Man o' War (race horse), 420, **553–554**
marathon dancing, 287, **554–555**
marathons (running), 287
Marconi Wireless Telegraph Company of America, 715, 773
margin buying, stock market crash, 829–830
Marin, John, 56, **555–556**
Marketing (magazine), 7
marketing, and advertising, 8
market research, A.C. Nielson Company, 3
marriage and dating, **556–557**; Asian brides in Canada, 134–135; companionate marriage, 930; literature addressing, **14–15, 32–34, 701–702**; marriage and retention bars to college, 924; slang, 802–803; social status effects on marriage, 557; women's citizenship, 60, **128–129**, 929–930
Married Women's Citizenship Act. *See* Cable Act of 1922
Married Women's Independent Nationality Act. *See* Cable Act of 1922
Marston, William, 689
Mart, Stam, 409
Martha Graham Center of Contemporary Dance, 359
Marx, Adolph, 557–559
Marx, Chico, 558
Marx, Groucho, 179–180
Marx, Harpo, 558
Marx, Herbert Manfred, 557–559
Marx, Julius Henry, 557–559

Marx, Leonard, 557–559
Marx, Milton, 557
Marx Brothers, **179–180, 557–559,** 833
Masses (newspaper), 726
mass production: advertising in the United States, 8–10; automobiles, 9–10
Masters golf tournament, 478
masturbation, sex development theories, 792
Maternity Act. *See* Sheppard-Towner Act
Mather, Stephen, 607–608
Mayer, Louis B., **1–2,** 339, 346, 572
Maytime (Romberg), 751
McAdoo, William Gibbs, 267, 715
McAlmon, Robert, 918
McCollum, Elmer, 899
McFadden, Louis Thomas, 559
McFadden Act of 1927, **559–560**
McKay, Claude, 384, 385, 684
McKaye, Benton, 45
McKenna, Joseph, 839
McKenzie, Fayette, 471
McKenzie, Roderick D., 169–170
McKinney, Nina Mae, 376–377
McKinsey, James Oscar, **560–561**
McLeod, John, 454, 566
McNary-Haugen Bills (1924 to 1928), 15, 262, 291
McNary-Woodruff Act of 1928, 615
McPherson, Aimee Semple, 208–209, **561–563,** 733
McReynolds, James, 576
McTeague: A Story of San Francisco (Norris), 366
Mead, Margaret, **184–185, 563–564**
meatpacking industry working conditions, 317, 801–802
medicine, **564–567**. *See also* health and medicine
mediums, spiritualism, **818–819**
Meighen, Arthur, 487–489, **567–568**
Mellon, Andrew, **568–569,** 736–737, 780
men: clothing and accessories, 293–294; gender discrimination,

516, 627–628, 667, 882; hairstyles of, 373, 374; as primary breadwinners, 882
Mencken, H. L., 37, 549, **569–571**, 671, 786, 814
Menuhin, Yehudi, 174, **571**
Men Without Women (Hemingway), 396
Meredith, Edwin T., 549
The Meriam Report, 610
Merriam, Charles E., 810, 811
Merry Widow, The (film), **572**
Messenger magazine, 720
Mexican Americans, 510, 515
Mexican Constitution of 1917, 574
Mexico, **574–576**; boxing, 109; immigration from, 441; recognition of Soviet Union, 816; U.S. foreign policy, 508–509, 574–575
Meyer, Adolph, 703
Meyer, Robert T., 576
Meyer v. Nebraska (1923), **576–577**, 680
MGM (Metro-Goldwyn-Mayer), **572–573**; Academy Awards, 1; Goldwyn Pictures merger, 354, 367, 572; movie theater evolution, 307, 329; "talkies," 847
Micheaux, Oscar, **577–578**
Mickey Mouse, 244, **823–824**
midterm elections. *See entries at* elections
migrant workers, 441
migrations (within U.S.), **578–580**. *See also* Great Migration
Milestone, Lewis, 428
military and war: aircraft manufacture, 246; arms control, Washington Naval Conference, **908–910**; Latin American operations, 507; pacifism, 730, 733; Thompson machine gun, **865–866**; Tomb of the Unknown Soldier, **870**; Washington Naval Conference, **908–910**. *See also List of Entries by Categories;* World War I

Milky Way galaxy, 61–62
Millay, Edna St. Vincent, 386–387, **580–581**
Miller, Marilyn, 486
Millikan, Robert Andrews, **581–583**, 633, 675, 676
Mills, Eleanor, 377
Mills, James, 377
Mims, Edward, 336
Mineral Leasing Act of 1920, 615
Mingo County, West Virginia coal strike, 499
minimum wage, 5–6
Minimum Wage Act, 5
mining. *See* coal industry
Minkowski, Oskar, 449
minority communities, Canadian, **132–136**
minority communities, United States. *See* African Americans; immigration; Native Americans
minor-league baseball, 84
Miss America pageants, **583–584**
Mississippi River Flood of 1927, **364–366**, 415, 613
Mitchell, Billy, **584–585**
Mitchell, Wesley Clair, 809, 811
Mix, Tom, **585–586**
Model A Ford, 65, 454, **586–587**
Model T Ford, 9, 64–65, 454–455
modernism: dance, 217–218, 359; interior design and architecture, 50, 51, 409, 775–776; Museum of Modern Art (MoMA), 54–55, **594–595**; poetry, 682–683
modular building, 50
money. *See* banking; credit and debt; currency and coinage
"Monkey Trial." *See Scopes* trial
Montessori, Maria, 588
Montessori method, **587–588**
Montgomery, Lucy Maud, 527
Montreal Group (poetry), 528
Moody, Helen Wills, **588–589**, 858
Moore v. Dempsey, 471, **589–590**, 840–841
Moorish American Community, 31–32

moral education, 794
morality code, film, 740
Moran, George "Bugs," 654, 655, 768–769
Morelli gang, 767
Morgan, Garrett, 874
Morgan, Julia, 393
Morgan, Thomas Hunt, **590–591**
Morrill Land Grant College Act of 1862, 923
Morrow, Dwight Whitney, 575
mortgage loans, 204
Morton, Jelly Roll, 380, **591–592**, 641
motels, **592–593**, 878
Mother Goose in Prose (Baum and Parrish), 666
Motion Picture Academy of Arts and Sciences, **1–2**
Motion Picture Producers and Distributors of America (MPPDA), 149, 307, 691
Mott, Lucretia, 629
Mount Rushmore, **593**
Mount Wilson Observatory, 61, 62, 63, 424–425
movie palaces, **594**
movies. *See* film
movie theaters, evolution in, 307, 329
Movietone, 846
moving-coil loudspeaker, 541–542
Mulholland, William, 537, **824–825**
Muller v. Oregon, 926
Museum of Modern Art (MoMA), 54–55, **594–595**
music: musical comedy, 92, 112, 597; popular, **595–598**; radio, 711; recorded sound, 271–272, 596–597. *See also List of Entries by Categories*
musical revue, 112–113. *See also* Ziegfeld Follies
music: people. *See List of Entries by Categories*
Music Box, The, 92
Muslims, 31–32
mutualistas, 884

NAACP (National Association for the Advancement of Colored People), **599-601**; antilynching crusade, 546; Clarence Darrow, 221; fight against Jim Crow laws, 471; founding, 11, 12; James Weldon Johnson, 475; W. E. B. Du Bois, 383

Nanook of the North (film), **599**

Nathan, George Jean, 549

National Academy of Science (NAS), 779, 780, 781, 782

National Amateur Athletic Federation, 819

National American Woman Suffrage Association (NAWSA), 516, 629, 927, 928, 929

National Association for the Advancement of Colored People. *See* NAACP

National Boxing Association (NBA), 108

National Bureau of Economic Research (NBER), 722, 809

National Conference on Street and Highway Safety (1924, 1926), **603-604**

national debt of the United States, **604-605**

National Football League (NFL), 360-361, **605-607**, 822, 867

national income during the period, 369, 444

nationalism, Canadian, 6-8, **136-137**

National League (baseball), 83-84, 658

National League of Women Voters. *See* League of Women Voters

National Origins Act of 1924, 191

national origins quota system for immigration, 441

National Parks of the United States, 403, **607-608**, 878

National Prohibition Act of 1919, 337

National Research Council (NRC), 47-48

National Romantic Style, Finland, 765

National Textile Workers Union (NTWU), 497-498

National Urban League (NUL), 11

National Woman's Party (NWP), 630, 667

National Woman Suffrage Association (NWSA), 629, 927

Native Americans, **608-611**; archaeology, 48-49; Art Deco movement, 53-54; in Canada, 135; citizenship, 171, **447-448**, 609; Inuit religion in Canada, 731; journalism, 306; photographs of, 674; Jim Thorpe, **866-867**

natural disasters, **611-614**; floods, 364-366, 415, 613, 638; hurricanes, 611-613, 638-639; tornadoes, 611-613. *See also* disasters

natural resources, exploitation of, **614-616**

nature as inspiration, 56

naval operations, 459, 483. *See also* Washington Naval Conference

Nazism, Emil Jannings' association with, 461

NBC (National Broadcasting Company), **601-603**; establishment of, 456; radio, 711, 714, 715; David Sarnoff, 601, **773-774**

NCAA (National Collegiate Athletic Association), 820

Negro History Week, **616-617**

Negro League Baseball, 89-90, 402, **617-619**, 822

Negro National League, 83-84, 617-618

Negro Project, 96

"Negro Speaks of Rivers, The" (L. Hughes), 430

"The Negro Woman and the Ballot" (Dunbar-Nelson), 630

Negro World (magazine), 340, 341, 889

Negry v Amerike (McKay), 385

Neighborhood Playhouse, 863

Neil, Florence E., 348

Nelles, Walter, 350

Nelson, Christian Kent, 278

Newberry v. United States, **619-620**, 901, 902

New Cascade Tunnel, 145

New Criticism, **620-621**, 683

New Deal, social science impact on, 811

New Found Land (MacLeish), 547

New History, The (Robinson), 398

New Negro, The (Locke), 383, 684

New School, The, 399, 809-810

newspapers: advertising in Canada, 6; advertising in the United States, 9-10; African American, 11-12; comic strips, **183-184**; crossword puzzles, **211-212**, 285-286, 403; gambling popularizing by, 337; tycoons, 151-152; in the United States, **621-624**. *See also List of Entries by Categories*

New York Daily News, 622, 623

New Yorker, The (magazine), 549, **624-626**, 755

New York Giants (baseball), 84, 657-658

New York Giants (football), 605-606

New York Philharmonic, 174

New York State Athletic Commission (NYSAC), 107-108

New York Stock Exchange, stock market crash, 829, 831

New York Times (newspaper), 750

New York Tribune (newspaper), 4

New York World (newspaper), 491

New York Yankees (baseball), 84, 342, **626-627**, 763-764

NFL (National Football League), 360-361, **605-607**, 822, 867

NHL (National Hockey League), 404

Nicaragua, U.S. occupation of, 507, 508, 509

Nielson, Arthur C., 2-3

Nigger Heaven (Van Vechten), 385-386

nightclubs, **627-628**

Night of the Hunter, The (film), 350
Nine-Power Treaty, 325, 909
Nineteenth Amendment, **628–631,** 928; African American women, 12, 13; passage of, 901; period following passage, 927–928, 930. *See also* suffrage
Ninety-Nines, 254
Nipkow, Paul, 853
Nivison, Josephine Verstille, 418
Nixon v. Herndon, **631,** 902
Nobel Prizes, 73, 81, **632–633,** 653
Normand, Mabel, **633–635**
Norris, Frank, 366
North American Indian, The (Curtis), 675
Notre Dame University: Fighting Irish, 322, 327; Four Horsemen of Notre Dame, 322, **327,** 747, 820–821; George Gipp, 347–348; Knute Rockne, 347, **746–748**
Novarro, Ramón, **635–636**
Noyes, Arthur A., 582
nudes and pornography, 690
numbers games during Prohibition, 337
Nurmi, Paavo, 644–646, 650
nutrition science, 319–320, 391, 456, 565

Obregón, Alvaro, 574, 575
obscene materials, pornography, 690
October Revolution, Russia, 724, 726, 815, 856–857
Ohio Gang, 208, 382
Ohio tornado of 1924, 611
oil and gas: drilling, 615; pollution, 615, **637–638;** Teapot Dome scandal, 238, 416, **849–851**
Oil Pollution Act of 1924, 615, **637–638**
Okeechobee Hurricane of 1928, 612, **638–639**
O'Keeffe, Georgia, **639–640;** art movements, 55, 56; marriage to Alfred Stieglitz, 639–640, 672, 828

old age pensions, 445
Oliver, Joe "King," 52, **640–642**
"Ol' Man River," 742, 800
Olmstead v. United States, **642–643,** 840, 844
Olympic Games, generally: amateur sports, 819–820; ice hockey, 405; Los Angeles Memorial Coliseum, **538–539;** Jim Thorpe, 867
Olympic Games of 1912 (Summer), 866
Olympic Games of 1920 (Summer), **643–645;** amateur sports, 821; swimming, 479; track and field, 663, 777; women athletes, 820
Olympic Games of 1924 (Summer), **645–647;** amateur sports, 821; soccer, 808; swimming, 255, 911; tennis, 858; track and field, 645, 663, 777
Olympic Games of 1924 (Winter), **647–648,** 821
Olympic Games of 1928 (Summer), **648–651;** amateur sports, 821; soccer, 808; swimming, 911; track and field, 754–755, 777
Olympic Games of 1928 (Winter), **651–652**
O'Neill, Eugene, **652–654;** *All God's Chillun Got Wings,* **33–34,** 862–863; *Anna Christie,* **42–43,** 653, 861; *Desire Under the Elms,* **239–240;** *Emperor Jones, The,* **276–277,** 653, 862; impact on theater, 530, 862; *Strange Interlude,* 653, **833–834,** 862
One of Ours (Cather), 146
one-piece bathing suits, 292
One Week (film), 481
Open Door Policy, China, 909
open shop drive, American Federation of Labor (AFL), 36–37
operettas, 112, 751–752, 834–835, 861
Opportunity, A Journal of Negro Life (magazine), 384

orchestras, classical music, 174–175
ore carriers, water transport, 875
organic chemistry, 159–160
Organic Synthesis (journal), 159
organizations. *See List of Entries by Categories; specific organizations*
organized crime, **654–656;** bootlegged and smuggled alcohol, 699; J. Edgar Hoover's focus on, 416–417; Roaring Twenties, 741; Saint Valentine's Day Massacre, 209; speakeasies, 817; Thompson machine gun, 865–866; Tong Wars of Chinatown, **871–872.** *See also* crime and scandals
organized labor. *See* unionism
Original Dixieland Jazz Band (ODJB), 463
Origins of the World War, The (Fay), 398
Orphans of the Storm (film), 348, 349, **657**
Orpheum theaters, 897, 898
Orteig Prize, 522–523
"Oscar" Academy Award, 1
Ostenso, Martha, 527
Ott, Mel, **657–658**
Ouija boards, 286, **658–659,** 818–819
Our Gang comedies, **659–661,** 740
Our Town (Wilder), 917
Owen, Chandler, 720
Owen, Robert Latham, 398
Owens Valley, California and Los Angeles Aqueduct, 537–538
Ozawa v. United States (1922), **661–662**

Pace, Harry, 98
Pacific and East Asia, Washington Naval Conference, **908–910**
pacifism, 730, 733
Pact of Paris. *See* Kellogg-Briand Pact of 1928
Paddock, Charles, 644, **663–664**
Paige, Satchel, 822
paleontology, **41–42**
Pal Joey (play, 1940), 387–388

Palmer, A. Mitchell, 416, 724–725
Palmer raids, **664–665**; J. Edgar Hoover, 185, 664, 724, 725–726; Red Scare, 416, 724–725
Palm Sunday tornado of 1920, 611
Pan-African Congress, 13
Pan-Africanism, 247–248
Panama Canal, and U.S. influence in the area, 507
Pancho Villa, 109
Papendick, Gustav, 110
Paramount Pictures, 114, 354, 898
Paris, as center for lost generation of writers, 103, 532, 539–540
Park, Robert E., 169–170
Parker, Dorothy, **665**
Parkinson, Donald, 539
Parkinson, John, 539
Parrington, Vernon Louis, 399, 552
Parrish, Maxfield, **665–666**
passports, 878
Paul, Alice, 629–630, **666–667**, 927
Pauling, Linus C., 159, 676, 677
Peace dollar, 214
peace initiative, Kellogg-Briand Pact (1928), **484–486**. *See also* Washington Naval Conference
Peace Prize (Nobel), 632
peanut butter and jelly sandwiches, **667–668**
Pearce, Louis, 564–565
Peer, Ralph S., 760
penicillin, discovery of, 565
per capita GNP, 368
Per Centum Law. *See* Immigration Act of 1921
performance surveys, by A.C. Nielson Company, 2–3
perfume. *See* cosmetics and fragrance
Perkins, Edwin, 494
Pershing, John, 668
Pershing Map, **668–669**
Persinger, Louis, 571
Phantom of the Opera (film), 154
pharmaceuticals, 316–317, 391, 456, 685
Philadelphia, PA, Sesquicentennial Exposition, **791–792**

Philadelphia Athletics (baseball), 372
Philadelphia Orchestra, 174–175
Phillips, C. Coles, **669**
Phillips, Ulrich B., 399
philosophy and philosophers, **669–672**
Phipps Act. *See* Federal Aid Highway Act of 1921
Phonofilm, 846
phonographs, 271–272, 410
photography, **672–675**; industry developments by George Eastman, **254–255**; of Native Americans, 674; portraits, by James Van Der Zee, **895–896**. *See also List of Entries by Categories*; Stieglitz, Alfred
physical attractiveness fads, 287
physical chemistry, 158–159
physics, 187–188, **675–677**
Physics Prize (Nobel), 633
Physiology or Medicine Prize (Nobel), 632–633
pianos (player), 410, **681**
Pickford, Mary, 348, 349, **678–679**, 886
pictorialism, 673
pictures, telephone transmission of, 852, 853
Pierce v. Society of Sisters, **679–680**
pilgrims on postage stamps, 692
Pinchback, P. B. S., 872
Piper, Watty, 103
Piston, Walter, **680–681**
Pitney, Mahlon, 839
Planck, Max, 675
planets, study of, 63
Planned Parenthood, 96, 772
player pianos, 410, **681**
playgrounds, 403
Playhouse, The (film), 481
Plessy v. Ferguson, 844
plumbing, indoor, 408
Poe, Edgar Allan, 835
poetry, **682–684**; Canadian developments, 528; female published poets, 851, 936; New Criticism, **620–621**, 683; U.S.

developments, 529–530. *See also specific poets and works*
Poetry (magazine), 529–530
police strike, Boston, 724
polio, **684–686**; developments in, 565; iron lung, 390, **457–458**; Franklin D. Roosevelt, 752
political activism: African Americans, 12–13; birth control, 772; First Lady Edith Wilson, 919–920; theory of evolution, 115–116; women's rights, 927, 928–929
political cartoons, **490–491**
political parties, **686–689**. *See also* Democratic Party; Republican Party
political science at University of Chicago, 810
Pollak, Walter, 350
pollution, oil, 615, **637–638**
polygraph, **689**
Ponzi, Charles, 204, 207
Ponzi schemes, 204, 207
Pooler, Frank, 345
Poplar Bluff tornado of 1927, 612
popular culture: African Americans, 11–12; baseball, 85; dances, **219–220**, 285, 403; highway culture, 300; music, **595–598**; obscene materials, 690; rural life, 759–760; yo-yos, **937–938**. *See also List of Entries by Categories*
population: of African Americans in North America, 231–233; in Canada, 231; of Mexican Americans, 510; in United States, 123, 231–232; urban, 889–890
pornography, **690–691**
Post, Emily, **691–692**
postage stamps, **692–694**
postal system: airmail, **22–23**, 24, 26, 876, 879; Canadian, 758–759; mail-order catalogs, 294; postage stamps, **692–694**; savings banks, 78
Potts, William L., 874

Pound, Ezra, **694–695**; T. S. Eliot, 273, 910; poetry, 682; William Carlos Williams, 823, 918–919
poverty levels and demographics, 446–447
pragmatism, 241–242
Pragmatism as philosophy, 610
Prairie School architecture, 50, 934–936
Pratt, E. J., 528
precisionism, 55–56, 237
Preface to Morals, A (Lippman), 526
prejudice. *See* discrimination and prejudice
President's Conference on Unemployment, **695–696**
President's Daughter, The (Britton), **696**
Principles of Chemical Engineering, The (Little), 160
Principles of Scientific Management, The (Taylor), 716
print censorship, 148–149
printing, labor strike in, 497
privacy rights, 397
process philosophy, 671–672
productivity, 368–369, 445
products and inventions. *See List of Entries by Categories*
professional sports: baseball, 821; boxing, 821; football, 322–323, 360–361, 821; golf, 355–357, 821–822; tennis, 821–822, 858–859. *See also specific sports, teams and athletes*
Professor's House (Cather), 146–147
Progressive Education Association (PEA), 258
Progressive Era: *Bailey v. Drexel Furniture Co.,* 74; birth control, 95–96; in Canada, 261; in education and schools, 257–258; end of, 687; political parties, 686; railroads, 716; Franklin D. Roosevelt, 753; in U.S. elections of 1920, 264; workers' education, 931
Progressive Party (Canada), 488–489

Progressive Party (U.S.), **500–501**, 688, **696–698**
Progressive Party of 1924, **696–698**
Prohibition, **698–701**; bathtub gin, 87; black-and-tan clubs, 97; Border Patrol, U.S., 105; gambling, 337; health dangers of illegal alcohol, 389; *Hester v. United States,* 397; nightclubs, 627; notable persons, 504–505, 778, 804, 805; organized crime, 654–656; religion in the U.S., 732–733; Roaring Twenties, **741–742**; slang, 803; social science focus, 809; Supreme Court rulings, 839; trade effects of, 452; urbanization, 891; women's liberation, 924
Prohibition Party, 688
property, income from, 369
Prophet, The (Gibran), **701–702**
propulsion, rocketry, **745–746**
prostitution, Wales Padlock Law, 149
protectionism, U.S., 451–452, 453
Protestant religion: in Canada, **729–732**; in the United States, **732–735**. *See also* fundamentalist Christians (Protestants)
Prouty, Olive Higgins, **827**
Provincetown Players, 652–653, 862
psychology, psychiatry, and psychoanalysis, **702–705**; behaviorism, 810–811; poetry, 682; psychological testing, 258; testimony in trials, Leopold-Loeb case, 518–519
PTSD (post-traumatic stress disorder), World War I veterans, 933
public health, science and technology, 781–782
public interest, Radio Act, 713
Publicity Act. *See* Corrupt Practices Act of 1925
Public Opinion (Lippmann), **705–706**
public works relief, 881–882
publishing houses, 102–103

publishing industry: books, **102–105**; newspapers, U.S., 621–624; science fiction, **784–786**; science journals, 779–780
Pueblo Lands Act, 610
Pueblos, 609–610
Puerto Rican immigrants, 510
Pullman Company, 114–115
pulp fiction, 103
Pure Food and Drug Act, 316, 317, 802, 887
Pyle, Charles C. C., 119, 606, 858

Q-tips (cotton swabs), 200–201
quantum energy, 676–677
Quebec: federal *vs.* provincial tensions, 136–137; Francophone theater in Canada, 859; religion in Canada, 729
quick-freezing method of food preservation, 94–95

raccoon coats, 286–287
racial composition of North America, 233
racial discrimination, **707–710**; *All God's Chillun Got Wings* (O'Neill), **33–34**, 862–863; baseball, 83–84, 617–619; birth control, 95–96; city development, 166; Dyer antilynching bill, **251–252**, 546, 600–601; Harlem Renaissance, 384; in industrialized North, 363–364; Jim Crow in the U.S. South, 363, 399, **471–472**; against Latinos, 510–511; NAACP, 599–601; nightclubs, 627–628; notable artists, 38–39, 75–76, 477; social science focus, 809; and "white" definition, 440. *See also* African Americans; Jim Crow in the U.S. South; KKK (Ku Klux Klan); *specific people*
racing: air, 253–254; auto, **67–68**, 821; horse, **419–421, 553–554**
radiation exposure among health care workers, 137–138, 139

radio, **710–713**; advertising in Canada, 6; advertising in the United States, 8–9, 10, 456; Anglophone theater in Canada, 860; broadcasting networks, 601–603; Canadian National Railroad, 718; college football, 821; comedy, **120–121,** 711, 712; comedy on, 120–121, 711, 712; electrification and, 272; Federal Radio Commission (FRC), **301–302**; food shows, 320; as major recreation activity, 401; music on, 596; popularity of, 410, 456; Franklin D. Roosevelt, 753; rural life, 760; David Sarnoff, 601, **773–774**; *Scopes* trial, 787; sportscasting, 711–712; telephone technology, 852–853; as tool for evangelism, 283–284; vaudeville *vs.*, 898. *See also List of Entries by Categories*
Radio Act of 1912, 712
Radio Act of 1927, 284, 301–302, 712, **713–714**
Radio Corporation of America (RCA), **714–715**; radio, 601–603, 710, 711, 713; David Sarnoff, 601, **773–774**; television, 855, 942
"radium girls," 137–138, 139
ragtime music, 463
railroad, **715–719**; Cascade Tunnel, **144–145**; labor strike, 498; rural life, 759–760; shipping industry, 875; tourism by, 878–879; transcontinental, 878–879
Railroad Labor Board, 498
Railroad Transportation Act, 715–716, 875
Railway Labor Act of 1926, 717, 718, **719–720**
rain, 613
Randolph, Asa Philip, 13, 114–115, **720–721**
Ransom, John Crowe, 814
Raphaelson, Samson, 466
rayon stockings, **721–722**
Razaf, Andy, 904–905

RCA. *See* Radio Corporation of America (RCA)
RCA Victor, 715
Reader's Digest, The (magazine), 549, 904
reading groups, books, 100–101
Reagan, Ronald, 347
real estate tycoons, 151–152. *See also* housing
realism: in art, 56, 417–418; in film, 366; in literature, 527, 530, 531, 532; in theater, 42, 861–862
recession of 1920–1921 ("the forgotten depression"), **722–723**; business and economics, **122–125**; effect on trade, 451; GNP and business cycle, 368–369; Harding administration, 381–382, 881; rural life, 759; unemployment, 881–882
recorded sound: music, 271–272, 596–597; phonographs, 271–272, 410. *See also* talking motion pictures ("talkies")
record setting, 287
recreation and entertainment. *See* hobbies and recreation; *List of Entries by Categories*
Redman, Don, 465
Red Scare, **723–726**; free speech right, 350; labor movement, 357, 358; Charles Lindbergh, 623; McCarthy-era (1950s), 725; Palmer Raids, 416, 724–725; unionism, 884
Reed, John, **726–727, 856–857**
refrigerators, 330–331, 334, **727–728**; frozen foods, 94–95, **278**, 319, **333–334**
refunding, 605
Regent Theatre in Harlem, 594
regulations: food and pharmaceuticals, 316–317; radio, 712; tariffs in international trade, 451–452, 453
rehabilitation, World War I veterans, 933
Rehn, Frank K. M., 418
Reid, Wallace, **728–729**

Reigh Count (race horse), 420
Reis, Johann Philipp, 541
religion in Canada, **729–732**. *See also* Jews in Canada
religion in the United States, **732–735**; conservative, 733–734; evangelism, **283–284**; Islam, 31–32; science, 779, 782–783; *Scopes* trial, 34–35, 116, 623; Al Smith Jr., 805; spiritualism, 286, **658–659, 818–819**; Thornton Wilder, 111. *See also List of Entries by Categories*
Remodeling Her Husband (film), 348, 349
"Renascence" (Millay), 580
Republican Party: Congress, 189–190; elections, midterm, 1922 and 1926, **262–264**; elections of 1920, **264–266,** 381; elections of 1922 (midterm), **262–264**; elections of 1924, **266–269,** 267, 268; elections of 1926 (midterm), **262–264**; elections of 1928, **269–271**; founding, 686–687; political parties, **686–689**; resurgence of, 190; women's rights, 928
reserve clause in baseball, 502
residential electrification, 272
residential segregation in cities, 167
restaurants, 320
restrictive covenants, *Corrigan v. Buckley,* **198**
"return to normalcy," 687, **735–736,** 922, 927
Revenue Acts of 1924, 1926, and 1928, **736–737**
revival style architecture, 49–50
Rhapsody in Blue (G. Gershwin), 344, 464, 596, **737–738,** 916
Rice, Chester W., 541
Rice, Elmer, **4–5,** 862
Richards, Vincent, 858
Richardson, Willis, 384–385
Rickard, George "Tex," 108, 109
rickets, 900
Riddle, Sam, 420, 553

Ringling, John, 739
Ringling Bros. and Barnum & Bailey Circus, 401, **738–739**
Rin Tin Tin films, **739**, 906
riots, race, 546, 707, 708, 724
river barges, water transport, 875
RKO (Radio-Keith-Orpheum), 307, 898
Roach, Hal, Sr., 511–512, 659–661, **739–741**, 768
road construction and safety, 298–300
Roaring Twenties, **178–179, 741–742**
Roberts, Charles G. D., 528
Robeson, Paul, 276, **742–743**, 800, 801
Robin Hood (1922), 288
Robinson, Doane, 593
Robinson, Edwin Arlington, 530, **743–745**
Robinson, James Harvey, 398
Robscheit-Robbins, Frieda S., 565
Rockefeller, Abby Aldrich, 594
Rockefeller, John D., 811
Rockefeller Foundation, 811
rocketry, 352, **745–746**
Rockne, Knute, 347, **746–748**
Rockwell, Norman, **748**
Rodgers, Jimmie, **749**
Roebuck, Alvah C., 788
Rogers, Richards, 378, 387–388
Rogers, Will, **749–751**, 940
Rogers, Will, Jr., 750
Rohwedder, Otto, 110, 668
USS *Roma* (airship), 26
Roman Catholics. *See* Catholics and the Catholic Church
Romantic American (Hoppé), 674
Romberg, Sigmund, 112, **751–752, 834–835**
Roosevelt, Eleanor, 752, 924
Roosevelt, Franklin Delano, **752–754**; James M. Cox, 202; defeat of Herbert Hoover, 882; polio, 685; and polio, 565; social science impact on the New Deal, 811; unemployment relief program, 881–882; Jimmy Walker, 903; Woodrow Wilson, 922
Rosenfeld, Fanny "Bobbie," **754–755**
Rosenfield, Joseph, 667–668
Ross, Donald E., 390
Ross, Harold, 549, 624, **755**
Ross, Nellie Tayloe, **755–757**
Ross, William Bradford, 756
Rothafel, Samuel, 594
Rothstein, Arnold, 337
Route 66, **757–758**
Royal Canadian Air Force (RCAF), **758–759**
Ruhr, occupation of, 226–227
rural life, **759–761**; agriculture in Canada, **16–18**; agriculture in the United States, **18–21**
Russia: Bolshevik Revolution, 724, 726, 815, 856–857; Soviet Union and North America, 282, **762, 815–816**; Union of Russian Workers, 664
Russian Famine Relief Act of 1921, **762**
Russian Imperial Conspiracy, 1892–1914, The (Owen), 398
Ruth, Babe, 84, 85, 626–627, **762–764**

Saarinen, Eliel, **765**
Sabin, Florence, 780
Sacco, Nicola, 709, **766–767**
Sacco and Vanzetti case, 709, **766–767**
Safety Last (film), 534, **767–768**
St. Denis, Ruth, 238–239
St. Francis Dam disaster, **824–825**
St. Louis Cardinals, 419
Saint Valentine's Day Massacre, **768–770**; gang violence, 141; organized crime, 209, 654–655; speakeasies, 817
Salk, Jonas, 685
Sally (play, 1920), 486
Samoa, Margaret Mead studies in, **184–185**
Samuel Goldwyn Productions, 354–355
Sandburg, Carl, **770–771**
Sandino, Augusto, 509
sandwiches: peanut butter and jelly, **667–668**; sliced bread, **109–110**, 668
Sanford, Edward Terry, 350, 839
San Francisco, Tong Wars, **871–872**
Sanger, Margaret, 95–96, **771–773**, 793
USS *Saratoga*, 71
Sarnoff, David, 601, **773–774**
Sartoris (Faulkner), **774**
Saskatchewan Wheat Pool (SWP), 17
SAT Scholastic Aptitude Test (SAT), **776–777**
Saturday Evening Post (magazine), **748**
Saturday Review, The (magazine), 549
saxophone, introduction of, 463
Schenck v. United States (1919), 408
Scherman, Harry, 100
Schiaparelli, Elsa, **774–775**
Schindler, Rudolph, 51, **775–776**
Schlesinger, Arthur, 400
Schmitt, Bernadotte, 398
scholarship. *See* education and scholarship
Scholz, Jackson, **777–778**
school-based sex education, **792–795**
Schultz, Dutch, **778–779**
science and technology, **779–784**; agriculture in Canada, **16–18**; agriculture in the United States, 20; automobile production, 123–124; bulldozers, 117–118; business and economics, 123–124; home innovations, 408–409; inventions, **454–457**; loudspeakers, **541–542**; music, 596–597; oil pollution, 615, **637–638**; rural life, 759–760; unemployment, 881; women in the workforce, 677, 780. *See also List of Entries by Categories*
science fiction, **784–786**
Scientific American (magazine), 780, 818

Scientific Monthly (magazine), 780, 782, 783
Scopes, John, 115–116, 257, 623, **786–788**
Scopes trial, **786–788**; ACLU, 34–35, 786–787; Agrarians, 814; William Jennings Bryan, 116, 623; Clarence Darrow, 221, 623; H. L. Mencken, 570, 623; political control of schools, 257; process philosophy, 671; science vs. religion, 733–734, 783
Scopes v. State, 788
Scott, Duncan Campbell, 528
sculpture, 56
seaman's strike [dock], 497, 723
Sears, Richard W., 788
Sears, Roebuck and Co., 409, **788–789**
Second World War. *See* World War II
securities, loans on, 203–204
segregation, Jim Crow in the U.S. South, 363, 399, **471–472**
Sennett, Mack, 313, 407, 503, 634, **789–791**
Sesquicentennial Exposition, Philadelphia, **791–792**
sex and sex education, **792–795**
sex development theories, 792
sexuality: and dating patterns, 556–557; pornography, **690–691**; prostitution, Wales Padlock Law, 149; psychoanalysis of, 703; sex symbols in film, 82, 106–107, 122–123, 635–636; slang, 802; Mae West, 912. *See also* birth control
sexually transmitted diseases (STDs), 792, **795–797**
Sexual Sterilization Act (Canada, 1928), **28–29**, 95–96, 133, 709
sexual themes, in DeMille films, 230
Shaker Heights, OH, suburbs, 837
sharecroppers, 12, 13, 363, 365, 366
Shaw, Louis Agassiz, 457
Shawn, Ted, 238–239

Sheeler, Charles, 673
sheet music and Tin Pan Alley, 869
Sheik, The (film), 306, **797**, 893
"shell shock," World War I veterans, 933
USS *Shenandoah* (airship) disaster, 27, 71, **797–799**
Shenandoah National Park, 607
Sheppard, John Morris, 22
Sheppard-Towner Act, 516, 630, **799**, 929
Sherlock, Jr. (film), 481
Sherman Antitrust Act, 887–888
shipping and freight industry: air transport, 876–877; labor strike in, 497, 723; railroad, 717–718, 875; trucking, 717, 875–876; water transport, 875
shoes, women's, 293
Shopmen's Strike, 716–717, 719
shopping centers, suburban, 837
Shotwell, James T., 484
Show Boat (stage musical), **800**; Oscar Hammerstein II, 378, 800, 861, 939; Jerome Kern, 486–487, 800, 861, 939; musical theater in the U.S., 861; Paul Robeson, 742, 800; Florenz Ziegfield, 111, 112, 113, 939
Shubert Brothers, 940
Shuffle Along (stage musical), **800–801**, 861
silent film: Academy Awards, 1–2; actor transition to talkies, 80–81, 83, 143; actresses in, 633–635; Cocoanut Grove nightclub, **178–179**; comedy, 155–157, 164–165, 480–482; cost of producing, 91; film in the era, **305–308**; flappers in, 106–107, 113–114; Keystone Kops, 790; revolutionized by sound, 90, 271, 328–329, 466–467, 780, 846, 906, 907; Roaring Twenties, 741; sex education films, 794; sex symbols in, 82, 121–122, 306, 635–636; successful transition to talkies, 83; William Desmond Taylor, 634, **848**;

theatrical makeup, 154. *See also specific actors, films and studios*
Simmons, William Joseph, 495
Sinclair, Upton, 317, **801–802**
Singstad, Ole, 405–406
Sissle, Noble, 800–801
"Sisters, The" (Lowell), 915
Skinner, B. F., 705
skyscrapers: architecture, 50; Chrysler Building, 162, **163–164**; Empire State Building, 50, 51, 54, 805
slang, **802–804**
sliced bread, **109–110**, 668
Sloan, Alfred P., 65
slot machines, 337
Smith, Alfred E., Jr. "Al," **804–806**; elections of 1928, **269–271**, 712, 804, 805; religion in the U.S., 733, 734; Franklin D. Roosevelt, 752–753, 805; Jimmy Walker, 903; World War I veterans, 933
Smith, Bessie, 464, **806–807**
Smith, Oswald J., 731
Smith v. Allwright, 902
smoke, air pollution controls, 24–26
smoking, impact of, 138–139
Snowden, George, 525
snowstorms, 613
Snyder, Homer, **447–448**
Snyder Act. *See* Indian Citizen Act of 1924
So Big (Ferber), 304
soccer, **807–809**
social class and women, 923–926
social Darwinism, 115, 279, 408
Socialist Party of America: Eugene V. Debs, 228–229; political parties, 687, 688; A. Philip Randolph, 720; Upton Sinclair, 801–802
social order, maintaining, and urbanization, 168–169
Social Science Research Council (SSRC), 809, 810, 811
social sciences, 169–170, **809–812**. *See also List of Entries by Categories*
Social Security Act of 1935, 445

Société Anonyme, **812**
Society for Human Rights (SHR), 412
Soldiers' Bonus Act of 1924, **99–100**
solid-fueled rockets, 352
Souls of Black Folk, The (Du Bois), 247, 383
Sound and the Fury, The (Faulkner), 295–296, 531, **812–813**
sound in film. *See* talking motion pictures ("talkies")
South, The: Jim Crow in the U.S. South, 363, 399, **471–472**; race relations in, 12, 13, 36–37; racial discrimination, 707–708
Southern Agrarians, 531–532, **620–621**, 683, **813–815**; *I'll Take My Stand*, 433, 814
Soviet Union: Bolshevik Revolution, 724, 726, 815, 856–857; and North America, 282, **762, 815–816**; Union of Russian Workers, 664
Spanish Renaissance architecture, 394
speakeasies, **816–818**; nightclubs, 627; organized crime, 655, 817; Prohibition, 699; slang, 803
speedways, auto racing, **67–68**, 821
Spirit of St. Louis, 69–70, 71, 523
spiritualism, 286, **658–659**, 818–819
sports, **819–822**; "Bunion Derby," 119–120; Canada, 404, **754–755**; fashions, 775; growth of as recreational activity, 401–402; radio, 711–712. *See also List of Entries by Categories;* Olympic Games; *specific athletes; specific sports*
sportscasting: radio, 711–712; writing, 821
Spring and All (W.C. Williams), **822–823**
Stafford v. Wallace, 844
Stag Canyon mine disaster of 1923, 614
Stallings, Laurence, 861
stamp collecting, 693
Stamper, Dave, 940–941

Stanton, Elizabeth Cady, 629
"Stardust" (song), 142
stars, study of, 62–63
STDs (sexually transmitted diseases), 792, **795–797**
Stead, Robert J. C., 527
Steamboat Willie (animated film), **823–824**
steel industry, 36, 498, 614, 723–724
Steenbock, Harry, 780, 899
Steichen, Edward, 555, 672–673, 690
Stein, Gertrude, 540, **825–827**
Stella Dallas (Prouty), **827**
Stephenson, David C., 495
sterilization: Alberta Sexual Sterilization Act (Canada), **28–29**, 95–96, 133, 709; *Buck v. Bell*, 116–117. *See also* birth control
Stevens, Henry, 377
Stevens, Wallace, 683
Stevens, William "Willie," 377
Steven's Pass Tunnel, 145
Stieglitz, Alfred, **827–829**; art movements, 56; John Marin, 555–556; marriage to Georgia O'Keeffe, 639–640, 672, 828; nudes, 690; photography, 672, 827–828
stock market crash, **829–831**, 882
Stone, Harlan Fiske, **831–833**, 839
Story of Philosophy, The (Durant), 250–251, 400
Stover, Russell C., 278
Strand, Paul, 673
Strange Interlude (O'Neill), 653, **833–834**, 862
Strauss, Herbert, 548
streetcars, 836–837, 890
strikes. *See* labor strikes
Strowger switch, telephone technology, 852
Student Prince, The (operetta), **834–835**
Studies in Classic American Literature (Lawrence), **835**
Sturtevant, Alfred H., **835–836**

submachine gun (Thompson machine gun), **865–866**
suburbs, **836–838**; automobile's contribution, 455; growth of, 423, 424; as response to urbanization, 890–891. *See also* urbanization
suffrage: for African American women, 12, 927, 928; Alice Paul, 629–630, 666, 927; for women, 516, 628–630, 901, 927–928. *See also* Nineteenth Amendment
Sullivan, Anne, 482
Sullivan, Mary Quinn, 594
Sun Also Rises, The (Hemingway), **838**; excerpt, 540; literary importance of, 395–396; in Paris, 103; social impact of, 532; Gertrude Stein, 825
Sunny (play, 1925), 486
Supreme Court, U.S., **839–841**. *See also List of Entries by Categories; specific justices*
surfing, **479**
Susan B. Anthony Amendment, 628–631
Sutherland, George, 839
Swanson, Gloria, **841–842**
swashbuckling films, 288
sweets, 319
Sweetser, Jesse, 356
Sweet trials, 221
swimming, Olympic, 255, 479, 911
swing in music, 464
synchronized-sound technology, 90, 846. *See also* talking motion pictures ("talkies")
syphilis, 565, 792, 794–796
Szent-Györgyi, Albert, 159

tabloids, 622–623
Taft, William Howard, **843–844**; child labor laws, 74; postal savings bank, 78; as Supreme Court chief justice, 381, 839, 840, 841, 843–844
Talented Tenth, 248
Tales of the Jazz Age (Fitzgerald), **845**
Taliesin (house), 935

talking motion pictures ("talkies"), **845–847**; Academy Awards, 2; *The Broadway Melody*, 573; comedy, 659–661; electrical recording, **271–272**; film in the era, **305–308**; Hollywood songs, 93; silent film actor transition to, 80–81, 83; silent films revolutionized by sound, 90, 271, 328–329, 466–467, 780, 846, 906, 907; Warner Bros., 466–467, 846–847. *See also specific actors, films, and studios*
Tammany Hall, 753, 804, 903
Tampa Bay hurricane, 611
tap dance, 218
tariffs in international trade, 451–452, 453
Tarkington, Booth, **32–33, 847–848**
Tarzan the Ape Man (film), 911
Tate, Allen, 335–336, 814
taxes. *See* income tax
tax rates, 446, 569, 736–737
Taylor, Frederick Winslow, 716
Taylor, William Desmond, 634, **848**
Teapot Dome scandal, 207, 238, 416, **849–851**
Teasdale, Sara, **851–852**
technical education, 258–259
Technicolor process, 307
technology. *See* science and technology
telephone technology and service, **852–853**; AT&T (American Telephone & Telegraph), 601–602; wiretapping, 642–643
telescope, Mount Wilson Observatory, 61, 62, 63, 424–425
television technology, **853–855, 941–942**
temperance movements, 698–699
Temptress, The (film), 339
Ten Commandments, The (film, 1923), 230, 507, **855–856**
Ten Days That Shook the World (Reed), 726–727, **856–857**
tennis, **857–859**; amateur, 857–858; professional, 821–822, 858–859;
woman in, 588–589, 646, 821–822, 857, 858
"territory bands," 465
Texas Democratic primary, 631
textile-block houses, Wright's, 934, 935
textile industry, 497–498, 884
Thalberg, Irving, 367, 572
Thayer, Scofield, 242–243
theater in Canada, **859–860**; English-language, 859–860; French-language, 859; vaudeville, 897
theater in the United States, **861–863**; African Americans in, 800–801, 861, 897–898; companies and troupes, 652–653, 862–863; developments in, 530; operettas, 112, 751–752, 834–835, 861. *See also List of Entries by Categories*
Theatre Guild, 863
There is Confusion (Fauset), 383
Thief of Bagdad, The (1924), 288, 678, **864**
This Side of Paradise (Fitzgerald), **864–865**
Thompson, John T., 865
Thompson machine gun, **865–866**
Thorpe, Jim, **866–867**
Three Soldiers (Dos Passos), **868**
Throop University. *See* California Institute of Technology (Caltech)
Tijuana Bibles, 690
Tilden, "Big" Bill, 821, 857–858, **868–869**
Time (magazine), 543–544, 549
Tin Pan Alley, 344, 463, 486, **869–870**
Toklas, Alice B., 825
Tomb of the Unknown Soldier, **870**
Tong Wars of Chinatown, San Francisco, **871–872**
Toomer, Jean, **872–874**
tornadoes, 611–613
Torrent, The (film), 339
Torrents of Spring, The (Hemingway), 40
tourism: by air, 876, 879; by automobile, 401, 455, 592, 878; by railway, 878–879; travel, **877–880**
Toward an Architecture (Le Corbusier), 935
toys: dolls and dollhouses, 403; yo-yo, **937–938**
track and field: amateur sports, 820; notable athletes, **663–664, 754–755, 777–778, 866–867**; Olympic Games (1920, 1924, 1928), 645, 646, 649, 663, 754–755, 777; women in, 650, 754–755
trade. *See* international trade
trade credit, 203
traffic signals, **874**
train. *See* railroad
Tramp character (Charlie Chaplin), 157, 164–165
transatlantic crossing, aviation, 69–70
transcontinental railroad, 878–879
transportation, **875–877**; Pershing Map, 668–669; traffic signals, **874**. *See also List of Entries by Categories; specific types of transportation*
travel, 877–880. *See also List of Entries by Categories;* tourism
travel agencies, 877–878
Treasury bonds, U.S., 78
tree rings (dendochronology), 48
Tri-State tornado of 1925, 611–612
trucking, 717, 875–876
Truman, Harry S., 882
Trumbull, Edward, 164
Trumpler, Robert J., 62–63
trust companies, failure of, 78
tryparsamide, 564
Tulsa, Oklahoma, race riot, 546, 707, 708
Tunney, Gene, 108, 234–235, **880**
Turner, Frederick Jackson, 331
Tutankhamen's tomb, 48
TWA (Trans World Airlines), 69
Twelve Southerners, 433, 814
Twenties, The: From Notebooks and Diaries of the Period (Edel), 921

Twenty-First Amendment, 733
Two Arabian Knights (film), 428

Ulmann, Doris, 673
unconscious in poetry, 682
unemployment, 124–125, **695–696, 881–883**
Uniform Motor Vehicle Code, 604
unionism, **883–886**; jobs and wages, 124; labor strikes, **497–500**; proportion of workers in unions, 445–446; railroads, 716–717; Red Scare, 724; support for Progressive Party in U.S., 501
Union of Russian Workers, 664
United Artists (UA), 155, 156, 368, 678, **886**
United Fruit in Guatemala, 508
United Mine Workers of America (UMWA): generally, 883–884; labor strike, 498–499; leadership, 519–520, 885
United States: advertising in, **7–11**; agriculture in, **18–21**; banking, **77–80**; birth control movement, 95–96, 117; book publishing industry in, **102–105**; currency and coinage in, **214–215**; elections (*See entries at* elections); food trends, 94–95; foreign policy, **324–327**, 574–575; housing, 118–119; national balance sheets of, 203; newspapers, 621–624; Olympic achievements, 644, 646, 647–648, 650, 651–652; population, 123, 231–232; power relationship with Canada, 132; recognition of Soviet Union, **815–816**; religion in the, **732–735**; trade with Canada, 131–132. *See also specific topics*
United States Census. *See* Census, U.S.
United States Railroad Administration (USRA), 715
United States v. Bhagat Singh Thind (1923), 106
United States v. Classic, 902
United States v. Ninety-Five Barrels Alleged Apple Cider Vinegar, **887**
United States v. United States Steel Corp., **887–888**
universal motor, invention of, 373
Universal Negro Improvement Association (UNIA), 11, 13, 340–341, **888–889**
Universal Negro Improvement Association and African Communities League (UNIA-ACL), 340–341
universe, discovery of, 61–62
university. *See* college
University of Chicago social sciences, 809, 810, 811
University of Illinois football, 821
Universum Film AG (Ufa), 307
Unknown Soldier: Harding's eulogy for, 381; Tomb of the Unknown Soldier, **870**
Urban, Joseph, 939
urbanization, **889–892**; air pollution, **24–26**; cities, **165–169**; housing market, **422–424**; medical care delivery, 389–390; in North America, 231–232; Sears, Roebuck and Co. department stores, 789; Al Smith Jr., 805; suburbs as response to, 890–891; traffic signals, **874**; urban planning, 891. *See also* suburbs
U.S. Bureau of Standards, science and technology, 780
U.S. Department of Agriculture (USDA), 760
U.S. Department of Commerce, 712
U.S. Department of Labor, 664
U.S. Forest Service, 615
U.S. National Championship (U.S. Open), 868–869
U.S. Postal Service (USPS): airmail, **22–23**, 24, 26, 876, 879; postage stamps, **692–694**
U.S. Public Health Service (PHS), 794, 796

USS *Lexington*, 71
USS *Los Angeles* (airship), 27
USS *Roma* (airship), 26
USS *Saratoga*, 71
USS *Shenandoah* (airship) disaster, 27, 71, **797–799**
U.S. Treasury bonds, 78
utilities, electric, 272

vaccines, 391, 456, 685
Valasek, Joseph, 676
Valentine's Day massacre. *See* St. Valentine's Day Massacre
Valentino, Rudolph, **893–894**; actor transition to talkies, 80; John Gilbert's career, 346; as sex symbol, 306; *Sheik, The*, 306, **797**, 893
Vallée, Rudy, **894–895**
"vamp" as slang, 802
Van Alen, William, 163
Vanderbilt University: Fugitive Poets, **335–336**, 620, 683, 813–814; Southern Agrarians, 531–532, **620–621**, 683, **813–815**
Van Der Zee, James, 674, **895–896**
Van Deventer, Willis, 839
Van Vechten, Carl, 385–386
Vanzetti, Bartolomeo, 709, **766–767**
Varley, Frederick, 370–371
vaudeville, **896–899**; Fatty Arbuckle, **45–47**; blackface, 476–477, 897; decline in, 861; Helen Keller in, 482; Babe Ruth, 764
Versailles, Treaty of, 398, 458, 514, 921–922
Veteran's Bureau, 933
veterans of World War I, **99–100**, 446, **932–934**
Victor Talking Machine Company, 715
Vidor, King, 376, **899**
Village of Euclid, Ohio v. Ambler Realty Co., 891
vitamins: C discovery, 159; D discovery, **899–900**; labeling and discovery of workings of, 391, 456

Vitaphone, 466, 846, 907
Voaden, Herman, 860
vocational education, 258–259
Voigt Act, 516
Volstead Act, 337, 698, 699, 701
von Stroheim, Erich, 366, 367, 572
voting rights (U.S.), **900–902**; African Americans, 12, 631, 927, 928; women, 12, 266, 628–631, 901. *See also* suffrage

Wadsworth, James W., Jr., 700, 701
wages. *See* income and wages
Wales Padlock Law, 149
Walker, Jimmy, **903**
Wallace, DeWitt, 549, **903–904**
Wallace, Lew, 91
Wallace, Lila, 549
Waller, Fats, **904–905**
Wall Street bombing, 207
Walsh, Thomas J., 849, 850
Walt Disney Company, 244–245, 401, 823–824
Walton, Izaak, 460
Waner, Lloyd, 85
Waner, Paul, 85
war. *See* military and war
Warm Springs Foundation, 565, 566
Warner, Albert, 905, 906, 907
Warner, Harry, **905–906**, 907
Warner, Jack, 905, 907
Warner, Sam, 905, **906–907**
Warner Bros., **907–908**; John Barrymore, 83; founding, as family business, 905–908; movie theater evolution, 307; sound development in film, 466–467, 846–847, 906, 907; studio aerial view, 907
Warren, Robert Penn, 814
Washington, George, 693
Washington Naval Conference, **908–910**; generally, 485; German reparations for World War I, 325; Warren G. Harding, 382; Charles Evans Hughes, 426; isolationism, 459
Wassily Chair, 409

Waste Land, The (Eliot), 273–274, 530, 682, **910**
water: as resource, 614; rights and navigation, 300–301, **537–538**; St. Francis Dam disaster, **824–825**; transport on, shipping industry, 875
Watson, James Sibley, Jr., 242–243
Watson, John, 703–705, 810–811
Watson, Thomas J., 450
Way Down East (film), 367
Weary Blues, The (L. Hughes), 429, 430, 683
Weissmuller, Johnny, 646, 650, **911–912**
Wellman, William A., 922–923
Well of Loneliness, The (Hall), 412
West, Mae, **912**
Western Electric Company: Bell Labs, **90**; film synchronized sound, 846; radio, 710; sound recording, 807; television technology, 854
Western Union, 830
Westinghouse Electric, 710, 711, 941
Weston, Edward, 673
West Virginia mining disaster, **912–913**
Wharton, Edith, **14–15, 913–915**
What Price Glory? (Anderson and Stallings), 861
What's O'Clock (Lowell), **915**
wheat, Canadian, 16–17
Wheeler, Burton K., 697
Whipple, George Hoyt, 565
White, Edward Douglass, 839, 843
Whitehead, Alfred North, 671–672
Whiteman, Paul, 463, 464, 596, **915–916**
"white primary" cases, 631
Whitman, Walt, 835
Wilder, Thornton, **110–111, 916–918**
Wilderness Act (1964), 346
wilderness area preservation, 345
Wild Geese (Ostenso), 527
Williams, Michael, 549
Williams, William Carlos, **918–919**;

Ezra Pound, 823, 918–919; works, **442**, 683, **822–823**
Wilson, Charles T. R., 633
Wilson, Edith Bolling, **919–920**, 921, 922
Wilson, Edmund, **920–921**
Wilson, Woodrow, **921–922**; League of Nations, 513; Henry Cabot Lodge, 535; railroads, 715; Treaty of Versailles, 281, 458
Wimbledon, 868–869
Winesburg, Ohio (Anderson), 530
Wings (film), **922–923**
wiretapping, 642–643
Within Our Gates (film), 577
Wolfe, Thomas, **536–537**
Woman of Affairs, A (film), 339
women in college, **923–925**, 924, 931
women in film, 82, 106–107, 122–123, 306, 635–636. *See also List of Entries by Categories*
women in literature. *See List of Entries by Categories*
women in sports: Olympic Games of 1920 (Summer), 820; tennis, 588–589, 646, 821–822, 857, 858; track and field, 650, 754–755
women in the workforce, **925–927**; *Adkins v. Children's Hospital*, **5–6**, 926, 929; aviation, 69, 70; fashion design, 175–176; "feminine" professions, 926, 930; film, 82, 106–107, 122–123, 306, 635–636; governor, 755–757; journalism, 303–304; participation increase, 445; postwar era, 93; scientific and technical field, 677, 780; World War I, 925, 933
Women's Christian Temperance Union (WCTU), 654, 699
Women's Citizenship Act. *See* Cable Act of 1922
women's issues: Asian brides in Canada, 134–135; cigarette smoking, 138; citizenship, **128–129**, 929–930; employment discrimination, 882; golf, 356;

hockey, 404; KKK, 708; marriage and citizenship, 60, **128–129,** 929–930; Roaring Twenties, 741; Rollin Kirby's support for, 491; Sheppard-Towner Maternity and Infancy Protection Act, 516, **799**; slang usage, 802–803; Mae West, 912. *See also* fashion and clothing; feminism; *List of Entries by Categories;* marriage and dating

Women's Joint Congressional Committee (WJCC), 799

women's rights, **927–931**; African American voting, 12, 927, 928; League of Women Voters' work against gender discrimination, 516; *Muller v. Oregon*, 926; voting, 12, 266, 628–631, 901. *See also* birth control; sterilization; suffrage

Women's Right's Convention of 1848, Seneca Falls, 923

Women's Suffrage Amendment. *See* Nineteenth Amendment

Women's Trade Union League (WTUL), 925, 929

Woodson, Carter G., 399, 616–617

Woollcott, Alexander, 30, 558

Work, Hubert, 610

workers. *See* employment; labor; unionism

workers' education, **931–932**

Workers Party, 185–186, 687

World Court, 326

World Series (baseball), 84, 337, 342, 712

World's Fair, Sesquicentennial Exposition, **791–792**

World War Adjusted Compensation Act of 1924. *See* Bonus Act of 1924

World War I: business and economics, **122–125**; college attendance, 924; ending, for U.S., 324; Europe after, 280–281; German reparations for, 226–227, 281, 325–326; Warren G. Harding's role in peace, 382; historical perspectives, 398; isolationism in U.S., 458; Prohibition, 699; radio, 710, 714–715; railroads, 715–716; Red Scare, 723–724; religion in Canada, 730; religion in the U.S., 732; "return to normalcy," 687, **735–736,** 922, 927; Robert La Follette on, 500–501; "shell shock," 933; STDs, 792, 794, 795; Sara Teasdale's poetry, 851; Thompson machine gun, **865–866**; *Three Soldiers* (Dos Passos), **868**; Tomb of the Unknown Soldier, **870**; trade effects of, 451, 452; Treaty of Versailles, 398, 458, 514, 921–922; Unknown Soldier commemoration, 381; U.S. foreign policy after, **324–327**; veterans, **99–100,** 446, **932–934**; women in workforce after, 925, 933; women's suffrage, 928

World War II: Josephine Baker in French resistance, 75–76; Soviet Union and U.S. relationship, 816

Wright, Frank Lloyd, 50, 776, **934–936**

Writer's Guild of New York, 383

Wylie, Elinor, **936**

Wyoming: Nellie Tayloe Ross as governor, **755–757**; Teapot Dome scandal, 207, 238, 416, **849–851**

Xochitl (dance), 359

X-rays and Compton effect, 187–188, 582, 583, 675–676

Yankee Stadium, 626

Yeats, William Butler, 682

yellow journalism, 392

Yellowstone National Park, 878

Yens, Otto, 566

Yerkes, Robert, 704

"You, Andrew Marvell" (MacLeish), 547

yo-yos, **937–938**

zeppelins. *See* airships

Ziegfeld, Florenz, Jr., 92, 93, 113, 486, **939**. *See also* Ziegfeld Follies

Ziegfeld Follies, **940–941**; Irving Berlin, 92, 93; on Broadway, 92, 111, 113, 114, 939; dancing, 219; Will Rogers, 750, 940

Ziegfield Girls, 940–941

Zukor, Adolph, 506–507, 678

Zworykin, Vladimir, 855, **941–942**

U-32 LIBRARY
MONTPELIER, VT